D1159523

Under the Editorship of MEYER F. NIMKOFF

The Florida State University

The Nature and Types
of Sociological Theory

A

DON MARTINDALE

UNIVERSITY OF MINNESOTA

HOUGHTON MIFFLIN COMPANY BOSTON

The Riverside Press Cambridge

The Riverside Press
Cambridge, Massachusetts
PRINTED IN THE U.S.A.

To EDITH

Preface

Notions are widespread that sociological theory is either an industrious activity on the drawing boards of the architects of fantasy or a branch of esoterics operating in a shadowy realm of semi-darkness. There are, to borrow Nietzsche's terms, Apollonian and Dionysian conceptions of sociological theory. Favorite descriptive adjectives for theory by persons holding the Apollonian conception are "abstract," "grand," "large-scale." To them, it appears, theory is an Odyssey through the Spice Islands of make-believe, with an occasional detour up the spiral staircase of the ivory tower. On the other hand, favorite descriptive adjectives for theory by persons holding the Dionysian interpretation are "elusive," "obscure," "ephemeral." To them, it seems, theory is a dangerous if exhilarating business where one makes one's way along the rat-infested waterfronts of the human spirit.

The present study holds neither of these conceptions of sociological theory and cannot even offer the reader the consolation of a middle road. If it were to liken theory to anything (and there is no particular reason for doing so), it would be to a light. As far as the present study is concerned, theory has only one function: to illuminate. The difference between one theory and another is in comparative candlepower. The power and reliability of a theory are not always evident all at once. A theory may have a power to explain what was not originally anticipated; it may also disclose the existence of problems it cannot explain. The inevitable process begins of attempting to improve the theory and of searching for alternatives to it. And periodically in a science it is of great value to review and bring up to date the general picture of its theories. In sociology this is long overdue.

We have come far enough from the original synthesis of positivism and organicism, which formed the first integration of sociology, to trace in perspective the dynamics of its inner tensions. The full implications of positivistic organicism become clear only with the disintegration of the formula itself. Similar observations hold for the later history of conflict theory in sociology, though here the transformations of the theoretical formula occurred in part as a result of pressures from socio-political movements. A third block of older sociological theory, sociological formalism, has also continued to develop and to display some rather unexpected forms.

Thus, the re-evaluation of the older schools of sociological theory is overdue. At the same time, there are blocks of materials formerly considered essential for sociological theory which no longer deserve serious consideration. The geographical theory of society and its many varieties of environmental and climatic interpretation of social institutions no longer require attention. Like various biologistic and racialistic theories of society, they deserve only to be dropped.

But, at the same time, other formations in sociological thought have long been in need of synthesis. The basic identity of a whole series of formulations running through the works of such American sociologists as Cooley and Mead and, in a somewhat parallel manner, through Weber in Europe have long deserved treatment as expressions of a single approach to the subject matter of sociology. In the present book, these will be summarized as variations of "social behaviorism."

Finally, an important segment of the modern sociological community, including such major students as Talcott Parsons and Robert Merton, have perceived new and distinctive affinities in their views. They have addressed themselves to the development of a special theory which they call "sociological functionalism."

One of the most difficult problems in the study of sociological theory is to determine what may be left out. Sociology first arose as a new point of view in Western philosophy. It was established as an independent field when exponents of the new point of view carved out spheres of influence from older disciplines. It became a science only when the new point of view and its special field were implemented by special methods, permitting it to develop its own facts and verify propositions on the basis of its own standards. There are also powerful ties between sociology and other disciplines of Western civilization. In the earlier stages, the interaction between sociology and other sciences was particularly close. One of the tasks of theory is the clarification of these ties. In pursuing this task, we are led step by step to areas ever more remote from sociology until we gradually enter the domain of a general history of ideas.

The present study has more modest aims. Because most schools of sociological theory, until recently, have drawn their inspiration from Western philosophy, their origins in this matrix have been traced, in order to clarify the main propositions and problems of the different sociological schools. To ignore these philosophical origins is to cut oneself off from insight into some of the most fundamental affinities of our discipline with others. At the same time, the primary interest has always been in the use sociologists have made of such philosophical beginnings, not what philosophers have made of them. Thus, at no time does the study become a history of philosophy.

Since interest attaches to particular schools of sociological theory, disciplines other than philosophy also repeatedly come into view. The earliest school of sociological theory had particularly strong ties with history and anthropology, as well as with philosophy. Later schools broke with either or both of these fields. After the early disrepute into which the comparative method fell, anthropology and sociology parted ways; only recently, with the development of sociological functionalism, have they tended to come together again. Between these periods, various special theories had other ties. Formalism, for example, which broke its ties both with history and anthropology, tended to establish close ties with jurisprudence. Social-action theory has developed ties with history and economics; pluralistic behaviorism has been allied with psychology and demography.

In examining the various schools of sociological theory, the properties of any particular school have determined both the areas and individuals who have been chosen for review. In treating the other fields with which a particular sociological theory has been connected, the aim has never been to achieve a comprehensive treatment of the non-sociological discipline. The only purpose has been to provide a full description of the primary features of the given school of sociological theory. It is in this manner that the study, for all its variety, becomes a special study of sociological theory rather than a general history of ideas.

Second in importance only to the problem of what to put in and leave out was the problem of apportioning space. One possible way of solving it would have been in terms of the influence of the individual thinker. But the influence of an individual is capable of different constructions. An individual can be important because his formulations have been used by many other persons. He can be important because he opened up new perspectives or pioneered new possibilities. These two kinds of importance are by no means necessarily identical. Any given kind of theory has both its heroic, its pioneering period, and its period of full development, its classic period. The thinkers of the classic period of a theory often have the most extensive influence, even though they may be far less creative than the pioneers of the heroic period. It is the classical theorists who give the ideas their finished form.

However, when we deal with a number of theories, we must also remember that they are usually not equally influential. And beyond the problem of allotment of space to individuals is allotment of space to systems of ideas. A study of theory is concerned with systems of concepts. Judgments of either quantitative influence or popular influence recede in importance before creativity. Moreover, attention necessarily attaches more completely to the theories as units rather than to the particular individuals who elaborated them. For this reason, the number of pages devoted to a given thinker must not be taken as a judgment of his importance in any other sense than in terms of his conceptual place in the particular theory under review. For example, the fact that about as much space is devoted to Vierkandt as to Tönnies and Durkheim is not intended to imply that Vierkandt is as quantitatively influential, nor is it intended to indicate that Vierkandt was for a long period the dominant sociologist of Switzerland. Rather, Vierkandt had a strategic position in the development of sociological formalism because of his attempt to solve the theoretical and methodological problems of neo-Kantianism. Vierkandt therefore marks the transformation within the school from neo-Kantianism to phenomenology. The importance of Tönnies and Durkheim is that of individuals belonging to a different phase of a different theory. Whereas Vierkandt is a pioneer in sociological formalism, Tönnies and Durkheim represent the classical phase of organismic positivism. Concretely, for every single person influenced by Vierkandt, there have probably been at least twenty influenced by Tönnies and Durkheim. The amount of space devoted to any given thinker is thus intended more to reveal strategic location in conceptual development than extent of popular influence. The only quantitative measure that has been employed in the present study is the devotion of approximately the same amount of space to each separate school of sociological theory. Even this does not mean that as theoretical formulations they are equally important.

There were other decisions flowing from primary interest in theoretical development. For example, in discussing the backgrounds of phenomenological formalism, some attention was devoted, not only to European philosophers, but to Santayana in America — this, despite the fact that no development of phenomenological formalism occurred in the United States. Why, then, should Santayana be mentioned at all? At times, the non-occurrence of a theoretical development has a special interest of its own. Although Santayana provided a thoroughly sound foundation for a development of phenomenological formalism on native grounds, it has remained a theoretical vein unmined in the quarry. In America the extension of the pragmatic tradition to sociology occurred at a time when Europe was inclined toward phenomenology. There is no better testimony to the power of pragmatism on the American scene than the frustration of this possibility. At the same time, it should occasion no surprise if an autonomous form of phenomenological formalism should arise in America when the pragmatic tradition weakens.

The one field outside sociology itself to which reference has most frequently been made is philosophy. In the case of every school of sociology to develop except the very last — sociological functionalism — discussion has begun with the philosophers. As systems of ideas, all the early schools of sociological theory originated as philosophic points of view. This cannot be taken to suggest that these origins had permanent importance for sociological theory. Often the philosophic parent model varies greatly from the sociological theory based on it. This is inevitable, for the precondition of the scientific development of an idea is its empirical fertility. The origins of a school quickly recede in importance. The possibilities and limitations of a point of view never appear more clearly than when the process by which they are shaped into something empirically relevant is traced. Positivistic organicism is made possible by the fusion of older forms of philosophic idealism and empiricism. Conflict sociology is the scientific extension of historical empiricism. Formalism was suggested by neo-Kantian empiricism and phenomenology. Pluralistic behaviorism and social-action theory found their point of departure in neo-idealism. Symbolic interactionism is the American form of social science proceeding most directly from pragmatism.

While the present study thus undertakes a new review of the traditional materials of sociological theory, it should not be assumed that it is without relevance for the new movement in sociological theory construction which has arisen under the stimulation of analytical philosophy and the philosophy of science. The task of formal theory construction (the transformation of a given theory into logically closed form on the basis of a calculus of propositions) cannot be accomplished directly without mediation. Though some of its proponents, like Hotspur, think it but "an easy leap to pluck bright honor from the pale-faced moon," either theory construction works with the explanations and data of the science or it turns into terminological pyrotechnics.

It is hoped that this study will be of value both to the traditionalists and philosophical radicals in sociological theory. However, I must confess that in these attempts to explore the nature, grounds, and explanatory powers of the various forms of sociological theory, I was guided by only one objective — to understand them myself.

In a work that has taken more than ten years to complete, it is no longer possible to remember all the persons who have given assistance and encouragement along the way. Elio D. Monachesi and John Sirjamaki have given much encouragement and advice. F. Stuart Chapin and George B. Vold have read sections of the manuscript and given me the benefit of their mature judgments. Mrs. Edith Martindale has spent many patient hours correcting the manuscript in its many stages. Mrs. Bette Soderstrom and Miss Louise P. Olsen did yeoman service in typing the manuscript. To Meyer F. Nimkoff I owe a debt of gratitude for perceptive criticism of the manuscript as a whole. Finally, I am grateful for the fact that the editors of Houghton Mifflin distrust stereotypes, are disturbed by errors and are dismayed by obscurity in all forms, while they are tolerant of human failing and patient in the face of the storms of temperament.

March 1960   D. M.

Contents

PART FIVE   Social Behaviorism

PART SIX   Sociological Functionalism

PART SEVEN   Conclusion

PART ONE

Sociology and the Sciences

1

The Road to Sociology

With all historical time to develop in, sociology is only about a hundred years old. As far as we can tell, our intelligence is no greater than that of men of previous societies. There is no greater potential incidence of genius. We have a broader culture at our disposal than any earlier society, but culture has accumulated in other epochs and times without the appearance of sociology. We can, of course, simply dismiss the problem of why sociology did not appear much earlier as a historical accident somehow related to the peculiar conditions of our era. But it is not an isolated event. Sociology is a continuing activity distinctive of our time. It is not the creation of one or a few men of genius but an on-going enterprise of research, study, and teaching. It provides careers for research workers and teachers. It offers knowledge and service to members of our society sufficient to justify their continuing support. If it did not, the entire enterprise would wither.

If we are to talk sensibly about sociology, we must first find out what it is that we are talking about. We might start out by defining sociology very generally as "a body of thought about man's interhuman life," but this does not carry us very far because, in many respects, the same definition might apply to folk wisdom and magic and religion. We come closer to the subject when we call sociology the "science" of man's interhuman life. But even if we beg the question of what science is, we have still not really isolated sociology from competing disciplines, for historically sociology has had to fight for its own place in a noisy circle of social sciences — a battle which even today leaves it preoccupied with its identity. Perhaps, then, the

3

best approach to a definition of sociology lies along the path of history. Sociology is a part of that great evolution of thought in Western civilization which passes from religion through philosophy to science. There are properties of modern sociology that can be accounted for only in terms of its birthright. The formula for the construction of science out of philosophy was in considerable measure fixed by the physical sciences, which pioneered the movement, and this fact has left a deep imprint on all the social sciences, including sociology. By tracing the primary relations of sociology to the other social sciences, and by exploring its ties with the intellectual and ideological movements from which it historically emerged, we can come closest to establishing the boundaries of the area that sociology claims for its own.

Sociology, Folk Wisdom, and Theology

Common-sense thinking about interhuman life occurs even in the simplest of societies. Life is made up of incidents and encounters which people reflect on and generalize. The proverbial lore or folk wisdom of a people is the essence of their "common sense," and it is important to them because of the contribution it makes to the maintenance of their particular social order.

The folk wisdom of a people is interpenetrated by the ethos of the local society. To be sure, people everywhere work and play, make a living, fall in and out of love, make friends, come into conflict, marry, raise children, bury their dead, and so on. All such things form the objects of the "common-sense" knowledge of the society. But the way the given social order organizes and distributes access to these things is unique. The common-sense lore of a people is time-bound and normatively local — in both of these respects it falls short of science.

There are other things men do, or perhaps things that happen to them, which fall outside the framework of everyday events. They have accidents, they become ill and die. They lose loved ones. Tragedies sometimes strike in the midst of what began as great happiness. Such things tend to defy the explanatory formulas of folk wisdom. How, furthermore, is one to explain the fact that, even if two members of a society are equally diligent in the conducting of the affairs of everyday life, the good fortune of one may be matched by the misfortune of another? Even without the unexpected and tragic or extraordinary event, feelings arise out of ordinary life that are not always easy to accept or explain. Every social order prescribes goals for its members and the means for attaining these goals. The stuff of life must be crammed into socially prescribed forms. The murderous or lustful impulse must be repressed. A man may be expected to go into battle knowing all too well that it may mean his life. The individual may in fact covet his neighbor's wife. Modern psychologists have familiarized us with the suppressed anti-social impulse that takes its secondary revenge in the form of guilt arising in the face of repression. Finally, no social order privileges all its members equally, a fact which does not make the frustrations generated within the order easier to endure.

The psychological roots of religion seem universal to mankind. They appear to lie in the demand for emotional and intellectual "closure." Man must explain and accommodate himself emotionally to the tragic, the unexpected, and frustrating events that take place within and around his life. He feels the need even to explain and adjust to the fact of his own death. At bottom, religions seem to be collective institutional solutions to these problems.

Thus, beside the common-sense thinking of a society, another type arises with various subtypes of magical, theological, and mixed forms. In various ways this thought, too, may be concerned with the incidents of everyday life. But its point of gravity is elsewhere, in the hidden, the extraordinary, the transcendent. And when such thought is concerned with everyday events, it is often because of the unpredictable or uncontrollable factors. The magical spell is added as a warrant for the success of a hunting expedition, its intent being to control the unforeseeable accident. Black magic is worked to injure an enemy who would be dangerous to face directly. Such thinking addressed to the extraordinary — the explanation of health and illness, life and death, chance and fate — may undergo various degrees of organization, development, and sublimation. In its "purer" form, it becomes a speculative, ethical probing into the ultimate meaning of life.

A number of older theories found such theological reasoning to be the first form of abstract thought and its bearers — the "magician-priests" — the world's first professional intellectuals. But even at this time there was a subdivision of intellectual roles, with the old man or woman — the "sage" — being thought of as the respected advocate of common-sense knowledge in contrast to the "magician-priest-philosopher," who was defined as the specialist in the esoteric. However this may be, theology is no more the counterpart of sociology than is folk wisdom. In fact, if one searches previous societies or contemporary preliterates for the equivalent of sociological knowledge, it is not to be found. Nor will the "sage" or "magician-priest" substitute for the sociologist. Sociology lies somewhere in between.

Like common sense, sociology is concerned with the everyday, the average, the ordinary, the recurrent social event. In this respect, it differs most widely from magic and theology. However, unlike common sense, sociology is not a discipline bound to uphold the ethos of some particular social order. It seeks maximum freedom from value suppositions. On the other hand, sociology shares with the various disciplines concerned with the extraordinary a speculative and intellectual intent, but, unlike magic and religion, its speculative motives are dominated by the concept of the "natural" rather than the supernatural. One may thus conceive of sociology as either extending the intellectual and speculative concerns proper to religion into the area of the ordinary; or, in reverse, as the rise from notions about the ordinary toward general, abstract explanation.

A peculiar combination of "naturalism" and "speculation" is almost the badge of a world in which the primary form of institutionalized thought is science itself.

Sociology and Philosophy

The relation between sociology and philosophy is at once more direct and more subtle than its relation to folk wisdom or theology. Sociology was one of the late offspring of philosophy. Comte even called the new field "positive philosophy" before he accepted the name "sociology" for it. It was some time before sociology was sufficiently established as an independent discipline beside its parent for the two fields to find special subject matter in each other. It has finally become possible for the "philosophy of the social sciences" to appear as a special project within philosophy and for sociology to contemplate the study of social factors important for philosophic systems as aspects of the "sociology of knowledge."

Because philosophy was the matrix which gave birth to sociology in the nineteenth century, and because of the continuing interaction between the two disciplines, it is important to differentiate them. But first we must consider the still earlier emergence of Western philosophy itself out of magic and theology — one of the foundation developments in Western civilization, preparing the way for all subsequent intellectual movements. Philosophy had first to become distinct from magic, theology, and folk wisdom before, much later, science and, still later, sociology could become distinct from it.

The effects of magic upon intellectual life were primarily in the direction of a stereotyping of form and content. The incantation does not invite analysis. Magical tabooing of words, such as the occasional absolute prohibition on uttering the name of God, hardly promotes analysis. Or compare the taboo on many words relating to sex in our own society and the effect this taboo has on the child's understanding of sexual matters. The requirement of letter-perfect rendition of an efficacious magical formula may even restrict expressive fluidity — to say nothing of fixing an upper limit on rational analysis. Intellectual life dominated by magic is fixed by requirements external to intelligence itself.

The step in thought from theology to philosophy was an important achievement of the human mind, one which has had its effect on human thought ever since. When speculation about the nature of man and the world occurs outside the protective confines of sacred institutions, the competition of alternative explanations becomes especially sharp. A religious institution has powerful sanctions at its disposal in securing intellectual conformity. The apostate may be punished or excommunicated. On the other hand, the believer who is challenged in his beliefs may retire to the protection of official doctrine. The very presence of official doctrine, "dogma," or a "party line" often involves many compromises and adjustments. If one observes a difference emerging between his personal beliefs and the official dogma, life is always easier if the dangerous thought is put aside. But all this is incidental to the most important point of all: so long as thought is controlled by sacred sanctions the criterion of acceptability tends to be external — outside thought itself.

All this is changed when the reasoning process takes place outside religious institutions. Viewpoints multiply, for there is no established dogma against which to measure acceptability of ideas. Most important of all, ideas are forced to stand "upon their own merit." It may become necessary to find criteria for the acceptability of ideas within the thought process itself. *The Socratic method formalized the procedure central to the transition of thought from theology to philosophy — the search for a procedure establishing the criteria of truth within the thought process itself.*[1]

Logic as an Example of the Rational Proof

It is the amusing estimate of Bertrand Russell in his somewhat whimsical *History of Western Philosophy* [2] that if Socrates actually practiced the dialectic in the manner described in the *Apology,* the hostility centering on him is easily explained, for all the "humbugs of Athens" would have combined against him. The dialectical method is an excellent way of establishing the truth whenever logical propositions are at issue. It leads to the formation of propositions into consistent logical systems and to the discovery of logical errors and inconsistencies.

Looking back from the standpoint of a scientific world, the Socratic method appears remarkably limited precisely at the point where things become crucial — the winning of new knowledge. Even logically it was limited. When it was pressed to the interpretation that contraries have some sort of capacity to generate higher truths, or that the truth-establishing process consists in the evocation of memories from previous lives, it was on the way toward mysticism. However, if one looks at the Socratic method from the standpoint of the magico-theological conceptions of a world still dominated by religion, the Socratic method is like an open window letting in light and fresh air. It marks the decisive point of transition from theology to philosophy, from an intelligence determined by external institutional criteria to an intelligence established on the basis of the principles of thought itself. There is a sort of poetic justice in the tradition that would transform Socrates from what he most probably was, the scion of an eminent family, into a "common man." Once one establishes truth as a property of the proper conduct of the thought process, anyone can establish truths. This important conceptual

---

[1] According to Plato in the *Parmenides,* Socrates did not stop with the dialectical method but went on to develop the fundamental "hypothesis" that behind every term with an unequivocal denotation there is an ideal object accessible only to thought. Such conceptual objects are "ideas" or "ideal forms." The objects of the ordinary world are then viewed as of secondary reality, becoming what they are by virtue of their temporary participation in a corresponding form.

[2] Bertrand Russell, *History of Western Philosophy* (New York: Simon and Schuster, 1945), p. 92.

function is emancipated from social class, and a commoner is as able to find truths as an aristocrat.

The development of the Socratic method testifies to the central place occupied in Greek philosophy by the search for a way of conducting the thought process that would provide dependable results. The magnificent discovery that resulted, to be transmitted on as an imperishable ideal of the West, was the *rational proof.* The two outstanding achievements of Greek thought were the foundations of logic and the demonstration of the nature of mathematical truth.

Aristotle is ordinarily given credit for having laid the foundations of logic. The most important of his logical works is the *Prior Analytics,* which presents the theory of the syllogism — a three-termed argument resting on the logic of classes. The syllogism consists of a *major premise,* a *minor premise,* and a *conclusion.* The conclusion necessarily follows from the premises, and if the premises are true, then the conclusion must be true. Thus, with the major premise "all men are mortal," and the minor premise "Socrates is a man," the conclusion necessarily follows that "Socrates is mortal."

The theory of the syllogism is not as simple as this, and Aristotle went on to analyze its properties in great detail, but these ramifications, significant as they are in the history of Western thought, are not immediately relevant to the present discussion. What is most important for our purposes is the impetus that Aristotelian logic gave to the notion that the criteria for establishing the truth of anything lie within the thought process itself.

Modern students have raised three main criticisms of the syllogism. (1) There are formal defects in the system. Statements such as "all Greeks are men" do not, as Aristotle assumed, necessarily assert that Greeks exist. When the ambiguity of such a statement is resolved, it is seen to contain two statements: (*a*) "there are Greeks," and (*b*) "if anything is a Greek, it is a man." The latter statement is purely hypothetical, involving no necessary assertion of existence. (2) The logic of Aristotle overestimated the importance of the syllogism — leaving, for example, the whole area of mathematical truth outside its framework and obscuring its character. Finally, (3) it overestimated the importance of deduction. In Aristotle's writings, where questions are raised which transcend the problems of the syllogism, the discussion tends to become metaphysically obscure. This may be seen in his doctrine of "essences" (qualities of a thing which cannot be changed without a loss of its identity) and his doctrine of "substance" (presumed ultimate subjects of properties). These studies transferred the task of obtaining the first premises of the syllogism to metaphysics.

Deductive inference was thought by Aristotle to be syllogistic. It was necessary only to state all knowledge in syllogistic form to avoid all fallacies. The historical fate of these brilliant logical beginnings was the transformation of Aristotelian logic into a medieval dogma and the continuance of this logical dogmatism into modern times, where it functioned as a stronghold of resistance against further development of logical analysis. The logical thought of the Greeks did not embrace the problem of deduction broadly enough to include mathematics.

Because of all these objections, many modern students are unwilling to accept Greek logic as one of the great achievements of the human mind and think of it rather as an obstacle to the general growth of logic. But such a judgment fails to take account of the sort of magico-theological thinking which Greek logic replaced. More impressive than the intrinsic logical limitations of the syllogism is the concrete demonstration which Aristotelian logic provided of the possibilities of rational proof and the dream to which it gave birth of a rationally ordered sphere which could encompass all knowledge. Syllogistic logic was a superb product of the drive in Greek philosophy toward rationality.

Mathematics as an Example of the Rational Proof

A much more universally acclaimed product of the same drive was the discovery of the nature of mathematical truth. The Greeks had inherited numerous mathematical propositions from Babylonia and Egypt. They transformed them into something quite new. The practical utilization of mathematics is reported of Thales, who is said to have measured the height of a pyramid by waiting until the time of day when the shadow of the king was the same height as the king and measuring the shadow of the pyramid. He is said also to have solved the problem of finding the distance of ships at sea. The Pythagoreans made numerous contributions to the development of mathematics and, incidentally, elevated mathematical reasoning to the status of a soul-purifying rite. They speculated on the meaning of "the square root of 2," the first irrational number to be discovered, and they devised methods to approximate its value. Pythagoras possibly discovered the theorem bearing his name.[3] As a product of the study of the square root of 2 and of other irrationals, Eudoxus (408–355 B.C.) developed a geometrical theory of proportion. He also developed the method of exhaustion later used with great skill by Archimedes.

The great work, however, was that of Euclid, slightly after Aristotle. He did for mathematics what Aristotle did for logic — to be sure with somewhat greater logical beauty. Euclid's elements begin with the definition of such basic concepts as point, line, plane, angle.[4] Next were presented certain principles or postulates or axioms which related the primitive terms. Finally a number of theorems (lemmas or corollaries) were proved by applying the postulates and definitions.

There were logical imperfections in the *Elements*.[5] Eventually the attempts to prove the postulate of parallels from other of Euclid's postulates led to

[3] Sir Thomas L. Heath, *A History of Greek Mathematics* (Oxford: The Clarendon Press, 1921), Vol. 1, p. 145.
[4] Strictly speaking, other terms used to define these basic concepts were left undefined. The clarification of them is somewhat comparable to the discovery of formal ambiguities in the syllogism.
[5] Corrected by David Hilbert and others.

important logical discoveries [6] and to the further evolution of mathematics. A variety of postulational systems have been explored, and it has been demonstrated that Euclid's system for plane geometry is satisfied by only one model. But all this should not obscure the tremendous importance of Euclid's system to the history of thought — the creation of a purely deductive system resting on undefined terms. It is another brilliant monument to the Greek drive toward rationality.

The great discovery of Greek philosophy so significant for the progress of Occidental thought was thus the rational proof. But this is not science, for science is more than logic. In fact, the very impressiveness of the logical discoveries of the Greeks strengthened the anti-empirical movements in the Greek world by reducing empirical knowledge to an inferior position. Euclid, for example, had a typical Greek contempt for the practical utility of his geometry. On the other hand, the discovery of rational proof was one of the essential steps toward science itself. Without the conception of an autonomous, rationally closed world of thought, the basis of which rests in the inner principles of thought itself, science could hardly have arisen. Furthermore, a major beginning was made toward the forging of mathematics into a powerful tool for the investigation of nature.

Greek Sophism as Protosociology

If science was not achieved, except whimsically and incidentally, in the Greek world, neither was social science. But philosophy in the West remained, thereafter, the guardian of bodies of thought which later separated into the special sciences. The first model for concept formation in the special sciences was often drawn from Aristotelian logic, and to this day the criticism is frequently directed against sociology that its conceptualizations rest on the foundations of an outmoded traditional logic.

The nearest approach to a social science in Greek philosophy was made by the Sophists, intellectuals originating as displaced persons who made their living by teaching. They included such men as Hecataeus of Miletus, Xanthus of Sardes, Hellanicus of Mytilene, Protagoras of Abdera. Xenophanes and Heraclitus had turned philosophic attention to religion and language; the Pythagoreans opened a tradition of the discussion of ethics and politics. Now these foreigners brought to philosophy an extensive comparative knowledge of customs and social forms. Sophism partly became a philosophy of civilization, studying man as a social being in terms of his language, religion, art, literature, and politics. Moreover, the Sophists had strong empirical inclinations and they sought to amass as much knowledge as possible from all areas of human life. Such comparative knowledge was made the basis for inferences about the progress of human civilization, the origin and structure of language, the most efficient arrangement of social institutions for the development of the individual. The concept of natural law was developed into a social critical formulation for the test of institutions, establish-

[6] Such as those of John Bolyai and Nikolai Lobachevski.

ing the view in Sophistic circles that society rests on natural laws. They even called the institution of slavery to critical account.

But in the end, the knowledge of the Sophists was more practical than theoretical, and Sophism increasingly aimed at teaching the art of the control of life. Sophism was oriented to the education of the young and to the control of opinion through popular education. It developed courses for promoting practical efficiency in the conduct of private and public life. Sophists became expert in teaching the techniques of debate and the conduct of argument. They were denounced by Plato as "shopkeepers with spiritual wares." [7]

As a genuine movement toward social science, Sophism had serious limitations, and, as time went by, it aspired more toward systematic moral education than the extension of objective empirical-social knowledge. Thus, in the end, the contribution of Greek philosophy to social science was not direct — through Sophism — but indirect, by way of its discovery of the rational proof, which as a basic element of science ultimately was important for sociology as well.

Sociology and History

Philosophy became the discipline in the West that in more or less logical form summarized the knowledge available to the intellectual. In this it was a most bountiful queen of the sciences, bequeathing intellectual grants to serve as starting points for particular disciplines, including the kind of knowledge potentially important for sociology. On the other hand, the assemblage of sociological knowledge by philosophy was subject to intrinsic restrictions as long as its primary aim was moral instruction. For the establishment of a science, the simple assemblage and preservation of traditional wisdom is not enough, even though this lore is partly transformed into logically consistent wholes.

Science lives by the extension of empirical knowledge, not in a discipline that may view such empirical knowledge as downright dangerous. The task of establishing and explaining new facts about society and developing criteria for ascertaining their authenticity fell to the lot of the historians of the Greek world rather than its philosophers. Indeed, if we desire a relatively full and accurate picture of the "facts" of the Greek world, we turn naturally to such persons as Herodotus, Thucydides, Xenophon, and Arrian. The Greek word ἱστορία meant "research" or "investigation." A progressive increase in the precision of investigation of social facts is the lesson of fundamental importance for social science contained in the development of historiography.

Some points of view in modern sociology have been determined by their opposition to history in all its forms. Some of the sociological formalists — for example, Leopold von Wiese — have felt that sociology could

[7] *Protagoras*, 313c.

emerge only to the degree that it freed itself from history. Moreover, the recent school of small-group sociologists of the "group dynamics" persuasion have been overwhelmingly of the opinion that any use by sociology of historical materials is evidence of medievalism. The formalists and small-group theorists undoubtedly have good reasons for their contempt for history, but it should not obscure the slow, difficult steps by which objectivity in the establishment of social facts was won. It is difficult to conceive the possibility of sociology without the prior developments of historiography, beginning in classical Greece.

Historiography and the Evolution of Empirical Methodology

There are shadowy figures such as that of Hecataeus behind the work of Herodotus. From Herodotus' comments it is clear that Hecataeus was interested in geography and ethnology. Herodotus began his own work as a report of his travels. Born in Halicarnassus about 484 B.C., he spent time on the island of Samos and traveled in parts of the Persian Empire, Scythia, and Egypt, and he visited Athens and Thurii in Magna Graecia as an Athenian colonist. Herodotus seems to have had the idea of systematizing geography and chronology and recording the myths encountered in his travels. He did not believe everything he reported. Once he began his account, the significance of the Persian wars for the appearance of Greek political freedom and the autonomy of the city-state became increasingly clear to him. Because Herodotus never abandoned a general religious interpretation of historical events, he was led ever and again to trace out the tragic sequence of well-being, insolence, folly, and disaster. But despite the ultimately religious character of his explanation and the errors of fact and even naïveté of reporting, his account ranges from climate to social custom, from geography to myth, meriting the characterization of Herodotus as the world's first ethnologist.

By contrast, Thucydides wrote about events occurring during his lifetime and in which he participated. He was one of the ten generals elected to direct political and military affairs and banished by the Athenians in 424 B.C. after his failure to relieve Amphipolis. Thucydides almost completely rejected Herodotus' type of theological explanation of social events. He opened his account with a quick synoptic history of Greece before the Peloponnesian War — an account marked by its thorough rationalism and skepticism. Hellas, he thought, was not regularly settled in ancient times. The original Greeks must have been migratory or semi-migratory. They had no walls around their settlements. The richest districts were most subject to attack. Before the Trojan War, he believed, there was no common action in Hellas; in fact, the country did not even have a name as a whole. In ancient times both Hellenes and barbarians, as well as inhabitants of the coast and islands, began to find their way to one another by sea and had recourse to piracy. They were commanded by powerful cities grown rich from war booty. As wealth accumulated, cities were built on the seashore and fortified;

peninsulas were occupied and walled off. As Hellas grew more powerful and the acquisition of wealth became more rapid, the revenues of the cities increased, and in many of them tyrannies were established where formerly there had been only hereditary kings with fixed prerogatives. Thus a political evolution parallels economic evolution.[8]

Thucydides rejects Herodotus' "external" cause of social events. The causes of economic and political events lie in the human sphere. Moreover, he distinguishes between biased opinion and observation, and he constantly specifies the need for first-hand information:

> Of the events of the war I have not ventured to speak from any chance information, nor according to any notion of my own; I have described nothing but what I either saw myself, or learned from others of whom I made the most careful and particular inquiry. The task was a laborious one, because eye witnesses of the same occurrences give differing accounts of them, as they remembered or were interested in the actions of one side or the other.[9]

A responsible social-scientific attitude is illustrated in the speeches that Thucydides put into the mouths of crucial actors in his account at critical times. He quite consciously separates his method of reporting such speeches from the methodology of the rest of his account:

> As to the speeches which were made either before or during the war, it was hard for me, and for others who reported them to me, to recollect the exact words. I have therefore put into the mouth of each speaker the sentiments proper to the occasion, expressed as I thought he would be likely to express them, while at the same time I endeavored, as nearly as I could, to give the general purpose of what was actually said.[10]

The conception of history contained in the works of Herodotus and Thucydides was dissipated in the work of the rhetoricians, such as Ephorus and Theopompus. But in the studies of Timaeus the Sicilian (fourth century) and even more in the work of Polybius (particularly his critique of Timaeus' use of controversial documents), a more adequate conception appears.

The Romans added practically nothing to historiography. Dionysius of Halicarnassus and Livy, while making a study of sources, reduced history to sketches from antiquity subordinated to literary aims. In the work of Cicero, the claims of Roman patriotism are everywhere predominant. And by the time of Suetonius (*Lives of the Caesars*), history had degenerated to the mere gossip of a court journalist.

In the medieval world, the conception of historiography degenerates still further. Eusebius of Caesarea introduced a world chronology that became basic for the Christian historians. In St. Augustine's *City of God*, philoso-

---

[8] Thucydides, *History of the Peloponnesian War*, tr. by Benjamin Jowett, in Francis R. B Godolphin (ed.), *The Greek Historians*, Vol. I (New York: Random House, 1942), p. 575 f.
[9] *Ibid.*, p. 576.   [10] *Ibid.*

phy of history on the grand scale was projected; but generally throughout the period the chronicle is typical, and it is dominated by fascination with the miraculous. The low level of historical responsibility is evidenced in outright historical forgeries such as the False Decretals and the Donation of Constantine.

The Renaissance carried with it a renewed sense of historical responsibility, as shown by Valla's attack on the Donation of Constantine. But it is only with the conflict between Protestantism and Roman Catholicism that the forces were fully set in motion for an increased responsibility in the writing of history. After the challenge presented by Luther and by the authors of the great Protestant ecclesiastical history known as the *Magdeburg Centuries* (1560–74), the collection of sources by Protestant writers began in earnest. Cardinal Baronius in *Annales Ecclesiastici* (1588–1607) began even more thorough source collections, and thereafter collections proceed from both groups. Leibnitz even proposed the formation of an organization specifically charged with collecting historical source materials. Such activities led on to the modern archives. The basis was being laid as well for more secular philosophies of history, such as began to appear in the eighteenth century. The importance of the so-called "philosophy of history" is found in the fact that it lifts out the conceptual element in historical thought, separating it permanently from the field of myth. However, formulations such as St. Augustine's — conceiving the history of mankind as the successive revelation of a divine plan — could only lead to the subordination of history to dogma. Augustine's philosophy received its last full statement by Bossuet (*Discours sur l'histoire universelle*, 1681).

The historians of the eighteenth century (Voltaire, Montesquieu, Hume, Robertson, and Gibbon) changed all this. The exclusive connection of history with theology was severed; traditional authorities were questioned; the concept of a universal history was projected; other objects took their place in the historical account alongside politics and religion; the concept of "progress" was projected as a historical theme, and the idea of the triumph of reason presented as its goal. However, there was a certain inevitable shallowness implicit in the Enlightenment approach to history. To a point, the critique of tradition is valuable; but carried to extremes it becomes a scorn of the past *per se*. The anchorage of interest in supposed "principles of human nature" can lead to the dismissal of the individual event as accidental.

When Vico phrased the idea of a fundamental value of every age (*Scienza Nuova*, 1725–44) and its function in preparing for the next, he emphasized the development of the historical series as a whole, posing the problem of its continuities and thus modifying the predominant interest merely in the "goal" of history. Winckelmann's study of Greek art left no doubt that there were periods of development which were unsurpassed in their own way, hence, not to be dismissed as mere stages in the progress of reason. Similarly, studies such as those of Justus Möser (1720–1794) lifted the examination of the locale to an importance equaling the study of universal human nature. Johann Gottfried von Herder (1744–1803) is particularly important in that he signalized a general shift from the historical interpretations of the Enlightenment to those of Romanticism. The principle of development became more important than "progress," and it was applied to cultural history (*Auch eine Philosophie der Geschichte zur Bildung der Menschheit* (1774); *Ideen zur Philosophie der Geschichte der Menschheit* (1784–91). Emphasis was on the whole historical series and not simply on the presumed "goal" of history.

As the new historical spirit fully emerged under the influence of the *Sturm und Drang* movement, new interests came to the fore. In contrast to the old emphasis on reason was the new appreciation of the role of the irrational in human affairs. Tradition was no longer dismissed out of hand as the irrational residue of the dead past, but treated with respect. Nationalism and the concept of the folk soul emerged as unifying concepts in place of universal human nature and the ideal of humanity. As already noted, development rather than progress became the watchword of the new history. In his concept of history as the realization of the absolute spirit in its dialectical struggle for freedom, Hegel summed up one aspect of the romantic theory of history.

Throughout the eighteenth and nineteenth centuries continuous gains in methodological exactness were registered. Editions of source materials were increasingly published during the eighteenth century. New historical tools were being forged. Philosophical criticism was applied to historical sources (Friedrich August Wolf, *Prolegomena ad Homerum*, 1795; Barthold Georg Niebuhr, *Römische Geschichte*, 1811–1812). The history of law was established as a special discipline (Savigny and Eichhorn). The synthesis of Enlightenment and romantic methods was secured and the establishment of the facts elevated to the status of the foremost historical duty (Leopold von Ranke, *Zur Kritik neuerer Geschichtschreiber*, 1824). The nation was proposed as a unit of historical analysis, particularly by Heinrich von Treitschke, *Deutsche Geschichte im neunzehnten Jahrhundert* (1879–94). The history of science was contemplated as a special discipline (Ranke) and social and intellectual history brilliantly projected (Jakob Burckhardt, *Die Kultur der Renaissance in Italien*, 1860). Meanwhile the interrelation between special social institutions was brought under investigation (as in the studies of Henry Thomas Buckle, *History of Civilization in England*, 1857–61, and in the work of Karl Marx).

Historiography and Sociology

This thumbnail sketch of the development of historical thought calls attention to two things. (1) Historical thought itself becomes fully possible only to the degree that objective secular knowledge of the actual world is possible and desirable. Historical thought appeared in the Greek world under the same general conditions that favored the discovery of the rational proof. Also, in parallel fashion, it went into comparative decline in the Roman world, where rhetorical and patriotic motives were dominant. Its deepest eclipse occurred in the medieval world, where the historical forgery testified to the domination of didacticism and propaganda over objectivity. It revived under the same circumstances as the rise of science, and indeed reached full development only as scientific history. (2) More important in the present context is the fact that to the degree that history makes its appearance and is extended to various areas of human life, an assemblage of dependable information about society occurs. Herodotus is sometimes called "the father of anthropology," and with justice: he recorded much of the varied data that an ethnological science finds indispensable. Or when Voltaire, in his *Essai sur les mœurs* (1754), attacked Bossuet's conception of history for its limitations and its reliance on miraculous procedure, he was performing two tasks essential to social science: (a) requiring dependable data, and (b) demanding a broader reporting of facts of social life than those narrowly relevant to a special theology.

Along the same lines, the movement from Enlightenment to romantic conceptions of history was also relevant for social science. A defective reporting of those social facts that some special philosophy would describe as "irrational" can hardly serve the full understanding of institutional phenomena. So, too, a social science will require information on the areas of social life isolated by romanticism: the developmental, the traditional, the local, and all the special cultural and institutional phenomena.

Philosophy, in its preoccupation with the good life, had traditionally been more concerned with the systematic cultivation of attitudes toward the world and man than with the patient assemblage of facts and the task of verifying them. In this last respect, the historian had more to teach the incipient sociologist than did the philosopher. (This is not to say, of course, that the system-building of the philosophers — a pioneering effort of thought — was not also essential for the growth of science.)

Philosophy and history together presided over the birth of sociology, as may be seen from the work of Auguste Comte (1798–1857), who has often been described as "the father of sociology." [11] Comte presented sociology as a polemic against traditional philosophy, which he denounced as "metaphysical." The very term "positivism" identifying the new field was intended to express this opposition. At the same time, the new "positive philosophy," or as Comte characterized it later, "sociology," relied directly upon history for its subject matter. The task of the new science was to establish laws of the regularities of social events. There was no doubt in Comte's mind that these events were supplied by history. "The historical comparison of the consecutive states of humanity is not only the chief scientific device of the new political philosophy. Its . . . rational development constitutes the substratum of the science, in whatever is essential to it." [12] The historians'

[11] Comte's work is discussed in detail in Chapter 3.
[12] *The Positive Philosophy of Auguste Comte*, freely translated and condensed by Harriet Martineau (London: J. Chapman, 1853), Vol. 2, p. 105.

The fundamental object of science is the advancement of empirical knowledge, the extension of knowledge of the facts of the actual world. The rational proof of philosophy is subordinated to this primary task of extending empirical information. With the advent of science, the mathematical achievements of philosophy cease to be an "end" of knowledge and become instead a means of empirical investigation. Only after this development is the ideal again restored of forming empirical concepts into logically closed systems.

Thus, from its earliest beginnings, science differed from philosophy in that it endeavored to find a systematic procedure for extending *empirical* knowledge, a general method of verifying statements about the empirical world. Only by generalizing the procedures of empirical proof could science hope to achieve the sort of autonomy which had been granted to philosophy by the discovery of the rational proof. Eventually such a procedure was found in the *experiment*, which performed the service for science which the rational proof had performed for philosophy. Science was thus emancipated from philosophy by a discovery equivalent to the one which had earlier freed philosophy from theology.

The interplay between thought, observation, activity, and thought once again, in such a way as to verify one's generalizations about the empirical world, was not new in human history. It has occurred in all societies, however primitive. The success of this movement is a measure of the progress of civilization. However, the transformation of the process into a conscious procedure is quite another matter. Isolated experiments are reported from the earliest days of Greek philosophy. But even the nearest approach to the modern scientist in the Greek world shows that science was still far in the future.

The closest foreshadowing of the modern synthesis of experiment and mathematics is provided by Archimedes of Syracuse (287–212 B.C.). The interplay between conceptualization and observation is illustrated by the principle that bears his name — that a body floating in a liquid displaces an amount equal to its weight. The principle is said to have occurred to Archimedes in his bath — showing the leap from observation to conceptualization. The trip back from conceptualization to manipulation is shown by his extension of this principle to the notion that equal weights of metals of different alloy will displace varying volumes of a liquid. Archimedes had, in fact, much of a scientist's delight in controlling things: he is said to have invented a screw for raising water for mining operations and irrigation; he moved great weights by systems of pulleys; he devised military equipment for the defense of Syracuse; he made great use of cut-out models in the service of his mathematical deductions. Furthermore, he employed experimental procedure, as shown in his use of the method of exhaustion in the measurement of a circle, leading to the discovery of the relation between the surface and volume of a sphere and its circumscribing cylinder within narrow tolerance limits. He proved that the ratio of the circumference to the

work was thus fundamental for sociology. For this reason Comte tried to promote the establishment of professorships of history in the French universities. His polemic against traditional philosophy, however, should not obscure an important fact: his basic point of view was derived from philosophy, and the new field was thought of as a philosophic movement.

Not only did the disciplines of philosophy and history preside over the birth of sociology, but in the early days of the development of sociology, when problems of a theoretical or methodological type arose for the new field, sociologists frequently turned to these disciplines for help. An extensive literature has developed on the interrelation of the fields; Dilthey and Rickert may be taken to illustrate the reaction of philosophy and history upon sociology at a later stage.

Dilthey, Windelband, and Rickert

To Wilhelm Dilthey (1833–1911), Comte's conceptions of society and human history seemed rather crassly materialistic. At the same time, he accepted the idea that empirical knowledge of historical materials is possible, and that these materials are precisely cultural in nature. He set about to examine the nature of knowledge in cultural history (*Geistesgeschichte*).

The materials of history are acts of spiritual agents, but these, contrary to Comte's assertion, are not understandable on the basis of the methods of natural science. Knowledge in history occurs through the isolation of spiritual forms (*geistige Gebilde*) present in cultural phenomena. The common ideas, feelings, and aims of a period of mankind constitute the spirit of an age (*Zeitgeist*), which determines the attitudes of men. The study of a historical period consists in the analysis of the structural system present in its various tendencies, discovering what these tendencies have in common and how they combine. The common element is the peculiar essence (*Eigenwesen*) of the period. The concepts which it expresses will apply generally throughout the period. These are historical categories.

In life the relation of whole to part is not mathematical but "meaningful." Meaning provides the relation between whole and part whenever this relation is grasped. The meaning of life episodes is determined by memories and future possibilities. The task of historical understanding is the grasp of meaningful relations between whole and part, between the elements of experience and the desires that inform them. In history, where we pass from the meaning of elements of our own experience to the experience of others as embodied not only in written texts but in all forms of expression, we utilize the various outer or external signs of activities as devices for inferring the inner meanings behind them.

Thus the comprehension of immediate experience of life is supplemented by "understanding," which grasps the nature of life through its external manifestations. The method of understanding consists in the act of thought moving from external forms (objectifications of life) to inner reality. This is done by "re-living"; such re-living consists in the imaginative reconstruc-

tion of another's experience in terms of one's own and passing to it by analogical inference. The method of history thus becomes a kind of empathic
technique.

When sociologists began to experience difficulties with their theories and
methods, one group turned to the discussions of Dilthey and his associates
for guidance. However, the effect of accepting Dilthey's formulations would
apparently have involved the abandonment of sociology as a natural science
and the fusion of it with history and the humanities. One would thus, it
seemed, be forced to abandon not only positivism but the science itself.
This was hardly a view to go unchallenged. The leaders of the opposition
to this view were Wilhelm Windelband (1848–1915) and particularly Heinrich Rickert (1863–1936). Both of these men, while admitting that the
sociology of Comte was inadequate, raised serious criticisms of Dilthey's
analysis, and the relation between sociology and history had to be re-
examined.

Windelband, a major German philosopher of the nineteenth century, assumed, with Dilthey, that the task of philosophy is to find the meaning of
life. This task, he maintained, is accomplished in the discovery of universally
valid norms of pure reason, embodied in human activities and actualized in
history. Their actualization in history is studied by the historical sciences
(*Geschichtswissenschaften*). The two fundamental ways of dealing with subject matter are by laying down laws (in which case knowledge is *nomothetic*)
or by describing individual facts (in which case knowledge is *idiographic*).
Natural science is a nomothetic type of inquiry; history is idiographic.

Dilthey had found the materials of history to be psychological, and in a
psychological method he located the procedure of history. However, Windelband argues, psychology is a nomothetic rather than an idiographic discipline. The methods of all nomothetic disciplines are similar, and psychology must be returned to natural science. And if this is done, it is quite
inappropriate for history.

The problem for historical understanding is found by Rickert in the determination of individuality. Historical knowledge attempts to grasp the meaning of a particular incident in its concreteness and individuality. The criterion
of indivisibility is needed as the source of its uniqueness. The historical
task is to trace the relation of individuals to values.

If one were to follow Dilthey, the problem of "meaningful" interpretations comes into prominence and the method of "empathic understanding" is
required. Moreover, a sharp division is accepted between the cultural and
natural sciences. If one follows Rickert, the results are different. Psychology
and sociology are conceived as sciences. But now the lines are sharply
drawn between science and history as alternative and antithetical forms of
thought. To the extent that sociology insists on being a science but accepts
the conceptual formulations of Rickert, it may well be set on the road toward abstract formalism.

The time was to come, as we have said, when sociology would experience

theoretical difficulties, and Dilthey and Rickert serve as starting points for
distinct schools of sociological theory.

Art, Natural Science, and Sociology

Like folk wisdom, sociology aspires to generalization about social events; unlike folk wisdom, it seeks abstract knowledge not bound by the normative
patterns of a local time and place. Like religious thought, sociology aspires
to abstract knowledge; unlike religious thought, it is neither metaphysically inclined nor subordinate to sacred institutions. Like philosophy,
sociology aspires to a body of knowledge resting on intrinsic rather than
extrinsic standards of validity — a knowledge formed into logically consistent wholes; unlike philosophy, it is empirical rather than social-ethical (as
in the case of traditional philosophy). Like history, sociology aspires to empirical knowledge of social events; unlike history, it aspires to a knowledge
of the general rather than the unique, for, when all is said and done, sociology is a scientific organization of knowledge.

But sociology did not immediately depart from traditional philosophy as
one of the special sciences. In time, it was to emerge and find a body of
data ready made in history, but this occurred only in an atmosphere in
which science was already a going concern. The separation of sociology from
philosophy was long anticipated by the departure of natural science therefrom. In fact, it was the great success attendant upon the separation of
physical science from philosophy that provided a major motive for the establishment of independent social science. For this reason, special interest
attaches to the factors promoting the independence of physical science.

As has already been indicated, the first step toward science was taken
when Greek philosophy discovered the rational proof. The logic of Aristotle,
however fragmentary from the standpoint of contemporary logic, represented
an important beginning, for, together with Euclidean geometry, it was bearer
of the ideal of a rationally organized world of thought. But Greek philosophy was primarily carried on by a stratum of thinkers remote from the
workaday world. Moreover, the spirit of empirical investigation declined
precisely with the rise of moral concerns. Nevertheless, the acquisition of
the rational proof permitted philosophy to acquire an autonomy, a self-
determination, which facilitated its separation from theology. When the
truth-establishing function was located in the thought process itself, no institutional hierarchy was required to fix the truth. Mythological, theological,
and magical types of thought were thoroughly undermined by the self-
correcting power of the new philosophy. Furthermore, this same autonomy
of thought was simultaneously being developed in the area of mathematics,
which was to become a fundamental tool of science. All this was transmitted directly on to science, which retains as a basic ideal of its own the
formation of its concepts as nearly as possible into logically closed systems.
Nevertheless, the point of gravity of science lies elsewhere.

diameter of a circle was between $3\frac{1}{7}$ and $3\frac{10}{71}$. From burning mirrors to weight-throwing machines for warfare, to attempts to determine the angle suspended by the sun's disk at the eye, an experimental mentality is evident.

But Archimedes was under the spell of the rational proof, and he never assigned to experiment anything like the importance which he attributed to rational demonstration. From a fascination with the lever, his interest quickly passed to the attempt to deduce its properties from a minimum number of axioms.[13] He attempted to deduce his observations on the relative density of bodies from the concept of a fluid as a substance yielding to the smallest shearing stress. Orderly logical deduction from a limited number of postulates was the aim of thought. Above all else, Archimedes minimized the importance of experiment. For Greek thought, science was remarkably close in possibility; and yet, psychologically, it was remote. Thus, for the person most completely approaching the modern synthesis, the elevation of experiment into a general method of thought was most completely out of the question. To achieve science, the enormous generalization of experimental procedure and its elevation to a position of prestige were required.

Science and Art

This increase of experimentation in prestige and the generalization of it into a rule of empirical procedure occurred in the workshops of the Renaissance artists. Both the social role of the artist and the nature of his activity were factors in the process. Art mediated the transition from philosophy to science.

The philosophers of ancient Greece were either eminent men or tutors in the households of eminent families. Their connection with the workaday world was indirect. The artist, on the other hand, is basically a craftsman — however high a value society may place on his type of craftsmanship. The artist finds himself in the center of an activity, operating with a material medium: metals, stone, wood, leather, glass, paint, sound.

Moreover, not only does artistic activity require a high level of skill; it also demands a novelty of product. Here, in contrast to many other areas of life, *originality tends to be rewarded rather than punished*.[14] To the degree to which art becomes a "play" activity or an "aesthetic" activity, it becomes peculiarly uncommitted or "free" from any limitations other than those it establishes itself. A combination of dedication and activity without external commitment tends to emerge. When his capacity to surprise and delight are rewarded, innovation may become one of the artist's fundamental goals. The Renaissance artist was thus inspired to experiment systematically with anything and everything the eye could see or the hand could touch.

There is no better illustration than Leonardo da Vinci (1452–1519). The

---

[13] He suggested two: (1) that equal weights placed at equal distances from the point of support balance, and (2) equal weights at unequal distances do not.

[14] At least this seems to be the case whenever artistic activity escapes from magical and religious contexts.

son of a lawyer and a peasant girl, Leonardo was educated by his father and served in a number of courts, including Florence, Milan, and Rome. He was a painter, sculptor, engineer, architect, physicist, and biologist among other things. Of all persons of the ancient world, it was Archimedes (not Aristotle) who fired Leonardo's imagination, and he noted the names of friends and patrons who could procure copies of Archimedes' work for him.[15] However, while sharing Archimedes' great respect for mathematics, Leonardo arrived at a very different estimate of its place and importance. Mathematics, he thought, concerned mental materials and provided certainty in its realm. Experience is another matter. For Leonardo, experience also potentially provided certainty. Experience, he argued, is never at fault. Only judgment is in error. Experience offers a realm of universal causation. Experiment is the procedure for determining causes. Once we understand the causes, we no longer have need for experiment.[16] Experiment is lifted by Leonardo to a level of importance parallel to that of mathematics. It is the only way of attaining certain knowledge of the actual world. One is not, under such circumstances, to be surprised by the fact that Leonardo's notebooks read like one continuous life-long collection of laboratory notes. Experiment after experiment is described. We learn that if we place the second finger under the tip of the third in a manner such that the whole of the nail is visible on the far side, any round object that is touched by the two fingers will seem double. To discover the north side of a magnet, fill a large tub with water and set the magnet floating in a wooden cup; it will turn toward the north star. A drop of dew with its perfect round affords an opportunity to observe the various functions of the watery sphere. A concave mirror, although cold when it receives rays of the fire, reflects them with undiminished heat. Experiments are recorded on how to measure the thinness of water, on making fire with mercury and a siphon, on flowing liquids, fire, waves in water and air. Innumerable experiments are described and inventions proposed. There are inventions for drying up the marsh at Piombino; for a clock showing hours, minutes, and seconds; for measuring how great a distance one goes in an hour with the current of the wind; for learning from the quality and density of air when it will rain; for reckoning mileage at sea; for an apparatus designed to lift weights with ropes and pulleys; for descending below the surface of the water; for an alarm clock and a drilling machine; for making concrete; for constructing a bellows without leather; for producing a wind, and so on.

A thoroughgoing spirit of scientific naturalism pervades all Leonardo's work: he knew the experimental impossibility of perpetual motion; he developed Archimedes' concept of the pressure of fluids; he traced analogies in wave theory in water, sound, and light; he treated the realm of astronomy, naturalistically conceiving the celestial world as a sort of machine; he

15 This interest in Archimedes was not peculiar to Leonardo. Some of Archimedes' works were published in Latin by Tartaglia at the time.
16 Edward McCurdy, *The Notebooks of Leonardo da Vinci* (New York: George Braziller, 1956), pp. 64 ff.

work was thus fundamental for sociology. For this reason Comte tried to promote the establishment of professorships of history in the French universities. His polemic against traditional philosophy, however, should not obscure an important fact: his basic point of view was derived from philosophy, and the new field was thought of as a philosophic movement.

Not only did the disciplines of philosophy and history preside over the birth of sociology, but in the early days of the development of sociology, when problems of a theoretical or methodological type arose for the new field, sociologists frequently turned to these disciplines for help. An extensive literature has developed on the interrelation of the fields; Dilthey and Rickert may be taken to illustrate the reaction of philosophy and history upon sociology at a later stage.

Dilthey, Windelband, and Rickert

To Wilhelm Dilthey (1833–1911), Comte's conceptions of society and human history seemed rather crassly materialistic. At the same time, he accepted the idea that empirical knowledge of historical materials is possible, and that these materials are precisely cultural in nature. He set about to examine the nature of knowledge in cultural history (*Geistesgeschichte*).

The materials of history are acts of spiritual agents, but these, contrary to Comte's assertion, are not understandable on the basis of the methods of natural science. Knowledge in history occurs through the isolation of spiritual forms (*geistige Gebilde*) present in cultural phenomena. The common ideas, feelings, and aims of a period of mankind constitute the spirit of an age (*Zeitgeist*), which determines the attitudes of men. The study of a historical period consists in the analysis of the structural system present in its various tendencies, discovering what these tendencies have in common and how they combine. The common element is the peculiar essence (*Eigenwesen*) of the period. The concepts which it expresses will apply generally throughout the period. These are historical categories.

In life the relation of whole to part is not mathematical but "meaningful." Meaning provides the relation between whole and part whenever this relation is grasped. The meaning of life episodes is determined by memories and future possibilities. The task of historical understanding is the grasp of meaningful relations between whole and part, between the elements of experience and the desires that inform them. In history, where we pass from the meaning of elements of our own experience to the experience of others as embodied not only in written texts but in all forms of expression, we utilize the various outer or external signs of activities as devices for inferring the inner meanings behind them.

Thus the comprehension of immediate experience of life is supplemented by "understanding," which grasps the nature of life through its external manifestations. The method of understanding consists in the act of thought moving from external forms (objectifications of life) to inner reality. This is done by "re-living"; such re-living consists in the imaginative reconstruc-

tion of another's experience in terms of one's own and passing to it by analogical inference. The method of history thus becomes a kind of empathic
technique.

When sociologists began to experience difficulties with their theories and
methods, one group turned to the discussions of Dilthey and his associates
for guidance. However, the effect of accepting Dilthey's formulations would
apparently have involved the abandonment of sociology as a natural science
and the fusion of it with history and the humanities. One would thus, it
seemed, be forced to abandon not only positivism but the science itself.
This was hardly a view to go unchallenged. The leaders of the opposition
to this view were Wilhelm Windelband (1848–1915) and particularly Heinrich Rickert (1863–1936). Both of these men, while admitting that the
sociology of Comte was inadequate, raised serious criticisms of Dilthey's
analysis, and the relation between sociology and history had to be re-
examined.

Windelband, a major German philosopher of the nineteenth century, assumed, with Dilthey, that the task of philosophy is to find the meaning of
life. This task, he maintained, is accomplished in the discovery of universally
valid norms of pure reason, embodied in human activities and actualized in
history. Their actualization in history is studied by the historical sciences
(*Geschichtswissenschaften*). The two fundamental ways of dealing with subject matter are by laying down laws (in which case knowledge is *nomothetic*)
or by describing individual facts (in which case knowledge is *idiographic*).
Natural science is a nomothetic type of inquiry; history is idiographic.

Dilthey had found the materials of history to be psychological, and in a
psychological method he located the procedure of history. However, Windelband argues, psychology is a nomothetic rather than an idiographic discipline. The methods of all nomothetic disciplines are similar, and psychology must be returned to natural science. And if this is done, it is quite
inappropriate for history.

The problem for historical understanding is found by Rickert in the determination of individuality. Historical knowledge attempts to grasp the meaning of a particular incident in its concreteness and individuality. The criterion
of indivisibility is needed as the source of its uniqueness. The historical
task is to trace the relation of individuals to values.

If one were to follow Dilthey, the problem of "meaningful" interpretations comes into prominence and the method of "empathic understanding" is
required. Moreover, a sharp division is accepted between the cultural and
natural sciences. If one follows Rickert, the results are different. Psychology
and sociology are conceived as sciences. But now the lines are sharply
drawn between science and history as alternative and antithetical forms of
thought. To the extent that sociology insists on being a science but accepts
the conceptual formulations of Rickert, it may well be set on the road toward abstract formalism.

The time was to come, as we have said, when sociology would experience theoretical difficulties, and Dilthey and Rickert serve as starting points for distinct schools of sociological theory.

Art, Natural Science, and Sociology

Like folk wisdom, sociology aspires to generalization about social events; unlike folk wisdom, it seeks abstract knowledge not bound by the normative patterns of a local time and place. Like religious thought, sociology aspires to abstract knowledge; unlike religious thought, it is neither metaphysically inclined nor subordinate to sacred institutions. Like philosophy, sociology aspires to a body of knowledge resting on intrinsic rather than extrinsic standards of validity — a knowledge formed into logically consistent wholes; unlike philosophy, it is empirical rather than social-ethical (as in the case of traditional philosophy). Like history, sociology aspires to empirical knowledge of social events; unlike history, it aspires to a knowledge of the general rather than the unique, for, when all is said and done, sociology is a scientific organization of knowledge.

But sociology did not immediately depart from traditional philosophy as one of the special sciences. In time, it was to emerge and find a body of data ready made in history, but this occurred only in an atmosphere in which science was already a going concern. The separation of sociology from philosophy was long anticipated by the departure of natural science therefrom. In fact, it was the great success attendant upon the separation of physical science from philosophy that provided a major motive for the establishment of independent social science. For this reason, special interest attaches to the factors promoting the independence of physical science.

As has already been indicated, the first step toward science was taken when Greek philosophy discovered the rational proof. The logic of Aristotle, however fragmentary from the standpoint of contemporary logic, represented an important beginning, for, together with Euclidean geometry, it was bearer of the ideal of a rationally organized world of thought. But Greek philosophy was primarily carried on by a stratum of thinkers remote from the workaday world. Moreover, the spirit of empirical investigation declined precisely with the rise of moral concerns. Nevertheless, the acquisition of the rational proof permitted philosophy to acquire an autonomy, a self-determination, which facilitated its separation from theology. When the truth-establishing function was located in the thought process itself, no institutional hierarchy was required to fix the truth. Mythological, theological, and magical types of thought were thoroughly undermined by the self-correcting power of the new philosophy. Furthermore, this same autonomy of thought was simultaneously being developed in the area of mathematics, which was to become a fundamental tool of science. All this was transmitted directly on to science, which retains as a basic ideal of its own the formation of its concepts as nearly as possible into logically closed systems. Nevertheless, the point of gravity of science lies elsewhere.

The fundamental object of science is the advancement of empirical knowledge, the extension of knowledge of the facts of the actual world. The rational proof of philosophy is subordinated to this primary task of extending empirical information. With the advent of science, the mathematical achievements of philosophy cease to be an "end" of knowledge and become instead a means of empirical investigation. Only after this development is the ideal again restored of forming empirical concepts into logically closed systems.

Thus, from its earliest beginnings, science differed from philosophy in that it endeavored to find a systematic procedure for extending *empirical* knowledge, a general method of verifying statements about the empirical world. Only by generalizing the procedures of empirical proof could science hope to achieve the sort of autonomy which had been granted to philosophy by the discovery of the rational proof. Eventually such a procedure was found in the *experiment,* which performed the service for science which the rational proof had performed for philosophy. Science was thus emancipated from philosophy by a discovery equivalent to the one which had earlier freed philosophy from theology.

The interplay between thought, observation, activity, and thought once again, in such a way as to verify one's generalizations about the empirical world, was not new in human history. It has occurred in all societies, however primitive. The success of this movement is a measure of the progress of civilization. However, the transformation of the process into a conscious procedure is quite another matter. Isolated experiments are reported from the earliest days of Greek philosophy. But even the nearest approach to the modern scientist in the Greek world shows that science was still far in the future.

The closest foreshadowing of the modern synthesis of experiment and mathematics is provided by Archimedes of Syracuse (287–212 B.C.). The interplay between conceptualization and observation is illustrated by the principle that bears his name — that a body floating in a liquid displaces an amount equal to its weight. The principle is said to have occurred to Archimedes in his bath — showing the leap from observation to conceptualization. The trip back from conceptualization to manipulation is shown by his extension of this principle to the notion that equal weights of metals of different alloy will displace varying volumes of a liquid. Archimedes had, in fact, much of a scientist's delight in controlling things: he is said to have invented a screw for raising water for mining operations and irrigation; he moved great weights by systems of pulleys; he devised military equipment for the defense of Syracuse; he made great use of cut-out models in the service of his mathematical deductions. Furthermore, he employed experimental procedure, as shown in his use of the method of exhaustion in the measurement of a circle, leading to the discovery of the relation between the surface and volume of a sphere and its circumscribing cylinder within narrow tolerance limits. He proved that the ratio of the circumference to the

thought the earth could be interpreted naturally, and the presence of fossils was taken as indicating that areas now dry were once covered by ocean; he dissected a number of human bodies, and made numerous anatomical drawings; he anticipated the theory of circulation of the blood; he knew how an image is formed on the retina of the eye. Though Leonardo was clearly one of the outstanding men of all time, his activities were not a departure from his day.

Science Outside the Artists' Workshop

The new faith in the possibility that experience could yield dependable knowledge if only method were sound diffused from the workshops of the artists to one area after another. Copernicus (1473–1543) revived the theories of Euphantus and Aristarchus from antiquity, maintaining that the earth revolves on its axis daily and around the sun yearly. He established the heliocentric theory, and Giordano Bruno was martyred for this and other opinions (1600). The study of animals was re-opened in the sixteenth century, and the science of ichthyology was founded. Theophrastus von Hohenheim, or Paracelsus (1493?–1541), broke away from the orthodox (Galenic) school of medicine, and opened the way to the application of chemistry to medicine. New studies in mineralogy and geology were opened by Agricola (1494–1555) and Jan Baptista van Helmont (1577–1644). Modern anatomy and physiology got under way with the work of Jean Fernel (1497–1558) and Andreas Vesalius (1514–1564). Vesalius particularly had seen many dissections, and extended knowledge of bones, veins, and abdominal organs. These developments led to the discovery of the circulation of the blood by William Harvey (1578–1657). Using the compound microscope (invented about 1590), Marcello Malpighi of Bologna (1628–1694) made numerous discoveries about tissues. Tycho Brahe (1546–1601) and Johannes Kepler (1571–1630) made systematic new observations in astronomy, providing — especially in Kepler's three laws of planetary motion — the theories and evidence that laid the foundation for Newton's great synthesis.

Galileo Models the Scientific Role

The full transition from art to natural science is evident in the work of Galileo Galilei (1564–1642). He invented a thermometer. From stories of a glass which magnified distant objects, he drew on his knowledge of refraction and constructed a telescope, observing the surface of the moon, and hitherto invisible stars. He experimented extensively with inclined planes and established the science of dynamics on an experimental and mathematical foundation. He studied the composition of forces, the pressure of liquids. In all his careful studies, Galileo constantly aimed at the establishment of exact laws. It is not difficult to see why he is often treated as the first modern scientist.[17]

[17] See, for example, Bertrand Russell, *The Scientific Outlook* (New York: W. W. Norton, 1931), Chapter 1.

Strictly speaking, of course, Galileo was not the first scientist. The extension of the scientific attitude to almost every conceivable area was better illustrated by Leonardo. And many of Galileo's predecessors and contemporaries not only observed and invented instruments for observation, but experimented as well. Galileo's importance lies not in his temporal priority but in the completeness or distinctness with which he represents the new scientific role. He is the very paradigm of the scientist. He demonstrates the value of systematic, continuous experimentation with limited aims, simultaneously motivated by the ideal of demonstrating mathematical relations between events and forming his ideas into a logically closed system. Copernicus and Kepler had shown that the motion of the heavenly bodies could be expressed mathematically. Galileo set out to discover the mathematical relations holding for falling bodies. Noting that bodies fall with increasing speed, he hypothesized that the increase is proportionate to the distance. Since measurement of bodies in free fall was beyond the scope of the available instruments, he designed special situations for studying slower rates of fall in inclined planes. He experimentally demonstrated that speed is proportionate to the time of fall. He also proved that a body running down an inclined plane will rise to an equivalent height on another except insofar as checked by friction, and that a body running down a plane will continue indefinitely in motion on a horizontal unless checked by friction. He proved that the swing of a pendulum is independent of the displacement, and that gravity increases the speed of the bob by equal amounts in equal times. Throughout this work, Galileo's aim was to arrive at the statement of the exact mathematical relations involved.

Newtonian Physics Models the Scientific Theory

If Galileo is the paradigm of the new man of science, the great achievement of Newtonian physics is the paradigm of the new scientific knowledge. Kepler had established his three laws of motion. Galileo had advanced a theory of the tides, and had developed some of the mathematical relations discoverable in motion. Sir Isaac Newton's *Principia* (1687) fused the two major elements of science — rational proof and experimental-observational evidence. From the three laws of motion and the law of gravitation, the movement of the solar system was explained by a system of mathematical deduction. So impressive was this logical schema that no fundamental criticism was carried through until Ernst Mach (1883) examined its logical structure and pointed out that Newton's definitions of mass and force were logically circular. But Newton had established the validity of terrestrial mechanics for celestial spaces. He annihilated, once and for all, the ancient and medieval view that the heavenly bodies are divine. In the course of his labors, like Leibniz, he invented infinitesimal calculus. He established the binomial theorem in mathematics. In astronomy he founded lunar theory. He also established hydrodynamics and the theory of the propagation of waves. Even his work in optics, had he done nothing else, was sufficient to place him in the forefront of science. But more than anything else, Newton's work emerged as a paradigm of organized scientific theory, much as Galileo supplied the paradigm of the scientific role.

Experimentation was therefore first established in the activities of the artists — activities which were peculiarly free and designed specifically for the creation of the aesthetically new. This area had invited systematization of the procedure by which the human mind moved into the unknown. The relevance of this for science was direct, for science itself can be conveniently described as a kind of *strategy of adventure*. It takes little insight to determine why the extension of experimentalism could be made from the workshop of the Renaissance artist to the physical world. For one thing, there was a coincidence of activity. Leonardo, like many of his contemporaries, was more than an artist. He was also an architect, engineer, and military expert. On occasion he sought work primarily as a civil and fortification engineer rather than as an artist. Techniques of procedure so useful in art were inevitably tried on other things.

But the reasons for the extension of experimentalism from art to physical nature are more than external and accidental. One could expect the extension of experimentalism only into areas relatively unencumbered by magical, religious, or traditional restrictions. Leonardo himself saw that unquestioned authority puts an end to thought. He suggested that whenever, in a discussion, authority is adduced, reliance is being placed on the memory rather than the intellect. He scorned the activities of the priests so far as they encouraged superstition and trade in miracles. At the same time, he recognized that religion claimed an unquestioned interpretation of the spiritual. But Leonardo did not fail to perceive that his researches could come into conflict with scripture. At the conclusion of his attempt to develop a natural theory of the origin of life, he observed that he spoke not against the sacred books which contain the supreme truth.

The extension of experimentalism to the physical world could only occur because at the time art was relatively outside magical and religious control. However, once science had been established as a procedure for dealing with physical events, its further extension was to be expected. Psychologists have proved than even a rat running a maze so complicated that it could not possibly comprehend will retain the favorable trials and gradually dismiss the unfavorable, until its behavior reduces to something approaching maximum economy. A creature's habits represent generalizations of its responses imposing a common behavioral form on a variety of particular situations. Habits form advance organizations of potential response. Only when these do not work does the rather painful process of readjustment occur.

Hence, there is no mystery about the fact that, when experimentation is once established as a method of exploring the physical world, it may expand beyond this sphere. Rather, at this stage the problem becomes one of explaining why it does *not* continue to spread, for the growth of science becomes largely self-perpetuating, and only repeated failure or the appearance of counter forces strong enough to overcome its momentum can halt its advance.

The very persons most directly involved with science have been the first to perceive the forces that oppose it. This is to be expected. Leonardo saw the potential conflict between his theories of the natural origin of life and the scriptures, and made an appeasing gesture in the direction of religion. The scientific role was not only fully established with Galileo, but the fact that it was not a role without limits was made clear as well. Galileo became unpopular and his lectures were booed; Einstein was to have a similar experience in his lectures in Berlin. When Galileo invited the professors to look at Jupiter's moons through his telescope, they refused: Aristotle had said nothing of such. And toward the end of his life, Galileo was called before the Inquisition, and forced to recant. However, by the time the forces basically inimical to science were thoroughly awakened to the threat it represented, it was too late. Science had become linked to new social forces which it helped to implement.

The Dream of a Social Science Takes Shape

The importance of Francis Bacon (1561–1626), Lord Chancellor of England, was not in the extension of scientific results, but in the generalization of the scientific program to make it coextensive with thought itself. Also, he helped to popularize the scientific point of view. For Bacon, medieval theology ceased to be the center of thought. He attributed the backwardness of thinking to three things: (a) resistance from antiquity, (b) resistance from the prestige of thinkers important in the history of philosophy, and (c) resistance of public opinion.

With respect to antiquity, Bacon maintained that the opinion men have of it is of negligible importance. The old people of the world, he argued, are its true antiquity. We expect greater wisdom from older men than from younger men, because they have experienced more. This and only this is an antiquity of value. In modern times, Bacon indicated, distant journeys have become frequent and have revealed the nature of things in a manner casting new light upon philosophy. And surely it would be a disgrace to open the material world of sea, earth, and stars while the intellectual globe remains closed. The obstacles to thought represented by antiquity, authority, and popular opinion must be eliminated. Bacon urged that the full extension of the new method of experimentation would infinitely expand the power of man. He proposed a general program of recording all available facts and the performing of all feasible experiments. The tabulation of results, he thought, would permit the discovery of general laws holding between facts. The full mastery of nature and the betterment of mankind was visualized and the possibility of a social science was conceived.

Summary

The entire structure of human culture is learned, and maintained, by habit. Its infinite plasticity is matched only by its amazing tenacity, for in the unceasing cycle of birth, learning, and death of individuals, the continuous introduction of individuals into the countless little acts that constitute culture make it incredibly adaptable in minor things but glacial in its responses to major things.

With all historical time to develop in, sociology is only about a hundred years old. For hundreds of thousands of years before this, men learned and transmitted to their children all the knowledge necessary for stability and successful life. The things essential for a science of social life were partly assembled in the folk wisdom of human societies. Other materials were refined and organized by theology. But neither the time-bound ethos of folk society nor the ethico-religious ethos provides the conditions for the secular pursuit of social generalizations. A significant step toward a general social science was taken by philosophy, which made general knowledge of a secular type possible.

The Greeks, however, who took this step, never quite achieved a clear social science. Where naturalistic attitudes were present, as in the Greek atomists, they were not applied to social phenomena. Where social phenomena were studied, as with the Sophists, they were subordinated to ethical and didactic requirements. For this reason, the great contribution of the Greeks to social science remained indirect by way of the discovery and elaboration of the rational proof. The real beginnings of Western mathematics and logic were laid by them. These beginnings formed basic elements in the imperishable heritage of rationalism which ever after remained fundamental components in Western philosophy and one of the primary factors in the rise of Western science.

For further insight into the sources of sociology and social science, one must therefore turn to history, where the accumulation of objective historical data about society was carried through. The development of historiography was also, in part, a development of objective empirical methods for assembling and evaluating social materials. The playback of historiography into social science continued into the nineteenth century, when Dilthey and Rickert pioneered special schools of sociology.

But the impulse for a genuine social science was to come from science itself. The scientific point of view needed, it seems, to have first proved its value by gains in non-social areas. Thus, sociology took its early points of view from philosophy, its first materials were supplied by history, but the model for its emergence was provided by natural science. Sociology comes into being with the extension of the scientific method (pioneered in art and confirmed in its applications to the physical world) to the social world of man himself.

SELECTED BIBLIOGRAPHY

(In the selected bibliographies at the end of each chapter, only the most readily accessible editions of a few principle works have been included. More complete bibliographical information is contained in the various footnotes within the chapters.)

BARNES, HARRY ELMER, "The Development of Sociology," in Harry Elmer Barnes, Howard Becker, and Frances Bennett Becker (eds.), *Contemporary Social Theory*. New York: D. Appleton-Century, 1940. Pages 3–16.

BARNES, HARRY ELMER, and HOWARD BECKER, *Social Thought from Lore to Science*. Second edition. Washington, D.C.: Harren Press, 1952.

BOSKOFF, ALVIN, "From Social Thought to Sociological Theory," in Howard Becker and Alvin Boskoff (eds.), *Modern Sociological Theory*. New York: Dryden, 1957. Pages 3–34.

CAIRNS, HUNTINGTON, "Sociology and the Social Sciences," in Georges Gurvitch and Wilbert E. Moore (eds.), *Twentieth Century Sociology*. New York: Philosophical Library, 1945. Pages 3–19.

ELLWOOD, CHARLES A., *A History of Social Philosophy*. New York: Prentice-Hall, 1938. Pages 3–129.

HOUSE, FLOYD N., *The Range of Social Theory*. New York: Henry Holt, 1929.

KILZER, E., and E. J. ROSS, *Western Social Thought*. Milwaukee: Bruce, 1954. Pages 1–178.

SOROKIN, PITIRIM, *Contemporary Sociological Theories*. New York: Harper, 1928.

TIMASHEFF, NICHOLAS S., *Sociological Theory*. Revised edition. New York: Random House, 1957. Pages 1–12.

2

The Birth of the Social Sciences

AT SEVERAL STAGES IN THE HISTORY OF WESTERN THOUGHT, MOVEMENTS arose which might have led to the establishment of the social sciences. At the end of the Renaissance period, Bacon had already visualized the general possibilities of social science. Repeatedly thereafter the extension from physical to social science was to be made, and not, of course, simply as a result of Bacon's influence. A hundred years later, George Berkeley's adventure into social physics in his essay *De Motu* (1713) is typical. Berkeley traced analogies between the action of physical force in the material world and moral or psychological force among people. Just as the bodies of the solar system attract one another, so do the minds of men. The power of moral attraction increases, like physical force, the nearer men are to one another. Systems emerge for the same reason in each case. At the same time, just as there are centrifugal forces in physical nature preventing the fusion of the heavenly bodies into a single mass, the operation of individual passions and desires in men prevent the coalescence of human minds.

However, such efforts in the direction of social science were premature. At least two basic conditions had to be fulfilled before a genuine social science could emerge in its own right: (1) naturalism — the doctrine that all phenomena can be explained in terms of cause-and-effect sequences occurring in the world of nature — had to be established in the sphere of *social* phenomena, and (2) systems of ethical evaluation had to be at least bracketed (if not ignored altogether) to permit the examination of social relations apart from values. The fulfillment of these conditions had been

29

anticipated many times in history, as we have seen, for example, in the discussion of Leonardo; but it was not until the seventeenth and eighteenth centuries, with the achievements of the new natural sciences fresh at hand as a model, that a significant number of great minds began to converge on a general conception of reality which would remove mental and social phenomena from the realm of the supernatural and view them instead as elements in the world of nature — elements which could be studied in the same manner as physical events.

The movement embodying the seventeenth- and eighteenth-century idea that, without recourse to supernatural or traditional assistance, the human understanding is capable of mastering the world, is generally described as the *Enlightenment*. The point of view was applied to ethics, philosophy, religion, history, law, and politics. *Rationalism*, the view that individual and social life can be interpreted and regulated in terms of a set of self-evident principles directly available to reason, was one of the major doctrines of the Enlightenment. The term "Enlightenment" refers to the movement; the term "Rationalism" refers to this major point of view held during the Enlightenment.

Eighteenth-Century Rationalism

When we trace the individual social sciences to their eighteenth-century origins, we are led back to the same persons: Voltaire, Condorcet, Montesquieu, Goethe, Gibbon, Ferguson, and their colleagues — the great thinkers of the Enlightenment. These men did not all think alike, but in retrospect we can abstract a few core propositions which were more or less common to eighteenth-century rationalism and naturalism:

(1) *Reason is the universally distinguishing property of man.* Good sense, as Descartes put it, is of all things most widely distributed among men. (2) *Human nature is everywhere the same.* Hence, variations in manifest human nature must be due to local conditions, historical accidents, the persistence of tradition, or penetration of irrationalities into conduct. (3) *Institutions are made for men, rather than men for institutions.* Institutions are instrumental and are to be valued in terms of their capacity to promote human personality. Man, as Rousseau phrased it, was born free, yet everywhere we find him in chains. (4) *Progress is the central law of society.* The striking feature of human society, as Condorcet saw it, is the continuous achievement of the human mind. Each age, to be sure, has its characteristic errors and problems, but it is a stage in progress as well. Hence, man must turn his eyes away from the past toward the progress in the present and the goals of the future. (5) *The guiding ideal of human kind is the realization of humanity.*

These were the general ideas current among the thinkers of the Enlightenment. They provided the rational basis for the freeing of social thought from the area of the supernatural, and it was out of this intellectual matrix that the individual social sciences began to take shape.

The intellectuals of the Enlightenment operated largely outside the universities. They came primarily from upper-middle-class families. When they were from the aristocracy (Montesquieu, Condorcet), they belonged to its newer, semi-commercial wing. Moreover, many of them had terms of service as secretaries and tutors in upper-middle-class homes. On the whole, they were not "institutionalized intellectuals" in the sense that they owed their living or their loyalties to particular institutions. They were relatively free spokesmen of the progressive trends of their times.

By the eighteenth century the religious intensity that had accompanied the Reformation and the passions aroused in the course of the struggles between Protestantism and Catholicism had receded. The political anchorage of these religious formations had been effected. Religious and political peace had been at least temporarily achieved. By and large, the intellectuals were not religious leaders, though they were at times concerned with religious phenomena and usually found themselves on the side of those forces in their social orders which were happy to see an end to the religious wars. Swift's scornful attack on religious "enthusiasm" expressed a basic theme of theirs. The intellectuals were weary of religious intensity. Whether they denounced evangelicalism as vulgar and in bad taste or as menacing and socially dangerous, there was no doubt of their disapproval of emotional excess.

This is not to say that the intellectuals of the Enlightenment ignored religion — quite the contrary. The Enlightenment thinker often saw traditional religion as his most worthy opponent. At the same time, with few exceptions, he was not ready to give up religion. It is quite unfair to treat him as an atheist. One of the most interesting aspects of Enlightenment thought was the movement that expressed both these elements — opposition to traditional religion and the attempt to arrive at a new and more appropriate statement — the movement known as Deism.

Deism and the Naturalization of Social Life for Scientific Study

Deism numbered among its adherents such persons as Voltaire, the Encyclopedists, Hume, the Earl of Shaftesbury, Benjamin Franklin, Thomas Jefferson, and numerous other intellectuals in France, England, and North America. No complete unity was ever achieved, but there was fair agreement among them on a number of general points: (1) they attempted to establish religion on the basis of reason rather than authority; (2) they rejected tradition except insofar as it was "reasonable"; (3) they restricted the sphere occupied in religion by "revelation" and "miracles"; (4) they were sharply critical of religious dogmas difficult to justify rationally (such as the doctrine of the Trinity); (5) they believed that there is a set of universal religious notions implanted in the minds of all men; (6) they thought that God does not continually interfere in the natural processes of the world, but permits the natural laws to operate once he has set them in motion.

Such a religion, with its careful avoidance of emotional excess, is designed for the style of life of restrained, tactful salon intellectuals. The Earl of Shaftesbury's observation that God surely had at least as much sophistication as an eighteenth-century gentleman neatly called attention to this. Moreover, such a religion could hardly be without appeal to responsible political administrators who had experienced the rebellions of religious sectarians. A religion which appeals to all people and calls for the calm search for a common meeting ground in the religious experience of all men could hardly be completely devoid of appeal to the "enlightened despots" interested in peace within their national boundaries.

Deism was bound up intimately with its social setting. Moreover, it had important consequences in its own right. It represented the penetration of rationalism into the innermost sphere of religious thought.

Through such penetration the "naturalization" of this most crucial area of human experience was largely secured. And if even the most sacred of all spheres — that of man's spiritual life — was subject to natural laws, there was no reason why even it should not be subject to scientific study. Deism epitomized the decisive extension of naturalistic modes of thought into the farthest reaches of the social sphere.

The fact that a decisive step was being taken toward the naturalization of social life, preparing it for scientific study, was manifest not only in Deism but in many areas which at the time were lumped together under the name of "social philosophy" — areas which would form the nuclei of the later social sciences. We now turn to some of the more important of these areas.

Nationalism and Capitalism as Milieux for Social Science

Among the great events of modern times, the rise of the national state and of the capitalistic economic order stand out as fundamental. They represent movements which occurred over considerable time, with beginnings in the late Middle Ages. Both nationalism and capitalism are social formations requiring considerable reorganization of the previous patterns of social order. Neither could advance except at the expense of the previous order. This automatically meant that they could only develop at the expense of tradition. Every advance was marked by the disintegration of traditional institutions and customs, and this occurred in part because they enlisted creative ideas into their service.

The eighteenth century was a kind of culminating point on the road toward modern nationalism and capitalism. Politically the first stage in the establishment of the modern state had been completed. A temporary political balance and integration had been achieved by the "enlightened despots" such as Frederick the Great in Prussia, Catherine in Russia, and Joseph II in Austria. Economically, too, it was a period of "leveling off." The great voyages of discovery of the Renaissance had done their work. Quantities of precious metal which had been brought back, particularly by the Spaniards and Portuguese, were poured into the traffic of Europe, and these were partly responsible for a long-range secular inflationary trend. The effects of colonial traffic were being felt, and the importation of raw materials and the export of manufactured goods was becoming typical of the relation between colony and parent country. The commercial revolution, as a great stage on the way toward modern capitalism, had been accomplished. More-over, enlightened despotism and commerce were linked phenomena, for not only did the national states create "free trade" areas within the boundaries of their states, but they pursued policies, called "cameralistic" or "mercan-tilistic," of promoting a "favorable balance of trade" — the export of manu-factures or other materials and the import of money as a device of building up the cash reserves of the political economy. Thus the fortunes of com-merce and nationalism were linked.

Political Science. Nationalism and capitalism were powerful anti-traditional systems of force. When they achieved a temporary stability in the eighteenth century, they provided spheres of activity that invited rationalistic and nat-uralistic explanation. Political science and economics were well on the way toward separation as special social sciences.

In political spheres the application of the assumptions of naturalism and rationalism resulted in the attempt to "derive" the state from a contractual agreement terminating a "state of nature" represented by individuals in a pre-political condition. The state had to be "rational." It was produced by a conscious and rational decision. It was made to rest upon "human nature" and the powers of the individual in yielding "rational consent." All political rights and duties were to be derived from this source. ("We hold these truths to be self-evident. . . . governments are instituted among men, deriving their just powers from the consent of the governed. . . .") Any variance from this principle in the actual observed course of political con-duct could only be due to factors preventing the full manifestation of hu-man nature and reason. Political reform was required to eliminate social abuse and restore the domination of reason in political affairs.

Economic Science. Economic thought freed itself from the applied ethics of medieval theology even as economic activity freed itself from the rela-tions of a feudal subsistence economy. The provisional organization of economic thought made by cameralists and mercantilists was rather narrowly bound up with the economic requirements of the rising national states and failed to attain the level of full scientific generality. Mercantilism did raise questions about the nature and source of economic value and the technique of economic husbandry at a national level, but at the same time it made economics into a branch of applied politics, preventing the emergence of an autonomous science. Enlightenment economics, which began with the doc-trines of the physiocrats and evolved into classical economics, made the same break from the past and employed the same basic ideas as social-contract doctrine in political thought.

Physiocratic theory operated on the assumption that economic behavior is subject to natural laws. Economic motivation is only a special aspect of universal human nature. Everyone pursues his self-interest and employs his reason to this end; hence the same regularities are displayed in economic conduct. Economic behavior is directed toward the increase of one's wealth. A most fundamental question is the source of new wealth (value). This can only be agriculture, for it alone, among human activities, constantly supplies new products, the consumption of which sustains and increases life. Other human activities merely change the form of location of true values or add nothing in the way of basic economic values to society: they can be thought of only as parasitical. The state, particularly, with its lawyers, administrators, and bureaucrats is composed of economic parasites. This may well be a component in the enormous economic irrationality that emerges whenever the state touches politics. Granted that taxes are necessary, they are rational only to the degree that they touch the production of new values. All taxes other than those on agricultural production are irrational, and as far as the relations of the state to agriculture, only a *laissez-faire* policy is legitimate — a policy of political hands off, permitting economic phenomena to obey their natural laws. Adam Smith took such reflections contained in the works of Quesnay, Turgot, and other physiocrats and generalized them into the foundations of classical economics.

Social Geography. A third sphere of social life in which the Enlightenment moved toward social science is illustrated by the work of Montesquieu in *De l'esprit des lois* (1748). If one believes that political and economic behavior obey natural laws resting on a universal human nature and a common faculty of reason, one can hardly observe the actual conduct of human kind without being faced by an important decision. In actual fact, human conduct is not as uniform as such theory would assume. Thus, one must either reject the theory or undertake radical extensions of it. Montesquieu was an intelligent observer. He was quite unwilling formally to abandon rationalism and naturalism. The only alternative was to assume that rational and naturalistic factors explained human social variability. Thus, the task shifted from the explanation of rational principles of conduct to the explanation of observed empirical regularities (and variations) in behavior. It was argued that a whole series of factors such as climate, soil, geography, and, of course, tradition, custom, public opinion, and so on, operate according to natural laws. It was assumed that any given kind of climate, soil, or geography would always produce the same effects. However, as a matter of fact such things as climate, soil, and mineral resources vary tremendously. And, for example, while hot climates have one effect on human temperament, cold climates have quite another; while barren soils have one kind of consequence, it is not the same as that of unusually rich soils. Moreover, there are not only variations in the factors that have different effects, but the ensemble of factors may vary. In Montesquieu's work, therefore, important strides were taken toward social sciences such as social geography.

Beyond a point, however, the Enlightenment could make no contribution to the development of social science. Enlightenment thought was brilliantly adapted to the need for clearing a jungle of traditions that obstructed the path of science. However, its rationalistic formulas were too superficial to constitute adequate principles of positive science. Enlightenment thought increasingly took the form of a program for political action. Once it had become identified as the philosophy of revolution it was exposed to the fate of all programs of action. In the wave of reaction following the revolutionary movements of modern society, it dropped out of favor.

The Nineteenth Century and the Emergence of the Social Sciences

Tocqueville observed that the French Revolution did more to consolidate the state in a few years than the monarchies had accomplished in centuries. The national conscript army appeared. Patriotism to the state emerged as a new configuration in communal sentiment as the state increasingly assumed a form in which every man has a stake. In the wave of the so-called "reaction" that followed the revolution, a new emphasis was placed on tradition, local custom, historical uniqueness, and the emotional and irrational factors of human conduct.

As a theory of the nature of human social conduct, adequate to the needs of its sponsors, rationalism had to give way. But men seem reluctant to abandon an idea once it has proved useful. While rationalism declined as a theory of human conduct of the middle classes, it assumed a more radical form and was advocated in the name of the working class. In this re-cast form scientific socialism picked up the remnants of the Enlightenment and pressed analysis forward in terms of it. Meanwhile, however, though there were repeated attempts to replace the naturalism of the previous epoch with a new mysticism, they never completely succeeded, and substantial segments of nineteenth-century thought retain it. So far as the attempt was made to replace naturalism with a new mysticism, this could only operate negatively on the possibility of a social science. It is here that many of the anti-scientific movements of the nineteenth century took their point of departure.

The eighteenth century established the assumptions of the lawfulness and naturalness of social phenomena. The nineteenth century made them empirical. All of the major social sciences — anthropology, economics, geography, jurisprudence, political science, psychology, and sociology — were established before the end of the century. In cases where the given social science was on the way toward formation before the end of the eighteenth century, there were direct continuities of development. In every case, to be sure, there were significant anticipations of the social science in question. But in all cases there were decisive re-definitions of the meaning and implications of the science. The social sciences were transformed into genuinely empirical disciplines, even when they were not created as distinct social sciences for the first time.

This transformation may be illustrated by the development of jurisprudence. There had been many anticipations of the study of the materials belonging to jurisprudence from the days of the great Roman jurists. Many of these students, from Grotius to Kant, made such brilliant contributions to the study of law that they remain permanently important in the history of jurisprudence. However, jurisprudence did not assume the properties of an autonomous social science until John Austin (1790–1859), under the influence of British utilitarianism (an heir of Enlightenment rationalism and naturalism), established the study of analytical jurisprudence. This treated the law as a rationally complete and logically closed body of precepts expressing the sovereign will. Jurisprudence was established as a rational science in the same manner as physiocratic economics or the social-contract theory of political science.

However, in German lands, in the wake of those complex social movements that followed the Napoleonic conquests, a different kind of legal study was founded which expressed the stirrings of an awakening national consciousness. Friedrich Karl von Savigny (1779–1861) and Karl Friedrich Eichhorn (1781–1854) began to study the law, not as a body of principles expressing the sovereign will, but as a social formation anchored "organically" in the customs of the people and expressing their historical development. One could not examine the law in one's armchair. It was essential to study its manifestations and residues in actual social conduct. Jurisprudence had been transposed from a rational to an empirical science, comparative observation of social fact had been instituted, the body of recorded materials had begun to accumulate, and the study of one decisive area of social relations had been brought to full scientific maturity. In a similar fashion, as closely interrelated phenomena, the other social sciences took empirical shape in the nineteenth century. It is useful to review even briefly the nineteenth-century movements in social science.

Anthropology

Anthropology began to take distinct shape with the work of Christoph Meiners (1747–1810), Gustav Klemm (1802–1867), and Theodor Waitz (1821–1864). The affinities of these thinkers with the thought of previous centuries was clear. Meiners saw Montesquieu as a predecessor, and Klemm conceived his work as the carrying out of Voltaire's program. Meiners examined man's bodily diversity and social characteristics and began to review some of his more unusual customs. He conceived of the need for a new discipline, the "history of humanity," which would study education, the treatment of women, the forms of government, the laws, customs, kinds of wealth, decorum, and honor. Klemm was an ardent collector of artifacts and a student of culture, which he conceived as comprising customs, information, skills, domestic and public life in peace and war, religion, science, and art. He thought that culture developed from savagery through tameness to freedom, with characteristic configurations of social relations at each period.

Waitz studied primitive mentality and tentatively reviewed the problems of a geographic determination of culture. In all these thinkers there is discernible the tendency to make the transition from the rationalistic armchair theorizing of the Enlightenment to the methodical empirical study of social facts.

This displacement in the direction of empiricism was intensified in the early nineteenth century. Slavery was abolished in England, and societies which were established primarily for the protection of aborigines began to assemble ethnological facts on the side. Similar societies soon appeared in France. The problem of the potential extinction of primitive peoples was perceived. Jacques Boucher de Perthes discovered flint instruments of great antiquity at Abbeville (1838–1846). Human bones were discovered together with those of extinct animals, and finds of ancient human skeletons were made at Neanderthal (1857). Theoretical formulations were recast in terms of such accumulating discoveries. Stone work by human beings was dated back to the Pleistocene (Boucher de Perthes). The evolution of human technology from a stone through a copper epoch to an iron age was conceived (Lauritz Vedel-Simonsen). With the publication of Auguste Comte's sociological theories in the 1830's, there was increased influence of sociology on anthropological development. Shortly thereafter the field was to feel the effects of Darwin and the growth of biological evolutionism. Moreover, the methodology and theories on comparative law (J. J. Bachofen's *Das Mutterrecht*, works by Henry Sumner Maine, and, in another way, Lewis H. Morgan) began to affect the field. With the work of Lewis H. Morgan and Edward B. Tylor anthropology came of age.

Economics

It has been observed earlier that with the publication of Adam Smith's *The Wealth of Nations* in 1776, economics had already emerged as a relatively distinct science. The classical school which he founded was rapidly developed by David Ricardo, Thomas Malthus, James Mill, and John Stuart Mill, who both assembled materials and extended and sharpened the theories. The guiding ideal of the classical economists was the development of a system of laws abstractly deduced. This objective took shape in the eighteenth-century matrix.

The full development of economics as a science and the establishment of its methodology on empirical grounds occurred only under further influences from the historical school of economics in Austria and Germany and marginal-utility economics in Austria and England. Influences were also felt from "scientific" socialism. As economics has become methodologically conscious, it has tended to be less deductive, becoming first historical and comparative, and later, once again, mathematical and statistical, sometimes showing a partial return to the ideal of its founders. Even today the mathematical-theoretical branch of economics is not completely integrated with the historical-empirical.

Geography

Geography was on its way to emergence in the eighteenth century, particularly with the work of Montesquieu. After the geographic theories of Montesquieu, perhaps the most important figure was Johann Gottfried von Herder (1744–1803) who, partly under the influences that led to the *Sturm und Drang* movement, conceived of the human race as subdivided into national individualities, who were in turn a product of other things, including climatic conditions.

From the time of the Renaissance, geographic information had been rapidly accumulating, beginning with the commercial activities of Henry the Navigator. Geographic exploration soon became self-conscious. Alexander von Humboldt (1769–1859) studied a whole variety of geographic factors in a series of scientific expeditions through Central and South America (1799–1804). Karl Ritter (1779–1859), who was acquainted with Alexander von Humboldt, made geography his life work and more than any other individual founded the science (*Die Erdkunde im Verhältniss zur Natur und zur Geschichte des Menschen*). He became the first professor of geography (University of Berlin, 1820). He thought that environment had been divinely provided with different habitats to accommodate different types of men. Ritter's influence was discernible throughout Henry Thomas Buckle's *History of Civilization in England,* which tried to establish the physical, moral, and intellectual laws of human society.

Friedrich Ratzel (1844–1904) came to geography from zoology and journalism. His conscious aim was the establishment of the science on more empirical foundations and on the basis of sounder methodology. In his *Anthropogeographie* he theorized about the conditions of culture as determined by environment, and formulated the problem of cultural diffusion. Thereafter the science rapidly came of age with the work of Frédéric Le Play (1806–1882), Edmond Demolins (1852–1907), and Paul Vidal de la Blache (1845–1918). The environmental determinism of Ratzel was modified. New techniques, such as that of the case study, were introduced. The establishment of geography as a social science was assured.

Jurisprudence

The rapid transformation of jurisprudence into a social science has been mentioned. Thibaut, a member of the law faculty at Heidelberg, proposed the adoption of a legal code — a suggestion inspired by Napoleon's imposition of his Code on the various "countries" of Germany. In reaction to this, the whole issue of code-making was re-examined in 1814 by Savigny, who argued that law originates in the peculiar character of a people and is fixed in the same way as their manners, language, and constitution. Symbolic acts are universally employed where rights and duties are created or extinguished. Such formal acts are the true grammar of the law. The program suggested by Savigny was the intensified study of the actual historical facts of the law. The method of such was to be historical and comparative.

Following the early movements toward analytical jurisprudence (Austin) and historical jurisprudence (Savigny), a whole series of developments occurred: social utilitarianism, neo-idealism, neo-Kantianism, and even, eventually, a school of sociological jurisprudence arose. Such developments had profound influence upon the surrounding social sciences.

Political Science

Political science has the oldest roots of the social sciences and, as has been seen, hardly a thinker of the seventeenth and eighteenth centuries is without influence on it, from Locke to Rousseau, from Hume to Montesquieu. But again, the nineteenth century worked major transformations in it. For all his mysticism, Hegel helped initiate new studies of the political aspects of life which he argued could be understood only when these were related to the complex of social and historical factors of a particular time.

By 1835 new studies by Friedrich Christoph Dahlmann (1785–1860) and Tocqueville illustrated a new kind of analysis, the detailed empirical examination of political phenomena in the rich context of social factors giving rise to them. Alexis de Tocqueville's *Democracy in America* (1835, 1840), for example, examined the problem of democratic quality on the American scene and the complex of social events bearing on it. He dramatized the rich rewards to be gained by empirical study. In Dahlmann's studies of the English constitution, his history of the English and French Revolutions, and his history of Denmark, he made use of the philological-critical method. These works mark the change from moral to political historiography.

Normative political theory — that is, political theory formulating the ideal state — is still to be found. But students have increasingly come to distinguish this kind of political theorizing from empirical theory. Moreover, as time goes by, there has been less tendency to account for political events (as did Marxian economic interpretations) on the basis of some single other area of social events. Increasing agreement locates the concerns of political science in the theoretical and empirical aspects of the state, law, state power, constitution, and sovereignty. Quite often the field has been visualized as the theory of the causes, formations, and transformations of power.

Psychology

The beginning of modern psychology may be traced back to such persons as Descartes, Leibnitz, and Hobbes. Descartes, for example, conceived the activities of men and animals as machines controlled by physical laws. He postulated the existence of "animal spirits" moving in the nerves to bring about bodily movement. Leibnitz thought the mind and body formed parallel but non-interacting spheres. Mental events were to be classified in terms of their degree of clarity. Perception was conceived as an internal condition representing internal things and apperception as consciousness or reflective images of this internal state. Thomas Hobbes conceived a thoroughgoing behavioristic and materialistic psychology. He assumed that conduct rests on a series of impulses: fear, the desire for honor and fame, and, above all, self-interest. The will itself was reduced to the last manifestation of appetite. The physiological sources of activity were hunger, sex, thirst. Ideas were simply sense impressions, and memories faded sense impressions brought into coherence with others.

A series of developments led from here through the eighteenth-century thinkers, particularly Locke and Hume, on into the nineteenth-century formation. David Hartley (1705–1757) described nerve processes as vibrations, and accounted for images in terms of them. This doctrine of associationism was systematically elaborated by James Mill, John Stuart Mill, and Alexander Bain. Here again psychology emerged as a full-fledged science only in the nineteenth century. James Mill's *Analysis of the Phenomena of the Human Mind* (1829) systematically carried out an uncompromising associationism devoid of all metaphysics. Johann Friedrich Herbart (1776–1841) tried to construct a psychology modeled on natural science: every experience was conceived as an expenditure of energy. Since the total volume of energy remains the same, formulas could be constructed for psychological energy transformations. If one impression gains in strength, another must lose it. An idea coming to attention has enough energy to lift itself above the threshold of consciousness. Attention, learning, and a new concept of the "unconscious" acquire new meaning.

Also in the nineteenth century through the works of such persons as Sir Charles Bell (*An Idea of the New Anatomy of the Brain,* 1811) and Johannes Müller (*Handbuch der Physiologie des Menschen,* 1833–40) an increased study of the physiology of the brain was undertaken. In 1811 the posterior roots of the spinal cord were determined to contain the sensory, and the anterior the motor nerves. This provided new information about functions. Müller formulated the principle of "specific nerve energy." Brilliant extension of the theory of psychophysiological events was made by E. H. Weber (1795–1878), who studied touch and temperature experimentally, and Gustav Fechner (1801–1887), who laid the basis for exact experimental laboratory methods along with Hermann Lotze (1817–1881).

Among the great students of psychology in the nineteenth century was Wilhelm Wundt (1832–1920), who institutionalized experimental method in his laboratory. The procedure was to conduct controlled introspection and attempt to reduce to quantitative form the content of consciousness. Mental life was conceived as compounds, blends, and reactions. The aim was to set up psychological experiments in the manner of physics. Wundt also studied the psychological record (*Geschichte*), and late in life began the study of folk psychology — the study of the psychological aspects of the cultural evolution of man. Wundt and his students exercised decisive influence in the development of new methods in the study of mental processes:

consciousness, discrimination, imagery, memory, judgment, and concept formation, all of which were posed as tasks for experimental examination. William James and Stanley Hall came under Wundt's influence, and in the course of transferring psychological research to America, they started new schools. In Germany, *Gestalt* psychology was a later experimental product.

If the experimental methods eventually institutionalized by Wundt were one source of modern psychological science, the rise of the concept of evolution was the other. Psychology as a study not of mental structure but of adjustment is typically American, a product of pragmatic psychology. William James's *Principles of Psychology* was a monument to this type of analysis. Stanley Hall, John Dewey, and James Angell furthered this approach. Evolutionism in psychology carried with it an emphasis on the genetic study of psychological problems. Influenced by it, animal psychology and comparative psychology were introduced. The concept of biological variation found its counterpart in the study of the range and distribution of psychological variation. And through the work of Sir Francis Galton and James Cattell, the field of psychological measurement was advanced. By this time psychology was established as a natural science both in content and in method.

Sociology

The special social sciences took shape only because the accumulation of empirical data and theory reached such volume as to require the disciplines of special sciences. Sociology was not the first of the social sciences to appear. By implication, it was present in eighteenth-century political science, economics, and geography. But eighteenth-century political science was too preoccupied with deriving all social forms from rational agreement (social contract) to permit the study of the full panoply of social forms. Eighteenth-century economics was too determined to explain economic behavior on the basis of rational self-interest to contemplate the full possibilities of the sociology of motivation. Social geography tended to shift attention from the social sphere *per se* to presumed factors external to social life that accounted for its variations.

More than anything else, historical jurisprudence seems to have pointed the most direct route to sociology. When Savigny argued against the reconstitution of jural life on the basis of a rationally conceived code by contending that human experience is not created by fiat but is, rather, a slow growth out of previous experience, he was automatically rejecting rational agreements as exhausting the array of social forms. Furthermore, an item of human experience ceased to be considered arbitrary simply because it was traditional or irrational. Every item of social experience was conceived as an incident in a causal series of human experience. Each stage of human experience was a function of previous stages.

As Albion Small observed long ago in his *Origins of Sociology*,[1] these

[1] Chicago: University of Chicago Press, 1924.

notions quickly led — already with Eichhorn in *German Constitutional and Legal History* (1810), and long before Ranke — to the attempt to recover historical source materials and to the conception that legal development occurs in a framework of particular social institutions. In the course of telling the story of legal history in relation to political history, the concept of the social subject matter was expanded until it became equivalent to social history.

By this time development was ripe for the work of Auguste Comte, to whom the field is conventionally traced. The *Cours de philosophie positive* (6 vols., 1830–42) sought to establish a general science of human life. Comte did not provide for separate subsciences at all, but conceived of society as an organic whole characterized by developmental stages during which every aspect of life was in typical relation to every other. Herbert Spencer continued the development from Comte with some shifts of emphasis, but made the transition to the conceptions of social subsystems, particular institutions, and more workable societal types.

However, the social and biological sciences continued to separate out during the nineteenth century with continuing importance for sociology. For example, Frédéric Le Play (1806–1882) technically belongs to social geography, but his work had so profound a bearing on sociology that he is often viewed as one of its founders with Comte and Spencer. He established the observational case-history method in *Les Ouvriers européens* (1855).[2] He visited nearly every country in Europe, and studied and wrote monographs on more than three hundred working-class families representative of characteristic industries and localities.

The playback on sociology of the developments in biology appears in Paul von Lilienfeld-Toailles' "Die menschliche Gesellschaft as realer Organismus," in *Gedanken über die Socialwissenschaft der Zukunft* (1873–81),[3] in which the social process is compared to the movement of free cells in the human body. A. E. F. Schäffle, in *Bau und Leben des socialen Körpers* (1875–78),[4] treated the cultural life of society as its nervous system.

The continuing influence of historical jurisprudence is shown by the work of J. J. Bachofen in *Das Mutterrecht* (1861),[5] which had a powerful influence on ethnology as well as sociology. Bachofen discovered many legal evidences that seemed to point to a frequent matriarchal stage of family organization prior to the historical patriarchal family. J. F. McLennan (*Studies in Ancient History*, 1876) maintained that many legal evidences point to a widespread marriage by capture in primitive societies and tribes. Lewis H. Morgan, in *Systems of Consanguinity* (1869) and *Ancient Society* (1877), transformed the methodology of ethnological study by the systematic use of kinship terminologies as a device for analyzing social structure.

[2] "The European Worker"; not available in English translation.
[3] "Human Society as an Actual Organism"; neither the essay nor the book in which it appears ("Thoughts on the Social Science of the Future") is available in English translation.
[4] "The Structure and Life of the Social Body"; not available in English translation.
[5] "The Mother Right"; not available in English translation.

But the single most important influence on sociology derived from the socio-legal studies of Henry Sumner Maine. He had been in contact with the legal customs of India. He was struck by similarities between them and the legal traditions of ancient Rome. He thought he could isolate a general socio-legal movement in modern society in which there was a fundamental transformation of individual situation from status (in the ancient family) to contract (in the modern state).

The present discussion does not strive for completeness. Such names as have been used in this quick review of the social sciences in the nineteenth century are intended primarily as illustrations of trends. The object has been to clarify the sense in which the nineteenth century may be thought of as *the age of social science.* The social sciences did not emerge in a neat sequence. In the community of disciplines that appeared, developments in any one area were almost immediately picked up and carried forward in others in a system of reciprocal reinforcement.

Because the social sciences emerged as a family of disciplines, the resemblances between them are great. Perhaps for this very reason passionate concern is often shown by them for their individual identity, and the impression is at times conveyed that between them there are only absolutely irreconcilable differences. The basic kinship of the social sciences is often recognized only negatively or by implication. At the time of Comte, soci ology lay claim to the entire field of the social sciences — an assertion of rights that could hardly be convincing apart from the idea that the phenomena analyzed by the social sciences were all of a piece. Psychology, at times, has also claimed to be the fundamental science in this area, and even today one sometimes encounters the idea that explanations in social science will be successful only when they are "reduced" to psychological form. Here, too, the basic identity of the materials of the social sciences is implied, for it is assumed that in the end "all is psychology."

On the other hand, great ambiguities have often appeared when the attempt has been made to find differences "in principle" between the social sciences. For example, it has been asserted that sociology studies the *forms* of social life, while other social sciences study their *content.* Unless the concept "form" is given some mystical meaning — which would locate it outside science — it must refer eventually to relations or patterns of relation holding among phenomena. If we accept this, it is difficult to decide which is the more incomprehensible, a science of relationless content or of contentless relations. One is reminded of the cat in *Alice in Wonderland* which disappears before its smile; to the kind of thinking just noted, this gives rise to two sciences: the science of vanished cats and a science of catless smiles. There are, to be sure, important historical and social reasons for the appearance of the separate social sciences. But these are extrinsic rather than intrinsic; they arise because of the external situation in which a discipline finds itself rather than out of inner properties of its structure.

All these considerations lead toward a single general conclusion — that the primary differences between the various social sciences lie in their content or subject matter. This is a rather poor way of distinguishing a science which in the nature of the case is more like a mining operation than a set of property claims. Just as a vein of metal may cross property lines, so a problem is no respecter of the niceties of academic departmental distinctions. Precisely for this reason the lines between the social sciences are extraordinarily fluid and at any given time their most exciting developments are likely to occur in the transitional zones.

Anthropology has been specialized in the past as a social science primarily by its concern with primitive cultures and prehistory. In turn, these concerns have led to emphasis on even more specialized areas — linguistics, for example. For similar reasons, the anthropologist has been particularly concerned with race. Finally, anthropology has worked with whole cultures often of small tribal units. Apart from these differences which emerge directly out of its peculiar historical content, it would be hard to say in what manner in the long run the theories of anthropology will differ from those of sociology. Meanwhile, anthropologists have carried out their researches with profit under the influence of theories and research in political science, economics, jurisprudence, sociology, geography, and psychology. The anthropologists in turn have often worked up bodies of material of great utility for comparative purposes for social scientists in other areas.

Both economics and political science are primarily differentiated as special social sciences by the fact of their interest in special categories of social relations (power and wealth-getting) and the special system of institutions relevant to these relations (the political and economic orders). The only real justification for the existence of political science and economics as special social sciences is the sheer quantity and importance of the phenomena they study. But political and economic institutions remain institutions still. There is something radically wrong when the explanations of economic institutions by economists are too much at variance with the explanations of the same institutions by sociologists or anthropologists. It is significant that at the very moment that the activity in the special area of the institution tends to become too remote from activity going on elsewhere, counter movements appear which tend to bring the various branches of study together. Institutional economics is a movement in economics that would bring the theory of economic institutions into closer accord with the general theory of institutions. The vigorous present interest of sociology in economic organization is the same kind of movement proceeding out of sociology. Similarly, the movement out of general sociology toward political science is epitomized by the vigorous development of political sociology (and the sociology of war); conversely, political scientists are developing the field of "political behavior," which moves toward sociology and psychology.

Jurisprudence, again, is clearly differentiated as a social science only by its specialized concern with legal relations and their place in the social matrix. But no full study of anthropology is complete without reference to primitive law. Many critical properties of economic, and even more, of political behavior can be explicated only by the study of the relation between law and economic and political spheres. Meanwhile, as a special form of social relations, law is so important to sociology that the sociology of law has appeared as a vigorous subdiscipline.

Social geography was most distinct as a social science at a time when everything common to human social behavior was thought to arise out of universal human nature. At this time psychology could be assumed eventually to account for everything in human social behavior that was common, and one or another feature of the natural environment could presumably account for everything that was different or various. The oversimplification of such single-factor explanations was rapidly replaced by a more plastic special social science assuming fluid relations between human society and the external environment.

As already indicated, psychology enjoyed the most comprehensive of claims in the eighteenth century, when all that was uniform in conduct was assumed to arise out of universal human nature. This undoubtedly accounts for the rather distinct rationalistic atmosphere that seems to cling to contemporary suggestions that social behavior can only be explained by "reduction to psychology." However, one of the most distinctive features of nineteenth-century social science was the rise of the idea that "society forms human nature," a notion that tended to reverse the rationalistic formula that "human nature forms society." At the same time, the rise of physiology tended to move one aspect of psychological study strongly in the direction of natural and biological science. In the space between, one of the most vigorous modern trends has been the growth of social psychology.

It thus becomes clear why sociology has so often in the past been claimed to be "the general social science." It is also clear why it has experienced rather unusual difficulties in defining itself as a special social science. Economics studies economic institutions, political science studies political institutions, jurisprudence studies legal institutions. But does not sociology study not only institutions other than these but economic, political, and legal institutions as well? Anthropology studies primitive society, but can sociology, in the long run, ignore the comparative evidence from primitive society and prehistory? Social geography studies the interaction of society and environment, and psychology studies human nature and the factors shaping and shaped by it; can sociology ignore these? It is easy to see why sociologists so often felt invited to conceive sociology as the *general social science*. Only with the gradual isolation of the concept of the study of the social *per se* has the idea been finally established that sociology studies materials that are also studied intensively by the other social sciences, but is, nevertheless, a special social science in its own right. The manner in which this special conception of sociology arose is coextensive with the whole of sociological theory and forms one of the general themes of this book.

Summary

By the end of the Renaissance, Francis Bacon had already visualized the possibility of applying the scientific method to every area of experience. About a hundred years later, George Berkeley formulated his social physics. Since then similar conceptions of a social science appeared at ever shorter intervals.

It is possible, in retrospect, to formulate the necessary preconditions of a social science. Naturalism had to be established as a principle of social phenomena, and systems of ethical evaluation had to be withdrawn from the objective judgment of social facts. These preconditions were generally realized in seventeenth- and eighteenth-century thought in the writings of such persons as Voltaire, Hume, Condorcet, Goethe, Gibbon, Kant, Ferguson, and others. The most dramatic area in which the spirit of rationalism was realized was natural religion, or Deism. The attempt was made to establish religion on the basis of reason rather than on a foundation of tradition, authority, or revelation. The result was the conception of all phenomena as natural and rational, for with the naturalization of religious experience itself, there was no good reason for withholding any other sphere of experience from the application of science.

The core ideas of eighteenth-century naturalism and rationalism were that reason is the distinguishing property of man, human nature is everywhere the same, institutions are made for men rather than men for institutions, progress is the law of society, and humanity is its ideal. Such ideas naturalized everything they touched, divested the traditional and magical halo from institutions, and welcomed social change.

Eighteenth-century rationalism was the ideological aspect of phenomena institutionally represented by nationalism and capitalism. The presuppositions of rationalism and the institutional requirements of nationalism provided the matrix for political science. The same ideology and the institutional demands of capitalism led to the origin of economic science. Similar combinations of factors give rise to jurisprudence.

The evolution of the same ideological tendencies under the expanding conditions of nationalism and capitalism in the nineteenth century led to the emergence of the galaxy of the social sciences. Rationalism and naturalism supplied the abstract principles of disciplines which were transformed into genuine empirical sciences. The programs of Montesquieu and Voltaire under the influence of Meiners, Klemm, and Waitz led to anthropology. The work of the physiocrats was transformed into an empirical science by Adam Smith, Ricardo, and the two Mills. Geography, visualized as a possibility by Montesquieu and Johann von Herder, was transformed into a science under the influence of Alexander von Humboldt, Ritter, and Ratzel. Jurisprudence became a science in the work of Austin in England, and Thibaut, Savigny, and others in Germany. Political science was transformed into an empirical discipline by the studies of Dahlmann and Tocqueville. Psychology was developed into an empirical science by Hartley, the two Mills, Alexander Bain, and Herbart. Sociology itself became a science under the influence of Auguste Comte and Herbert Spencer.

In the course of this development, the social sciences played back upon one another in a mutually up-building cycle of development.

What is sociology? Where did it come from? Who influenced it? In what direction is it most likely to grow? These questions cannot be completely answered by the location of it among other disciplines. But neither can they be completely answered without examination of the stage on which the drama occurred.

SELECTED BIBLIOGRAPHY

BARNES, HARRY ELMER, *Sociology and Political Theory*. New York: Alfred A. Knopf, 1924.

BARNES, HARRY ELMER, *The New History and the Social Studies*. New York: Century Company, 1925.

CAIRNS, HUNTINGTON, *The Theory of Legal Science*. Chapel Hill, N.C.: University of North Carolina Press, 1941.

CAIRNS, HUNTINGTON, "Sociology and the Social Sciences," in Georges Gurvitch and Wilbert E. Moore (eds.), *Twentieth Century Sociology*. New York: Philosophical Library, 1945. Pages 3–19.

FRIEND, JULIUS W., and JAMES FEIBLEMAN, *The Unlimited Community: A Study of the Possibility of Social Science*. London: George Allen and Unwin, 1936.

GOLDENWEISER, ALEXANDER, "The Relation of the Natural Sciences to the Social Sciences," in Harry Elmer Barnes, Howard Becker, and Frances Bennett Becker (eds.), *Contemporary Social Theory*. New York: D. Appleton-Century, 1940. Pages 93–142.

LYND, ROBERT S., *Knowledge for What?* Princeton, N.J.: Princeton University Press, 1939.

OGBURN, WILLIAM F., and ALEXANDER GOLDENWEISER, *The Social Sciences and Their Interrelations*. Boston: Houghton Mifflin, 1927.

3

The Social and Philosophical Origins of Positivistic Organicism

TWO THINGS TEND TO BE TRUE OF A SCIENTIFIC DISCIPLINE IN TH[ ]
stages of its development: (1) it depends extensively on the surr[ ]
intellectual context, and (2) its ideas become organized into "sch[ ]
is inevitable that a new discipline will be more dependent on the in[ ]
context from which it emerges than an older, better established d[ ]
At the time of its origin, the new discipline has rarely invented [ ]
the ideas which will eventually become central to it, and it will [ ]
have acquired few of the facts which it seeks to explain throug[ ]
research resources. Indeed, the first form of a new discipline is [ ]
a new point of view in one of the older disciplines. Psycholog[ ]
origins in the epistemological branch of philosophy and in some [ ]
aspects of political explanation; economics took shape out of [ ]
ancient philosophy, applied medieval theology, and out of mate[ ]
oped in large measure in the course of practical statecraft. Socic[ ]
sented a new departure among the ideas traditionally forming[ ]
philosophy. Many of the materials for sociology had been a[ ]
history. In part, sociology took over programs from reforn[ ]
Both Comte and Spencer originally approached sociology fron[ ]
point of philosophy. Comte even called his study "positive[ ]
before he adopted the term "sociology," and Spencer approach[ ]
of his "synthetic philosophy."

Once a discipline is organized it begins to institute standard[ ]
late materials, and to verify ideas on its own. It become[ ]

autonomous. Recourse to outside disciplines diminishes and new points of view occur as departures within the context of the new science itself.

A second characteristic of the early stages of a science is the organization of its thought into "schools." The fertility of the human mind seems constantly to exceed the particular requirements of its time. The appearance of a new discipline depends not on this fertility alone but on a situation requiring the new thought. When social needs confirm the new discipline, the accumulation of knowledge and systematic research in one general direction can go forward. Social recognition and honors accrue to the persons satisfying the new demand. Competition for this recognition begins. And since the new area is, at first, unsettled in its theories, problems, materials, or methods, a variety of claimants appear. Thus in the early stages of a discipline alternative constructions of the basic ideas into "schools" is to be expected. The only person inclined to deny this fact is the partisan of some particular school: it seems to be normal to deny the very existence of every other than the one true faith.

Just as with the gradual maturity of the science the discipline becomes intellectually "self-sufficient" or "autonomous," although never completely so, there also tends to be a decline in the number of schools. We do not hear of "schools" of physical theory; we do hear of schools of psychology and sociology. This is to be expected in sciences of such different degrees of maturity. It is possible, of course, to grieve over the fact that sociology is still divided into schools; it is also possible to ignore this fact. Neither of these alternatives, however, is of any particular value to social theory, which must discover what the schools are and how they differ. Furthermore, it is unthinkable that any theorist should ever ignore the stimulation afforded by contrasting ideas.

The first theoretical construction of the new discipline of sociology may be designated as "positivistic organicism." It represented, in part, a fusion of opposed tendencies in philosophy. One could hardly find a more dramatic way to announce the appearance of a new discipline than in a formula combining previously opposed philosophic principles. The nature of these principles and the points at which they are in potential conflict is one of the most dramatically interesting problems in early sociological theory.

Organicism and Philosophical Idealism

The potential tension between "organicism" and "positivism" may be seen even in the most simple formulations of them. *Organicism* refers to that tendency in thought which constructs its picture of the world on an organic model. By an organismic metaphysics is meant the attempt to explain reality, or the world, or the universe, or the totality of everything as if it were a kind of organism or had properties like an organism such as being "alive," having a "vital principle," or displaying relations between parts like those between the organs of a living body. *Positivism*, on the other

PART TWO

Positivistic Organicism

hand, refers to that tendency in thought which rigorously restricts all explanation of phenomena purely to phenomena themselves, preferring explanation strictly on the model of exact scientific procedure, and rejecting all tendencies, assumptions, and ideas which exceed the limits of scientific technique. Nothing is more immediately obvious than the fact that organicism commits one to assumptions about the nature of phenomena that exceed the limits of what is immediately presented in experience as well as the limits imposed by scientific technique. Organicism and positivism should have been in tension from the start. The fact that they were put together and accepted by the learned world of the time is demonstration of the need for a new discipline, for the learned world will not overlook contradiction unless it has good reasons for doing so.

Origins of Sociological Organicism in Philosophical Idealism

Popularly, *idealism* tends to refer to visionary and prophetic attitudes toward human affairs. It also tends to refer to the optimistic frame of mind. The person who dreams of a better future or better world, who looks at the bright side of every issue and who stoutly maintains cheerfulness in the face of difficulty tends to be described as an "idealist." Philosophically, "idealism" does not require this hopeful and forward-looking attitude toward human affairs, though many philosophical idealists have retained it. Philosophical idealism refers to the view that reality itself is somehow in the nature of ideas or, in more moderate forms, to the view that, among all the kinds of realities, ideas are the most significant.

Idealism has played an important role in the history of Western thought.[1] It was deeply imbedded in that tradition in ancient Greece which was summarized in the philosophies of Plato and Aristotle. Plato's doctrine of ideas is typical. Ideas are the only things that really exist. Each thing is what it is only through the presence of the idea in it or through its participation in the idea. An idea as the "one" stands in opposition to the "many" — the plurality of actual things. For example, one idea "horse" refers to many actual horses. The world of actual things is constantly changing or becoming something else. The "many" are changeable; the "idea" remains always the same. All becoming, including human conduct, has its end and aim in a being. These ends can only be in the realization of that in which thought recognizes the unchanging primary patterns of things — ideas. Despite his many objections to Plato's theory of ideas, Aristotle accepted all its essentials. With Plato, he thought that only necessary and unchangeable forms can be objects of knowledge.

The idealistic traditions expressed in Plato and Aristotle became the domi-

[1] See Guido de Ruggiero, "Idealism," in the *Encyclopædia of the Social Sciences* (New York: Macmillan, 1931), Vol. 7, pp. 468–72. Among general works, see R. F. Alfred Hoernlé, *Idealism as a Philosophy* (New York: Doran, 1927); John Theodore Merz, *A History of European Thought in the Nineteenth Century* (Edinburgh: 1896–1914), Vol. 3, Ch. 5; and Josiah Royce, *Lectures on Modern Idealism* (New Haven, Conn.: Yale University Press, 1919).

nant ones from the Greek world. They formed the basis for the theologies of the Middle Ages, which were established first on the basis of Platonism and Neo-Platonism, later on the basis of Aristotelian metaphysics. The theological idealism of the medieval world sharpened the distinction between heaven and earth. The activity of human kind became a pilgrimage toward eternal goals. The ultimate source of reality was the idea in the mind of God.

Modern forms of idealism appear most clearly in the more theologically inclined philosophers. Leibnitz, for example, conceived the world as a complex of individual monads. The soul of man is a single monad which does not stand alone in nature. According to the law of continuity, by which there are no leaps in nature, we must assume infinite degrees of the kind of existence found in ourselves. *C'est partout et toujours la même chose, aux degrés de perfection près.* The law of continuity for Leibnitz originates in the principle of sufficient reason. The appearance of consciousness in nature can only be explained in terms of more obscure forms and degrees of psychic life, of impulse and efforts which awake to full consciousness in the higher forms of life.

Transcendent Idealism and Subjective Idealism. Ancient idealism may be described as "transcendent idealism," since it located the *idea* in some world beyond the world of the senses. Modern idealism as typified by George Berkeley may be called "subjective," for it tends to relocate the idea at the core of experience. Berkeley arrived at it by way of a critique of the empiricist tradition he shared. Philosophers since Locke had tended to make experience the starting point for the analysis of the world and the mind. Experience was believed to show properties that belonged to each: there were some qualities like weight, extension, existence in time, that belonged to real things; there were others like smell, color, etc., that were subjective. Berkeley, however, argued that this distinction of qualities cannot be maintained. The experience of weight is just as subjective as the experience of color. We have no more basis for assuming the existence of a real thing corresponding to a weight than we do the existence of a real thing in nature corresponding to a color. In fact, if we stick purely to what experience gives, the world consists of ideas. To account for the fact that when we awake day after day it is to the same sights, sounds, smells, and weights, Berkeley urged that there must be a Divine Mind where things exist when they are not present in the individual mind.

Objective Idealism. While a kind of personalized and subjective idealism was developed in the work of Leibnitz and Berkeley, a modern form of "objective idealism" appeared in the work of Hegel. Like the subjective idealists, Hegel was strongly theological in orientation. His philosophy represents a new departure in idealistic philosophy attempting to overcome some of the individualistic and atomistic characteristics of subjective idealism. Hegel maintained that ordinary consciousness develops into speculative thought by stages. The truth is a process in which substance and subjectivity are phases. The individual consciousness is an incident in the development of the world spirit. History itself is the development of the consciousness of mankind. Nature is rational, and the task of philosophy is to grasp the reason contained in it. The ethical world is the state of social affairs representing reason as actualized self-consciousness. Thought is the last product of a world process. Reflection itself is a sign that an epoch is drawing to a close. The Owl of Minerva takes its flight only when the shades of night are gathering. The mind of mankind develops in much the same manner as that of a single individual from infancy to intellectual maturity.

Irrational Idealism, Idealism of the Will. Another important form of idealism that developed in the nineteenth century along somewhat different lines was a kind of negative or irrational idealism. It remains idealistic in the most basic of all senses — the world is ultimately conceived as a living process. However, instead of discovering the world to be modeled after the more rational actions of the human mind, this model of the world is conceived after man's feelings and will. Schopenhauer argues that the world as immediately given corresponds to changes in our bodies. Space, time, and causality are various ways in which the immediately given sensation is comprehended. Science deals with this world. Science can do nothing other than present a materialistic explanation of phenomena. However, Schopenhauer believes the world as idea is only a surface manifestation, a relatively superficial level of existence. There must be a thing-in-itself that is a substratum of all this. The will is the essence of man as a thing-in-himself. The will must also represent the essence of the world. This makes striving, wishing, experiencing pleasure, pain, hope, fear, love, and hate as the most important aspects of man and the world. These are only the infinitely varied, different forms of the will to live, which in nature is manifest as the crude force. Here is a type of idealism taking not rationalism but blind irrational will to explain what the world is really like.

Modern types of idealism thus have a threefold source. From subjective and personal idealism like that of Berkeley, from objective idealism like that of Hegel, from irrational idealism like that of Schopenhauer, the modern world has also witnessed new versions of irrational idealism, illustrated by Henri Bergson.

All types of philosophic idealism have been represented as an extension of the organic analogy.[2] Once the analogy is applied, it leads to such characteristic results as: (1) the teleological concept of nature; (2) the view that nature, society, history, and what not are integral wholes which lose their peculiar property (their "life") when dissected (analyzed); and (3) the idea that the relation between the sub-parts of nature, society, history, or civilization are like the relation between the organs of a living body. From

[2] Harald Høffding, *A History of Modern Philosophy*, trans. by B. E. Meyer (New York: Macmillan, 1935), Vol. 1, p. 348.

idealism, early sociology took the organismic concept of society, history, and civilization.

The Philosophical and Social Background of "Positivism"

Positivism is that movement in thought which rests all interpretation of the world exclusively on experience.[3] Since science has been the mode of thought most successful in the modern world in dealing with the data of experience, positivism takes its point of departure from natural science, seeking a unified view of the world of phenomena, both physical and human, through the application of the methods and extension of the results of the natural sciences. Positivism arose as a reaction to traditional philosophy, being an attempt to cut through its complexities and variations and to establish thought on a definite foundation.

Ancient Positivism

In the ancient Greek world the closest approaches to a positivistic orientation are found in the atomists and the Sophists. Democritus, for example, conceived all changes in nature as due to the ceaseless joining and separation of uncreated atoms. Qualities were thought to depend on the size, shape, and arrangement of the atoms. Love, hate, and the other emotions were conceptualized as motions of the primary substance. Thinking was viewed as changes in the soul-body. Knowledge was thought to be derived from observation, and the imperfections of sense-perception were one of the primary sources of error.[4]

These ideas of Democritus could appear remarkably promising to a modern positivist. However, Democritus' ideas were not established on the basis of observation, nor were his notions of such things as atoms and primary motions confirmed by scientific procedures. He seems rather to have deduced them from his central principles. Democritus' sensualism did not lead him to oppose the existence of the gods but to a naturalistic explanation of them. He thought that beings of human form inhabit space. They are superior to men in size and length of life. The images which they send out appear to men in waking and sleep, and are believed to be gods.

Actually much closer to modern positivism was the sophistical movement

---

[3] See Guido de Ruggiero, "Positivism," in the *Encyclopædia of the Social Sciences*, Vol. 12, p. 260. For various historical forms of positivism, see the works of Comte (cited further on in this chapter) ; T. H. Huxley, "The Scientific Aspects of Positivism," in *Lay Sermons, Addresses, and Reviews* (3d ed.; London and New York: 1870) ; Marcel Boll, *La Science et l'esprit positif chez les penseurs contemporains* (Paris: Larousse, 1921) ; Ernst Mach, *The Science of Mechanics*, trans. by Thomas J. McCormack (La Salle, Ill.: Open Court Publishing Co., 1942) and *The Analysis of Sensations and the Relation of the Physical to the Psychical*, trans. by C. M. Williams and Sydney Waterlow (Chicago: Open Court Publishing Co., 1914) ; and John Dewey, *Experience and Nature* (Chicago: Open Court Publishing Co., 1925; New York: Dover Publications, 1958).
[4] Eduard Zeller, *Outlines of the History of Greek Philosophy* (13th. ed., rev. by Wilhelm Nestle and trans. by L. R. Palmer; New York: Meridian Books, 1955).

in Greek thought. In the long run, the major philosophic traditions in Greece, while not eliminating observation, relegated it to second place. This was not the case with the Sophists. The Sophists abandoned metaphysical inquiries, and taking their stand on experience, they sought to amass the greatest amount of knowledge in all departments of life. They developed ideas on the possibility of knowledge, on the beginning and progress of human civilization, on the origin and structure of language, on the appropriate and efficient arrangement of the life of the individual and society. Their method was empirico-inductive. Sophism tried to maintain its analysis strictly on the foundation of experience itself; furthermore, like modern positivism, it showed an inclination to extend its method to the solution of everyday problems and to social life. Another impulse typical of positivism appears in sophistic enterprise: the practical twist given to knowledge. For the Sophists, "knowledge was only valuable in so far as it formed a means to the control of life. The sophist cannot be thought of without pupils. His aim was not primarily to make sophists of them, but he wished to give the layman a general education which he could use in life. His aim was therefore predominantly practical: the art and control of life." [5] However, despite somewhat greater promise than that of the atomists, the Sophist program is not altogether equivalent to modern positivism. If the program of Democritus and that of the Sophists could have been fused, the result would have amounted to a full-scale positivism.

Modern Positivism

Only in recent Western thought has it been possible to bring together the kinds of conceptual tendencies present in the ancient atomists with those present in the ancient Sophists. The tremendous gains of natural science in the last three centuries of the modern period increasingly make possible the conception of the complete reconstruction of thought on the basis of science and the extension of its procedures to society and civilization. Ruggiero justly speaks of a more or less latent positivism from the beginning of the seventeenth century on, reflecting the increasing success of science in the modern world.[6]

It is conventional to trace modern positivism to the writings of Francis Bacon. His *Novum Organum* appeared in 1620. It was an investigation of the imperfections of the sciences and the obstacles to knowledge which were located in the constitution of the human mind and the situation in which it finds itself. In the *Advancement of Learning* Bacon sketched the branches of knowledge to clarify the achievements and further problems of science. In the *New Atlantis* he portrayed the lot of humanity under the guidance of the new aristocracy of science, in which the domination of man by man is replaced by the domination of man over nature.

The Early Positivistic Program. If a general positivistic program — the application of science to the regeneration of humanity — is presented by

5 *Ibid.*, p. 94.   6 *Op. cit.*, p. 261.

Bacon, a much more concrete, if more limited, program is contained in empiricism. The anti-metaphysical tendencies of science are focused in the problem of constructing knowledge out of the data of experience without appeal to transcendent principles of any kind. Locke argued that "men, barely by the use of their natural faculties, may attain to all the knowledge they have, without the help of any innate impressions." [7] The manner in which this occurs is set down generally as follows: "The senses at first let in particular ideas, and furnish the yet empty cabinet; and the mind by degrees growing familiar with some of them, they are lodged in the memory, and names got to them. Afterwards the mind, proceeding farther, abstracts them, and by degrees learns the use of general names." [8]

The development of empiricist epistemology is a well-known story, of only incidental importance here. Through Locke, Berkeley, and Hume, the derivation of knowledge from experience and the consequences of this derivation were explored. It became clear that, when traditional ideas were put to the test of experience, an extensive liquidation occurred. Bishop Berkeley demonstrated that one could not justify the existence of a physical world on the basis of experience. The world could be reduced to ideas in the minds of men and God, a conclusion very agreeable to him. Hume in a famous argument showed that even the principle of causality could not stand the test of experience. "Let men once be fully persuaded of these two principles, *That there is nothing in any object, consider'd in itself, which can afford us a reason for drawing a conclusion beyond it; and, That even after the observation of the frequent or constant conjunction of objects, we have no reason to draw any inference concerning any object beyond those of which we had experience. . . .* [9] When these principles are applied, it is soon discovered that we have no apparent grounds for accepting some very significant traditional ideas such as God, the self, the physical world, causality. The significance of empiricism for positivism has been phrased with unusual cogency by a modern anti-positivist:

> the last bridge which still joined the new empiricism with the old metaphysics was broken, and the natural world was reduced to a complex of phenomenal data bound up with relations equally phenomenal; the corresponding subjective and mental world also was resolved into a bundle of sensations held together by empirical bonds of an associative nature. The mind, fortress of traditional metaphysics, was reduced to the level of nature and thus became, at least potentially, subject to the application of the same scientific methods which proved so fecund in the study of nature. [10]

In France Voltaire early in the eighteenth century had begun to popularize Newtonian science. The philosophy of Locke began to gain adherents. The

[7] John Locke, *Selections*, ed. by Sterling P. Lamprecht (New York: Scribner's, 1928), p. 96.
[8] *Ibid.*, p. 99.
[9] David Hume, *Selections*, ed. by Charles W. Hendel (New York: Scribner's, 1927), p. 43.
[10] Ruggiero, "Positivism," *loc. cit.*, p. 262.

ideal of progress of the individual and mankind received expression in Condorcet's *Esquisse d'un tableau historique des progrès de l'esprit humain* (1795). This, however, was more rationalistic than positivistic. Closer to the core of positivism was the utilitarianism of Helvétius in France and Bentham in England. The main epistemological theorists of the French Enlightenment were Condillac (1715–1780), a tutor and head of an abbey, and Helvétius (1715–1771), who was farmer-general.

Condillac attempted, by deductive rather than inductive means, to establish the principle that everything in consciousness consists in transformations of simple sensations. Memory is treated as an after-effect of sensation. Abstraction consists in singling out one sensation from others. All analysis proceeds by the assignment of signs to sensory elements discovered by analytical differentiation, and by the use of speech to combine and analyze signs, thus developing a calculus of signs. Helvétius adopted Condillac's doctrine of the transformation of sensation. He tried to apply the theory to the development of our faculties through experience and external influence. He argued that even self-love is acquired. We do not feel love unless we first feel pleasure and pain. This is a datum of nature. Pleasure and pain arouse and sharpen attention and determine our actions. What will attract our attention depends on education — which includes everything in the environment and circumstances that influences personal development.

English Utilitarianism. In England Jeremy Bentham (1748–1832) developed a most influential form of positivistic utilitarianism. In Bentham's theory, all ethics, thought, and psychology rest on the fundamental principle that pleasure is preferable to pain. Only prejudice was thought to stand in the way of recognition of the principle; men do, in fact, follow it regardless of what they say. The greatest happiness of the greatest number is *utility.* In his most important work, *Introduction to the Principles of Morals and Legislation,* (1789) Bentham argued that not only are feelings of happiness preferred above others, but some importance must be attached to the certainty, strength or intensity, and "purity" of pleasure as well as to the "fecundity" of any given pleasure. The principle of utility was employed as a device for measuring motives. Those motives are good which lead to a harmony of the individual's interests with others; bad motives lead to a separation of interests. On this basis, the older teleological and natural-law conceptions were submitted to radical criticisms as metaphysical constructs; the principle of utility was offered in place of them. Bentham and his followers also advocated an extensive reform of administration and law (finding a foremost advocate in John Austin) on the basis of utilitarian principles. It was argued, for example, that the aim of criminal law is to prevent crime. It is more important for a punishment to be certain than severe. Furthermore, the punishment must fit the crime. For, if a whole series of crimes of different seriousness are subject to the same penalty, not only will juries tend to refuse conviction when they think a given penalty excessive, but the criminal will be encouraged always to commit the more serious of the offenses. The basic principle for testing any given law or administrative act is a calculus of pleasures and pains.

Positivism and Social Reform

The critical point for social science in the development of empiricism was aptly put by Ruggiero: the mind reduced to the level of nature became subject to the application of scientific methods. One irreplaceable component of early sociology was its positivism, which consisted in the fulfillment of the scientific program made possible by the "naturalization" of mind and society.

This property of empiricism led it inevitably down the road toward reform. Locke's researches led him toward the theory of the state and civil society. Berkeley's led him to a theory of *Social Physics* and the concept of human love as a unifying force in society (moral attraction), binding people together in a lawful manner as a sort of social gravitation. Voltaire and the Encyclopedists visualized reconstruction in many social areas. Bentham and the utilitarians were led toward the reconstruction of administration and law.

The latter part of the eighteenth century saw the success of the American Revolution. Many of the American revolutionaries were trained in the doctrines of the eighteenth-century rationalists and empiricists. The linkage of rationalism, empiricism, and reform was also apparent in France. It is not surprising under such circumstances that the social reaction following the French Revolution, the eleven months of Robespierre's Reign of Terror, and the dictatorship of Napoleon should take the form of a reaction to empiricism, which was blamed for these events. But however intense the reaction following the Revolution, basic social tendencies remained. The program of social reform on the basis of science was pressed forward again, now by socialist-reformers.

Comte Henri de Saint-Simon (1760–1825), for example, is often called the father of French socialism. He was one of the first writers on a new style of social reform. He entered the army at the age of seventeen, fought with the French expeditionary forces under de Grasse in the American army, and was present at the surrender of Cornwallis at Yorktown. He did not take part in the French Revolution, but made a fortune speculating in confiscated church estates. He was in prison during Robespierre's Terror. Later he devoted himself to the problem of social reform. His *Introduction to the Scientific Work of the Nineteenth Century* was published in 1807. Other works include *The Reorganization of European Society* (1814), *The Industrial System* (1821–22), *Political Catechism for Industrialists* (1822), *New Christianity* (1825). Saint-Simon proposed the scientific reorganization of society and the promotion of science, since, he believed, progress depended on it. In the new society, idlers would be punished, and people would be paid according to the wealth they produced. The industrial class, the only useful one, would prosper. The new political state would be confined to the maintenance and protection of the industrial organization. In time the national states of Europe would disappear. A new religion would give men a sense of unity in the world. Until they parted company, Comte was a disciple, secretary, and friend of Saint-Simon and was thoroughly familiar with these proposals.

That Saint-Simon did not represent an isolated phenomenon is shown by the fact that a school quickly gathered in his name, and he influenced such diverse persons as Proudhon, Marx, Owen, Blanc, John Stuart Mill, and Rodbertus. Robert Owen (1771–1858), the son of an iron monger and a successful industrialist, may be taken to illustrate parallel social ferment in England. William Godwin, with his belief in the perfectibility of human nature, was one of the inspirations of Owen. Owen's ideas were expressed in his essays, *A New View of Society* (1813–1814). Eventually he tried to carry out his theories of the effect of environment and education on character by forming model communities, organized on a cooperative model. Several attempts to put the theories into practice were tried. Other social reformers with schemes for social betterment included Charles Fourier (1772–1837), Étienne Cabet (1788–1856), Louis Blanc (1811–1882), and Pierre Joseph Proudhon (1809–1865).

Idealistic Organicism and Social Conservatism

Social reformism and utopia-building were the early nineteenth-century counterpart of the liberal and revolutionary movements of the eighteenth century. The conservative reaction to the course of events, on the other hand, may be seen in such persons as Burke, de Maistre, and de Bonald. Edmund Burke ((1729–1797), who was born in Ireland and studied law, practiced as a journalist for a time in London. He gained fame as a Whig member of the British parliament. In 1775 he pleaded for a liberal policy toward the American colonies. The course of the French Revolution increasingly was a source of alarm to Burke, who eventually expressed a conservative reaction in *Reflections on the French Revolution* (1790) and *An Appeal from the New to the Old Whigs* (1791). He argued that society and the state are not created by man's conscious reason in the form of a contract; they emerge as an organic growth. Traditions and customs are ancient and important; they embody a wisdom more profound than reason. Institutions must be adapted to new situations, but the changes must be organic and from within, not violent and from without. Religion is the necessary basis of social stability. The hierarchy of society is a natural order difficult to improve. The doctrine of progress is dangerous.

Joseph de Maistre (1753–1821) was an *émigré* Savoyard nobleman and Sardinian ambassador to Russia. His reaction to the Revolution appears in his *Considerations on France* (1796) and *The Essay on the Generating Principle of Political Constitutions and Other Human Institutions* (1814). The idea that individuals rationally and voluntarily create society and government was rejected. These are thought rather to be products of natural organic growth. In fact, intelligence, religiousness, and sociability are human faculties dependent on life in society. Society is presupposed for the development of the highest elements of the individual. Language, for example, was not invented by individuals or groups of men but was of divine origin. It was, however, a capacity that could emerge only in society. Individual reason and experience must be justified in terms of the collective historical experience of mankind. Social structure can be modified; it cannot be created or destroyed.

Louis de Bonald (1754–1840), a nobleman of the French court, had at first welcomed the Revolution. Its excesses, however, gave him pause, and he was eventually forced to flee to Heidelberg. There he wrote *The Theory of Political and Religious Authority* (1796). Later he added his *Analysis of the Natural Laws of the Social Order* (1800), *Primitive Legislation Considered by the Sole Light of Reason* (1802), and *Philosophical Demonstration of the Constitutive Principles of Society* (1830). De Bonald agrees with de Maistre that society does not originate in agreement like a trading group. It is divine in origin and a product of nature. Individuals do not create society; society creates the social individual. Like de Maistre, he believed the origins of language can reveal much about society. Words are necessary to make thinking and reasoning possible. But men could not have invented language itself; hence, it too must be of divine origin. The laws of society may best be studied among people who have preserved primitive revelation. Society necessarily rests on tradition and is most stable when hierarchical in structure. The professions (like the medieval guild) should be organized as corporations which are natural social institutions.

The Comtean Synthesis

A social contrast corresponding to contrasting intellectual traditions appears characteristic of the situation in which sociology made its appearance. The positivistic program of the reorganization of society on the basis of science was anchored in liberal and reformist circles. The idealistic program with its organic conceptions of society and history was anchored in conservative strata, opposed to planned social change. In taking over the socially conservative, idealistic-organismic concept of society and subordinating the positive method to it, Auguste Comte (1798–1857) may be seen to have been providing a conservative answer to socialism.[11] Comte was a success not because of a freakish combination of intellectual and

---

11 Comte's first major work was *Cours de philosophie positive*, 6 vols. (Paris: 1830–42), which was freely translated and condensed, with Comte's approval, by Harriet Martineau and published as *The Positive Philosophy of Auguste Comte*, 2 vols. (London: J. Chapman, 1853). The quotations in the present work are from this translation. Comte's other major work was *Système de politique positive, ou traité de sociologie, instituant la religion de l'humanité*, 4 vols. (Paris: 1851–54), translated by John Henry Bridges as *System of Positive Polity*, 4 vols. (London: Longmans, Green, 1875–77).

social elements but because his epoch had a need for precisely this combination. His simultaneous idealistic and conservative definition of subject
matter is evident in his treatment of social phenomena. According to Comte,
ideas govern the world or throw it into chaos. Social mechanism rest on
opinion. "The great political and moral crisis that societies are now undergoing is shown by a rigid analysis to arise out of intellectual anarchy.
While stability in fundamental maxims is the first condition of genuine
social order, we are suffering under an utter disagreement which may be
called universal." [12] However, Comte does not proceed from this point
to an analysis of public opinion as one might think, but to a classification of
the sciences as a first step in the institution of an intellectual, moral, and
social order. A beginning of order in society is thus made by setting one's
house in order.

The field of social order or structure was described by Comte as *social
statics*.[13] Society was conceived as an organic whole analyzable into three
elements: the individual, the family, and society. In his study of the
individual the phrenologist Gall was followed, chiefly, it seems, because
Comte thought Gall had proved basic social behavior to be biologically
inherent. (It may be noted that the conservatives de Bonald and de Maistre
had thought this.) While society is anchored in human nature, Comte does
not agree that the individual is the simplest unit of society. The organs
of society are institutions. The family is the smallest potentially self-
sufficient unit — a sort of suborganic whole; it is the basic social unit.
Other social forms arise out of it, be they tribes or nations. This permits
the assertion of the organic wholeness of mankind: "the whole human race
might be conceived of as the gradual development of a single family." [14]
With the conservatives, the family is seen as a control institution arising
out of the ordered and disciplined satisfaction of sex. Comte seems to feel
that the family has undergone some deterioration, for he argues wistfully
that the society of the future ought to have families founded on "the natural
subordination of woman." [15] Only in this way can women be kept in "a state
of perpetual infancy."

The real unit of sociological analysis is society. It is superior to the
individual organism. It includes "the whole of the human species, and
chiefly the whole of the white race" [16] The structure of society, its complexity and integration, rest on the divison of labor. Because this source of
its strength can, in the case of overspecialization, become a weakness,
it is important to maintain the idea of the whole and a feeling of common interconnection. The most important of all the properties of society,
beyond cooperation and division of labor, are its basic subordination and
tendency toward government. Subordination is both material and social,
and arises out of the natural differences of individuals. The individual must
be subordinate to those above him. Such subordination is the basis for a

---

[12] *Positive Philosophy*, I, p. 3. [13] *Ibid.*, II, Chapter 5.
[14] *Ibid.*, I, p. 145. [15] *Ibid.*, p. 134. [16] *Ibid.*, p. 137.

"natural" tendency toward government, which arises because of the greater fitness, by nature, of some men to command. Comte had great admiration for the Indian caste system, which seemed to him a paradigm of social stability.

One of the most important properties of the modern conservative-idealistic formula is its reception of the principle of development. This was its answer to the social-critical conception of progress. Conservatism, too, could accept development; in fact, it was its true heir! Progress was broken out of the revolutionary context and reset at the very core of the conservative position. In the course of this conversion it suffered a sea-change, for it became the principle of immanent development; it is inevitable; it can only be spurred on or checked by such things as climate, race, social boredom, or population density. The conservative content of this *coup* is clear only when the stages of progress are set down. Mankind, it is said, has developed from a theological, through a metaphysical, toward a positivistic stage. The metaphysical stage of social development is identified with the period of the French Revolution and the philosophy of rationalism. Metaphysical philosophy to Comte meant the ideas of social contract and natural rights; it referred to rationalism and Deism.

However, the real ingenuity in the converted progress formula is seen in the idea that each stage has made its permanent contribution to social and intellectual development. Even the primitive theological period produced a permanent speculative class, a system of common opinions to control individual eccentricity, and hence the substratum of government. The primitives developed a leisure class which is the precondition of intellectual progress. A value is even found for the metaphysical period, which is said to have familiarized men with the idea of regularities or laws in social affairs, thus paving the way for science. The conservative argument maintains that the philosophy of revolution has made its contribution to progress and has been surpassed. In the same manner various institutions are vindicated: slavery inculcated (along with militarism) habits of regularity and discipline; industry is a major pacifying and civilizing influence of mankind; ancient astrology was a step toward science. Conservatism thus receives and surmounts the dangerous principle of change.

Comte had a stormy emotional nature, which, spurred by a stormy marriage, led to severe nervous crises. At one time in a letter to Stuart Mill he said he thought his sanity was in danger. About this time he fell deeply in love with a young woman, who died within a year. His love for her seems to have been central to the later synthesis of his ideas in *System of Positive Polity*. Comte prepared himself for this work by the practice of "cerebral hygiene," abstaining from reading anything he disagreed with, thus excluding all disturbing thoughts and insuring the unity and harmony of his ideas. He proposed a new religion of humanity, and saw himself as high priest of it. He conceived of the most elaborate and minute systematization of life. The functions of the sociological priesthood which would rule the new society were to exercise systematic direction over education. Domestic life, however, was to be left in the hands of women in their three roles as moral guardians, as mother, wife, and daughter in accordance with his theory of the brain, each corresponding to three altruistic instincts of veneration, attachment, and benevolence.

In the religion of the new society Humanity becomes the object of worship. Humanity includes all dead, living, or future beings who have labored for the blessedness of man. A calendar was drawn up in which each day of each month was named after heroes who had furthered the development of Humanity. The caste of priests in charge of education will not only have encyclopedic wisdom, but they will be poets and physicians as well. Every animal kind will be conceived as a human species whose growth was stunted. In the new religion, world space is the great medium and the earth the great fetish. The great medium, the great fetish, and the great being — space, the world, and mankind — are the positivistic trinity. In the sociocracy no one will have rights, only duties. The ruling power in external affairs will reside with the captains of industry, but they will be so rich they will feel no greed. They will conduct industrial life in such a way as to make family life possible as the basis of blessedness. Men are in charge of rational life, and women are in charge of feeling.

Spencer's Reformulation

Comte was born in France on the heels of the French Revolution, and was reared in an atmosphere torn by the extremes of socialism and conservative reactionism. In fact, he received much of his intellectual stimulation from one of the first of the French socialists. Herbert Spencer (1820–1903) was born in England in quite a different atmosphere, living through one of its freest and most optimistic periods. Spencer's father educated the boy outside the school system, and Spencer grew up as a confirmed individualist. The religious and political attitudes of his family encouraged critical suspicion of all attempts at social legislation and state interference. Spencer was raised on Adam Smith's moral philosophy. He was fascinated by Lyell's *Geology*, and was impressed by its theory of natural development. In Spencer's first important work, *Social Statics* (1850),[17] he conceived social development by analogy with organic development, and he never gave up the idea. The form of positivism developed by Bentham was transmitted to Spencer by way of the Mills. He worked his way through some of its problems in his *Principles of Psychology* (1855).

There is little doubt that Spencer's fusion of positivism and organicism

---

[17] Since the original publication dates of Spencer's chief works are given in the exposition, a full bibliographical note will not be attempted here. Quotations have been taken from the following editions: *Social Statics* and *The Man Versus the State* (New York: D. Appleton, 1904) ; *First Principles of a New System of Philosophy* (New York: DeWitt Revolving Fund, 1958) ; *The Study of Sociology* (New York: D. Appleton, 1929).

again operates in an essentially conservative manner. It is also clear that Comte and Spencer arrived at this requirement in quite different ways. Comte came to sociology from the standpoint of a profoundly unsettled personal emotional life and developed a message for an unsettled social order, the intellectual life of which was pulled between socialistic utopias and the conservative emphasis on tradition. In Comte's personal life he performed for himself a settling action in his "cerebral hygiene" like the one he wished to perform for society with his sociocracy. Comte, to be sure, did contemplate social legislation, a new society, and a new religion, but they were all in the interest of a traditionalistic, authoritarian social order, organized into permanent castes, with women back in permanent subordination in the home.

The impression Spencer conveys is very different; there are certainly no equivalent signs of inner torment. He seems to have been a man satisfied with himself and with his time and social order. He apparently feared that the educational reformers might be right; he felt he must by all means refute public education. The empiricists, in emphasizing the origin of all individual thought in experience, underlined the importance of education. They argued that since everything we know comes from the environment, by proper education (manipulation of the environment) any kind of society can be developed. We may be one generation away from utopia, but we are one generation away from barbarism as well. Spencer could not accept the idea that a society he liked so well could be disposed of so easily. The idea that a social order can be changed in a generation by education must at all costs be rejected. This was the basic thesis of his psychology: it is impossible to explain individual consciousness in terms of the individual's experiences alone. Spencer feared the social consequences if one could. Mental development, he asserted, takes place slowly. Modifications due to the environment gradually lead to the establishment of new forms. In the case of the individual mind, the experience of the race must be taken into account. Tradition, the structure of the mind, the manner in which ideas are associated, the form of development of the feelings and instincts, and hereditary tendencies are all important. Such was Spencer's answer to all who would change the world by education.

The concept of evolution [18] that came so handily into use in the *Principles of Psychology* (1st ed., 1855) was broadened in *Progress: Its Law and Cause* (1857), and was given general form in *First Principles* (1862): "Evolution is an integration of matter and concomitant dissipation of motion; during which the matter passes from an indefinite, incoherent homogeneity to a definite, coherent heterogeneity; and during which the retained motion undergoes a parallel transformation." [19] This formula was believed to apply to the universe, to the evolution of the earth, and to the development of biological forms, the human mind, and human society.

Society for Spencer was an entity formed of distinct units characterized

---

[18] Darwin, in *The Origin of Species* (1859), mentioned Spencer as one of his predecessors.
[19] *First Principles*, p. 394.

by a relatively permanent arrangement in some specific area. The arrangement of the various parts of society are analogous to the arrangement of the parts of the living body. Among the basic properties of society as an organism are the facts that: (1) society undergoes growth; (2) in the course of its growth, its parts become unlike (that is, there is a structural differentiation); (3) the functions of society are reciprocal, mutually independent, and interrelated; (4) like an ordinary organism, the society may be viewed as a nation of units; and (5) the whole may be destroyed without at once destroying the life of the parts. There are, however, some contrasts between the ordinary living organism and society: (1) whereas the social organism is a discrete whole, the biological organism is a concrete whole; the units of the social organism are free and may even be widely dispersed; (2) the agencies of cooperation are more important for society; these are the languages of emotion and intelligence, which create a living whole of the social aggregate; however, (3) while consciousness in the individual organism is concentrated in a small part, in society it is diffused, as are capacities for happiness and misery.

In his study of the problems of social growth and social structure, Spencer traced out more detailed comparisons. Like living bodies, societies begin as small units — germs — and grow to great size. They grow in aggregates of varying degrees. There is both an enlargement of groups and the fusion of groups of groups. Integration is discernible in the formation of masses and the increasing coherence of the parts of the mass. Growth as an increase of mass is accompanied by an increase in structure. As growth occurs from simple to compound and doubly compound, the unlikeness of parts increases. As the unlikeness of parts becomes greater, owing to the development of coordinating agencies, there is an increase in independence of unlike parts. Differentiation proceeds from general to specific. Moreover, the organic in animals and in societies is based on the same principle. There are, in both cases, instruments for conveying nutriment to its parts and bringing out waste products. There are regulative activities. In both societal and organic forms, in the most primitive of units there is no subdifferentiation of specialized functions.[20]

Just as in the case of growth there is a specialization of structure, so, too, there is a specialization of function. In little developed aggregates, actions are very little interdependent and the various parts of the social organism may easily exchange functions. With the advance of organization, however, every part comes to have a very special function which it performs in a relatively inelastic and irreplaceable manner.

Social differentiation begins with broad contrasts at first, showing the effects, respectively, of the primary external and then of internal conditions of society. Thus, for example, in the early stages of society the masters are warriors carrying on defensive and offensive activities, representing the societal agency in direct response to external conditions. At the same time

[20] *Ibid.*, Sections 228–232.

the slaves carry on the internal activities of subsistence, serving first the masters, then themselves. The external and internal systems have been differentiated. A distributing system operates between the two and ties them together. In the simplest of social orders there is no distributing system, for the two original classes are in contact; in time, however, industries are localized and devices for transfer of goods appear. As society grows, new functional and industrial classes appear.

In all developed societies, thus, there are three systems of organs, even though in the simplest of societies at least one of these has little distinctness. (1) The *sustaining* system represents that organization of parts carrying on elimination in a living body, productive industries in society. In large societies built of smaller ones, industrial structures may extend without reference to political divisions. (2) The *distributing* system is required as a special integration of parts whenever the various parts of society are no longer in close contact. It is required by the division of labor. It appears between the original systems, and carries out that essential function of transfer among interdependent parts. (3) The origin of the *regulating* system is found in wars between societies, when the governmental-military organization comes into being. The subordination of local governing centers to the general governing center accompanies cooperation of components of the compound aggregate in its conflict with other aggregates. As in the individual organism, this takes the form of the appearance of a dominant center over subordinate centers, with an increase in the size and complexity of the dominant center.

Spencer suggested that societies may be arranged either in terms of their composition (as simple, compound, double-compound, etc.) or in terms of the dominance of a kind of system (predominantly military or predominantly industrial). The militant society is one where the external system predominates; the industrial society is one where the internal system dominates. In the militant type of society there is strong centralized control, an identity of the command for war and peace, a hierarchical ordering of authority. Religion in this society tends to be militant, and the ecclesiastical order is like the military. Even the sustaining system is a military-like ordering. All life is subject to discipline. The individual is subordinated to the whole, and life is compulsorily coordinated. In the industrial society commerce has more importance than war; there is a development of free political institutions; freedom extends to the religious and industrial structures. The ideas of the relation between citizen and state are transformed. It becomes a duty to resist an unpopular government. Society is conceived as the instrument of individual action. Cooperation becomes voluntary.

The specific parts of society, the "organs" of the social organism are *institutions*. There are six types: domestic, ceremonial, political, ecclesiastical, professional, and industrial. Paralleling the general development of societal energy and structure from incoherence to coherence and from diffuseness to specificity has been a development of institutions. The *family*, for example, developed from a primitive state, where it barely served the need of sheer perpetuation of the race, to the free family of the present, in which there is a conciliation of the needs of young and old alike and a maximum of individual freedom. In form it evolved through promiscuity, polyandry, and polygyny, to monogamy. *Ceremonial* institutions compass the whole body of custom. Ceremony was the most primitive form of social control, regulating interhuman conduct before the appearance of institutions of control. Rites of the grave, for example, were attempts to propitiate the ghost and anticipated the rise of religion. Ceremonies include mutilations, trophies, presents, visits, obeisances, titles. The trend in evolution is toward replacement of ceremonies by more definite institutions. *Political* institutions also represent an evolution of structures from primitive anarchism through various types of domination by one or a few persons, to modern democratic and parliamentary structures. Especially important are the processes by which political institutions take over the functions of control. In turn, this is a product of conquest and the rapid evolution of political institutions which occurs with war and the emergence of a dominant class. *Religious* institutions originate in the rational misunderstanding of primitive man: his interpretation of phenomena like shadows, dreams, and reflections as real persons. His terror of these ghosts is the motive power of religion. Religion represents a gradual evolution of such primitive ideas and sentiments beginning in ancestor worship. The *professions,* which originally function in the defense of tribal life, later serve national life. They represent the products of the specialization and differentiation of original social organization. *Economic* institutions, too, have gone through a slow evolution from primitive slavery through serfdom to free labor and contract.

In the social organism, structure is adapted to activity. The outer (regulating) and inner (sustaining) systems are increased or diminished by activities. Where societies descend from one another in a series, a type is established which undergoes development, maturity, and decay. When it resists metamorphosis, a society will tend to revert to an earlier state. Of especial importance, is the transformation of militant into industrial society. When industry is not checked by war, non-coercive regulating systems become more important. However, it is quite possible for an industrial society to become more militant.

Ward and the Introduction of Sociological Organicism in America

Lester F. Ward (1841–1913), the first systematic sociologist in America, brought out his first and in some ways his most important study in 1883 between the publication of the first and last volumes of Spencer's *Principles of Sociology.* He added five additional major volumes to this statement.[21] Ward brought the various ideas of Comte and Spencer into a peculiar synthesis of his own.

Ward divided his sociological ideas into those concerning the *genesis* of social structures and functions and those concerning social *telesis* — the application of social science for social improvement. The extensive organicism of his theory may be seen even in the very choice of terms that characterize the nature and development of social structure. Social development is "sympodial"; it develops like those plants which after growing to some degree give off a branch or sympode. Such social development displays creative synthesis; that is, each combination represents something new in nature. Ward's particular term was taken from Wilhelm Wundt, but he was clearly referring to what modern students describe as "emergence." (This is the theory that there are, so to speak, "leaps" in nature, points at which new syntheses occur with properties not explainable in terms of their components.) Any such new synthesis represents the working together of antithetical forces of nature. Ward describes it with the term "synergy." It is crucial to his concept of the spontaneous development of society. In this development, socio-organic forces follow the principle of least resistance of the law of parsimony.

Life itself originated by the creative synthesis of chemical compounds in the process of "zooism," of which mind itself was an emergent product. "Awareness" was an irreducible new element, characterized by the capacity to distinguish pleasure and pain. Feeling and desire, the dynamic elements of mind, had an earlier origin than intellect, a directive faculty.

Spencer and Comte had established the division of sociology into social statics and social dynamics. Ward took these over. *Social statics* was taken as dealing with equilibration and the formation of social structure. Synergy is the most important principle in the formation of successful structure, which emerges in the processes of collision, conflict, antagonism, and opposition, eventually to collaboration, cooperation, and organization. Synergistic development occurs through "social karyokinesis" which, like fertilization in biology, is evident in the amalgamation and synthesis of different social groups.

Social dynamics deals with social process. Three basic principles are operative in it: difference of potential, innovation, and conation. In the contact

---

[21] Ward's major works are: *Dynamic Sociology*, 2 vols. (New York: D. Appleton, 1883; 2d. ed., 1897); *The Psychic Factors of Civilization* (Boston: Ginn, 1893; 2d. ed., 1906); *Outlines of Sociology* (New York: Macmillan, 1898); *Pure Sociology* (New York: Macmillan, 1903; 2d. ed., 1925); and *Applied Sociology* (Boston: Ginn, 1906). For details on Ward's personal life, see Emily Palmer Cape, *Lester F. Ward* (New York: G. P. Putnam, 1922). A general sketch of Ward's work may be found in Harry Elmer Barnes, "Lester Frank Ward: The Reconstruction of Society by Social Science," in Barnes (ed.), *An Introduction to the History of Sociology* (Chicago: University of Chicago Press, 1948), pp. 173–190. See also Samuel Chugerman, *Lester F. Ward: The American Aristotle* (Durham, N.C.: Duke University Press, 1939).

of different cultures, the development of social sports or mutations and social effort are operative. The basic social forces involved in the process are ontogenetic or preservative, phylogenetic or reproductive, and sociogenetic or spiritual. The theory of "gyneocrocracy" explains the peculiar primacy of these forces, for the female sex was original in nature and in human society.

Social telesis refers to the conscious control and direction of social development by the human mind. It is immensely superior to the operation of the blind forces of nature. The telic (purposive) control of social forces is characteristic of human social life. The state was created as the primary agent of conscious manipulation of the social process. It cannot, however, operate with any degree of precision until there is a general diffusion of basic knowledge. A general system of education, thus, is a basic prerequisite for the full realization of social telesis.

In a way it is perhaps too bad that the publication of *Dynamic Sociology* occurred before the appearance of Volume II of Spencer's *Principles of Sociology.* Inasmuch as Spencer had great influence on Ward's initial formulations, the major part of Spencer's investigations of institutions and structure were not a part of this influence. Moreover, Ward never changed in essentials the scheme of *Dynamic Sociology.*

For Ward, as for Comte and Spencer, "society" was the object of sociological analysis. However, he did no better job than his colleagues in formulating the peculiar properties of a society. Comte treated society as equivalent to humanity, but there is obviously no such entity which operates as a single working social unit. Humanity includes the living as well as the dead and people whose activities will never have any effect on the activities of others. Spencer realized that it was necessary to be more specific than this. He defined a society as a plurality of people occupying a specific territory and between whom various common features obtain. This definition of Spencer's, however, does not differentiate "society" and "the state." Ward's concept of society was even vaguer. He assumed that society is some kind of entity organized in accord with the principles of "synergy" and "equilibrium." But this was also, from Ward's position, true of any group.

The principles of "synergy" and "equilibrium" are of less value for the study of institutions than examination of a series of specifically delimited forms. At bottom, institutions are conceived by Ward as constructive equilibria of antagonistic forces. They are ultimately products of human wants. The social classes are three in number: producers, accessories to production, and parasites. Ward's entire discussion of structure is dominated by his reformist interests. This may be illustrated by the following: ". . . long before history began the earth was decked with costly temples, and within them a well-fed and comfortably clothed priesthood sat enjoying, all unearned, the luxuries vouchsafed by toil and credulity. . . . When we consider the universality of this hierarchic system, it presents one of the most extensive drains which are made upon the productive industry of the world." [22]

Ward did far more than simply repeat Comte and Spencer and add new biological and botanical terms to the analysis. Both Comte and Spencer in different ways elevate the value of the "organic" above the artificial. Comte, to be sure, dreams of a utopian society to be established, but it is thoroughly organic in character: caste-like, authoritarian, and fixed. Spencer at all times elevates the organic property of society into a principle opposed to social legislation. "Thus admitting that for the fanatic some wild anticipation is needful as a stimulus, and recognizing the usefulness of his delusion as adapted to his particular nature and his particular function, the man of the higher type must be content with greatly moderated expectations, while he perseveres with undiminished efforts. He has to see how comparatively little can be done, and yet to find it worth while to do that little: so uniting philanthropic energy with philosophic calm." [23] How different this counsel of utmost caution in instituting any social change is from the impetuous revisionism of Ward. Spencer's list of interdicted activities for the state — which should remain merely a joint stock company for the mutual protection of individuals — was famous: commercial regulation, state religious establishments, charitable activities, state education, colonization, sanitation, coinage of money, postal service, provision of lighthouses, and improvement of harbors.[24] For Ward, by contrast, the whole meaning of civilization lies in the triumph of the artificial over the natural. He wants neither the conservative utopia of Comte nor the rugged individualism of Spencer. His principle was "meliorism," the improvement of social conditions through the application of scientific intelligence. "There is one form of government that is stronger than autocracy or aristocracy or democracy, or even plutocracy, and that is sociocracy. The individual has reigned long enough. The day has come for society to take its affairs into its own hands and shape its own destinies." [25] Sociocracy is not considered to be identical with socialism. It is argued that, while individualism creates artificial inequalities, socialism seeks to create others. Sociocracy, however, recognizes natural inequalities and abolishes artificial ones. Whereas individualism confers benefits on those who obtain them by power, cunning, intelligence, or position, socialism would confer benefits on all equally. But sociocracy would confer benefits strictly in proportion to merit, determined in terms of equality of opportunity. In contrast to his conservative European colleagues, Ward was beginning to disintegrate the conservative synthesis and restore the combination of liberalism and positivism of the eighteenth-century rationalists.

---

[22] *Dynamic Sociology*, I, p. 589.
[23] Spencer, *The Study of Sociology*, p. 403.
[24] *Social Statics*, pp. 206 ff.
[25] *Psychic Factors in Civilization*, p. 323.

Positivistic Elements in the Sociology
of the Founders of Positivistic Organicism

Positivism, the view that the methods which had proved their worth in the physical sciences were appropriate to the study of social phenomena, was inseparably built into Comte's sociology. Sociology was, in fact, Comte's substitute for metaphysical philosophy, traditional common sense, and theology. Sociological knowledge is not in principle different from other forms of scientific knowledge; it is merely more complex and less general. Moreover, Comte argued, the more general knowledge of the physical sci- ences is essential as a foundation for biological and, eventually, sociological knowledge. Comte's classification of the sciences with sociology at the apex expressed these notions.

As sociology assumes its place in the hierarchy of sciences, Comte main- tains, its means of investigation must be partly peculiar to it ("direct") and partly "indirect," or arising from sociology's relation to the other sciences. According to Comte, the three direct methods of sociology are observation, experiment, and comparison. To be effective, *observation* must be guided by theory:

> No real observation of any kind of phenomena is possible, except in as far as it is first directed, and finally interpreted, by some theory. . . .
> Scientifically speaking, all isolated, empirical observation is idle, and even radically uncertain. . . . science can use only those observations which are connected, at least hypothetically, with some law.[26]

Experimentation, the second of the methods, has only incidental applica- tion to social science materials:

> If direct experimentation had become too difficult amidst the complexities of biology, it may well be considered impossible in social science. Any arti- ficial disturbance of any social element must affect all the rest, according to the laws both of co-existence and succession.[27]

Since everything in society is related to everything else, it follows that to change one thing, whether for experimental purposes or not, is to change everything. Since one cannot know everything, experiment can yield no knowledge; it can only render the world more irrational. However, Comte opines, the situation is not completely hopeless, for one can always observe pathological states of society, using them as a kind of spontaneous experi- ment.

It is on *comparison* that sociology must rely for its successes. In part, it is possible to compare contemporary with primitive society. "By this method, the different states of evolution may all be observed at once." [28]

[26] *Positive Philosophy,* II, p. 97.
[27] *Ibid.,* p. 100.   [28] *Ibid.,* p. 103.

However, the truly significant comparisons are always historical:

> The historical comparison of the consecutive states of humanity is not only
> the chief scientific device of the new political philosophy. Its . . . develop-
> ment constitutes the substratum of the science, in whatever is essential to
> it.[29]

Herbert Spencer shared Comte's positivism. He assumed that scientific
knowledge is the highest form of knowledge available. Its peculiarities lie
in the rejection of metaphysical pretenses and in rigidly confining itself to
the demonstration of the laws of phenomena.

> Ultimate Scientific Ideas . . . are all representative of realities that can-
> not be comprehended. After no matter how great a progress in the colli-
> gation of facts and the establishment of generalizations ever wider and
> wider . . . the fundamental truth remains as much beyond reach as ever. . . .
> The man of science sees himself in the midst of perpetual changes, of which
> he can discover neither the beginning nor the end.
> Supposing him in every case able to resolve the appearances, properties,
> and movements of things into manifestations of Force in Space and Time,
> he still finds that Force, Space and Time pass all understanding.[30]

Unknown causes work known effects, which we call phenomena, and between
these phenomena likenesses and differences may be discovered. Space and
time are the "modes of cohesion" under which such manifestations invariably
appear. The manifestations themselves are perceived as forms of matter and
motion:

> Over and over again it has been shown in various ways, that the deepest
> truths we can reach are simply statements of the widest uniformities in our
> experience of the relations of Matter, Motion, and Force; and that Matter,
> Motion, and Force are but symbols of the Unknown Reality. A Power of
> which the nature remains forever inconceivable, and to which no limits in
> Time or Space can be imagined, works in us certain effects. These effects
> have certain likenesses of kind, the most general of which we class together
> under the names of Matter, Motion and Force; and between these effects
> there are likenesses of connection, the most constant of which we class as
> laws of the highest certainty.[31]

Among the most general of such laws is evolution, representing an integration of matter and dissipation of motion.[32] Spencer believed that the change
from incoherent homogeneity to coherent heterogeneity is at work throughout
the universe:

> . . . there is habitually a passage from homogeneity to heterogeneity, along
> with the passage from diffusion to concentration. While the matter compos-
> ing the Solar System has been assuming a denser form, it has changed from

[29] *Ibid.*, p. 105.   [30] *First Principles*, pp. 78–79.
[31] *Ibid.*, pp. 548–49.   [32] *Ibid.*, p. 289.

unity to variety of distribution. Solidification of the Earth has been accompanied by a progress from comparative uniformity to extreme multiformity. In the course of its advance from a germ to a mass of relatively great bulk, every plant and animal also advances from simplicity to complexity. The increase of a society in numbers and consolidation has for its concomitant an increased heterogeneity both of its political and industrial organization. And the like holds of all super-organic products — Language, Science, Art, and Literature.[33]

Thus the same laws obtain within all classes of phenomena, each science merely establishing them in its particular sphere. The method by which sociologists do this for social phenomena is ultimately comparative:

By making due use not so much of that which past and present witnesses intend to tell us, as of what they tell us by implication, it is possible to collect data for inductions respecting social structures and functions in their origin and development: the obstacles which arise in the disentangling of such data in the case of any particular society, being mostly surmountable by the help of the comparative method.[34]

Lester Ward, who was a scientist in his own right as well as a careful reader of Comte and Spencer, agreed with them in the location of social science knowledge in a context of the physical sciences. He rested his case for sociology on the comparative method:

It is the function of methodology in social science to classify social phenomena in such a manner that the groups may be brought under uniform laws and treated by exact methods. Sociology then becomes an exact science. In doing this, too, it will be found that we have passed from chaos to cosmos. Human history presents a chaos. The only science that can convert the milky way of history into a definite social universe is sociology, and this can only be done by the use of an appropriate method, by using the data furnished by all the special social sciences, including the great scientific trunks of psychology, biology, and cosmology, and generalizing and coördinating the facts and groups of facts until unity is attained.[35]

One need never doubt the basic positivism of the founders of sociology.

Summary

Sociology became manifest first as a new point of view within traditional philosophy. The conceptual resources at its disposal were as deep and as rich as Western philosophy itself. At the same time, there was no doubt about the novelty of the new point of view, fusing as it did tendencies in Western thought that had hitherto been opposed. The characterization of this point of view as "positivistic organicism" immediately calls attention to the potential conflict within it.

[33] *Ibid.*, pp. 535–36.
[34] *The Study of Sociology*, pp. 101–102.
[35] *Pure Sociology*, p. 62.

Organicism is that tendency in thought which constructs its picture of the world on an organic model. An organismic metaphysics refers to the attempt to explain the world, or reality, or the universe, as a kind of organism. This organismic tendency is anchored in the idealistic philosophies of the West. Plato and Aristotle, for example, advocated a kind of transcendent idealism, conceiving true reality to be a kind of living world beyond this world. Modern forms of idealism tend to relocate reality at the very core of experience. The philosopher Berkeley, for instance, thought that reality was as it was experienced to be, a subjective structure whose objective properties were sustained by the mind of God. A position somewhere between the subjective idealism of Berkeley and the transcendent idealism of the ancient Greeks was developed by Hegel, for whom reality represented the processes of history and the development of civilization through time. The development of civilization was conceived as the maturation of an objective mind. Finally, an irrational idealism or an idealism of the will was developed by Nietzsche and Schopenhauer, who went so far as to conceive the very law of gravitation as a kind of hungry will force.

Positivism is that movement in thought which attempts to explain the world exclusively in terms of experience or what experience eventually reduces to — facts, forces, energies, or something of the sort. The strong naturalism we tend to identify as positivistic was present in the Greek world in various ways in the atomists and the Sophists, but they were never able to bring it to full expression. Positivism has only come into its own with the rise of science. In the modern world it is almost synonymous with the attempt to make the procedures of science the norm of all effective thought. Thus the true beginnings of modern positivism trace to the *Novum Organum* (1620) and other writings of Francis Bacon, with the proposal to extend science to every area of social and personal experience. Further developments of a positivistic empiricist spirit appear in the work of the British empiricists (Locke, Berkeley, and Hume) and the French and English utilitarians (Condillac, Helvétius, Voltaire, Bentham, and John Stuart Mill).

These philosophical points of view, idealism and positivism, have tended to have a characteristic social anchorage. Idealism has almost always been associated with philosophies of social conservatism. In the ancient world Plato and Aristotle were conservatives. In the modern world both the objective idealists and the irrational idealists were conservative. Hegel, for example, thought the state was the march of God through the world; and Nietzsche and Schopenhauer were even opposed to science itself. The positivists, on the other hand, both in the ancient and modern world tended to line up on the side of social reform. The Sophists were feared by Plato and Aristotle for this reason. In the modern world a whole series of reformist programs have been begun in the name of science from the time of Bacon's *New Atlantis*.

Following the events of the French Revolution in the closing days of the eighteenth century, the linkage of idealism with social reaction became particularly strong, as manifest in the writings of Edmund Burke, Joseph de Maistre, and Louis de Bonald. Meanwhile, the positivistic program became linked to the programs of scientific socialism, as may be seen in the works of Saint-Simon, Proudhon, Marx, Owen, Blanc, John Stuart Mill, and others.

It was under these circumstances that sociology made its appearance. It was dramatic as a spark across the positive–negative intellectual and social poles of the time. The fact that its contradictions were not seized upon as representing an impossible confusion testifies to the social need for such a new discipline. The world was unwilling to abandon either the idealistic and conservative image of society or the program of science. The Comtean synthesis of these two intellectual and social tendencies was so significant that the new point of view spread, was copied, and soon became an independent discipline.

The three great original founders of sociology adapted the synthesis of organicism and positivism to the social and intellectual environments of their respective countries: Comte for France, Spencer for England, and Lester F. Ward for the United States. In this adaptation different features of the point of view were emphasized. In the case of Ward, there is indication of a tendency for the synthesis to come apart at the seams. There was already little doubt that the inner tensions of these opposed modes of thought were going to become the dramatic element in the evolution of positivistic organicism.

SELECTED BIBLIOGRAPHY

BARNES, HARRY ELMER, (ed.), *An Introduction to the History of Sociology* Chicago: University of Chicago Press, 1948.

BOOTH, A. J., *Saint-Simon and Saint-Simonism.* New York: Longmans, Green, 1871.

COMTE, AUGUSTE, *The Positive Philosophy of Auguste Comte.* Two volumes. Freely translated and condensed by Harriet Martineau. London: J. Chapman, 1853.

ELLWOOD, CHARLES A., *A History of Social Philosophy.* New York: Prentice-Hall, 1938.

EWING, A. C., *Idealism.* London: Methuen, 1934.

MISES, RICHARD VON, *Positivism: A Study in Human Understanding.* Cambridge, Mass.: Harvard University Press, 1951.

SPENCER, HERBERT, *The Study of Sociology.* New York: D. Appleton, 1882, 1908.

4

The Classical Period of
Positivistic Organicism

EVERY SCHOOL OF THOUGHT THAT MANAGES TO SURVIVE MUST FIRST GO through a pioneering or heroic phase. Comte, Spencer, Ward, and their immediate associates did their work well, and positivistic organicism went on to higher things. Before it could reach its full richness, however, this first school of sociology had to adapt itself to the changing requirements of its *milieu*. For a while, it was strongly deflected toward pure biological organicism, reflecting the powerful claims of nineteenth-century biology on the times. For sociology, however, this was a dead end, and the new field had to shake itself free of such influences to find its proper field.

Extreme Bio-organicists

The organismic theory of society has ancient origins in idealistic philosophy. The biological form of idealistic theory, on the other hand, is a relatively modern phenomenon, a product of the imitation of the splendid gains of nineteenth-century biology. Sorokin, who has given some thought to the matter, quite correctly argues that the organic conception of society has everywhere been most popular among philosophers.[1] He distinguishes three types of organicism: (1) philosophical, conceiving society as a super- or trans-individual reality; (2) psychosocial, conceiving society as a super-individual organism of ideas, representations, minds, and volitions; and (3) bio-organismic, conceiving society as like a biological organism in its

[1] Pitirim Sorokin, *Contemporary Sociological Theories* (New York: Harper, 1928).

nature, functions, origin, development, and variations. Sorokin is also quite correct in his assertion that organismic theories of one sort or other have been held by ancient Hindu, Chinese, Greek, and Roman writers. The dramatic development in biology culminating in the work of Darwin led to the special development in the latter part of the nineteenth century of a new series of bio-organismic theories.[2]

Paul von Lilienfeld (1829–1903), a Russian of German stock who had a place in the aristocracy and had held a number of political offices, seems to have arrived at his organicism independently of Spencer. His biological theories were elaborated in three books written between 1870 and 1900.[3] Society was conceived to be a living organism composed of smaller ones. The nervous system of the individual and society is argued to be similar. There is an inter-cellular substance binding the social organism together. There were three stages of social evolution from savagery through barbarism to civilization and every individual recapitulates these stages. Lilienfeld invented the term "social pathology" to refer to the study of maladjustments of society — disorders of industry, politics, justice, which operate in society like insanity, disease, and paralysis in the individual. The chief source of contemporary social pathology was seen to be the conflict between science and religion, which social science should mediate.

Albert Schäffle (1831–1903), who taught as an economist at Tübingen and Vienna, shows in his work [4] the influences of Spencer, Lilienfeld, and Darwin. The divisions of sociology were presented as social morphology, social physiology, and social psychology, which study individuals, national positions, social tissues and organs, and the mental life of society. His five types of social tissue homologous to biological tissue include somewhat direct organic comparisons such as settlements, buildings, and roads; protective tissues like the epidermal tissues of the body, including clothing, roofs, safes, the army, police; economic arrangements like nourishing tissues of the body; technical social structures for the application of social power (army, police) like the muscular tissues; and psychosocial tissues similar to the nerves, compassing all institutions concerned with intellectual and authoritative activity, the school, the state, science, and the church. The social organs are made up of the social tissues. For Schäffle, group life was the unit of conflict, mutual

---

[2] A review of the bio-organismic group can be found in Albion Small, *General Sociology* (Chicago: University of Chicago Press, 1905, 1925), pp. 109–167; Pitirim Sorokin, *op. cit.*, pp. 194–208; Harry Elmer Barnes and Howard Becker, *Social Thought from Lore to Science* (2d. ed.; Washington, D.C.: Harren Press, 1952), pp. 664–691; and E. Kilzer and E. J. Ross, *Western Social Thought* (Milwaukee: Bruce, 1954), pp. 340–347.

[3] None of Lilienfeld's works are available in English translation. The three books referred to here are: *Gedanken über die Socialwissenschaft der Zukunft* ["Thoughts on the Social Science of the Future"] (Mitau: 1873–81); *La Pathologie sociale* ["Social Pathology"] (Paris: 1896); and *Zur Vertheidigung der organischen Methode in der Sociologie* ["In Defense of the Organic Method in Sociology"] (Berlin: 1898).

[4] English translations are not available for Schäffle's major sociological works: *Bau und Leben des socialen Körpers* ["Structure and Life of the Social Body"], 4 vols. (Tübingen: 1875–78) and *Gesammelte Aufsätze* ["Collected Works"] (Tübingen: 1885–86).

aid, and survival. In Small's estimate, "Schäffle even elaborates some bio-logical parallels more minutely than Spencer does. . . . The difference, as I see it, reduces to this: Spencer does not succeed in making his interpre-tation of society . . . more than an *organization of mechanisms.* Schäffle's central conception of society is of an *organization of work.*" [5]

Alfred Fouillée (1838–1912), the French philosopher, has special interest among the bio-organicists. In his main works,[6] he makes the unique attempt to combine the ideas of social contract and organism. The doctrines of con-tract theory had been anchored in circles holding a mechanical conception of the state. Social-contract theory had implemented the notion of society as a purely rational arrangement for instrumental purposes. Fouillée's fusion thus has special interest. For Fouillée, society was a "contractual organ-ism." It had both natural and artificial causes. The psychological character of social organization rests on the spontaneous attraction of people for one another, resting on sympathy. This becomes the basis of sociability. Society and the organism have five characteristics in common: concurrence of dis-similar parts; a functional distribution of members; organic subunits; spon-taneity of movement; and the property of growth and decay. Society emerges as a new organism when men meet in assembly and when in their thinking they symbolize society as an independent form. Society arises because it has been thought and desired. It is born of an idea and is thus a con-tractual organism.

Another French scholar, René Worms (1869–1926), developed the bio-organismic thesis in a number of works.[7] Society was conceived to be an enduring aggregation of living beings, exercising activity in common. In both the organism and society, external structures vary in time and are irregular in form; internal structures undergo constant change through assimilation and integration, dissimilation and disintegration; there is a coordinated dif-ferentiation of parts; and both have power of reproduction. Detailed analo-gies are traced with regard to structure, function, evolution, and pathology.

There were many other extreme bio-organicists such as Jacques Novicow (1849–1912), the Russian industrialist from Odessa, Guillaume de Greef (1842–1924), the first sociologist of the University of Brussels, and the Scottish philosopher J. S. McKenzie (1860–1935). But it would serve no particular value to trace the views of these and others. Small put the matter very compactly. *"Not merely in sociology, but in every department of*

---

[5] Albion Small, *General Sociology*, p. 167.

[6] Fouillée's main sociological works, none of which are available in English translation, are: *La Science sociale contemporaine* ["Contemporary Social Science"] (Paris: 1880) ; *La Psychologie des idées-forces* ["The Psychology of Ideal Forces"], 2 vols. (Paris: 1893) ; and *Le Mouvement positiviste et la conception sociologique du monde* ["The Positivist Movement and the Sociological Conception of the World"] (Paris: 1896).

[7] René Worms' sociological works, none of which are available in English translation, include: *Organicisme et société* ["Organicism and Society"] (Paris: Giard & Brière, 1896) ; *Philosophie des sciences sociales* ["Philosophy of the Social Sciences"], 3 vols. (Paris: Giard & Brière, 1903–1907) ; *Les Principes biologiques de l'évolution sociale* ["The Biological Principles of Social Evolution"] (Paris: Giard & Brière, 1910) ; and *La Sociologie* (Paris: Giard, 1921; 2d. rev. ed., 1926).

knowledge, the organic concept is the most distinctive modern note. . . . The most intimate and complex and constructive coherence of elements that we discover, previous to our study of society, is the coworking of part with part in vital phenomena. About a generation ago, men who wanted to understand the social reality more precisely began to make systematic use of ascertained vital relationships as provisional symbols of societary relationships." [8] The bio-organismic school retained strong affinities with the positivistic point of view. It sustained, in fact, strong "reductionistic" tendencies, and despite the occasional admission that there is no complete identity between the individual and social organism, it assumes that, by and large, the laws of society are merely a special application of the laws of biology.

Bio-organicism has disappeared rather completely. When one asks what permanent residue of findings it left to sociology, it is remarkably difficult to come up with anything. In the perspective of the present, its importance lies at a semi-ideological rather than conceptual level. During the time when sociology was emerging, biology underwent spectacular development — it was the bright new star in the nineteenth-century firmament. Bio-organicism in sociology represented an attempt to link the fortunes of the two disciplines. It was made plausible by the older "organicism" which sociology had derived from its idealistic components. Bio-organicism actually served the function of "protecting" the new field of sociology by camouflaging it. Among prevailing nineteenth-century trends, it added a protective armor around the discipline until it became strong enough to fend for itself. In time, the grotesque analogies to which it led became offensive and it was dismissed as the "big animal" theory of society.

The Classic Phase of Positivistic Organicism

There has been a somewhat unfortunate tendency to define the organismic theory in such narrow terms as to obscure the extent of its theoretical assemblage of ideas. For example, in many works "organicism" is confined to the persons sketched in the previous section. Comte, Spencer, and Ward are treated as a sort of pre-organismic type of theorist and the organismic school proper is dismissed as if it terminated with Worms, de Greef, and Novicow. However, this is to shift attention away from precisely those organicists who left the most decisive mark on sociology. The organismic framework is shared not only by Comte, Spencer, and Ward but also by such persons as Tönnies and Durkheim. Both of the latter thinkers restylized and developed organismic ideas in a manner that gave them long-range importance for sociology, having influences into the present.

Ferdinand Tönnies

Ferdinand Tönnies (1855–1936) was born on a farm in Eiderstedt on

---

[8] Albion Small, *General Sociology*, pp. 74–75. This was Small's statement of the case in 1905. (Italics in the original.)

the coast of Schleswig-Holstein. He received his doctor's degree from the University of Tübingen in 1877, and became a lecturer at the University of Kiel in 1881, where he remained until ousted by the Nazis in 1933. The most influential of Tönnies' works was his *Gemeinschaft und Gesellschaft* (1887), translated into English as *Community and Society;* it is the only one of his works generally appreciated in America, although in his later works he applied the influential concepts first developed in *Community and Society* to various social phenomena, among which might be singled out his study of folkways and mores in *Die Sitte* ["Custom"] and of public opinion in *Kritik der öffentlichen Meinung* ["Critique of Public Opinion"].[9] Among empirical studies conducted by Tönnies was the review of the social situation of the longshoremen in Hamburg and other ports after the strike in Hamburg, the study of relationships between socio-economic conditions and ideological phenomena in Schleswig-Holstein, and the study of cyclical changes in marriage rates and the sex ratio.

Tönnies divided sociology into three disciplines: (1) pure sociology, (2) applied sociology, and (3) empirical sociology. *Pure* or general sociology aspires to develop a system of concepts of "normal" or ideal types essential for the description and understanding of empirical phenomena. *Applied* sociology consists in the application of these concepts to contemporary and historical phenomena. As with Comte, sociology is the study of history. This discipline studies society dynamically and developmentally. *Empirical* sociology proceeds by inductive empirical methods utilizing the concepts of pure sociology as basic orientation devices. In his own work, Tönnies approached these areas by way of the *Gemeinschaft–Gesellschaft* dichotomy which he made famous.

All the facts of society and social relationship are viewed by Tönnies as products of the human will. "Social relationship or bond implies interdependence, and it means that the will of the one person influences that of the other, either furthering or impeding, or both. . . . The collective will can remain the same for an indefinite period, but it can also from time to

---

[9] Only two of Tönnies' books are presently available in English translation: *Gemeinschaft und Gesellschaft* (Leipzig: 1887; Berlin: K. Curtius, 1926) has been translated by Charles P. Loomis and published, first, as *Fundamental Concepts of Sociology* (New York: American Book Company, 1940) and, later, as *Community and Society* (East Lansing, Mich.: Michigan State University Press, 1957); and *Thomas Hobbes Leben und Lehre* (Stuttgart: F. Frommann, 1925), the third revised edition of a study first published in 1896, has been translated and published under the title *The Elements of Law, Natural and Political* (Cambridge, England: The University Press, 1928). Important works which are not available in English include: *Die Sitte* (Frankfurt am Main: Rütten & Loening, 1909); *Marx: Leben und Lehre* ["The Life and Teachings of Marx"] (Jena: E. Lichtenstein, 1921); *Kritik der öffentlichen Meinung* (Berlin: J. Springer, 1922); *Soziologische Studien und Kritiken* ["Sociological Studies and Critiques"] (Jena: G. Fischer, 1925–26); and *Einführung in die Soziologie* ["Introduction to Sociology"] (Stuttgart: F. Enke, 1931). An excellent review of Tönnies' sociology is Rudolf Heberle's "The Sociological System of Ferdinand Tönnies: 'Community' and 'Society' ", in Harry Elmer Barnes (ed.), *An Introduction to the History of Sociology* (Chicago: University of Chicago Press, 1948), pp. 227–248.

time undergo change by renewed acts. . . . Such a collective person consists of single persons." [10]

The organismic core of Tonnies' thought could not be more clearly formulated. All interaction is at bottom the expression of acts of will. The result of acts of will is the development of a collective will. This collective will is very like a person. Fundamental to Tönnies' whole view is the concept of different types of will.

The simplest way of approaching the problems of Tönnies' sociology is through the interrelationships involved in exchange or barter. When we barter, two objects are involved in such a way that each is a means to the other considered as an end. An act of barter or exchange consists in carrying out an interrelationship in such terms. One can imagine an entire system of social life in which all acts are carried out in this manner. In contrast, there are situations in which one's motives to satisfy his aims and desires take the form of satisfying those of another person or of groups. Such a volition, of this latter type, rests not on a calculation of means and the appropriateness of means to ends; rather, it is unconditional, like the love of a mother for an infant. Such unconditional relationships are not necessarily positive. Between man and woman, love may turn to hate, which becomes a kind of inverted love. Thus we have two kinds of social relationship, resting on two types of human willing. In the first case, we can speak of a rational will (*Kürwille*), in the second, of a natural will (*Wesenwille*).[11]

The simplest and most general unit of social life is the *social relationship*. Sociology as a special science is interested in the products of social life. These social products result from human thinking and exist only for human thinking. Social relationship is the most elementary of these things. Social relationships cannot be other than the embodiments of one of the two fundamental forms of the human will — *Kürwille* or *Wesenwille*. One total complex of social relationships (society) may differ from another as a result of the type of will predominant in it. In terms of the kind of will involved, two ideal types (also called "normal concepts") of society are possible. A society or total complex of social relationships which embodies the rational will is called a *Gesellschaft;* a complex embodying the natural will is a *Gemeinschaft*. A collective has the character of a *Gemeinschaft* insofar as its members think of the grouping as a gift of nature created by a supernatural will. On the other hand, to the degree that consciousness of authority arises from class relationships, the collective tends to assume the characteristics of a *Gesellschaft*.

Social entities of lesser scope than the entire society may be characterized in similar terms. The corporation is a social body or union. It can emerge from natural relationships, as does the kinship group, the gens, or the clan. Common relation to the soil tends to associate people, and the neigh-

---

[10] *Fundamental Concepts of Sociology*, pp. 9–10.
[11] In making this contrast, Tönnies seems to have had Wilhelm Wundt's contrast between *Zweckwille* and *Triebwille* partly in mind.

borhood may be the product of such an association. On the other hand, in the development of the state — the mightiest of all corporate bodies — or in the development of the characteristic corporations of capitalistic, middle-class society, the original qualities of the *Gemeinschaft* may be lost.

Tönnies thus distinguishes three main types of social units: social relationships, groups, and societies. All of these units are characterized by their volitional components. However, the manner in which these volitional components differentiate total societies has attracted greatest interest, for from this base Tönnies developed his famous contrast of societal types, tracing out multiple lines of contrast through such things as the dominant social relationship, theory of personality, central corporate group, and many others. The accompanying table shows some of the more interesting contrasts which Tönnies developed — or, in some instances, summarized from his predecessors — to compare *Gemeinschaft* and *Gesellschaft* societal types.

| SOCIAL CHARACTERISTIC | SOCIETAL TYPE: | |
	Gemeinschaft	*Gesellschaft*
Dominant Social Relationship	Fellowship Kinship Neighborliness	Exchange Rational calculation
Central Institutions	Family law Extended kin group	State Capitalistic economy
The Individual in the Social Order	Self	Person
Characteristic Form of Wealth	Land	Money
Type of Law	Family Law	Law of contracts
Ordering of Institutions	Family life Rural village life Town life	City life Rational life Cosmopolitan life
Type of Social Control	Concord Folkways and mores Religion	Convention Legislation Public opinion

The mentality basic to the *Gemeinschaft* is characteristic of the woman, and operates through sentiment. The mentality basic to the *Gesellschaft* is characteristic of the man, and operates through intention. The first appears through the mind and consciousness, the second through calculation and conscious behavior. Moreover, the same contrast appears between youth and old age, and the common people and educated classes. The *Gemeinschaft*, thus, is typical of the woman, the young, the masses. The *Gesellschaft* is typical of the man, of old age, and of the educated classes.

It has already been observed that having developed the contrast between the *Gemeinschaft* and the *Gesellschaft*, Tönnies applied it to the societal sub-units — social relationships and social corporations or groups. In the case of the corporation, the social body is thought of as a person possessing a rational will to which it can give validity through functionaries. But in any case, all three categories of social entity (*Wesenheiten*) were thought to be determined primarily either by *Wesenwillen* or *Kürwillen*. The same scheme was applied to social norms and values. The main classes of norms distinguished by Tönnies are order, law, and morality. The kinds of social will by which they are created are *gemeinschaftliche* (including unanimity or concord, custom, or religion, the last based on faith in supernatural powers) or *gesellschaftliche*, based on convention, legislation, or public opinion. *Order* is the most general and complex of norms, based primarily on concord or convention. *Law* is the complex of norms enforced by judicial decision; it is created by either custom or intentional "legislation." *Morality* is the complex of those norms the interpretation and application of which are the work of an imaginary judge (God or conscience); the norms of morality are sanctioned either by religion or public opinion.

The public opinion of a country or nation is an expression of group will and not, as popularly conceived, a conglomeration of contradictory views. Public opinion as politically valid opinion must be distinguished from local or apolitical opinion. Public opinion can be more or less fixed, fluid, or gaseous, depending on the issues involved.

The idea of developing conceptions of contrasting types of society was by no means new in Tönnies' day. There is no value in reviewing early forms, for dualistic constructions of human society are as old as mythology. Tönnies himself was familiar with a number of them. The eighteenth-century rationalists had advanced the idea of the origin of society in a contract and the rational agreements this implied. An extreme form of the rationalistic and contractual conception of society was expressed by Thomas Hobbes, with whom Tönnies was thoroughly familiar. The opponents of eighteenth-century rationalistic conceptions, among them the romantic conservatives of the nineteenth century, developed organic conceptions of the state. Tönnies specifically intended in his typology to represent the Hobbesian concept of society in the *Gesellschaft*, the romantic concept in the *Gemeinschaft*.

A somewhat similar set of ideas was familiar to Tönnies from Henry Sumner Maine. In his *Ancient Law*,[12] Maine traced, by means of the law, the development of ancient society. On the basis of the evidence of Roman law, Maine advanced the patriarchal theory of society — the idea that in antiquity society was organized into households in which the eldest male was supreme, having dominion extending to life and death over his children and slaves. Maine believed that one can trace, in Roman legal develop-

---

[12] Henry Sumner Maine, *Ancient Law* (London: 1861). References here are to the 1906 edition (New York: Henry Holt).

ment, the gradual decline in the authority of the father. Thus, for example, first the son was freed from the father's influence — a phenomenon attributable to the Roman army and civil administration, which required that the state receive the primary loyalty of its servants. Under later systems even the woman gradually achieved freedom. In ancient society, thus, Maine urges, the individual's life chances were fixed by his status in the family. The patriarchal origin of society allowed little room for the idea of contract. In its earliest form one family could contract with another only in the most ceremonious of manners. But in time contractual relationships spread to wider and wider spheres. "If then we employ Status . . . to signify these personal conditions only . . . we may say that the movement of the progressive societies has hitherto been a movement *from Status to Contract.*" [13]

These distinctions, too, were taken up into Tönnies' typology. Moreover, he was not only familiar with Wundt's contrast of mentalities in *Zweckwille* and *Triebwille* and Hegel's conception of the development of history as the evolution of the human spirit from the ancient world, in which only one (the despot) is free, to modern situations, where all are free, but with the contrast of societal types employed by Comte and Spencer. Comte believed that society evolved through three major types: theological, metaphysical, and positivistic. The metaphysical, corresponding to the eighteenth century, was little more than a transitional type. Spencer, on the other hand, reduced the major types to two: religious-militaristic and modern industrial-peaceable. All these and many other conceptions of contrasting social types were familiar to Tönnies. However, he did far more than merely summarize. He pulled together all the main ideas into a systematic form. He developed the notion of an underlying integral mentality. He systematized the contrasts. He identified them with social development. The organismic character of the system is all-pervasive, but this is not its only important property. So long as one employs simply an over-all conception of society, organismic or not, made up of little-differentiated parts, analysis cannot proceed far. But a dichotomous typology made up of carefully itemized elements can, however crude, at least serve as a device for comparative review. It is for this reason that all modern societal typologies — such as Durkheim's distinction between "mechanical" and "organic" solidarity, Park's "sacred–secular" distinction, Redfield's "folk–secular" distinction — take Tönnies' conceptualizations as a starting point.

Émile Durkheim

The very utility of Tönnies' formulations for later sociological purposes seems to have obscured the anchorage of his ideas in organicism. The same appears to be true of the theories of Durkheim. Émile Benoît-Smullyan invented the term "agelicism" to epitomize Durkheim's theories:

---

[13] *Ibid.*, p. 165. (Italics in the original.)

By "agelicism" we mean the general sociological doctrine which maintains the reality *sui generis* or the causal priority of the social group *qua* group. Agelicism in its modern form was introduced into the stream of French social thought by de Bonald and de Maistre, who maintained that the social group precedes and constitutes the individual, that it is the source of culture and all the higher values, and that social states and changes are not produced by, and cannot be directly affected or modified by, the desires and volitions of individuals.[14]

Quibbles over terminology have no interest here. By "agelicism" Benoît-Smullyan means precisely the "organismic thesis" in social science, no more, no less. The importance of Benoît-Smullyan's statement lies in its correct relocation of Durkheim's thought at the very core of the organismic school.

Émile Durkheim (1855–1917), the son of a Jewish rabbi, entered the École Normale Supérieure of Paris in 1879, and after three years' study there began to teach philosophy. It is significant for his organicism that one of the works which aroused his interest in sociology was Schäffle's *Structure and Life of the Social Body*. In 1885 and 1886 he studied in Germany. In 1887, he inaugurated the first course in social science to be offered in France at the University of Bordeaux.

Durkheim's first book, his doctoral dissertation on *The Division of Labor in Society*, was published in 1893.[15] Because of his familiarity with Comte, Spencer, Schäffle, Tönnies, Wundt, Alfred Espinas, and Evgeni de Roberty, Durkheim was in a position to ask precise questions. Taking (in *The Division of Labor*) the fact of social solidarity as the essential property of society, he divided societies into two primary types in a manner suggestive of Tönnies: those in which social solidarity was *mechanical,* or dominated by a collective consciousness; and those in which it was *organic,* or characterized by specialization, division of labor, and interdependence. Durkheim devoted thought both to the problem of how a transformation of social solidarity occurs and how one is to determine its state or degree. He believed

---

[14] Émile Benoît-Smullyan, "The Sociologism of Émile Durkheim and His School," in Barnes, *An Introduction to the History of Sociology,* p. 499.

[15] Almost all of Durkheim's major sociological writings have been translated into English: *De la Division du travail social* (Paris: F. Alcan, 1893) has been translated by George Simpson as *The Division of Labor in Society* (Glencoe, Ill.: The Free Press, 1947); *Les Règles de la méthode sociologique* (Paris: F. Alcan, 1895) has been translated by Sarah A. Solovay and John H. Mueller as *The Rules of Sociological Method* (Chicago: University of Chicago Press, 1938; Glencoe, Ill.: The Free Press, 1950); *Le Suicide* (Paris: F. Alcan, 1897) has been translated by John A. Spaulding and George Simpson as *Suicide* (Glencoe, Ill.: The Free Press, 1951); *Les Formes élémentaires de la vie religieuse* (Paris: F. Alcan, 1912; 2d. ed., 1925) has been translated by Joseph Ward Swain as *The Elementary Forms of the Religious Life* (New York: Macmillan, 1915; Glencoe, Ill.: The Free Press, 1954); *Éducation et sociologie* (Paris: F. Alcan, 1922) has been translated by S. D. Fox as *Education and Sociology* (Glencoe, Ill.: The Free Press, 1956); *Sociologie et philosophie* (Paris: F. Alcan, 1924) has been translated by D. F. Pocock as *Sociology and Philosophy* (Glencoe, Ill.: The Free Press, 1953); and *Leçons de sociologie* (Paris: Presses Universitaires de France, 1950) has been translated by Cornelia Brookfield as *Professional Ethics and Civic Morals* (London: Routledge & Kegan Paul, 1957). For an evaluation of Durkheim's sociology, see Harry Alpert, *Émile Durkheim and His Sociology* (New York: Columbia University Press, 1939).

that as population grows in size, more complex societies develop. The division of labor was thought to be in direct ratio to the volume and density of society. Moreover, social growth in part takes place by condensation of societies. Such formations require greater division of labor.

The manner in which one is to determine the state of social solidarity led Durkheim to pick up from Maine and Tönnies the idea of the value of law for social analysis. In primitive society, Durkheim believed, solidarity is mechanical, for people are little differentiated and are held together by friendliness, neighborliness, and kinship as if by an external force. At this stage the law of the people will be dominated by *repressive* sanctions. The chief purpose of the law will be to satisfy an outraged collective sentiment. However, when society becomes more complex and its solidarity rests on a differentiation of people, one can no longer afford the luxury of simply giving vent to one's rage. A new motive enters the law — the restoration of the social system to a workable state and the repair, insofar as possible, of any damage done to the injured parties. Law becomes *restitutive* rather than repressive. Thus the law becomes a major index to this most crucial of all social facts — social solidarity.

The drive for a precision of concepts evident in *The Division of Labor* was continued in *The Rules of Sociological Method* (1895). Social solidarity had been conceived as the ensemble of beliefs and sentiments common to the average members of a particular society. This set of beliefs was thought to form a system and have a life of its own. In this further study, Durkheim set out both to give a more precise statement of the nature of sociological facts and to establish the criterion of method. One result was the achievement of one of the best statements of positivistic method to his time. The other achievement was to analyze social solidarity into its component elements. The data of sociology were said to be *social facts*. These are any "ways of acting" capable of "exercising an external constraint on the individual"; they are, moreover, "general throughout" a given society. Societies may be most simply viewed, for Durkheim, as integral complexes of such social facts. The society has a "collective consciousness" which creates values and imposes them as imperative ideals on the individual.

One novel extension of these ideas occurred in Durkheim's study, *Suicide* (1897). He divided suicides into three types: (1) *altruistic* (where the suicide occurs in the interest of a group, as, for example, a war hero); (2) *egoistic* (due to a defect in social organization and search for an escape from the group); and (3) *anomic*, where social adjustment is disrupted (by economic changes such as sudden wealth, economic depression, the rise or fall of a social class). The idea of *anomie* is introduced as a strict counterpart of the idea of social solidarity. Just as social solidarity is a state of collective ideological integration, anomie is a state of confusion, insecurity, "normlessness." The collective representations are in a state of decay.

Another form of the elaboration and extension of these ideas came in *The Elementary Forms of the Religious Life* (1912). Collective representations are again taken as the starting point for analysis. In general, in a manner strongly suggestive of the old empiricists who attempted to derive every basic idea from the data of experience, Durkheim attempts to derive every major social form from the collective representations. Asking, in such manner, what is the object of religious sentiment and the source of its institutions, Durkheim discovers that it cannot be other than the social group itself. The world is divided into the sacred and the profane; the sacred consists of the collective representations of the group itself. Religious representations are those aspects of the collective representations expressing the collective realities. Religious rites are a manner of acting arising in the midst of the assembled group, destined to excite and maintain certain mental states in this group. Religious phenomena are of two classes, dogmas and rites, deriving their force from the social substance or the group within which they are obligatory. From this starting point, Durkheim proposes a sociology of knowledge. Moral facts have a kind of duality. They inspire respect and a feeling of obligation, but we must assume the content of morality is good even if it does not correspond to personal desires. The moral rule cannot emanate from the individual, since no act is moral which has as its exclusive end the conservation and self-development of the individual. The moral fact can only represent a value higher than the self. This higher moral fact is God, which is only society conceived symbolically. Thus religion and the moral life have the same origin.

Durkheim argued that thought depends on language and language depends on society. Thus society produces the basic instrumentality of thought. Moreover, he argues, the fundamental categories of cognition are merely the transformed and refined categories of society itself. The ultimate origins of the concept of "time" are found in the rhythms of group life; the idea of "space" is supplied by the territory occupied by society; the idea of "causality" is supplied by the control which a group exercises over its members.

During the course of his development, Durkheim's underlying organicism grew ever more pronounced:

> Around 1898, Durkheim entered on a new and distinct phase of his work. It is characterized, in the first place, by a more idealistic conception of the social group, with more emphasis on "collective representations" and less on the internal social milieu; and, in the second place, by adventurous speculation concerning the social origin of morals, values, religion, and knowledge. The social group is successively endowed by Durkheim with the characteristics of hyperspirituality, personality, creativity, and transcendence.[16]

But here again the basic organicism of Durkheim's work tends to be forgotten in the face of the fact that his ideas had great utility in later

[16] Benoît-Smullyan, *loc. cit.*, p. 510.

sociology. Durkheim and Tönnies illustrate the conceptual precision possible within the organismic framework.

Positivistic Aspects of the Theories of Tönnies and Durkheim

As positivistic organicism was being brought to its classical stage in the works of Tönnies and Durkheim, the first signs of possible tension between its positivism and its organicism began to appear. All the original exponents of positivistic organicism subscribed to the comparative method. However, this method operated so loosely that a variety of partly contradictory conclusions could be drawn from the same facts. For example, conflicting constructions were made of the evolutionary sequences of societies and social institutions.

Under these circumstances both Tönnies and Durkheim began to employ statistical material in their interpretations of social phenomena. In his study of suicide, Durkheim made extensive use of official statistics; in his study of institutions, he drew upon field data of ethnographers. Tönnies undertook a survey of the socio-economic situation of longshoremen and seamen at various north German ports, investigated the relation between moral and socio-economic conditions in Schleswig-Holstein, studied statistical and other materials collected in the provincial prisons, as well as suicide and marriage rates.[17]

The methodological crisis that was beginning to loom for positivistic organicism not only drove its classic representatives on to the employment of new methodological devices, but forced upon them a new level of methodological self-consciousness. The most impressive attempt to salvage positivistic methods was made by Durkheim in *The Rules of Sociological Method*. Durkheim urged that, while there is a distinction between natural and social science, the methods of natural science are applicable to the social field. Social facts are ways of acting and feeling. The criteria for judging whether given items are to be classified as "social fact" are whether they are capable of exercising constraint over the individual. Durkheim sought to lay down the rules for the observation of social facts. There are, he believed, two types of social facts: normal and pathological. Those facts which are most generally distributed are "normal," others are "pathological."

> A social fact can . . . be called normal for a given social species only in relation to a given phase of its development. . . . we must also take special care to consider them at the corresponding phase of their evolution.[18]

Moreover, Durkheim argues, since a social fact can be construed as normal or abnormal only in relation to a given social species, one branch of sociology must be devoted to the creation and classification of social types. There are rules for the explanation of social facts and rules for establishing

[17] See Rudolf Heberle, *loc. cit.*, pp. 230 ff.
[18] *The Rules of Sociological Method*, p. 57.

sociological proofs. Most of John Stuart Mill's methods, he believed, were not applicable. One can explain a social fact only by following its complete development through all social species. Moreover, societies must be compared at the same period of development, and the sociologist must avoid preconceptions and distinguish between normal and pathological conditions.

Somewhat more clearly than Durkheim, Tönnies glimpsed the potential tension between positivism and organicism:

> As human beings we are able to produce only inorganic things from organic materials, dividing and recombining them. In the same way things are also made into a unity through scientific manipulation and are a unity in our concepts. Naive interpretation or attitudes and artistic imagination, folk belief, and inspired poetry lend life to the phenomena. This creative element is also apparent in the fictions of science. But science also reduces the living to the dead in order to grasp its relations and conditions. It transforms all conditions and forces into movements and interprets all movements as quantities of labor performed, i.e., expended energy, in order to comprehend processes as similar and commensurable. This last is true to the same extent that the assumed units are realities, and the possibility for thought is unlimited. Thus understanding, as an end, is attained and therewith other objectives.
>
> However, the tendencies and inevitableness of organic growth and decay cannot be understood through mechanical means. In the organic world the concept itself is a living reality, changing and developing as does the idea of the individual being. When science enters this realm it changes its own nature and develops from a logical and rational to an intuitive and dialectic interpretation; it becomes philosophy. However, the present study does not deal with genus and species, i.e., in regard to human beings it is not concerned with race, people, or tribe as biological units. Instead, we have in mind their sociological interpretation, which sees human relationships and associations as living organisms or, in contrast, mechanical constructions.[19]

This passage is noteworthy, not only for its confusion between things and the thought about things ("in the organic world the concept itself is a living reality, changing and developing as does the idea of the individual being" — presumably the concept of a man, like an actual man, gets up in the morning, puts on its pants, shaves, and in other ways prepares for a busy day), but for its treatment of science as analysis, analysis as dismemberment, and dismemberment as the destruction of life. Hence, when science deals with living and spiritual matters, we are told, it ceases to have the form of natural science: "it changes its own nature and develops from a logical and rational to an intuitive and dialectic interpretation."

There is little doubt that Tönnies was inclined toward a break with methodological positivism. The same inclination was evident in his handling of "types."

> In living, the organism proves its fitness for life, i.e., the appropriate (correct, good) condition, organization, and order of its focuses or parts.

[19] *Community and Society*, pp. 36–37.

The form, as a whole, is constituted of its elements, which, in relation to it, are of a material character and maintain and propagate themselves through this very relationship. For the whole as a lasting form, each of its parts will always represent a more transitory modification of itself which expresses its nature in a more or less complete manner.

The intuitive and purely intellectual understanding of such a whole can be made easier and more readily grasped through classification by types, each of which is conceived as comprising the characteristic of all examples of the respective groups before their differentiation was made. Thus the types are more nearly perfect than the individuals because they embody also those forces and latent capacities which have withered away through lack of use. But they are also more imperfect, in that they lack the qualities which have been developed to a higher degree in reality.[20]

It is clear that, with other of his colleagues and predecessors, Tönnies retains the view that comparison is the proper method of sociology. Methodologically, the formation of types is the device by which comparisons in the social sciences are made precise. Tönnies, like Durkheim, was thus attempting to tighten up the comparative method inherited by the school from Comte, Spencer, and Ward. However, in his new emphasis on intuition and in assigning types an ontological status such that "types are more nearly perfect than . . . individuals," he is again on the threshold of a radical break with positivism.

Robert Redfield

Undoubtedly the single most able exponent of the classic phase of positivistic organicism in the contemporary period was Robert Redfield (1897–1958). Born in Chicago, he was associated most of his academic life with the Department of Anthropology of the University of Chicago. He received his doctorate in 1928, becoming instructor in anthropology in 1927, and professor in 1934. For some years (1934–1946) he served as Dean of the Division of Social Sciences and was later Chairman of the Department of Anthropology. He was a research associate in charge of ethnological field work for Yucatan and Guatemala for the Carnegie Corporation between 1930 and 1947. Among his major works are *The Folk Culture of Yucatan* (1941), *The Primitive World and Its Transformations* (1953), and *The Little Community* (1955).[21]

[20] *Ibid.*, pp. 172, 173.
[21] For a complete bibliography, see Fay-Cooper Cole and Fred Eggan, "Robert Redfield," *American Anthropologist*, Vol. 61 (August 1959), pp. 652–662. Redfield's best-known works are: *Tepoztlan: A Mexican Village* (Chicago: University of Chicago Press, 1930); *Chan Kom, A Maya Village*, written in collaboration with Alfonso Villa R. (Washington, D.C.: Carnegie Institution of Washington Publication No. 448, 1934); *The Folk Culture of Yucatan* (Chicago: University of Chicago Press, 1941); *A Village That Chose Progress: Chan Kom Revisited* (Chicago: University of Chicago Press, 1950); *The Primitive World and Its Transformations* (Ithaca, N.Y.: Cornell University Press, 1953); *The Little Community* (Chicago: University of Chicago Press, 1955); and *Peasant Society and Culture* (Chicago: University of Chicago Press, 1956).

Redfield observed that he and a number of other social scientists received their introduction to the main stream of sociological ideas from Robert E. Park at the same time.[22] The contrast between what Redfield and some of Park's other students did with this heritage is instructive; their works represent the best and worst possible uses that can be made of societal typologies. One of Redfield's contemporaries reduces ideas designed to deal with the richness of entire societies to the barren contrast between response to the new and response to the old. Even the fact that there are dozens of different ways of responding to the new and the old is ignored. The oversimplified formula that results is advanced as sufficient to account for the differences between entire societies. Next, the *Gemeinschaft–Gesellschaft* typology (or, as it is variously designated, "sacred–secular" or "folk–secular") has been divided into subtypes and these into so many sub-subtypes that it is difficult even to find examples of all of them, indicating the extent to which a great sociological tradition may degenerate into empty verbalisms.

Moreover, the startling suggestion has even been advanced that one can construct a *"Gemeinschaft–Gesellschaft* continuum." [23] "Continuum" is a pertinent concept in geometry and the theory of functions. A straight line may be said to be continuous when between any two points on it there is a third and whenever the line is separated into two pieces there is always an extreme point on one of the pieces which may be taken to define the separation. But the idea that these properties obtain between such complex, multidimensional phenomena as societies is pseudo-science. Quite in keeping with this surrealistic atmosphere, some individuals making this kind of use of the type have argued that they wish to use a typological method to determine how far their types deviate from reality.

Redfield's studies are in refreshing contrast to this. With his first study of the Mexican village of Tepoztlan on the plateau of South Central Mexico, Redfield showed his capacity to use the societal typology of classical positivistic organicism as a skillful tool in field research. Tepoztlan, he felt, was typical of the peoples intermediate between "folk" and "demos." They had even developed an intermediate type of literature in the ballad form known as *corrido*.[24] The *corrido* is no longer the folk song of a truly primitive people, but lies on the threshold of news, public opinion, or propaganda. The folk culture producing these forms is neither Indian nor Spanish but a transitional type.

The fusion of elements from these two sources was traced through the material culture, the organization of community and village, the rhythms of social life, and religion. In its peculiar adjustment to its intermediate

[22] *The Little Community*, p. 143.
[23] It would be unfair to single out for illustration any one individual among those who have made this proposal. The issue is one of the adequate or inadequate use of ideas and not one of personalities.
[24] *Tepoztlan: A Mexican Village*, p. 8.

situation, the community finds its symbolic self-consciousness in songs known as *alabanzas* and *corridos:* the traditional, sacred, ritualistic songs on the one hand and the ephemeral, secular, and historical songs on the other. The *alabanzas* are songs of celebration of the *santos;* the *corridos* recount the exploits of the military heroes, the *veteranos.* The *santos* are local patron saints still found in every rural hamlet like the *barrios* of Tepoztlan. Each has its *santo,* represented by a particular effigy. While the *santo* tends to become a sacred effigy, the *veterano* also tends to become a symbol rather than a particular person. Both are symbols of the ideals and wishes of the ideologically as well as economically self-sufficient group.

The sharpest cultural differences in Mexico, Redfield observed, are not between one region and another, but between the city people (*los correctos*) and the country people (*los tontos*). *Los tontos,* even despite the revolutions that have swept Mexico, tend to live in the mental world of folk culture. However, *los correctos* develop an intelligentsia who live in two worlds. A developing group consciousness is produced by the conflict between these elements, becoming most acute in individuals who, coming to live in the city, look back on the world of the folk. The frontier of change is thus located between *los correctos* and *los tontos.* The diffusion of city traits from their origin in the *plaza* comes into conflict with the traditions of the *barrios.* It is *los correctos* who promote the carnival with its secularized commercial aspects; but in the end, *los tontos* control the religious *fiestas* commemorating *santos.* In fact, the nearer a birth occurs to the *plaza,* the less the proportion of merely ritualistic and expressive behavior that attends the occasion. While the difference between *los correctos* and *los tontos* increases in times of disorder, it is always decreased in times of peace, showing the constant quiet erosion of the old ways.

Between *Tepoztlan* (1930) and *The Folk Culture of Yucatan* (1941), a considerable increase in conceptual subtlety and empirical skill is evident. Conceptually, the characteristics of isolated communities are grouped into a "type." These are: isolation, cultural homogeneity, organization of conventional understandings into a single unit, adjustment to local environment, predominantly personal character of social relations, relative importance of familial institutions, relative importance of sacred sanctions, development of ritual expression of belief and attitude, and a tendency for the behavior of the individual to involve his familial or local group. These traits were quite consciously derived from Maine, Durkheim, and Tönnies.[25]

Such a careful construction of types was made the basis for the development of a number of hypotheses: (1) primitive and peasant societies have characteristics of the first type; (2) when such societies come into contact with urbanized society, they tend to change in the direction of the opposite of these characters; (3) there is some natural or interdependent relation among various of these characters in that change with regard to some of them tends to bring about change in others.

[25] *The Folk Culture of Yucatan,* p. 343.

This is no empty verbalism, but responsible social science. The major cultural contrast in Yucatan was found between the Spanish area of the northeast, particularly the city of Merida, and the Indian hinterland of the southwest. A comparative study of four communities was carried out along the lines of contrasting culture: a tribal village (Tusik), a peasant village (Chan Kom), a town (Dzitas), and a city (Merida). These communities were progressively less isolated and homogeneous, progressively less traditionally organized; they were also more individualized and secular. Disorganization, individualization, and secularization were found not simply to be directly caused by the city but interrelated with mobility and heterogeneity and with one another. Lines of division already appear between the tribe and the peasant village. In the former (Tusik), people were most economically independent of the city. They were hostile to the national government and suspicious of the ways of the urbanite. But in Chan Kom the government was accepted and the ways of the urbanite had prestige. In general, the principles of tension were represented by race and class. Spanish and Indian cultures were concentrated in the extremes. The nearer one approached Tusik, the more completely an isolated Indian culture was manifest, while the city tended to supplant the original racial and cultural differences with a series of classes. Similar contrasts were found in every major area of life.

The less isolated and more heterogeneous societies were found to be more secular, individualistic, and disorganized. In the city, division of labor becomes more complex, less sexually defined, less cooperative, and more specialized. The stability of the elementary family declines with a decline in patriarchal and matriarchal authority; a disappearance of family customs occurs, a reduction in the strength of conventions of respect takes place, more unconventionality toward relatives is manifest, and a restriction in the application of kinship terms is evident. The pagan elements of religion give way. The symbols of saints and of God are most venerated in the remotest community. A secularization of Catholicism, turning it into a formal church, self-consciously organized and maintaining itself in competition with other interest groups, occurs. The festivals cease to be holy days, becoming holidays. The secularization of medicine and magic shifts healing functions from male shaman-priests to curers. Magic increases in the city, perhaps as a product of increased individual insecurity.

In a series of studies in the 1950's,[26] Redfield developed his ideas into a general theory of civilization, quite in the manner of the classical representatives of positivistic organicism. He takes the world historical event in the development of humankind to be the emergence of the city. The urban revolution created a new type of man, a new type of outlook. Prior to this, each little group was largely self-contained, self-supported, without writing, composed of one kind of people, with a strong sense of group

[26] *The Primitive World and Its Transformations, The Little Community,* and *Peasant Society and Culture.*

solidarity, preliterate, precivilized, and morally ordered. The most striking property of preliterate society was a predominance of the moral order over the technical order.

In civilization the moral order becomes small before the expansion of the technical order. In fact, the later histories of folk societies already show the influence of civilization. The developing city requires a wider area of production, it extends its influence by creating new cities, taxation is imposed on a tribal people, sending them on the road toward peasanthood, the moneylender makes his appearance, the institutionalized resident stranger appears, local authority is transformed by the presence of alien political power, migratory professional entertainers appear, destroying the autonomy of local cultural life, literacy grows, and in many additional ways a society appears which is transitional between the isolated community and the city.

The city makes world wide and conspicuous the self-conscious struggle to maintain a traditional ethos. Traditional morality is attacked and broken down. The moral order becomes managed by an elite or functional class. The family declines before the public hearth. Religion is on the way to creating citizens. Literacy produces speculative thinkers, and skepticism is not uncommon. Proletariats, internal and external, appear. The technical order extends its influence to all areas.

In such fashion, with suggestions drawn from Maine, Tönnies, Durkheim, Sumner, Toynbee, Ogburn, and many others, Redfield advanced a special theory, first, of peasant society as a type between the isolated tribe and the city and, second, of civilization, the most dramatic events of which are formed in terms of the tense interplay of technique and moral order. Redfield developed a type of world-historical culture-lag theory. In contrast to such persons as Toynbee, Sorokin, and Spengler — who clearly influenced his thinking — Redfield never abandoned the positivistic aspects of positivistic organicism. His theories thus remain within the framework of the classic tradition.

Summary

Positivistic organicism, the first school of sociological thought, was established by a series of great pioneering minds in Europe and America. It weathered the hazards that face every new discipline, and adapted itself to the changing intellectual *milieu* of the late nineteenth century.

The most important intellectual development in the last half of the century was the rise to popularity of biological theory. Sociological organicism, to be sure, was of a pre-biological type, drawn from idealistic philosophy. But the rise to popularity of biological theories led to a penetration of biological forms of organicism in sociology. Lilienfeld pursued biological analogies at great length, arguing for the existence of a social nervous system, an intercellular substance binding the social organism together, and inventing the term "social pathology." Schäffle distinguished five types of social tissue thought to be homologous to biological tissue. Fouillée attempted to synthesize mechanical and organismic theories of society in his strange conception of society as a contractual organism. René Worms drew out detailed analogies of structure, function, evolution, and pathology between society and biological organisms.

The overdrawn analogies of the extreme bio-organicists almost inevitably fell into disrepute as thinkers with clearer heads and a keener sense of humor appeared on the scene. The mechanical spinning of analogies can never take the place of science. Nevertheless, bio-organicism served sociology well. It camouflaged the new discipline, tied it in with a dominant nine-teenth-century trend, and gave it the opportunity to find its proper field. By the time sociologists were ready to reject the "big animal" theory of society, sociology had come to stay.

Positivistic organicism was brought to its classical stage of development by a series of imaginative scholars, numbering in the early period Henry Sumner Maine, Ferdinand Tönnies, and Émile Durkheim, and in the modern period, Robert Redfield.

These thinkers developed the idea that the core of society is formed by a peculiar psychology, will (Tönnies), mentality (Durkheim), philosophical outlook (Redfield). Accepting total society as a primary object of analysis, the classic theorists developed a conception of contrasting types: societies based on status in contrast to those based on contract (Maine); societies characterized by mechanical solidarity in contrast to those based on organic solidarity (Durkheim); *Gemeinschaft* and *Gesellschaft* (Tönnies); folk society and secular society (Redfield).

In terms of such concepts the classic members of the school not only developed tools for the institutional analysis of actual societies, but laid the foundation for general theories of social and civilizational change.

SELECTED BIBLIOGRAPHY

BENOÎT-SMULLYAN, ÉMILE, "The Sociologism of Émile Durkheim and His School," in Harry Elmer Barnes (ed.), *An Introduction to the History of Sociology*. Chicago: University of Chicago Press, 1948. Pages 499–537.

DURKHEIM, ÉMILE, *The Division of Labor in Society*. Translated by George Simpson. Glencoe, Ill.: The Free Press, 1947.

DURKHEIM, ÉMILE, *The Elementary Forms of the Religious Life*. Translated by Joseph Ward Swain. Glencoe, Ill.: The Free Press, 1954.

HEBERLE, RUDOLF, "The Sociological System of Ferdinand Tönnies: 'Community' and 'Society'", in Harry Elmer Barnes, *op. cit.*, pp. 227–248.

MAINE, HENRY SUMNER, *Ancient Law*. Everyman's Library. New York: E. P. Dutton, 1936.

REDFIELD, ROBERT, *Tepoztlan: A Mexican Village*. Chicago: University of Chicago Press, 1930.

REDFIELD, ROBERT, *The Folk Culture of Yucatan.* Chicago: University of Chicago Press, 1941.

REDFIELD, ROBERT, *The Primitive World and Its Transformations.* Ithaca, N.Y.: Cornell University Press, 1953.

REDFIELD, ROBERT, *The Little Community.* Chicago: University of Chicago Press, 1955.

REDFIELD, ROBERT, *Peasant Society and Culture.* Chicago: University of Chicago Press, 1956.

SMALL, ALBION, *General Sociology.* Chicago: University of Chicago Press, 1905, 1925. Pages 109–167.

SOROKIN, PITIRIM, *Contemporary Sociological Theories.* New York: Harper, 1928.

5

The Transformation and Eventual
Disintegration of Positivistic Organicism

FROM THE VERY BEGINNING, POSITIVISTIC ORGANICISM WAS STRICKEN WITH an inner conflict. Its organismic view of society tended to make it non-positivistic; its positivism of method tended to make it anti-organismic. Whenever its members were not united to fight external enemies, their relations tended quickly to degenerate into civil war.

The dissatisfaction with the early view of society was already manifest in the speed with which sociologists accepted biological organicism. But the claims of science are not to be satisfied with mere figures of speech. Another position was current among the romantics and irrational idealists of the nineteenth century, who viewed society as a manifestation of emotion and will rather than reason. While this appeared to accord with the facts, it was also linked to strong anti-rational and anti-scientific sentiments.

The early sociologists were by no means ready to abandon their positivism, for this appeared to them as the foundation of their claim to science. However, if the anti-scientific and anti-positivistic features of irrational idealism could once be eliminated, the view was available for a new kind of theoretical construction.

Voluntaristic Positivism

Among the types of idealistic philosophy developed in the nineteenth century, irrational idealism was a not unimportant form. It is "idealistic" in the sense that it, too, models the world, society, history, and civilization on the analogy with human psychology. It is "irrational" in the special sense that it gives primacy in its picture of the world to the feeling-life of man, to the impulses or the will and not to man's reason.

Initially, irrational idealism was in no shape to supply a foundation for a movement in sociological theory. In emphasizing the importance of emotion and will at the expense of reason, the irrational idealists often felt called upon to treat reason as relatively superficial. Science was dismissed as a shallow affair, dealing with superficialities, while a true analysis penetrated "deeply" into human feeling. This point of view appears in the works of Schopenhauer and Nietzsche.

Schopenhauer and Nietzsche

For Arthur Schopenhauer (1788–1860) it was a source of unrelieved pessimism to conceive of nature and society as moved by a will to power, which in nature was the source of all movement and which in man gave rise to every variety of pain and suffering. In society the only thing of particular interest to Schopenhauer was the possibility of release from pain and grief. The meaning of the arts was found in the temporary relief they offered from the struggle. But ultimately the only answer for society lay in extensive renunciation of will and desire (on an Oriental model).

Nietzsche (1844–1900) very correctly perceived himself as the successor of Schopenhauer. He did not, however, conceive the omnipotence of the will in a negative sense, but as the source and criterion of all values.[1] With his interest not in metaphysics but in historical criticism, literature, and ethics, Nietzsche illustrated many of the ways in which irrationalistic idealism could possibly apply to social events.

With Schopenhauer, he accepted the *will* as the most important fact of man. Value was conceived to be the expression and realization of the will. Evil is whatever is opposed to or which limits its expression. Nietzsche had the greatest admiration for war, force, and physical and military prowess, but he also admired art, philosophy, and literature. One of the most influential teachers of Nietzsche was Jakob Burckhardt, from whom he derived a picture of those Renaissance figures who fused these two kinds of phenomena, art and war, in their lives and experiences.

In his critique of Greek philosophy and culture, Nietzsche thought he could trace the rise of tragedy out of the primitive dithyramb. He saw parallels between the romantic music of Germany, particularly that of Wagner, and the ecstasy of the Greek Dionysian masses of Pan, god of resurrection and death. In terms of these contrasts, he conceived of two fundamental forms of the realization of the will: the human will as expressed in the idealized, remote, philosophic calm of the Apollonian image, and the will as expressed in the passionate, ecstatic frenzy of Dionysus. In his early period, Nietzsche thought human greatness was revealed in culture in the saint, creative artist, and philosopher.

[1] Friedrich Wilhelm Nietzsche, *Complete Works*, translated by W. A. Haussman and others, and edited by Oscar Levy, 18 vols. (Edinburgh: 1909–14).

As time went by these thematic materials came to be expressed by Nietzsche with increasing bitterness. He came to denounce most religions, particularly Christianity in all its forms. Humility and Christian charity were increasingly imagined to be the resentful images of helots, a cancellation of true values. True virtue, he thought, was possible only for an aristocratic minority. The fundamental social fact of every civilization, he thought, was the conquest of the stupid masses of men by a horde of blond beasts who installed themselves as masters of the weaker civilization, reducing its members to slavery. There always were and always will be masters and slaves. Only a warlike ethic is appropriate to the masters. When this master group has to struggle to maintain itself, it develops a true nobility, with the chivalrous values of the true aristocrat. The slaves develop a religion and morality of humanity and — out of resentment for the aristocracy — of equality. Nietzsche was a passionate individualist, perceiving as the only legitimate ideal the emergence of the superman in a new aristocracy of supermen. He was little impressed by science and its methods. In his opinion science operated with a mechanistic conception of the universe and man. He feared that science dealt a death blow to belief in geniuses, heroes, and saints. Nietzsche became an ardent opponent of the Darwinian type of biology. The evolutionary process was for him a blind, impulsive, teleological development.

While there is nothing particularly attractive about the social interpretations of Schopenhauer and Nietzsche, it is quite clear that a sociological program could be projected on such grounds. Schopenhauer had applied his conceptions to art and to the relation of the individual to social life. Nietzsche had applied them to social change, to religion, to mass sentiments, and to the problems of the social classes. Schopenhauer had treated rationality and science as dealing only with the more superficial areas of experience. Nietzsche responded to the methods and suppositions of science with scorn. They formulated, thus, a platform for one of the anti-scientific movements of the century and, as such, did not initially recommend themselves to the new social sciences.

Vilfredo Pareto

Even before Nietzsche's death, Vilfredo Pareto (1848–1923) had begun to work out a fusion of irrational idealism and positivism, making this form of theoretical orientation available for social science.[2] His method-

---

[2] Pareto's chief sociological work, *Trattato di sociologia generale* (Florence: G. Barbéra, 1916; 2d ed., 1923), is available in an English translation by Andrew Bongiorno and Arthur Livingston, edited by Arthur Livingston, under the title *The Mind and Society*, 4 vols. (New York: Harcourt, Brace, 1935). For studies of Pareto's work, see: Georges Henri Bousquet, *The Work of Pareto* (Hanover, N.H.: The Sociological Press, 1928); Max Sylvius Handman, "The Sociological Method of Vilfredo Pareto," in Stuart A. Rice (ed.), *Methods in Social Science* (Chicago: University of Chicago Press, 1931), pp. 139–153; and George C. Homans and Charles P. Curtis, Jr., *An Introduction to Pareto* (New York: Alfred A. Knopf, 1934).

ology was a form of extreme positivism. He argued that sociology must become a logico-experimental science based on observation and experiment to the exclusion of all reasoning and speculation going beyond the observed facts. The propositions of sociology should include nothing beyond a description of the facts and their uniformities. So rigorously did Pareto argue his case that his favorite illustrations of the sins against a logico-experimental method were taken from positivists like Comte and Spencer. For example, in his discussion of the rationalization of non-logical conduct in *The Mind and Society*, Pareto uses Comte and Spencer to illustrate pseudo-science:

> In his *Lectures on Positive Philosophy* . . . Comte seems to be decidedly inclined to ascribe the predominance to logical conduct. He sees in positive philosophy . . . "the one solid basis for that social reorganization which is to terminate the critical state in which civilized nations have been living for so long a time."
>
> After quoting Comte's dictum that ideas govern and upset the world, Herbert Spencer advances a theory that non-logical actions alone influence society. "Ideas do not govern and overthrow the world: the world is governed or overthrown by feelings, to which ideas serve only as guides. . . ."
>
> Then a curious thing happens: Comte and Spencer reverse positions reciprocally! In his *System of Positive Polity* . . . Comte decides to allow sentiment to prevail. . . . Comte becomes a prophet. The battle of ideas is over. He imagines he has won a complete victory. So now he begins proclaiming dogma, pronouncing *ex cathedra*, and it is only natural that nothing but sentiments should now be left on the field — his own sentiments of course.
>
> Spencer, on the other hand, after admitting, even too sweepingly, the influence of non-logical actions, eliminates them altogether. . . . Says he: "Our postulate must be that primitive ideas are natural, and, under the conditions in which they occur, rational." [3]

Among Pareto's special arguments for positivism were: that sociology must operate with conceptions of mutual dependence, functional relationship, regularities, uniformities, and correlations in space and time, and quantitative measurements; it must exclude ideas of one-sided dependence, cause and effect, uniqueness and irregularity, and qualities. In this manner sociology will be able to obtain formulas which approximate the complexities of social reality more closely.

A society for Pareto is a system of forces in equilibrium. A number of types of factors are ultimately involved in this system: physical (such as soil, climate, flora, fauna, geography), external (other societies with which it may come into contact), and internal (including race, sentiments and feelings, ideologies). Pareto was particularly interested in the study of the internal factors. Internally — as a system of behavior — the character of society is determined by the properties of the actions and the individuals

[3] *The Mind and Society*, I, pp. 188, 189, 191.

who act. Since these individuals are illogical, illogical factors lie at the core of society. Quite an extensive part of Pareto's treatise is devoted to the task of showing that the explanations ordinarily given to explain human conduct do not in any way touch its essence.

The most fundamental classification of actions for establishing sociology as a science is that between logical and non-logical types of action. It was Pareto's belief that almost the whole of human effort that has gone into the explanation of conduct is misguided. Most of the theological, philosophical, and even scientific explanations of human conduct have tended to ignore its non-logical elements. Examples to prove this are found in the works of Aristotle and Plato, Polybius, Fustel de Coulange, Comte, and Spencer.

The starting point of a logico-experimental sociology appears in the recurrent features of action (*residues*) rather than the variable elements (*derivations*) they display. The residues are non-logical constancies; they are manifestations of sentiments. For all intents and purposes, Pareto's "residues" are identical with what Schopenhauer and Nietzsche describe as "manifestations of the will." The residues are thought to be the real forces underlying the social equilibrium. They are grouped into six classes: (1) residues of combination, (2) residues of persistence of aggregates, (3) residues of manifestations of sentiments through external acts, (4) residues of sociability, (5) residues of individual integrity, and (6) sex residues.

Residues of *combinations* are sentiments expressed by the combining of things. The taking of signs in dreams as indications of luck, the astrological casting of horoscopes, the multiple forms of magic and prophecy, the belief that good is associated with progress, democracy, and universal suffrage, all are examples. There is often no logical reason for the combination; in fact, opposites are often the preferred components. The residue of *persistence of aggregates* refers to the tendency of aggregates once formed to persist. The survival of all customs even beyond the conditions of their appearance is characteristic. The cult of the family is an example. The residue of *manifestation of sentiments in external acts* is illustrated by all phenomena such as religious exaltation and political agitation. The residues of *sociability* are basic to the drive to be like everyone else. Such residues are manifested in style, fashion, and standardization of all sorts. Pity, cruelty, and neophobia appear to be sentiments bound up with sociability. The residues of *integrity of personality* refer to the drive to preserve one's self against any thing tending to upset it or detract from it. Such residues cause us to resent every attack on ourselves or on our group, social status, or society. Finally, in connection with the *sex* residue, it is observed that various residues often enter into combination, as in the union of asceticism with the sex residue.

Of special interest for Pareto's sociology is the relation of the derivations to the residues. Derivations consist in the ways men dissimulate and explain their acts. Derivations are of various kinds: (1) *simple affirmation* — statements of real or imaginary facts; (2) *authority* — the pseudo-explanation of events by citing the authority of the past, of tradition and custom, or of the Divine Will; (3) *accord with sentiments or principles* — derivations which attempt justifications of conduct on the basis of the presumed fact that it is for the benefit of others; and (4) *verbal proofs* — consisting in using terms not in accordance with the facts, allegories, metaphors, and so on. The "derivations" correspond closely to what students often prefer to describe as "ideologies." They are pseudo-reasons for conduct.

The stability of society depends not on the derivations but the state and distribution of the residues. The derivations may be useful as instruments in the service of the residues, but they cannot take their place. Of the residues, the first two are of greatest importance for society. The residues are not equally distributed among individuals and social classes. There are individuals and groups with strong residues of combination, others with strong residues of the persistence of aggregates. Two principal social types of persons and of social classes rest on these residues. The social type concentrating the residue of combinations are the *speculators;* those concentrating the residue of persistence of aggregates are the *rentiers.* To the first class belong combiners, entrepreneurs, schemers, inventors of all types. They are also the reformers, sentimentalists, and radicals. The second type represents the conservatives, persons with a strong sense of duty and a narrow determined will. In democratic and plutocratic governments the speculators are usually dominant. They are clever at combining. They are full of trickery and usually succeed in deceiving the masses. They are corrupt. Eventually they will be succeeded by the *rentiers.* But history is the graveyard of aristocracies, and if the *rentiers* are in the saddle, they are easily penetrated by the ingenious, subtle combiners from below. If the latter penetrate too deeply, the result is a wholesale weakening of the position of the *rentiers.*

Thus, history typically shows a "circulation of the elite." In any situation composed predominantly of a ruling group resting on residues of combination, the situation rapidly arrives in which the man of force is the only answer to the need for social stability. The lions oust the foxes. Once in power, however, it is easy for the elite, resting on residues of persistence, to maintain power by combinations of force and trickery. In such fashion the foxes penetrate the conservative circles and weaken the unity of the conservative elite. There is an upper and lower class in every society showing a difference in distribution of the residues. There is also a circulation of individuals from upper to lower classes and vice versa. Although the intensity of circulation varies from society to society and in a given society over a period of time, it is nonetheless inevitable that any aristocracy is destined some day to disappear. All of the devices of an aristocracy to maintain its position — including the elevation of dangerous leaders from the lower to the upper classes, the use of bribery, corruption, imprisonment, and extermination — will not prevail in the long run. Pareto's voluntarism adds new dimensions to organicism.[4]

[4] Certain aspects of Pareto's organicism will be explored further in Chapter 18.

Sigmund Freud

If one were to locate the sociological formulations springing from Freud-ianism, it could not be more accurately placed than as a form of sociological theory which fused voluntaristic organicism and positivism very similar to Pareto's theory. Sigmund Freud (1856–1939) was a thoroughgoing posi-tivist by training and inclination. He assumed that, fundamentally, mental life is structured by underlying forces which always produce the same effects under the same conditions. Even his method of analysis was typical of his positivistic orientation: he observed the events of everyday life, taking care-ful note of slips, errors, and omissions of all sorts. He assumed that these are not accidental but rather the result of constant causal agencies. Constant forces are assumed to distort systematically in characteristic ways the little doings of everyday life. This was the burden of argument in *The Psychopa-thology of Everyday Life*.[5] Similarly, Freud assumes that dreams are pro-duced by constant features of human nature and that even the very content of the dream is capable of interpretation in terms of constant forces. So, for example, the mechanisms of distortion of dream content are thought to result from displacement, dramatizations, symbolization, and secondary elab-oration.

Freud's affinities with the irrationalistic idealism of Schopenhauer and Nietzsche were as fundamental as were Pareto's. He, too, maintained that more basic than man's rationality (his "derivations," according to Pareto) is his emotional and instinctive life (his "will," his "residues" — Pareto). Freud did not work out the basic drives in the same way as Schopenhauer or Nietzsche or Pareto. In the first form of his theory, the psychology of the individual was divided into a conscious, an unconscious — containing the more basic factors of emotional life, strongly sexual (libidinous) in nature — with a censoring mechanism operating between the two spheres. Later Freud conceived the central elements of the personality to consist of the id, the ego, and the superego, the id taking over many of the phenomena

---

5 Translated by A. A. Brill from *Psychopathologie des Alltagslebens* (Berlin: S. Karger, 1904) and included in A. A. Brill, translator and editor, *The Basic Writings of Sigmund Freud* (New York: Modern Library, 1938). Those works of Freud which have special relevance for sociology are readily available in various editions; cited here are only the particular editions of translations that were consulted for the present discussion: *Totem und Tabu* (Leipzig: H. Heller, 1913), translated by James Strachey as *Totem and Taboo* (New York: W. W. Norton, 1952); *Massenpsychologie und Ich-analyse* (Leipzig: Inter-nationaler Psychoanalytischer Verlag, 1921), translated by James Strachey as *Group Psychology and the Analysis of the Ego* (London: Hogarth Press, 1948); *Die Zukunft einer Illusion* (Vienna: Internationaler Psychoanalytischer Verlag, 1927), translated by W. D. Robson-Scott as *The Future of an Illusion* (Garden City, N.Y.: Doubleday, 1957); *Das Unbehagen in der Kultur* (Vienna: Internationaler Psychoanalytischer Verlag, 1930), translated by Joan Riviere as *Civilization and Its Discontents* (London: Hogarth Press, 1946); although the first two parts of *Der Mann Moses und die monotheistische Religion* appeared in German in *Imago*, Vol. 23 (1937), the first edition of the book in its entirety was the translation by Katherine Jones, *Moses and Monotheism* (London: Hogarth Press, 1939).

of the original unconscious and the superego taking over many of the functions of the former censor. Still later, Freud conceived man's emotional life
to consist of life and death instincts. One institution, the family, was conceived by Freud to be absolutely essential to the development of personality.
The libidinous impulses of man even in an infantile state were crucial to
the stylization of behavior. Freud assumed that each new social achievement
by the individual corresponded to the molding of the libidinous impulses as
the infant passes through states from auto-eroticism through oral and anal
eroticism to hetero-eroticism. Of particularly profound importance were the
later stages of libidinous molding. In the course of development the child
tends to anchor its love impulses on the parent of the opposite sex. This
takes the form of the Oedipus model in the boy, the Electra model in the
girl. For full normal development the child will have to transfer its sex
interests to some member of the opposite sex other than the parent. If
this final transfer fails, there is a tendency for the individual to regress to
some previous stage of libidinous development.

The difference between Freud and other irrational idealists is clear enough.
Schopenhauer and Nietzsche find the locus of man's voluntaristic life in the
will, particularly in the will to power. Pareto found it in the residues of
combinations and persistence of aggregates. Freud found the sex drive particularly important. From all appearances, he had less reason than they to
move out to a general theory of society, but precisely this step was taken —
the attempt to develop a Freudian theory of society.

A general theory of primitive society and explanation of the origins of
social structure and morals was projected in *Totem and Taboo* (1913).
Taboo customs were identified by Freud with the manifestations of the symp-
toms of compulsive neurosis, in their lack of apparent motivation, their
enforcement through an inner need, their capacity for displacement, and in
the causation of ceremonial actions emanating from the forbidden.

A peculiar system of taboos characterizes totemism, which Freud takes to
be the oldest form of religion and social structure. Totemism displays taboos
on the killing and eating of the totem animal and on sexual intercourse
with totem companions of the other sex. Freud assumes that this system
of taboos arose in the following way. There was an original unstruc-
tured primitive horde under a primal father, who was envied and feared
by his sons. The ancient father-beast monopolized the sexual services of
all the women for himself. The sons banded together and killed him. They
were then seized by guilt and remorse, and in their anxiety they substituted
a symbol (a totem animal) for the primal father, making it taboo to kill
and eat the totem. They denied themselves intercourse with the women of
the horde (originating clan exogamy). In ceremonies once a year the totem
animal was killed and eaten — ceremonial re-enactment of the ancient crime.
The structure of ancient society thus is determined as a racial form of the
Oedipus drama.

In *Moses and Monotheism* (1939), Freud analyzes the origins of Christianity and Judaism along the broad lines laid down in *Totem and Taboo.* He sets forth and defends the hypothesis that Moses was originally an Egyptian, transformed by myth into a Jew. Moses is assumed to have been a noble Egyptian, accepting the monotheism of the Pharaoh-dreamer Ikhnaton. However, when the regime of Ikhnaton fell, Moses, who was a protector of the Jews, led them out of Egypt. In this new sect the custom of circumcision was taken over, and the Levites were the original, partly-Egyptian practitioners of the new cult. However, in the course of the difficulties of leading the people out of Egypt, Moses was murdered. This operated to fix monotheism on the Jews in much the same manner that the murder of the primal father fixed totemism on the primitives. Later the triumph of Christianity represented a renewed victory of the Amon priests over the God of Ikhnaton after an interval of a millennium. "The great deed and misdeed of primal times, the murder of the father, was brought home to the Jews, for fate decreed that they should repeat it on the person of Moses . . . an eminent father substitute." [6] The murder of Christ was a repetition of the same theme and, for Freud, the reason for the profundity of Christianity.

In *Civilization and Its Discontents* (1930), Freud presented the individual's instinctive life as standing in the sharpest antagonism with civilization. The ordinary man's relation to his religion, for example, is conceived as a duplicate of his relation to the family. "The ordinary man cannot imagine this Providence in any other form but that of a greatly exalted father, for only such a one could understand the needs of the sons of men, or be softened by their prayers and placated by the signs of their remorse. The whole thing is so patently infantile, so incongruous with reality, that to one whose attitude to humanity is friendly, it is painful to think that the great majority of mortals will never be able to rise above this view of life." [7] By its very nature civilization imposes privations on man. Men cannot tolerate the degree of privation society imposes; they cannot help becoming neurotic. So long as society remained at the level of the primitive family, with its direct controls and gratifications, we were relatively safe. But "civilized society is perpetually menaced with disintegration through this primal hostility of men towards one another." [8] There is no escape. Civilized man is inevitably frustrated, hostile, and neurotic.

In *Group Psychology and the Analysis of the Ego* (1921), Freud attempted to explain crowd psychology. The typical crowd was treated as an organized group with a leader, such as the Christian church with Christ as its head or an army with its commander. The relation between the members of the group and the leader was visualized as being like that between a patient and hypnotist, or lover and his beloved. Older theories of the crowd, such as those of Le Bon, saw the physical contact and common stimulation of the

[6] *Moses and Monotheism*, p. 143.
[7] *Civilization and Its Discontents*, p. 22.
[8] *Ibid.*, p. 86.

group as the context generating leadership. Freud's formulation reverses this order.

In *The Future of an Illusion* and *Civilization and Its Discontents,* Freud attempted to go beyond the mere tension of man with society to the analysis of culture. The source of religion is taken as fear of the unknown. The primitive god-father was a product of this fear. The task of the gods is to exorcise the terrors of nature, reconcile men to the cruelty of fate, particularly death, and make amends for the suffering imposed by communal life. Religion is an instance of the "omnipotence of thought," for it is an illusion, a wish-fulfillment, a mass delusion comparable to the personal delusions of the neurotic. The struggle of man's nature against culture is inevitable. Nature and culture are menacing powers to which man must adjust. To accept society, it is necessary for man to recognize his limitations and accept social aims. Restrictions are placed on sex, the drive for power and aggression. Man submits to society, and his own superego functions as a censor. Because impulses for aggression arise, the superego and culture brush aside the ego's claim for happiness. The price of progress is a sense of guilt.

The limitations of a Freudian theory of society are not difficult to locate. Primitive society, the great religions of the world, modern civilization — all are modeled after a narrow conception of the family drama. To make the basic arguments plausible, mythological reconstructions of human history, often on the basis of disputed authorities, were presented.[9] Arbitrary decisions were made, such as treating the crowd and the organized group as identical — a practice which no sociologist will accept. Further unacceptable assumptions were made, such as the existence of racial memories (without which the primitive taboo ceremonial, as Freud presents it, could not be maintained).

Some of the one-time associates of Freud also showed some inclination to develop a voluntaristic positivism. Alfred Adler made his point of attack on psychological problems through organ inferiority. He noted that any defect or weakness — a missing limb, poor motor ability, ugliness — places a person in a position where he must either fight for a place in life or give up. The process set in motion by reaction to inferiority leads to compensation or even overcompensation. Inferiority feeling, overcompensation, and lust for power were made the basic categories for analysis of individual and social events.

Carl Gustav Jung, who was also at one time an associate of Freud, was closer to Freud's own position. Libido, a general sexual energy according to Freud, was subject to repression, transformation, and sublimation. Jung broadened the idea still more to include all psychic energy, in fact, all energy

---

[9] For example, in his study of *Totem and Taboo,* Freud relied on anthropological authorities who had been rejected by their colleagues. Similarly, in the study of *Moses and Monotheism,* reliance was placed on questionable research. This is not responsible social science but poetic license.

in animals and men responsible for biological and social evolution itself. Jung also contributed to the study of personality by his typology of introvert (a personality inwardly oriented, self-occupied, thoughtful) in contrast to the extrovert (an out-going type of personality, objective, oriented toward action). Moreover, even in the early days, Otto Rank and Hanns Sachs suggested the application of psychoanalysis to mythology, religion, ethnology, and linguistics.[10]

Among repeated attempts to explain social phenomena on the basis of the voluntaristic positivism of Freud, some stand out. Harold D. Lasswell in *Psychopathology and Politics* [11] tried to trace the influence of infantile experience on political careers. Politicians were divided into agitators, administrators, theorists, and men of political convictions. A series of case histories was examined to discover the experimental foundation of each type. Typical findings were that early forms of animosity were compensated for by love of humanity and that feelings of uncertainty tended to produce an exaggerated vehemence in the assertion of principles. Franz Alexander and Hugo Staub in *The Criminal, the Judge, and the Public* [12] proposed nothing less than the reform of criminological procedure by the use of psychoanalytic concepts. They urged that when the individual finds himself neglected or abused by society, any protest against cultural impositions tends to be violent. Social justice is always felt repressively. When it breaks down, antisocial forms of individual protest are likely to take criminal form. Responsibility for crime commonly associated with free will has been shown by psychology to be determined by behavior lying in the unconscious id. Hence a new classification of criminals is needed in which the normal are distinguished from neurotic and acute. One must isolate, for example, the neurotic who may commit criminal acts to secure the punishment demanded by his superego for inclinations of a criminal type arising out of the id.

A parallel trend to that of the Freudian forms of voluntaristic positivism appears in the ethnological school of culture configurationism. Its roots extend back to linguists and philosophers like Moritz Lazarus and Heymann Steinthal, who developed a form of the folk-soul notion taken from Hegel. In modern times the doctrine has been revived by Ruth Benedict in *Patterns of Culture*,[13] though her specific inspirations were found in Nietzsche (the concepts of Apollonian and Dionysian mentality) and the Gestalt psychology conception of "wholes." For Benedict a culture is like an individual, displaying a more or less consistent pattern of thought and action. In each

[10] Otto Rank and Hanns Sachs, "The Significance of Psychoanalysis for the Mental Sciences," *The Psychoanalytic Review*, Vol. 2 (1915), pp. 297–326, 428–457; Vol. 3 (1916), pp. 69–89, 189–214, 318–335. Other early extensions of psychoanalysis to social phenomena include Karl Abraham, *Dreams and Myths*, tr. by William A. White (New York: The Journal of Nervous and Mental Disease Publishing Co., 1913) ; Oskar Pfister, *Some Applications of Psycho-analysis* (London: George Allen and Unwin, 1923) ; and Géza Róheim, *Social Anthropology* (New York: Boni and Liveright, 1926).
[11] Chicago: University of Chicago Press, 1930.
[12] Translated by Gregory Zilboorg (New York: Macmillan, 1931).
[13] Boston: Houghton Mifflin, 1934.

culture, characteristic purposes appear which at least in their peculiar assemblage are not shared by any other. All items of behavior tend to
assume contours with reference to these. This cultural-psychological whole
is no mere sum of its special parts; it determines the parts in their relation
and nature. Using Nietzsche's Apollonian and Dionysian types, Benedict
analyzed three tribal groups — the Zuni of the Pueblos, the Dobuans of
Northwestern Melanesia and the Kwakiutl of the Northwest Coast — to illustrate psychocultural forms.

A similar type of analysis appears in the work of Margaret Mead,[14] in
whose work the conception of psychocultural wholes is shifted back toward
a more distinctly Freudian type of explanation. The road back to Freud
becomes still more clearly marked in modern students such as Abram
Kardiner, Karen Horney, and Erich Fromm. Voluntaristic positivism seems
by no means to have played itself out as a trend.

The Separation of Organicism from Positivism

In reviewing the various formations of positivistic organicism, one must
never lose sight of the fact that they contain opposed principles. Positivism
attempts to maintain knowledge on the level of experience; organicism at
every point tends to exceed the limits positivism would impose. If one
once denies the organic analogy, all the special claims of the point of view
disappear; and if one once takes his positivism seriously, the organic analogy
must go.

The maintenance of a condition in which one accepts two antagonistic
principles at the same time can only be explained by the presence of reasons
good enough to cause one to overlook all the contradictions inherent in the
principles. These reasons have already been identified. The exponents of
early sociology wished to realize two major objectives in their discipline:
(a) to maintain a position of unshakable social conservatism (which was
secured by their particular interpretation of organicism) and (b) to remain
scientific (which was secured by way of their positivism). Voluntaristic
positivism had the same essential requirements. The moment one was willing
to accept modification and tolerate a liberal social outlook (as in the case
of Lester Ward), the formula of positivistic organicism tended to fall to
pieces. The same was true for Alfred Fouillée, with the barbarism arising
from his attempt to fuse the ideas of social contract (anchored in liberalism)
with organicism and his outlandish proposal of a "contractual organism"
to account for society. As in the case of Ward, the formula was breaking
down.

Positivistic organicism thus was maintained not by its inner composition
but by the presence of a set of external requirements imposed on sociology.
The first form of sociological theory contains a set of internal contradictions

[14] See, for example, her *Sex and Temperament in Three Primitive Societies* (New York:
William Morrow, 1935).

precisely because it was socially responsible. But it follows that the moment the external situation changes, and the forces which led to the simultaneous acceptance of positivism and organicism are no longer present, positivistic organicism should decline. When the decline sets in, there are two major possibilities: the development of organicism relatively unmodified by positivism or vice versa. The first possibility may be illustrated by three interesting persons: Oswald Spengler, Arnold Toynbee, and Pitirim Sorokin.

Oswald Spengler

Oswald Spengler's *Decline of the West* [15] appeared at the turning point of four years of war, July 1918. It fitted the growing general mood, and the large and rather turgid work became a best seller. It was significant that the author was not a recognized scholar but a simple high school teacher (*Oberlehrer*), a fact accentuating his appeal.

The keynote of the work is found in an unrestricted, aggressive organicism, with a powerful anti-positivistic bias. No ideal is more dear to the positivist than the mathematical analysis of experience; no notion is more savagely attacked by Spengler. "The means whereby to identify dead forms is Mathematical Law. The means whereby to understand living forms is Analogy. By these means we are enabled to distinguish polarity and periodicity in the world." [16] This distinction between mathematical law and analogy corresponds to a distinction drawn between the world as history and the world as nature and between the appropriate methods for understanding the one and the other. Nature is organic, civilization is mechanical; the one is represented by picture and symbol, the other by formula and system; the one is in the domain of chronology, the other in mathematical number; to the one applies the concept of causality, a logic of space, to the other, destiny, the logic of time. Only chronology and the idea of destiny are sufficient for ordering the facts of society, culture, and history as living things. The positivistic method is adapted only to superficialities, to surfaces, to evidence of the world of the senses. The true aim of cultural historical study is to penetrate to the living core or soul of phenomena where "imagination seeks comprehension of the living existence of the world in relation to . . . life." [17]

The unrestricted organicism of Spengler's view appears over and again. What diaries and autobiographies are to an individual, historical research and every kind of psychological comparison and analysis of alien peoples, times, and customs, are to the soul of culture. Only by such means do we discover, for example, that Indian culture has a perfectly ahistorical soul, expressed in Brahma Nirvana. Hence we learn the implications of the fact

[15] The first volume of *Der Untergang des Abenlandes* was published in 1918 (Vienna: Braumüller); not until 1922–23 were both volumes published together (Munich: C. H. Beck). The book was translated by Charles Francis Atkinson as *Decline of the West* (New York: Alfred A. Knopf, 1926).
[16] *Decline of the West*, I, p. 4.
[17] *Ibid.*, p. 8.

that there is no pure Indian astronomy, no calendar, no history. And while the Indian forgot everything, the Egyptian forgot nothing, for the Egyptian's soul was historical in texture and impelled by primitive worship of the past and future of the world.

In developing his theory, Spengler draws sharp distinctions between culture (the organic living entity) and civilization (the dead external shell and monuments of a one-time living culture). The two phenomena, organic growth and death, are expressed in the peasantry, bound to the soil and lying outside history, and in the urban citizenry, the agents of history and civilization. History and society represent "the drama of a *number* of mighty cultures, each springing with primitive strength from the soil of a mother-region to which it remains firmly bound throughout its whole life-cycle; each stamping its material, its mankind, in *its own* image; each has *its own* idea, *its own* passions, *its own* life, will and feeling, *its own* death. . . . Here the Cultures, peoples, languages, truths, gods, landscapes bloom and age as the oaks and the stone-pines, the blossoms, twigs, and leaves. . . . Each culture has its own new possibilities of self expression which arise, ripen, decay, and never return." [18]

The ideological mood to which Spengler's argument is addressed is very different from that of early sociology. Not conservativism and science, but reactionary regression and anti-scientific bias are its properties. While it was a German schoolteacher's rebellion against the doom to which the authorities, including the scientists, seemed to be leading his society, the rural mysticism present in it corresponded to the universal disillusionment following World War I. The world of the twentieth century has shown repeated preoccupation with the problem of the "death of civilization." In all such studies, a semi-religious tone is maintained and an anti-positivism is discernible. Toynbee's work is a famous example.

Arnold Toynbee

A less extreme form of organicism of the same general type as Spengler's is found in the work of the English historian, Arnold Toynbee (1889–   ). Toynbee argues, in *A Study of History*,[19] that if we explore the distribution of social facts in space and time — for example, those represented by English history — the conclusion is inescapable that we are dealing with a developing whole. His arguments at this point are not dissimilar from those by which Spengler set up culture as a unit of study. He claims "that the intelligible unit of historical study is neither a nation state nor (at the other end of the scale) mankind as a whole but a certain grouping of humanity

---

[18] *Ibid.*, p. 20.

[19] Arnold J. Toynbee, *A Study of History*, 10 vols. (New York: Oxford University Press, 1934–54). Oxford University Press has also published an excellent two-volume abridgment of the entire work by D. C. Somervell; the first of these, covering Volumes 1–6 of the original, was published in 1947, the second, covering Volumes 7–10, was published in 1957; both bear the same title as the original. References here are to the first of Somervell's abridgments.

which we have called a society." [20] Not only does analysis prove the existence of a unit which one may designate as Western European Society but also that there are at least four other living societies of the same species today: (a) an Orthodox Christian Society in Southeastern Europe and Russia; (b) an Islamic Society with its focus in the arid zone from North Africa to the Middle East and from the Atlantic to the outer face of the Great Wall of China; (c) a Hindu Society in India; and (d) a Far Eastern Society in the subtropical and temperate regions between the arid zones and the Pacific.

We know that Western European society developed out of the Greco-Roman world, and we can ask about the pertinent characteristics of Hellenic society just prior to its decline. There were three: (1) it developed a universal state; (2) when the Roman Empire fell there was a kind of interregnum during which there was a tremendous expansion of the Christian Church; moreover, (3) during this same period there were extensive movements of peoples both in the form of an internal and external proletariat. "The Church, a survival from the dying society, became the womb from which in due course the new one was born." [21] The fact that our society arose out of a previous one and that there were characteristic factors which signaled its decline opens up two possibilities. We should be able to study the factors in the growth, expansion, and death of a society. We are also able to build up a picture of the total array of such societies that have historically appeared. We are even able to develop information on various fossil societies of the parent society from which the living specimens are derived. In all, according to Toynbee, we are able to discover nineteen societies: the Western, the Orthodox, the Iranic, the Arabic (the last two now united in the Islamic), the Hindu, the Far Eastern, the Hellenic, the Syriac, the Indic, the Sinic, the Minoan, the Sumeric, the Hittite, the Babylonic, the Egyptiac, the Andean, the Mexic, the Yucatec, and the Mayan. Moreover, it is useful to divide Orthodox Christian Society into the Orthodox-Byzantine and Orthodox-Russian and the Far Eastern into a Chinese and a Korean-Japanese Society. These societies, twenty-one in all, are all species of a single genus. It is customary to describe them as civilizations to distinguish them from primitive societies as a special genus. About 650 primitive societies are registered, most of which are alive today.

There are three different methods for studying such phenomena. The first is the ascertainment and recording of "facts"; the second is the elucidation, through a comparative study of the facts ascertained, of general "laws"; the third is the artistic recreation of the facts in the form of "fiction." Toynbee points out that it is usually assumed that the technique of ascertaining and recording facts is the method of history, the elucidation and formulation of general laws is the technique of science, and the use of fiction is the technique of drama. He feels, however, that this is a mistake: these methods are not to be kept in watertight compartments. To be sure, his-

[20] *A Study of History*, I, p. 11.   [21] *Ibid.*, p. 13.

tory does not concern itself with everything. "It leaves alone the facts of social life in primitive societies, from which anthropology elucidates its 'laws'; and it hands over to biography the facts of individual lives; . . . but besides recording facts, history also has recourse to fiction and makes use of laws. . . . History, like the drama and novel, grew out of mythology." [22] Thus it is clear that Toynbee, while not a rabid anti-positivist in quite the same sense as Spengler, adds methods to his procedure, like fiction, which the positivists cannot tolerate.

Toynbee's whole treatment of civilization as a genus of society is characterized by a thoroughgoing organicism. He rejects the idea that primitive societies and civilizations differ because of the presence or absence of institutions in some which are not found in others, or because of a difference in the division of labor between them. They differ, he maintains, because of the quality of their inner subjective life. *Mimesis,* or imitation, is treated as a generic feature of all social life, operating both in primitive societies and in civilizations, in every activity "from the imitation of the style of film stars by their humbler sisters upwards." It operates differently in the two species of society. In primitive societies mimesis is directed toward the past. In such a society custom rules and the society remains static. On the other hand, in societies in process of civilization, mimesis is directed toward creative personalities who command a following because they are pioneers.

Primitive societies are compared by Toynbee to a people asleep on a mountain ledge with a precipice below and a mountain above. Civilizations are like the companions of the sleepers who have started to climb. Toynbee maintains that this contrast between active and passive societies was anticipated by the Chinese conceptions of *yang* and *yin.* What launched society in the movement from a *yin* (passive) to a *yang* (active) state? The attempt to account for the movement from primitive society to civilization on the basis of race and environment fails to deal accurately with a living thing. We are far better off, he suggests, in looking for the starting point of civilization in an encounter between two superhuman personalities. A society is confronted in the course of its life by a succession of problems. Each problem is a challenge to undergo an ordeal. The personal ordeals of Job and Faust represent, in the intuitive language of fiction, "the infinitely multiple ordeal of mankind." The same idea of an encounter of superhuman forces is portrayed in the Book of Genesis and the New Testament. The expulsion of Adam and Eve from Eden follows the encounter between Yahweh and the Serpent. In the New Testament the passion of Christ is nothing less than Man's Redemption. The story opens with a perfect state of *yin.* Faust is perfect in Knowledge, Job is perfect in goodness and prosperity, Adam and Eve are perfect in innocence. The Virgins (Gretchen, etc.) are perfect in purity and beauty. In the astrologer's universe the sun is the perfect orb, and the *yin* state is complete in its peace before it is ready to pass into a *yang* state.

[22] *Ibid.,* p. 44.

Auguste Comte

Herbert Spencer

Lester Ward

Ferdinand Tönnies

Émile Durkheim

Vilfredo Pareto

Sigmund Freud

Robert Redfield

Oswald Spengler

Arnold Toynbee

Pitirim Sorokin

George Lundberg

Into this perfect *yin* state some factor is intrusive, the Serpent in Genesis, Satan in the Book of Job, Mephistopheles in Faust, Loki in Scandinavian mythology, the divine lovers in the virgin myths. Some factor intrudes, serving as a stimulus of a kind best calculated to evoke potent creative variations.

When a civilization arising as the successful response to a challenge begins to lose its creative force, a differentiation occurs. The ailing civilization disintegrates into a dominant minority, which rules with increasing oppressiveness but no longer leads, and a proletariat (internal and external) which responds to this challenge by becoming conscious that it has a soul of its own and by making up its mind to save its soul alive. A conflict between these two wills continues, while the declining civilization verges toward its fall until, when it is *in articulo mortis,* the proletariat at length breaks free from what was once its spiritual home but has now become a prison-house and finally a "city of destruction." When this occurs the result is the genesis of an affiliated civilization.

When society has suffered its breakdown and the "creative minority" has ceased to be creative, becoming merely "dominant," a creator is called upon to play the part of a conqueror who replies to a challenge with a victorious response; in a disintegrating civilization, he is called upon to play the part of a savior. "The savior-archaist will try to reconstruct an imaginary past; the savior-futurist will attempt a leap into an imagined future. The savior who points the way to detachment will present himself as a philosopher taking cover behind the mask of a king; the savior who points the way to transfiguration will appear as a god incarnate in a man." [23]

Pitirim Sorokin

Undoubtedly the most brilliant of all sociological exponents of a purified organicism is Pitirim A. Sorokin (1889–   ). He was born in a village of northeastern Russia, studied at the University of St. Petersburg, and had entered upon a career of teaching and research at the time of the outbreak of the Revolution. By 1914 he had published a major monograph on crime and punishment, and a system of sociology by 1919. He served as secretary to Alexander Kerensky in 1917, and was later arrested by the Communists, sentenced to death, but had the sentence commuted to exile. At the University of Minnesota, where he came after two years in Czechoslovakia, he completed *Social Mobility* (1927), which was long the undisputed major work in this field, and *Contemporary Sociological Theories* (1928), perhaps the finest single systematic study of sociological theory that America has produced. In 1930, he became professor of sociology at Harvard, where he continued to develop the sociological theory which will be our concern here.[24]

[23] *Ibid.,* p. 534.
[24] Sorokin's two Russian works referred to above are not available in English translation: *Prestuplenie i kara, podvig i nagrada* ["Crime and Punishment, Meritorious Deeds and

The core of original theory around which Sorokin's work is constructed consists of a form of idealistic organicism, and is most systematically expressed in *Social and Cultural Dynamics* (1937–41) and *Society, Culture, and Personality* (1947). For him, the basic facts of sociology are "mentalistic in nature," and can only be understood in terms of "man's sociocultural universe as a whole." [25] This is true not only for "a minor phenomenon such as suicide," but for the cause of crime, revolution, war, and practically all sociocultural phenomena. Sorokin takes his stand on a platform of superorganic mentalistic wholes.

One of the surest indications of the serious critique of positivism that is intended by Sorokin is the relativization of truth as ordinarily understood. There are at least three distinct systems of truth, cognition, and knowledge.[26] *Ideational* truth is revealed by the grace of God through his prophets or oracles. It is absolutistic, non-utilitarian, and non-pragmatic. *Idealistic* truth represents a synthesis of sensory and supersensory forms. The role of the sense organs in verifying sensory truth is recognized, but supersensory truth coming from God is also accepted. *Sensate* truth finds the only true value to be sensory, and cognition is derived only through the sense organs. It denies supersensory reality altogether. It favors the study of the sensory world in its physical, chemical, and biological relations.

In *Social and Cultural Dynamics,* where these topics were treated extensively, Sorokin made a case for the existence of a kind of truth rising above and replacing all of these. He urged that each of the three main systems of truth and reality may be either entirely true, entirely false, or partly true or false. For this reason, the only adequate system of truth will embrace all three. Furthermore, one must recognize that the truths of intuition are the most profound of all. "All great religions explicitly declare that they are the *corpus* of the revealed, super-rational, superempirical, supersensory truth granted by grace of the Absolute to charismatically gifted persons — prophets, saints, mystics, oracles. . . . The experience of these instruments is always super-rational or mystic." [27]

Integral truth is not identical with any of the three forms of truth, but embraces all of them. In this three-dimensional aspect of the truth — of faith, of reason, and of the senses — the integral truth is nearer to the absolute truth than any one-sided truth of one of these three forms. "The

---

Rewards"] (St. Petersburg: 1914) and *Sistema sotsiologii* ["System of Sociology"] (Petrograd: 1920). Sorokin's principal writings in English are: *Social Mobility* (New York: Harper, 1927); *Contemporary Sociological Theories* (New York: Harper, 1928); *Social and Cultural Dynamics*, 4 vols. (New York: American Book Company, 1937–41); *Sociocultural Causality, Space, Time* (Durham, N.C.: Duke University Press, 1943); *Society, Culture, and Personality* (New York: Harper, 1947); *Social Philosophies in an Age of Crisis* (Boston: Beacon Press, 1950); and *Fads and Foibles in Modern Sociology* (Chicago: Henry Regnery, 1956).
[25] *Society, Culture, and Personality*, p. 5.
[26] *Ibid.*, p. 607 f.
[27] *Social and Cultural Dynamics*, **IV**, p. 758.

empirico-sensory aspect of it is given by the truth of the senses; the rational aspect, by the truth of reason; the super-rational aspect by the truth of faith." [28] Thus it seems that Sorokin has not moved into the circle of positivism after all. He is, by his own admission, extraordinarily close to the Absolute.

Sorokin's particular type of organicism is most evident in his conception of the great supersystems. These are all said to be products of intuition, the initiator of all original conceptions in religion, ethics, philosophy, aesthetics, and even mathematical logic and scientific thought. No group, however, is encyclopedically creative. The central achievement of Greece was in the fine arts and philosophy, that of Rome in the creation of a political empire, a military system, and a system of law; the Hebrews in religion, ethics, and literature; medieval society expressed its creativity in organization and the development of Christianity; the Western World is creative in science, technology, philosophy, and the fine arts. It is precisely at this point that Sorokin both identifies his thought with — and distinguishes it from — that of Danilevsky, Spengler, Toynbee, and F. S. Northrop. They claim a great culture is creative in only one field. Sorokin sees them creative not in all but a few.[29]

A new system of meanings takes form first as a mere mental conception. "It must first somehow be objectified through vehicles and then socialized through becoming known to other human beings. If the conception of an ideological system may be compared to the conception of an organism, its objectification may be likened to the birth of an organism." [30] Some of the systems so invented and for which vehicles are found and socialization secured grow into great supersystems. If a petty system possesses three characteristics, it may evolve into a great system: (1) it must contain the potentialities of unfolding into a vast system, meaningfully and practically important; (2) as a minor ideological system, it must correspond to some genuine *need on the part of a given population*; and, finally, (3) to be durable, a minor system must be related to some *"perennial reality and value."* In order for a system to grow, ideas must be developed as they are exchanged in meaningful interaction; quantitative and qualitative accumulation of meanings, vehicles, and processes must occur; there must be attacks by other ideological systems and survival of the given one; there must be cross-fertilization and merging of congenial minor systems; and, while unfolding under attacks and becoming more generalized and spontaneous, the great systems must be stimulated by good luck and incidental genius.

Some great supersystems have emerged that have integrated the vast majority of cultural elements of a time. These most vast of all supersystems are based upon the most "general of all the ontological principles, namely, *the one defining the ultimate nature of reality and value.* Ontologically there

28 *Ibid.*, pp. 762–763.
29 *Society, Culture, and Personality*, p. 548.
30 *Ibid.*, p. 555.

are no more all-embracing concepts than the three following definitions of the ultimate nature of reality and value: (a) true reality and true value are sensory — the major premise of the sensate supersystems. (b) True reality and value consist in a supersensory, super-rational God, Brahman, Atman, Tao, or its equivalent — the major premise of the ideational super-system. (c) True reality and value are an infinite manifold, partly super-sensory and super-rational, partly rational, and partly sensory — the premise of the idealistic supersystem." [31]

Around one of these three central definitions of reality and conception of value, in true organismic fashion, all or most of the other phenomena of culture are arranged: religion, arts, the state, politics, philosophy, criticism — in fact, all the aspects of human society and culture. Moreover, again like organisms, a supersystem may decline. This may occur chiefly quantitatively without loss of quality, it may occur qualitatively and not, at first, quantitatively, it may decline in both respects simultaneously, and it may become petrified. The three great supersystems have tended to alternate successively between sensate and ideational forms. The idealistic super-system is conceived of as an intermediate type.

The Separation of Positivism from Organicism

As the examples of Spengler, Toynbee, and Sorokin indicate, once the formula of organismic-positivism disintegrated, organicism was free to go its way unhindered. One inevitable result was that organicism turns upon positivism itself. Spengler launched a frontal attack on science. Toynbee introduces alongside the ordinary methods of scholarship the methods of intuitive mythology as more appropriate to the cultural historian. Sorokin relativizes truth in its ordinary sense, turning it into an ideology and setting up a new system of truth, integral truth, beyond all others.

But this is only one possibility flowing from the divorce. Positivism was free to go its own way as well. The result was, eventually, the development of an active movement known as "technocracy." It sought to synthesize the principles found in the writings of various engineers, economists, and students of science. The basic arguments of the technocrats centered in the conception that social phenomena are measurable and hence laws of social control can be deduced from these measurements. It was argued, with principles drawn from Veblen, that the phenomenon of machine production has made it impossible any longer to measure values in terms of a single commodity like gold. The engineers have destroyed the price system. The expansion of credit under the capitalistic system was said to have so disturbed the relative claims of capital and labor that capitalism had in fact already collapsed. Finally, the economic processes of the social order are too complex to be understood and controlled by politicians. The engineers and scientists are the only legitimate agents of control in modern society. In

[31] *Ibid.*, p. 590.

its milder and more methodological forms, the development appears as "operationalism," but whenever its social claims are developed in unimpeded fashion, it inclines toward technocracy.

The outstanding American representatives of this development in sociology are Stuart S. Dodd and George A. Lundberg. Dodd's *Dimensions of Society* [32] appears clearly to be neither a theory nor a method (which it claims to be) but a system of notation. It is of no interest here except as an example of the danger always facing pure positivism of degenerating into an empty formula.

George Lundberg

The most able and influential of the positivists is George A. Lundberg (1895–   ), who has been professor of sociology at the University of Washington for a number of years. The works embodying his position most fully are *Foundations of Sociology* and *Can Science Save Us?* [33]

The central category in Lundberg's theory is "adjustment." Sociology is conceived of as dealing with communicable techniques of adjustment developed by groups in relation to each other and their environment. Science itself is an adjustive technique and, as such, a subject of sociology. Adjustment represents the state of experience that terminates an imbalance or tension. It is a state of equilibrium. It is also the state of maximum probability in any organism or social situation. As such it is normal. When tensions are formulated verbally they take the form of a question. Scientific questions are hypotheses. A verified hypothesis is a "law" or equilibrium in thought — the mind in a state of rest.

Lundberg not only makes a concerted attempt to avoid the use of all terms such as "organic" or "spiritual" or "mental," but conceives the entire history of science as the expansion of the realms of the natural and physical at the expense of the mental and spiritual: "One by one 'spiritual' phenomena have become 'physical'. . . . The evolution of the concept of the 'soul' is especially relevant, because its final state of transition or translation by way of the 'mind' into purely 'physical' concepts is still underway." [34] The aggressive anti-organicism expressed here is typical.

On the other hand, Lundberg advocates an extreme positivistic operationalism of method. The data of science are the experiences of organisms or responses of organisms to environment. Symbols are also such responses. They are the data of communicable knowledge and science. All propositions or postulates regarding more ultimate "realities" than these are inferences, generalizations, or abstractions from such symbols. Extrapolations are merely new symbols. Any other statements are unverifiable phenomena. As far as science is concerned, all that exists is words; science is words about words.

[32] New York: Macmillan, 1942.
[33] *Foundations of Sociology* (New York: Macmillan, 1939); *Can Science Save Us?* (New York: Longmans, Green, 1947).
[34] *Foundations of Sociology*, p. 8.

At the same time, Lundberg makes one vast metaphysical postulate: namely, that whatever it is that evokes our words or precipitates our responses exists. Behind the phenomenal world is the world of things in themselves.

Since the ultimate subject matter for study in Lundberg's view is responses or at least the words designating them, these responses come into central focus. Meanings are responses to words. Such phenomena as *"divisions, categories, classifications,* and *groupings* of phenomena of the universe are *words representing* differential responses of man." [35] Frames of reference and universes of discourse are "merely comprehensive ways of responding to large configurations of data."

A technology of word manipulation is presented as the solution to the most crucial of all human problems:

> Personal, community, and international relations constantly reflect the tensions resulting from an inadequate symbolic system of communication. Whole nations frequently fall upon each other with great ferocity because of word-systems or ideologies through which they attribute to each other characteristics, "motives," and behaviors entirely fantastic and demonstrably devoid of foundation in fact. Untold nervous energy, time, and natural resources are wasted in warfare upon or protection against entirely imaginary monsters conjured up by words. Widespread mental disorders result from constantly finding the world different from the word-maps upon which we rely for guidance to adjustments. Social problems cannot be solved as long as they are stated in terms as primitive and unrealistic as those which attributed diseases to demons and witches.[36]

The problem of the international world is due to words.

Furthermore, the backward state of sociology is due to words. The development in science attributed to Galileo, Newton, Lobachevski, and Einstein is attributed to their use of better symbol systems. In sociology we need "the selection of significant behavior — segments and . . . their representation by symbols which lend themselves to operational representation of relationships." [37] In the new order so created, all questions such as what an attitude really is will disappear. Like all other facts, theory will disappear into the words that designate it. The attitude will be defined as the behavior evoked by the particular test. And all such concepts as "racial," "liberal," "happiness," "social status," "intelligence" will vanish or become equally clear. It will be increasingly recognized that all phenomena of scientific concern consist of energy transformations in the physical cosmos manifest as various forms of motion.[38] Sociology is concerned with "the behaviors of those electron-proton configurations called societal groups, principally human groups." [39] These operate on the basis of the conversion of energy into human behavior — a conversion which "takes place through the well known metabolic process of the combustion of fuel, in this case called food." [40]

---

[35] *Ibid.*, p. 25.   [36] *Ibid.*, p. 47.   [37] *Ibid.*, p. 58.
[38] *Ibid.*, p. 203.   [39] *Ibid.*, p. 204.   [40] *Ibid.*, p. 206.

If we will do all these things, most of our problems will clear up, for "as a result of scientific knowledge, men will not want impossible or mutually exclusive things. They will not seek to increase foreign trade and at the same time establish more comprehensive and higher tariffs. They will not seek to reduce crime but at the same time maintain a crime-promoting penal system. They will not destroy the productive power of a nation and still expect it to be peaceful, prosperous, and democratic." [41]

All this and much more will be produced by a coherent system of symbols operationally defined. A coherent and consistent system of symbols

> is important not only to science but also from the standpoint of mental health and practical social administration. A very large proportion of the population . . . are . . . carrying on a major part of their lives in an impersonal machine culture to which they adjust according to the assumptions and rules (word-systems) of science. Another important part of their lives (linguistic and otherwise), having to do with their social adjustments, is carried on according to vitalistic, animistic, primary-group assumptions . . . of a bygone age. . . . Our schizoid societal behavior resides largely . . . in the inadequate and inconsistent symbolic systems according to which we attempt to steer our course. [42]

Let no man say that Lundberg is a peddler of gloom who leaves man without hope. An equivalent amount of word magic has not been found in Anglo-Saxon countries since Merlin the Magician was active in King Arthur's courts. This, it must be noted, has nothing to do with Lundberg personally, but is a property of the popular semantics which he attempted to turn to sociological account. Sometimes the value of a theorist for his time is the vigor with which he explores conceptual alternatives rather than the ultimate defensibility of any one. Lundberg has one of the challenging minds of his generation. The forthrightness with which he has pursued a purified type of positivism has forced a higher level of theoretical understanding upon his time.

Summary

Positivistic organicism drew its original intellectual materials from two philosophic sources of profound significance in Western thought. Its organicism came originally from idealistic philosophy, which extends in an unbroken tradition back to classical Greece. Such idealistic philosophy tended to serve as an ideological bulwark to conservative sections of society. The other conceptual source was from empiricism, which had been evolving in the West since the seventeenth century. Empiricism increasingly carried out the naturalization first of knowledge, then of society, and paved the way for the demand for the fullest possible scientific analysis of society. It tended to become the philosophy of reform. One branch of it became the

[41] *Can Science Save Us?*, p. 29.
[42] *Foundations of Sociology*, pp. 76–77.

philosophy of the French Revolution. And in the opening days of the nineteenth century, it became a plank in the platform of scientific socialism.

Sociology arose in an atmosphere characterized by the conservative reaction to revolution. Sociology was supported by conservative groups. In fusing organicism to positivism, sociology proposed to convert the empiricist-positivistic tradition of the West to conservative ends. The early schools of sociology, as a result, have important ideological dimensions which were often only thinly disguised. Internally they found themselves faced with opposed principles which were difficult to reconcile. Even in the early days (as in the work of Ward), the formula of positivistic organicism tended to disintegrate.

The first major adaptation of positivistic organicism came with the rise to popularity of nineteenth-century biology. The new social science partly vindicated itself by assuming a bio-organismic form. This, however, did not persist for long. Meanwhile, the possibilities of a concept formation in terms of the principles of positivistic organicisms were explored with unusual brilliance by Ferdinand Tönnies and Émile Durkheim. Many of the permanent gains for sociology made by its first theoretical form were due to them.

The second major adaptation of organicism came from the freeing of voluntaristic or irrational idealism from the strongly anti-scientific bias it had assumed under the influence of Nietzsche and Schopenhauer. A voluntaristic positivism was explored by Pareto and in another way by Freud, the configurationists, and the neo-Freudians. The major additions to social theory by this form of positivism were due to the new perspectives on the emotional life of man developed by these schools.

The ideological atmosphere that sustained the fusion of organicism and positivism has passed away. The result has been the disintegration of the early theoretical formula. Under pure organicists such as Spengler, Toynbee, and Sorokin, organicism has been developed in an unrestricted manner, and radical modifications have been proposed for positivism. On the other hand, positivism, freed from the organismic context, has tended to transform itself into an anti-theological, anti-spiritual, anti-organismic metaphysics of instruments. Its variations range from relatively mild operationalism to extreme forms of technocracy.

SELECTED BIBLIOGRAPHY

FREUD, SIGMUND, *General Introduction to Psychoanalysis.* Translation of the revised edition by Joan Riviere. Garden City, N.Y.: Garden City Publishing Company, 1943.

FREUD, SIGMUND, *The Future of an Illusion.* Translated by W. D. Robson-Scott. Garden City, N.Y.: Doubleday, 1957.

FREUD, SIGMUND, *Moses and Monotheism.* Translated by Katherine Jones. New York: Vintage Books, 1955.

LASSWELL, HAROLD D., *Psychopathology and Politics.* Chicago: University of Chicago Press, 1930.

LUNDBERG, GEORGE A., *Foundations of Sociology.* New York: Macmillan, 1939.

NIETZSCHE, FRIEDRICH, *Beyond Good and Evil.* Translated by Marianne Cowan. Chicago: Gateway Editions, 1955.

SOROKIN, PITIRIM A., *Society, Culture, and Personality.* New York: Harper, 1947.

SPENGLER, OSWALD, *Decline of the West.* Translated by Charles Francis Atkinson. Two volumes. New York: Alfred A. Knopf, 1926.

TOYNBEE, ARNOLD J., *A Study of History.* Two-volume abridgment by D. C. Somervell. New York: Oxford University Press, 1947, 1957.

PART THREE

Conflict Theory: The Paradox of Maturity

6

The Foundations of Conflict Theory

THE IDEOLOGICAL REQUIREMENTS IMPOSED ON EARLY SOCIOLOGY DICTATED
that it be both scientific and conservative. Positivistic organicism was both.
Its positivism pulled the teeth of anti-conservative liberal and socialist programs, turning an instrument of reform into a weapon of defense. Meanwhile,
the organic conception of society was almost foolproof. What should one
add to a living whole? What organism needs two heads or a spare leg?
What should one cut out of a living whole — its liver, or lungs, or
stomach? Even change does not present any problems when it is identified
with organic growth — artificially forced, reformist, or revolutionary
change must give way before immanent change proceeding out of the inner
nature of the social organism. To anyone concerned with issues in the
present, there was counsel of patience. Ancient injustices often sustained
important values: ancient theology nourished intellectuality, ancient excesses in leisure based on exploitation made independent thought possible,
ancient war taught men discipline, even ancient slavery was a step in
progress. By the same token, great good must be contained in present injustices. When positivistic organicism was so brilliantly adjusted to the
ideological atmosphere of the nineteenth century, why was it ever given up?

It is unnecessary to remind the reader that sociology is not an ideology —
a set of ideas defending a social position or promoting a program of social
action. Sociology is a science — a set of ideas attempting to explain social
life. Positivistic organicism was given up in part because it was seen to be
ideological. Ideological factors may have a *causal* effect on inquiry, molding

127

its direction and form. But the acceptability of a set of scientific ideas is determined by the application of the criteria of science.

By its very nature, science is a self-correcting enterprise. Hence, it did not matter, in one sense, where the science started. In the long run it was going to cast off its ideological moorings, for sociology is neither revolutionary nor reactionary, neither liberal nor conservative; it is a science — an objective enterprise in empirical knowledge. External requirements might incline sociology to fuse organicism and positivism; internal requirements, conformity to scientific and logical criteria, would determine the acceptability of the fusion.

The first result of the application of more exacting scientific standards to sociological propositions was a speed-up in the turnover of ideas. This only made matters worse, for no scientist needs to be told that if there are ten equally plausible explanations of a body of facts, any one is practically useless. The sure sign of a growing sense of crisis in sociology was an increased preoccupation with method. By the time of the classical stage of early organismic positivism, this preoccupation with method became increasingly apparent. Tönnies, for example, took his stand on the importance of "normal" concepts or "ideal types" for estabishing sociological proofs. Durkheim devoted an entire book to the *Rules of Sociological Method*. Pareto addressed almost a quarter of his four-volume study of *The Mind and Society* to method. But anxiety was hardly confined to method. As the rival theories began to compete for acceptance, inadequacies in the content of early sociology were forced to attention.

Weaknesses of Positivistic Organicism

The most glaring of all content deficiencies in positivistic organicism was its apparent inability to handle the issues bound up with interhuman conflict. Comte feared social conflict so much that he dreamed of a caste-like society organized in an authoritarian manner. So far as possible, Spencer assigned the major forms of social conflict to the militaristic societies of the past, predicting that the advance of industrial society would render war impossible. Tönnies located the more significant forms of conflict in the social type of which he most disapproved — the *Gesellschaft*. It is surprising even to find reference to conflict in Durkheim's work; when it occurs it is treated as a form of social sickness.

The one form of positivistic organicism that recognizes the role of conflict is the voluntaristic type. Pareto approves the forceful tactics of the conservative "lions" who do not hesitate to use the most ruthless means to keep themselves in power. Freud builds his picture of personality out of a tension between emotional and social life; he constructs his picture of man and culture in terms of further tensions and the dark inclinations of individuals as actors on the social stage. There is little doubt that part of the reason why voluntarism was introduced into positivistic theory was the attempt to account for conflict. But the evolution of voluntarism has tended — in the configurationists and neo-Freudians — to return to the more typical organismic model in which conflict has no place.

The failure to account for the facts of conflict turns up at every point. Positivistic organicism could hardly maintain its claims as a form of scientific theory in the face of this discrepancy. Every society has its conflicts. No society can survive without individuals who face up to them. In all societies some strata face conflicts more directly than others. Every society, for example, attempts to protect its young against conflict. One of the most universal meanings of "adulthood" or "maturity" is reception into the stratum of those who are expected to face up to the conflicts of the society in which they live. This is true even in our own society, where youth is protected from full admission to conflict situations, a fact that makes the act of growing up a "bitter pill." It is assumed that youth in its enthusiasm wishes to "make the world over." One of the paradoxes of maturity in our society is the forcing of the young into life situations with high ideals and no experience. By the time the young have acquired experience adequate for a realistic course of action, their ideals are often compromised. One sociologist has taken this fact to be the major clue to the understanding of the age differences in our society,[1] finding irresponsibility, the glamor pattern, and the cult of sports to be the result.

In any case, once the idea was accepted that it was a legitimate objective to develop a social science to explain interhuman life, the most obvious difficulty of early sociology to the minds of mature students was its relatively complete failure to recognize and explain the facts of conflict. This also suggested a new grouping of the materials available in Western thought.

Conceptual Sources of Conflict Theory

If we adopt the notion that conflict and its resolution are a central fact of society, and search tradition for materials relevant to it, a great richness is available. Every society requires a minimum realism about its conflicts to survive. The analysis of society from the standpoint of its typical conflicts is neither new nor confined to the West. For objective "realism" Kautilya's *Arthashastra* has never been surpassed.[2] Han Fei Tzu in ancient China was the teacher of Li Ssǔ, the prime minister of Shih Huang Ti — the great dictator of the ancient state of Ch'n. He taught that the essence of society is power. People by themselves are cowardly and lazy. Fear of the

---

[1] Talcott Parsons, "Age and Sex in the Social Structure of the United States," in *Essays in Sociological Theory Pure and Applied* (2d. ed.; Glencoe: Ill.: The Free Press, 1954).

[2] Kautilya is identified by many scholars with Chanakya, the Brahman minister of the Maurya emperor Chandragupta, who reigned from about 321 to 296 B.C. The *Arthashastra*, long lost but recovered in 1909, deals with the art of government, including civil law and the science of warfare. Kautilya, *Arthashastra*, tr. by R. Shamasastry (Mysore: Wesleyan Mission Press, 1923).

law makes men good; fear of punishment puts them to work. In ruling the world one must act in accord with human nature, distributing rewards and punishments addressed to their likes and dislikes.

In classical Greece, Heraclitus (c. 544–484) of Ephesus, scion of a noble family with hereditary claims to the royal office of the sacrificial priest of the Eleusinian Demeter, was impressed by the instability of all things. He made conflict the law of the visible universe, conceiving everything as in process of transformation into its opposite. Strife is the justice of the world, and war, which is common to all, is the father and king of all things. Heraclitus was not alone among the ancient Greeks to isolate conflict; the Sophists, who methodologically were strongly positivistic, also held conflict theories. Protagoras of Abdera (c. 481–411 B.C.) held a theory of knowledge resting on the Heraclitean doctrine of flux. Gorgias of Leontini (485?–?380 B.C.) recognized the manipulation of illusion as a means of controlling the minds of men. Callicles derived the concept of right from political strength, arguing that morals and law are the work of a majority of weak men who, through uniting, tame the natures of stronger individuals, who are like beasts of prey. Critias viewed the law as instruments for taming the beast in man, while religion operated through fear to keep men good. Thrasymachus of Chalcedon (c. 427 B.C.) argued that, nonsense aside, might makes right.

The conflict doctrines of the Sophists were transmitted on to Epicurus (342?–270 B.C.), who fused them with the conceptions of atomic structure of the atomists and the concept of eternal change of Heraclitus. Epicurus thought that in his wild state man was savage as a beast. The movement from savagery to civilization occurred in the course of the struggle with nature. The struggle with nature is followed by an interhuman struggle. The purpose of all laws is to secure society against injustice. The mass of men are deterred from harmful actions only by the fear of punishment.

Conflict Theories of Polybius

The fullest interpretation of society from the standpoint of conflict was advanced in antiquity by Polybius (c. 205–125 B.C.), the son of a statesman of the Achaean League and one of the thousand leading Achaeans who surrendered on demand of the Roman government in 167 B.C. and were interned in Italy as hostages for sixteen years. He imagined, like Plato, that a great catastrophe had destroyed all human communities, leaving only a few individuals. The impulse that causes impotent and defenseless animals to live in herds also works in man, whose weakness leads him to form into communities with the strongest and bravest individuals as leaders. *Monarchy,* the rule of the strongest, is the first form of the human community. The virtue of this theory of the state, according to Polybius, is its concentration on essentials: power relations. The second step in the formation of society is the transition from the monarchy, which is based on force, to *kingship,* which is based on justice and legitimate authority. Kingship arises out of the sense of obligation on the part of the strong to keep the peace. This is the origin of the sentiment of justice, enforced on recalcitrant and unjust members, and sustained by the majority, who out of gratitude retain the ruler even when he grows old and fails in physical strength.

However, the descendants of the king often become haughty and over-bearing, forgetting the need to sustain justice. The kingship turns into a *tyranny*. When the tyranny becomes unendurable, the most high-minded and noble of the subjects conspire to overthrow the monarchy, and they are supported by the people. But, alas, the *aristocracy* in turn becomes heredi-tary, forgets its lessons, loses its sense of mission, and gets to be unendurable. The *democracy* that replaces it will also work for a time. But people become used to liberty and equality; individuals and groups begin to conspire for influence. Demagogues appear, paying people out of their own pockets. It is time for the government to revert to a monarchy to restore law and order. The only way of bringing this cycle to an end is developing a kind of government combining the best elements of kingship, aristocracy, and democracy. Such a mixed constitution was designed by Lycurgus of Sparta. Such a one grew up gradually in Rome, where the consuls represented kingship, the senate aristocracy, and the people de-mocracy. The state thus arises out of anarchy by the imposition of power which is stabilized by being made legitimate.[3]

Polybius has rather special importance among the early conflict theorists both because he collected so many of the previous ideas into his own theories and because he in turn transmitted his ideas to others. The later Epicurean school among the Romans added Polybius' doctrines to their own. Lucretius and Horace maintained that all things originate in conflict. and Livy sang the praises of Roman expansion, taking conflict as critical in the process of absorbing smaller states and, through the cen-tralization of power, bringing the blessings of peace.

After the fall of Rome, conflict theories went into eclipse in the West, for the theologians of the medieval world found them inconsistent with their ideas. The one place where the conflict theory of society and the state continued to receive expression was in the Arab world.

Conflict Theories of Ibn Khaldun

Abu Zaid 'Abd-al-Rahman Ibn Khaldun was born in Tunis in 1332 of a family originating from Hadramaut of the agricultural region of southern

[3] For an outline of ancient Chinese conflict theory, see Fêng Yu-Lan, *A Short History of Chinese Philosophy*, ed. by Derk Bodde (New York: Macmillan, 1948). The conflict doctrines in classical Greece are expounded in Milton C. Nahm, *Selections from Early Greek Philosophy* (New York: F. S. Crofts, 1934); Eduard Zeller, *Outlines of the History of Greek Philosophy*, 13th ed., rev. by Wilhelm Nestle and tr. by L. R. Palmer (New York: Meridian Books, 1955); and J. B. Bury, *Ancient Greek Historians* (New York: Macmillan, 1909; Dover Publications, 1958), Chapter 6. For a recent analysis of Polybius, see Kurt von Fritz, *The Theory of Mixed Constitutions in Antiquity: A Critical Analysis of Polybius' Political Ideas* (New York: Columbia University Press, 1954).

Arabia. His family had played a leading part in the civil wars of the ninth century and members of the family for four centuries had occupied leading positions in the administration and army. Ibn Khaldun had much political experience in Spain and North Africa, serving in a variety of capacities, eventually as Chief Justice of the Malikite rite. He died in 1406 at the age of 74.

Ibn Khaldun has special interest to sociologists, for he was brought to the attention of the modern world by Gumplowicz and treated with great respect by Franz Oppenheimer. Some persons have viewed him as the first true sociologist. Khaldun believed that social phenomena obey laws like those found in natural phenomena. He believed that they operate on masses and cannot be significantly modified by isolated individuals, maintaining, for example, that a reformer trying to rejuvenate a corrupt state will hardly achieve any success, for powerful social forces are against it. He thought that social laws can only be discovered by gathering a large number of facts and observing comparable cases. Both past and present events can supply such facts. Social laws operate the same way in the same kinds of structure. For example, the laws of nomadic behavior apply to Arabic Bedouins, Berbers, Turkomans, and Kurds indifferently. Moreover, societies change and evolve under contact of people or classes as a result of imitations and intermixtures.[4]

The core of Ibn Khaldun's sociology is found in his concept of "social solidarity" (asabiyya), the distinctive property of society. Human society originates out of necessity. Each individual in nature by himself is hardly able to stay alive "unless he join with his fellow men, for he cannot, unaided, make the many tools needed. . . . Cooperation, however, secures both food and weapons, thus fulfilling God's will of preserving the species." [5] Ibn Khaldun was certain that no sooner do men band together and solve the problems of nature than

> there arises the need of a restraining force to keep men off each other in view of their animal propensities for aggressiveness and oppression of others. Now the weapons with which they defend themselves against wild beasts cannot serve as a restraint, seeing that each man can make equal use of them. Nor can the restraint come from other than men, seeing that animals fall far short of men in their mental capacity. The restraint must therefore be constituted by one man, who wields power and authority with a firm hand and thus prevents anyone from attacking anyone else, i.e., by a sovereign. Sovereignty is therefore peculiar to man, suited to his nature

---

[4] The references to Ibn Khaldun's works here are from the translation by Charles Issawi, *An Arab Philosophy of History* (London: John Murray, 1950). An earlier edition of his writings is the translation by Duncan B. Macdonald, *A Selection from the Prolegomena of Ibn Khaldun* (Leiden: E. J. Brill, 1905). Since this section of the book was written, a new American edition of his works has appeared, translated by Franz Rosenthal, *The Muqaddimah: An Introduction to History*, 3 vols. (New York: Pantheon Books, 1958). See also Mushin Mahdi, *Ibn Khaldûn's Philosophy of History* (London: George Allen and Unwin, 1957).

[5] *An Arab Philosophy of History*, p. 100.

and indispensable to his existence. . . . The state is . . . to society as form is to matter, for the form by its nature preserves the matter and, as the philosophers have shown, the two are inseparable.[6]

The state and society emerge together as form and substance of the same thing. The really important phenomenon is *solidarity*, which is traced to its origins in kinship and blood ties, uniting smaller societies. But such blood ties mean nothing unless accompanied by neighborly contact and common life. These mutual interactions generate a solidarity as powerful as kinship. The relations between aliens, clients, patrons, slaves, and masters may all lead to wider solidarity. Social solidarity is strongest in tribal society, because of the nature of nomadic life. Nomads constantly require mutual assistance. Because the poverty of the desert frees them from ties to the land, to them all countries are equally good. They are more manly, upright, and self-reliant as a result of their way of life. One consequence of this is numerous conquests of populated empires by the smaller, more solidary tribes.

A state can be established only by conflict in which victory goes to the more cohesive and compact group. Similarly, a new religion can establish itself only by strife, but it will succeed only if it enlists the help of a powerful social solidarity. Once established, a religion can reinforce social solidarity, even replacing the cohesiveness of the tribe by centering emotion and thought in a common purpose. Religion is the most powerful cohesive force in a large sedentary people. The sweeping conquest of the Muslim Arabs in the seventh century was made possible by the fusion of tribal and religious solidarity. Tribal solidarity can solidify or weaken empires. It is easy to rule Egypt with its large sedentary population; it is almost impossible to rule Morocco because of the plurality of its tribes.

There must be some original basis of solidarity for a state to arise in the first place; but once established, its solidarity decreases. The presence of unquestioned authority leads to acquiescence and obedience by the subjects. In the early stages the state is cohesive; in time, change and decay set in. Sedentary life and luxurious living take their toll. Power is then concentrated in the hands of the rulers. A division and estrangement occur between ruler and subject. Growing luxury leads to heavier taxes. The state is ready for a change, and soon falls prey to internal or external aggression.

Machiavelli's Conflict Theory

However impressive the writings of Ibn Khaldun, they had no effect on Western European thought before the nineteenth century. When conflict as the key to the interpretation of social and political events was picked up again in the West after Roman times, it was in connection with work of French jurists and the Italian Niccolò Machiavelli (1469–1527), the son of a Florentine jurist. Machiavelli had served as a clerk at the time of the ex-

[6] *Ibid.*, p. 101.

pulsion of the Medici in 1494, and in 1498 he became second chancellor of
the republic, remaining in the post for fourteen years. He headed the
correspondence bureau, went on diplomatic missions, and organized the
Florentine militia. When the Medici returned to power in 1512, Machiavelli
was first imprisoned, then exiled. He spent the rest of his life writing.[7]

His best-known work, *The Prince,* and his more profound *Discourses on
the First Ten Books of Livy* were written from quite different points of view.
The first is a handbook for dictators and the second the thoughtful statement
of an Italian patriot dreaming of the unity of Italy. However, the theories
of human nature and the state that inform them are the same. Human
nature is basically evil. "Men are bad and ever ready to display their vicious
nature, whenever they may find occasion for it." [8] In *The Prince,* this is
interpreted to mean that the desire for conquest is most natural among
men. Men are good only when they are constrained. If the evil disposition is concealed for a time, it must be due to unknown reasons, and
"we must assume that it lacked occasion to show itself." It is observed that
"poverty and hunger make men industrious, and law makes men good."

Initially men were few in number, living dispersed like beasts. When the
human race increased, men came into contact and the need for defense
against one another was felt. By necessity, men "chose the strongest and most
courageous from amongst themselves and placed him at their head,
promising to obey him. Thence they began to know the good and the
honest, and to distinguish them from the bad and vicious." [9] Machiavelli
traces justice to the same source as Polybius — the attempt to constrain those
who do injury to others. There is no difficulty so long as princes are wise
and just. However, once sovereignty becomes non-elective, there is no
guarantee against inferior stock. Excessive luxury in a prince is an occasion
for envy of others. This leads to conspiracy. The fear this generates in the
prince turns him into a tyrant. The rise of the conspirators against the
tyrant establishes an aristocracy. It in turn is corrupted and replaced by
democracy, which in turn moves step by step toward anarchy, hurrying the
day for a new dictatorship.

Machiavelli was not a systematic theorist, yet a clear plan was present in
both *The Prince* and the *Discourses.* In the former work he brought
under review all those properties of the political landscape which seemed
to him to be either conditions or instruments of political activity. In the
Discourses, these same properties assume a more general meaning, becoming

[7] Many editions are available in English of the two works of Machiavelli's with which
we are chiefly concerned — *Il Principe* and *Discorsi sopra la prima deca di Tito Livio.*
References here are to Luigi Ricci's translation "The Prince" and Christian E. Detmold's
translation "Discourses on the First Ten Books of Titus Livius"; both appear in a
single volume: Niccolò Machiavelli, *The Prince and the Discourses,* ed. by Max
Lerner (New York: Modern Library, 1948).
[8] *The Prince and the Discourses,* p. 117.
[9] *Ibid.,* p. 112.

the component forces, as he saw them, of political society. Among the
forces at work on the state he discovers tradition, religion, popular ideology,
social classes (at least the nobles and people), military institutions, and the
person of the dictator. Machiavelli agrees with Polybius not only in viewing
the state as a kind of equilibrium of forces, but also in his idea of a
balance of forces as the source of a stable and durable state. Very probably
he thought a unified state could be established only by the aggressive
action of a dictator. However, only when the various forces are given recognition and the interests of prince, nobles, and people are all realized, will
liberty be maximized.

Conflict Theories of Bodin

Jean Bodin (1530–1596), the most powerful social and political writer
in sixteenth-century France, and thought by many to be the most significant
of the century, contributed much to the conflict theory of society and the
state. Little is known of his family. It is thought that his father was a
French lawyer, his mother a Spanish Jew. He knew Hebrew and was
familiar with Jewish writing on the Old Testament. Trained for the law, he
taught for twelve years at the University of Toulouse. He settled in Paris as
an advocate, and later (1576) he was elected to the States-General at Blois.
He also occupied the post of magistrate at Laon. His first book, *Method
for the Easy Comprehension of History* (1566), dealt with problems of
politics in general and with the foundation of the French constitution. Here
he sought a means of studying history which would at the same time constitute a method of analyzing society. His solution was a theory of historical
stages. In his next work, he turned to the study of the economic conditions of
France, *The Response of Jean Bodin to the Paradoxes of Malestroit*
(1568). His great work, the *Six Books of the Commonwealth* appeared in
1576. His strange *De la Démonomanie des sorciers* ["On the Demono-
mania of Sorcerers"] was written in 1580 to defend magic and witchcraft
against skeptics and to provide a practical manual for magistrates; Bodin
was convinced that man lives constantly under the influence of spiritual
beings who work good and evil.[10]

At the time Bodin wrote, the French monarchy was weakened by the

---

[10] The standard edition of Bodin's works is: Jean Bodin, *Œuvres philosophiques*
(Paris: Presses Universitaires de France, 1951). The *Methodus ad facilem historiarum
cognitionem* was translated by Beatrice Reynolds as *Method for the Easy Comprehension
of History* (New York: Columbia University Press, 1945). A recent edition of *La
Response de Jean Bodin aux paradoxes de M. de Malestroit* is the translation by
George Albert Moore, *The Response of Jean Bodin to the Paradoxes of Malestroit*
(Chevy Chase, Md.: The Country Dollar Press, 1946). *Les Six livres de la république*
is available in an abridged translation by M. J. Tooley as *Six Books of the Commonwealth*
(Oxford: B. Blackwell, 1955). There appears to be no available English translation of
De la Démonomanie des sorciers. An excellent account of Bodin's work may be found
in J. W. Allen, *A History of Political Thought in the Sixteenth Century* (2d. ed.;
London: Methuen, 1941).

religious conflict between Catholic and Huguenot. Bodin supported the monarchy against such religious factions. The basis of society, he believed, lies in the family, founded on the inevitable association of man and woman and involving children, property, and rightful authority. Man is naturally the ruler of woman, because of woman's moral and intellectual inferiority. It would be a disaster to emancipate her. The family is the first and only "natural" form of society. The state is an association of families recognizing "sovereign power."

The formation of civil societies precedes the formation of the state. Families group around advantageous sites, being drawn to trade and cooperation for defense and common worship. A union follows among the loose associations, in which war and conquest play a part.

While the family precedes any form of complex social structure, the state arises from conquest. Many social phenomena, such as class distinctions, can ultimately be traced to the superiority–subordination relation of conquerors and conquered. A stable social structure consists in a process of continuing dissolution and reorganization in which conflict plays a part. The lack of conflict is fatal, as is evident in agriculturalists who lack fighting vigor. Discipline which is imposed by scanty natural resources is advantageous. Bodin also observes that trading cities are often located so as to be safe from attack; city dwellers are more adaptable than isolated peoples.

At the core of Bodin's thought there always appears the conception of *sovereign power* as the essence of civil society. Sovereignty, however, is never clearly separated by Bodin from legal prerogatives. Law is treated as the command of the sovereign. Customary law is valid only so long as sanctioned by the sovereign. Sovereignty has unlimited authority to make law.

Bodin was modern in far more ways than his anticipation of the contemporary problem of sovereignty. He broadened the trend already present in Machiavelli toward an empirical method. He attempted the systematic and critical use of historical materials. He proposed the systematic comparative study of law. He takes as accepted that a law of nature conditions all human relations and he does not identify such a law with the law common to all nations (*ius gentium*). Furthermore, in the course of reviewing historical materials he advanced many ideas necessary to a general sociology: he thought that every association of men involves subjection of some members to others; he conceived of mankind as organized in a series of associations from the family to the state; he thought nobility was a significant social and political institution; he believed that a man's occupation is important for determining his position in society and the state; he distinguished two types of state — the commonwealth and the city; he wished to keep property inviolate against unjust seizure by political power; he formulated theories about the relation of law and custom; he conceived revolutions as changes in the location of authority.

Hobbes' Conflict Theory

Bodin, in some respects, is more modern in spirit than his greater successor in conflict theory, Thomas Hobbes (1588–1679), who did his work in the face of conditions very similar to those that faced Bodin sixty years earlier. *De Cive* was written in 1642, *Leviathan* in 1651.[11] The English Puritans were as opposed to English tyranny as the Huguenots were to the French. Hobbes' political treatises were published in exile. In Paris he lived in close relation to the royalist colony and was identified, like Bodin, with the royalist cause in times of civil dissension. On the other hand, whereas Bodin borrowed much from other authors and from historical and contemporary events and arrived at inconsistent hypotheses, Hobbes carried through a deductively consistent argument from a basic set of premises about human nature.

Hobbes accepted a materialistic conception of man and nature and a rigorously empirical conception of knowledge. All thoughts of man begin with the senses and everything else is derived from this: memory, dreams, apparitions, or visions. Understanding and imagination work with these ultimate materials. They have no others. Language is important, for it consists of "named" sense materials. It must work with definitions.

The essence of the animal is found behavioristically in two kinds of motions: vital (like the course of the blood or breath) and animal (voluntary). Endeavor (or will) consists in the small beginnings of motion, which, directed toward something, is appetite or desire; directed away, it is aversion.[12] All emotions reduce to these. Deliberation consists in the alteration in the individual of desire and aversion. The last appetite or aversion adhering to the action or omission of action is what is called the will.

On this basis Hobbes attacks the problems of the nature of society and the state. The mainspring of human action is formulated as follows: "In the first place, I put for a general inclination of all mankind a perpetual and restless desire of power after power, that ceaseth only in death." This operates in two ways, in king and subject alike. The desire for power is insatiable.

> Hence it is that kings, whose power is greatest, turn their endeavors to the assuring it at home by laws, or abroad by wars: and when that is done, there succeedeth a new desire; in some, of fame from new conquest; in others, of ease and sensual pleasure; in others, of admiration, or being flattered for excellence in some art, or other ability of mind. . . . Desire of ease, and sensual delight, disposeth men to obey a common power: because by such desires, a man doth abandon the protection that might be

---

[11] The editions consulted here are: *De Cive, or The Citizen* (New York: Appleton-Century-Crofts, 1949) and *Leviathan* (New York: Macmillan, 1947). Other works of Hobbes which are of special interest are: *The History of the Civil Wars of England* (1679), *Behemoth* (1679), and *The Art of Rhetoric* (1681).

[12] *Leviathan*, p. 31.

hoped for from his own industry and labor. Fear of death, and wounds, disposeth to the same; and for the same reason.[13]

The main forms of strife appear in the competition to gratify identical appetites, in fear lest each surpass the other in power and in craving for recognition and admiration. The natural relations of an individual to every other are competition, distrust, and the struggle for prestige. In a state of nature men are in a state of war, and life is "solitary, poor, nasty, brutish, and short." In the state of nature there is no distinction between right and wrong; there are no standards by which passions may be morally judged. There is no distinction between the just and unjust. Natural right means no more than the right to do anything that preserves one's existence.

The state originates in the need for self-preservation — the need to escape the natural condition of war. The state is a real individual replacing the many. Every act of disobedience by a subject is unjust regardless of the grounds for the act. Nor can the sovereign set up grounds for violation of the contract by the subject. This would be an injustice by the sovereign, for it would violate the covenant. There is, moreover, no justification for resistance by the minority of the community on the grounds that it did not select the sovereign, who has entire power for prescribing laws as well as unrestricted power over property; he has the power to determine all controversies between subjects; sole authority to make war or peace, appoint magistrates, and distribute wealth, honors, and privileges. However, in the case of anarchy, when the sovereign can no longer protect the subject, one owes no obligation to the sovereign. Nor does one owe any obligation to the sovereign if captured in war or molested in a foreign country. Morality and justice are creations of the state. Even the church should be subordinated to the state.

Conflict Theory Acquires an Empirical Foundation

David Hume

The shift in conflict theory from a purely rational to an empirical foundation may be seen in the work of David Hume (1711–1776). Hume came from a well-to-do family, and was able to devote himself to the study of literature, philosophy, and law. He tried his hand at business. During a sojourn in France, he wrote *A Treatise of Human Nature* (1739–40). His social and historical views appear primarily in the *Philosophical Essays* (1748), *Dialogues Concerning Natural Religion* (written about 1750 and published in 1779), and his *History of England* (6 vols., 1754–63). Hume served for two years as secretary in France, where he became acquainted with Montesquieu and Helvétius. He brought Rousseau back to England,

[13] *Ibid.,* p. 64.

but they soon fell out. For a time Hume acted as under secretary of state for Scotland.

In his essay "On the First Principles of Government," Hume presents the picture of a state in remarkable contemporary terms. Nothing, he says, appears more surprising "than the easiness with which the many are governed by the few; and the implicit submission with which men resign their own sentiments and passions to those of their rulers. When we inquire by what means this wonder is effected, we soon find that, as force is always on the side of the government, the governed have nothing to support them but opinion.[14] Right is right to power and right to property. "When men act in a faction, they are apt, without shame or remorse, to neglect all the ties of honor and morality, in order to serve their party." [15] At the same time, nothing is more obstinate than a faction endowed with a sense of right. Opinion of right to property is fundamental (though not absolutely essential) to all government.

> Upon these three opinions, therefore, of public *interest*, of *right to power*, and of *right to property*, are all governments founded, and all authority of the few over the many. There are indeed other principles which add force to these, and determine, limit, or alter their operation: such as *self-interest*, *fear*, and *affection*.[16]

Thus, government is presented by Hume as a kind of complex equation in which force and public opinion are involved. The transition has been made by Hume to the concept of "legitimate power" as the critical phenomenon of the state, which rests basically on force.

The problem of the origin of government was handled in a common-sense and empirical-minded manner. Man, Hume thought, was born in a family, and is compelled to maintain society from necessity, from natural inclination, and from habit. In his further progress he is led to establish political society in order to establish justice, without which there can be no peace, safety, or mutual intercourse. Government probably began casually and imperfectly with the ascendancy of one man over multitudes during the states of war where superiority of courage and genius is most quickly seen and where concert is requisite, for the effects of disorder are sensibly felt. However, the transition to peacetime ascendancy must have been slow. "If the chieftain possessed as much equity as prudence and valor, he became, even during peace, the arbiter of all differences and could gradually, by a mixture of force and consent, establish his authority." [17] But the problems of force and freedom or authority, and liberty, are not solved all for one.

> In all governments, there is a perpetual intestine struggle, open or secret, between authority and liberty; and neither of them can ever absolutely pre-

[14] David Hume, *Essays: Moral, Political, and Literary,* ed. by T. H. Green and T. H. Grose (London: Longmans, Green, 1907), Vol. 1, pp. 109–110.
[15] *Ibid.,* p. 110.   [16] *Ibid.,* p. 111.   [17] *Ibid.,* p. 113.

vail in the contrast. A great sacrifice of liberty must necessarily be made in every government; yet even the authority, which confines liberty, can never, and perhaps ought never, in any constitution, to become quite entire and uncontrollable.[18]

Hume insists that some combination of force and consent are operative in social structure. Since men are nearly equal in bodily force, mental powers, and faculties until cultivated by education, we must allow — if there ever was an original contract — that nothing but "their own consent could, at first, associate them together, and subject them to authority." [19]

Adam Ferguson's Conflict Theory

A member of the same circles of the Scottish Enlightenment, Adam Ferguson (1723–1816), a friend of Hume and an admirer of Montesquieu, tried to carry through the critical principles of Hume on the empirical foundations of Montesquieu. Ferguson was professor of psychology and moral philosophy at the University of Edinburgh. His ideas appear in *Institutes of Moral Philosophy* (1769), *Principles of Moral and Political Science* (1792), and particularly in the greatest of his works, *An Essay on the History of Civil Society* (1766).[20] With Montesquieu he believed that external and unwilled elements determine social growth; natural causes rather than speculations of the philosophers determine the state. "No constitution is formed by concert, no government is copied from a plan." [21] With Hume and Bodin, Ferguson believed that mankind never lived in a kind of pre-social individual state, but in groups. Also with Hume, he thought that while man is born in society, some of his important institutions originate in force. He believed that conflict in human communities is a genuine benefit and necessary concomitant to progress. "Without the rivalship of nations and the practice of war, civil society itself could scarcely have found an object or a form." In fact, we cannot even understand our fellows unless we have struggled ourselves: "he who has never struggled with his fellow creatures is a stranger to half the sentiments of mankind." [22] The various forms of strife and conflict appear in the competition of the economy as well as in politics; they appear in war and international relations. Economic prosperity is founded in political and military strife. Instinct and habit operating on their products create social forms. Natural right lies only in the right of a man to use his own faculties. Out of the efforts of man to secure values arises the order and authority of society. The forms and powers of government are established by the incidents of struggle. Also like Hume, Ferguson believed that consent is a component in the in-

[18] *Ibid.*, p. 116.   [19] *Ibid.*, pp. 445–446.
[20] There is no recent edition of Ferguson's works. References here are to: *An Essay on the History of Civil Society* (Edinburgh: 1767) and *Principles of Moral and Political Science*, 2 vols. (Edinburgh: 1792). For a fuller exposition of Ferguson's views on society, see William Christian Lehmann, *Adam Ferguson and the Beginnings of Modern Sociology* (New York: Columbia University Press, 1930).
[21] *Essay on the History of Civil Society*, p. 188.
[22] *Ibid.*, p. 36.

stitutions of government,[23] though it is only one component. He doubts that peace is the goal of society.

Turgot and Conflict Theory

In France, views essentially similar to those of Hume and Ferguson were developed by Anne Robert Jacques Turgot (1727–1781) under the influence of Montesquieu. Turgot had studied theology for a time, but instead of becoming an ecclesiastic he became a member of the French state bureaucracy, where he was concerned with problems of finance and taxation. In 1750, while holding an honorary office in the Sorbonne, he delivered his famous lecture *Tableau philosophique des progrès successifs de l'esprit humain*.[24] Later, under the influence of Quesnay, he wrote his *Réflexions sur la formation et la distribution des richesses* (1766).[25] Following Montesquieu, Turgot developed the conception of a plurality of influences on mankind (climate, custom, soil, etc.). He assumed, as a rationalist, that the human mind is everywhere the same. This casts into central focus the value for social science of comparative social and historical evidence, since every variety of barbarism and culture is to be found on earth and could be employed to reveal the laws of mind and society. Isolated nations, at present, show almost the same degree of barbarism as must once have characterized the human race. As culture develops, educational and religious institutions play an increasing role in fixing behavior. Migration and culture play a role in social change. However, without the effects of war and conflict in liquidating fixed customs, the human race would have remained in mediocrity.

Turgot believed that the relations between nomadic and sedentary-tillage peoples undergo typical sequences. Rulers holding agricultural peoples in subjection in turn reach a point where they become surrounded by barbarous tribes. When they become feeble, the barbarians, out of greed and ambition, attack. The barbarians in time adopt the culture of the conquered people, but as they become more domesticated, their fate is eventually the same as that of the rulers they supplanted. Conflict, the great liquidator, is the source of all real progress.

The Significance of Early Conflict Theories

This review of the highlights of the historical antecedents of conflict theory indicates the nature and richness of the material available to the new school of sociological theorists, and it supplies evidence of the sociological relevance of conflict theory.

The historical forms of conflict theory are not simple historical curiosities;

[23] *Principles of Moral and Political Science*, p. 244.
[24] Translated by McQuilkin DeGrange as *On the Progress of the Human Mind* (Hanover, N.H.: The Sociological Press, 1929).
[25] Translated as *Reflections on the Formation and Distribution of Wealth* (New York: Macmillan, 1898). See also W. Walker Stephens (ed.), *The Life and Writings of Turgot* (London: Longmans, Green, 1895) and Douglas Dakin, *Turgot and the Ancien Régime in France* (London: Methuen, 1939).

they form a developing tradition. Polybius, for example, was familiar with various conflict interpretations in the Greek world. He synthesized these into his own. The Roman, particularly the Epicurean tradition, was in turn familiar with the views of Polybius. When conflict theory was vigorously advanced in the Renaissance world by Machiavelli, his preferred model was found in Polybius, though indeed he was also familiar with Latin authors in part also influenced by Polybius. From Machiavelli conflict tradition was passed on into the theories of seventeenth- and eighteenth-century students. Thus, the conflict theorists are no matter of historical curiosity; they constitute a fairly unified tradition. To be sure, the Chinese legalists and the Indian Kshatriya writers lie outside the Western traditions; they show that other societies, too, have had their "realists." Similarly, the theories of Ibn Khaldun, while influenced by the classical Greek discussions, perhaps even by Polybius, lie outside the developments in the West until the nineteenth century; not until they were introduced into Western discussions by Gumplowicz did they acquire interest for sociological conflict theory. Conflict theory is an ancient form which underwent expansion and internal differentiation, supplying a rich tradition available to modern students. As one comes into recent times, conflict theory is given rationally coherent form (Hobbes) and made empirically and methodologically conscious (Bodin, Hume, Ferguson, and Turgot).

The social anchorage of its exponents is of special interest. Conflict theory is the creation of men of affairs. Heraclitus was the scion of a political and priestly family. The Sophists were displaced persons who had usually belonged to the ruling circles of their home cities. Plato, by contrast, as leader of a genteel sect, was passionately opposed to their views. Polybius was a statesman and political hostage. The Romans who adhered to a conflict interpretation of society were trained in the law and politically responsible. Machiavelli was an exiled politician; Bodin was a lawyer and magistrate, Hobbes a political secretary. Hume had served as a political secretary and ambassador, and Turgot was one of the more brilliant administrators of pre-revolutionary France.

When sociology turned to the conflict theorists, it is evident that it was appealing to the realistic analyses of mature men of affairs. However, before conflict theory emerged in sociology, it was to undergo rapid evolution in some of the near-by social sciences. In the course of this odyssey, conflict theory was considerably enriched.

Classical Economics and the Evolution of Conflict Theory

In the seventeenth and eighteenth centuries the primary anchorage of conflict theory was in circles concerned with the problems of political science. However, in the eighteenth century some propositions central to conflict theory were adapted to the explanation of economic phenomena. Physiocracy, the product, was the first step toward modern economics.

Important works of the physiocrats include Pierre Samuel Du Pont de Nemours' *De l'Origine et des progrès d'une science nouvelle* (1768), François Quesnay's *Le Droit naturel* (1765), Paul Pierre Mercier de la Rivière's *L'Ordre naturel et essential des sociétés politiques* (1767),[26] and the works of Turgot.

Adam Smith

The physiocrats believed that there is a natural order in society which man can analyze rationally and control. The peculiar property of land is its capacity to produce an excess of value, forming a fund from which all classes of society live. Only the agricultural class can add new value; the other classes are all sterile and parasitical. All revenue for the support of government must come from the net produce of land. There should be a single tax, resting directly on land. The proprietors have a peculiar role in economic affairs. The advantages emerging from trade and commerce are of indirect value to agriculture, enabling the cultivators to concentrate on raising crops. For this reason the trades and commercial pursuits should be entirely free from obstruction of any kind in order best to serve agriculture. The duty of the state is to furnish instructions about the natural order, to protect it, to assist it by such things as roads, bridges, and harbors needed by the economy. In all other matters the state's activity should be curtailed. These ideas were taken over, expanded, and modified by Adam Smith, in *The Wealth of Nations* (1776), which traced the source of all value to labor and modified the idea of the agriculturalists as the sole productive class. The crucial ideas that emerged from Smith's re-working of physiocracy were: (1) that competition in economic affairs should be completely free: only in this manner could a maximum productivity be achieved; and (2) that the sphere of government should be correspondingly reduced; natural forces will reconcile the requirements of both individual and group.

> As every individual . . . endeavours as much as he can both to employ his capital in the support of domestic industry, and so to direct that industry that its produce may be of the greatest value; every individual necessarily labours to render the annual revenue of the society as great as he can. He generally, indeed, neither intends to promote the public interest, nor knows how much he is promoting it. By preferring the support of domestic to that of foreign industry, he intends only his own security; and by directing that industry in such a manner as its produce may be of greatest value, he intends only his own gain, and he is in this, as in many other cases, led by an invisible hand to promote an end which was no part of his intention. Nor is it always the worse for the society that it was no part of it. By pursuing his own interest he frequently promotes that of the society more effectually than when he really intends to promote it.[27]

---

26 "On the Origin and Progress of a New Science"; "Natural Law"; and "The Natural and Essential Order of Political Societies." None of these is readily available in English translation.
27 Adam Smith, *The Wealth of Nations* (New York: Modern Library, 1937), p. 423.

Traditional conflict theory had made the state the central object of analysis, conceiving of it as the institution equilibrating the stress arising out of the conflicts of individuals or groups. The physiocrats shifted the focus: to them the most fundamental of all phenomena in human society is the struggle for the necessities of life. Even the conception of conflict as having positive value is not new; Turgot and Ferguson attributed positive effects to political conflict. In fact the positive functions of a form of conflict are formulated in terms of widest generality. Economic competition is the great agency of efficiency in the production of the basic necessities of life. The state is an institution resting on force but hardly productive in the manner of economic competition; like a great bird of prey, it tends to interfere with normal productive process. Between the physiocrats and Adam Smith the foundations of classical economics were laid. Moreover, Malthus soon showed that the conflict formula located at the heart of classical economics was capable of expansion.

Thomas Malthus

Thomas Robert Malthus (1766–1834), the son of a country gentleman, had been trained at Jesus College, Cambridge, and took holy orders. He became in 1805 professor of history and political economy at the East India Company's College at Haileybury. The first form of the *Essay on the Principle of Population* was printed in 1798, the second in 1803.[28] In these, the competition formula was rephrased in more general form.

One can, of course, look at competition positively as the basis for an increase in precision and competence. One can also look at it negatively, as the struggle for scarce value which everyone cannot have. Insofar as competition produces values, it is positive; but it loses this property the moment there is greater need for values than competition can produce. This last is precisely Malthus' addition to the argument on the basis of demographic facts.

There is, according to Malthus, a constant tendency in all animated life to increase beyond the nourishment available to it. Nature scatters the seeds of life about in great abundance, but it is comparatively miserly in its provision of nourishment for them. In the plant and animal world, some balance is preserved by the fact that different life forms prey on each other. These same forces operate in man. The population has a constant tendency to increase beyond the means of subsistence. On the basis of statistical calculations available to him, Malthus urged that conservatively it may be assumed that the population, when unchecked, will tend to double itself every twenty-five years, or increase in a geometric ratio. Meanwhile the basic soil is being depleted. It is doubtful, he believed, whether the amount of subsistence can be doubled in any number of years. He predicted that

[28] References here are to the Macmillan edition of 1894, which contains both the first and second editions of the *Essay*. All of the quotations here are from Malthus' later version.

in America the Indians would be driven farther into the country, until the whole race was exterminated. Under the best management, it is questionable whether the food supply can be increased faster than in an arithmetic ratio.

> Taking the whole earth, instead of this island, emigration would of course be excluded; and supposing the present population equal to a thousand millions, the human species would increase as the numbers 1, 2, 4, 8, 32, 64, 128, 256, and subsistence as 1, 2, 3, 4, 5, 6, 7, 8, 9. In two centuries the population would be to the means of subsistence as 256 to 9; in three centuries as 4096 to 13, and in two thousand years the difference would be almost incalculable.
> In this supposition no limits whatever are placed to the produce of the earth. It may increase for ever, and be greater than any assignable quantity; yet still the power of population being in every period so much superior, the increase of the human species can only be kept down to the level of the means of subsistence by the constant operation of the strong law of necessity, acting as a check upon the greater power.[29]

The most general preventive check that can be conceived is rational abstinence from having children. If birth control did not produce vice, it would be just about the least evil that could arise from population. However, it is usual for a corruption of morals to result, particularly degrading the female character. There are clearly serious risks.

> When a general corruption of morals, with regard to sex, pervades all classes of society, its effects must necessarily be, to poison the springs of domestic happiness, to weaken conjugal and parental affection. . . .[30]

Moreover, a preventive check on population would operate most efficiently precisely on the most worthy elements of the population, while it increased unchecked on the part of the less worthy. Of course, it never increases quite unchecked:

> The positive checks to population are extremely various, and include every cause, whether arising from vice or misery, which in any degree contribute to shorten the natural duration of human life. Under this head therefore may be enumerated, all unwholesome occupations, severe labour and exposure to the seasons, extreme poverty, bad nursing of children, excesses of all kinds, the whole train of common diseases and epidemics, wars, pestilence, plague, and famine.[31]

Competition, as a central concern of economic theorists, has indeed been given a grim turn.

All competition in the end becomes a competition to survive. This inevitably drives wages down to that point where they are just sufficient to permit the laborer to live and reproduce himself. In other areas, also,

---

[29] *Ibid.,* p. 86.   [30] *Ibid.,* p. 89.   [31] *Ibid.,* p. 89.

Malthus introduces a grim note, calling into question any and all programs for reform, which are doomed unless the population growth is checked.

> . . . it seems evident, that no improved form of government, no plans of emigration, no benevolent institutions, and no degree or direction of national industry, can prevent the continued action of a great check to increase in some form or other; it follows, that we must submit to it as an inevitable law of nature. . . .[32]

The most important argument against Malthus is that he completely underestimated the gain in productivity made possible by the industrial revolution. For example, the United States in 1790 was only about 5 per cent urban. The ordinary American farm was able to raise only enough food for its own and perhaps one other family At present the population is over 60 per cent urban, and the farmer is able to produce enough for himself and seventeen others. We are at the moment embarrassed by a tremendous farm surplus. However, it is by no means clear that this proportionate increase in productivity can continue indefinitely, and the argument may belong to the Malthusians in the long run. All this aside, however, the central concern here is with the sharp, hard turn given to the meaning of competition as a form of conflict central to economic behavior, and with the consequences of this conflict for the conduct of society, the standard of living, the condition of labor, and the social classes.

Malthus' conclusions were a very severe blow to the kind of rationalistic optimism of persons like Helvétius, Condorcet, and Godwin. But more important than this was the influence of Malthus on biology, and particularly on Darwin.

The Conflict Theory Receives Biological Support

Great gains had been made in biology toward the end of the eighteenth century and in the early nineteenth century. The cell theory was established by Bichat, Schleiden, and Schwann. Embryology had been established by Karl Ernst von Baer (1792–1876). The evolutionary hypothesis had been advanced in various ways by such men as John Ray (1628–1705), Georges de Buffon (1707–1788), and Alexander von Humboldt (1769–1859). The effects of geographic factors on the distribution of flora and fauna had been studied by Carl Linnaeus (1707–1778). Attempts to state the mechanism of evolution began to make their appearance in the work of Étienne Geoffroy Saint-Hilaire (1772–1844), Erasmus Darwin (1731–1802), and Jean Baptiste Lamarck (1744–1829), but it was a conflict theory taken from classical economics, and particularly from Malthus, that provided the spur to nineteenth-century biology. Charles Darwin was led through the influence of Malthus to a re-statement of the mechanism of evolution:

[32] *Ibid.*, p. 97.

In October, 1838, that is, fifteen months after I had begun my systematic inquiry, I happened to read for amusement, *Malthus on Population*, and being well prepared to appreciate the struggle for existence which everywhere goes on, from long continued observation of the habits of animals and plants, it at once struck me that under these circumstances favorable variations would tend to be preserved, and unfavorable ones to be destroyed. The result would be the formation of new species. Here, then, I had at last got a theory by which to work.[33]

Darwin took for granted the fact that variation occurs in all animal species. However, it was the idea of the struggle for existence and the survival of the fittest that provided the needed formula.

On a biological level, a parallel had been reached to the conception of the social benefits of struggle, conflict, and war. Conflict and the struggle to survive now appeared at the very heart of biological phenomena. A mechanism had been achieved that placed supreme importance on efficiency. All recourse to a teleological explanation of biological development became unnecessary. Thus an idea born in the sphere of politics migrated to economics, was specialized in demography, and taken over and applied to biology. It was now ready to return to the field of general sociology, serving as the basis for one of the main types of conflict theory in modern times.

Summary

Although positivistic organicism was adapted to the two main demands of the nineteenth century — its conservatism and the demand for the application of science to society — tension between these two sets of requirements could not be permanently avoided. If one actually did apply science to society, the results were certain to upset tradition; if one did not apply science to society, one could hardly pretend that the new discipline was a science. Moreover, the assemblage of information by the new discipline led to the rapid evolution of alternative ideas. This created the requirement for a dependable method. In various ways Tönnies, Durkheim, and Pareto all illustrate a growing concern with scientific standards.

The institution of more exacting standards, however, quickly revealed a major weakness of positivistic organicism — its apparent inability to handle issues of interhuman conflict. So glaring was this deficiency that the phenomena of social conflict became the point of gravity for reconstruction of the science.

Once conflict was accepted as a central fact of society, a rich intellectual tradition was available for its interpretation. Every society has its conflicts; every society has persons who face up to them. In classical Greece a series of thinkers from Heraclitus to the Sophists treated conflict as *a* primary, perhaps *the*, primary social fact. The best developed conflict theory

[33] Francis Darwin, *The Life and Letters of Charles Darwin* (New York, Appleton, 1887).

of antiquity was that of Polybius, for whom it was the fundamental fact in the evolution of political institutions. In fact, he visualized the state as a kind of stabilized system of power. In the medieval Arabic world, Ibn Khaldun developed a conflict theory of society based on the assumption that the struggles between the nomad and the tiller were fundamental to the evolution of civilization.

While Ibn Khaldun's ideas did not affect Western thought until the nineteenth century, Polybius' conceptions were transmitted directly to Niccolò Machiavelli, who found the origin of the state and its key institutions in the same place. These ideas were expanded by Jean Bodin, who became a harbinger of the modern theories of sovereignty. They were also transmitted to Thomas Hobbes, who developed them into a materialistic rationalism.

Modern conflict theory was pulled out of its rationalistic context and turned into an empirical investigation by David Hume and Adam Ferguson. In treating conflict as an empirical fact, Hume laid the foundations for the contemporary theory of the political party. Ferguson turned these ideas into a general account of political institutions and government, conceived as arising out of struggle. Parallel theories appeared in France in the works of Turgot.

The idea of universal competition taken from modern conflict theory became central to classical economics. Competition, in turn, was transformed from the central law of economic behavior by Thomas Malthus into a general competition to survive. It became the basis of his population theories. Conflict theory was now ready to migrate to biology, where, in the works of Darwin, it became the foundation for a reconstruction of biological science.

The theory of social conflict has had a richly colorful career in the West. At one time it had been turned into a very particular explanation of special events; at another it had been turned into a general examination of human affairs. A treasure of experience and insight was available to the new school of theory.

SELECTED BIBLIOGRAPHY

ALLEN, J. W., *A History of Political Thought in the Sixteenth Century*. Second edition. London: Methuen, 1941. (See the discussion of Jean Bodin.)

FERGUSON, ADAM, *An Essay on the History of Civil Society*. Edinburgh: Bell, 1767.

FRITZ, KURT VON, *The Theory of Mixed Constitutions in Antiquity: A Critical Analysis of Polybius' Political Ideas*. New York: Columbia University Press, 1954.

HOBBES, THOMAS, *Leviathan*. New York: Liberal Arts Press, 1948.

HUME, DAVID, *Selections*. Edited by Charles W. Hendel. New York: Scribner's, 1927.

IBN KHALDUN, *An Arab Philosophy of History.* Translated by Charles Issawi. London: John Murray, 1950.

MACHIAVELLI, NICCOLÒ, *The Prince and the Discourses.* Translated by Luigi Ricci and Christian E. Detmold. New York: Modern Library, 1948.

MALTHUS, THOMAS, *An Essay on the Principle of Population.* Everyman's Library. New York: E. P. Dutton, 1941.

POLYBIUS, *The Histories.* Translated by W. R. Paton. Loeb Classical Library. Cambridge, Mass.: Harvard University Press, 1954–55.

STEPHENS, W. WALKER, (ed.), *The Life and Writings of Turgot.* London: Longmans, Green, 1895.

7

Major Conflict Ideologies of the Nineteenth Century

IF WE COMPARE THE EARLY CONFLICT THEORISTS WITH THE THINKERS WHO laid the foundations of the organismic view of society, some interesting similarities and contrasts are evident. The ancient intellectual was nearly always drawn from the upper social strata. This was almost inevitable, since except for unusual circumstances only these strata had access to the literary educations of their times. In their social-class positions, then, the predecessors of both schools were roughly equivalent.

However, among the founders of conflict theory there was a far greater preponderance of secular men of affairs than among the idealistic predecessors of positivistic organicism. Even in ancient China and India, Kautilya, Han Fei-Tzu, and Li Ssǔ were active men of affairs. And in the West, Heraclitus was from a political and priestly family, Polybius was the son of a statesman and a political hostage, Ibn Khaldun was a chief justice, diplomat, and administrator, Machiavelli was an exiled statesman and patriot, Jean Bodin was a practicing lawyer. By contrast, Plato was the leader of a semireligious genteel sect with only a tangential (and inept) political experience, Aristotle was a tutor and school head, and in modern times the idealist has been much more likely to be a clergyman (Berkeley) or professor (Hegel) than a man of affairs. The differences in social realism between conflict theory and positivistic organicism are partly to be accounted for by the social roles of their founders.

In working closer to secular affairs, the conflict theorists of the past tended to develop ideas more immediately based on actual social experience and less "out of this world." However, such close involvement in actual affairs has its own risks. The man of affairs tends to be skeptical of abstract conceptualization, which appears to him to be speculative armchair philosophizing. His thinking is likely to be dominated by the crises of the day. Much of his thought turns, automatically, to the task of getting the job done rather than pondering its meaning. It is not without significance in this connection that the thought of the man of affairs frequently rises to the level of truly general formulations only when circumstances have isolated him from action. Polybius was a captive hostage, Machiavelli an exiled statesman, and Hobbes shared the exile of his royalistic sponsors.

Conflict theory tends to be only a step away from *ideology*, which may be defined as the organization of ideas for the promotion of social movements or for the defense of social institutions. An ideology is a system of ideas intended to serve practice rather than to promote the aims of understanding. It may, to be sure, raise the level of understanding, but this is not its primary function.

Three major forms of conflict ideology arose in the nineteenth century: Marxian socialism and two forms of social Darwinism. It is of great importance for the understanding of conflict theory to distinguish between ideology and scientific theory. For one thing, whatever their similarities, ideology and scientific theory are essentially different. For another thing, the major conflict ideologies of the nineteenth century raised a host of extremely vital problems that the social sciences eventually had to solve.

From Romantic Idealism to Marxian Socialism

It was observed in tracing the backgrounds of positivism that nineteenth-century socialism was the true heir of the peculiar combination of scientific method and social reform of the eighteenth century. Sociology took over the scientific method, but set aside social reform. Indeed, in pressing science into the service of conservative social ends, sociology assumed the character of a conservative answer to socialism; for this reason it is not hard to understand the remarkably restricted influence that Marx had on early sociology. It is rare to find a sociologist who even mentions Marx or, for that matter, socialism — except, perhaps, to dissociate himself from it, like Ward, for example. At the same time, to characterize socialism as combining scientific claims with social reform is insufficient to identify the peculiarities of Marxism, despite its claims to being the "only scientific form of socialism." Therefore, we must characterize socialism more fully before differentiating Marxism.

Human society is not completely arbitrary, with unlimited possibilities of combining anything with anything. Societies are as incapable as people of eating their cake and having it too. Hence, basic institutional arrangements in one area have consequences for other areas of societal life. Whatever value there is in the "economic interpretation of society" lies here. It is a good point, but the Marxians rode it into the ground. The institutional possibilities are not so limited that only economic arrangements determine the rest. Nevertheless, it remains true that various other social arrangements tend to consolidate in a manner in which property and economy play a very significant role. In the feudal system, with its nobility, who claimed the right to bear arms and monopolized the games of war, and with its clergy and peasantry, the system of landed property held in hereditary entailment was critical. The basis for support of the bourgeoisie, who launched a series of revolutions against the feudal world, was found in economic institutions centering in private property. The revolutions that freed these new classes from the feudal system also had multiple influences on other than economic areas. The right to bear arms was secured; formal legal freedom of individuals was attained; and a class system replaced the system of estates. The new world created by the bourgeoisie extended formal legal freedom to the lower levels of society, tearing them out of systems of hereditary bondage, bringing them into dependence upon the new industries that were arising, and in which their fates were now determined by sale of their services on the labor market. The homeless and uprooted masses of modern times — the peculiarly modern proletariat — found no protection in "private property" but only exposure to the whims of the bourgeoisie. Insofar as it has advanced its own interests, the proletariat has found the point of gravity of its interests in socialized property. Whether private and socialized property should be considered to be absolutely antithetical — as some thinkers have assumed — is of no concern here. The only point of interest is that modern society has created groups quite without economic protection except for various kinds of socialized property and services. This is a structural development in the Western world. Among the kinds of property and services which have been socialized are: education; the postal and, at times, other communication systems; various types of transportation facilities — roads, bridges; and often other kinds of facilities. Unemployment insurance, old-age benefits, social security, all have appeared. Socialized medicine has many times been demanded and partly carried through. The common starting point in all systems of socialist ideology is their attempt to guarantee the economic security of all segments of society. In this lies their motive force, for proletarian groups have as undeniable claims as did the bourgeoisie in the feudal world. No modern nation has found it possible not to socialize some services and utilities. In England, France, Spain, the United States, and Germany, the common element of the socialistic argument has been found in the attempt to satisfy the needs of working groups. The differentiation of German-Marxian socialism from other types starts from this common base. Marxian socialism developed, first of all, against a background of German romanticism.

No mysterious dialectic of the spirit is necessary to see that for nearly every point in the rationalistic credo of the eighteenth-century intelligentsia, the conservative intellectuals of the nineteenth century tended to develop a counter point. The rationalists discovered the universal equivalence of human nature; the romantics discovered the genius of the particular race. The rationalists asserted cosmopolitanism as a principle of culture; the romantics discovered the national, the parochial, the bucolic. The rationalists conceived of history as the record of folly and error; the romantics discovered in history only profundity and depth. The rationalists found the essence of man in reason; the romantics found it in spirit.

Hegel and Romantic Idealism

In Hegel's great synthesis of the modern idealistic argument, the ego was located at the center of existence, credited with moral and aesthetic creativity. The ego and the moral or aesthetic world it creates appear as unified against a transpersonal psychic background. The processes of individual experience are paralleled in the process of nature.

Georg Wilhelm Friedrich Hegel (1770–1831), who advanced these ideas, was the son of a civil servant at Württemberg. Hegel received theological training at Tübingen. His philosophy was developed between 1793 and 1801, when he served as a private tutor. From 1808 to 1816 he edited a newspaper. In 1818 he was called to the University of Berlin, where he became a favorite of the government.

When mind is placed at the core of reality, change is transformed into an act of thought.[1] Hegel was convinced that thought does not consist of eternally fixed forms; it is a process. As a process any particular idea cast up by thought (*thesis*) necessarily calls out its opposite (*antithesis*). Now thought must reconcile the conflict (*synthesis*). This process is dialectical. The way we think is also an expression of the innermost essence of existence. Every state of reality is a thesis which passes into its negation, or antithesis. The negation brings a new synthesis into being. Further development of the same process negates the negation, lifting thought to a higher unity. This dialectical evolution of concepts represents the self-development of existence. Every phenomenon points beyond itself to a greater whole. The appearance and synthesis of opposites, light and darkness, life and death, are conceived as the creative rhythm of the world of process. The innocence of childhood is canceled by unrest and doubts and synthesized in the adult character. The seed must perish for the plant to appear.[2]

[1] William Wallace, *Prolegomena to the Study of Hegel's Philosophy and Especially of His Logic* (2d ed.; Oxford, England: The Clarendon Press, 1894, 1931). A complete bibliographical note on Hegel will not be attempted. The works of chief importance for the present discussion are: *The Philosophy of History*, tr. by J. Sibree (New York: Dover Publications, 1956); *Science of Logic*, tr. by H. W. Johnston and L. G. Struthers, 2 vols. (New York: Macmillan, 1929); *Hegel's Doctrine of Formal Logic*, tr. by Henry S. Macran (Oxford, England: The Clarendon Press, 1912); *Hegel's Logic of World and Idea*, tr. by Henry S. Macran (Oxford, England: The Clarendon Press, 1929); and *The Philosophy of Right*, tr. by S. W. Dyde (London: George Bell, 1896).
[2] Harald Høffding, *A History of Modern Philosophy*, tr. by B. E. Meyer (New York: Macmillan, 1935), II, p. 181.

The dialectical process has its first forms in nature in a first realization of the *logos* as a world-creating, world-ordering principle. Nature works its way up through a series of states from pure externality to inwardness of spirit. The most important stages are those from mechanism to the physical stage and on to the organism. The philosophy of the spirit also falls into three parts: the subjective mind, the spiritual life of the individual subject, and the objective mind. The last, the spiritual life displaced by the *logos* in social forms and institutions of history, covers the problems of law, morality, the ethical life of the family, and the state.

In Hegel's *Philosophy of Right*, he proposed to demonstrate the process by which the idea of the state was formed. The starting point for analysis was the will, conceived as pure intelligence — as eternal, universal, self-conscious, self-determining, as *Geist*. Freedom is the essence of the will. Freedom is the idea of the free will that wills the free will.[3] The absolute idea is only realized by the state. Law is the form of the will in which personality, property, and contract are realized. A living creature is a person so far as it freely wills to be so. An object determined by the will of a person becomes property. A human being is a slave (property) only when he does not will to be free. The free will is also realized in subjective morality, which includes those aspects of self-determination in which the individual is affected by the consciousness of others. Purposes, responsibility, motive are manifestations of will at this level. The full relation of individual will to universal will occurs in customary morality or social ethics. The customs and habits of mankind express the working of universal cause at the same time that they embody individual choice.

The institutions embodying social ethics are the family, civil society, and the state. The family is a natural foundation for the order of reason which culminates in the state, but at the same time it represents such a foundation only in so far as it dissolves. However, the family has eternal reality in property, which destroys the family. Children grow up and establish property-holding families of their own. Thus the family unit breaks into a multitude of competing proprietors striving for their egoistic advantage. These groups prepare the way for civil society.[4]

Civil society rests on two principles: that individuals aim only at their private interests, and that individual interests are so related that the satisfaction of one depends on the satisfaction of the other. As a competition of egos, the civil community appears only to disappear in a "spectacle of excess, misery, and physical and social corruption."[5] This competition leads to the accumulation of wealth and the growing impoverishment of the working class.

---

[3] *The Philosophy of Right*, Introduction, Section 27.
[4] *Ibid.*, Sections 177 and 182. An excellent summary of Hegel's importance for social theory is found in Herbert Marcuse, *Reason and Revolution* (New York: Oxford University Press, 1941); for his comments on the present issues, see pp. 200 ff.
[5] *The Philosophy of Right*, Section 185.

By generalizing the relations of men by way of their wants, and by generalizing the manner in which the means of meeting these wants are prepared and procured, large fortunes are amassed. On the other side, there occurs a repartition and limitation of the work of the individual laborer and, consequently, dependence and distress in the artisan class. . . .

When a large number of people sink below the standard of living regarded as essential for the members of society, and lose that sense of right, rectitude, and honor which is derived from self-support, a pauper class arises, and wealth accumulates disproportionately in the hands of a few.[6]

Civil society is devoted to the satisfaction of economic needs. The satisfaction of economic needs requires the protection of property through the administration of justice and the protection of the general welfare by the police and the corporation. The administration of justice makes abstract right into law and introduces a conscious universal order into the contingent processes of society. The police represent the interest of the whole against social forces that are strong enough to disrupt the function of the civil process. The police, as a basic civil institution, are complemented by the corporation (conceived somewhat along the lines of the old guild system), which brings unity to competing economic interests and activities and champions the organized interests of civil society against the state.

The state is the highest of the ethical communities combining the essence of family and civil society. The state is the realized socio-ethical idea. Spirit reaches its greatest perfection here. The state is the progression of God in the world, and must be honored as semi-divine. The idea of the state manifests itself as the constitution or internal public law, as external public law, and as world history. In each of these areas there is an unfolding of freedom. The basic property of a particular state is the political consciousness of a people. This consciousness determines the constitution. Three powers are indispensable to the state, the legislative, the administrative (including the judicial), and the monarchic. Monarchic power is highest, being the unifying force of the other two. The legislative power is conceived as an organ where prince, administration, and people have a role. The most popular element of the assembly, the people, are to be represented by the classes (*Stände*).

The final channel through which the state is revealed as the expression of the spirit is world history — the process of events in the unfolding of the universal spirit. The culture of a people, including its art, religion, and political institutions, expresses a stage in the self-realization of the absolute. Each age represents a level in the realization of the absolute spirit.

The History of the World is the discipline of the uncontrolled natural will, bringing it into obedience to a Universal principle and conferring subjective freedom. The East knew and to the present day knows only that *One* is Free; the Greek and Roman world, that *some* are free; the German

[6] *Ibid.*, Sections 243 and 244.

World knows that *All* are free. The first political form therefore which we observe in History, is *Despotism*, the second *Democracy* and *Aristocracy*, the third *Monarchy*.[7]

If one ignores all of the mystical aspects of Hegel's arguments, observing only their surface features, two general properties appear. The first of these is the tendency toward a rather complete organicism, which is present in every step. It is little wonder that Comte immediately recognized his kinship with Hegel. Comte's first work was well received by Hegel, and that Comte saw Hegel's point of view as a more metaphysical form of his own may be seen in his letter to his friend A. M. D'Eichtal in Berlin:

> Je suis bien aise d'avoir fait connaissance avec Hegel, et je regrette que votre extrait ne soit pas plus étendu; il est bien moins fort que Kant, mais c'est, sans aucun doute, un homme de mérite. Il me semble encore trop métaphysique; je n'aime point du tout son *esprit*, auquel il fait jouer un rôle si singulier. Mais je trouve, comme vous, un esprit positif dans les détails. . . .[8]

Hegel, thus, had a very direct effect upon the founding of sociology.

But the career of organicism and positivism in social theory has been traced. Interest here attaches primarily to the second major property of the idealism of Hegel and his predecessors. There is an almost pathological concern with conflict running through this school of idealists. Conflict, opposition, strife, the appearance of contradictions, appear over and over. There is conflict in the state, in civil society, in the family, between individuals, and within the individual. The most fundamental method of thought is a dialectic, the casting up and surmounting of oppositions. A whole series of stages appears in the dialectic of nature. The phenomena of art, literature, manners, institutions are to be understood as produced in the dialectic of history. All these forms of opposition, strife, or conflict are eventually transformed into a kind of debate of the Absolute with itself. In the end, all conflicts turn into a mere war of words.

Marxian Socialism as a Conflict Ideology

Karl Marx

With these ideas, much that was conceptually essential to Marxism was already present. Karl Marx (1818–1883) came as a student under the influence of Hegel, and with Bruno Bauer, Arnold Ruge, and Ludwig Feuerbach, he interpreted Hegelianism in a militant atheistic form. Failing to get a

---

[7] *The Philosophy of History*, p. 104.
[8] Émile Littré, *Auguste Comte et la philosophie positive* (2d ed.; Paris: L. Hachette, 1864), p. 157. ["I am very much pleased to have made Hegel's acquaintance, and I regret that your excerpt was not more extensive; he is not nearly so strong as Kant, but without any doubt he is a man of merit. He still seems to me to be too metaphysical; I am not at all taken with his notion of *spirit*, to which he assigns such an extraordinary role. But I find, like you, a practical mind in the details . . ."]

university position, Marx became a journalist, contributing to and later editing the *Rheinische Zeitung*, an organ of radical bourgeois opinion, established in 1842 and suppressed fifteen months later. In 1844 he embarked on the study of economics in Paris, continuing in Brussels after his expulsion. After a second attempt at political activity in 1848, cut short by the counter movement against the revolutionary action, Marx resumed his studies in London, continuing in them until his death.

Friedrich Engels (1820–1905) was Marx's closest friend and collaborator. He was born in Barmen of a prosperous commercial family. In 1842 he left Germany to take a position with a firm in Manchester, England, and acquired a knowledge of *laissez-faire* economics. His friendship with Marx dates from their meeting in Paris in 1844, though they had met in 1842. In 1849 Engels took part, with Marx, in the republican insurrection in Baden. After 1850 he returned to England to engage in business, supporting Marx in his researches and the writing of *Das Kapital*.

The physiocrats and classical economists had come to the conclusion that there is one form of struggle at once universal and operating for human good: economic competition. Malthus had showed under what conditions this competition could turn into a grim downward spiral in which a good part of mankind is just able to stay alive. Hegel found a peculiarly ordered conflict of oppositions to be central to personality, society, the state, and mankind. Not without interest is the fact that Hegel had himself conceived the dialectic of civil society to be due to the egoistic struggle of each man to pursue his own good. Hegel had suggested that this inevitably sharpens the distinction between classes, separating the wealthy from those depressed in poverty. In the course of this, Hegel advanced another idea often attributed to Marx — that law and property are inseparable; in fact, the sharpening of the social classes goes on under the rule of law. By the time Marx and Engels wrote *The German Ideology* (1846), they were thoroughly familiar with and critically oriented toward both the Hegelian and *laissez-faire* ideas.[9]

The influence of Hegel was fundamental:

> The great basic thought that the world is not to be comprehended as a complex of ready-made *things*, but as a complex of *processes*, in which things apparently stable no less than their mind-images in our heads, the concepts, go through an uninterrupted change of coming into being and passing away, in which, in spite of all seeming accidents and of all temporary retrogression, a progressive development asserts itself in the end — this great fundamental thought has, especially since the time of Hegel, so thoroughly permeated ordinary consciousness that in this generality it is scarcely ever contradicted.[10]

[9] Although the basic ideas contained in *The German Ideology* were more highly elaborated in the later writings of Marx and Engels, for present purposes this early formulation is adequate.

[10] Friedrich Engels, *Ludwig Feuerbach and the Outcome of German Classical Philosophy* (New York: International Publishers, 1941), p. 44. (*Ludwig Feuerbach* was written in 1886 and first published in 1888.)

It was not with Hegel's dialectical logic that Marx and Engels took issue, but rather with what they called the "idealist trammel" of his philosophy. Men distinguish themselves from animals, according to Marx and Engels, the moment they begin to produce their means of subsistence, a phenomenon determining their nature. "As individuals express their life, so they are. What they are . . . coincides with their production, both with what they produce and *how* they produce. The nature of individuals thus depends on the material conditions determining their production." [11] The break with the Hegelians was expressed in this assertion that the starting point of all understanding lies in the facts of material existence rather than in the spirit. They expressed the same point sarcastically: "Once upon a time an honest fellow had the idea that men were drowned in water only because they were possessed of the idea of gravity." [12] By contrast with this — and very close to the classical economists — Marx and Engels take the production of goods to stay alive as the basic social fact. "As soon as a need is satisfied . . . new needs are made; and this production of new needs is the first historical act." [13]

As with Hegel, the family is assumed to be the first and only natural human relationship. "The family which to begin with is the only social relationship, becomes later, when increased needs create new social relations and increased population new needs, a subordinate one." [14] The fact of human association creates language and consciousness of a human type. "Man's consciousness of the necessity of associating with the individuals around him is the beginning of the consciousness that he is living in society at all." [15] There are, in this argument, echoes of the development from Fichte to Hegel — every development of consciousness is bound up with the appearance of some new distinctions and oppositions. "Division of labor only becomes truly such from the moment when a division of material and mental labor appears. From this moment onwards consciousness *can* really flatter itself that it is something other than consciousness of existing practice; that it is *really* conceiving something without conceiving something *real*." [16] Division of labor is correlated with a division of consciousness. With "the natural division of labor in the family and the separation of society into families opposed to one another, is given simultaneously the distribution . . . and unequal distribution . . . of its labor and its products." [17] There is a latent slavery already present in the family. An actual slavery quickly emerges. From this time on, society is divided into conflicting groups. Division of labor implies a contradiction between the interest of the separate individuals or individual family and the communal interest of all individuals. "This consolidation of what we ourselves produce into an objective power above us, growing out of our control, thwarting our ex-

[11] Karl Marx and Friedrich Engels, *The German Ideology* (New York: International Publishers, 1947), p. 7.
[12] *Ibid.*, p. 2.   [13] *Ibid.*, pp. 16–17.   [14] *Ibid.*, p. 17.
[15] *Ibid.*, p. 20.   [16] *Ibid.*   [17] *Ibid.*, pp. 22–23.

pectations, bringing to naught our calculations, is one of the chief factors in the historical development up till now. And out of this very contradiction between the interest of the individual and that of the community the latter takes an independent form as the State, divorced from the real interests of individual and community."[18] Classes, determined by the division of labor, become the agents of the opposition. "It follows from this that all struggles within the State, the struggle between democracy, aristocracy, and monarchy, the struggle for the franchise, etc., are merely the illusory forms in which the real struggles of the different classes are fought out among one another."[19]

The Communist Manifesto

German workers living abroad had been organized into the League of the Just since 1836, with headquarters in London since 1840. In 1847 the League sent a representative to Brussels to learn more about Marx. The League later became the League of Communists, and held its first Congress in London in the summer of 1847. At the meeting of 1848, Marx and Engels prepared the *Communist Manifesto,* formulating a new program for the League. In this document, the ideas developed earlier were emphatically expressed. "The history of all human society past and present has been a history of class struggles."[20] It was urged further that the West was on the threshold of another revolution, for when modern bourgeois society arose out of the ruins of feudalism, it simplified class antagonisms, splitting society into two great hostile camps: the bourgeoisie and the proletariat.

The earlier class struggles under slavery and feudalism terminated either in the revolutionary reconstruction of society at large or in the ruin of the contending classes. Capitalism, which appeared with the opening of Asia and the discovery of America, replaced the guild system with the manufacturing system and supplanted hand power with steam power. The capitalist class has played the most recent revolutionary role in the world. It shattered feudal relationships, leaving no relation between man and man other than "crude self-interest and unfeeling 'cash payment.' "[21] It has drowned the most heavenly ecstasies of religious fervor, of chivalrous enthusiasm, of Philistine sentimentalism, in the icy water of egotistical calculation. It has resolved personal worth into exchange value, and in place of numberless indefeasible chartered freedoms, has set up that single, unconscionable freedom — free trade. "In a word, it has replaced exploitation veiled by religious and political illusions, by exploitation that is open, unashamed, direct and brutal."[22] On the other hand, the positive achievements of capitalism were more wonderful than the Egyptian pyramids, Roman aqueducts, or Gothic cathedrals.

[18] *Ibid.,* p. 20.   [19] *Ibid.,* p. 23.
[20] Karl Marx and Friedrich Engels, *The Communist Manifesto* (New York: International Publishers, 1930), p. 25.
[21] *Ibid.,* p. 28.   [22] *Ibid.*

Class conflict is taken as central to society. The conflict between the capitalists and the proletariat is central to our own society. All such conflicts assume the form of an increasing consolidation of the sides involved. The capitalist class has agglomerated population, centralized means of production, and has concentrated production in a few hands. The bourgeoisie has created more productive forces than all generations of previous history. But its own classes also are turning against one another. "More and more, society is splitting up into two great hostile camps, into two great classes directly facing each other: bourgeoisie and proletariat." [23]

Basic to the Marxian analysis is the conception of political power as an adjunct to class power and political struggles as a special form of class struggles. The administrative structure of the modern state is but a committee for managing the common affairs of the bourgeoisie. A number of general predictions are made about the future course of these conflicts. It is predicted that the middle class will disappear. Tradesmen, shopkeepers, handicraftmen will sink into the proletariat because petty capital will not be able to compete with mass capital or more efficient methods of production. "Thus the proletariat is recruited from all classes of the population." Distinctions will be obliterated between the workers, and as conflicts become more frequent between the two classes, the workers will begin to form combinations. "The workers begin to form coalitions against the bourgeoisie, closing their ranks in order to maintain the rate of wages; they found durable associations which will be able to give them support whenever the struggle grows acute. . . . This struggle . . . turns . . . into a national contest, a class struggle." [24] The proletarianization of sections of the bourgeoisie supplies the proletariat with elements of enlightenment and progress, increasing its revolutionary potential. When the class struggle nears the decisive hour, the process of dissolution within the bourgeoisie accelerates, providing leadership for the revolutionary class, the class that holds the future in its hands.

The Uniqueness of Marxism

The uniqueness of Marxism does not lie — as its proponents have maintained — in the fact that it is the "only scientific form of socialism." Its claims to scientific standing are usually based on the use of the dialectic and on the thoroughness with which all phenomena in society are explained economically. The dialectic, which treats scientific method, logic, life growth, physical change, and innumerable other things as if they were identical, is outright mysticism. Similarly, the claim to be scientific because every phenomenon conceivable is reduced to economics can only be put down to a complete failure to distinguish between metaphysics and scientific theory. The proposition is not treated as a hypothesis to be tested, but as a foregone conclusion to be illustrated. The very things claimed to be most scientific represent points farthest removed from science. They are

[23] *Ibid.*, p. 26.   [24] *Ibid.*, p. 32.

unique, however, to Marxian socialism. It was the only type of socialism to spring from the heart of organismic romanticism. It was the only type so completely to subordinate every phenomenon to economically based class conflicts. It was the only form of socialism so completely utopian, so completely convinced that the destruction of the entire existing world was the prior step to its own realization.

There is little doubt that the socio-political events in nineteenth-century Germany gave the final reinforcement to the uniqueness of German socialism. The liberal movements expressed in the revolutionary stirrings of 1848 were accompanied by reform in other European states. In Germany they were largely suppressed, and the Prussian state entered upon an extreme program of suppression of both socialism and the labor movement while trying to pull the teeth of the revolutionary argument by paternalistic state measures. Hence, in Germany more completely than anywhere else in Europe, the socialist program was not permitted to work within the existing order. Once one presses a force out of its normal sphere of manifestation, one does not destroy it; one merely forces it into a context where the ordinary limiting forces cannot react upon it. German socialism had profound ties with organismic romanticism in the first place. The political policy that outlawed it redoubled these properties. German socialism was forced to become utopian — its goals, frustrated in the present, could only lie in the future. It necessarily became revolutionary; being prevented from working within the society, it required bloody revolutions to clear space for action. As these forms became fixed, the hatred between orthodox old-line communists and revisionists such as Bernstein [25] was inevitable. It is noteworthy that when the program of suppression of the labor movement and socialism was abandoned in Germany and it became possible to work legally within the society, membership in old-line communist organizations rapidly declined. It was also true that Marxian socialism, having gained a utopian revolutionary form, was inclined to carry out a kind of monistic analysis in which everything was reduced to economics: religion, the state, art, culture, thought itself. Here was the foundation for its peculiar windy bombast and easy stereotypes.

One of the functions of extreme exaggeration of a point of view is its tendency to force into the open problems which might otherwise have passed unnoticed. Marxism was a socialistic conflict ideology. But in the passionate analysis of all problems into economically based class, class organization, class conflict, and in the attempt to reduce all phenomena — art, music, literature, philosophy, religion, the state, etc. — to forms dependent on economics, it played a major role in forcing these phenomena to the attention of the modern social scientist. In the long run these problems had to be faced if for no other reason than to answer the Marxians. The twentieth century has witnessed the emergence of a number of problems in some measure forced to attention by the Marxians: the problem of class, the

[25] Eduard Bernstein, *Evolutionary Socialism* (New York: Huebsch, 1909).

problems of the sociology of music, art, culture, and knowledge, and the problem of the interrelation of economic and other social phenomena.

Social Darwinism as a Conflict Ideology: Phase I

Marxism represents a form of conflict ideology developed in the name of the proletariat. Social Darwinism represents a form of conflict ideology developed in the name of business groups of modern society. It is significant that Marxism was practically without influence on early sociology, making its effect only belatedly by indirect routes. Social Darwinism, on the other hand, lies close to the main stream of sociological development.

As we have observed, the ideal of universal competition was made the foundation of economic life by the physiocrats and classical economists. The notion of competition was deepened into the concept of survival in the demographic reflections of Malthus. These notions formed one of the spurs to Darwinian biology — one of the outstanding scientific gains of the nineteenth century. So successful was biology that positivistic organicism for a time modeled itself on biology. Now it was time to make the return from biology to society.

Darwin and Social Darwinism

Darwin was quite ready to apply his own theories to man. In such an extension, Malthus always seems to be in the background of his thinking. All creatures are in competition to survive. There must, Darwin argues, be a natural selection of the most fit. This is also true for man.

> The early progenitors of man must also have tended, like all other animals, to have increased beyond their means of subsistence. They must, therefore, occasionally have been exposed to a struggle for existence, and consequently to the rigid law of natural selection. Beneficial variations of all kinds will thus, either occasionally or habitually, have been preserved, and injurious ones eliminated.[26]

Implicit also in this passage is the idea that mankind has repeatedly found itself on a level of pure subsistence, at which time the laws of natural selection operate.

> Man in the rudest state in which he now exists is the most dominant animal that has ever appeared on this earth. He has spread more widely than any other highly organized form: and all others have yielded before him. He manifestly owes this immense superiority to his intellectual faculties, to his social habits, which lead him to aid and defend his fellows, and to his corporeal structure. The supreme importance of these characters has been proved by the final arbitrament of the battle for life. Through his powers of intellect, articulate language has been evolved; and on this his wonderful advancement has mainly depended. As Mr. Chauncy Wright remarks: "a

[26] Charles Darwin, *The Descent of Man* (New York: D. Appleton, 1880), p. 48.

psychological analysis of the faculty of language shows that even the smallest proficiency in it might require more brain power than the greatest proficiency in any other direction." He has invented and is able to use various weapons, tools, traps, etc., with which he defends himself, kills or catches prey, and otherwise obtains food. He has made rafts or canoes for fishing or crossing over to neighboring fertile islands. He has discovered the art of making fire, by which hard and stringy roots can be rendered digestible, and poisonous roots or herbs innocuous. This discovery of fire, probably the greatest ever made by man excepting language, dates from before the dawn of history. These several inventions, by which man in the rudest state has become so preeminent, are the direct results of the development of his powers of observation, memory, curiosity, imagination, and reason. I cannot, therefore, understand how it is that Mr. Wallace maintains that "natural selection" could only have endowed the savage with a brain little superior to that of an ape.[27]

A subtle, but important, distinction is implied here. The laws of natural selection and survival of the fittest gave man his intelligence. But man's intelligence made possible language, a complex social life, tools, and fire. Thus the whole area of culture would not be necessarily explainable in terms of natural selection directly but indirectly. It is incidentally worth noting that Darwin's estimate concerning what is peculiar to mankind has a remarkably modern sound.

Darwin is not altogether consistent about when and where one should not apply the principles of his biological theory. He does, it seems, think that a group with a solidary ethic has increased survival value.

When two tribes of primeval man, living in the same country, come into competition, if . . . the one tribe included a great number of courageous, sympathetic, and faithful members, who were always ready to warn each other of danger, to aid and defend each other, this tribe would succeed better and conquer the other.[28]

However, Darwin approached the view that even for the primitive, bravery and moral sense may have been individually dysgenic:

The bravest men, who were always willing to come to the front in war, and who freely risked their lives for others, would on the average perish in larger numbers than other men.[29]

Despite the interesting suggestion by some students that Darwin was not a "social Darwinist," by extending the point of view just noted to the problem of natural selection in civilized nations, Darwin comes to the usual conclusions.

We civilized men . . . do our utmost to check the process of elimination; we build asylums for the imbecile, the maimed, and the sick; we institute poor-laws; and our medical men exert their utmost skill to save the life of

27 *Ibid.*, pp. 48–49.   28 *Ibid.*, pp. 130–131.   29 *Ibid.*, p. 130.

everyone to the last moment. There is reason to believe that vaccination has preserved thousands, who from a weak constitution would formerly have succumbed to smallpox. Thus the weak members of civilized societies propagate their kind. No one who has attended to the breeding of domestic animals will doubt that this must be highly injurious to the race of man. It is surprising how soon a want of care, or care wrongly directed, leads to the degeneration of a domestic race; but excepting in the case of man himself, hardly any one is so ignorant as to allow his worst animals to breed.[30]

And worse, we not only keep the weak alive, but eliminate the fit:

In every country in which a large standing army is kept up, the finest young men are taken by conscription or are enlisted. They are thus exposed to early death during war, are often tempted into vice, and are prevented from marrying during the prime of life. On the other hand, the shorter and feebler men, with poor constitutions, are left at home, and consequently have a much better chance of marrying and propagating their kind.

Nor is this the end.

The children of parents who are short-lived, and are therefore on an average deficient in health and vigor, come into their property sooner than other children and will be likely to marry earlier, and leave a larger number of offspring to inherit their inferior constitutions.[31]

Natural selection operating on individuals produced a superior animal. This superior animal creates a society tending to destroy its own biological superiority.

Spencer's Social Darwinism

Herbert Spencer has been treated as an organicist because of the primary structure of his sociological theory. His organicism goes back to a period before the appearance of Darwin's *Origin of Species*. The play back of Darwin's findings on Spencer is evident in his increased concern with conflict in his later works. Particularly as he turned attention to social issues, Spencer tended to welcome the conception of a natural process of conflict and survival which operates as a kind of biologically purifying process. Spencer gave a novel twist to social Darwinism, urging not that it does in fact operate in society but that it ought to!

It seems hard that widows and orphans should be left to struggle for life or death. Nevertheless, when regarded not separately but in connexion with the interests of universal humanity, these harsh fatalities are seen to be full of beneficence — the same beneficence which brings to early graves the children of diseased parents, and singles out the intemperate and the debilitated as the victims of an epidemic.[32]

Spencer's attitude toward the poor laws is typical of his approach to all meliorative legislation.

---

[30] *Ibid.*, pp. 133–134.   [31] *Ibid.*, pp. 134–135.
[32] Herbert Spencer, *Social Statics* and *The Man Versus the State* (New York: D. Appleton, 1908), p. 150.

By suspending the process of adaptation, a poor-law increases the distress to be borne at some future day; and here we shall find that it also increases the distress to be borne now. For be it remembered that of the sum taken in any year to support paupers, a large portion would otherwise have gone to support labourers employed in new reproductive works — land-drainage, machine-building, etc. An additional stock of commodities would by-and-by have been produced, and the number of those who go short would consequently have been diminished.[33]

Spencer was opposed to practically every form of state interference with private activity, justifying his opposition on the grounds of a social Darwinism. The list of his complaints includes state-supported education, sanitary supervision, regulation of housing conditions, state protection of the ignorant from medical quacks, tariffs, state banking, and government postal systems.

Spencer's theories were as agreeable to some business groups as Marx's were to some labor elements. Hofstadter has assembled an interesting series of quotations to this effect from some of the business magnates of the time. James J. Hill, the railroad magnate, for example, argued that "the fortunes of railroad companies are determined by the law of the survival of the fittest." John D. Rockefeller took no less an occasion than a Sunday-school address to identify the survival of the fittest with the law of God. "The growth of a large business is merely a survival of the fittest. . . . The American Beauty rose can be produced in the splendor and fragrance which bring cheer to its beholder only by sacrificing the early buds which grow up around it. This is not an evil tendency in business. It is merely the working out of a law of nature and a law of God." Andrew Carnegie reports the reading of Darwin and Spencer to have been a source of great peace of mind. "I remember that light came as in a flood and all was clear. Not only had I got rid of theology and the supernatural, but I had found the truth of evolution. 'All is well since all grows better' became my motto, my true source of comfort. Man was not created with an instinct for his own degradation, but from the lower he had risen to the higher forms. Nor is there any conceivable end to his march to perfection. His face is turned to the light; he stands in the sun and looks upward." [34]

Sumner's Social Darwinism

A practical and applied social Darwinism appears also in the work of William Graham Sumner, described by Hofstadter as "the most vigorous and influential social Darwinist in America." Sumner (1840–1910) was the

[33] *Ibid.*, pp. 154–155.
[34] An excellent review of Spencer's social Darwinism is found in Richard Hofstadter's *Social Darwinism in American Thought* (rev. ed.; Boston: Beacon Press, 1955), pp. 31–50. The foregoing quotations, all from Hofstadter's book, were drawn originally from: James J. Hill, *Highways of Progress* (New York: Doubleday, Page, 1910), p. 126; Rockefeller was quoted in William J. Ghent, *Our Benevolent Feudalism* (New York: Macmillan, 1902), p. 29; and Andrew Carnegie, *Autobiography of Andrew Carnegie* (Boston: Houghton Mifflin, 1920).

son of an immigrant English artisan. He was born in New Jersey, studied at Yale University, and spent three years at Geneva, Göttingen, and Oxford. He became a tutor in mathematics and Greek at Yale in 1866. As an ordained Protestant minister, he became assistant pastor at New York Church. In 1872 he was offered a professorship of political and social science at Yale, and remained in that position until his death. Sumner tied together the Protestant ethic, the doctrines of classical economics, and Darwinian natural selection.[35]

In his early essays, Sumner took a position with respect to economic and social issues that the original human situation was a struggle for existence. "The struggle of man to win his existence from nature is one which he begins with no advantages at all, but utterly naked and empty-handed. He has everything to conquer. Evidently it is only by his achievements that he can emancipate himself from the difficulties of his situation." [36]

Spencer conceived the ruthless elimination of widows and orphans as a first step by nature in maintaining the quality of the race. Sumner contemplates the elimination of the old in primitive society with equal equanimity: "The killing of old people by their children among savage tribes seems to us inexpressibly shocking, but this custom means something very different from the selfishness of the young; it testifies to the fact that the first liberty of all, the liberty to exist, becomes an unendurable burden to the savage man when he becomes old." [37]

In Sumner's thought it is only a step from the struggle for existence to the permanent importance of property for civilization. The first advance of mankind is the production of capital, increasing the fruitfulness of labor and making possible the advance of civilization. Primitive man withdrew from the competitive struggle, ceased to accumulate capital, and was reduced to permanent backwardness.[38] The captains of industry and capitalists are the great competitors of the present, the true creators of wealth and worth every cent they cost. "The captains of industry and the capitalists . . . if they are successful, win, in these days, great fortunes in a short time." There are, according to Sumner, "no earnings . . . more legitimate or for which greater services are rendered to the whole industrial body." [39] The burden of proof lies on those who affirm that our social situation needs radical regeneration. "The greatest folly of which a man can be capable" is "to sit down with a slate and pencil to plan out a new social world." [40] The impoverished have brought their situation on themselves.

[35] Sumner's most famous work, *Folkways* (Boston: Ginn, 1906), will be discussed in the next chapter, where his more strictly sociological contribution is taken up. Sumner's many essays appeared in various editions; the references here, unless otherwise noted, are to *Essays of William Graham Sumner*, edited by Albert Galloway Keller and Maurice R. Davie, 2 vols. (New Haven, Conn.: Yale University Press, 1940).
[36] *Essays*, I, p. 293.   [37] *Ibid.*
[38] *The Challenge of Facts and Other Essays*, ed. by Albert Keller (New Haven, Conn.: Yale University Press, 1914), p. 40.
[39] "The Absurd Effort to Make the World Over," *Essays*, I, p. 97.
[40] *Ibid.*, p. 106.

At present, poverty is correlated with ignorance, vice, and misfortune — the slow and tedious processes which we have hitherto been invited to employ and trust, have aimed to abolish poverty by working against ignorance, vice, and misfortune. If we can abolish poverty by a device or contrivance introduced into the social organization, then we can divorce poverty from its correlation with ignorance, vice, and misfortune. We can let those things stand and yet escape their consequences.[41]

At the other end of the social scale are the millionaires who

are a product of natural selection, acting on the whole body of men to pick out those who can meet the requirement of certain work to be done. . . . They may fairly be regarded as the naturally selected agents of society for certain work. They get high wages and live in luxury, but the bargain is a good one for society. There is the most intense competition for their place and occupation. This assures us that all who are competent for this function will be employed in it, so that the cost of it will be reduced to the lowest terms. . . .[42]

The fundamental fact of all societies is a peculiar ratio of men to land. It is this ratio that determines the possibilities of human development and what man can attain by way of civilization. Standards of living reflect the type of resolution of the problem. A population of high intelligence, great social ambition, and self-respect will increase economic power and the average level of comfort, and it will *not* increase its numbers. When institutions have outlived their usefulness, they become an abuse. Wars and revolutions that overthrow them are a comparative good.

For Sumner the inequality of the social classes is normal. The "superstition of democracy" applies to the unusual case:

Democracy itself, the pet superstition of the age, is only a phase of the all-compelling movement. If you have abundance of land and few men to share it, the men will all be equal. Each landholder will be his own tenant and his own laborer. Social classes disappear. Wages are high. The mass of men, apart from laziness, folly, and vice, are well off.[43]

The moment this condition does not exist, social classes appear and the competitive struggle sharpens. While within the society social distinctions grow tense, the state, as a whole, discovers a "manifest destiny" in the acquisition and holding of land.

There is . . . some truth to be admitted in the doctrine of "manifest destiny," although the doctrine is, like most doctrines in politics, a glib and convenient means of giving an appearance of rationality to an exercise of superior force. The truth in the doctrine is that an incompetent holder will not be able, as a matter of fact and in the long run, to maintain possession

[41] "The Abolition of Poverty," *Essays*, I, p. 108.
[42] *The Challenge of Facts*, p. 90.
[43] "Earth Hunger or the Philosophy of Land Grabbing," *Essays*, I, p. 185.

of territory when another nation which will develop it according to its capacity is ready to take it.[44]

It is rather startling to hear, about so indefatigable a defender of the *status quo,* that the Republican press and Republican alumni of Yale periodically urged his dismissal — a demand which became general when Sumner announced his opposition to the Spanish-American War.[45] It is a comfort to realize, however, that not all of Yale's alumni missed the point. "One old fashioned benefactor of Yale doubled his donation because Sumner's presence had convinced him 'that Yale College is a good and safe place for the keeping and use of property and the sustaining of civilization when endangered by ignorance, rascality, demagogues, repudiationists, rebels, copperheads, communists, Butlers, strikers, protectionists, and fanatics of sundry roots and sizes.' " [46]

Social Darwinism: Phase II

Social Darwinism as illustrated by Sumner was primarily a defensive position — a vindication of the successful business groups of nineteenth-century European and American society and a defense of the *status quo* against all types of reform, whether internal or revolutionary. But there was no good reason why social Darwinism should not develop a "positive" program of its own as the strict counterpart of the activism of Marxism. Even before Darwin's great work on the origin of species, the foundations of racism were being laid — a position that could potentially claim Darwin's support.

Arthur de Gobineau

Count Joseph Arthur de Gobineau (1816–1882) was one of the upper-class Frenchmen disgusted with the political development of France. His essay on *The Inequality of Human Races* (1853–57) [47] was dedicated to George V of Hanover, the blind German king who had just swept away the liberal constitution granted by his father to the people. The specific object of his anger was the revolution of 1848. He was one of the founders of a periodical to work for the establishment of a republic led by aristocrats. De Gobineau had been cabinet secretary, minister to Persia, and representative of the government on missions to Brazil and many European capitals.

The problem upsetting to de Gobineau was the disintegration of the aristocratic society he had known. He found race to be the key to history, and inequality of races sufficient to explain the entire enchainment of

---

[44] *Ibid.,* p. 197.   [45] Hofstadter, *op. cit.,* p. 64.   [46] *Ibid.,* p. 64.
[47] *Essai sur l'inégalité des races humains,* 4 vols. (Paris: 1853–55; 2d ed., 1884). The first volume was translated by Adrian Collins and published as *The Inequality of Human Races* (New York: G. P. Putnam, 1915). See also Maurice Lange, *Le Comte Arthur de Gobineau* (Strasbourg: Librairie Istra, 1924). For a recent critique, see Ruth Benedict, *Race: Science and Politics* (rev. ed.; New York: Viking, 1943), pp. 112 ff.

the destinies of peoples. He urged that "everything great, noble, and fruitful in the works of man on this earth, in science, art, and civilization, derives from a single starting point, it belongs to one family alone, the different branches of which have reigned in all the civilized countries of the universe." [48] The decline of aristocratic Europe was seen by de Gobineau to lie in the loss by the "Aryans" of their position of dominance.

H. S. Chamberlain

In the work of Houston Stewart Chamberlain and G. Vacher de Lapouge, the racialist position was shifted in the direction of Darwinism. There was also the development of a nationalistic cast to the doctrines, an emphasis on anti-Semitism, the establishment of the doctrines on a pseudo-quantitative foundation. Wagner's son-in-law, Houston Chamberlain (1855–1927), the son of Admiral William Charles Chamberlain, received a foreign education. He traveled extensively, and published several works. His most famous was *Foundations of the Nineteenth Century*,[49] a book with great influence on German thought. The Kaiser read two volumes of the work aloud to his sons; he had them distributed to army officers, and displayed in all libraries and bookshops in Germany.

Modern civilization was thought by Chamberlain to be derived from four sources: from Greek, Roman, Jewish, and Teutonic civilizations. It received poetry, art, and philosophy from the Greeks, statecraft, order, and the idea of citizenship from the Romans, Judaism and, indirectly, Christianity from the Jews. The fusion of these three traditions was the contribution of the Teutons. For Chamberlain, the Teutons included not only the Germanic tribes described by Tacitus, but the Celts and Slavs as well — all were descended from a presumed single pure stock. Mixture of blood between these subgroups prevented sterility, and accounts for German greatness. This race understands leadership, and gives unfaltering loyalty to it. The incidence of the leadership trait among the Italians and French — insofar as it is found in them at all — is due to the presence of Teutons among them. Chamberlain had little doubt that persons such as Louis XIV, Dante, Michelangelo, Marco Polo, and Jesus Christ were really Teutons.

Georges Vacher de Lapouge

The French anthropologist, Georges Vacher de Lapouge (1854–1936), in three works written at the turn of the century,[50] sharpened the Darwinian elements of this type of racism and provided a pseudo-quantitative basis for

[48] *The Inequality of Human Races*, pp. xiv–xv.
[49] *Die Grundlagen des neunzehnten Jahrhunderts* (Munich: F. Bruckmann, 1900), translated by John Lees as *Foundations of the Nineteenth Century* (London: John Lane, 1911).
[50] *Les Sélections sociales* ["Social Selection"] (Paris: A. Fontemoing, 1896); *L'Aryen: son rôle social* ["The Aryan: His Role in Society"] (Paris: A. Fontemoing, 1899); *Race et milieu social* ["Race and Social Milieu"] (Paris: M. Rivière, 1909). English translations of these three works are not available.

it. Lapouge was too sophisticated to assume that there are any pure races. Traced back to the time of Christ, every man has no less than 18,000,000,-000,000,000 ancestors. It was his opinion, however, that many incidental crossings would not appreciably alter the race. The population of Europe has three principal races: *Homo Europæus* or Aryan (tall of stature, blond, conspicuously dolichocephalic); *Homo Alpinus* (of moderate stature, brown in pigmentation, and having a cephalic index of 85 and above as opposed to the Aryan index of 76 and below); and *Homo contractus* or Mediterranean (of low stature, dark color, and cephalic index of about 78). Character and temperament were thought to be related to these traits. When the cranium is small, the race lack energy. The brachycephalic race (that is, with a high cephalic index) is deficient in individuality and initiative. Intellectual power is correlated with the breadth of the anterior part of the brain. The Nordic or Aryan race are leaders in every creative activity.

As Lapouge saw it, education can work no long-run influence on temperament and character, hence on civilization. Selection argued on Darwin's principles represents the elimination of the unfit and survival of the fittest. Among men, natural selection is replaced by social selection. In present society, such selection is primarily negative in its biological effects. Thus, the Aryan race is rapidly disappearing, and it will disappear altogether unless a natural aristocracy is created on the basis of the innate qualities of individuals and through greater procreation and organization of a new dominant racial caste.

There were many additional contributors to the fusion of racism, Darwinism, and nationalism, but these are sufficient to illustrate what was occurring. Such individuals provided the rationale for one type of social Darwinistic nationalism and imperialism.

Francis Galton

One form of social Darwinism, as we have seen, buttressed the imperialism and expansionism subscribed to by a whole series of American statesmen and educators. A second form led to various programs of racial improvement as the only effective means of solving social problems. A more scholarly version of this second form than the master-race theories of Chamberlain and Vacher de Lapouge was the work of Darwin's cousin, Sir Francis Galton (1822–1911), who did much to inaugurate the eugenics movement. Galton was a grandson of Erasmus Darwin. He studied medicine at Birmingham Hospital and King's College, London, and in 1844 he graduated from Trinity College. His work on *Hereditary Genius* may serve to illustrate the tenor of Galton's books.[51]

---

[51] Galton's principal works are: *Hereditary Genius* (London: 1869; 2d ed., 1892); *English Men of Science: Their Nature and Nurture* (London: 1874); *Inquiries into Human Faculty and Its Development* (London: 1883; 2d ed., 1907); *Natural Inheritance* (London: 1889); *Finger Prints* (London, 1892); and *Finger Print Directories* (London, 1895).

Individuals differ from one another in bodily and psychological characteristics: stature, weight, health, energy, sensitivity, gregariousness, intelligence, and so on. Physical and mental characteristics differ according to typical frequency distributions. For example, if we grade the intelligence of one million individuals, we will find the greatest number of them concentrated in the group classified as mediocre and a great rarity of individuals with commanding ability. There are fixed limits to educational development. Inheritance fixes these limits; talent and ability are inherited. Able fathers produce able children in much greater proportion than do others. Galton's study of English men of science, of genius, and Fellows of the Royal Society convinced him that families with two or more eminent men produce more famous men of genius than families with only one. There is a rapid decrease in the frequency of noteworthiness as distance of kinship from eminent men increases. Abilities such as those of mathematician, musician, judge, and statesman are inherited. Social hindrances cannot impede men of high ability from becoming eminent. Galton's study of twins, he thought, bore the same conclusion. There was no escaping the conclusion that nature prevails enormously over nurture when the differences of nurture do not exceed what is commonly found among persons of the same rank of society and in the same country.[52] What holds for individuals also holds for races. Just as upper and lower strata differ in regard to ability, the upper strata producing more men of genius and talent, so the races are unequal. This is to be judged by their ability to produce men of genius per given population number. The ancient Athenian Greeks produced one genius to 4,822 population. He argued that there were other groups that have not been able to produce a genius in their entire history.[53]

Karl Pearson

Karl Pearson (1857–1936) carried on Galton's work. Educated in mathematics at University College and at King's College, Cambridge, he was called to the bar in 1882, and later became an authority on eugenics. He was appointed Galton Professor of Eugenics at London University and Director of the Francis Galton Laboratory of National Eugenics. From 1902 until his death in 1936 he edited the journal *Biometrika*, and from 1925 on he was editor of *The Annals of Eugenics*. Quite apart from his great contributions to the science of statistics[54] was his development of the eugenic branch of social Darwinism. He believed that biological factors "are dominant in the

[52] *Inquiries into Human Faculty and Its Development.*
[53] *Hereditary Genius*, pp. 325–337.
[54] See his famous *Tables for Statisticians and Biometricians* (Cambridge, England: The University Press, 1914; 2d ed., 1924; 3d ed., 1945). Pearson's other principal writings are: *The Ethic of Free Thought* (London: 1883; 2d ed., London: A. and C. Black, 1901); *The Grammar of Science* (London: W. Scott, 1892; 3d ed., London: A. and C. Black, 1911; New York: Macmillan, 1911); *The Chances of Death* (London: E. Arnold, 1897); *National Life from the Standpoint of Science* (London: A. and C. Black, 1901; 2d ed., 1905); and *The Scope and Importance to the State of the Science of National Eugenics* (London: Dulau, 1909).

evolution of mankind; these and these alone, can throw light on the rise and fall of nations, on racial progress and national degeneracy." [55]

Like that of animals, man's development rests on natural selection. Characteristics are variable and inherited. There is a selective death rate. The earlier a person dies, the fewer offspring he leaves. Pearson was shocked by the differential fertility of present society, where the physically and mentally superior social classes have a lower rate of reproduction than inferior stock. He proposed that education should vary for different individuals and groups according to their ability.

Among the works in the United States which tremendously popularized the eugenics movement was Richard Dugdale's *The Jukes* (1877), a study of the descendants of a group of sisters who had lived in New York State in the eighteenth century, and which argued that disease, pauperism, and immorality are largely controlled by inheritance. Eugenics, in fact, grew with such rapidity that by 1915 it had reached the dimensions of a fad. The early eugenicists identified the "fit" with the upper classes, the "unfit" with the lower. They railed against multiplying morons. The poor were thought to be held down by biological deficiency rather than environmental conditions. Pearson set the tone for the eugenics movement by his estimate that nine-tenths of man's capacity was determined by heredity. Henry Goddard studied successive generations of a family whom he called the Kallikaks, and concluded that feeble-mindedness is largely responsible for criminals, prostitutes, and drunkards. David Starr Jordan thought that poverty, dirt, and crime were due to poor human material, while Lewellys F. Barker, a distinguished physician, thought the birth and death of nations was due to the relative fertility of fit and unfit elements.

Lothrop Stoddard

Where this all leads is developed fully by Lothrop Stoddard (1883–1950), in his proposals for race-building, "multiplication of superiors," and "elimination of inferiors" or "race cleansing." [56] These processes are termed "positive" and "negative" eugenics. The starting point is in race cleansing. This begins with the segregation of the insane and feeble-minded in public institutions, awakening society to the gravity of the situation, and tracing the relation between the "degenerate classes" and others "all the way from the unemployable 'casual laborer' right up to the 'tainted genius.'" [57] The eugenic ideal is that of "an ever-perfecting super-race." Not the "superman" of Nietzsche — "that brilliant yet baleful vision of a master *caste*, blooming like a gorgeous but parasitic orchid on a rotting trunk of servile degradation, but a super *race*, cleansing itself *throughout* by the elimination of its defects, and raising itself *throughout* by the cultivation of its qualities." [58] The neo-aristocracy so created will need a new philosophy more adequate

---

[55] *The Scope and Importance*, p. 38.
[56] Lothrop Stoddard, *The Revolt Against Civilization* (New York: Scribner's, 1922).
[57] *Ibid.*, p. 245.   [58] *Ibid.*, p. 262.

than democracy. "Now I believe, *for the time being at any rate*, the new philosophy should be called 'Neo-Aristocracy'; because it involves first of all the disestablishment of the democratic *cult* and the rehabilitation of the discredited aristocratic idea." [59]

Nazism

The further full development and practical application of the kind of program indicated by Stoddard occurred in Germany, with beginnings before the date of his book (1922). Hitler outlined future German policy in *Mein Kampf*. National policy was to be based on racist theories, following Chamberlain. The Jews were held responsible for the national defeat. This became the core of National Socialism. In the Nazi program of 1920, citizenship and public office were proposed only for those of German blood, and everyone of alien blood was to be deported or eliminated. Upon Hitler's assumption of power in 1933, laws began to be passed to these various ends, and anti-Semitic persecutions began. In 1935, with the Nuremberg Laws, full-scale actions began in earnest. All Jews were deprived of the right of citizenship, and marriages and extramarital relations between Jews and German non-Jews were prohibited. All Jewish children were removed from elementary schools. In 1936 the expropriation without recompense of Jewish property and banking accounts began and continued through 1937 — this measure aimed at eliminating Jews from trade and commerce. In 1938 outbursts against Jews became general, and mass arrests occurred in Berlin. Pogroms took place throughout Germany. By an edict, the Jews were assessed for all damage done during such outbreaks, plus a fine of a billion marks.

In 1939 the Jewish community in Berlin received orders from the police to produce daily the names of one hundred Jews who would receive two weeks' notice to leave the country. No provisions were made to finance the emigration. Racism in the Third Reich was beginning to spread to other areas. Alfred Rosenberg, editor-in-chief of official newspapers, pronounced the Christian Church to be a menace to true Nordics, and discovered racial antipathy of the Nordics in the decadent words of the Sermon on the Mount. This all terminated in the mass murders, the gas chambers, and the death factories of the concentration camps.

Summary

The three major forms of conflict ideology, which must not be confused with conflict theory as a sociological school, were Marxian socialism and two forms of social Darwinism.

Marxism was unique among the various types of socialism of the nineteenth century in that the starting point for its development was found in the romantic idealism of Fichte (who developed the dialectic of the moral

[59] *Ibid.*, p. 266.

experience), Schelling (who developed a dialectic of artistic experience), and Hegel (who developed a spiritual dialectic of human history and civilization). These idealistic and romantic philosophers popularized the concept of human society as a developing spiritual process in which every aspect was related to every other in an evolving whole. Although this process was mystically conceived, it did lead to the systematic search for new interrelations between social phenomena. There was, in fact, a very direct kinship between Comte and Hegel.

Marxian socialism transformed the spiritual dialectic of civilization into the material dialectic of opposed economic classes. This gave a new significance to the concept of class. Moreover, in the attempt to explain every other social phenomenon as class based and economically caused, the Marxians raised a whole array of new issues. The special developmental conditions of German socialism, with its prohibition by law of socialism and the social democratic movement, thrust the development of German socialism outside the working context of events, forcing it to assume a revolutionary and utopian form. German socialism came to envision the apocalyptic destruction of existing society.

While Marxian socialism represented a conflict ideology advanced in the name of the proletariat, both forms of social Darwinism were developed as ideologies of the business groups of modern society. The first form of social Darwinism, already partly evident in the writings of Charles Darwin, conceived human society as a product of the struggle for existence and the survival of the fittest. In the works of Spencer, William Graham Sumner, and others, this led to the notion that the captains of modern industry represented the fittest members of society. It also led to the assumption that social welfare activities, in aiding the socially underprivileged, were destroying the biological potential of the race. The rich thus merited their wealth; the poor, by biological inferiority, deserved their fate.

Marxism was a conflict ideology projected in the names and interests of the proletariat. Social Darwinism was a conflict ideology projected in the name of the upper strata of bourgeois society. Marxism's external program was the world-wide union of the proletariat; social Darwinism's external program was imperialism ("manifest destiny," the "white man's burden"). Marxism's internal program was the overthrow of capitalistic society, the temporary dictatorship of the proletariat, and the withering away of the state. Social Darwinism's internal program was an active eugenic policy aimed at race improvement, mass sterilization, and the rooting out of socialism as if it were a genetic defect. It was left to the Germans, with typical Teutonic thoroughness, to demonstrate fully the implications of consistent social Darwinism.

Just as Marxism left a residue of problems behind it for objective social science, so too did the ideological forms of social Darwinism. The problems of nationalism and imperialism were posed. The problems of racial and other minority groups were phrased. The possible relevance of individual differences to social conduct was formulated, and great strides were made in the study of individual differences. The fact was established that there are certain ultimate limits fixed for society in the nature of biological materials. As in the case of Marxism, these problems were posed for sociology — not solved.

SELECTED BIBLIOGRAPHY

DARWIN, CHARLES, *The Origin of Species* and *The Descent of Man.* One-volume edition. New York: Modern Library, no date.

GALTON, FRANCIS, *Hereditary Genius: An Inquiry into Its Laws and Consequences.* New York: Horizon Press, 1952.

HEGEL, G. W. F., *The Philosophy of Right.* Translated by S. W. Dyde. London: George Bell, 1896.

HEGEL, G. W. F., *The Philosophy of History.* Translated by J. Sibree. New York: Dover Publications, 1956.

HOFSTADTER, RICHARD, *Social Darwinism in America.* Revised edition. Boston: Beacon Press, 1955.

MARCUSE, HERBERT, *Reason and Revolution.* New York: Oxford University Press, 1941.

MARX, KARL, and FRIEDRICH ENGELS, *The German Ideology.* New York: International Publishers, 1947.

MEAD, GEORGE HERBERT, *Movements of Thought in the Nineteenth Century.* Edited by Merritt H. Moore. Chicago: University of Chicago Press, 1949.

SPENCER, HERBERT, *Social Statics* and *The Man Versus the State.* One-volume edition. New York: D. Appleton, 1908.

STODDARD, LOTHROP, *The Revolt Against Civilization.* New York: Scribner's, 1922.

SUMNER, WILLIAM GRAHAM, *Essays of William Graham Sumner.* Edited by Albert Galloway Keller and Maurice R. Davie. New Haven, Conn.: Yale University Press, 1940.

8

Sociological Conflict Theories

Marxism and social Darwinism were ideologies — sets of ideas vindicating particular social positions and spurring particular action programs. Sociological conflict theory, though some of its propositions coincide with those appearing in the ideologies, is scientific, resting its hypotheses on the scientific standards of the discipline. Nevertheless, when sociologists began to turn to conflict theory in the late nineteenth century, the general ideological atmosphere that gave birth to positivistic organicism was still effective, as is evident in the fact that they found many more affinities with social Darwinism than with Marxism. If there had not been a predisposition toward one rather than the other ideology, we would expect equal receptivity or equal indifference.

The ideological atmosphere sustaining early sociology required a combination of conservatism and scientific method. However, positivistic organicism, though brilliantly adapted to both requirements, did not give stable results. It was a fluctuating compound, yielding to the whims of every student. Ultimately it could not satisfy the demand either for a conservative image of society or for a dependable method. It is not surprising, then, that a sober search for "realities" made its appearance.

Although positivistic organicism proved in the end to be inadequate, the need for scientific method and a conservative picture of society remained. Conflict theory was able to fulfill both needs. The sociological conflict theorists are, as a whole, even more positivistic than their organicist colleagues. They can afford to be: they have not had to close their eyes to whole blocks of empirical facts. While it is possible, as shown by Marxism and social Darwinism, to develop conflict theory into an aggressive ideology, it is by no means necessary. There is a milder ideological conclusion that may be drawn whenever one takes as the most obvious fact of society the occurrence of conflict. The normal task of on-going society can be seen as a constant movement toward what is variously called adjustment, stability, equilibrium, or the termination of conflict. Hence, bad as things sometimes seem, it is conservative wisdom not to make matters worse, nor to make the world over, nor to interfere with "the normal processes of society," but rather to leave well enough alone and keep whatever peace is possible. *Conflict sociology emerged as the second form of sociological theory precisely because while correcting positivistic organicism in a realistic manner it was conformable to the same ideological requirements.*

Walter Bagehot

The re-stylization of traditional conflict theory in Darwinian terms, with a theoretical rather than a practical (moralistic) intent, is presented by the work of Walter Bagehot (1826–1877), son of an English banker. Bagehot took his degree at London University in 1848, and was called to the bar in 1852. He entered his father's banking business, Stuckey and Company, for many years managing its London agency. Bagehot was also an underwriter at Lloyd's. He married the daughter of James Wilson, the first editor of the *Economist,* and began a long connection with the journal. His main books were *The English Constitution* (1867), *Physics and Politics* (1869), and *Lombard Street* (1873). For conflict theory, *Physics and Politics* was most important.[1] It attracted the favorable attention of Darwin. The subtitle, "Thoughts on the Application of the Principles of 'Natural Selection' and 'Inheritance' to Political Society," are a clue to Bagehot's theory of society, which rests on a fusion of biological and political considerations. He was familiar with Henry Sumner Maine's *Ancient Law,* and inclined to accept Maine's ideas about the original state of society.[2] Bagehot was also familiar with Darwin's theories, and was convinced that natural selection plays a part in the development of human society equivalent to its role in the evolution of animal species.

The peculiarity of our age to Bagehot is found in the rapidity of change: "by it everything is made 'an antiquity.'"[3] The function of science, by its eternal prying and continuous recording, is to turn everything rapidly into an item of the past while thought moves restlessly on. This, for Bagehot, is in thematic contrast with past ages, which were marked by a stability based on unreflective habit. Prior to historical times, society was organized into patriarchal families; only the germs of the state were present in the

[1] References here are to: Walter Bagehot, *Physics and Politics,* introduction by Jacques Barzun (New York: Alfred A. Knopf, 1948).
[2] For a brief discussion of Maine, see Chapter 4, pp. 85–86.
[3] *Physics and Politics,* p. 4.

patriarch. Behavior was automatic and arbitrary. Maine thought that the origins of political society occurred with the shift from the patriarchal family to local contiguity as a principle of organization. Bagehot saw this as superficial, for he thought Darwin's principle of natural selection was more adequate. "When once politics were begun, there was no difficulty in explaining why they lasted. Whatever may be said against the principle of 'natural selection' in other departments, there is no doubt of its predominance in early human history. The strongest killed out the weakest, as they could. And I need not pause to prove that any form of policy is more efficient than none." [4] The most fundamental of all problems for early political society was achieving order and obedience. This was obtained through the fusion of church and state. "To gain . . . obedience, the primary condition is the identity — not the union, but the sameness of — what we now call Church and State." [5] The object of such fusion was to create what may be called a "cake of custom." All the actions of life were to be submitted to a single rule for a single object — gradually creating the " 'hereditary drill' which science teaches us to be essential." [6] The early recorded history of the Aryan race shows that a king and a council were required to solve early conflicts. Rome and Sparta were "drilling" aristocracies, succeeding for this reason. This phenomenon of "drill" or discipline is a component in all societies and extends to the writers. "What writers are expected to write, they write; or else they do not write at all." While men vainly assume that they choose what they like, they are actually dominated by "received opinion" which prescribes what they ought to like; "or if their minds are too marked and oddly made to get into the mould, they give up reading altogether. . . . the principle of 'elimination,' the 'use and disuse' of organs . . . works here." [7]

This process of disciplining and customary consolidation of habits in terms of the social order gives rise to national character. "I believe that what we call national character arose in very much the same way. At first a sort of 'chance predominance' made a model, and then invincible attraction, the necessity which rules all but the strongest man to imitate what is before their eyes, and to be what they are expected to be, moulded men by that model. This is, I think, the very process by which new national characters are being made in our own time." [8]

Bagehot perceived the dynamics of society as the tension between customary behavior and intrusive elements which conflict with it.

"Whoever speaks two languages is a rascal," says the saying, and it rightly represents the feeling of primitive communities when the sudden impact of new thoughts and new examples breaks down the compact despotism of the single consecrated code, and leaves pliant and impressible man — such as he then is — to follow his unpleasant will without distinct guidance by hereditary morality and hereditary religion. The old oli-

[4] *Ibid.*, p. 26. [5] *Ibid.*, p. 28. [6] *Ibid.*, p. 29.
[7] *Ibid.*, p. 38. [8] *Ibid.*, pp. 38–39.

Adam Smith

Karl Marx

Charles Darwin

William Graham Sumner

Walter Bagehot

Gustav Ratzenhofer

Ludwig Gumplowicz

Albion Small

Franz Oppenheimer

George Vold

garchies wanted to keep their type perfect, and for that end they were right not to allow foreigners to touch it." [9]

From this theoretical base — a tension between customary and intrusive factors — Bagehot was in a position to present conflict as the central phenomenon in social development and structure.

> Three laws, or approximate laws, may . . . be laid down. . . . First. In every particular state of the world, those nations which are strongest tend to prevail over the others; and in certain marked peculiarities the strongest tend to be best.
>
> Secondly. Within every particular nation the type or types of character then and there most attractive tend to prevail; and the most attractive, though with exceptions, is what we call the best character.
>
> Thirdly. Neither of these competitions is in most historic conditions intensified by extrinsic forces, but in some conditions, such as those now prevailing in the most influential part of the world, both are so intensified. [10]

In developing the significance of conflict, Bagehot maintained that the "progress of the military art is the most conspicuous, I was about to say the most showy, fact in human history." [11] Taken as a whole, the fighting capacity of mankind has ever grown more immense. Military vices decline as military strength increases. For example, it is no longer true that living in cities makes people unwarlike and effeminate. The primitive could have withstood the attack of ancient civilized men in the past; the primitive in the present cannot withstand ours. In history the strongest nation always conquers the weaker, always prevailing over it. Every intellectual gain, so to speak, that a nation possessed was in the earliest times made use of — was invested and taken out in war. Moreover, conquest improved mankind by an intermixture of strength. Even civilization grows by coalescence of strengths and by the competition of strengths. The conflict of nations was at first a main force in their improvement.

Bagehot structures human history into three great ages: (1) the prehistorical age of custom, (2) the age of war and nation-making, in which warfare and militarism were the primary constructive force, and (3) the age of discussion or science, which has built a social order open to the intrusive ideas of science. In the course of his elaboration of these themes, numerous stereotypes are disposed of. For example, he objects to the idea that progress is a general feature of history. The Greeks and Oriental nations knew nothing of the idea. A large part of mankind lived outside it. Bagehot also opposes the stereotype that mankind wants to be original. "At this very moment there are the most rigid Comtists teaching that we ought to be governed by a hierarchy — a combination of savants orthodox in science. Yet who can doubt that Comte would have been hanged by his own hierarchy?" [12] Nor is Bagehot sure that the academies are sources of original ideas. "The academies are asylums of the ideas and the tastes of the last

---

[9] *Ibid.*, p. 42.   [10] *Ibid.*, p. 46.   [11] *Ibid.*, p. 48.   [12] *Ibid.*, p. 61.

age. . . . I have heard a most eminent man of science observe, 'by the time a man of science attains eminence on any subject, he becomes a nuisance upon it, because he is sure to retain errors which were in vogue when he was young, but which the new race have refuted.' " [13]

Bagehot's theoretical statement may serve as further illustration of the difference between conflict theory as a theoretical explanation and as the basis for a practical or applied program. Bagehot does not feel compelled to advocate the conquest of the world by the various English-speaking nations, nor does he seem unhappy if he cannot sterilize about three-quarters of mankind. He is certainly about as far removed from sentimental reformism as one can imagine, but he seems not to have felt obliged, for this reason, to embrace some special form of idiocy.

In Jacques Barzun's opinion, Bagehot explored two fundamental paradoxes of socio-political life. "The first was the *moral* paradox that the public good is not to be achieved by following the rules of private good. Now we face the *psychological* paradox that stability and change are equally necessary though diametrically opposed. But are men capable of being at once quiescent and active, habit ridden and original?" [14] Human nature is conceived as basically plastic. Training and "custom," or the "cake of custom," rigidify man's original flexibility. The plastic mind of a boy can be molded into a merchant, barrister, butcher, baker, surgeon, or apothecary. Once make him an apothecary, however, and he will never again bake bread. Make him a butcher, and he will kill too extensively ever to be a surgeon. Acquired habit is the source of stability in professional man and citizen. Bagehot maintains that good government rests on this stability. Paradoxically, the true source of the strength of English government is the stupidity of the population. All the way up to Parliament a few invaluable members think, but the best English people keep their minds in a state of decorous dullness. The stolid attention to business makes for steadiness, and once committed to free government it is effective there. If everyone were to do what he thinks is right in Parliament, there would be 657 amendments to every motion and no motion could be carried. "There never was an election without a party. You cannot get a child into an asylum without a combination. At such places you see 'Vote for Orphan A' upon a placard, and 'Vote for Orphan B (also an Idiot! ! !)' upon a banner, and the party of each is busy about its placard and banner." But if the first need of government is order, arising as habit in the unthinking mass, the second requirement is "agitation." In the modern world, with its newspapers and speeches, the ideas of the few are pounded into the minds of the many.

Ludwig Gumplowicz

Ludwig Gumplowicz (1838–1909) was perhaps the most influential of the conflict theorists of his time. Son of a prominent family of Polish Jews

---

[13] *Ibid.*, p. 63.   [14] From Barzun's introduction, *ibid.*, p. xiv.

in Cracow, he was educated and found a career in the Austro-Hungarian Empire. The powerful forms of anti-Semitism and multiple inter-ethnic and inter-class conflicts, and the political control of the Dual Monarchy, are thought to have been the most important influences on his sociology. Gumplowicz began his career as a journalist, later teaching law at the University of Graz. In 1909 he committed suicide. His most important books are *Rasse und Staat* (1875), *Philosophisches Staatsrecht* (1877), *Der Rassenkampf* (1883), and *Sozialphilosophie im Umriss* (1910).[15]

Gumplowicz worked with a narrow specific definition of the materials of sociology and a strongly positivistic conception of method. "The function of sociology consists in showing that universal laws apply to social phenomena; in pointing out the peculiar effects produced by them in the social domain, and finally in formulating the special social laws." [16] Social phenomena consist in the operations of groups and aggregates of men. Sociology at bottom is always a study of groups and the interrelations of groups. The behavior of groups is orderly. "Social groups persist in their actual social condition and cannot be made to 'pass' into another without adequate social cause. . . . In other words, each alteration in the social condition of a group must always have a sufficient social cause." [17] Such a sufficient cause can only be found in the influence of other social groups. Intergroup causes and effects constitute a social event or process. "When two or more distinct (*heterogen*) groups come into contact, when each enters the sphere of the other's operations, a social process always ensues." [18] Social laws concern such process. "All social laws, indeed all universal laws as well, have one characteristic in common: they explain the becoming, but never the beginning, of things, the ultimate origin." [19] The question of ultimate origins of groups, strictly speaking, lies outside the sphere of sociological science.[20]

In explanation of social life, the antithesis of individual and group and the supposition that every individual is an active center of influence, are false leads. As a matter of fact, even what the individual thinks is a product of the influences to which he has been subject from childhood. The individual

---

[15] Only one of Gumplowicz's works is available in English — *Grundriss der Sociologie* (Vienna: 1877; Innsbruck: Wagner, 1926), which was translated by Frederick W. Moore as *The Outlines of Sociology* (Philadelphia: American Academy of Political and Social Science, 1899). His other books are: *Rasse und Staat* ["Race and State"] (Vienna: 1875); *Philosophisches Staatsrecht* ["Philosophy of Constitutional Law"] (Vienna: 1877); *Der Rassenkampf* ["The Conflict of Races"] (Innsbruck: 1883); *Die sociologische Staatsidee* ["The Sociological Conception of the State"] (Graz: 1892); *Allgemeines Staatsrecht* ["General Constitutional Law"] (Innsbruck: 1897); *Soziologische Essays* ["Sociological Essays"] (Innsbruck: 1899); *Geschichte der Staatstheorien* ["History of Theories of the State"] (Innsbruck: 1905); and *Sozialphilosophie im Umriss* ["Social Philosophy in Outline"] (Innsbruck: 1910). See also *The Letters of Ludwig Gumplowicz to Lester F. Ward*, edited by Bernhard J. Stern (Leipzig: C. Hirschfeld, 1933).

[16] *The Outlines of Sociology*, pp. 82–83.

[17] *Ibid.*, p. 84.   [18] *Ibid.*, p. 85.   [19] *Ibid.*

[20] Despite Gumplowicz's explicit rejection of the search for origins as a legitimate sociological task, the powerful currents of evolutionism and historicism of his day drew his work in their course, and his studies are permeated with the quest for origins.

is like a prism that receives rays of influence from the surrounding social world and transmits them according to fixed laws. In his actions in the aggregate or the group, the individual has a sheep-like character.

Not only did Gumplowicz reject the notion that sociological science can fruitfully concern itself with the problem of social origins; he also rejected theories of society based on the assumption of rationalistic individualism. Gumplowicz's views were quite in accord with those of Bagehot, who was also suspicious of all theories of the total progress of humanity. Moreover, just as Bagehot's great emphasis on customary behavior led him to the counter principle of "agitation," so Gumplowicz's theory of the sheep-like character of individuals in assemblies requires — in order to explain the dynamics of a society — a variety of groups in conflict. He states:

> If mankind is conceived to be a unit, the condition necessary for the action of opposing forces is by supposition absent. Besides, nowhere on earth, and at no time either in the present age or in remotest antiquity has mankind been found to be a simple substance. It always consists in a countless number of distinct (*heterogen*) ethnical elements. Hence I was led to seek the starting point of sociological investigation in the hypothesis that there was originally an indefinitely large number of distinct (*heterogen*) ethnical elements; and it gives me satisfaction to note that good authorities consider the polygenetic hypothesis established.[21]

The polygenetic hypothesis — that mankind must have had a pluralistic origin — was argued at great length in *Der Rassenkampf,* where the attempt was made to reconcile it with Darwinism.

The natural tendency of men in aggregates is to mill about like sheep. In the simplest situations men must have lived in a herd or horde — "a group of men who are still dependent upon the simplest animal impulses, whose conditions of life and social constitution show no social change." Because sexual satisfaction was promiscuous, and biological paternity could not be recognized as such, the children were the mother's property. The family and the institution of property are both traced to intergroup conflict. Within a single promiscuous horde, wife-stealing would not have been possible. If a man wanted a woman for his own, he had to steal her from another group. In this way, marriage-by-capture and exogamy appeared, together with the father-family, with the woman as property of her lord. As the sovereignty of men was established, the overthrow of matriarchy was inevitable. These institutions, then, originated in intergroup conflict, but they were not the only ones. Rape was not only an occasion for early intertribal hostilities, but the plunder of property must also have been an incentive, just as it has always been and still is. Simple forms of irregular plunder must have occurred first; later expeditions led to the permanent subjection of the foreign horde and the acquisition of territory. The first

[21] *The Outlines of Sociology,* p. 92.

form of property in land must have consisted of tracts for common use. Movable property must also have originated in conquest, at the time when one horde overpowered another and used its labor force. Some persons, the subjects, were excluded from enjoyment of goods produced by their own labor in favor of the ruling class.

The most striking social institution to emerge in the course of this pursuit of the women and property of another group was the *state*. The state was a social phenomenon obeying natural laws. The first step toward it was the subjection of one social group by another and the establishment of a sovereign minority in control. Numerical inferiority was supplemented by mental superiority and greater military discipline. The sovereign class required compulsory acquiescence of a subject class. Its objectives were defense against attacks, increase of power, and territory. The superior class also sought to make profitable use of the subject classes. In the organized control of a minority over a majority, the state was "not a union or community for securing the common weal, for realizing justice. . . . No state was ever founded with one of these ends in view." [22] States have only arisen in the subjection of one stock by another in the economic interest of the latter.

Once an order is established by force, a process of amalgamation gradually occurs. Labor must always be organized under compulsion. Training and discipline presuppose the state, which in the beginning demands untold sacrifices of life and health. Finally, in a rising civilization, even laborers become participants in material and moral possessions, and the whole interest of the subject class becomes devoted to expanding its privileges.

The origins of rank are in warfare, but the creation of classes does not stop here, for a complex of economic and historical facts continues to create a multitude of subclasses. The merchant comes as a guest, and he is permitted to come, for he has new things to sell. He is personally free, and knows how to maintain his freedom. He is identified with neither lords nor vassals, but soon becomes necessary to both. Such an intrusive autonomous middle class between the old classes introduces social stress in the order. Basically, therefore, the classes have a twofold origin. "Some classes, the ruling, the peasant and the merchant classes . . . arose from the union . . . of different . . . ethnological elements. . . . There are others . . . the priesthood, large industry as contrasted with small, scholars, jurists, officials, and so forth, which arise from the others by a process of differentiation." [23]

Gumplowicz insists that individual conscience and morality have nothing to do with the social struggle. Individuals have a conscience; societies do not. The social struggle is carried on, not by individuals, but by societies. This is the basis for the establishment of a sharp distinction between *morals* and *right*. The social group is the source of opinions, feelings, and morals. At bottom, morality is nothing but the conviction implanted by the social

[22] *Ibid.*, pp. 118–119.   [23] *Ibid.*, p. 134.

group in the minds of its members of the propriety (*Statthaftigkeit*) of the manner of life imposed by it on them. Whereas morals are a product of the relations between the simple social group and the individual, rights are a product of the unions of different social elements. Rights never arise except in the union of societies, no matter how simple they may be; organized sovereignty is always presupposed. Morals, on the other hand, arise in the most primitive social element, in the simple aggregate or horde. This may be illustrated by some of the most fundamental rights. The rape of women from another tribe developed the first family right, the right of the man over his wife; also, by reducing the foreign element to servitude, the right of the lord over his slave was evolved; and from the resulting distinction between the lord, to whom the fruits of the soil belong, and the slave who cultivates the soil for his master, arose the right of property. Gumplowicz concludes: "Rights can arise only in the state and nowhere else for they are eminently political institutions . . . containing as it were a particle of political sovereignty." [24]

The concept of "inalienable human rights" rests on an unreasonable self-deification of man and an overestimation of the value of life as well as a misconception of the basis and existence of the state. "This fancied freedom and equality is incompatible with the state and is a direct negation of it. But the only choice for men here below is between the state with its necessary servitude and inequality, and — anarchy." [25]

Gustav Ratzenhofer

Gustav Ratzenhofer (1842–1904) was influenced not only by Gumplowicz but by the same socio-political situation in the Dual Monarchy. Ratzenhofer was born in Vienna in 1842. The early death of his father, who was a clock-maker earning a modest income, forced the family into dire economic straits. This was the beginning of a series of difficulties that led Ratzenhofer to join the Austrian army. He became a lieutenant in 1864, and saw active service. After four years in an advanced military academy, he was promoted to the general staff in 1872 and placed in charge of the army archives, where he began systematic research and writing on military subjects. In 1898 he was made field marshal lieutenant and president of the military supreme court in Vienna. He retired from active service in 1901. Among his sociologically important works are *Wesen und Zweck der Politik* (1893), *Die sociologische Erkenntnis* (1898), and *Soziologie* (1907).[26]

[24] *Ibid.*, p. 179.   [25] *Ibid.*, p. 180.
[26] Ratzenhofer's chief works, none of which has been translated into English, are: *Die Staatswehr* ["National Defense"] (Stuttgart: J. G. Cotta, 1881); *Wesen und Zweck der Politik* ["The Nature and Aim of Politics"] (Leipzig: F. A. Brockhaus, 1893); *Die sociologische Erkenntnis* ["Sociological Knowledge"] (Leipzig: F. A. Brockhaus, 1898); and *Soziologie* (Leipzig: F. A. Brockhaus, 1907). A partial translation and paraphrase of important sections of *Wesen und Zweck der Politik* and *Die sociologische Erkenntnis* are contained in Albion Small, *General Sociology* (Chicago: University of Chicago Press, 1905), pp. 189–394.

Though Ratzenhofer has never been translated into English (except in fragments), he has rather special interest in the development of conflict theory, not only for his influence on Albion Small, the major early American student of conflict theory, but also because he presents a position midway between the individualistic conflict theory of classical economics and the social Darwinists and the collectivistic theory of Gumplowicz. For Ratzenhofer, the units of the social process are neither individuals nor groups but *interests*.

Interests arise on a biological foundation. Among the basic biological properties of life are: movement because of inner impulses; propagation; avoidance of alien conditions and growths; a tendency toward individualization; and capacity for perception.[27] These biological properties are also important to social structures, which operate under the same laws of life and death as the organism.[28] Nature thus outfits the individual with a number of basic drives. *Interests* may be defined as the social reconstitution of biological drives. Although the fate of the individual is drawn into and fulfilled in the stream of social development, it must never be forgotten that social development is possible only by means of the strivings of individual men. Individuals find self-fulfillment in society; society is produced by individuals seeking self-fulfillment. "The strivings of the individuals, in whom inherent interests are rooted, are either private (*rein subjektiv*) or public (*subjektiv im sozialen Wege*)." [29]

The social process is the product of interests which, depending on the circumstances, cause men to pull together or to pull apart. This may be seen in Ratzenhofer's eighteen-item outline of his theory of the social process: [30]

1. The preservation and propagation of humans is the basis for all association.

2. The individual's impulses of self-preservation and sex are modified by and adapted to the life conditions which he faces.

3. Every disposition in the individual is an imperative which he tends to obey without restriction.

4. When population presses against natural conditions, individuals and groups are forced into a struggle for existence.

5. Though men (like all creatures) would prefer to live and propagate at peace with others of the same species, the pressure of population on natural conditions gradually forces the interests of individuals and groups into a condition of absolute hostility toward others.

6. There are some advantages in common self-preservation by a number

[27] *Die sociologische Erkenntnis*, pp. 108–112.
[28] *Ibid.*, p. 115.
[29] *Soziologie*, p. 17.
[30] See *Die sociologische Erkenntnis*, pp. 244–250. A translation of this section appears in Small's *General Sociology*, pp. 189–199. What we present here are summaries of the main argument Ratzenhofer advances under each of his eighteen points. Much greater clarity is possible by freely rendering the main argument rather than translating the key sentences, which often contain terms and concepts which themselves need further explanation.

of persons; moreover, sex interests force people into association. Thus, the first natural group is based on sex and kinship. However, the very success of the blood group in satisfying these interests permits population to increase and press against the food supply. Kin groups split and come, in time, to be different in culture and race. Contact between differentiated groups leads to flight or to battle. The conquest of one such group by another leads to more complex social formations, held together by common traditions and institutions of control, rather than by kinship.

7. Social structures arising from biological relationships are simple; those arising from conquest are complex.

8. The social process is a rhythm of *individualization* of structures by which new structures arise out of others already in existence, and of the *socialization* of structures already in existence.

9. *Differentiation*, or the impulse toward individualization, is limited only by the number of individuals. The limit of individualization is the atomization of society. *Socialization*, or the formation of a number of individuals into a collective unit, reaches its theoretical upper limit in the formation of all mankind into a single structure of *humanity*.

10. Differentiation frees men from social restraints, permitting free expression and satisfaction of inborn interests; socialization restrains men in order that they may achieve the cooperation necessary for securing natural or supposed interests.

11. For the social processes of socialization and differentiation, social necessity may be either *internal* (determined by the inborn capabilities of men) or *external* (determined by natural or social conditions).

12. The more men are spread out over the available space capable of sustaining life, the greater the social variations. Organization under such conditions increasingly assumes a formal and coercive character. Moreover, interests arising in other spheres tend to assume a political form.

13. The kinds of controls in the state depend upon the stage of social evolution. In the early stage of the formation of a state, controls are arbitrary and coercive; in time, customary and peaceable controls appear.

14. Conflicts consolidate social structures and create aggregations of power; culture and commerce, as sources of social differentiation, tend to dissipate aggregations of power.

15. Social differentiation creates complicated social structures in superordination, coordination, and subordination.

16. As social structures grow more complicated, the occasions for war and violence are reduced, for every disturbance in a complicated social structure sets in motion the counter activity of many opposed interests.

17. The potential absolute hostility embedded in individuality tends to emerge whenever unlike social structures confront one another.

18. To the extent that the state resting on tradition (Ratzenhofer's "culture" state) takes the place of the state resting on force (the "conquest" state), differences among men in the satisfaction of interests tend to equalize.

In brief, biological requirements are the foundation of drives. When re-stylized by the presence of other persons, drives may be characterized as interests. Depending on the circumstances, interests may drive people into associations or cause them to differentiate within associations. The tribal horde resting on kinship was the first successful collaboration of human beings. However, its very efficiency permitted men to increase, caused them to differentiate into multiple tribal hordes, and eventually brought these hordes into group conflict. Thus, the principle of absolute hostility, which was kept under control so long as men lived in kin groups, broke out in the wars between kin-based groups. In time, the new structures tended to grow more peaceable. Interests, thus, are the basis for both association and dissociation of people. The peculiar intersection of interests with the conditions for their fulfillment gives them a constructive or destructive form in the given case. There is thus a rhythm of conflict and peace, during which men are pressed to form social structures of increasing comprehensiveness.

Conflict led men to form into the successively more comprehensive structures of (1) the horde and race, (2) the settled race, (3) the state as an exclusive society, (4) the hegemony with world control, and (5) the coalition and the balance of power and aggressive combination of states across state boundaries.[31] If by ethics one refers (as Ratzenhofer does) to the peaceable resolution of conflicts of interests rather than their resolution by further conflict, an ethical development accompanies each stage of social structure. These ethical stages are: (1) care of fellow beings, (2) community of interest, (3) political self-restraint for the sake of peace, (4) universal freedom, with equality of legal rights, (5) diplomacy between states, and (6) international peace.

Sumner as a Conflict Theorist

Ratzenhofer has a rather special interest, because he was a transitional figure between European conflict sociology and American, as represented by Sumner and Small. In fact, he had a distinct influence on both.

American forms of conflict theory are more individualistic than the European. Sumner, who developed a highly individualized form of conflict theory, has already been discussed as a social Darwinist. We have drawn a distinction between conflict *ideologies* — propaganda weapons in the interests of special class formations — and conflict *theory;* the term "social Darwinism" has been employed to refer to one of the major developments in conflict ideology. This terminology is used in the attempt to keep normative and empirical theory distinct. The ideological, social Darwinistic phase of Sumner's thought is found in the essays, written for the most part while he was still close to the ministry and under the influence of Spencer and Julius Lippert.[32] These essays display a most ardent apologist's enthusiasm for the middle class. Their very titles show propagandistic intent: "The Forgotten Man," "What the Social Classes Owe Each Other," "The Absurd

---

[31] *Wesen und Zweck der Politik*, I, Sec. 12.
[32] Julius Lippert (1839–1909) was an ardent proponent of social evolution. His *Kulturgeschichte der Menschheit in ihrem organischen Aufbau*, 2 vols. (Stuttgart: 1886–87) has been translated and edited by George Peter Murdock and published as *The Evolution of Culture* (New York: Macmillan, 1931). His history of the priesthood, *Allgemeine Geschichte des Priesterthums* (Berlin: 1883–84), and his history of the family, *Die Geschichte der familie* (Stuttgart: 1884), are not available in English translation.

Effort to Make the World Over," "The Power and Beneficence of Capital-ism." However, there is little doubt that Sumner was a conflict theorist as well as a conflict ideologist. Around 1893 he began to confine himself to sociology. His work thereafter displays a deepening sense of empirical re-sponsibility, and he began with great energy a collection of comparative cultural materials on an immense scale. His plan for a comprehensive sys-tem of sociology was well under way at the time of his death; the first volume was drafted in rough form, and the notes were systematized. A. G. Keller completed this work, which appeared as the four volumes of *The Science of Society* in 1927.[33] The one major work Sumner completed was *Folkways* (1906), which was destined to become a classic. In this, the in-fluence of Malthus, Spencer, Lippert, Gumplowicz, and Ratzenhofer is mani-fest.

However, before he came under the influence of the conflict theorists he was first influenced by the organic evolutionists, and his first attempts at a synthesis of sociology date from this earlier phase. *Folkways* was developed as an incident during the time when he was moving from the first to the second phase of his development. It is hard to say what might have hap-pened had Sumner lived to bring out the synthesis he desired. As things stand, there are numerous incompletenesses and even contradictions between *Folkways* and the more ambitious *Science of Society* finished by Keller. For example, the conflict theorists were generally rather critical of unilinear evo-lutionism. It is significant that most of *Folkways* will stand even if unilinear evolutionism is abandoned; not so the work published later. The clearest statement of a conflict position appears in the former work. The argument is roughly as follows.

Men act because they cannot help it to satisfy their needs. These are of four basic types: hunger, sex, vanity, and fear of ghosts. (Some persons have assumed that W. I. Thomas got the four wishes here. There is no doubt that this statement in Sumner's account is closely modeled upon the theories of Ratzenhofer.) The most fundamental of all elements of the social process is the tendency of individuals to repeat actions which have been successful in satisfying recurrent needs. These are stereotyped as habits of individuals. When they arise out of the interhuman struggle for existence, they are social habits or customs.

Group habits have a special property: they arise in the minds and actions of the stronger members of the group, and are then imitated by others and spread by suggestion, which is at the base of mass phenomena. Invention and imitation are the second and third most important factors (after custom formation) of the social process. Inventions which are imitated are *folkways* (solutions to common problems which have become customary). Folkways

---

33 William Graham Sumner and Albert Galloway Keller, *The Science of Society*, 4 vols. (New Haven, Conn.: Yale University Press, 1927). A recent edition of *Folkways* was brought out by Dover Publications (New York: 1959). For further bibliographical information on Sumner, see Footnote 35, Chapter 7.

are subject to a strain toward improvement and toward consistency. The formation of folkways is guided and checked by the principles of pleasure and pain. Moreover, there is an element of chance in human affairs. Those folkways thought to be right and true are enforced by fear of ghosts and powerful taboos. The differentiation of folkways into the general *folkways* and the *mores* is the next major element in the social process.

The folkways are the source of philosophy and ethics. They constitute the structure of roles, professions, classes, religions, and sects. They are the basis of group solidarity. They give rise to institutions, which consist of a concept and a structure. Institutions are simply collections of folkways and mores about a dominant interest — a formation that may occur gradually and unconsciously (*crescive* institutions) or consciously (*enacted* institutions). Laws are conscious regulation in areas of conduct originally covered by custom.

It may be seen that the social process ultimately is anchored in the relation of men to men and men to land — the man–land ratio. Sumner urged that for any given level of adjustment of men to land there is a specific appropriate arrangement of social institutions. The agents of social development are not individuals but total groups. Only the fittest survive. One of the most significant of distinctions is between "we-groups" and "they-groups" or "in-groups" and "out-groups." The in-group is a peace group of an intimate type bearing strong ethnocentric attitudes of its own superiority. In the past, when any group was widespread it was because of its "survival value." Over time the tendency has been to expand the size of the peace group. Slavery, for example, was once universal. It taught men to "labor" and was only displaced when advanced technical development occurred. War has characterized all stages of the development process. It has been important as a source of social discipline, social stratification, government, and efficiency. Religion, with its origin in the fear of ghosts, has been a powerful source of social cohesiveness. But throughout, primary importance attaches to maintenance institutions, which form the basis of the institutional order.

Sumner, consciously or unconsciously, tried to reconcile the individualistic conflict position (derived from *laissez-faire* economics and Malthus) with the tradition of group conflict (derived from Gumplowicz). The distinctions between in- and out-group clearly follow Gumplowicz; the conception of an evolution of a peace group of ever increasing size comes from Ratzenhofer; and his location of ultimate importance in the achievement of stability — placing maintenance institutions at the heart of the institutional order — is a central phenomenon of conflict theory.

Albion Woodbury Small

Albion Woodbury Small (1854–1926) was perhaps the most balanced conflict theorist to appear on the early American scene. He was trained in theology at the Newton Theological School (1876–1879), and continued his studies in Germany at Leipzig and Berlin (1879–1881). There he came under the influence of the German social economists, Gustav Schmoller and Adolf Wagner. After teaching for some years at Colby College in Maine, Small attended Johns Hopkins University (1888–1889), coming in contact with the Adams school of historians, hot in the pursuit of theses based on the Teutonic and Aryan theories. Small worked out a conflict position of his own.

Small influenced sociology in a number of ways, for he brought to the field intellectual interests in history, political science, and economics. At Colby he introduced the second course in sociology to be given in the United States. (The first was Sumner's at Yale.) In 1892 he left Colby for the University of Chicago, and became chairman of the first graduate department of sociology in the world. In 1894, in collaboration with George E. Vincent, he produced the first textbook in sociology: *An Introduction to the Study of Society*.[34] He founded *The American Journal of Sociology* in 1895 and remained its editor until his death. Small's publications reflect the variety of his interests: *General Sociology* (1905) was one of the most sophisticated reviews of theory in its time; *Adam Smith and Modern Sociology* (1907) and *The Cameralists* (1909) reflect his combined interests in economics and sociology, and *The Meaning of Social Science* (1910) and *Between Eras: From Capitalism to Democracy* (1924), in sociology and socio-political problems. *Origins of Sociology* (1924) was a sophisticated derivation of sociology from its nineteenth-century intellectual context. The theoretically most solid of all Small's work was *General Sociology*, where he gave fullest systematic expression to conflict sociology.

In the early *Introduction to the Study of Society*, the effort was made to delimit the field of sociology and present its main problems. The book outlined the field and development of sociology and described the evolution of society from an isolated agrarian form to modern metropolitan groups. Organic analogies were employed in the analysis of social structures and functions. The basis for a social psychology was tentatively sketched. In *Adam Smith and Modern Sociology* the attempt was made to free the field from the exclusive sphere of Comte. The beginnings of sociology were traced to Smith's theory of sympathy as developed in the *Theory of Moral Sentiments*. *The Wealth of Nations* was treated as a sociological study emphasizing economic process. "If one were to come upon *The Wealth of Nations* for the first time, with a knowledge of the general sociological way of looking

[34] Albion W. Small and George E. Vincent, *An Introduction to the Study of Society* (New York: American Book Company, 1894). Small's other books are: *General Sociology: An Exposition of the Main Development in Sociological Theory from Spencer to Ratzenhofer* (Chicago: University of Chicago Press, 1905, 1925); *Adam Smith and Modern Sociology* (Chicago: University of Chicago Press, 1907); *The Cameralists: The Pioneers of German Social Polity* (Chicago: University of Chicago Press, 1909); *The Meaning of Social Science* (Chicago: University of Chicago Press, 1910); *Between Eras: From Capitalism to Democracy* (Kansas City, Mo.: Inter-collegiate Press, 1913); and *Origins of Sociology* (Chicago: University of Chicago Press, 1924).

at society, but with no knowledge of economic literature, there would be not the slightest difficulty nor hesitation about classifying the book as an inquiry in a special field of sociology." [35]

In Small's view, sociology merely carried out the program of analysis implied in Adam Smith's moral philosophy. The tendency of the economists has been to exaggerate the significance of economic interests in isolation from other social interests of society. Sociology is a correction of this tendency. In *The Cameralists* Small examined the German analogue of British mercantilism. To him, cameralism was a forerunner of synthetic social science and an example of the exploitation of social science for guidance of social policy. Cameralism aimed at the subordination of everything in society to the problems of the state. *The Meaning of Social Science* attacked the kind of departmentalization of social science which leads to narrowness and incomplete analyses of social situations. Here Small maintained that the knowledge of society must be unified as well as specialized, for it is necessary to take account of the interaction of phases of social life upon one another. The aim of social science is to arrive at a valid appraisal of human values. In *Between Eras: From Capitalism to Democracy,* Small criticized conventional capitalism of his day from the point of view of nature and labor as the ultimate factors in productivity. He thought profit economics was ethically bankrupt, as evident in its waste, inefficiency, and injustice. The inheritance of immense fortunes was attacked, as was the conception of unlimited private property. In place of the profit economy, Small urged production for human service. Inheritance should be limited, and labor given a greater share in industrial enterprise and social policy.

Origins of Sociology traces the various phases of the development of social science in terms of the successive gains transmitted from field to field. From the Savigny–Thibaut controversy came a heightened concept of continuity in social and historical process; Eichhorn added the concept of the complexity of social and historical factors; Niebuhr advanced the scientific evaluation of historical sources; Leopold von Ranke raised the level of adequacy in documentation of historical generalizations; the organization of source and archival material was improved by Pertz, Waitz, and the editors of the *Monumenta;* cameralism proposed objectivism in social science, as did the systematic economics of Smith and the classical school; Wilhelm Roscher promoted comparative economic history; Karl Menger advanced the psychological point of view in economics; Karl Knies advocated the study of ethical factors in economic science; and Schäffle and Schmoller promoted the ameliorative point of view in economic and political activity. These and other influences contributed finally to the rise of the sociological movement.

In *General Sociology* (1905), Small attempted both to summarize the main development of sociological theory and to present his own. Sociology, he thought, had gone through three major stages, represented respectively by Spencer, Schäffle, and Ratzenhofer. In his opinion, the ideas of Spencer,

[35] *Adam Smith and Modern Sociology,* p. 1.

and Schäffle had served their purpose and had been by-passed. "We have
. . . taken brief account of two conceptions which have been prominent in
the history of sociological theory: the conception of social structure, and
that of social functions. These concepts have been, in turn, centers for
ambitious sociological systems. Those systems are no longer regarded as
serious competitors for leadership in social theory. They have served their
day. . . ." [36] The time had come, Small maintained, to drop analogical
procedures and approach scientific precision. "We want an explanation, not
of men's crystalline formations, not of their machineries, not of their institutional remains. We want an account of the intimate process of their lives,
in terms that will assign their actual meaning and value to the chief and
subordinate factors concerned in the process. . . . No larger contribution to
explanation in this spirit has been made than that of Ratzenhofer." [37]
Small then took over the major bulk of Ratzenhofer's sociological theory,
reformulating it wherever necessary to fit his own requirements. For our
purposes, it is important to note the clear demand for positivism and realism.

For his own purposes, Small developed a framework of ideas around formulations very similar to those of Ratzenhofer. The central concept of the
system is "social process." Society as interaction occurs against a background
of conditions, ultimately those supplied by nature. At one level, human
activity is devoted to the constant business of staying alive. Most of the
goods produced by human economic activity are not in great supply. "Put
an effective blockade around England for three months, and Westminster
Hall and St. Paul's Cathedral would look like grinning skulls in a graveyard." [38] Life is an affair of adjustment to "material, matter-of-fact, in-
exorable nature." The various materialistic and mechanical theories of human history have attempted to find the secret of human development in the
inevitable operations of nature. They are not completely wrong. They have
merely overstated the absolute value of one fundamental factor. If nature
represents one ultimate condition of the social process, biology is another.
For Small, the same forces that reduced the universe from formless star
dust to an organized system of process are still the undercurrents of every
human life.

> Through the facts of food and sex, for example, we are indissolubly united,
> from the past and toward the future, with the ceaseless operation of the
> physical forces that have laid course after course in the structure of the
> worlds, and of the organic products upon the world. We may never unravel
> the methods of the physical forces that make the ultimate conditions of
> life, but we may know them as facts, and may make somewhat appropriate
> accounts of them in our calculations of the possibilities of practical con-
> duct.[39]

[36] *General Sociology*, p. 176. Small draws a distinction between subtypes of organismic
positivism which was not found useful in the present account. In one basic respect,
it is necessary to agree with Small: by this time positivistic organicism had seen its
best days, and the future of sociological theory lay elsewhere.
[37] *Ibid.*, p. 188.   [38] *Ibid.*, p. 407.   [39] *Ibid.*, p. 414.

The requirements and possibilities of what will occur in the social process are set by the properties of the natural environment and biology. The social process as a conflict and coordination of forces is already established by environment and heredity. As objects of scientific study, however, biology and the natural environment are, according to Small, the subject matter of other sciences. The social sciences have as their object of study the manifestation, operation, and causes of forces as they appear in the social sphere. Here science requires an ultimate unit of study just as it does in other sciences. The notion of interests serves the same purpose in sociology as the notion of atoms in physical science. They are the last elements to which we can reduce the actions of human beings. "*Interests are the simplest modes of motion which we can trace in the conduct of human beings.*" [40] The most basic of interests — the health interest — is shared by men with animals and plants. It is common to all forms of vital energy. It typifies all bodily organisms and has a specific content in a clover plant, an oak tree, an insect, and a man. The biological study of man does not advance beyond the study of this interest. To the psychologist, however, the individual is interesting as a center of knowing, feeling, and willing. To a sociologist he begins to be interesting as knowing, feeling, and willing *something*. Throughout, the idea of "interest" provides the central clue. "*An interest is an unsatisfied capacity, corresponding to an unrealized condition, and it is predisposition to such rearrangement as would tend to realize the indicated condition. . . .* Human interests . . . are the ultimate terms of calculation in sociology. *The whole life-process, so far as we know it, whether viewed in its social phase, is at last the process of developing, adjusting, and satisfying interests. . . .* We have several times named the most general classes of interests which we find serviceable in sociology, viz.: *health, wealth, sociability, knowledge, beauty,* and *rightness.*" [41] And sociology becomes first of all a technique for detecting, classifying, criticizing, measuring, and correlating human interests with reference to their past and present manifestations and their indications for the future.

A general property of conflict theory is its tendency either to ignore or to play down the importance of the individual. Bagehot derived the stability of society in large measure from the sheep-like behavior of the great mass of individuals. Gumplowicz not only agreed but added ramifications of his own, maintaining that the individual is a prism of social influence, and that the group rather than the individual thinks. One of the special properties of Small's re-stylization of conflict theory is its attempt to take the individual into account. Small tried to accommodate insights taken from Baldwin's *Social and Ethical Interpretations,* Cooley's *Human Nature and the Social Order,* and Royce's *The World and the Individual.* In Small's opinion, sociology has reached a stage where it cannot get along without a concept of the individual, but has no completely adequate concept of him.

[40] *Ibid.,* p. 426.
[41] *Ibid.,* pp. 433–435.

Today's sociology is still struggling with the preposterous initial fact of the individual. He is the only possible social unit, and he is no longer a thinkable possibility. He is the only real presence, and he is never present. Whether we are near to resolution of the paradox or not, there is hardly more visible consensus about the relation of the individual to the whole than at any earlier period. Indeed, the minds of more people than ever before are puzzled by the seeming antinomy between the individual and the whole. . . . *the human individual is a variation of the sixfold interests, i.e., desires (subjective); and . . . the conditions of human satisfaction consists of variations of the sixfold interests, i.e., wants (objective).*[42]

The sociologist, Small maintains, takes the individual for granted, and pursues the explanation of associations. Everything that occurs in association is a function of elements in individuals in reaction to variable factors in the external conditions making up the individual's environment. Quite consistent with the idea that the basic property of man as moved by interests which are the same in all is Small's assertion that there is or can be an equality of men. One of the most fundamental problems, in view of the concept of common human nature, is how this human nature and society are differentiated. Small introduced a number of basic concepts to account for such variations. These include (1) spiritual environment, (2) contacts, (3) differentiation, (4) group, (5) conflict, and (6) social situation. One of the reasons why individuals and groups vary is that man responds to a *milieu* or spiritual environment. "Just as every portion of space has its physical atmosphere, so every portion of society has its thought-atmosphere. This mental envelope largely explains habit and custom, impulse and endeavor, power and limitation, with the society."[43] The basic incidents in the life of the human individual are contacts between individuals and with physical conditions. Contact is important in accounting for differences in kinds of character and of social life, since they are infinitely varied from case to case. The social process is varied, moreover, because as part of the world process it is a collection of historically distinct combinations. In the first instance, the interests are differentiated, and with this follows a corresponding differentiation of social structures and functions. The term "group" refers to any larger or smaller number of persons between whom relations are discovered such that they must be thought of together. A family, a mob, a picnic party, a trade union, a city precinct, a corporation, a state, a nation, all are illustrations. Individuals nowhere live in utter isolation. The moment they begin to adjust to a condition outside society, they die. It is critical to know to what groups a person belongs, the interests of the groups, and the means they use to promote their interests. Social life cannot be explained without this knowledge. Social life varies as an endless formation and destruction of groups. The social process is a perpetual action and reaction between group-based interests. "Conflict" is the basic and universal social process. Social life will be structured locally

---

[42] *Ibid.*, pp. 443, 445.   [43] *Ibid.*, p. 486.

by whatever particular conflicts the individual faces. Finally, social variation is due to "social situation"; that is, to "any portion of experience brought to attention as a point in time or space at which a tension of social forces is present." [44]

The social process assumes a variety of forms in terms of spiritual environment or *milieu*, contacts, differentiation, groups, conflict, and social situation. The social process *"is a collection of occurrences, each of which has a meaning for every other, the whole of which constitutes some sort of becoming."* [45] The social process always realizes some essential human interests. Some specific wants are present. When many persons are involved, there may be several classes of wants with relations between them. When these wants are realized, they leave a situation different from the one before the process occurred. "If we are justified in drawing any general conclusions . . . from human experience . . . it is safe to say that the social process tends to put an increasing proportion of individuals in possession of all the goods which have been discovered by the experience of humanity as a whole, and that all social programs should be thought out with a view to promotion of this tendency." [46] The concepts "social structure," "social function," and "social environment" have come into being for dealing with specialized aspects of the social process. *Social structure* is useful in accounting for the formation of elements in an activity. Whenever men act together some arrangement between persons emerges. Superiority and subordination, for example, are universal. Social structure refers to such instrumental arrangements. *Social function* refers to the various kinds of work done by any social group in the course of the social process. This is determined by group structure.

Herbert Spencer had divided institutions into six types: domestic, ceremonial, political, ecclesiastical, professional, and industrial. Every society, however primitive, has at least minute portions of these. But institutions, to Small, are only the shell of social activities. The analysis of them is preliminary to the study of actual working social arrangements and the social content they actually serve. According to Small, the ideas of "social forces" and "social ends" are also useful for analyzing the workings of the social process, but greatest interest attaches to his idea of "subjective environment." "Every individual begins to be a repository of feelings, notions, ideas, prejudices, beliefs, theories, purposes, so soon as he begins to be conscious." [47] Subjective environment refers to "a state of mind primarily in the individuals, and then diffused throughout the association, consisting first of perception that the group exists." [48] *Esprit de corps*, patriotism, ethnocentrism, all represent expressions of subjective environment.

Small sums up his whole position compactly. "The social fact is the incessant reaction between three chief factors: (1) nature; (2) individuals; (3) institutions, or modes of association between individuals. Each of these

[44] *Ibid.*, p. 500. [45] *Ibid.*, p. 513. [46] *Ibid.*, p. 522.
[47] *Ibid.*, p. 544. [48] *Ibid.*, p. 548.

factors is composite, but at this point we may disregard that phase of the situation. *The social process is the incessant evolution of persons through the evolution of institutions, which evolve completer persons, who evolve completer institutions, and so on beyond any limit that we can fix.*" [49]

Franz Oppenheimer

The most prominent European conflict theorist of the recent past is Franz Oppenheimer (1864–1943). The son of a poor but liberal Jewish rabbi of Berlin, Oppenheimer had little chance under normal circumstances of becoming a professor. He studied medicine, and became a practicing physician in Berlin. His practice led him to an awareness of the correlation between the problems of disease and moral decline, between housing and ground rent. He began to read the socio-economic literature on such problems. A high level of ability and personal courage is quite apparent in his actions. He became so interested in his studies that he abandoned medical practice, and supported his wife and child by writing articles. In 1909 he became *Privatdozent* of economics at the University of Berlin. As an unsalaried lecturer receiving only students' fees, he was still required to support himself by his publications. Oppenheimer was employed as economic adviser by the war office during World War I. In 1919 he became *Ordinarius* (the German equivalent of a full professor), teaching economic theory and sociology at the University of Frankfurt. Ill health caused him to retire in 1919. He took up residence in a rural settlement cooperative that he had founded before World War I. After 1933 he was guest lecturer in Paris, Palestine, and the United States. He died in Los Angeles in 1943.[50]

Society was conceived by Oppenheimer as an organism with an ascertainable "normal" state. This state is one organized and dominated by justice. Just as there are factors in human nature leading to conflict and mutual help, so there is a sense of justice originating in the pressure brought to bear on conflicting persons or groups by third persons or groups. Justice represents the limitation of the sphere of freedom of an individual made

[49] *Ibid.*, p. 552.
[50] Very little of Oppenheimer's work in German has been translated into English. *Der Staat* (Frankfurt am Main: Rütten & Loening, 1907; 4th ed., Stuttgart: G. Fischer, 1954) was translated by John M. Gitterman as *The State* (Indianapolis: Bobbs-Merrill, 1914; 2d American ed., New York: Vanguard Press, 1928). Other sociologically important works, not available in translation, are: *Die Siedlungsgenossenschaft* ["The Communal Association"] (Leipzig: Duncker, 1896; 3d ed., Jena: G. Fischer, 1922); *System der Soziologie*, 4 vols. (Jena: G. Fischer, 1922–33); and *Die Volkswirtschaftslehre der Gegenwart in Selbstdarstellung* ["The Self-Portrait of the Present System of Political Economy"] (Leipzig: F. Meiner, 1929). Biographical details may be found in *Mein Wissenschaftlicher Weg* ["My Scientific Course"] (Leipzig: F. Meiner, 1921). Reviews of Oppenheimer's theories and influence appear in Harry Elmer Barnes and Howard Becker, *Social Thought from Lore to Science* (2d ed.; Washington, D.C.: Harren Press, 1952), pp. 712–726; and Paul Honigsheim, "The Sociological Doctrines of Franz Oppenheimer: An Agrarian Philosophy of History and Social Reform," in H. E. Barnes (ed.), *An Introduction to the History of Sociology* (Chicago: University of Chicago Press, 1948), pp. 332–352.

necessary in practice by the reciprocal interaction of individuals. Practically, justice always represents a limitation of the sphere of individual freedom. In every society deviations from the norm are due to social, economic, or political factors. Anthropology, history, psychology, and sociology study these factors.

Among the fundamental laws of sociology is that of systematic uniformity in the origin and development of state, the law, social classes, property, monopoly, and surplus value. In working out this law, Oppenheimer distinguishes between economic and political means. Economic activity consists in the satisfaction of economic needs through economic means, which include some of the means of achieving a livelihood. Political means such as conquest and subjugation may also appear. Primitive economic inequality arose out of the employment of political means for economic ends: the ruling group introduced uniform institutionalization to make permanent their favorable situation, and the state and a system of law were thereby established. One of the first of such means was the introduction of a land monopoly — the first of all monopolies and basic to class stratification and surplus value. From a monopoly of land there developed a monopoly of tribute.

A second group of laws concerns the uniformity governing subjective evaluation of economic groups. The main one of concern to Oppenheimer states that satisfaction derived from consumption decreases with each additional unit of a given commodity until it reaches zero. Commodities are valued in terms of the last smallest unit in the available supply. Applied to the wages of the worker, "marginal utility" means that the amount of wage is determined by the value attached to the least useful worker whom it is necessary to employ in production.

The law of the ratio between quantity of emigrating rural population and the distribution of property arises in the following manner. The quantity of emigrating rural population is in direct proportion to the amount of land owned by the landed gentry and organized in estates. It is in inverse proportion to the land owned by peasants and worked by the peasant in his family. When population is increasing, the profit rate of industrial products rises and that of agricultural products falls. This trend is compensated for by the immigration of the rural population to the city, intensifying competition and bringing prices of industrial products down. Meanwhile, the prices of rural products go up because of the increased demand for them. This is modified by peasant properties, however, for the surplus income created by the rise of the prices of primary products is distributed among the entire population. Also, one could expect rural workers to raise their demands for higher wages. But where there are larger estates, land monopolies are powerful enough to prevent a rise in the wages of the agricultural workers. Then the advantage in the decrease in prices of industrial products accrues to the holders of large estates.[51]

[51] This is no place to trace all the virtues and limitations of Oppenheimer's particular attempt to account for the influence of the rise of capitalism on the problems of agricul-

These laws explain the increase in supply of urban factory workers and the decline in wages of the group. They also account for emigration from countries where large estates are the predominant form of rural property. The lowest level of wages paid to the lowest type of agricultural worker determines the amount of existing supply of urban factory workers and is the cause of the excess of supply over demand. It is the cause of the low wages paid to the urban factory workers in industrial Europe and elsewhere. Thus, there are ultimate relations between political means and the absence of justice in the modern world. The low wage level of the agricultural workers on the feudal estates of eastern Europe is a product of the land monopoly. The land monopoly is the ultimate cause of the existence of a proletariat and the absence of justice in the world. And by the first group of Oppenheimer's laws, land monopolies were basically established by political means or force.

Oppenheimer's general sociology was an extension of the principles which he first developed in *The State,* a brilliant synthesis of European conflict sociology. In Oppenheimer's opinion, the conventional theories of the state from Plato to Rousseau and Karl Marx give no insight into its genesis, essence, or purpose. He maintains that "every state in history was or is *a state of classes,* a polity of superior and inferior social groups, based upon distinctions either of rank or of property." [52] The Marxian theory that the state arose by way of an internal differentiation of classes is a fairy tale. Oppenheimer maintains that at the time of the migration of barbarians (350–750 A.D.) in Europe, an able-bodied man was able to cultivate about twenty acres of land (at least one-third of which was uncultivated in any given year). What remained was sufficient to feed immense German families. Marxian theory holds that when the available space was fully taken up in the natural increase of families, a restructuring of families had to occur. But if we assume that it requires about twenty-five acres to support a family of five persons, Germany, with an agricultural area of about 84,000,000 acres, would still not have reached a stage where the differentiation of classes would begin. Thus Oppenheimer maintains that purely economic and demographic causes have not brought about the differentiation of classes and the growth of a propertyless laboring class. Hence, if it is true that the class state can arise only where all the fertile acreage has been completely taken up, then it follows from the historical fact that class states *have* arisen in territories where the population was not large enough to account for all the fertile acreage that this pre-emption of land must be *political,* rather than strictly economic. "Therefore the State, as a class-state, can have originated in no other way than through conquest and subjugation." [53] In its genesis

---

ture, labor supply, and the like. Oppenheimer's arguments are outlined here merely to call attention to the fact that among the conflicts he thought to be central to the modern world are those between workers and capitalists. His basic theme is that the capitalists, both urban and rural, are usually exploiters.
[52] *The State*, p. 5.
[53] *Ibid.*, p. 14.

and essence, the state is a social institution forced by a victorious group on a defeated group, and its original purpose was the economic exploitation of the vanquished by the victors.

The state develops in distinct stages. (1) There is first robbery, killing, and border fights, marked by killing of men, carrying off of women and children, looting of herds, and burning of dwellings. During this period, the differentiation of peasant and herdsman grows increasingly clear. (2) This gives way to a second stage in which the peasant has accepted his fate and ceased resistance. The herdsman, having discovered that a fruit tree cut down will not bear and that a murdered peasant does not work, lets the tree stand and the peasant live. He kills a few peasants and burns enough fields to enforce wholesome respect and to break isolated resistance. Like the bee-keeper, he leaves the bees enough honey to carry them through the winter. The herdsman has learned to "capitalize." The peasant has obtained a semblance of *right* to the bare necessities of life. It becomes wrong to kill an unresisting man or strip him of everything. This is the germ of the process of external amalgamation out of which small hordes are formed into nations. (3) A third stage arrives when the "surplus" obtained by the peasantry is regularly brought by the peasant to the tents of the herdsmen as "tribute." The strains of the former method of taxation are mitigated. Fewer men are knocked on the head, fewer women violated, fewer farmhouses burned. The herdsmen now have full time and energy free for the "extension of the works" — subjugating other peasants. (4) In the next stage there is the union on one territory of both ethnic groups. This is significant, since no jural definition of a state can be arrived at without the concept of a state territory. Such territorial union may be forced by foreign influence (strong hordes from the outside) or economic pressure. Perhaps it has become necessary for the conquering group to protect subjects by keeping a levy of young warriors in the neighborhood. At this stage, there is physical presence of the two groups in the same place, but not a single system of institutions. From particular centers the lords control their "subjects," mainly for the purpose of gathering their tribute, and pay no attention to them in other respects. They let them administer their affairs, carry on their religious worship, settle their disputes, and adjust their methods of internal economy in their own way. Their autochthonous constitution, their local officials, are, in fact, not interfered with. However, the logic of events quickly presses beyond this, for (5) quarrels arise between neighboring villages or classes which the lords cannot permit, since service would be impaired. The lords assume the right to arbitrate. And, step by step, movement is toward a new internal unity, (6) the development of "nationality." In customs, habits, speech, and worship the groups begin to amalgamate. In almost all cases the master class picks the handsomest virgins from the subject races for concubines. A race of bastards develops, which is sometimes taken into the ruling class. With the blood of the masters in their veins, they become the born leaders of the subject race.

George Bryan Vold

Perhaps the foremost conflict theorist in present-day North America is George Bryan Vold (1896–   ), who was born at Platte, South Dakota. Vold took his M.A. degree at the University of Chicago (1924), and his Ph.D. degree at the University of Minnesota (1930). He was assistant professor of sociology at Macalester College from 1924 to 1927, joining the faculty at the University of Minnesota in 1927. He has been a full professor since 1937. In 1946–1947 he was with the United States Occupation Forces in Japan as a consultant on criminological problems for the occupation army. For years Vold has taught a course in the sociology of conflict in the classic tradition of Albion Small. Many of his reflections have been embodied in *Theoretical Criminology*,[54] his most important publication to date. Uniquely among the current theorists, Vold formulated the problem of crime in a manner leading directly into conflict theory.

> If criminal behavior, by and large, is the normal behavior of normally responding individuals in situations defined as undesirable, illegal, and therefore criminal, then the basic problem is one of social and political organizations and the established values or definitions of what may, and may not, be permitted. Crime, in this sense, is political behavior and the criminal becomes in fact a member of a "minority group" without sufficient public support to dominate and control the police power of the state. Criminals often become involved in the serious business of politics and the control of the police power of the state for their own protection. This is "pressure politics" in the interest of organized crime.[55]

The basic suppositions of conflict theory, according to Vold, are that man is a "group-involved being whose life is . . . a product of group associations." It is assumed, furthermore, that society is "a congeries of groups held together in a shifting but dynamic equilibrium of opposing group interests and efforts." The social process consists of the interaction of groups "in an immediate and dynamically maintained equilibrium." The end result is "a more or less continuous struggle to maintain, or to defend, the place of one's own group in the interaction of groups." "Conflict is . . . one of the principal and essential social processes upon which the continuing on-going of society depends." [56]

The relative stability of conflicting group forces in uneasy equilibrium is social order or organization. The constantly changing adjustment of group interests of varying strength is the essence of society as a functional reality. Groups are formed where members have common interests and common needs that can be most effectively pursued through collective action. New groups, thus, are continually formed as new interests arise, while existing groups weaken and vanish. Whenever group interests overlap or encroach on one another, they become competitive. Conflict arises when they cannot

---

[54] George B. Vold, *Theoretical Criminology* (New York: Oxford University Press, 1958).
[55] *Ibid.*, p. 202.   [56] *Ibid.*, p. 204.

be kept out of each other's territory. A group must be constantly alert to defend itself, for one of its basic objectives is to prevent displacement. Only where this possibility of displacement appears is there the risk of conflict between nations, races, religions, economic systems, labor unions, or any type of organization.

For the members of the group, participation in group activity and in its values and dis-values, makes the individual into a self-conscious person. Group identification and loyalty become intense psychological actualities, of a transrational nature. Conflict between groups tends to intensify these loyalties to highest degree, developing *esprit de corps* or morale. The individual is most loyal to the group he has to die for. Patriotic feeling runs high in wartime, for example. The finest ideals of character are products of group conflict, where individuals serve the common purpose and not merely selfish ends. The consequences of group conflict are complete destruction of the other side, or flight of one's own, or some compromise between. Generally there is no compromise with a position of weakness. As a rule, the weak are overwhelmed, subjugated, and integrated with the victors in a subordinate capacity.

From this formulation of conflict, Vold approaches other sociological areas. Politics, for example, "as it flourishes in a democracy, is primarily a matter of finding practical compromises between antagonistic groups in the community at large." The law is a formula expressing a ratio of strength. "Thus the familiar cry, 'there ought to be a law,' . . . to suppress the undesirable is understandable as the natural recourse of one side or the other in a conflict situation." [57] And quite in accord with this modernized "might makes right" formula, Vold assures the reader that the law always asserts the dominant interests. The application to crime of this theory is direct. "The whole political process of law making, law breaking, and law enforcement becomes a direct reflection of . . . fundamental conflicts between interest groups and their . . . struggles for the control of the police power of the state." [58] The winners of the struggle decide "who is likely to be involved in violation of the law." The principle of compromise from positions of strength is said to operate at every stage of the conflict process from bargaining in the legislature to get the law passed, to bargaining between prosecution and defense in the conduct of the trial, to bargaining between prison official and inmate, parole and parole agent. From this standpoint, Vold urges, criminological theory is merely a special application of the general theory of conflict. There may, of course, be criminal behavior arising from defectiveness or abnormality or even impulsive irrational acts. Much "criminality" represents the normal, natural response of normal, natural human beings struggling in natural situations for the maintenance of the way of life to which they stand committed. The behavior of some individuals is incidental to the course of action required for the group to maintain its place in the struggle with other groups.

[57] *Ibid.*, p. 208.   [58] *Ibid.*, pp. 208–209.

To phrase Vold's theory of crime in a sentence: so far as criminal acts do not arise from defectiveness, abnormality, or irrational impulse, so far, in short, as they are genuinely "social," they are best explained by conflict theory.

Theoretical Criminology, if one may hazard a prediction, should live as a classic of contemporary conservatism. Superficially, it is a review of criminological theory; actually, the discussions of crime are merely illustrative material. The book represents a theoretical interpretation which quite obviously could apply to any area of social life. Classical conflict theory in Vold's formulation is reduced to an economical model: individuality is played down in a worthy tradition extending in western thought from Polybius to Hobbes and in sociological conflict theory from Bagehot to Oppenheimer — the sheep-like character of the individual is emphasized. The primary flow of influence is from group to personality, not otherwise. The *social process* stands in contrast to the *socialization process*. Socialization is the molding of the individual into the image of the group, committing him to it, blowing up the thin bag of his ego with group pretensions and ethnocentrism until he finds the highest of all individual values in his patriotic readiness to die for the group. It is noted that some kinds of crime represent, essentially, failures of socialization either because the individual is biologically defective, pathological, or socially substandard — impulsively unable to mold his actions to social requirements. These are among the least important forms of crime. The *social process* in contrast to the *socialization process* is the contact of groups — conceived of as an endlessly changing kaleidoscope of force-ratios. The laws are peace treaties intended to secure the permanent ascendancy of the victors in the social process, preferably in "hereditary" form, holding for all generations. In all these respects, *Theoretical Criminology* is a synthesis of the classic conflict tradition.

A good deal of crime is seen not as failure in the socialization process but as incidents of the *social process*. This is in accord with the view that individual behavior is primarily "sheep-like"; hence, if crime amounts to anything at all, it will be group behavior. It is argued, in fact, that crime is "minority group behavior." The evidence of a great number of students of crime and delinquency — Clifford Shaw and Henry McKay, Sheldon and Eleanor Glueck, William F. Whyte, Solomon Kobrin, Frederic Thrasher, Herbert Asbury — is cited to the point that most crime is committed in association with others. Vold's theme is then expanded to include the "fact" that much criminal behavior is political in nature. It is maintained that a successful revolution makes criminals out of government officials previously in power; an unsuccessful revolution makes its leaders traitors and subject to exile or execution. Moreover, "murder, sabotage, seizure of private property, and many other offences against the ordinary criminal code are commonplace accompaniments of political rebellion." [59] Not quite as extreme, but of the same type, are the personal dishonesty, bribery, perjury,

[59] *Ibid.*, pp. 214–215.

burglary, and theft occurring in the course of winning political elections and keeping political control. To this configuration belong all the incidents in the clash of interests of company management and labor unions. So, too, in this category are the "numerous kinds of crimes" which "result from the clashes incidental to the attempt to change, or to upset the caste system of racial segregation in various parts of the world, notably in the United States and in the Union of South Africa." [60]

It is only a step from the occurrence of all sorts of so-called crimes in connection with normal group process to the study of "The Organization of Criminals for Profit and Power." Vold observes that there is "general acceptance of the idea of crime as an organized business, conducted for business profit." [61] It is maintained that the incentive in normal society to earn a living, to improve one's profits, and to combine with others if profits are thereby increased, is the key to understanding the organization in the field of crime. Crime is transformed into syndicates or combinations only partly outside the law. A terminology for crime partnerships, groups, and institutional arrangements appear with teams, mobs, fixes, and fences. Profits are computed in some rational "pay-off." The criminal syndicate may become a relatively stable business organization which organizes its rackets and pins down its flanks through political graft and corruption. Here as elsewhere, lucrative opportunities encourage rivals, teams, mobs, gangs, or syndicates, resulting in the lurid phenomena of underworld competition and gang war. Finally, the relations of underworld and upperworld tend to be integrated. "From the standpoint of the problem of control, organized crime seems to be more significantly affected by economic facts of supply and demand, and the fads and foibles in consumer habits, than by much legislation and sporadic attempts at formal control." [62]

Vold not only brings an extensive amount of evidence into an able synthesis in terms of group conflict, but in deliberate, carefully reasoned steps sets about to annihilate opposed interpretations. The idea that crime does not necessarily arise because of some atavistic throwback to an earlier evolutionary state, or because of mental or biological deficiency, or psychological abnormality, is not new. The idea that it is socially caused had received clear formulation by Gabriel Tarde among others. It has been generally recognized that the major modern heir to Tarde's approach is the late Edwin H. Sutherland's "differential association" theory of criminality. The commonsense element lying back of this view is that if criminality is not primarily caused by biological deficiency, psychological abnormality, or some other such thing, it must be "social" — specifically, it must be a special category of learned behavior. Since most learning takes place in association with others, Sutherland argues that criminal learning must be the product of "differential association": a person learns to be a thief in much the same way that he learns to be a Methodist or a Roman Catholic. Since, however, not everyone who associates with criminals becomes a criminal, the attempt is made

[60] *Ibid.*, p. 217.   [61] *Ibid.*, p. 220.   [62] *Ibid.*, p. 242.

to tighten up the idea by adding that *frequency* and *consistency* of association are important. Systematic criminal behavior occurs when criminality
becomes a way of life like that of the professional thief, the circus grafter,
the card sharp. A major application of these ideas was Sutherland's extension of the general theory to the special case of white collar crime.[63]

Vold's general argument against the "differential association" theory is that
it is so general and non-specific that it "reaches far into the margin of un-
reality." [64] Crime is a *mélange* of behavior, having in common only the fact
that it is "in violation of the criminal law." The theory of differential association is undiscriminating. This fact should not obscure the significant
point that, *at this very general level,* Vold and Sutherland agree on essentials.
Most significant types of criminal behavior are of the same type as non-
criminal behavior. The critical difference between the two thinkers emerges
over Sutherland's *White Collar Crime.*

Barnes and Teeters, in *New Horizons in Criminology,*[65] described a large
variety of commercial transactions of questionable ethics as "white collar
crime," and placed them in the same context as racketeering and organized
crime. Sutherland's interest in crimes of the well-to-do was life-long. The full
fruit of his theories appeared in the 1949 volume. He urged that the conception of the criminal as an economically underprivileged lower-class person is
false. Even the robber barons of the early period — Ivar Kreuger, William
Whitney, Samuel Insull, Albert B. Fall, Harry Sinclair — show that this is
not the case. White collar criminality occurs as misrepresentation in financial
statements of corporations, manipulations of the stock exchange, bribery of
public officials, misleading advertising and salesmanship, embezzlement and
misuse of trust funds, dishonest bankruptcies. Evidences of a similar type
were assembled by Marshall Clinard, in his study of the black market,[66]
for violations by reputable businessmen of the government's rationing and
price control program in World War II. Sutherland made the most able
analysis of the idea. Citing violations of the law on the part of seventy major
American corporations, Sutherland argued that they should be treated as
crimes, because they were recognized in the law as injurious to the public,
there were legal sanctions against such violations, and the behavior involved
was willful or intentional rather than accidental.

At first blush, the theories of Sutherland and Vold might seem to be
identical: both treat crime as social, both treat criminal and non-criminal
behavior as arising in the same way; both extend the conception of criminal
behavior from acts of individuals to acts of complex organized groups.
Sutherland extends his concept of crime to acts of corporations, and Vold to
the incidents accompanying all group struggles and the organization paral-

[63] Edwin H. Sutherland, *White Collar Crime* (New York: Dryden, 1949).
[64] *Theoretical Criminology,* p. 199.
[65] Harry Elmer Barnes and Negley K. Teeters, *New Horizons in Criminology* (New York: Prentice-Hall, 1946; 2d ed., 1951).
[66] Marshall B. Clinard, *The Black Market: A Study of White Collar Crime* (New York: Rinehart, 1952).

leling and partly involving the upperworld by the underworld. Nevertheless, Vold finds Sutherland to be his most important opponent.

Vold's answer to Sutherland springs from the core of conflict theory. He
argues: "There is an obvious and basic incongruity involved in the proposition that a community's leaders and more responsible elements are also its
criminals." [67] Business leaders and corporation executives by and large play
important roles in civic and community affairs. More often than not they
constitute an important source of the imaginative leadership for community
enterprise of all kinds. The very fact of reputable community standing is
therefore one of the more confusing and inconsistent aspects of the concept
of "white collar crime." And quite succinctly to the point, he argues:
"The label results in good part from the semantic device of calling all
violations of law or regulations 'crime' and all the persons involved
'criminals.' " [68]

The peculiar properties of the conflict point of view could hardly be more
ingeniously contained in a single formula. The common property of crime is
found originally in the fact that it is a violation of the law. But law is a formula expressing a force-ratio of dominant to minority group. Do then all violations of the law constitute crimes? To maintain this, it is said, is a semantic
device. Violations of the law constitute crimes and the violators criminals
only if they belong to the minority group. Two major arguments are assembled in defense of this. Eighty-five per cent of the law violations in
America are traffic violations by average citizens, but this, it is said, does not
make their violations crime nor make them criminals. The second major
argument against treating violations of the law by "reputable sections of
society" as crimes is the unassailable integrity of Robert A. Taft of Ohio. "It
seems clear that the American effort at price control and rationing was
something less than completely successful . . . because a large and influential portion of the population simply did not believe in or accept as valid
any such conception of the proper role of government activity. Persons of the
caliber and character of the late Senator Robert A. Taft of Ohio may not
lightly be accused of having raised their voices in defense of crime and
criminal practices" [69]

The clinching argument against Sutherland has special interest, since it
sounds a basic theme in conflict theory as old as Sumner's "The Absurd
Effort to Make the World Over." Vold argues that Sutherland "was not
really seeking a reformation of criminological theory as much as he was
urging a reformation in the mores and culture of America so that violation
of laws regulating business transactions would be viewed as 'crime' rather
than a misconduct of a less serious sort." [70] When is a given act a crime,
since sometimes it is and sometimes it is not? It depends on whose ox is being
gored.

[67] *Theoretical Criminology*, p. 253.
[68] *Ibid.*, p. 254. [69] *Ibid.*, pp. 257–258. [70] *Ibid.*, p. 259.

Summary

No attempt has been made to cover all possible combinations of conflict theory. For example, Jacques Novicow (1849–1912) analyzed the concept of social conflict into four phases — physiological, economic, political, and intellectual. Benjamin Kidd (1858–1916) employed the idea to justify just about everything in the *status quo* as good because it has survived. Peter Kropotkin (1842–1921) introduced special considerations in his attempt to universalize mutual aid and cooperation to parallel universal conflict. And Thomas Henry Huxley (1825–1895) pursued social Darwinism into a series of social-ethical and cultural areas.

Generally the attempt has been made to trace conflict sociology as the second wave of sociological theory, arising in the same atmosphere as positivistic organicism. As the major failures of organicism became apparent, some modification of theory was inevitable. At the same time, the same general ideological demands which shaped positivistic organicism from the outside remained.

The first effect of the movement toward a new formation of theory was a return to the rich intellectual treasures of Western civilization. A stock of ideas was available, established by men of affairs of the past. In an atmosphere that demanded "realism," these were precisely the thinkers consulted. A brief sketch was made of the development of conflict theory in the West from the days of the Sophists, Epicureans, and Greek historians to the political writers from Machiavelli to Bodin and Hobbes, to the specialized form of economic conflict theory embodied in the works of the physiocrats and the classical economists.

It was noted that precisely because conflict theory comes from men who are close to actual affairs, re-enlistment in the social struggle is often invited. When this occurs, conflict theory is transformed into a conflict ideology and shaped to the special interests in the name of which it is designed. Two major forms of conflict ideology were sketched because of the number of problems they cast up for modern social science: Marxism and social Darwinism.

Conflict sociology, on the other hand, aspires to be an explanation rather than a social program. The development of modern sociological conflict theory has been traced from Walter Bagehot to George B. Vold. Its general properties may be seen throughout to be such as to satisfy the ideological requirements imposed on early sociology. Conflict theory was more empirically positivistic even than organismic positivism. At the same time, in somewhat more subtle fashion, it did not violate the need for a conservative position. By and large, sociological conflict theory has found its lodestar in stability. Precisely because of its acceptance of the universality of conflict, the vindication of society is found in achieved order.

The sociological gains as one moves from organismic positivism to conflict theory are immense. The conception of society as a big tame animal is abandoned. Analysis shifts to infinitely variable relations of groups. Grand schemes of evolution drop away; a whole range of processes takes their place. One cuts below the surface of institutional formulas to the stabilities of custom and the factors that may disrupt it. The problem of the interrelation of economic and other institutions is posed and, above all, the interrelation of political and other institutions. The problem of social class is formulated as are the problems of "ideology," the "sociology of law," and "political sociology." Even the problem of the social shaping of the individual has made its appearance.

There can be no doubt about the significance of the conflict theory of sociology as a step toward mature science. The subtitle to Part Three, "The Paradox of Maturity," was phrased, however, to call attention to the ideological significance of the early forms of sociological conflict theory — the last link to ideology before sociology became a fully autonomous discipline. The conflict theorists were more realistic than their organismic predecessors and colleagues. But if they were a bit less hysterical about it, they shared their conservatism. The ideological formula that sociological conflict theory supplied its adherents was precisely this — the paradox of maturity: "If you know enough to carry out a reform, you know better."

SELECTED BIBLIOGRAPHY

BAGEHOT, WALTER, *Physics and Politics*. Introduction by Jacques Barzun. New York: Alfred A. Knopf, 1948.

GUMPLOWICZ, LUDWIG, *The Outlines of Sociology*. Translated by Frederick W. Moore. Philadelphia: American Academy of Political and Social Science, 1899.

HEADLEY, FREDERICK W., *Darwinism and Modern Socialism*. London: Methuen, 1909.

KELLER, ALBERT G., *Reminiscences of William Graham Sumner*. New Haven, Conn.: Yale University Press, 1933.

KIDD, BENJAMIN, *Principles of Western Civilisation*. New York: Macmillan, 1902.

LIPPERT, JULIUS, *The Evolution of Culture*. Translated by George Peter Murdock. New York: Macmillan, 1931.

OPPENHEIMER, FRANZ, *The State*. Second American edition. Translated by John M. Gitterman. New York: Vanguard Press, 1928.

RATZENHOFER, GUSTAV, *Die sociologische Erkenntnis*. Leipzig: F. A. Brockhaus, 1898.

SMALL, ALBION, *General Sociology: An Exposition of the Main Development in Sociological Theory from Spencer to Ratzenhofer*. Chicago: University of Chicago Press, 1925.

SUMNER, WILLIAM GRAHAM, *Folkways*. New York: Dover Publications, 1959.

VOLD, GEORGE B., *Theoretical Criminology*. New York: Oxford University Press, 1958.

PART FOUR

The Formal School of Sociological Theory

9

The Philosophical Foundations of Sociological Formalism

ORGANISMIC POSITIVISM AND CONFLICT SOCIOLOGY ARE THE TWO OLDEST schools of sociological theory. They both drew deeply on ancient philosophic traditions in Western thought. Both brought a new integration, a new emphasis, and a new direction to the analysis of society. Their exponents cut out a territory from the established disciplines. Positivistic organicism laid down the outlines of the new synthesis, and conflict theory brought a density, specificity, and maturity of outlook. These schools established sociology as a recognized field of scientific endeavor. Two of their representatives, Sumner and Small, established, respectively, the first course and the first department of sociology in North America. Small collaborated in writing the first college sociology textbook.

Sociology was carried by the early schools to a stage where it was ready to be professionalized and institutionalized; the process was beginning. Beside the teaching of courses and the establishment of sociology departments in the colleges and universities, sociology was soon to have a professional society and two professional journals: in the United States, Small was active in establishing the *American Journal of Sociology;* in France, Durkheim played an equivalent role in connection with *L'Année sociologique.*

In all areas, professionalization and institutionalization have had sweeping effects. A new professional role has appeared. Materials have been integrated and interpreted for teaching purposes. Scholars are now systematically trained in sociology, and a wider public is being given some systematic instruction in it. Its journals serve as a platform for the expression of its ideas. Its societies serve as a meeting point for its members. The discipline as a whole begins to acquire a recognized prestige among others. It competes in university and college settings for the presentation of its own viewpoint and for student enrollment.

The phenomena of professionalization and institutionalization affect the intellectual structure of the discipline. Materials are accumulated specifically for teaching purposes. A teacher feels that he must present other points of view than his own as a part of his "responsibility" toward his students and the field. The field must be justified in the context of other disciplines; at least equivalent standards must be established. Last but not least, the discipline cannot afford to be too imperialistic. Emphasis shifts from the enterprise of carving out new territories in the intellectual domain to holding and justifying the discipline and establishing boundaries around it. In sociology, the initial wave of this movement led to the development of a new school of sociological thought drawing upon different sources in the philosophic traditions of the West.

Older Forms of Philosophical Rationalism

Sociological formalism drew its primary inspiration from some special aspects of Western philosophical rationalism. Although the older forms of rationalism enter the picture only incidentally, they are significant for the understanding of those nineteenth-century forms which directly affected the social sciences. Groethuysen has called attention to the dual aspect of rationalism as explanation and action orientation. "Rationalism is a comprehensive expression applied to various theoretical and practical tendencies which aim to interpret the universe purely in terms of thought, or which aim to regulate individual and social life in accordance with the principles of reason and to eliminate as far as possible or to relegate to the background everything irrational." [1]

In philosophy, rationalism promoted the conception of a world forming a coherent whole analyzable by reason; in science, it promoted the concept of a logical and mathematical universe; in human conduct, it led to the conception of self-evident principles regulating behavior. Any given form of rationalism involves a conception of reason and of the irrational, but there are different forms of rationalism, depending on whether the irrational is located in nature or human nature.

---

[1] B. Groethuysen, "Rationalism," *Encyclopædia of the Social Sciences* (New York: Macmillan, 1931), Vol. 13, p. 113. Especially useful studies of rationalism are: W. E. H. Lecky, *History of the Rise and Influence of the Spirit of Rationalism in Europe* (London: 1865; New York: G. Braziller, 1955); Wilhelm Dilthey, *Weltanschauung und Analyse des Menschen seit Renaissance und Reformation*, Vol. 2 of *Gesammelte Schriften* (2d ed.; Stuttgart, Teubner, 1957); Ernst Cassirer, *The Philosophy of the Enlightenment*, tr. by Fritz C. A. Koelln and James P. Pettegrove (Princeton, N.J.: Princeton University Press, 1951); and A. W. Benn, *The History of English Rationalism in the Nineteenth Century* (London: Longmans, Green, 1906).

Greek rationalism conceived the irrational as manifest in the changeable world of sense. By contrast, the world of reason was populated by perfect, unchangeable forms. Aristotle directed his philosophy to the study of these permanent and unchangeable forms accessible to reason. His logic was intended to develop the relations between the forms, enabling man to achieve rational comprehension of them. Human and world reason were conceived as unified in divine reason. It was, however, not nearly as important as pure reason.

> The nature of the divine thought involves certain problems; for while thought is held to be the most divine of things observed by us, the question how it must be situated in order to have that character involves difficulties. For if it thinks of nothing, what is there here of dignity? It is just like one who sleeps. And if it thinks, but this depends on something else, then ... it cannot be the best substance, for it is through thinking that its value belongs to it.

> Evidently, then, it thinks of that which is most divine and precious, and it does not change; for change would be change for the worse, and this would be already a movement.

> Therefore it must be of itself that the divine thought thinks (since it is the most excellent of things), and its thinking is a thinking of thinking.[2]

The Greek forms of theoretical rationalism had little appeal for the Romans. What was of interest to them, however, was the fusion by the Stoics of rationalism and ethics. The school was founded by Zeno of Citium in Cyprus around 334–262 B.C. Of Semitic extraction, Zeno came to Athens in his twenty-second year and attached himself to the Cynic Crates. About 300 B.C. he became a teacher and philosopher. His studies were called Stoicism, from the *stoa*, or colonnaded porch, where the group met. The Stoics held that without knowledge true morality is impossible. They opposed the dualism of Plato, preferring the monistic materialism of Heraclitus and the atomists. They thought that dualism endangers the absolute rule of reason in human life, that everything obeys universal laws. Man by his reason is able to know these laws, and follow them consciously. In fact, through his rationality, man sees himself as part of the universe and pledged to work for the whole. He knows he is related to all rational beings in nature. They are similar to him with equal rights under the same law of nature and reason. In Stoicism, cosmopolitanism takes the place of politics.

These Stoic doctrines, transmitted to the Romans, became an important basis for rational legal action. As a city-state with dominion over an empire, Rome was placed in the position of having to legislate for the changing needs of a variety of peoples. Reason became for the Romans an instrument for the control of life. The theory that some moral and rational insights are basic to all human beings undergirded the idea of universal legislation as the basis of a political and social world order. These ideas were popular-

[2] Aristotle, *Metaphysics*, Book XII, Chapter 9.

ized by Cicero. With respect to the individual, the ideal arose of the wise man, guided by reason, with an independent and self-contained personality, preserving his equanimity in the face of all the trials of the world.

In the medieval world, this doctrine went into eclipse. St. Augustine held that the instincts and will had independent existence and were not controlled by the intellect and reason. As a result of his fall, man was unable to carry out decisions on the basis of rational insight. Hence, because of the impotence of human reason, man needed divine grace. Human life and the world constituted a meaningful whole, not in terms of man's reason but in terms of God's divine plan — a plan which could be known only through divine revelation. Thus the reason of antiquity was subordinated to a superrational, divinely inspired whole.

Modern Rationalism

In the Renaissance, in place of the medieval notion of divine providence, the idea of "fortune" again appears from antiquity. The casual impudence of Renaissance man toward what was formerly piously regarded as divine providence is visible in Machiavelli's formulations:

> I certainly think that it is better to be impetuous than cautious, for Fortune is a woman, and it is necessary, if you wish to master her, to conquer her by force; and it can be seen that she lets herself be overcome by the bold rather than those who proceed coldly. And therefore, like a woman, she is always a friend to the young, because they are less cautious, fiercer, and master her with greater audacity.[3]

In the Renaissance the individual again was left to his own devices. He looked for security in the development of his individual reason as the means of escaping the tumult of life.

Renaissance man was quite aware of the variety of things and events defying reduction to reason. There was an intensified sense of the individual, the particular, the unique. The problem of knowledge was reformulated. Its task was no longer one of reducing the variety of events to changeless forms but of discovering the rational principles for organizing and regulating the multiplicity of things. The ancient world was dominated by the dream of types, ideas, and forms. The new world was concerned with functions and laws. Not static conceptual classifications, but dynamic causal relations, typified the new. This was basic to the scientific rationalism of the seventeenth century, with its ideal of a mathematically understandable universe analyzable on the basis of a universal mathematical language. The ideal was formulated by Galileo. It was central to the philosophic systems of Descartes, Spinoza, and Leibnitz.

Parallel to this scientific rationalism was the rationalization of social life

[3] From Luigi Ricci's translation of *The Prince*, in Niccolò Machiavelli, *The Prince and the Discourses* (New York: Modern Library, 1948), p. 94.

on the basis of self-evident, universal principles. The state was conceived as the instrument of reason in the control of individual arbitrariness and irrational instincts, just as, it was assumed, a man's mind is in control of his material body. In the state, the various domains of human life were to be regulated by definite principles on the basis of the decisions of a single sovereign will embodying the so-called *raison d'état*. Such an equation of rationalism and political absolutism soon declined, however, as the middle classes learned to shape life on the basis of their own foresight. The fundamental differences between the rationalism of the seventeenth century and that of the eighteenth were correlated with a relocation of reason in individual activity and the fusion of the mental and the physical into a single unit. In the former period, reason was regarded as a compulsory force imposed from above, curbing the various irrational manifestations of individual life and coordinating them in such a way as to make social life possible; in the latter period, there was growing confidence in the rational endowments of every individual, endowments which could be developed through education and enlightenment. Of the contrast between the two centuries, Cassirer stated: "The difference in the mode of thinking does not mean a radical transformation; it amounts merely to a shifting of emphasis. This emphasis is constantly moving from the general to the particular, from principles to phenomena. But the basic assumption remains; that is the assumption that between the two realms of thought [the mental and the physical] there is no opposition, but rather complete correlation — except for Hume's skepticism which offers an entirely different approach." [4] Methodologically, the counterpart was a fusion of the logical and the empirical. Thus, the eighteenth century proposed to carry out an integration on three fronts: between the group and the individual; between the mental and physical in the individual; and between the logical and the empirical in the individual's methodology.

Descartes

The idea of a synthesis of logico-mathematical and empirical thought dominates the forms of rationalism important to the development of modern science since Galileo. Descartes, for instance, saw no inconsistency in applying the principle of doubt to knowledge as the device most quickly designed to uncover the immutable principles it contains. His aim was to arrive at those truths presented by the good sense found in all men. The mental operations giving certain knowledge were intuition and deduction — the direct perception of indubitable truths and the deduction of concepts from them. One could, therefore, build an absolutely certain structure of thought. Descartes' development of analytical geometry occurred in response to his assumption that the world could be mathematized.

Descartes presented a rationalism quite different from that of the Greeks, who conceived the world of the senses to be irrational, over and against the world of thought. True, Descartes wanted to start with intuition and work

[4] Ernst Cassirer, *The Philosophy of the Enlightenment*, p. 22.

with deduction, rather than rely on "the fluctuating testimony of the senses" or the "misleading judgment that proceeds from the blundering constructions of the imagination." [5] However, he posed no absolute antithesis between them; he did not conceive the purpose of reason to be the overcoming of the irrationality of the sensory world. Descartes could thus become a common starting point for either empiricism or further forms of rationalism. Later development in thought has a way of re-classifying its ancestors. In one respect, the philosophers who have come to be known as "empiricists" (Locke, Berkeley, and Hume) and those who are now thought of as "rationalists" (Descartes, Spinoza, Leibnitz) were similar: they both perceived a difference between logical and empirical knowledge, and both believed that these forms of knowledge would ultimately be brought into synthesis. They had different strategies for the solution of their problems, to be sure: the empiricists proposed to start with empirical facts and unify thought; the rationalists sought this unity by way of logical principles.

Both Descartes and Locke subscribed to the division of "primary" and "secondary" qualities. Descartes thought that sense knowledge was notoriously variable. He also thought that some forms of sense knowledge contain very real information about reality. Sense qualities were divided into "secondary," which to a large degree depend for their character on the mind itself, and "primary," which correspond directly to properties of nature. Our senses can deceive us about the smell or color of a thing, but they are very accurate about its extension and weight. It was not until the distinction between primary and secondary qualities collapsed that logical and empirical knowledge ended up in apparently irreconcilable spheres. Knowledge applying to reality had no certainty, and certain knowledge no application to reality. This was precisely what Immanuel Kant (1724–1804) thought had happened when Hume logically carried out the program of empiricism. He reported that Hume had awakened him from his dogmatic slumbers. To Kant, Hume's critique of the concepts of the "self," "God," and causality not only brought ethics and religion to a state of crisis but threatened the foundation of science itself.[6]

Kant's Rationalism

Kant's startled reaction to Hume can only be explained in terms of his rationalistic assumption. He had originally shared the idea of the ultimate unity of empirical and logical knowledge. The task of science was thought to be the attainment of knowledge at once logically certain and empirically accurate. Since the knowledge of science concerned causal laws, in Kant's view Hume had dissolved the very foundations of science itself by the acid of his wit. Kant's surprise at Hume's argument is a tribute to the clarity of his perception of the assumptions of rationalism and empiricism and his sensi-

5 René Descartes, *Selections* (New York: Scribner's, 1927), p. 46.
6 Immanuel Kant, *Critique of Pure Reason*, tr. by Norman Kemp Smith (New York: Macmillan, 1953).

tivity to the critical state to which they had been brought. Kant's intellectual solidity appears in his formulations, which were made in such full awareness of the crisis that he became one of the main points of departure for many movements in modern thought.

By way of a series of distinctions, Kant proposed to save science from the skepticism of Hume. The first of these was the distinction between *synthetic* and *analytic* statements. A synthetic statement is any statement which adds some new item to the stock of knowledge about the world. It is a statement about the world, a statement of fact. Generally, there is only one way to arrive at a bit of factual knowledge; that is, to obtain it from experience. Synthetic knowledge is empirical knowledge. Analytic statements, on the other hand, do not require factual investigation. They are not statements arrived at in this manner. They are deduced from other statements already made. The conclusion of an Aristotelian syllogism is analytic. Such knowledge is not known after the fact (*a posteriori*) but before, or without appeal to facts (*a priori*). These two kinds of knowledge in terms of the manner in which they are known are as follows:

How Known?	Types of Knowledge	
	Analytic	*Synthetic*
A Priori	X	
A Posteriori		X

Kant did not invent this distinction. It is found in the writings of Hume and Leibnitz, and even suggested by some of Locke's arguments. Kant, however, sharpened the distinction and called it to attention. Furthermore, he posed his problems in terms of it.

Hume had shown that the causal knowledge of science is synthetic, and had presented the case for its being purely *a posteriori*. He denied logical necessity to the laws of science. Thus if science is to be saved from the skepticism of Hume, it is necessary to demonstrate, in addition to these categories of knowledge, the existence of a special type, a kind of scientific knowledge that is at once "synthetic," representing factual, but at the same time necessary knowledge. How can science be saved? By demonstrating that at least some synthetic knowledge is *a priori* possible.

Kant's second set of distinctions concerns the object of knowledge. We know that we have experience. We assume it refers to a real world. The world as experienced is called by Kant *phenomenon*. The thing in itself is the *noumenon*. Our knowledge of the world, including all our scientific knowledge, is concerned with things as experienced. However much one might wish it, science does not apply to *noumena*, but only to *phenomena*. Kant made a tremendous concession to the empiricists: the identification of the objects of synthetic knowledge with phenomena.

But if knowledge of phenomena is synthetic and *a posteriori*, Hume's critique of causality holds. Kant therefore introduced a third set of distinctions. The knowledge of phenomena may be divided into two main types: *form* and *content*. Kant argued that the *forms* are fundamental, serving as conditions for anything becoming an object of knowledge in the first place. More simply, the forms are the missing *synthetic a priori*. The forms under which anything is known were assumed by Kant to be supplied by the faculty of knowledge itself. The content of experience is produced by external influences. Kant distinguished the activities of the mind into perceiving and conceiving. Perception, too, has its forms. When we perceive anything, it is in space and time. Location and duration characterize everything experienced. When all sense qualities are abstracted from things experienced, extension and succession remain. Space and time, then, are the fundamental forms of perception. Similarly the activity of conceiving and thinking may be analyzed. If we abstract every item of content from thought, something still remains in one's comprehension. Or, by reverse, whenever we understand anything, we do so by binding it together in certain relations, the most important of which are quantity and cause. By means of a judgment, a combining activity, we understand one phenomenon as cause or effect of another. The same form of synthesis may be employed, whatever the content.

There were for Kant three groups of forms. (1) *Forms of Perception.* Space is the form of all perception in the sphere of outer experience, time the form of all perception in the sphere of inner experience. They are forms, because every single experience presupposes them. (2) *Forms of Understanding.* Perception and conception are conjoint activities. Perception without conception is blind; conception without perception is empty. In perception, a manifold is directly united into a whole. In conception, combination is consciously performed. Unity and self-identity of consciousness are the necessary conditions for conceiving any content. Only by the application of the causal conception can we apprehend such phenomena as the freezing of water, the transition from fluidity to solidity as an objective event. In all, Kant recognized twelve fundamental categories of conception. (3) A third type of form is found in the *Ideas of Reason,* which refer to the whole of the faculty of knowledge. Reason, in its narrow sense, refers to the faculty of knowledge in performing unconditioned syntheses. Perception fashions sensation into spatial and temporal form. Understanding arranges them into conceptual wholes in terms of such forms as quantity and causality. But reason demands an absolute beginning and limit to space and time, an absolute maximum to causal series. This is the continuation and consumption of the combining activity of perception and understanding. Concepts designating an absolute conclusion are *Ideas.* There are three such ideas: the Idea of the Soul, the Idea of the World, and the Idea of God. These ideas proceed from the nature of reason itself. No objective deduction of the Ideas is possible. They refer to an unconditioned ultimate. The Ideas have a subjective origin in the need of *Reason* for unity.

Kant was a child of the Enlightenment as much in his ethics as in his metaphysics and epistemology.[7] If Hume dominated his conception of scientific knowledge, Rousseau exercised an influence on his ethics. The problem of knowledge was solved, to Kant's satisfaction, by means of his forms. He attempted to solve the problem of ethics by the discovery of a law of right action in man's inner nature. From Rousseau he took over the idea of the dignity of man as a personal being. Following the pattern of his epistemology, he searched for the universally valid element of ethical knowledge in a distinction between form and content. The moral law expresses itself as conscience. It consists of the injunction to act in such manner that one's action could be universally extended to every human being; moreover, it requires that each man be treated as an end, never as a means. An ethical action depends not on outer facts but on the inner will. Nothing is good in itself except the good will. Moral law, or duty, is not an anticipation of the goal of historical development, but, as *a priori* principles, prefigures experience. The ideal derived from experience and human need is that of a free society of human personalities.

Kant's central place in modern thought derives in part from his attempt to link two great traditions: the rationalistic and empirical. Kant yielded to the empirical criticism of concepts everything he thought it required. He made a tremendous sacrifice to empiricism when he restricted the application of reason to phenomena, in principle excluding it from analysis of the thing in itself. All this, however, was done in the name of science, to achieve that necessary knowledge he thought science required. In a similar way, Kant fused the principle of individual freedom from the eighteenth-century rationalistic tradition with the principle of order taken over from the conservative position. He performed the same type of synthesis in his socio-ethical philosophy as in his technical philosophy.

The idea of "freedom" was thrust into central focus. History was conceived as the development of the principle of freedom. Perhaps the entire history of the human race represents the fulfillment of nature's secret plan through the development of a system of government as the condition for the full realization of the nature of man. The central problem for mankind is that attainment of a universal system of law for civil society founded not on the relation of ruler to ruled, or force, but on interhuman relationship in which every individual is an end in himself. As a free agent, man participates in a constitution on the basis of laws he helped to develop.

The ideas of the eighteenth-century contract thinkers (particularly Rousseau) were reflected in Kant's notion that society rests on social contract. This was not, however, a historical fact but an ideal of reason, binding every law-giver to make laws in such ways that they express the united will of the entire people, compelling regard for every subject so far as he wishes to be a citizen. Natural right has a different origin from the laws of nature; it arises

[7] Kant's ethical philosophy was expounded in the *Critique of Practical Reason,* tr. by Lewis White Beck (Chicago: University of Chicago Press, 1949).

from the noumenal world of the moral self, while the laws of nature apply only to the phenomenal world. Natural right is the contribution of the noumenal self acting in opposition to the principles of the sensory world. In this manner, Kant attempted to reconcile the problems of individual autonomy and freedom with the lawfulness and stability of society.

It is essential to keep these facts in mind if we are not to be faced with a solemn mystery in accounting for the unusual importance of Kant for later thought. After all, what had Kant done beside draw a distinction between form and content? In deriving ideas of form and content from two fundamentally different sources — form from the *noumenal* self and content from experience — he would seem to have created tremendous problems. The categories are contributions by the noumenal self to the world of phenomena. Yet they do not refer back to the noumena. If we try to make such an application, we fall into self-contradictions. Or again, when we turn to the problem of moral life, our first discovery is the contradictory requirements of the ethical and the scientific worlds. Morality requires freedom; science requires necessity. Our actions thus have two different constructions: scientifically as necessary and causal, ethically as free and "responsible." Does it really help us to ascribe these different characterizations to a phenomenal and noumenal world, respectively, since the problems then appear as a relation between the two spheres? Or, if we ask what new values the position makes possible, the most immediately obvious fact is the withdrawal of scientific thought permanently from the investigation of things in themselves. Science is saved, but is this not at the price of making it trivial? It does not take any great acumen to discover serious problems in the Kantian position. What would seem most in need of explanation is why science is so important.

The most important reason has already been stated. Kant's formulations were addressed to major problems of Western thought. He tried to reconcile the values of both the rationalists and the empiricists. Socially he tried to reconcile the theories of a free world with those of a lawful world. We do not solve Kant's problems by throwing out his solutions as shallow or inadequate. Kant had summarized these problems and sharpened them. Thus, good sense dictated that one start with Kant's formulations.

In the nineteenth century, Kant became one of the perennial starting points for new departures of thought: for absolute idealism, for irrational idealism, and even for extreme positivism. It was perhaps inevitable that when any given trend in thought broke down, a natural tendency was to return to Kant. Neo-Kantianism was also one of the ground movements in social science in the late nineteenth and early twentieth centuries.

Neo-Kantianism

Friedrich Albert Lange (1828–1875), philosopher and social reformer and foremost historian of materialism in the nineteenth century, founded the neo-Kantian movement.[8] He saw materialism as the most comprehensive explanation available of the physical world. At the same time he felt that it was basically deficient in its account of the human spirit. But this was no difficulty to be repaired by the arbitrary insertion of spiritual activity into the framework of materialism. "On the Atomic theory we explain today the laws of sound, of light, of heat, of chemical and physical changes in things in the widest sense, and yet Atomism is as little able today as in the time of Demokritos to explain even the simplest sensation of sound, light, heat, taste, and so on. In all the advances of science, in all the presentations of the notion of atoms, this chasm has remained unnarrowed."[9] On the other hand, the question may be asked what reality a thing has other than that of the representation of a subject. There is no fundamental reason why dissolving the world into the facts of consciousness should be preferable to reducing consciousness to physical things. There must be a third reality transcending the physical and the psychical. This is found in poetry:

> Kant would not understand, what Plato before him would not understand, that the "intelligible world" is a world of poesy, and that precisely upon this fact rests its worth and nobleness. For poesy, in the high and comprehensive sense in which it must be taken, cannot be regarded as a capricious playing of talent and fancy with empty imagination for amusement, but it is a necessary offspring of the soul, arising from the deepest life-roots of the race, and a complete counterbalance to the pessimism which springs from an exclusive acquaintance with reality.[10]

Lange's analysis starts from Kant's division into the spheres of physical and psychical. He tries to solve their relation in a Kantian manner. Poetry provides the reconciliation of the creativity of the spirit and the determinism and skepticism produced by physical fact.

Among other early students developing the neo-Kantian point of view were Otto Liebmann (1840–1912) and Alois Riehl (1844–1924).[11] Drawing the distinction between subjective consciousness and objective knowledge of science, Liebmann tried to resolve their relation by distinguishing between the conception of space and time given in empirical intuition and a pure transcendental conception of space and time. But where was one to obtain the criteria of the transcendental conception of space and time? One cannot turn to consciousness, for it only gives the empirical conception. But the empirical conception is merely phenomenal and not real. By shifting one's point of view,

[8] Friedrich Albert Lange, *The History of Materialism*, tr. by E. C. Thomas (New York: Humanities Press, 1950).
[9] *Ibid.*, p. 23.   [10] *Ibid.*, pp. 231–232.
[11] See Otto Liebmann, *Kant und die Epigonen* ["Kant and His Followers"] (Stuttgart: 1865) and *Zur Analysis der Wirklichkeit* ["On the Analysis of Reality"] (Strassburg: 1876). Riehl's chief work was *Der philosophische Kriticismus und seine Bedeutung für die positive Wissenschaft* ["Philosophical Criticism and Its Significance for Positive Science"], 3 vols. (Leipzig: 1876–87; 3d ed., Leipzig: A. Kröner, 1924–26); Part Three of this work (1887 edition) was translated by Arthur Fairbanks as *Introduction to the Theory of Science and Metaphysics* (London: 1894). For an excellent review, see Guido de Ruggiero, *Modern Philosophy*, translation of the first edition (1912) by A. Howard Hannay and R. G. Collingwood (New York: Macmillan, 1921).

Liebmann thought one could arrive at the telelogical conception of thought passing from nature to "ethos."

For Liebmann, the Kantian dualism is located in the field of knowledge. Riehl locates it in being, and attempts a transition from the reality outside thought to consciousness. Starting with the fact of consciousness, Liebmann attempted to account for science. On the other hand, Cohen[12] did not take consciousness as the center of reference or reality; consciousness was treated rather as the pure form of modal reflection, establishing the possibility rather than the reality of the objects of thought. Thought is conceived by Cohen as a self-dependent production and a reality in itself. The mathematical science of nature is an illustration of the self-dependent production of thought. The quantitative reality of mathematics is spontaneously generated starting from infinitesimal calculus, which resolves the lacuna created in the antithesis of the continuous and discrete. The categories are integrated according to the inherent teleology of the mathematical science of nature.

This same idea is essentially continued by Ernst Cassirer, for whom the mathematical concept is an absolute *a priori* element in knowledge, expressing the rules of any possible scientific experience. This, Cassirer claims, supplants Kant's principle of pure apperception.[13] In its development from Hermann Cohen to Ernst Cassirer, neo-Kantianism becomes the search for a mathematical concept to provide a regulative unity for the multiplicity displayed in experience. Mathematics becomes the universal science of form, containing the rule of all possible experience. The knowledge of natural science centers in number as an *a priori* form. Concepts such as substance and cause are constructions determined by *a priori* requirements of number. In these formulations the *a priori* and the scientific construction differ only in their degree of generality, insofar as the first is the more general law and includes the other.

The neo-Kantian philosophy of value starts from the subjectivity of consciousness and attempts to establish the objectivity of science by means of the concept of value. This is the essence of the theories of Windelband and Rickert, whom we have already had occasion to discuss. Accepting the traditional distinction of man's psychological life into thought, will, and feeling, Windelband attempted to use the theory of values to unify the logical, ethical, and esthetic. Moral consciousness supplies the criteria for the universal valuations of philosophy. The central property of philosophy is its inquiry into the standards of thought, ethics, the will, and esthetics. The basic dualism in Windelband's thought is between ideal standard and empirical being, which is also a dualism between the immanent and transcendent.

[12] Hermann Cohen, *Logik der Reinen Erkenntnis* ["The Logic of Pure Knowledge"] (Berlin: B. Cassirer, 1902).

[13] Ernst Cassirer, *Substanzbegriff und Funktionsbegriff* (Berlin: B. Cassirer, 1910). A full bibliography of Cassirer's work will be presented in Chapter 14, where his importance for the sociological movement known as symbolic inter-actionism is taken up.

Rickert accepts the doctrine of immediate experience, maintaining that being does not exist except as the content of consciousness. Immanent in consciousness is immediate reality as representation. The immanence of being, as found in consciousness, is that of the universal, the concept of formal logic in its representation. However, the objective of knowledge cannot be obtained from formal logic. All that is given in consciousness is the play of representations, and between representations there is no universal and necessary validity. To establish the objectivity of knowledge, it is necessary to get away from consciousness and to devise a transcendent standard that has required validity. The transcendent is not a content of consciousness; it is not being, for "to be" is to be in consciousness. It is an "ought to be." This "ought" is the standard of logical valuations. The feeling of self-evidence is the only indication of its presence. Such self-evidence is the ultimate criterion of truth. In the further development of his ideas, Rickert abandons the abstract doctrine of "ought" and replaces it with "value," or the ideal, to which the doctrine of "ought" is a stepping stone.

This last form of neo-Kantianism was critically central to the neo-Kantian conception of history. Generally the form this took was somewhat as follows. History is conceived not as the field of mechanical interaction of forces but as a spiritual process. A dualism is then found between history as a spiritual process and science. History is the science of individualities, but these contain elements of human universality outside time. Historical development has no meaning without *a priori* conditions that surmount the temporal.

One of the most interesting phenomena of nineteenth-century thought was the movement beyond Kant in the early part of the century, then back to Kant in the later part of the century.

The reasons for the speed with which thought traveled beyond Kant are clear enough. The distinction between the phenomenal and noumenal world was used by Kant to salvage science, the ethical life of man, and his religious life. This was all well and good, but it was achieved only by tremendous concessions. Science was "saved" by confining it in principle to phenomena. The world of the really real, the noumena, was placed forever outside science. The ethical life of man was saved, but among other things it was permanently, so it seemed, deprived of the possibility of claiming a scientific foundation. And so with other formulations.

One trend in early nineteenth-century thought addressed to these problems posed by Kant, organismic idealism, leads from Johann Gottlieb Fichte (1762–1814) to Comte. Fichte's problem arose in the attempt to unite the self in its phenomenal and noumenal aspect. The moral personality of the individual is a noumenal fact belonging to the "kingdom of ends" not determined by phenomenal things. Does conscious moral experience have no relation to the noumenal self? Does not the "kingdom of ends" supply the very principles that structure the world of conscious ethical action? Fichte proposed the idea of the "ethical self" which imposes its forms on the phenomenal world of action. Ethically the self establishes ends to which action is a response. The ethical quality of mankind is revealed thus in response to a self-created world. Ethically the limits of the self are transcended and fully realized in society.

Friedrich Schelling (1775–1854) expanded a similar argument to account for the creative activity of the artist, and Hegel generalized the arguments of Fichte and Schelling to apply to all areas of experience. The essence of man and mankind is located in the human spirit, which has two spheres of manifestation: the conscious world of phenomena and the deeper, more profound, world of noumena. As with Kant, the idea is accepted that conscious life constantly presses against the limits of experience, and when it does, it is caught in contradictions (antinomies). But after all, the spirit of man and of mankind is "one." By this very process the spirit realizes itself ethically (in the manner of Fichte) and artistically (in the manner of Schelling). Human history is the history of progressive self-realization of the free spirit that constantly presses against the limits of its applicability, casting up antinomies and surmounting them in new syntheses. In the idea of history as the dialectical self-realization of the free spirit, Hegel tried to solve Kant's problem.

That this was not the only possible solution to the Kantian problems was shown by Schopenhauer and Nietzsche. They, too, started by accepting the distinction between the phenomenal world of experience and the noumenal world of what really exists. Morality belongs to the world of action, hence it is, as Kant said, a noumenal fact. The world of science, on the other hand, is concerned with the explanation of phenomenal events. This means, said Schopenhauer and Nietzsche, that man's rationality and science are confined to relatively superficial aspects of reality. In the self on which action depends, emotional life is fundamental. The real essence of man is will. Anti-scientific movements were launched from this platform.

The reasons for the movement beyond Kant are thus clear enough. This hardly explains why there should be a return to formulations that had proved to be so unstable. The various forms of organismic idealism had been very important to the rise of the social sciences, but they had problems of their own. The absolute idealism of Hegel, for example, tended to turn into a kind of panlogism. It led to pantheistic religiosity and a mystic sense of wholeness. This is no way to arrive at the hard-headed hypotheses necessary to science. Nor did it help matters that the Marxians self-consciously took over the "dialectic" and turned it into a weapon of class struggle. Moreover, the other branch of the movement, voluntaristic idealism, by elevating man's emotional life and will to the center of interpretation and reducing rationality (science) to mere instruments of the will, became paramount critics of science. Schopenhauer cynically offered his generation the self-negation of the orient. Nietzsche not only slashed away at science (including Darwinism, which he despised), but offered his world a race of amoral supermen. Under such circumstances it is clear why there should be some attempt to return to fundamentals.

But the battle cry, "Back to Kant!" was heard not only in philosophical circles. It formed one of the ground movements in the social sciences toward the end of the nineteenth century and in the early decades of the twentieth. It may be recalled that sociology itself had emerged as a new field with the daring fusion of apparently contradictory areas of nineteenth-century thought: organicism and positivism. The tension between these areas provides much of the motive power for the early development of sociology. But one can also say that the day of reckoning, while it may be postponed, must arrive. Sooner or later the new discipline must face up to the problem of how objective knowledge is to be achieved when its subject matter is defined "subjectively." Ideas, Comte had maintained, either rule the world or throw it into chaos. Not inconsistently with this, sociologists at a later date were to define the subject matter of sociology as collective representations (Durkheim), ideas and beliefs (Tarde), the imaginations people have of one another (Cooley), definitions of the situation (Thomas), consciousness of kind (Giddings), and so on. The moment sociological enterprise was not directed primarily toward extending its territories but justifying its existence and consolidating its method, the problems implicit in its origins had to be faced.

One product of this ferment was the emergence of conflict theory alongside of organismic positivism. Conflict theory added a sobering realism to sociological discussion. It rejected large-scale, loosely defined entities as units of analysis. It called various schemes of unilinear evolution into question. It exposed the value premises of progress theories. It showed organismic positivism to be superficial and biased. However, by supplying still new systems of explanation alongside those already competing for acceptance, it added to the babble of voices. Moreover, conflict theory was not easy for everyone to accept. Many persons shrink from a point of view placing conflict in central focus. There seems to be a sort of impiety about it. The function of conflict theory was primarily to call organismic positivism into serious question. The self-examination that resulted coincided with the professionalization of the field. Sociology could not continue forever to draw checks on an unbalanced account. Neo-Kantianism, representing a re-examination of the general trends of nineteenth-century thought, offered itself as one of the most direct means for the self-survey.

Before turning to the neo-Kantian movement in sociological theory, however, it will be useful to review another rationalistic development in late nineteenth-century thought that was to produce effects in sociology somewhat parallel to those of neo-Kantianism.

Phenomenology

Charles Renouvier

Charles Renouvier (1815–1903) was the founder of a theory, based on the study of Kant, known as "phenomenalism" or "neo-criticism." [14] Reality,

---

[14] See Charles Renouvier, *Essais de critique générale. Premier essai: Traité de logique générale* ["Essays in General Criticism. First Essay: Treatise on General Logic"] (2d ed., Paris: 1875).

he held, is the fact of consciousness and the system of relations between the facts of consciousness. Renouvier thought in this manner to eliminate the noumena, thus reversing the usual attempt to reduce phenomena to noumena.

Whereas for Kant the categories were brought to experience by the subject, for Renouvier they were already present in phenomena as the most general relations. Number, for instance, was thought to be the relation of plurality to quantitative unity. Similarly, Dauriac [15] applied the notion of contingency to the Kantian categories, treating them not as necessary but conditional. Renouvier attempted to solve the antinomies of pure reason on the basis of phenomenal relations. For example, the antinomy of the finite and infinite is approached from the point of view that an actual infinite is impossible. The world is internally finite, with a definite measurable size beyond which there is nothing. However, it cannot actually be measured by the beings who are a part of it, for they can only investigate relations less than the whole — relations subordinate to other relations. Ruggiero not unfairly observes that the contradiction which Kant had tried to avoid with his distinction between noumena and phenomena has obscurely crept back, now appearing as a contradiction of method.

Renouvier gradually abandoned his phenomenalism. Organic forms increasingly appeared to him to be genuine individualities, not mere aggregates. In the study of personality, he came to recognize that the individual possesses a unifying power he had originally denied to it. There is a connection between volitional acts and personality, making it impossible to view the self as a mere aggregate of sensations. Increasingly he saw the presence of freedom as the thing that binds a being in countless relations to other beings. Eventually, in *The New Monadology*, he conceived the person as the center of spontaneity, a representative power endowed with the faculty of producing representations.[16]

Edmund Husserl

The phenomenalism of Renouvier took its point of departure from Kant. So also did the phenomenology of Edmund Husserl (1859–1938). Renouvier attempted to dispose of the noumena by taking phenomena as ultimate. But he was led step by step from this position, through his interest in living being, personality, and individual consciousness, eventually to an idealistic position reminiscent of that of Leibnitz. Husserl, too, seems to have had Kant in mind when he advanced his formulations. He did not, however, as did Renouvier, attempt the reduction of all reality to phenomena, but rather took the intuition of phenomena as fundamental to the approach to any and all forms of reality.[17]

[15] Lionel Dauriac, "Essai sur les catégories," *L'Année philosophique, 1900* (Paris: F. Alcan, 1901), pp. 29–63.

[16] Charles Renouvier and L. Prat, *La Nouvelle monadologie* (Paris: A. Colin, 1899). See Ruggiero's summary of Renouvier's position in *Modern Philosophy*, pp. 141–147.

[17] Edmund Husserl, *Ideen zu einer reinen Phänomenologie und phänomenologischen Philosophie* (Halle: Niemeyer, 1913); translated by W. R. Boyce Gibson as *Ideas: General Introduction to Pure Phenomenology* (New York: Macmillan, 1931).

Husserl assumed that there is a real external world which can be known. Experience, which must be consulted for access to this world, consists of both objects and essential objects or essences. The sense qualities of an object consist of its essences. Corresponding to these are cognitive relationships. The existence and meaning of objects are independent of the subject and act of cognition. These, existence and meaning, yield themselves in special modes of experience. All knowledge is based on experience in which objects are presented. The central problem of Husserl's epistemology is the investigation of how objects are known by immanent inspection, since they are known only when they become part of pure consciousness. His method is that of phenomenological reduction.[18]

Like Renouvier, the starting point for Husserl's position is the assumption that understanding may operate with phenomena without need to appeal to an "unknowable." Kant's fundamental error, according to Husserl, was his assumption that the only objects of experience and cognition are those of a sensory character. Instead, it was Husserl's opinion that there are many kinds of experience. Phenomena are not, as for Kant, constructions of consciousness; they are essences (Greek "eidos") forming the content of pure consciousness.

Husserl's aim was to establish phenomenology as an "eidetic" science, as the theory of the essentiality of the transcendentally purified consciousness. His method is a special kind of "reduction" as a refined analysis of the properties of conscious experience. Husserl believed that there are two kinds of experience: natural and eidetic. The content of knowledge consists of natural objects and their intrinsic phenomenal essentiality.

There is an important difference between the naturalistic and the phenomenological attitude. As natural human creatures, we will, judge, and feel. We are aware of the world in space and time as a becoming without end. We are aware of our selves and others in a world of nature and events. The phenomenological method consists in the analysis of experience to discriminate within it its various properties. It involves an eventual reduction of experience to pure consciousness and its correlates. The method assumes that every experience has essences accessible to intuitive apprehension. Husserl's ultimate objective was the investigation of pure consciousness and its correlative realm of eidetic being. To arrive at this, it is necessary that the world of objects and the "I" as a psychophysical organism be "put aside" or "bracketed" for the purpose of gaining an intuitive vision of the pure sphere of transcendental subjectivity.

The first step in the application of the phenomenological method of reduction is the differentiation of the natural and eidetic realms. The second major step is distinguishing between "immanent" and "transcendent" essences. Transcendent essences include such essences as "thing," "spatial shape," "movement," "color of a thing," and "quality of character."

---

[18] For an excellent analysis of Husserl's phenomenology, see E. Parl Welch, *The Philosophy of Edmund Husserl* (New York: Columbia University Press, 1941), especially pp. 203–204.

The transcendent essences are required for knowledge of the physical objects of nature. The second act of bracketing holds the transcendent essences apart from analysis and moves on to the immanent essences of pure consciousness. Within the world of immanent essence one may arrive, by further successive acts of bracketing, at a pure ego.

George Santayana

On the American scene, an analysis very similar to Husserl's was developed by George Santayana (1863–1952), who also argued that the complex world of ordinary existence involves many inferential elements. "Existence . . . not being included in any immediate datum, is a fact always open to doubt." [19] One may, however, by "a difficult suspension of judgment" deprive "a given image of all adventitious significance, when it is taken neither for the manifestation of a substance nor for an idea in a mind nor for an event in a world, but simply if a color for that color and if music for that music." When this is done, "scepticism at last has touched bottom, and my doubt has found honorable rest in the absolutely indubitable. Whatever essence I find and note, that essence and no other is established before me. I cannot be mistaken about it, since I now have no object of intent other than the object of intuition." [20]

Husserl and Santayana are not altogether similar, for Husserl seems to feel that for every phenomenon that can be known there is some corresponding essence, while Santayana suggests that one rises from essence to existence by a leap of imagination. The leap is taken when one hypostatizes an essence into a fact, locating it in relations not given within it. This rests not on essence, but on animal faith. The existence of things and one's self is not founded on reasons, but on action. It is a faith which does no "violence to a sceptical analysis of experience; on the contrary, it takes advantage of that analysis to interpret this volatile experience as all animals do and must, as a set of symbols for existences that cannot enter experience." [21]

Each essence has a character distinguishing it from all others. It has an inalienable individuality which renders the essence a universal. However, essences do not exist. The realm of matter is the second realm of being. It is the field of action. It is essentially dynamic. The existence of this realm is a matter of animal faith. The third realm of being is the realm of truth, of things seen under the form of eternity. Beyond this is the realm of the spirit.[22]

[19] George Santayana, *Scepticism and Animal Faith* (New York: Scribner's, 1923), pp. 39–40.
[20] *Ibid.*, p. 74.
[21] *Ibid.*, p. 106.
[22] Santayana develops these ideas not only in *Scepticism and Animal Faith* but also in *The Realm of Essence* (1927), *The Realm of Matter* (1930), *The Realm of Truth* (1938), and *The Realm of Spirit* (1940), all published by Charles Scribner's Sons, New York.

Summary

Sociology was not invented by academic men. The early phases of the two oldest schools were the work of journalists and men of affairs. They were imaginative men with capacities for synthesis, drawing material for their new points of view from wherever it could be found. They did their work well, establishing the field as an independent discipline.

The professionalization and institutionalization of sociology were accompanied by a heightened intellectual ferment. Material had to be organized for teaching purposes. Teachers had to be trained to deal with all points of view. A wide public had to be informed about the new field. Sociology had to be defined in ways that did not lead to endless boundary disputes with other disciplines. It had to develop standards if it was to achieve respectability in the family of sciences.

These new professional and institutional demands were felt both in the old disciplines and in the emergence of new schools of sociological theory. The professionalization of sociology coincided with the classic stage of positivistic organicism. A strong methodological consciousness was present in Tönnies and Durkheim. Similarly, in conflict theory, methodological and professional responsibility was a significant factor in the theories of Gumplowicz and Albion Small.

There were a number of reasons why the new intellectual ferment could not be confined to the old theories. For one thing, the number of alternatives had increased. When there are many possible explanations, one needs standards in order to choose among them. Moreover, in the social sciences, no one as yet had made full use of the rationalistic traditions of Western thought.

While rationalism has often been combined with idealism, there is no necessary connection between them. There are forms of materialistic rationalism and irrational forms of idealism. Rationalism as a philosophy has always promoted the conception of the world as a coherent whole, analyzable by reason. In science it promoted the concept of a logical and mathematical universe. In human conduct it led to the conception of self-evident principles which regulate behavior. Wherever rationalism appears it leads to the search for special forms, rules, or principles.

A significant form of rationalism was advanced by Immanuel Kant, intended to salvage empiricism from a skepticism which he thought would destroy it. Kant agreed with the empiricists that science aspires to a knowledge of phenomena. However, he disagreed with the apparent critical conclusion of Hume that if knowledge is confined to phenomena based only on experience, no general knowledge is defensible except on grounds of habit or prejudice. Kant argued that knowledge of phenomena is of two kinds: of *forms* which are *a priori* and certain, and of *contents* which are merely contingent.

Kant attempted to integrate the rationalistic and empirical traditions of the eighteenth century, to maintain science on an empirical level and still supply it with universal, rational concepts. In his theories of the social world, he tried to reconcile the ideas of a free and simultaneously lawful world.

But Kant made an unusually great sacrifice to empiricism. By confining science purely to experience and urging that every time knowledge aspires to extend beyond experience it breaks down into antinomic contradictions, Kant seemed to have saved science, but at the price of sacrificing everything that made science worth while. The repeated neo-Kantian movements of nineteenth-century thought constantly returned to the Kantian formulations and attempted to avoid these sacrifices. Among the major neo-Kantians was Lange, who found in poetry the reconciliation of the creativity of the spirit and the determinism of physical fact. Liebmann located the Kantian dualism in the field of knowledge, seeking to reconcile it in a teleological conception of thought. Other neo-Kantians like Riehl, Hermann Cohen, and Cassirer located it elsewhere. Windelband and Rickert attempted to establish the objectivity of science by means of the concept of value.

One trend in nineteenth-century thought which was rooted in neo-Kantianism and which achieved the status of a distinct sub-school was phenomenology, as founded by Charles Renouvier. Reality was defined by him as consisting of the facts of consciousness and the relations holding between them. In this way Renouvier thought to eliminate the difficult problem of the noumena — the "really real," which Kant's philosophy was in principle prevented from touching. This reversed the usual attempt by neo-Kantianism to rise from the phenomenal to the noumenal by reducing phenomena and noumena to one another. Despite his attempt to develop a theory of phenomenal relations, Renouvier gradually abandoned his phenomenalism.

The problems of phenomenalism were taken up by Edmund Husserl in Germany and George Santayana in the United States. Husserl took the intuition of phenomena as fundamental to the approach of any and all forms of reality. He advanced phenomenology as an eidetic science, as the science of essentiality of the transcendentally purified consciousness. He proposed a special method of "reduction," a successively controlled analysis of the objects of experience proceeding through various levels of depth to the pure ego itself.

In America, Santayana proposed the treatment of all forms of existence other than that included in any immediate datum of experience as always open to doubt. He proposed a method of suspension of judgment, which sheared away from any given image all adventitious significance, treating it merely for what it was. Such essences so discovered are universal, but they do not exist. The realm of matter, as the dynamic field of action, is a second realm of being. The existence of this realm is a matter of animal faith. A third realm of being is that of truth, things seen under the form of eternity. Santayana's radical skepticism and Husserl's "bracketing" are roughly equivalent.

The multiplicity of partly conflicting theories in sociology, which by now had split into two major branches, each of which embraced a variety of alternatives, invited the institution of more precise methods. In fact, a growing methodological anxiety was discernible even in the older schools, as illustrated by Tönnies, Durkheim, and Gumplowicz. Moreover, sociology was being transformed into an academic subject. It was imperative that it find a limited definition of its subject matter. Under such circumstances it is hardly strange that many sociologists repeated the battle cry of the nineteenth century, "Back to Kant!" The rationalistic traditions of Western thought, particularly the Kantian, were explored by some sociologists in the effort to arrive at a more special and limited definition of the field.

Neo-Kantianism in sociology developed first with the attempt to find a special definition of subject matter for sociology in the same way that Kant had for epistemology. However, it appears to have been almost unavoidable that a neo-Kantian sociology should soon reach the stage when it would chafe against self-imposed limitations, as did the Kantians. As sociology grew restless under these limitations, one could anticipate that various expedients would be tried.

The single most important of these alternatives was phenomenology. The dynamics of its inner tensions drove some neo-Kantians on to this new step. While today only minor remnants of neo-Kantian formalism remain in sociology, the phenomenological branch of sociological formalism is still vigorous.

The philosophical bases for phenomenological formalism were laid by Husserl in Europe and by Santayana in the United States. While foundations were laid on native grounds, an American variant of phenomenological formalism did not develop. A sociological development from American pragmatism prevented this. Phenomenological sociology has remained an unexploited possibility in America and a testimony to the strength of other forces.

SELECTED BIBLIOGRAPHY

CASSIRER, ERNST, *The Philosophy of the Enlightenment.* Translated by Fritz C. A. Koelln and James P, Pettegrove. Boston: Beacon Press, 1955.

HUSSERL, EDMUND, *Ideas: General Introduction to Pure Phenomenology.* New York: Macmillan, 1952.

KANT, IMMANUEL, *Critique of Pure Reason.* Abridged edition. Translated by Norman Kemp Smith. New York: Modern Library, 1958.

KANT, IMMANUEL, *Critique of Practical Reason.* Translated by Lewis White Beck. Chicago: University of Chicago Press, 1949.

LANGE, FRIEDRICH ALBERT, *The History of Materialism.* Translated by E. C. Thomas. New York: The Humanities Press, 1950.

LECKY, W. E. H., *History of the Rise and Influence of the Spirit of Rationalism in Europe.* New York: G. Braziller, 1955.

RICKERT, HEINRICH, *Die Grenzen der naturwissenschaftlichen Begriffsbildung* ["The Limits of Concept Formation in the Natural Sciences"]. Revised edition. Tübingen: J. C. B. Mohr, 1921.

SANTAYANA, GEORGE, *Scepticism and Animal Faith.* New York: Scribner's, 1923.

WELCH, E. PARL, *The Philosophy of Edmund Husserl.* New York: Columbia University Press, 1941.

10

The Neo-Kantian Branch of Sociological Formalism

IT COULD PERHAPS HAVE BEEN PREDICTED THAT AT THE TIME SOCIOLOGY became established as an independent science some reaction would set in against the influence of ideological conservatism upon the theory of society. The effects of conservatism appear over and again. Society, not the individual, is made the unit of analysis. It is insisted that institutions, not persons, are the units of society. When the individual is considered at all, as in some of the conflict theories, his sheep-like character is emphasized. Again it is insisted that groups, not men, are the units of social analysis. Moreover, the central property of society is found in such things as stability, order, solidarity — the conservative values.

The liberal theory of society, on the other hand, places emphasis on the individual rather than the group. It is more concerned with opportunity than with solidarity. Kant had received the liberal theory of society from his eighteenth-century predecessors. Society for him was not an organic form but an ordered community of independent wills. "Freedom," not "stability," was the watchword. History represents the development of the principle of freedom. At the same time, Kant attempted to formulate the principle of freedom in terms of the requirements of interhuman order. Hence, Kant suggested, one need not consider the external system of government as the antithesis or enemy of the individual. This external system may provide the very condition for the full realization of the nature of man. The central problem for mankind is the attainment of a universal system of law for civil society founded on the nature of man rather than on a rule of force.

These conditions are applied only in a system of interhuman relationships
in which every individual is an end in himself. As a free agent, man participates in a constitution on the basis of laws he helps to create. This is a
long way from the conception of law as a peace treaty ceremonially confirming the dominance of one group over another. It is more subtle than the
usual eighteenth-century rationalistic conception of society as a mere contractual agreement. It locates law in central position as the condition for an
ordered liberal society. Kant provided the basis for a theory of jurisprudence
very different from that of the conflict theorists.

Rudolf Stammler

For Rudolf Stammler (1856–1938), theoretical jurisprudence is concerned with the law as a set of rules formulating the means for achieving
human aims; it inquires into the means by which human aims are realized
and the justification of rules for achieving them.[1] Stammler's "critical"
method is modeled on Kant's procedures; it draws a distinction between
form and content and seeks to discover the pure forms of law irrespective
of their particular content of matter. A distinction is also drawn between
the concept of law and the idea of justice. "Law" sums up the ways in
which means are related to ends in social volition; "justice" provides the
criteria of just law.

There are two ways in which order is introduced in consciousness: perception and will. *Perception* forms sense impressions, in terms of categories,
into objects in an order. The *will* orders materials in terms of a goal to be
achieved in the future. Law is a form of volition in which we are concerned
with means to bring about an end. A legal principle formulates an end to
be achieved.

Not all forms of will are legal. One form, which represents the ordering
of means to achieve the ends of the individual personality, is "isolated
volition" (*getrenntes Wollen*). This is the sphere of morals. Isolated volition
is distinguished from the "binding will" (*verbindendes Wollen*), implying
a social relationship in which one will makes use of the purposive acts of another as a means to its own ends. Society is a group of wills functioning as
means and ends to each other. Through cooperative effort society attains
common ends. Law as the binding will is concerned with the external form
of the acts of men in social relationships.

Not every volition is right. The rightness of a volition is determined in
two ways. (1) Some means may be essential to the achievement of a par-

[1] Stammler's basic works are: *Wirtschaft und Recht nach der materialistischen
Geschichtsauffassung* ["Economy and Law According to the Materialist Conception of
History"] (Leipzig: Veit, 1896; 5th rev. ed., Berlin: W. de Gruyter, 1924); *Theorie
der Rechtswissenschaft* (Halle: Waisenhaus, 1911; 2d ed., 1923); and *Lehrbuch der
Rechtsphilosophie* ["Textbook in the Philosophy of Law"] (Berlin: W. de Gruyter,
1922). The present discussion follows *The Theory of Justice*, translated by Isaac Husik
(New York: Macmillan, 1925). For an evaluation of the place of Stammler in the
theory of jurisprudence, see Morris Ginsberg, "Stammler's Philosophy of Law," in [no
author], *Modern Theories of Law* (London: Oxford University Press, 1933).

ticular aim or end. If the end is willed, so too the means must be. (2) The claim to universal validity arises out of the idea of justice. Over and above the conditional validity of appropriate means is a criterion of unconditional validity. Justice rests on the harmony of all striving and endeavor, requiring us to subordinate the particular to the universal and to view all particular ends in terms of the maximum harmony possible for all ends.

It is the distinction between the particular and the binding will that locates morality. Morality is concerned with inner life and the expression of personality. Law, however, is concerned with the external relations of men and the binding character their wills have on each other. The ideal of justice applied to morality leads to the idea of the "pure will," requiring truthfulness and honesty with one's self and the principle of perfection. In the sphere of law, the idea of justice gives rise to the concept of the "pure community." A community has a pure will when its order is based on principles of universal validity. The principles of right law are *respect* (no act of will is subject to arbitrary control of another, and people remain ends in themselves) and *cooperation* (no person may be arbitrarily excluded from a community if he is legally a part of it).

A rule is a just law or right law or a law of nature when it passes certain tests. These tests are found in a volition purged of all subjective elements in the service of an ideal harmony represented by a community based on objective purposes. In such a community of free willing men, everyone is both bound and free, each person is an end in himself. Everyone is bound by his respect for the purposes of others, but at the same time no one is subject to the caprice of another nor can anyone be arbitrarily excluded from the benefits arising from membership in society. Law is not derived from the state. Rather, the state is one type of legal order presupposing the notion of law in general. The obligations of international law do not rest on the existence of a league of states; they derive from the idea of justice. The ultimate appeal is always to the social ideal. "We obtain the formula of a *community of men willing freely,* as the final expression which comprehends in unitary fashion all possible purposes of persons united under law. I call this *the social ideal.*" [2] This is not an empirical issue:

> In undertaking to work out the universal principles which are to span the bridge between the idea of just law and its significance for specific legal questions, we must take notice of a two-fold danger and try to avoid it: (1) The principles must not be gathered at random from historical observation. . . . (2) We must keep out of the content of our principles everything that is merely empirical and pertains to the material. . . .[3]

This conception of society lies at the opposite end of the scale from Comte's. The true units of society are individuals. Society exists for them, not they for society. The dream of a caste-like order has no place in this scheme

[2] *The Theory of Justice,* p. 153.
[3] *Ibid.,* p. 158.

There are both comparisons and contrasts with the conflict theorists. Like them, Stammler places great importance on the contrast between morality and law. However, while, for the conflict theorists, morality was the sphere of a peculiar type of group, the in-group or we-group, morality is here conceived as the sphere of personality. Furthermore, law is not peculiar to the conquest group, but to the external order of society. This re-alignment of distinctions introduces the individual as a genuine social agent in many capacities other than that of a sheep-like follower.

Such a rational and liberal model of society was taken over by Georg Simmel, the foremost sociological exponent of neo-Kantianism. Simmel goes beyond such general distinctions to develop a more detailed sociology.

Georg Simmel

Georg Simmel (1858–1918) was born in Berlin, the son of a chocolate manufacturer. After his father's death, a friend of the family and founder of an international musical publishing house was appointed Simmel's guardian. He left Simmel a considerable fortune, enabling him to live as an independent scholar. He entered the University of Berlin in 1876 at the age of eighteen, studying with such scholars as the historians Theodor Mommsen, Johann Droysen, Heinrich von Sybel, and Heinrich von Treitschke, the philosopher Eduard Zeller, the ethnologist Adolf Bastian, and the art historian Herman Grimm. He received his doctor's degree in 1881 with a dissertation of Kant's concept of matter. From 1885 to 1900 he was *Privatdozent* in philosophy, and for another fourteen years he was *ausserordentlicher Professor* in philosophy at Berlin. In 1914 he was called to Strassburg as full professor (*Ordinarius*).

The two main theories of society in the eighteenth and nineteenth centuries were the mechanical-atomistic (developing in the sixteenth and seventeenth centuries) and the organic. In the one theory, individuals were conceived as independent and self-sustaining units, and the community as a mechanical summation of them. (This appears very clearly in John Stuart Mill and is reflected in Stammler.) The organismic theory sees society as something distinct from and opposing the individual. It was already suggested by Rousseau; it was systematically developed by Hegel and Fichte. In the nineteenth-century historian Lorenz von Stein it was transmitted directly to sociology,[4] receiving typical expression in the idea of the *Volksgeist.* Theodore Abel very justly observes [5] that Tönnies' work can be conceived as an attempt to fuse the two concepts of society (organic and mechanical) into one formulation. Society as an organic group is represented in the *Gemeinschaft;* society as an association resting on interests is represented in the *Gesellschaft.* The organismic point of view was retained by Tönnies through

[4] See especially von Stein's history of social agitation in France, *Geschichte der socialen Bewegung in Frankreich, von 1789 bis auf unsere Tage,* 3 vols. (Munich: Drei Masken Verlag, 1921).
[5] Theodore Abel, *Systematic Sociology in Germany* (New York: Columbia University Press, 1929), p. 14.

the expedient, discussed earlier in Chapter 4, of having these two societal forms spring forth as manifestations of different kinds of will, *Wesenwille* and *Kurwille.*

Simmel made a new approach to the problem of the nature of society, bringing forward the concepts "relation" and "function." He had the liberal's objection to the organic theory, particularly its frequent postulate of a group mind. Society seemed to him to be a function manifested in dynamic relations among individuals and in interactions between individual minds. Society exists wherever a number of individuals enter into reciprocal relationships. It is a process. There exist only relations and actions between individuals of whom it may be said that in interaction they form a unity.

This was all stated in thoroughgoing Kantian manner. Kant had tried to reconcile the epistemological requirements of rationalism and empiricism. Simmel attempts to reconcile the sociological requirements of the social theories of organicism and mechanism. Theoretically one of the most interesting of all Simmel's essays was the one in which he directly posed the Kantian question and discussed it in a manner paralleling Kant's procedure in the *Critique of Pure Reason:* "How Is Society Possible?" [6]

Kant's fundamental question in the *Critique of Pure Reason* was how is nature as the object of science possible? According to Simmel, Kant could propose an answer because "nature" was taken to be the *representation* of nature. Nature is the special way our intellect assembles, orders, and forms sense perceptions. Nature is a kind of cognition, a picture growing in and through our cognitive faculties. Simmel proposed the analogous question for society: what are the *a priori* conditions making society possible? Here too there are individual elements always remaining in their discreteness (as in the case of nature as content) yet undergoing a synthesis into the unity of society through a process of consciousness which puts the individual

[6] Georg Simmel, "How Is Society Possible?", translated by Albion Small from "Exkurs über das Problem: Wie ist Gesellschaft möglich?" in *Soziologie* [see below], pp. 27–45, and appearing in *The American Journal of Sociology,* Vol. 16 (November 1910), pp. 372–391. Simmel's main sociological works are: *Philosophie des Geldes* ["Philosophy of Money"] (Leipzig: Duncker & Humblot, 1900; 5th ed., 1930) ; *Kant* (Leipzig: Duncker & Humblot, 1904) ; *Soziologie* (Leipzig: Duncker & Humblot, 1908; 3d ed., 1923) ; *Hauptprobleme der Philosophie* ["Chief Problems of Philosophy"] (Leipzig: G. B. Göschen, 1910; 6th ed., Berlin: W. de Gruyter, 1927) ; *Philosophische Kultur: Gesammelte Essais* ["Social Philosophy of Culture: Collected Essays"] (Leipzig: Kröner, 1911; 2d enlarged ed., 1919) ; and *Grundfragen der Soziologie* ["Fundamental Problems of Sociology"] (Berlin: W. de Gruyter, 1917; 2d ed., 1920).

English translations of some of Simmel's essays, many of which were included by Simmel in *Soziologie,* were made by Albion Small and published in early issues of *The American Journal of Sociology.* Some of these have been reassembled and retranslated by Kurt Wolff and published, together with other selections from Simmel, in *The Sociology of Georg Simmel* (Glencoe, Ill.: The Free Press, 1950). Two other essays from *Soziologie* have appeared in English: *Conflict,* translated by Kurt Wolff, and *The Web of Group-Affiliations,* translated by Reinhard Bendix, published in a single volume with a foreword by Everett C. Hughes (Glencoe, Ill.: The Free Press, 1955). In the following discussion, some of the references will be made to Small's translations rather than to those of Kurt Wolff in order to call attention to the dates at which Simmel's work became generally available, through English translation, to American sociologists.

existence of several elements into definite relationship through *forms*, in accord with definite laws.

There is, however, a difference between the unity of society and that of nature. While nature becomes a unity in the contemplation of the subject, societal unity is realized by its elements without further mediation. The societary connection is directly realized in the individual's experiences. Society does not acquire an objective unity through an outside observer. It does not need to. By its nature, it is a direct unity between observers. Society is my representation, posited in the activity of consciousness. The soul of another has for me the same reality as I have myself. Within consciousness, Simmel continues, one distinguishes between the fundamental character of the ego and the contents of consciousness. Thus the question "How is society possible?" has a different meaning from the question "How is nature possible?" The answer is given by an *a priori* residing in the elements themselves, while the *a priori* of nature rests in the observer.

When we discover the sociological apriorisms, Simmel continues, they will have the same double significance as those which make nature possible: they will more or less completely determine the actual process of sociation as functions of psychical occurrence and, on the other hand, serve as logical presuppositions of the perfect society. Specifically, then, the task is to investigate the conditions of "sociation" [7] as the conscious association of beings. The task is to discover the *a priori* effective conditions or forms of sociation.

The first discovery that is made is that sociation represents the intersection of two dominations. To enter into society is in some degree to be generalized. Yet every man has in himself a deep individuality, a nucleus that cannot be subjectively reproduced. From the complete singularity of personality, we form a picture of it that is not identical with its reality, but still is not a general type. Within a sphere which has any sort of community of calling or of interests, every member looks upon every other not in a purely empirical way but on the basis of an *a priori* which this sphere imposes on each consciousness having a part in it. From the common basis of life originate suppositions in terms of which people look at one another as through a veil. This does not conceal the peculiarity of individuality, but gives personality a new form. To enter into society, individuality must undergo a kind of generalization into a new form required by sociability. This generalization is always more and less than individuality. Thus every element of a group is not only a societary part, but also something else. With respect to certain sides of his personality, the individual is not an element of the group.

[7] The term "sociation" is Kurt Wolff's rendering of the German *"Vergesellschaftung."* The most literal translation would perhaps be "societalization," and Albion Small consistently translated the word as "socialization." Since the literal translation is awkward, and since the word "socialization" has come to have a more specific meaning in sociology, Wolff's practice has been followed and the word "sociation" will be used throughout this discussion. (See Wolff's introduction to *The Sociology of Georg Simmel*, pp. lxiii–lxiv.)

To be received into a group in any form, therefore, an individual must become at once more and less than an individual personality. The truth of this appears decisively in the fact that even the person who is shut out of the group — the stranger, the enemy, the criminal, the pauper — is simultaneously partly formed by the group. In the commerce of men in societary categories, men are confronted with each other in the character that belongs to each in the role for which he is responsible. The individual can enter society only by forgoing some of his individuality and exchanging it for the generality demanded by the role. At the one extreme are individuals giving up so little of their individuality that they can hardly function in societal life; at the other are individuals in whom the whole tone of the total personality has disappeared, being merged into the function to such a degree that almost all traces of individuality have disappeared.

One of the most important sociological formations rests on the fact that the societary structures are composed of beings who are at the same time inside and outside them. Sociation brings the individual into a double situation. The individual has his setting in the sociation and is at the same time in antithesis to it. The meaning of the *a priori* peculiar to society is revealed in the fact that between individual and society the "within" and "without" are not two determinations, but rather they are properties of a unitary social being. One may generalize this insight to society as a whole. Society may be conceived as a body of officials who have a definite ordering of positions, a preordination of performances which are detached from their personnel of a given moment. Within this series, every newcomer finds an unequivocally assigned place which, so to speak, waited for him and with which his energies harmonize. The individual need not be aware of the *a priori* which creates the possibility of his belonging to a society. Each person, by virtue of his own quality, is automatically referred to a determined position in his social milieu. This position ideally belonging to him is also actually present in the social whole.

The *a priori* condition making society possible is found in the category of vocation (*Beruf*). To the individual, society begets and offers in itself a position which in content and outline differs from others, but which in principle may be filled by any man. It is therefore anonymous. At the same time, despite its generality, the particular position is grasped by the individual on the ground of an "inner call." Empirical society becomes possible only through the *a priori* category of *vocation.*

This is undoubtedly as amazing a piece of pure theoretical brilliance as modern sociological theory displays. Simmel's problem was identical with that of Stammler — to account for the problem of order while conceiving society as an association of independent persons. The phrasing of the Kantian question was a device for exploring the inner nature of this order. In society both individual and group are surmounted. The idea of vocation is introduced as the point where the inner content of individual motivation, the "inner call," and the external requirements of interhuman action, the "position" or "office," are fused. The entire discussion is a brilliant anticipation of modern role theory. At the same time it permitted Simmel to develop a more special definition of sociology.

Simmel distinguished three problem areas of sociology: general sociology — the study of historical life from the standpoint of sociology; philosophical sociology — the study of the epistemological and metaphysical problems that border sociology; and formal or pure sociology. He found the true area of sociology in the study of societal forms. Pure sociology is compared to geometry. "Geometrical abstraction investigates only the spatial forms of bodies, although empirically, these forms are given merely as the forms of some material content. Similarly, if society is conceived as interaction among individuals, the description of the forms of this interaction is the task of the science of society in its strictest and most essential sense." Such societal forms "are conceived as constituting society . . . out of the mere sum of living men." And sociology, which isolates them "inductively and psychologically from the heterogeneity of . . . contents . . . proceeds like grammar, which isolates the pure forms of language from their contents." [8]

Simmel's analysis of "sociability" may illustrate formal sociology. In any human society one can, he believes, distinguish between form and content of interhuman action. The form and content of human interaction are separable: knowledge, for example, initially appears as a means in the struggle for existence, but it comes to be cultivated for its own sake autonomously, as happens in science. This is also true for law: the requirements of social life compel or legitimate some types of behavior simply because they meet these requirements; however, such requirements may then recede into the background and the rule assume functional autonomy, remaining "law" regardless of the specific requirements that gave rise to it. Generalizing from such examples, Simmel continues:

> This complete turnover, from the determination of the forms by the materials of life to the determination of its materials by forms that have become supreme values, is perhaps most extensively at work in the numerous phenomena that we lump together under the category of *play*. Actual forces, needs, impulses of life produce the forms of our behavior that are suitable for play. These forms, however, become independent contents and stimuli within play itself or, rather, *as* play. There are, for instance, the hunt; the gain by ruse; the proving of physical and intellectual strength; competition; and the dependence on chance and on the favor of powers that cannot be influenced. All these forms are lifted out of the flux of life and freed of their material with its inherent gravity. . . . Here lies whatever may justify the analogy between art and play. In both art and play, forms that were originally developed by the realities of life, have created spheres that preserve their autonomy in the face of these realities. [9]

This process illustrates the separation of the form and content of societal existence. The forms may gain a kind of life of their own. The form exists,

[8] *The Sociology of Georg Simmel*, pp. 21–22.   [9] *Ibid.*, pp. 42–43.

then, for its own sake and for the sake of the fascination due to liberation from the ties with content. This is true for the phenomena of *sociability,* which Simmel defines as "the play-form of sociation." Sociability is the association of men for its own sake, not for loot (as hordes of bandits) or supernatural purposes (as a religious society) or for gain (economic association). Sociability is association for its own sake and for the delight in association without the restrictions of practical purposes. The conditions providing delight to the process of sociability are separate from the particular person involved. The character of the gathering is determined by personal qualities like amiability, refinement, and cordiality. Everything depends on the personalities of the participants, not upon other interests. Tact is here of peculiar significance, for no external or immediate egotistic interest directs the self-regulation of the individual in the relation to others. Moreover, the individual possesses many attributes — wealth, social position, erudition, fame, exceptional capability, and merit — which are not permitted to play a part in sociability. One can, for this very reason, speak of "sociability thresholds." A person enters the association as an individual with complex ideas, forces, and possibilities. He is capable of sociability only so far as he is able to neutralize these factors. The moment interaction is converted into an intentional form with objective content and purpose (to rise in the social scale, to make a sale, to obtain a job), sociability ceases. There are, thus, upper and lower limits to the individual's capacity for sociability — sociability thresholds which are passed either when individuals interact from motives of objective content and purpose or when their entirely personal and subjective aspects make themselves felt.

It is perhaps possible to find the positive formal motive of sociability which corresponds to its negative determination by limits and thresholds. In explaining law, Kant posited the axiom that each individual should possess freedom to the extent that it is compatible with the freedom of others. The same principle, says Simmel, may be applied to sociability. Each individual ought to have as much satisfaction of his sociability drive as is compatible with its satisfaction on the part of others. Therefore, as Kant's law is democratic, one sees here the democratic structure of all sociability. It is, however, a democracy that can be realized only within a given social stratum. Sociability between different strata can be inconsistent and painful. At the same time, the democracy of sociability even among social equals is only something played. It is an artificial world composed of individuals with no desire other than to create pure interaction with others. We do not enter sociability as full men but as men divested of various aims, goals, and intentions. In primitive society, sociable men did not have to be wrested from so many objective claims. The form appeared more distinct in contrast with the individual's personal existence. Behavior at social gatherings was more ceremonial than it is today. As abstracted from sociation through art or play, sociability is the purest kind of interaction. It is the game in which one acts as if all men were equal. The game becomes a lie only when the sociable action and speech are mere instruments of intentions of a practical sort. Apparently Simmel would not have numbered himself among the followers of Dale Carnegie.

The connection between sociability and play explains why sociability covers all phenomena which are conventionally thought of as sociological play-forms, particularly games as such. All forms of interaction in which men exchange or form parties are outside the framework. However, each of these areas may experience the penetration of sociability so that any one or all are played in the form of a game.

> ... even where the game involves a monetary stake, it is not the money (after all, it could be acquired in many ways other than gambling) that is the specific characteristic of the game. To the person who really enjoys it, its attraction rather lies in the dynamics and hazards of the sociologically significant forms of activity themselves. The more profound, double sense of "social game" is that not only is the game played in a society . . . but that, with its help, people actually "play" society.[10]

Almost any area of social life may have its play form. In the sociology of sex, the play form of eroticism is coquetry. The erotic question between the sexes is that of offer and acceptance or refusal (its objects are infinitely varied and by no means purely physiological). The nature of feminine coquetry is to play up alternately allusive promise and allusive withdrawal: to attract the male, always stopping short of decision; to reject him, but never deprive him of all hope. Behavior shifts back and forth between "yes" and "no," stopping at neither. Coquetry has the character of suspension, distance, ideality; and it is quite correct to speak of its "art," not merely of its "artifices." To develop as a form of sociability, coquetry must meet specific behavior on the part of the male. Coquetry unfolds its charms at the height of sociable civilization, leaving behind the reality of the erotic desire, consent, or refusal, becoming the interplay of the silhouettes of their serious import. As sociability plays with the forms of society, so coquetry plays with those of eroticism.

The full extent to which sociability abstracts the forms of interaction from their contents becomes evident in conversation, the most general thing men have in common. People talk seriously about some content they wish to communicate or come to an understanding about. At a social gathering, however, they talk for the sake of talking. Talk becomes its own purpose, and is fully realized in an "art of conversation," obeying its own laws. The topic of conversation is merely the medium of a lively exchange of speech, in which all the forms are recognized by the participants — quarrel, appeal to norms recognized by all, pacification by compromise, grateful acceptance of the new, covering up anything on which no understanding can be hoped. Talk presupposes two parties; it is two-way. Among all sociological phe-

[10] *Ibid.*, p. 50.

nomena, talk is the purest and most sublimated form of two-wayness. It is the fulfillment of a relation that wants to be nothing but a relation, in which the mere form of interaction becomes its self-sufficient content.

Another problem to which Simmel gave some thought was that of how one arrives at theories. A further illustration of his social forms and his conception of the method of arriving at them may be seen in his study of superiority and subordination. There are two steps in the analysis: (1) the bringing together of contents in which the form is manifest, and (2) the abstraction of the form. Simmel argues that we gain knowledge of the forms of sociation by bringing together actual historical manifestations. We must collect and exhibit the element of form which these historical manifestations have in common, abstracted from a variety of material (economical, ethical-ecclesiastical, social-political, and so on). Geometry has the advantage of finding within its field very simple figures to which the most complicated forms may be reduced. Truths respecting these simple figures are therefore widely applicable. From relatively few fundamental truths all possible arrangements of form may be interpreted. In the case of social forms, however, reduction to simple elements has not been made. "Social phenomena are too immeasurably complicated and the methods of analysis are too incomplete. . . . Long and patient labor will be necessary before we can understand the concrete historical forms of socialization [i.e., "sociation"] as the actual compounds of a few simple fundamental forms of human association." [11]

In developing the meaning of superiority and inferiority, Simmel maintains that it is one of the forms in which "society" comes into being. Despite appearances, it is by no means a one-sided relation. There is an often unnoticed but no less significant influence of inferior on superior, as well as the reverse. One of the basic sources of the differences in cases of superiority and inferiority is found in the relative amount of spontaneity which subordinates and superiors bring to bear on the total relation. At one extreme, absolute despotism, the ruler attaches to his edicts the threat of penalty or promise of reward. However, the inferior still has a claim on the superior — for example, the implied promise of protection. In law, there seems to be the connotation that he who gives the law is unqualified superior. But as the Romans knew, the relation is always reciprocal. Where all spontaneity on the part of the subordinate is excluded, there is no longer sociation. The orator confronting the assembly or the teacher confronting the class seems to be the sole temporary superior. But the mass is not really passive, for it has a limiting and leading reaction. Even in hypnotism it has been suggested that the hypnotized person exercises a not easily defined influence on the hypnotist.

Superiority may be exercised by an individual, a group, or an objective

[11] Georg Simmel, "Superiority and Subordination as Subject-Matter of Sociology," tr. by Albion Small, *The American Journal of Sociology* (September and November, 1896), p. 168.

principle. The subordination of a group to a single person has consequences for the unification of a group — a generalization which holds even in the case where the group is opposed to the head. The transformation in the political life of a people may occur not merely in the case of a complete abolition of monarchy but in the gradual limitation of its power. The Christian religion is credited with attuning men's souls to peaceableness. In fact, it is a case of subordination to a divine principle. Unification may take the form of leveling or gradation. There is a considerable difference in the distribution of power in the two cases.

The imaginative charm with which Simmel explored his materials may be seen in his discussion of secrecy as a social form.[12] He pointed out that a precondition of relationship between people is that they know something about each other, whether it be between a buyer and seller, a teacher and student, or what not. One must, first of all, know with whom he must deal. In part, social relationships depend upon the completeness of knowledge of each other. At the same time, no one can know everything about the other. Various possibilities arise between people in terms of the limitations and aberrations to which our knowledge of each other is subject. Ordinarily we cherish only so much truth, so much science, as is useful for practical purposes.

In the relation between people, men may voluntarily reveal the truth about themselves or dissimulate and deceive each other. Sociological structures are differentiated by the measure of mendacity operative in them. This may vary from simple relations, in which a lie is relatively harmless, to complex relations, where it may be disastrous. Not only is there a relative permissibility of lying as between different types of relationship, but various positive utilities reside in lying. For example, the lie may be useful in bringing about organization, stratification, and centralization of the group, bringing the physically less weak and intellectually less crafty under control. Simmel, who had a vein of old-fashioned socialism in his make-up, observes that, at the other extreme, when they reach a certain stage of development, wholesale and retail trade may arrive at a point where they can act in accordance with complete integrity in marketing their goods.

Without tracing all the additional ramifications, this is sufficient to illustrate the imagination and delicate surprise with which Simmel developed his sociological forms.

Not the least significant aspect of every school of thought is the manner in which it is able to receive the materials of alternative or opposed schools. Without attempting to do justice to the subtlety, range, and penetration of his discussion, it is interesting to note that Simmel received the concept of "conflict" into his system as a social form.

> ... it must appear paradoxical to the ordinary mode of thinking to ask whether conflict itself, without reference to its consequences or its accom-

[12] "The Sociology of Secrecy and of Secret Societies," tr. by Albion Small, *The American Journal of Sociology*, Vol. 11 (January 1906), pp. 441–498.

paniments, is not a form of socialization ["sociation"]. . . . If every reaction
among men is a socialization, of course conflict must count as such. . . .
The actually dissociating elements are the causes of the conflict — hatred
and envy, want and desire. If, however, from these impulses conflict has
once broken out, it is in reality the way to remove the dualism and to arrive
at some form of unity, even if through the annihilation of one of the
parties.[13]

In developing this theme, Simmel points out that, even in so organic a
system as India with its caste system, the hierarchy of castes rests directly
on their reciprocal repulsion. Competition is merely a formal relation of
tension. Entirely apart from its results, it determines the form of the group,
reciprocal position, and distance of the elements. In the city, the whole
internal organization of interhuman commerce rests on complicated gradations of antipathies, indifferences, and aversions. Antipathy protects us
against typical dangers of city life: being smothered under its multiple impressions and shattered by the too extensive engagement of our sympathies.
Erotic relationships are often woven out of love, respect, and contempt at
once. Almost unavoidably an element of community weaves itself into a
hostility. As a social form, conflict ranges in its manifestations all the way
from the inner-subjective processes of personality to the affairs of great
states.

The real cunning of Simmel's position is nowhere more clearly demonstrated than in the handling of conflict. By reducing it to one of a multiplicity
of social forms, many of its decisive properties are transformed. While it is
a form that can range in manifestation from inner-subjective spheres to
international war, it can hardly function *solely* as a device to subordinate
individuals to the group. The teeth have been pulled from the conservative
position and its key idea pressed into the service of liberal ends.

At times Simmel turned his attention away from what he called "sociological forms" to factors or conditions affecting social forms. Such were
his analyses of the "Persistence of Social Groups" and "The Number of
Members"[14] as a determining factor in social forms. A few ideas from the
latter essay may illustrate this kind of analysis.

Simmel asserts that some aspects of the form and inner life of a social
group are determined by its numerical relationships. A very large number
of people can form a unity only on the basis of a division of labor, but division
of labor is not essential for a small group. A large group without structure
will tend to split into smaller segments. A previously calculated, mechani-
cally working life system, regulated in every detail, can be applied only to

---

13 "The Sociology of Conflict," tr. by A. W. Small, *The American Journal of Sociology,*
Vol. 9 (January 1904), p. 490.

14 "The Persistence of Social Groups," tr. by Albion Small, *The American Journal of
Sociology,* Vol. 3 (March and May, 1898), pp. 662–698, 829–836; Vol. 4 (July, 1898),
pp. 35–50; "The Number of Members as Determining the Sociological Form of the
Group," tr. by Albion Small, *The American Journal of Sociology,* Vol. 8 (July and
September, 1902), pp. 1–46, 158–196.

a small circle, and cannot work on a large scale. A group organized on such a scheme will remain minute. It is not surprising, then, that there are such tightly organized group formations of an ecclesiastical sort which permit no application to large numbers. Again, an aristocratic body can have only a relatively narrow compass. When an aristocratic body gives way to democratic forms, centrifugal tendencies and fatal contradictions develop in its life principles.

Simmel did not carry out a systematic analysis on the basis of his *forms*, despite his obvious suggestion that this should be done. Raymond Aron quite accurately summed up this aspect of Simmel. "The reader becomes lost in an interminable succession, not so much of historical examples, as of theoretical cases and possible combinations. These dazzling exercises often seem like an elaborate game. The book (*Soziologie*) has thus brought its author many admirers, but few disciples." [15] Simmel achieved his results in part by the vague use of the concept "form." Abel has made a careful inventory of some of the main things included as forms: characterizations of complex situations (slavery, legal contests, exchange); characterizations of norms (law, custom, mores, honor); definitions of groups (family, secret society, political party); characterizations of social types (the stranger, the poor, the teacher, the middleman); characterizations of social relations (conflict, superiority–subordination); characterizations of social structures (hierarchy, stability, elasticity); and even generalizations about the social process.[16] This is to say nothing about the legitimacy of separating form from content in the first place — a point of especial importance, since most of Simmel's more brilliant analyses are secured by ignoring it.

However, all such criticism should not obscure the very significant point that Simmel developed a worthy liberal counterpart to the conservative theory of society of the two previous types of sociological theory. This is implicit in Aron's estimate. He had noted that Simmel made the reduction of the whole to its elements into a theoretical principle of his method. "Only those laws which regulate atomic movements are valid. A natural unity is defined by the reciprocal action of the parts. Thus sociology discovers individuals in the crowd." [17]

In this reduction of society to individual behaviors, Simmel stands sharply opposed both to organismic positivism and to conflict theory. This makes him a "sociologist of democracy."

> The dissolution of the idea of society as a real entity corresponds to a period in which the hostile classes are no longer united except by the fiction of one society. Crowds play a decisive role in democratic civilizations, and in the social sciences "the sociological spirit" expresses the individual's realization of the power of collectivities. . . . Simmel regarded crowds and institutions,

---

[15] Raymond Aron, *German Sociology*, tr. by Mary and Thomas Bottomore (Glencoe, Ill.: The Free Press, 1957), p. 6.
[16] Theodore Abel, *Systematic Sociology in Germany*, pp. 24–25.
[17] Raymond Aron, *German Sociology*, p. 7.

not as superior beings, but as monstrous realities created blindly by men as a result of the collective life itself . . . . Simmel's sociology expresses a double antinomy, that between atomism and holism and that between individualism and the rule of the masses.[18]

Simmel stands in between worlds — perceiving a similar type of danger from the aristocratic society of the past and a society resting on mob action. In either case the individual is threatened.

Because Simmel was a contributor to *L'Année sociologique*, his ideas early came to the attention of French thinkers. Albion Small, as we have mentioned, translated many of Simmel's pieces and published them in *The American Journal of Sociology*, bringing them to the attention of the American audience. The imagination and charm they contained touched many minds. Moreover, they corresponded to the need both for a more professional definition of sociology and for one which avoided the extremes of conservative ideologies.

Célestin Bouglé

Célestin Bouglé (1870–1940) was perhaps the foremost sociologist in France to show Simmel's influence. He was professor of social philosophy at the University of Toulouse, later taking over Durkheim's position at the Sorbonne.

In a pleasant essay on the nature of sociology,[19] he invites us to imagine a little village, let us call it Saint-Pol, with all its ongoing social life: its people, its events, its institutions. What would the sociologist wish to know about it? What would be the object of his study? As with Simmel, Bouglé defines sociology as the study of social forms. He quickly adds, however, that sociology is no mere classification of empty categories. He closely approximates Simmel's suggestion that form and content should be separated.

The materials with which sociology works are to some considerable degree historical in nature. But Bouglé rejects the search for social origins as a vain task. He rejects also the historical task and the task of turning sociology into a philosophy of history. It aspires merely to be a science. As a science it must examine historical phenomena; how else could it judge the

---

[18] *Ibid.*, pp. 7–8.
[19] *Qu'est-ce que la sociologie?* ["What Is Sociology?"] (Paris: F. Alcan, 1907). Only one of Bouglé's books is available in English — *Leçons de sociologie sur l'évolution des valeurs* (Paris: A. Colin, 1922) — which was translated by Helen Stalker Sellars as *The Evolution of Values* (New York: Henry Holt, 1926). Also available in English is a lecture which Bouglé delivered at Columbia University, *The French Conception of "Culture Generale" and Its Influence upon Instruction* (New York: Bureau of Publications, Teachers College, Columbia University, 1938). Bouglé's principal works are: *Les Sciences sociales en allemagne* ["The Social Sciences in Germany"] (Paris: F. Alcan, 1896); *Les Idées égalitaires* (Paris: F. Alcan, 1899); *Essais sur le régime des castes* ["Essays on the Caste System"] (Paris: F. Alcan, 1908); *La Sociologie de Proudhon* (Paris: A. Colin, 1911); *Chez les prophètes socialistes* (Paris: F. Alcan, 1918); *Doctrine de Saint Simon* (Paris: M. Rivière, 1924); *Le Solidarisme* ["Solidarity"] (2d ed., Paris: M. Giard, 1924); and *Humanisme, sociologie, philosophie* (Paris: Hermann, 1938).

consequences of social forms? And in becoming a science, sociology inevitably passes over into the search not only for the consequences of the forms but their causes. "Il ne faudra pas sans doute qu'elle se contente de montrer les *conséquences* des formes sociales, il faudra encore qu'elle en découvre les *causes*." [20]

On occasion Bouglé was able to isolate a configuration and trace its various aspects through diverse situations with a learning and imagination at least equivalent to that of Simmel. Such was his book on the caste system (*Essais sur le régime des castes*), which was so much in advance of the ordinary thinking on the subject of the time (1908) as still to be worth examining.

That caste was hereditary had been widely noted. Also, it was widely observed that race and military occupation were coupled in caste. But Bouglé was impressed by a phenomenon that had come to Simmel's attention where caste reigns: the different groups are repelled rather than attracted to one another. A man refuses to look for a wife outside the traditional circle. He refuses food from all except his own confreres. Contact with strangers is avoided as impure. While caste crumbles the societies it penetrates, it divides them into superimposed layers, and sets up groups separated by elementary repulsion. Thus Bouglé thought that the three elements of repulsion, hierarchy, and hereditary specialization were required to define caste completely. Where the system is found, the society is divided into a large number of hereditarily specialized groups, hierarchically superimposed and mutually opposed. In principle neither upstarts, hybrids, nor deserters of a profession are tolerated. Mixtures of blood, conquests of rank, and change of occupation are avoided.

Once we have isolated these three constituent elements of caste, we may inquire into the civilizations where caste is found to discover the social forms connected with caste. Many tendencies toward caste were present in occidental civilization: horror of misalliance, fear of impure contact. Statistics show that there are some occupations whose members willingly intermarry, others where intermarriage is rare. There are customs showing that different worlds do not mix; there are districts, cafés, schools frequented by exclusive categories of the population. There are villages where the same industry has been performed for centuries.

On the other hand, when the medieval clergy was described as a caste (Guizot), this was inaccurate. It was no hereditary stratum; its magistrates were celibates. The feudal system fell short of caste organization in many ways. The principle that land determines status is negative to the exclusive determination of status by birth. In systems of fiefs, a man might be a vassal to some, suzerain to others. Social rank ceases to be clearly defined. In the ancient world, one of the nearest approaches to caste was found among the Egyptians, who, according to Herodotus, were divided into several orders: priests, warriors, cowmen, herdsmen, merchants, interpreters, and

[20] *Qu'est-ce que la sociologie?*, pp. 22–23.

river pilots. However, the priests and warriors alone enjoyed marks of distinction, special land, and exemption from taxes. All strata were riveted to the profession of their ancestors. When a priest died he was replaced by his son. A warrior did not have the right to practice an occupation other than that of arms. The extent of endogamous marriage is known in some cases. The coffins of thirty generations of priests attached to the Theban god Mentu show that nearly all belonged to two or three families, marrying among themselves or taking wives from the family of the priests of Ammon. One family of royal architects kept the post for several centuries under all Egyptian dynasties. On the other hand, during the hieroglyphic periods, a sort of bourgeois class appears with members not confined to any particular profession. In a famous anthem, a scribe tells of placing himself in the bureau of supplies and of becoming auctioneer, later tax collector, finally chief of bailiffs, master auctioneer, and director of the royal line. He was soon placed at the head of a village, then a city, and finally a province. He finished by being head of the occidental porte (the institution from which justice was administered). He enjoyed full honors, and possessed several fiefs, which were endowed his family and placed under his sons. Social stratification was not petrified; still the spirit of division and opposition was widespread in Egyptian society.

The full development of caste, however, takes place in the traditional system of India. The process of economic production remains relatively simple and so far as possible is allocated in the form of occupational tasks of local groups. Since even the professional group has subgroups, one may distinguish six castes of merchants, three of scribes, forty of peasants, twenty-four of journeymen, nine of shepherds and hunters, thirteen of liquor-makers, and so on. A caste may be distinguished by its members' abstaining from certain technical procedures, not using the same materials, not making the same products. From top to bottom of traditional Hindu society, plurality of occupations is prohibited in principle, change of occupation illicit. Functions are divided once and for all by birth. Heredity of profession is the rule.

Of all the castes, the Brahmans have the most varied profession, for they are not confined to sacred books but appear as plowmen, soldiers, merchants, and cooks. Their very superiority reserves to them more possibilities than for common mortals. Superiority implies purity. Purity excludes many modes of action. The doctrine of *ahimsa* prohibits wounding the smallest creature. The priest may not open the earth with a plow share. Most of the unusual trades of the Brahman are due to his right to practice different trades in time of distress. After the crisis is over, the Brahmans often retain the emergency profession. Thus the system of hereditary specialization admits more mobility than appears at first sight. However, mobility is collective rather than individual. The individual does not leave the occupation of his ancestors; rather, groups detach themselves collectively. When groups change professions they depart clandestinely, or seek to justify themselves by some legend. How hard it is to move even then is shown by a group of weavers of

Western Bengal. It took 30 per cent mortality in a trade under ruin by English imports before they decided to look for a new livelihood.

The traditional Hindu society is hierarchically organized with the pariahs at the bottom. They are permitted to cultivate the earth for their needs. They are obliged to hire themselves to other tribes. Their masters can beat them when they wish without their being able to demand reparation. A Nair meeting a pariah has a right to kill him. At the other end of the scale are the Brahmans, in principle sustaining themselves from alms. Their superiority is as uncontested as the absolute inferiority of the pariahs. Between these extremes is a multitude of castes ranked in terms of purity of blood, fidelity, abstinence from prohibited foods. Practically, rank is determined by social distance from the Brahman caste. The key question is, will a Brahman accept gifts from a man of this caste?

Between the castes the principle of mutual repulsion holds. A self-respecting Hindu would die of thirst rather than drink from a glass served to a "mleccha" (foreigner). Much trouble was experienced in setting up a canalization of water in Calcutta: how could people of different castes be served by the same water pipe? Contacts with pariahs inspire horror. They have to carry bells to reveal their presence. Some persons are forced to go nearly naked for fear of being touched by flowing clothes. When two friends, daughters of a Gahapati and a Purohita, played in the gateway of a city, two Tshandal brothers appeared. When they were noticed, the children ran to save themselves and to wash their eyes. A stranger must not touch the food of a Hindu. At times his look is enough to contaminate it. If a pariah looks into the kitchen, all of the utensils must be smashed.

Meanwhile, the effects of endogamy tend to be redoubled by internal exogamy. Caste forms a narrow circle, and within it there are restrictions. In immigration of the Brahman caste, the caste is often divided into "gotras." Members of the same gotra cannot marry one another. The rules are complex, and vary with the castes. While there are breaches of the rules, a pure marriage can only be secured within the caste.

All in all, Bouglé thought that it was fortunate for sociological curiosity that the caste system triumphed in India over the forces that suppressed or thwarted it elsewhere. In this civilization it was realized in about as complete and pure a form as possible. It makes possible the observation of the characteristic properties in a more or less pure state. For those who wish it, India forms a kind of crucial experiment.

Bouglé's study of caste shows that he was at least as capable of carrying out a brilliantly articulated study of social forms as Simmel. However, he seems to have been as little inclined as Simmel to organize the existing body of sociological knowledge on the basis of forms. This task was clearly visualized by E. A. Ross.

E. A. Ross

Ross did not add anything new to the theory of social forms nor did his use of forms or formally conceived processes constitute the most significant of his theoretical contributions. He did, however, conceive the problem of utilizing forms as a device for the systematic presentation of sociological knowledge.

Edward Allsworth Ross (1866–1951) was born in Illinois. He received his doctorate at Johns Hopkins University in history, politics, and economics in 1891, and studied for a year at the University of Berlin. He taught economics at Indiana University and Cornell before going to Stanford University in 1893. There he was dismissed for his public stand on the use of Chinese labor in building the Central Pacific Railroad. From 1901 to 1906, Ross was professor of sociology at the University of Nebraska. He went to Wisconsin in 1906, where he remained until his retirement in 1937. With John L. Gillin, Ross built an effective department there that produced such notable students as Joyce O. Hertzler, Reuben Hill, D. E. Lindstrom, Lowry Nelson, and John Useem, among others. Ross published a total of twenty-nine books, the most useful for theoretical purposes being *Social Control* (appearing first as articles from 1896 to 1898) and *Social Psychology* (1908). From the standpoint of the attempt to systematize sociology by a review of basic social forms, the works of importance here are *The Principles of Sociology* and *New Age Sociology.*[21]

Ross had a journalist's nose for news and a sense of the current need. In the early decades of the twentieth century, the demand for a systematic sociology was widely felt. The evolutionary trends had fallen into disrepute and in the growing departments of sociology in the schools there was need for systematic coverage of the field. Simmel had indicated that one of the most direct ways of doing this was through an inventory of basic social forms. Small had introduced many of Simmel's discussions to the American public through translations in *The American Journal of Sociology.*

In *The Principles of Sociology*, Ross carried out a formalistic program. He divided the volume into five parts: Social Population, Social Forces, Social Processes, Social Products, and Sociological Principles. In this arrangement social population and social forces represented the raw materials of society. The social forces, for example, included the instincts, the interests resting on instincts, race, and geographic conditions affecting these. As Ross handled them, they were presupposed before anything really social was discussed. The sociological focus of the study was, therefore, in the social processes.

Ross did not come to the processes with any refined concepts of form and content. In fact, he did not betray any philosophic sophistication. Simmel's forms and Small's processes seem to have been all one to him. Yet he was clearly interested in the processes as a kind of general or recurrent pattern of phenomena. The most fundamental of the social processes were treated as four in number: (1) association, (2) domination, (3) exploitation, and (4) opposition. Just as Simmel had examined the "form" in various contexts, so Ross examined these processes in the same manner. *Domination,* for example,

21 E. A. Ross, *Social Control* (New York: Macmillan, 1901; Boston: Beacon Press, 1959); *Social Psychology* (New York: Macmillan, 1908, 1929); *Principles of Sociology* (New York: The Century Company, 1920; rev. ed., 1930); *New-Age Sociology* (New York: D. Appleton-Century, 1940).

was found to occur in parent over offspring, older over young, husband over wife, men over women, foremen over workers, one ally over the rest, and conquerors over conquered. *Exploitation* was found to be characteristic of the relations of parents and their offspring, of men and women, of the rich and the poor, of the intelligent and the ignorant, of priests and the laity, of the ruler and the ruled.

In addition to the four general processes, thirty-two others were isolated and discussed; they included such things as stimulation, personal competition, sex antagonism, class struggle, adaptation, cooperation, stratification, gradation, equalization, selection, individualization, commercialization, professionalization, and ossification.

The operation of the social processes was thought to produce various social products, such as uniformities, standards, groups, and institutions. Finally, a number of principles such as anticipation, stimulation, individualization, and balance were thought to be at work.

In Ross's last systematic statement, *New Age Sociology*, the same basic materials are present. The four fundamental processes are retained: association, communication, domination, and exploitation. The same subgroupings are presented of the remaining processes, which appear as conflict and adaptation, cooperation and organization, class and caste, processes involving society and the individual, those centering in occupation and social function, and finally those concerned with social repression and progress. Except for minor changes and additions, the general pattern is the same.

Ross stood astride two of the basic theories of sociology. His early and most creative phase was under the influence of that form of social behaviorism identified with Gabriel Tarde (to be discussed later). Two of his most important works, *Social Psychology* and *Social Control*, were produced under its influence. His actual theoretical contribution to sociological formalism was negligible, but he did much to popularize the view. In mid-career, Ross shifted perspective and devoted himself to carrying out the program implied in sociological formalism. Although there was some eclectic carry-over from his first position, it was too unconscious to lead to theoretically new formulations. A somewhat parallel phenomenon is observable in the textbook by Park and Burgess.

Robert E. Park and Ernest W. Burgess

Park and Burgess worked out their famous textbook, *Introduction to the Science of Sociology*,[22] at the University of Chicago in the shadow of the conflict tradition established by Small. Their statement represented a movement from conflict theory to formalism in somewhat the same manner that Ross's statement represented the movement from social behaviorism to formalism. Despite the fact that this work was perhaps the most famous socio-

---

[22] Robert E. Park and Ernest W. Burgess, *Introduction to the Science of Sociology* (Chicago: University of Chicago Press, 1921; 2d ed., 1924). References here are to the second edition.

logical textbook to appear in the United States, both Park and Burgess are more significant for other things — Park for developing the studies of the city, race relations, and the immigrant press, Burgess for the study of the family.[23]

Robert Ezra Park (1864–1944) studied at the University of Michigan. For a time (1887–1898) he served as a journalist. He received his M.A. degree in philosophy at Harvard in 1899 under William James and Josiah Royce, and from there went to Berlin, where he studied under Windelband and Simmel. He was an assistant in philosophy at Harvard in 1905 and 1906. From 1905 to 1914 he was engaged in educational work, mostly with Negroes. In 1914 he joined the faculty of the University of Chicago as a lecturer in sociology. He was professor of sociology at Chicago from 1923 to 1933, the time of his retirement.

Ernest Watson Burgess (1886–   ) was born in Canada. He received his Ph.D. degree in sociology at Chicago under Small in 1913. He taught at Toledo University (1912–1913), the University of Kansas (1915–1916), and the University of Chicago from 1916 to his retirement in 1951.

With his background in philosophy and his training with and under two such notable neo-Kantians as Windelband and Simmel, one might have expected Park to carry forward the theoretical aspects of neo-Kantianism in sociology. Moreover, Park had been strongly influenced by James and Dewey and the tradition of sociology identified with Albion Small. The tradition of Windelband and Simmel remains, but is encrusted with many other things. Simmel and Windelband had played an important part in the differentiation of sociology and history. Park and Burgess simply accepted this:

> Historically, sociology has had its origin in history. History has been and is the great mother science of all the social sciences. Of history it may be said nothing human is foreign to it. Anthropology, ethnology, folklore, and archaeology have grown up largely, if not wholly, to complete the task which history began and answer the questions which historical investigation first raised. [24]

Simmel had defined society (as content) as interaction. In essence, Park and Burgess accepted this definition:

> While it is true that society has this double aspect, the individual and the collective ... the thing that distinguishes a mere collection of individuals

[23] In addition to the *Introduction to the Science of Sociology*, Park's works include: *Old World Traits Transplanted*, with Herbert A. Miller (New York: Harper, 1921); *The Immigrant Press and Its Control* (New York: Harper, 1922); *The City*, with Ernest W. Burgess, Roderick D. McKenzie, and Louis Wirth (Chicago: University of Chicago Press, 1925); and *Race and Culture*, ed. by Everett C. Hughes (Glencoe, Ill.: The Free Press, 1950). Burgess's other books include: *Predicting Success or Failure in Marriage*, with Leonard S. Cottrell, Jr. (New York: Prentice-Hall, 1939); *The Family: From Institution to Companionship* (New York: American Book Company, 1945); and *Engagement and Marriage*, with Paul Wallin (Philadelphia: Lippincott, 1953).

[24] *Introduction to the Science of Sociology*, pp. 42–43.

from a society is not like-mindedness, but corporate action. We may apply the term social to any group of individuals which is capable of consistent action, that is to say, action, consciously or unconsciously, directed to a common end. This existence of a common end is perhaps all that can be legitimately included in the conception "organic" applied to society.[25]

With Windelband and Simmel it was argued that "history is the concrete, sociology is the abstract, science of human experience and human nature." The difference between sociology and the other social sciences is that they "are, to a greater or lesser extent, applications of principles which it is the business of sociology and of psychology to deal with explicitly." [26]

Park and Burgess seem primarily to have been responsible for introducing the distinction between realistic and nominalistic sociology. Moreover, they broke down the development of sociology into three periods:

1. The period of Comte and Spencer; sociology, conceived in the grand style, is a philosophy of history, a "science" of progress (evolution).

2. The period of the "schools"; sociological thought, dispersed among the various schools, is absorbed in an effort to define its point of view and to describe the kinds of facts that sociology must look for to answer the questions that sociology asks.

3. The period of investigation and research, the period which sociology is just now entering.[27]

Park and Burgess agree with both Simmel and Small that the common object of reference of sociology is found not in society as a structure but in the social group. Social process is taken as the general name for all changes in the life of the group. Sociology is said to be interested in "original nature" only insofar as it supplies the raw materials out of which individual personalities and social order are created. Out of these same materials every group is thought to create its own type of character which becomes a component part of the social structure. Under these circumstances, society becomes merely a kind of descriptive term. "Society now may be defined as the social heritage of *habit and sentiment, folkways and mores, technique and culture,* all of which are incident or necessary to collective human behavior." [28]

Park and Burgess built up a kind of sociological superstructure of elements taken from Le Bon, Cooley, Tarde, Small, Giddings, and many others. However, when all is said and done, their hearts belonged to Simmel, for the central integrating ideas of their sociological system were composed of processes, formally conceived. Actually, Park and Burgess presented two different approaches to social processes. In the first, the social processes were analyzed in terms of degree of involvement. Isolation, social contact, and social interaction were reviewed successively. This phase of the discussion terminated in an investigation of social forces which, in the long run, were

[25] *Ibid.,* p. 42.   [26] *Ibid.,* p. 43.   [27] *Ibid.,* p. 44.   [28] *Ibid.,* p. 165.

identified with interests, sentiments, and attitudes. In effect, this amounted to a separation of form and content.

Once this review was completed, Park and Burgess undertook a second systematization of materials. Rather than degree of involvement, the basis of systematization was now in terms of the amount of conflict and cooperation involved. The social processes were divided into four: competition, conflict, accommodation, and assimilation. In this context competition was conceived as a less social form of interaction, for it was identified with the biological struggle for existence. *Competition* was, in fact, conceived as interaction without social contact. It was viewed as the pre-social struggle to survive that eventually initiates conflict, accommodation, and assimilation and hence creates sympathies, prejudices, and personal and moral relations. By contrast, *conflict* is a social process; it represents competition lifted to a conscious and social level. The authors summarize the interrelations among the social processes and their relation to social structure as follows:

> Conflict is . . . to be identified with the political order and with conscious control. Accommodation, on the other hand, is associated with the social order that is fixed and established in custom and the mores.
>
> Assimilation, as distinguished from accommodation, implies a more thoroughgoing transformation of the personality — a transformation which takes place gradually under the influence of social contacts of the most concrete and intimate sort.
>
> Accommodation may be regarded, like religious conversion, as a kind of mutation. The wishes are the same but their organization is different. Assimilation takes place not so much as a result of the changes in organization as in the content, *i.e.*, the memories, of the personality. The individual units, as a result of intimate association, interpenetrate, so to speak, and come in this way into possession of a common experience and a common tradition. The permanence and solidarity of the group rest finally upon this body of common experience and tradition. It is the role of history to preserve this body of common experience and tradition, to criticize and reinterpret it in the light of new experience and changing conditions, and in this way to preserve the continuity of the social and political life.
>
> The relation of social structures to the processes of competition, conflict, accommodation, and assimilation may be represented schematically as follows:

Social Process	*Social Order*
Competition	The economic equilibrium
Conflict	The political order
Accommodation	Social organization
Assimilation	Personality and the cultural heritage [29]

Park and Burgess may not have added anything new to the theory of social forms or of formal processes, but their work belongs along with that of E. A.

[29] *Ibid.*, p. 510.

Ross among the major attempts in the early American period to systematize sociological knowledge from this point of view. Their *Introduction to the Science of Sociology* has been described as the most influential sociological textbook ever produced in America. It has even, on occasion, been listed among the four or five most important books of early American sociology. These judgments may be taken as indicative of the wide reading public to whom, through this work, the formalistic tradition was transmitted. To this day there are persons who do not feel they have covered the basic subject matter of sociology until they have discussed competition, conflict, accommodation, and assimilation.

Leopold von Wiese

Leopold von Wiese (1876–   ) was born in Glatz, Silesia. He received his doctorate from the University of Berlin. In 1915 he was appointed professor of economics at the School of Commerce in Cologne. (This school became the University of Cologne in 1919.) Except for the long interruption during the Nazi regime, von Wiese has remained a professor of sociology at Cologne, where, among his other duties, he has served as editor of the *Kölnische Zeitschrift für Soziologie*. After World War II, Wiese headed a revival of German sociology. His tradition at Cologne is presently being carried on by René König (1906–   ), who succeeded him in the department in 1949. His best known work is his *Allgemeine Soziologie* ["General Sociology"], published in two volumes in 1924 and 1929, and revised in 1933.[30]

Simmel formed the starting point of Wiese's reconstruction of sociology. One of the first changes worked in Simmel's scheme was the abandonment of the terminology of "forms" and the formulation in terms of relations. The formal character of relations, however, is made basic. "Sociology . . . must deal with interhuman relations without immediate reference to ends, norms, or purposes; it involves a wholly different kind of abstraction." [31]

---

[30] Leopold von Wiese, *Allgemeine Soziologie*, Vol. 1, *Beziehungslehre* (Munich: Duncker & Humblot, 1924); Vol. 2, *Gebildelehre* (Munich: Duncker & Humblot, 1929). The second revised edition, published in 1933 by Duncker & Humblot, was called *System der Allgemeine Soziologie*. *Allgemeine Soziologie* was translated, adapted, and amplified by Howard Becker and published as *Systematic Sociology on the Basis of the Beziehungslehre and Gebildelehre of Leopold von Wiese* (New York: John Wiley, 1932); this was later reissued with new title page and 1950 preface by the Norman Paul Press, 1148 St. Joseph Street, Gary, Indiana, 1950. Dr. Becker points out in a personal communication of December 1959 that an abridged version, stressing wherever possible those parts of the original treatise for which Wiese rather than Becker was primarily responsible, will shortly appear as: Howard Becker, *Systematic Sociology as Based on Wiese* (New York: Dover Publications, 1960). Also available in English are a collection of articles and a lecture by von Wiese, translated by Franz H. Mueller, and published under the title *Sociology* (New York: Oskar Piest, 1941) and *Sociology: Its History and Main Problems* (Hanover, N.H.: The Sociological Press, 1928), a translation of *Soziologie: Geschichte und Hauptprobleme* (Berlin: W. de Gruyter, 1926). Other works of Wiese's, not available in English translation, are: *Die Weltwirtschaft als soziologisches Gebilde* ["The World Economy as a Sociological Structure"] (Jena: G. Fischer, 1923); *Gesellschaftliche Stände und Klassen* ["Societal Estates and Classes"] (Bern: A. Francke, 1950); and *Abhängigkeit und Selbstständigkeit im sozialen Leben* ["Dependence and Independence in Social Life"] (Cologne: Westdeutscher Verlag, 1951).

[31] *Systematic Sociology*, pp. 72–73.

The isolation of the relation from the things related is assumed as in the case of Simmel's separability of form and content.

> ... The delimiting principle of sociology as a special social science is not based upon any of the purposes of sociation, as are all the other social sciences. Direction and rhythm of motion are often the same where the purposes in view are entirely different; contrariwise, efforts to achieve identical purposes may utilize social relations following widely discrepant paths. The sociologists therefore delimit according to *direction* (approach or avoidance) and *rhythm* of motion; economics, jurisprudence, linguistics, etc., delimit according to the *purposes* served by social relations.[32]

One tremendous advantage potentially offered by the concept of relations over that of forms is the fact that there is less danger of their reification. From ancient times, "forms" have been thought of as independently existing things with the power to act as independent causes. The concept of relation has been much less abused in this manner, for the idea of a relation existing independently of any items that are actually related is a bit absurd.

A second major difference between Wiese's formulation and Simmel's has been Wiese's strong positivism. After all, Simmel showed pronounced idealistic tendencies and intuitive proclivities. By contrast, Wiese insists that *"Our methodological starting point is the single human being as known to our naïve sense perception;* we began simply by observing what is 'given' in concrete behavior. . . . we do not begin with an abstraction, but with direct observation; the basis of the system here set forth is empirical."[33]

Strong positivistic inclinations also appear in the fascination with physical analogies.

> Relations as they occur in physical phenomena are based upon more or less rapid motion between magnitudes — upon interaction. In order to get a clear picture of such interaction and its effects, let us think of the magnitudes as molecules which are made up of atoms. A stream of energy flows between these molecules and produces relations. Many molecules must give up atoms in the process, but nevertheless do not disintegrate completely. The stream of energy carries the detached atoms to other molecules; these therefore change and grow through the combination of the new with their old atoms. At many places where a cluster of molecules forms, where a plural number of them accumulates, there results a structure or pattern of more or less definite configuration. Such structured clusters may be termed *plurality patterns.*[34]

Before any mistakes are made, it should be noted that Wiese is talking about society, and not chemical transformation. Lundberg must be forgiven

---

[32] *Ibid.*, pp. 41–42.

[33] *Ibid.*, p. 21.

[34] *Ibid.*, pp. 25–26. Howard Becker points out in a personal communication that the term "plurality pattern" is his "somewhat arbitrary rendering of the German original, *Gebilde*, for which 'structure' is not an exact equivalent. A perhaps more apt translation would be 'constellation,' for this makes it clear that the parts of the *Gebilde* are separately distinguishable, and when the definition of *Gebilde* is altered, may be viewed as parts of *other* constellations."

his tendency to clasp Wiese to his bosom and feel hurt when his love is unrequited.[35]

Nor does Wiese's positivism stop with physical figures of speech. The ideal method of analysis of social process is set forth in pseudo formulas:

> Every social process implies a plurality of participants, sometimes quite large, but the simplest process takes place in an occurrence directly involving but two persons, and we shall here assume that this is what the formula indicates:
>
> $$P = A \times S$$
>
> That is, every social process is the result ("product") of a personal attitude (A) and a situation (S). In thus calling attention to the observable fact that in every social process both attitude and situation exert influence, there is no claim that both always exert it in the same degree.
>
> Attitude and situation are composite factors. A is the resultant of (1) the socially relevant native equipment, or N (including, among other things, the temperamental attitudes described by Thomas); and (2) previous experiences, or E. The inherited *and* the experienced are to be taken into account. Therefore $A = N \times E$.
>
> The situation, S, also yields two components: (1) the extrahuman environment, the physical basis, or B; and (2) the attitudes of the other participant in the process in question, or A_1. Here also one factor must not be disregarded for the sake of the other. Hence $S = B \times A_1$.
>
> The factor A_1 offers the same possibility of separation into component elements. . . .
>
> The various minor formulae used in analysis combine into the following major formula:
>
> $$P = N \times E \times B \times (N \times E)_1.[36]$$

But, alas, all this quantification is only make-believe. It is almost with regret that von Wiese admits "all plurality patterns are intangible, incorporeal; they are nothing more than neuropsychic patterns — and nothing less!"[37] The situation, of course, is not as yet completely hopeless, for they could still be specific quantities of nervous energy — that is, if that has any meaning. But the problem, it seems, is worse even than that. "The strictly mechanistic task of measuring (or of stating numerically) the path of motion involved in interaction is only one stage and not the final goal of sociological knowledge, for that goal lies beyond the mechanistic. *The behavior of human beings, when all is said, is something qualitative.*"[38]

Over and beyond these discussions, von Wiese advanced the cause of formal sociology by bringing the entire field together as he perceived it. Sociology, the science of interhuman relations, is divided in two: the systematics of

---

[35] See George Lundberg, *Foundations of Sociology* (New York: Macmillan, 1939), pp. 36, 87, 102, 111, 132, 248, 261, 267, 280, 281, 348, 371, 374.
[36] Wiese-Becker, *Systematic Sociology*, p. 73.
[37] *Ibid.*, p. 31.   [38] *Ibid.*, p. 52.

action patterns and the systematics of plurality patterns or social structures. Social relations are the basic elements of both divisions; they are of two types — common human relations and circumscribed relations. Relations, so far as delimited by the presence of social groups, are circumscribed. Common human social relations are studied as existent and as functional. They are sociative in three possible ways: associative, dissociative, or mixed. Social structures are divided into three main categories: crowds (patternings of lowest order), groups (patternings of intermediate power), and abstract collectivities (patternings of highest power). Sociation, the total social process, comprises all social relations: association or dissociation, circumscribed and common human. The two fundamental processes of association and dissociation may be divided into subprocesses, and these in turn into single processes subsuming concrete social actions. In the systematics of action patterns, all-inclusive and single processes are conceptually delimited and described; assigned places within the total system; analyzed as objective or subjective phenomena; ranked; and compared with other action patterns. Wiese's actual procedure was far more of an arm-chair operation than his positivistic formulas would imply. It consisted in the patient collection of terms that seemed to have social import. This was followed by long conferences to assess the amounts of association they represent. Once this was done, the task for systematic sociology consisted in the assembly of the known sociological materials in tables. Whether von Wiese's followers in the school he established will manage to find their way back to empirical reality remains to be seen.

Hans Kelsen

Has the neo-Kantian brand of sociological formalism completely run its course in sociology proper? Certainly it is still alive in jurisprudence, supplying now as in the past a juridical theory of society. Hans Kelsen (1881–) is a primary representative of contemporary neo-Kantian jurisprudence. A native of Prague, he became lecturer (*Privatdozent*) at the University of Vienna in 1911. In 1919 he was appointed to the Chair of Public Law and Philosophy of Law at Vienna, and in 1930 he became Professor of International Law at the University of Cologne. Because his views were incompatible with the Nazi ideology, Kelsen was forced to leave Germany in 1933. For the next seven years, he divided his time between the University of Geneva and the University of Prague, where he taught international law and jurisprudence. In 1941 he was invited to Harvard University as research professor and lecturer on international law. From 1942 to 1952 he taught international law and jurisprudence at the University of California at Berkeley, where, since 1952, he has been University Professor Emeritus.[39]

[39] Kelsen has written both in German and in English. His main works with sociological import include: *Hauptprobleme der Staatsrechtslehre* ["Main Problems of Constitutional Law"] (Tübingen: J. C. B. Mohr, 1911); *Das Problem der Souveränität und die Theorie des Völkerrechts* ["The Problem of Sovereignty and the Theory of International Law"] (Tübingen: J. C. B. Mohr, 1920); *Allgemeine Staatslehre* ["General Political Science"]

Kelsen's method is essentially Kantian, though he is critical of some features of Kant's legal theory. He believes that knowledge is no mere passive picture of the objective world. Knowledge creates its objects in terms of its inherent forms of the material presented to the senses. Law, as such a creation, is a product of a mental operation, but not one that belongs to the world of nature. Law belongs to the category of essence (*das Sollen*), not to the category of existence (*das Sein*). One essential property of law is the possibility that it will not be observed. A rule of law is a special kind of hypothetical proposition. If one defined set of factors occurs, another involving compulsion ought to follow as a matter of law, though not necessarily as a matter of experience. Law is an imperative in a hypothetical sense. Law is a branch of the normative rather than natural sciences. The legal rule is concerned with what positive law shall be, not with why positive law ought to be.

A law in the domain of natural science is an application of the principle of causality. It reveals certain events as the necessary consequence of others. The man-made law, on the other hand, lays down rules of right conduct. A norm can not be explained by reference to the acts of existence. The question as to why a legal rule is established in fact is social-psychological and outside legal science. The question as to why a legal rule is binding is the proper study of jurisprudence.

A legal rule is binding only by reference to another, higher, legal rule. But must this legal rule then be based on another, and so on without end? There must, of course, be some stopping point. The regress from legal rule to legal rule must end somewhere upon some ultimate proposition from which a legal system is traced. The initial hypothesis of a legal system is its fundamental norm (*die Grundnorm*). The reasons for accepting the fundamental rule are meta-legal. The jurist goes back to the fundamental rule; he does not go beyond it. Thus, at the summit of every legal system there is a rule providing that the final legislative organ in the form it takes from time to time is to have the power of determining the process by which all other rules are maintained. The birth of a legal system is in this "hypothetical constitution." It is this hypothesis that transforms might into right, force into law.

Legal duty is the central and only essential property of a legal system. The essence of a compulsory ordering is that it binds those subject to it. The

---

(Berlin: J. Springer, 1925); *Probleme der Rechtsphilosophie* ["Problems of Legal Philosophy"] (Berlin: Rothschild, 1927); *The Legal Process and International Order* (London: Constable, 1935); *Law and Peace in International Relations* (Cambridge, Mass.: Harvard University Press, 1942); *Society and Nature: A Sociological Inquiry* (Chicago: University of Chicago Press, 1943); *Peace Through Law* (Chapel Hill, N.C.: University of North Carolina Press, 1944); *General Theory of Law and the State*, tr. by Anders Wedberg (Cambridge, Mass.: Harvard University Press, 1945); *The Law of the United Nations* (London: Stevens, 1950); and a collection of essays, *What Is Justice?* (Berkeley: University of California Press, 1957). Summaries of Kelsen's views may be found in J. Walter Jones, *Historical Introduction to the Theory of Law* (Oxford: Clarendon Press, 1940), pp. 222–234; and H. Lauterpacht, "Kelsen's Pure Science of Law," in [no author], *Modern Theories of Law* (London: Oxford University Press, 1933), pp. 105–138.

fact of being bound is expressed through the conception of duty. Every legal rule establishes a legal duty. Subjective right obtains only so far as it is laid down in objective law. A "person" is a bundle of legal duties and rights. The physical person is the personification of the total of legal rules applicable to one person. The juristic person is the personification of legal rules applicable to a plurality of persons.

The phenomenon of delegation from the fundamental hypothesis is essential for the relation between the pure objective fact of law and positive law. There is a descending process of delegation from the "constitution" to legislation, administration, judicial decisions, and private transactions. Legislation is only relatively law-creative; it applies the fundamental rule of law embodied in the constitution.

Once the distinction between the creation and application of law is clear, one may understand the distinction between private and public law in a new way. Kelsen rejects the idea that there is any principled difference. The very fact that the legal order protects a private interest shows that it is of public interest to do so. Any rule of criminal or administrative law can ultimately be traced to the individual person or persons in whose interest it has been created. The duty to observe certain conduct is grounded not in the will of one person but in agreement. The breach of legal duty thus created evokes compulsion not from the other party but from the state.

Moreover, just as private law and public law collapse and form one system, so too are the law and the state found to be identical. Negatively, this is seen in the fact that the other sciences cannot dispense with the legal conception of the state, but must assume it. The state assumed by sociology, for example, is a unity such as is posited by legal science. Positively, the state may be seen to be a normative ordering coextensive with the ordering of the legal system. Only by perceiving the state as *a system of norms* can it be seen as an authority, and the relation of the individual to the state can be seen as one of subordination. Moreover, the state can only be understood so far as duties issue from it, and individuals are bound to observe certain rules of conduct. The apparatus of compulsion, called the state, turns out to be simply the legal order. The legal norm is the rule through which the attribution of acts to the state occurs. It consists of the condition posited by law and the legal consequence. The power of the state is not its guns, ships, forts, prisons, and gallows; these are inanimate objects. They derive their significance from the human use made of them. This use results from the ideas dominating men. The state is a product of personification. Human thought finds it inconvenient to deal with the unity of the legal system except by a hypothetical device that embodies a multitude of abstract norms. The state is only the expression of the demand for logical completeness and inner consistency of a system of legal norms.

In somewhat the same fashion that Kelsen tends to fuse public and private law, there is a clear tendency to fuse the sovereignty of the individual state in the single unity of international law. Sovereignty is reduced to the expression of the unity and exclusiveness of the legal system. The assumption of such unity is essential for law as a science. But, asks Kelsen, do not the demands of that science press beyond the limits of the individual state? Kelsen's reasoning seems to run as follows. The sovereignty of the state implies that the legal order of the state is independent, self-existent, and self-sufficient. When the exclusiveness of the individual sovereign state is necessarily asserted, other sovereign states exist only so far as recognized. However, so far as recognized, they are included within the legal order of the recognizing state. One must now either abandon the sovereignty of the state or accept the primacy of international law in which the legal system of the individual state is a partial legal order, deriving its validity by delegation from the fundamental rule of the world legal order. The world legal order is already in existence as a result of the existence of international law. The primacy of international law subordinates the state to a higher authority and deprives it of absolute superiority over the corporate entities within its territorial units.

Kelsen's objection to Kant arose from his view that Kant, as a personality rooted in Christianity, was led in his capacity as a legal philosopher to abandon his transcendental method, making his metaphysic of morals into a perfect expression of the classical natural-law doctrine. Kelsen's estimate is quite correct. Kelsen made the central point of his own position the break with natural-law doctrines. Natural law was, he thought, based on the assumption of a natural order with rules valid because they are not made by human authority, but are rather a product of God, nature, or reason. By rejecting natural law, Kelsen believed he was affirming the dignity and autonomy of man. The central concept in the pure science of law is the rejection of natural law. The foundation is located, as already noted, in the fundamental constitution which is placed in international law.

Kant had, indeed, drawn a distinction between the spheres of morality and causality. Kelsen, in effect, accuses Kant of having violated his own distinction, mistakenly assigning law to the realm of causality. Kelsen may thus claim to have carried out the original Kantian program.

Kelsen's criticism of Kant should not obscure his basic Kantianism. In both Kant and Kelsen, the liberal and rationalistic conception of society is maintained. Both men resist the idea of the absolute subordination of the individual to the group. Individual freedom is simultaneously limited and made possible by the group, which is merely another name for inter-individual behavior. Both men find their highest personal value in the dignity of the free personality.

In view of these agreements, Kelsen's accusation that Kant confused morality with causality may seem odd. But if one notes the frequency and passion of his rejection of the idea of a "natural" law, his accusation may have a simple explanation. The plastic eighteenth-century meaning of "natural" as "universal" permitted its application both to morality and to empirical regularities. To be sure, this ambiguity invites misunderstanding. While Kant nearly always kept it clear, his followers often did not. Kelsen, in fact, reasons like a "natural law" theorist of Kantian type. Like Kant, he dissolves the state into the law conceived as a binding inter-individual arrangement. He sounds a Kantian note approximating the idea that nothing is ultimately good other than the good will. Kelsen thus places Kantian legal formalism and the sense of duty on the broadest possible base, such that the validity of every rule — every rule, eventually, of the human world — is derived from some other legal rule deriving eventually from a kind of "hypothetical constitution" of mankind. (This is Kelsen's counterpart to the Enlightenment's "reason.") In a sense, the Kantian formula, "so act that one's action can become a universal law," never received a more general formulation.

Kelsen has not stopped his reflections with these formulations, but has extended his analysis to sociology in his book *Society and Nature: A Sociological Inquiry* (1943). In this work he employs the dualism between society and nature and between normative order and the principle of causality in quite a new manner, to account for the evolution of men's conceptions of nature and society. Here Kelsen's argument is that primitive man was dominated by feeling and emotion rather than by rationality. The primitive man's concept of nature was also dominated by feeling, hence the initial form of his conception of nature was determined by evaluations establishing a normative order of human behavior. (This accounts for the lack of causal thinking and the dominance of magic among primitives.) It also accounts for the primitive man's lack of ego-consciousness and his belief that animals cannot be killed against their will, and that there are tongues in trees and spirits in running brooks. Autocratism, conservativism, and traditionalism rule among primitives, and, generally, primitive thought about everything is dominated by the principle of retribution — an idea appropriate to society — that applies to all things and all areas of natural events. Thunder and lightning, natural catastrophe, other natural events, all are given the form of retribution. This idea of retribution, Kelsen maintains, was still dominant in the religion and arts of the ancient Greeks.

Beginning with the Greeks, however, a new idea appeared, particularly in the doctrines of the atomists, of the existence of a principle of absolutely valid causality. The idea continued to grow in clarity until Hume performed the final act of shearing the last remnants of the idea of retribution from the concept. Kant completed the emancipation. The importance of the discovery of causality, however, tended to lead to its overemphasis and the reverse process of the incorporation of society into the order of nature.

> Together with the emancipation of the law of causality from the principle of retribution occurred the divorce of the notions of nature and society. Nature appeared to be part of society when it was interpreted according to the principle of retribution.[40]

From this vantage point, Kelsen summed up the central point of his thought:

> With the emancipation of causality from retribution and of the law of

[40] *Society and Nature*, p. 264. (Copyright 1943 by the University of Chicago.)

nature from the social norm, nature and society prove to be two entirely different systems. The idea of a system of norms regulating human behavior and constituting society as an order totally different from the laws of nature is possible without the fiction of freedom of will and therefore without contradiction to the principle of causality. . . .

The idea of natural law . . . presumes a dualism within nature conceived as a universal society; the real, inadequate human society is contrasted with the ideal cosmic society. It is the antagonism of man and God, of the empirical and the transcendental. With the emancipation of the causal from the normative interpretation of nature . . . the antagonism of the empirical and the transcendental disappears from the sphere of science. Hence there is no longer room for a natural [law] behind or above a positive legal order.[41]

And with this formulation, Kelsen relinquishes to sociology all those aspects of human society in which it is a part of the order of nature. "After the complete emancipation of causality from retribution in the modern notion of law, society is — from the point of view of science — a part of nature."[42]

However comforting it may be to have a liberal image of society as a legally ordered plurality of independent wills, many problems are buried in neo-Kantian theory. By drawing the line between phenomena and noumena and making the former the sphere of science, the latter the sphere of morality — and incidentally, society — extraordinarily tough problems are posed for a science of society. Strictly speaking, a science of society seems to have been made impossible. Freedom, for example, belongs to action and morality; it does not belong, as does "causality," to phenomena. But if the thing of interest in society is its "freedom," does not the study of society lie outside science? If we study society causally, do we not miss precisely its most significant element? Kelsen is therefore very traditionally Kantian when he appropriates everything socially significant for jurisprudence, leaving to sociology the study of everything that does not matter.

Nor do our woes stop here. Kant had "saved" science on the basis of a distinction between form and content. But forms are mind-given. Clearly we do not discover a mind-given "form" by the methods appropriate to the discovery of content. If the forms are really *a priori*, we need no experience to discover them. Not inductive study of facts, but mental inspection, is suggested as the proper method for this most important element. To the degree to which sociology seriously follows this lead, *it for the first time launches a fundamental attack on methodological positivism*. Since it represents the attempt to face up to the inner difficulties of neo-Kantian formalism, phenomenological formalism is more profound.

Summary

The two earliest schools of sociology were predominantly conservative in orientation. They were interested in groups rather than individuals. The

[41] *Ibid.*, pp. 265–266.   [42] *Ibid.*, p. 266.

values of stability, order, and solidarity repeatedly appeared as social objectives.

One could well have expected some change with the professionalization and institutionalization of sociology. Once the role of sociologists became established among the accepted academic positions, recruitment could take place purely in terms of the role itself rather than in terms of prevailing ideological atmospheres. Sooner or later, liberals would appear among the ranks of sociologists with the demand for a theory of society more suited to their requirements.

Neo-Kantianism was one of the first examples of a liberal theory of society in sociological circles. Kant had been heir to eighteenth-century liberalism. Society was not, for him, an organic form that swallowed up the individual, but an ordered community of independent wills. Kant shrank from the view that the external system of government had to be the antithesis of the individual. Rather, this system might provide the very condition for the full realization of the nature of man. Law was thrust into central position as the basis of an ordered liberal theory of society and the new school of sociological formalism developed ties with jurisprudence, as may be illustrated by the social theories of Rudolf Stammler.

The new school of sociological formalism came into its own with the theories of Georg Simmel. He even attempted to carry out a Kantian type of analysis directly in his study, "How Is Society Possible?" He tried to deduce the *a priori* condition making society possible as an entity in which the individual is simultaneously realized and surpassed. The concept of "calling" or "role" was thought to be this form. This was Simmel's only attempt to deduce a system of *a priori* forms. For the rest, he rejected the organismic concept of society, treating it merely as interaction analyzable into form and content. The systematic study of social forms was set down as the objective of sociological study. Simmel carried out many intuitively rich studies of forms such as sociability, coquetry, secrecy, superiority, and subordination and conflict.

The neo-Kantian position migrated to France, where it found its most imaginative exponent in Bouglé, who also posed the task of sociology in formalistic terms. Like Simmel, Bouglé had the capacity for unusually subtle analysis of social events as revealed in his study of *caste*. More than any other single study, this essay laid the basis for the modern theory of caste.

In America, neo-Kantian formalism found able exponents in E. A. Ross and Park and Burgess, who utilized a mechanism of forms as the foundation for the most nearly systematic general sociology to be achieved at the time. The fullest development of neo-Kantian formalism was the work of Leopold von Wiese, who tried to integrate the entire field of sociology in formalistic terms. Though this enterprise was bolstered by elaborate positivistic analogies and pseudo-mathematical formulas, the actual procedure consisted in a patient collection of terms with apparent social importance. These terms were then consolidated in lists and assembled in tables in terms of the presumed type and amount of association they were thought to signify.

Meanwhile, so far as neo-Kantian formalism remains a vital position in the contemporary world, its ablest exponents are found not in sociology but in jurisprudence, as illustrated by Hans Kelsen.

SELECTED BIBLIOGRAPHY

ABEL, THEODORE, *Systematic Sociology in Germany.* New York: Columbia University Press, 1929.

ARON, RAYMOND, *German Sociology.* Translated by Mary and Thomas Bottomore. Glencoe, Ill.: The Free Press, 1957.

BOUGLÉ, CÉLESTIN, *Qu'est-ce que la sociologie?* Paris: F. Alcan, 1907.

JONES, J. WALTER, *Historical Introduction to the Theory of Law.* Oxford: The Clarendon Press, 1940.

KELSEN, HANS, *Society and Nature: A Sociological Inquiry.* Chicago: University of Chicago Press, 1943.

PARK, ROBERT E., and ERNEST W. BURGESS, *Introduction to the Science of Sociology.* Second edition. Chicago: University of Chicago Press, 1924.

ROSS, EDWARD ALLSWORTH, *Principles of Sociology.* Revised edition. New York: The Century Company, 1930.

SIMMEL, GEORG, *The Sociology of Georg Simmel.* Translated, edited, and with an introduction by Kurt H. Wolff. Glencoe, Ill.: The Free Press, 1950.

WIESE, LEOPOLD VON, *Sociology.* Articles and a lecture translated by Franz H. Mueller. New York: Oskar Piest, 1941.

Modern Theories of Law. No author. London: Oxford University Press, 1933.

11

The Phenomenological Branch of Sociological Formalism

IN THE NEO-KANTIAN PROGRAM FOR KNOWLEDGE AND SCIENCE, THE SEARCH for the general, the objective, and the universal sooner or later became a search for the formal. From its sources in Kant, this formalism had been derived from a twofold distinction: (1) one that separated phenomena from the thing in itself, rejecting the latter as an object of cognition, and (2) from a distinction between the form and content of phenomena, with forms seen as objective and universal, representing the mind-supplied universal element of knowledge. Things were different for phenomenology.

The procedure of the two approaches was distinct. The point of departure in the analysis of the objective aspects of scientific knowledge for Kant was made through the question: how is nature *a priori* possible? Simmel, as was seen, paraphrased this in his neo-Kantian sociology with the question: what are the *a priori* conditions that make society possible? In the Kantian framework there is only one possible answer: forms. Husserl had Kant in mind when he insisted that phenomena are the object of immediate experience and the data of cognition. He maintained that Kant's error was to assume that only objects of experience and cognition can be of a sensory character. He maintained that phenomena as essences are the contents of pure consciousness. He argued that the objects of ordinary experience are constituted as "essences" which are objects of immediate intuition. Every object, whether factual, actual, natural, imaginary, or essential, is at least a potential object of some kind of experience. Whenever something is experienced, it is experienced by virtue of the fact that it is in some relation to consciousness and the ego. The two basic subdivisions of experience are the natural and eidetic, referring respectively to the natural world of events and to the essences directly intuited. Husserl was interested in the second, for in the last analysis all meaning assigned to the natural is derived from its relation to the essences. To analyze the latter, Husserl proposed a special method of bracketing or reduction: a progressively focused and controlled concentration of attention on experience to reveal the levels in depth it displays. For our purposes, the only thing that is of interest in all this is *the possibility it offered for a special kind of sociological formalism in which directly intuited essences are assumed to supply the element of generality in social life.*

Alfred Vierkandt

Alfred Vierkandt (1867–1953) had made his reputation in his study of culture history and ethnology, *Naturvölker und Kulturvölker* (1896) and in the study of cultural change, *Stetigkeit im Kulturwandel* (1908), before he undertook the fusion of the formalistic tradition in sociology with Husserl's phenomenology.[1] In his earlier work, Vierkandt anticipated Clark Wissler's concept of "culture area" and Ogburn's conception of "cultural lag." In this early stage, sociology had been conceived as the generalizations of ethnological and historical materials. However, under the growing demand to make sociology into a special science, Vierkandt rejected this historical approach to sociological problems and the use of historical materials, and in his *Gesellschaftslehre* (1923) he proposed a form of sociological formalism. The object of his study, Vierkandt maintained, was to examine the last forms, powers or forces, and facts of societal life which reveal the patterns free of all historical change but which emerge from the character of society. Though this scientific goal had been established by Simmel and Tönnies, Vierkandt believed it was not obtainable in Simmel's terms. It becomes fully attainable only through the development of phenomenology, which permits us in a quite new manner to isolate the final *a priori* circumstances that make society possible.[2]

Vierkandt objected to the lack of precision in the concept of sociology which was characteristic of a whole series of disciplines applying to human groups, their life, spiritual activity, products, and culture. Like Simmel, he wished to confine the term "sociology" to the study of the peculiarities of the group and the theory of social interaction and its products. Also like

1 None of Vierkandt's major sociological works are available in English translation, including: *Naturvölker und Kulturvölker* ["Natural Peoples and Cultural Peoples"] (Leipzig: Duncker & Humblot, 1896); *Die Stetigkeit im Kulturwandel* ["The Order in Cultural Change"] (Leipzig: Duncker & Humblot, 1908); *Gesellschaftslehre: Hauptprobleme der philosophischen Soziologie* ["The Study of Society: Main Problems of Philosophical Sociology"] (Stuttgart: F. Enke, 1923; 2d rev. ed., 1928); and *Kleine Gesellschaftslehre* ["Small Studies of Society"] (Stuttgart: F. Enke, 1949). A review of Vierkandt's sociology appears in Theodore Abel's *Systematic Sociology in Germany* (New York: Columbia University Press, 1929), pp. 59–79.

2 *Gesellschaftslehre*, Foreword, p. 1. (References are to the 1923 edition.)

Simmel, Vierkandt did not stop here, but insisted that the sociologist is interested in the innermost actualities of societary facts, and not simply the objective external manifestations of interaction. Precisely for this reason, sociology is different from naturalistic investigation. Man lives in a world of biological and cultural relations but also in a world of social relations, a realm with qualities of its own and different from those of the cultural and biological spheres. These qualities are *mental states,* emerging in the process of living together. Thus, while studying interaction, formal sociology is not behavioristic. And it is not attempting to isolate behaviors, but rather the mental states presupposed by these behaviors. Similarly, the investigation of products of interaction has no concern for their external manifestations but only for their utility in the isolation of the ultimate unchangeable aspects. Only when the interplay of the forces of interaction is the object of study, rather than the totality of the cultural complex, is the investigation sociological. The relation of formal sociology to the cultural sciences and practical life is similar to the relation between mathematics and physics or technology.[3]

Vierkandt thought the systematization of social phenomena to be the primary task of sociology. This could be achieved by reducing social phenomena to their ultimate *a priori* forms. Simmel, he felt, had failed in this by burdening his writing with too many examples and displaying too much fascination with concrete social content. Domination is a social form, but any concrete manifestation of domination (as between social classes, for example) is historical. Simmel remained at this level and did not develop sociology into a true theory of pure forms or categories. This task, Vierkandt believed, was made possible only by the newly developed phenomenological method. This is applicable to sociological problems, because societal life is directly given in experience as all mental life.[4] Thus, the argument develops that, through the phenomenological method, and through it alone, is a true formal sociology possible.

The phenomenological method consists in controlled examination of the process of awareness itself. It requires the focus of attention on aspects of conscious experience and not upon external manifestations. It represents a kind of "immanent reflection" and concentration upon the inherent meaning of things as given. The phenomenological method attempts, through the analysis of experience, to uncover certain fundamental social dispositions assumed to lie at the foundation of common life. These fundamental dispositions or essences are discoverable only through this method of progressive discrimination and reduction. Among other things, it may indicate that apparently similar experiential processes are intrinsically different. "Shame," for instance, differs from "fear of undesirable consequences." If one attends only to externals, such a distinction will never be discovered. In fact, this was the mistake made by Simmel. Through the inductive review of historical events, one may discover the basis for historically determined

[3] *Ibid.,* p. 18.   [4] *Ibid.,* p. 15.

individual differences, but not irreducible essences. No inductive procedure of inference involving either repeated observation or the consideration of various cases is required. Potentially, the insight may be gained in a single act of intuition. Simmel's procedure is a relatively crass kind of induction, destined to fail because it attempts to arrive at the form by mistaken methods. The dispositions discovered by phenomenology, on the other hand, are essences, *a priori* properties of interhuman mental life.

Examples of phenomenological analysis are found in the disposition of *self-respect,* which simultaneously calls forth a deep inner sense of superiority and instills respect. It displays the presence of an inner bond expressed as submission to the values of the group. At times it is manifest as a will to power for the purposes of achieving distinction and of being recognized as better than others. When satisfied, it is the source of the feeling of dignity. Frustrated, it becomes the source of the feeling of hurt and shame.

The phenomenological study of *submission* [5] shows that it is not due to fear or other ulterior motives but may imply a voluntary inner surrender. It is accompanied by psychological states such as timidity, embarrassment, and a feeling of the need for contact with the superior personality. Characteristic attitudes associated with it are adoration, devotion, and respect. But its course is a kind of participation in the greatness of the other, an instinct which manifests itself in the cult of power, the desire to follow the leader, the feeling of duty and blind submission to an inner command.

The general issues to which Vierkandt addressed his sociology were: (1) the historical character of human mental life, (2) the nature of society, (3) the power of the environment, (4) relations as fundamental categories of sociological thought, and (5) the concept of social wholes. Human nature is not universal; there are only particular historically influenced configurations. The possibility of historical influences on the individual is due to the plastic conditions affecting the innate dispositions. Society is a group of men, so far as they are the bearers of inwardly established interrelations. The social relations that hold in society are among the powerful forces molding, controlling, and conditioning the expression of the dispositions.

Society,[6] in fact, is easily defined, since the individual is not enclosed within himself but participates in the life of other people and derives self-awareness as well as ideals, affections, and desires from others. Social life implies at least a minimum of reciprocity. The internal bond is the fundamental characteristic of society. The community is its ideal form. Only in community do social dispositions flourish. In no case is society to be assumed to be an organism. The inner character of societal materials bears the imprint of the forms of relations which must be presupposed from the outset.

Within this framework, sociological analysis was thought to begin with the

[5] *Ibid.,* pp. 68–87.
[6] *Ibid.,* pp. 560–562.

phenomenological investigation of the innate dispositions or instincts. In addition to the two referred to — the dispositions of self-respect and of submission — Vierkandt examines the parental drive and the dispositions of struggle, sympathy, imitation, expressiveness, and sociability. Probably the single most important source for the materials of these particular discussions was William McDougall's *Introduction to Social Psychology* (1908). Vierkandt also made use of discussions by William James, James Mark Baldwin, Gabriel Tarde, Karl Groos, and Simmel.

After completing this phase of his study, Vierkandt turned his attention to fundamental societal relations. The general formula for this phase of the study was provided by Tönnies' typology of *Gemeinschaft* and *Gesellschaft*, representing, respectively, a relatively compact and a relatively loose form of interhuman life. An understanding of both was said to be essential to the comprehension of human affairs. *Gemeinschaft* was the original form of society, *Gesellschaft* a later dissolution of the early form. The most important historical forms of the *Gemeinschaft* were the family, the sib and locality groups, the men's club, the status group, class, political party, and the cultural unities of folk, lineage, nation, and the state. Vierkandt completed his study with the examination of collective phenomena of the group, such as morale, collective consciousness, and group self-consciousness.

The phenomenological study of social relations also concentrates on mental process, or "inner" life. All social relations affect the inner life of the participating individuals. Social relations are sought not only for external advantage but in the anticipation of inner experience. One may enter into a social relation with others for external reasons or for inner stimulation or some combination of both. This is most clearly the case in the establishment of union (*Gemeinschaft*) with others; one expects sympathetic response. But relations of dominance, mutual recognition, and conflict also offer inner satisfaction. This is a product of the specific qualities of experience each relation offers. *Gemeinschaft* offers, in the surrender to the whole, an enhanced and expanded sense of self; conflict affords the pleasure of achievement and exhilaration due to the exertion of one's powers. The inner bond in human intercourse is fundamental. It is most pronounced in primary-group relations, resting on awareness of the mutual benefit of the union and presupposing like-mindedness and we-feeling. In other social relations, the basis of the inner bond is found in the regulation of the activities present in all the relations. The inner bond is here expressed in the mutual recognition of norms. Regulation results from the demands of the group, imposed on inborn motives. Regulation originates in the primary group, where the dependence of the individual or the group most quickly leads to the acceptance of discipline. Moreover, the *Gemeinschaft* prevails in three other fundamental relations: those based on agreement (keeping of agreements or contracts), those based on dominance, and those based on conflict (the recognition that the conflict takes place according to rules, presupposing a moral community). Therefore, there is an inner bond or degree of *Gemeinschaft* in all social relations.

According to Vierkandt, not only does phenomenological sociology give the first adequate account of the innate dispositions out of which society is constructed, and the *only* adequate account of social relations, but it makes possible, for the first time, the full understanding of the group. The group is thought to be more than the mere sum of individuals composing it. Moreover, it develops new properties in its individual members. It creates a set of external forms which act as a constraining force on them. Such forces emerge from the group as a whole. The group possesses a spirit of its own that forces the individual to think, feel, and act in a definite way. The group is self-conscious and manifests a life-urge and life-organization, acting like a person.[7]

For the adequate explanation of the group, we need a new theory of social wholes. Gestalt theory is an instance of this new theory. The external and constraining force exercised by the group is explained by the fact that the members at any time may divide into actors and spectators. The spectators watch and control the behavior of the actors. The group is in reality the spectators. Its will is their will. Conformity of the actors is due to the change of roles to which every group is subject. The individual is actor at one time and spectator at others. The actor is at other times a spectator, in which role he controls the actors. The group spirit embodies the ideas, attitudes, and values shaped by all. It is external to each, for it is not a product of the individual mind but results from the interaction between the individuals and their circumstances. Group self-consciousness is the awareness of each individual of the inner bond uniting him to others. Each member is conscious of belonging to a whole of which he is a part. It is a consciousness of common elements. The life-urge of the group is a product of each member's desire to maintain intact the group to which he belongs. The objectivity of the group is the constancy of functions of collective representations, which are independent of any particular individual and appear as a uniform, causal, and purposeful system.

Thus, the phenomenological method, the method of pure sociology, discovers the essences of society, social behavior, and social relations. It is not to be confused with the inductive-empirical approach to social materials, although the latter may consist in the specialized research that applies the principles and discoveries of the phenomenological method. In fact, the inductive-empirical and phenomenological methods are not simple alternatives, for the latter is more profound, establishing results more basic than the former. The phenomenological method, in contrast to induction, may arrive at judgments of absolute certainty and finality. Through use of this method, one discovers the ultimate, *a priori* facts of social life, the inborn but plastic dispositions. These dispositions — to fondle, to help, to fight, to sympathize, to imitate, to receive suggestions, to be sociable, to

[7] *Ibid.*, pp. 241–242.

trust, and so on — are the *a priori* preconditions of human society, and social life is reducible to the development of them. Because they are inborn, they are discoverable directly — if only one has the proper method. As original qualities of mental experience, they are susceptible only to phenomenological analysis, which discovers them and reduces all other qualities of experience to them.

The adherence by phenomenologists to the Enlightenment model of society is nowhere more completely shown than in the treatment of society and the group. They are not treated as external coercive structures. While they may exercise a "constraint" over the individual, it is a constraint exercised by one aspect of a man's mind over others.

Max Scheler

The chief importance of Max Scheler (1874–1928) for modern sociology is his popularization of the sociology of knowledge (*Wissenssoziologie*). Theoretically, however, he belongs to the phenomenological branch of sociological formalism and deserves consideration here from that standpoint. Scheler was a student of Dilthey and Simmel and became professor of sociology and philosophy at the University of Cologne, thus having many-sided contact with the formalists, for at Cologne he was a colleague of von Wiese.[8]

Fundamental to all aspects of Scheler's thought was the distinction characteristic of the phenomenologists between the realm of ideal value — essence — and the realm of existential fact. While they partly parallel one another, they must not be identified.[9] Real existence consists in factual relationships changing in time; the realm of values is a sphere of timelessly

---

[8] Only two of Scheler's works are currently available in English translation: the second edition of *Wesen und Formen der Sympathie* (Bonn: F. Cohen, 1923) was translated by Peter Heath as *The Nature of Sympathy* (New Haven, Conn.: Yale University Press, 1954); and *Philosophische Weltanschauung* (Bonn: F. Cohen, 1929) was translated by Oscar A. Haac, *Philosophical Perspectives* (Boston: Beacon Press, 1958); included in *Philosophical Perspectives* is Scheler's earlier book *Die Formen des Wissens und die Bildung* ["Forms of Knowledge and Culture"] (Bonn: F. Cohen, 1929). Works which have not been translated include: *Schriften zur Soziologie und Weltanschauungslehre* ["Writings in Sociology and Philosophy"], 3 vols. (Leipzig: P. Reinhold, 1923–24); *Versuche zu einer Soziologie des Wissens* ["Essays Toward a Sociology of Knowledge"] (Munich: Duncker & Humblot, 1924); *Die Wissensformen und die Gesellschaft* ["Forms of Knowledge and Society"] (Leipzig: Neue-Geist Verlag, 1926); and *Bildung und Wissen* ["Culture and Knowledge"] (Frankfurt am Main: G. Schulte-Bulmke, 1947). His collected works have now been edited by Maria Scheler, *Gesammelte Werke* (Bern: Francke, 1954).

For reviews of Scheler's work, see: Howard Becker and Helmut Otto Dahlke, "Max Scheler's Sociology of Knowledge," *Philosophy and Phenomenological Research*, Vol. 2 (March 1942), pp. 309–322; H. O. Dahlke, "The Sociology of Knowledge," in H. E. Barnes, Howard Becker, and Frances Bennett Becker (eds.), *Contemporary Social Theory* (New York: D. Appleton-Century, 1940), pp. 64–92; Robert Merton, "The Sociology of Knowledge," *Isis*, Vol. 27 (November 1937), pp. 493–503, reprinted in *Social Theory and Social Structure* (Rev. ed.; Glencoe, Ill: The Free Press, 1957); and Maurice Mandelbaum, *The Problem of Historical Knowledge* (New York: Liveright, 1938), pp. 147ff.

[9] *Die Wissensformen und die Gesellschaft*, pp. 347–348.

valid, intuited meanings. This metaphysical distinction is essential to the contrast between cultural sociology and the sociology of real factors. Cultural data are "ideal," existing in the realm of ideas and values. Real factors are part of changing events in time. Cultural data are defined by ideal goals or intentions; real data form an impulse structure around such things as sex, hunger, and striving for power. It is wrong to assume that real factors such as race, political power, and economic production exclusively determine meanings. It is also wrong to assume that external events of experience consist in the unfolding of spiritualistic and personalistic ideas. Ideas do not become concrete and actualized unless bound up in some fashion in collective tendencies and incorporated in institutional structures. The peculiar problem of historical knowledge for Scheler is the explanation of how these two realms are jointly effective.

The goal of cultural sociology is the apprehension of the ideal — the object matters of the artist, musician, and scientist who address themselves to the comprehension of ideal ends. Cultural sociology studies religion, philosophy, scientific thought, and art. Empirical sociology, on the other hand, is directed to the study of the drives which produce changes in actuality. There is a sort of selective affinity between the *real* basis of society and the ideal. Real factors encourage or discourage the exploration of ideal values. Hence, a fundamental task is the discovery of the successive ways in which real and ideal factors interact. There is a sequence of stages of integration of these realms from domination of blood and kinship, to influence by political structure, to determination by economic facts. This sequence of stages is substituted for Comte's theological, metaphysical, and positivistic stages in the development of human mentality.

Scheler was able, on occasion, to display great virtuosity in the conduct of phenomenological analysis, as in his qualitative differentiation of apparently similar feeling states in the study of *The Nature of Sympathy*. A series of feeling states normally identified as "sympathy" is discriminated into subunits. One may, for example, isolate *sympathy*, or emotional solidarity (*Miteinanderfühlen*), from other forms. This is identified as the immediate sharing of the same emotion with someone, as when persons participate in a common joy or grief. *Mimpathy*, or emotional imitation (*Nachfühlen*), is very distinct, inasmuch as the feeling does not arise from the same base. Both these forms, in turn, are distinguished from *propathy*, or emotional participation (*Mitgefühl*), found in cases where one participates in another's emotional state. However, this in turn is not automatic, like *emotional contagion* (*Gefühlsansteckung*), but more conscious. These are distinguishable from *empathy*, or emotional introjection (*Einfühlung*), and *unipathy*, or emotional identification (*Einsfühlung*). In this last type of formation one sees the basis for the ecstasies of the mystery cults in which the worshiper feels himself to be one with the god.

But despite such analyses, the major trend in Scheler's thinking was away from the elaboration of distinctions in the realm of essences and toward

Georg Simmel

Rudolf Stammler

Edward A. Ross

Célestin Bouglé

Ernest Burgess

Robert E. Park

Hans Kelsen

Leopold von Wiese

Alfred Vierkandt

Max Scheler

Georges Gurvitch

the comprehension of socio-historical meaning complexes, the problem that cast the sociology of knowledge into focus. History as the fusion of vitalistic and normative spheres reveals the intrusion of norms into otherwise undirected organismic events. Mind affects events both by guiding and directing, restraining and releasing, dispositional impulses. This interaction of vital and normative events is mediated by an elite, a small number of persons taking the lead in the fusion of ideal and factual events. They grasp the phenomenological essences. Their insights in turn are diffused by imitation through the masses. History thus is a product of the drive structure of the leaders of society and its ethos. The essence of a culture becomes conscious in its elite.

Cultural sociology stands in contrast to real sociology in that it deals with ideal factors (deriving from goals and aspirations) rather than real factors (resting on drives). Ideal factors have an influence on cultural development when they are anchored in interests and incorporated in institutional forms; otherwise, they remain epiphenomenal.

There are a number of forms of knowledge, the most basic of which are the fundamental cultural axioms of the group, which form the climate of opinion. The most fundamental of all the tasks of the sociology of knowledge is to isolate these basic suppositions and their transformations. Such basic cultural suppositions constitute an organic growth more fundamental than any body of mere theories. They are possibly transformed by the mixture of races, languages, and cultures.

Once this fundamental task has been accomplished, the sociology of knowledge analyzes more superficial forms of knowledge resting on these: technological information, scientific and mathematical knowledge, philosophical knowledge, mystic knowledge, religious knowledge, folk wisdom, and legendary knowledge. The more technical and rational the form of knowledge, the more rapid its rate of change. Each type of knowledge has its own peculiar rate.

The sociological character of forms of knowledge (of thought, intuition, and cognition) is unquestionable, according to Scheler. Nevertheless, neither the content nor the objective validity of knowledge is determined by social structures. Knowledge *per se* consists of a realm of essences. From this realm of essences, one or another set is selected. Hence, the different types of knowledge are tied up with the particular forms of groups. Plato's theory of ideas, for example, was the ideal counterpart of the Platonic academy. Every type of social movement or structure has forms of knowledge peculiarly appropriate to it. The *Gemeinschaft*, as a type of society, has a traditionally defined fund of knowledge. Far from being concerned with discovery or the extension of knowledge, even the effort to test traditional knowledge is a blasphemy. The prevailing mode of thought is one of demonstration rather than testing, and the methods of thought are ontological and dogmatic. Thought is realistic rather than nominalistic, and its categories are organismic.

Between ideas and institutional forms, for Scheler there was a relation of selective affinity, a parallelism or structural identity. The rise of modern industrial civilization of a *Gesellschaft* type, for example, was related to a new individualism in contrast to the old collectivism; a principle of competition rather than cooperation became central to the ethos, and scientific and technical knowledge rather than a treasure house of wisdom became the objective; a movement to science in place of theology and philosophy occurred.

Georges Gurvitch

The phenomenological branch of sociological formalism still has active representatives, as may be illustrated by Georges Gurvitch (1894–   ). Gurvitch, a Russian sociologist, became a naturalized citizen of France in 1928. He was appointed to a chair of sociology at the Sorbonne in 1949. He was founder and first director of the Centre d'Études Sociologiques, established after World War II under the auspices of the Centre Nationale de la Recherche Scientifique, and he is editor of the *Cahiers internationaux de sociologie*. During the war years (1940–1945), Gurvitch taught at the New School for Social Research and other colleges in North America. Among the major influences on Gurvitch are the phenomenology of Scheler and sociometry.[10]

In Gurvitch's view, the sociological positivism of Comte had two basic features: the attempt to build a positive science of social facts and the conception of sociology as a total science or science of sciences. After Comte, sociological positivism renounced the identification of sociology with philosophy and with a theory of progress. It tended to become social naturalism, reducing sociology to a kind of mechanics, a theory of energy, geography, demography, and biology. Only organicism (Spencer and Schäffle) took account of the problem of societal regulation. Social psychologism (Lester Ward and Tarde) began to react against mechanical naturalism. Sociological formalism and American behaviorism (Simmel, von Wiese) limited sociology to the study of pure forms, excluding from sociology all study of spiritual content. More promising were the various kinds of recognition of the role of organization and control in human

[10] Gurvitch's chief sociological works have not been translated: *L'Idée du droit social* ["The Concept of Social Justice"] (Paris: Sirey, 1931); *Morale théorique et science des mœurs* ["Theoretical Ethics and the Science of the Mores"] (Paris: F. Alcan, 1937; 2d rev. ed., Paris: Presses Universitaires de France, 1948); *Essais de sociologie* (Paris: Sirey, 1938); *Éléments de sociologie juridique* ["Elements of Sociological Jurisprudence"] (Paris: Aubier, 1940); *Industrialisation et technocratie* ["Industrialization and Technology"] (Paris: A. Colin, 1949); *La Vocation actuelle de la sociologie* ["The Real Vocation of Sociology"] (Paris: Presses Universitaires de France, 1950; 2d ed., 1957); and *Déterminismes sociaux et liberté humaine* ["Social Determinisms and Human Liberty"] (Paris: Presses Universitaires de France, 1955). During the war years, Gurvitch published two books in English: *Sociology of Law* (New York: Philosophical Library, 1942) and *The Bill of Social Rights* (New York: International Universities Press, 1946).

affairs (Sumner, and particularly E. A. Ross). Cooley, with his analysis of the organic wholeness of society, was particularly valuable for a fully developed sociology. The self and social unit are abstract forms of this organic unity. Another basic contribution to sociological development occurred with Max Weber, who helped give logical precision to the problem of the sociology of spiritual meaning. Durkheim began to divide social reality into distinct levels: (1) on the surface social reality consists of a geographic demographic unity; (2) underneath this Durkheim located re-established collective behaviors; (3) a third level was found in symbols corresponding to institutions; (4) below symbols are collective values, ideas, and ideals symbolized by symbols; (5) finally we arrive at the deepest level of social reality, states of the collective mind, collective representations, collective memory, collective feeling, tendency, aspiration, and volition. It was on the basis of these distinctions that Durkheim distinguished various branches of sociology, including (1) social morphology, the study of the social surface; (2) social physiology, studying institutions, symbols, values, and ideas; (3) collective psychology; and (4) general sociology, studying the integration of all levels. In various ways, especially through Durkheim, the sociology of spiritual materials was developed. Particularly important for this were Wilhelm Dilthey, Max Scheler, and Karl Mannheim. The discussion of social symbols and noetic collective mentality was advanced by Ernst Cassirer, Lucien Lévy-Bruhl, and George Herbert Mead. Finally, Robert MacIver and Pitirim Sorokin and the philosopher, Elijah Jordan, have focused attention on the relation between social reality and spiritual meaning. In such fashion Gurvitch conceives the relation of the sociological tradition to his own theoretical position. Actually, most of such attributions are secondary reflections arising out of the extensions of the phenomenological point of view. They are interesting indications of the manner in which a modern phenomenologist organizes the whole field of theory.

The real final core of sociology is to be found in the study of the noetic mind or of the human spirit. Only the phenomenological method, Husserl's reduction, or Bergson's "method of inversion," is appropriate. What is needed is the immanent downward reduction of experience through successive stages toward whatever is most directly experienced as social reality.[11] The various levels of social reality correspond in part to those attributed to Durkheim. (1) The surface of social reality is made up of individuals and directly perceptible things, such as the demographic and geographic facts of society, including buildings, means of communication, etc. This material surface is social only to the extent that it is transformed and organized by collective human actions and penetrated by symbols and values given by the mind. It is a sort of external manifestation of man's spiritual life. (2) The next level of social reality is made up of organizations, superstructures, or collective conducts, hierarchized and centralized according to pre-fixed

[11] *Déterminismes sociaux et liberté humaine,* pp. 103–104.

patterns. (3) Below this is a level of patterns of standardized images and collective conducts. They need not — as with the second level — be rigged or pre-fixed. They may be flexible, ranging from rites and traditions to changing fashions. However, a sharp distinction must be drawn between technical or economic patterns and symbolic-cultural patterns linked to spiritual values. The latter form a part of the noetic or spiritual realm. (4) Beneath these patterns lie unorganized collective conducts. Their spontaneity is limited by standardization. They are habitual conducts. (5) Beneath these in turn is a layer of social reality constituted by social symbols. Without them, organization, cultural patterns, and collective conduct are impossible, since they guide such patterns. Such symbols are neither simple expressive signs nor illusions. The symbols mediate between appearances and things in themselves. Social symbols are inadequate expressions of the spiritual realm adapted to concrete social situations. Social symbols are simultaneously conditioned by social reality and the spirit. They can take varied forms. They are not necessarily connected with patterns and not necessarily standardized and generalized, for they may be images valid for a unique behavior. (6) Below the level of symbols are collective behaviors, which innovate, disrupt old patterns, and create new ones. These innovating social behaviors are unforeseeable. But they are manifest in times of revolution, epochs of reform, religious disturbance, and war. They conceal some symbols, weaken or change others, and create new symbols. (7) Below creative and unforeseeable social conduct is a real level of values and collective ideas which inspire this unforeseeable conduct and serve as the spiritual basis of symbols. Only at this level of social reality do we encounter the spiritual realm proper, the realm of values and ideas which are irreducible to acts which realize them and to states of the collective mind which grasp them. At various epochs and in different cultural spheres they appear and vanish. The study of the particularization of spiritual values defines the framework of the sociology of the noetic mind. (8) Spiritual values and ideas particularized with reference to social epochs and structure must be grasped, tested, and experienced. Thus, one must assume the existence of collective mentalities aspiring toward such values and ideas, enlightening itself with them. This is the deepest level of social reality — the level of the collective mind — the collective psyche which displays itself at every level of social reality. It may be studied in a state of greater or less detachment from its content. The study of the human spirit or noetic mind is the study of cultural patterns, social symbols, and collective spiritual values and ideas in their functional relations with social structures and concrete historical situations of society. Only a sociological method interpreting inner meanings, or *"verstehen,"* is appropriate to this type of study.[12]

12 *Ibid.*, pp. 99–161. For a brief statement, see *Sociology of Law*, pp. 33–40.

Summary

The first two systems of sociological theory, organismic positivism and conflict theory, took shape before sociology had become an institutionalized and professional discipline. Institutionalization standardizes a set of social relations and fixes social roles. Sociology as an intellectual discipline may be said to have become an institutionalized discipline when it achieved a standard form with an autonomy separate from that of any single person who might become a "sociologist." One of the surest signs of the social crystallization process called institutionalization is the speed with which sociology became a recognized department in the colleges and universities, taught by specially trained personnel.

For practical purposes, professionalization implies a peculiar kind of institutionalization characterized by the extensive self-determination of the activity by its own members. When the conditions of work, standards of performance, and standing of members are determined by some outside agency (as in the case of the wage worker, where these things are determined by industry, or the conditions of a civil service worker, where such affairs are determined by the administrative bureau), we do not speak of a profession. The establishment of recognized scientific societies and journals was an aspect of the professionalization of sociology. To an extensive degree, sociologists themselves had usurped the right to say who was and who was not a sociologist and what is and what is not good sociology.

One of the conditions of institutionalization and professionalization was the necessity for sociology to abandon the imperialistic claims to areas and material of the founders. One could not maintain such claims and expect to live at peace with other disciplines. Institutionalization and professionalization thus coincided with the demand for a more restricted definition of sociological subject matter. Besides, as already noted, organismic positivism was beginning to disintegrate into its component parts, and the "progress" and "evolution" formulas were producing contradictory findings. Furthermore, while adding a powerful note of realism, conflict theory could hardly have universal appeal. The line between empirical theory and ideology was not clearly drawn. Some forms of social Darwinism could only appear to be crass justifications of current social abuses: racism was partly linked to political and economic imperialism, partly to class exploitation; eugenicism in part implemented a dangerous class snobbery. In terms of its normal anchorage, Marxism could only appear to the average sociologist of the times as an apocalyptic vision of social chaos. Conflict theory was thus too near to ideology to satisfy modified professional claims. Besides, the imperialistic compass of sociology was largely maintained among the conflict theorists.

The early formalists like Simmel and Vierkandt were quite self-consciously searching for a special and precise definition of their field. This search coincided with ground movements in nineteenth-century thought, in the neo-Kantian reaction to idealistic and romantic excesses. The ferment was not confined to sociology, but was a product of the late nineteenth century, appearing in philosophy, history, jurisprudence, and all the social sciences. In sociology, it meant, among other things, that the search of the traditions of Western thought for new approaches was undertaken once again, and a whole new body of relatively unexploited sources was brought to bear upon sociological theory construction. The rationalistic traditions of Western philosophy came into prominence for sociological theory at this time. Of especial importance were the traditions of Kant, the neo-Kantians, and the phenomenologists. In sociology, all this took the shape of an attempted establishment of a "pure" or formal sociology.

The solution to the problem of obtaining a more restricted but more exact definition of the field by the neo-Kantians was to find the true nature of pure sociology in the study of forms. The great prestige the term "form" derived from Kantian philosophy was a component in the attractiveness of this term for various social sciences. Simmel himself saw that there were differences between his sociological forms and Kant's categories. He was unable to supply a convincingly exact explanation of just what the difference was. Moreover, he achieved his most imaginative brilliance precisely when he undertook the comparative study of the most varied social situations, disregarding the distinction between form and content. Simmel was by no means clear about the method to be followed in the discovery of forms. He wavered between the idea that they were only to be found by introspection and the notion that they were to be established by comparative study and induction.

The early American formalists perceived one tremendous advantage in the formalistic approach: it could serve as a vehicle for the systematization of all aspects of sociological knowledge without the need to appeal to older ideas (like progress and evolution) that had fallen into disrepute. But such students as Ross, Park, and Burgess, tended to lose sight of the theoretical problems posed by the formalists. In their zeal to carry out sociological systematization, such issues were cast aside. Judgment day was merely postponed.

Von Wiese shows one type of vigorous response to the methodological ambiguity of Simmel. The concept of form is re-expressed in the more anonymous language of relations. Moreover, the problem of method is posed in terms of pseudo-mathematical equations, and the elaborate dream of a thoroughgoing positivism of procedure is entertained. But the proposals for extreme empiricism were never carried out, and von Wiese presents a rather barren scheme of "relations" without any real justification for schematizing them in terms of "approach" and "avoidance." When systematization is carried out for its own sake, the results may be a kind of scientific curiosity. Such seems to have been the case with von Wiese, for he did not particularly promote the formation of those further hypotheses critical to the growth of science.

The close ties between the neo-Kantian and phenomenological branches of formalism are clear. Vierkandt, the phenomenologist, in part took Simmel's formalism as a starting point. Scheler, the phenomenologist, was the student of Simmel. Gurvitch, the phenomenologist, was also powerfully influenced by Simmel.

One could thus take Simmel as the common starting point for two types of later formulations: the extremely positivistic interpretation of von Wiese and the extremely subjectivistic interpretation of the phenomenologists. In a sense, the phenomenologists solved the problem of Simmel's methodological ambiguity in precisely the opposite way from von Wiese. Here the pretense that in the search of the immanent structure the *a priori* socio-psychic conditions that make society possible are performed inductively is dropped.

There is little doubt that Vierkandt's phenomenological sociology is a far more theoretically consistent solution to the problems of Simmel's neo-Kantianism than is von Wiese's *relational* formalism. The artificiality of von Wiese's procedure could not be more dramatically demonstrated than by the development of pseudo mathematical formulas which are set down as ideals, lamely admitted to be quite empty, and ignored in practice. This means that, in fact, no method adequate to relational formalism has been provided, and the theoretical basis of the system is obscure. By contrast, Vierkandt is quite correct. If the real point of stability for sociology is to be found in *a priori* forms, we are likely to obscure them by reviewing varied historical circumstances. The theory that established the "forms" also consistently requires a method really appropriate to their discovery. Phenomenological method recommends itself as the true means of arriving at absolute knowledge of the forms in a single act of immediate intuition.

The formalists developed a liberal conception of society as a legally ordered plurality of independent wills to counterbalance the conservative image of society of their predecessors. But as the inner course of the evolution of formalism from neo-Kantianism to phenomenology demonstrates, there was an implicit rebellion against the positivism of the previous theories as well as against their substantive social theory. The full implications of this for theory only gradually become clear. It increasingly grows necessary for the phenomenologists to decide whether their propositions about essences or spiritual forms or aspects of the noetic mind are testable scientific hypotheses or whether they lie outside the sphere of science.

SELECTED BIBLIOGRAPHY

ABEL, THEODORE, *Systematic Sociology in Germany*. New York: Columbia University Press, 1929.

ARON, RAYMOND, *German Sociology*. Translated by Mary and Thomas Bottomore. Glencoe, Ill.: The Free Press, 1957.

DAHLKE, HELMUT OTTO, "The Sociology of Knowledge," in Harry Elmer Barnes,

Howard Becker, and Frances Bennett Becker (eds.), *Contemporary Social Theory.* New York: D. Appleton-Century, 1940. Pages 64–92.

GURVITCH, GEORGES, *Sociology of Law.* New York: Philosophical Library, 1942.

GURVITCH, GEORGES, *Déterminismes sociaux et liberté humaine.* Paris: Presses Universitaires de France, 1955.

MANDELBAUM, MAURICE, *The Problem of Historical Knowledge.* New York· Liveright, 1938.

MERTON, ROBERT, *Social Theory and Social Structure.* Revised edition. Glencoe, Ill.: The Free Press, 1957. "The Sociology of Knowledge."

SCHELER, MAX, *Versuche zu einer Soziologie des Wissens.* Munich: Duncker & Humblot, 1924.

SCHELER, MAX, *Die Wissensformen und die Gesellschaft.* Leipzig: Neue-Geist Verlag, 1926.

VIERKANDT, ALFRED, *Gesellschaftslehre: Hauptprobleme der philosophischen Soziologie.* Second revised edition. Stuttgart: F. Enke, 1928.

PART FIVE

Social Behaviorism

12

The Conceptual Foundations
of Social Behaviorism

SOCIAL BEHAVIORISM WAS THE RIVAL SCHOOL TO FORMALISM TO ARISE IN
sociological theory at the time when sociology was undergoing professionalization and institutionalization. The term "social behaviorism" is borrowed from George Herbert Mead and applied to the whole school of
which Mead occupied only one branch. The school worked with a behavioral
definition of the materials of sociological science, in contrast to the
structural definition of organismic positivism and conflict theory, on the
one hand, and to the relational definition of the formalists, on the other.
It attempted to devise new empirical methods of sociological study, avoiding
both the methodological weaknesses of the early schools and the anti-
empirical tendencies in formalism. While this general characterization holds
for the whole school, three separate branches of social behaviorism can be
distinguished by their special analyses of social behavior and their special
methodological emphases.

The Problem of the Formalists

The demand for a delimited and precisely defined subject matter in
sociology called forth sociological formalism. The new formula for
sociology bore many interesting contrasts to organismic positivism and
conflict theory. Organismic positivism claimed to be the general science
of the social; formalism claimed to be a very special science. Organismic
positivism found the basic units of sociological analysis in entire societies;

formalism rejected such units as fictitious, finding its basic units in subjectively apprehended "forms." Organismic positivism advanced a conservative image of social phenomena; formalism was deeply rooted in the liberal traditions. Organismic positivism combined a conservative image of society with a positivism of method; formalism at first tried to fuse a liberal idea of society with a positivistic method in a manner which quickly proved to be unstable. The basic anti-positivism of the formalists could not be permanently concealed. The clarification of its presence and implications in considerable measure accounted for the internal evolution of formalism and the transition from a neo-Kantian to a phenomenological form.

There were, in fact, two fundamental problems that quickly emerged to haunt the formalists. Neither has ever been satisfactorily solved. (1) The separation of form and content has not been adequately justified, and (2) sociological formalism shows the repeated tendency to turn into a non-empirical discipline. In any case, it modified early positivism without supplying a defensible substitute.

The dualisms of phenomena and noumena and form and content were critical to the Kantian synthesis of modern philosophic thought. No one remained happy with the distinctions for long. The attempt to solve the problems they created led to the mysticism and panlogism of Hegel. When the neo-Kantians developed a modified Kantianism, a half-dozen interpretations of form appeared. In neo-Kantian treatments, the form–content dualism was transposed from a metaphysical into a methodological type.

When Simmel applied the form–content dichotomy to sociological problems, it carried with it a host of new issues. Simmel himself recognized that the distinction between form and content had new significance when applied to social data, but he offered no solutions to the new issues he raised. To make matters worse, many of Simmel's most brilliant results were attained by ignoring the distinction between form and content, comparing a wide variety of different situations. But by implication, if one established the forms by inductive analysis of comparative events, the sociological forms were not of a different character from the contents of interhuman life. Simmel suggested that in contrast to the Kantian "forms" of "nature," which are imposed on nature as experienced by the observer, the "forms" of "society" are parts of the internal structure of the matters they shape. The forms of nature are imposed from the outside; the forms of society arise from within.[1]

But the implications of this difference were not explored. This means either that there is no methodological difference between form and content after all, or that both, though different from each other, are "subjective" and outside the "externalistic" procedures of natural science. In any case there is no doubt of the validity of Vierkandt's judgment: Simmel did not achieve a purely formal analysis.

---

[1] There are shades of Dilthey in this argument. Dilthey had drawn the distinction between knowledge in the natural sciences, which is "external," and knowledge in the cultural sciences, which is "internal."

To the degree that one retains the distinction between form and content and attempts to carry out a "pure" formal analysis, one's enterprise tends to turn in a non-empirical direction. If the fundamental forms are actually *a priori*, one need not analyze a wide variety of diverse experiences to discover them. Vierkandt again has a point: one does not discover "forms" in this manner, at least if one accepts the distinction in the Kantian manner. Vierkandt proposed phenomenology as the missing method which would make a "pure" sociology possible. Formal sociology was simultaneously transformed into a non-empirical discipline. But what is the status of findings made by use of the phenomenological method? If these are treated as hypotheses and solved by inductive study, there is no difference between phenomenological and inductive method after all. However, if one can do this, one has not truly applied the phenomenological method.

A series of tough problems is left over for both versions of formal sociology, neo-Kantian or phenomenological. It is no help to cast up a smoke screen over the issue, as von Wiese did in offering a schema of pseudo-mathematical formulas, or to bury them, as Gurvitch does, under an elaborate mechanism of depth levels of sociological analysis. Thus for all its splendid gains in elevating to paramount consideration the theory of social relations, formal sociology left a veritable mare's nest of new issues. The demand that gave rise to formal sociology remained unsatisfied. The process of professionalization was still going on, and the requirement of a precise definition of sociological subject matter only became more urgent.

Neo-Idealism

In the continued search for an adequate definition of sociological subject matter, some possibilities had been eliminated. Total organic units had proved to be too vague to serve precise analysis. Biologistic entities had led to the multiplication of analogies that began to appear a bit silly. Besides, with the downfall of evolutionism they lost much of their original appeal. Conflict definitions were uncomfortably close to social ideologies. Formalistic definitions of sociological subject matter were also proving to be inadequate. There was strong inclination to search Western thought for points of view allowing one to avoid relapsing into empty formalism or dilution into vague all-inclusive psychic entities of one sort or another.

Rudolf Hermann Lotze

Some forms of idealism were being developed that did not take anti-scientific form. Rudolf Hermann Lotze (1817–1881) was in the forefront of this development. He was born in the Bautzen district, from which Lessing and Fichte had come. He had studied philosophy, medicine, and physics under E. H. Weber, A. W. Volkmann, and Gustav Fechner, making first-hand acquaintance with scientific methods. He graduated as doctor of philosophy and medicine, and after working some years at Leipzig, he succeeded Johann Friedrich Herbart in his professorship at Göttingen. Important works include *Mikrokosmus* and *System der Philosophie.*[2]

Lotze's training in philosophic idealism and scientific materialism bore fruit in his attempt to fuse them. Moreover, as a medical writer, he tried to maintain physiology as a mechanical science of nature. Natural forms appear in organisms as everywhere in nature. Organic life is not something higher than mechanics, but merely a particular way in which mechanical forces operate. However, mechanism is only one aspect of nature, and in *Microkosmus* Lotze attempted to develop a psychology which would harmonize with physiology, the history of culture, cosmology, and the philosophy of religion.

To Lotze, the spiritual was the highest aspect of man. He theorized that mechanical laws and causes are necessary for the realization of these highest spiritual ideals. A plurality of elements in reciprocal interaction is the foundation of a mechanical conception of nature. However, the mechanical conception of nature cannot encompass all aspects of nature, for it cannot go beyond a manifold of atoms in reciprocal action; it results in a pluralism. Beyond the relations of atoms are relations of elements and their interconnections. Thus, for Lotze, the concepts of causal relation and reciprocal action (basic to the mechanical conception of nature) lead to the idea of an original substance, or all-embracing principle, which he called the "ultimate postulate" or "ultimate fact of thought." This, he believed, was presupposed even in the simplest case of reciprocal action.

Lotze was an atomist, but he did not think of the atoms as material. Extension and other sensory qualities in themselves result from the reciprocal action of atoms. The atoms must not possess such qualities. Like life, the sensory fact of extension emerges from the cooperation of points of force. The atoms must be conceived as starting points of the inner working of infinite primal being.

The mechanical conception of nature explains only the mutual relation of elements, not inner nature. To arrive at the notion of the inner nature of elements, we must conceive of these elements by analogy with our own inner nature. Atoms must be feeling beings in a more primitive form. We must assume that the elements of the universe are animated in various degrees. Inner states are bound together into a unity. Our own inner spiritual life is the only example known to us of the possibility of the preservation of unity in the midst of fluctuating states. Thus the world

---

[2] *Mikrokosmus: Ideen zur Naturgeschichte und Geschichte der Menschheit* (Leipzig: 1856–64), translated by Elizabeth Hamilton and E. E. Constance Jones as *Microcosmus: An Essay Concerning Man and His Relation to the World* (4th ed., New York: Scribner's, 1897). *System der Philosophie* (Leipzig: 1874–79) is not available in English translation. A complete bibliographical note on Lotze will not be attempted. Studies of his work are contained in: G. Stanley Hall, *Founders of Modern Psychology* (New York: D. Appleton, 1912); E. E. Thomas, *Lotze's Theory of Reality* (New York: Longmans, Green, 1921); and Harald Høffding, *A History of Modern Philosophy*, tr. by B. E. Meyer (New York: Macmillan, 1935), Vol. 2, pp. 516–524.

principle is to be conceived as absolute personality. Absolute being must be personal, for personality alone possesses inner independence and originality. Personal life involves resistance to be overcome and the faculty of suffering.

In summary, on such bases, Lotze developed a spiritualistic psychology. He argued that psychical phenomena must either be derived from a soul or explained by the cooperation of physical forces. But the second alternative is excluded by the fact that reciprocal action of physical forces cannot explain the unity of even the simplest expression of psychical life. There are areas in which the soul is influenced by physical events; outside these, it is determined by its own laws. The material organisms work in service of spiritual activities by supplying the material on which the soul exercises its force. Given the material, spiritual activities such as memory, thought, and aesthetic and moral feeling can operate. Despite all the unpromising aspects of Lotze's view, there is one aspect of basic importance for further development: the psychical and physical are being brought together in a way that particularly invites investigation. The basis is being laid for a scientific psychology. An idealistic philosophy and a wide-ranging scientific knowledge are being brought together.

Gustav Fechner

This integration of idealism and science opened the way for a new departure in scientific psychology, which was as significant for psychology as positivistic organicism was for sociology. The potential was already evident in the work of Lotze. The actual transition to a quantitative psychology was made by Gustav Theodor Fechner (1801–1887). Fechner, born at Lausitz, also studied medicine and physics. In 1835 he became professor of physics. In 1839–1840 he contracted a disease of the eyes which eventually forced the abandonment of his professorship. His interests turned at this time to philosophy.[3]

Høffding compares Fechner to Kepler in the employment of bold, imaginative speculation which led to positive exact results. Fechner was led to the conviction that there is a definite quantitative relation between the mental and material. In working out the idea, he became the founder of psychophysics or experimental psychology.

Fechner's general theory is very similar to Lotze's. The mechanical and

[3] Fechner's best-known book is *Elemente der Psychophysik* ["Elements of Psychophysics"] (Leipzig: 1860). For Fechner's views on religion, see Gustav Fechner, *Religion of a Scientist,* edited and translated by Walter Lowrie (New York: Pantheon Books, 1946). General accounts of his theories as set forth in such books as *Elemente der Psychophysik, Die drei Motive und Gründe des Glaubens* ["The Three Motives and Bases of Belief"] (Leipzig: 1863), *Über die physikalische und philosophische Atomenlehre* ["Concerning the Physical and Philosophical Doctrine of the Atom"] (Leipzig: 1864), and *Vorschule der Aesthetik* ["Introduction to Aesthetics"] (Leipzig: 1876), can be found in: Harald Høffding, *op. cit.,* Vol. 2; G. Stanley Hall, *op. cit.;* and John Theodore Merz, *A History of European Thought in the Nineteenth Century* (Edinburgh: 1896–1914), Vol. 2, Ch. 11.

non-mechanical worlds must differ in degree rather than in kind, for the
phenomena of mind and animation could not be derived from a purely
mechanical world when this is conceived as the antithesis of mind. The
consciousness of plants must be as much lower than that of animals as
that of animals is below that of men. There is no good reason why the
heavenly bodies should not also be animated. Lower souls may be related
to higher ones, as are ideas and motives to particular souls. All souls
must be part of the highest embracing soul, whose life and reality are
manifest in the causal law, the principle of interconnection and order in the
world.

The program of a psychophysics is visualized. The difference between
mental and material, Fechner reasoned, cannot be that between two beings.
The material world is the outer, the spiritual the inner side of events. The
difference between them is phenomenal, depending on the standpoint of the
spectator. It is like the concave and convex side of the same circle. Consciousness is in reciprocal relation to external events. The sum total of physical
energy at our disposal is sometimes used one way, sometimes another.
Physical energy may be consumed when we do physical work or when
we think. Both cannot be done equally well at the same time. There
must be a mathematical-functional relation between the two sides of existence. The mental does not rise or fall in simple proportion to the material,
but changes in the former correspond to proportional changes in the latter.
The change in intensity of a mental state is determined by the relation
between the change of energy in the corresponding material state and
previously existing energy. (The intensity of a sensation equals a constant
times the logarithm of a stimulus, or, symbolically, $S = K \log R$.) [4] Formulations had now been made which could be phrased as exact hypotheses
subject to experimental test. Fechner found that the intensity of the sensation of a light does not increase as quickly as the intensity of a physical
stimulus. Fechner called this "Weber's Law," after its discoverer. He
tried experimentally to investigate the relation between activities of the
mind and corresponding events of the brain. Serious laboratory testing had
begun!

Eduard von Hartmann

A third member of this group was strongly influenced by Schopenhauer,
forming a transition between Schopenhauer and Freud. Eduard von Hartmann (1842–1906) was born in Berlin, the son of an army general.
Though slated for a military career, he devoted his leisure to music, painting, and philosophy. When, in 1865, a knee infection forced his retirement
from military service, he began to occupy himself with philosophizing and
essay-writing. His most famous book was his *Philosophie des Unbewussten*

---

[4] This general concept is expressed in various formulas; see *Elemente der Psychophysik*,
Vol. 2, pp. 96 ff.

(1869); of nearly thirty additional works, *Phänomenologie des sittlichen Bewusstseins* (1879) is most important.[5]

Whereas Lotze and Fechner took the scientific mode of explanation as fundamental and attempted to establish their thought on a scientific basis, Hartmann partly represents a neo-romantic reaction. His aim was to show that scientific explanation is not sufficient. Beside the causes assumed by the mechanical conception of nature, we must assume a spiritual principle. Matter, to be sure, must be conceived as a system of atomic forces. But interconnection and coherence require an additional principle such as the striving of a will and the unconscious idea of an end. Force at bottom is a will. In organic growth an unconscious will is manifest, for the organism realizes an unconscious end. Between organic and instinctive action there is only a difference in quantity. Instinct is neither an automatic mechanism nor conscious reasoning but a manifestation of will. All mental life ultimately rests on feelings and motives produced by the unconscious.

> Conscious reasoning is only denying, criticizing, controlling, correcting, measuring, comparing, combining, classifying, inducing the general form from the particular, ordering the particular case according to the general rule, but it is never creatively productive, never inventive. Here man is entirely dependent on the unconscious, and were he to lose the faculty by which he receives inspiration from the unconscious, he would lose the spring of his life, without which he would drag out a monotonous existence entangled in the dry schematism of the general and particular. Hence the unconscious is *indispensable* to him, and woe to the age which, in one-sided over-estimate of the consciously reasoned, listens to the latter only, and violently suppresses the unconscious.[6]

In the attack and defense that *Philosophy of the Unconscious* called forth, Hartmann made many concessions to his critics. He admitted that he had underrated mechanical causes. He also provided more place for the scientific method, though he tended to limit it to the task of filling in gaps in his theories and confirming the results his speculation had turned up. In his ethical studies Hartmann developed a peculiar type of pessimism and attempted to reconcile the philosophies of Hegel and Schopenhauer by combining Hegel's "absolute idea" with Schopenhauer's "will."

One effect of this continued evolution of idealistic philosophy upon sociology has already been noted. The modification of the anti-scientific aspects of early voluntaristic idealism made possible a major subdivision of the development of organismic positivism. However, the influence did not stop here. New syntheses of idealism and scientific methodology were opening up the possibilities of a laboratory psychology. Hence, when sociology be-

[5] *Philosophie des Unbewussten* (Berlin: 1869) was translated by William Chatterton Coupland as *Philosophy of the Unconscious* (New York: Harcourt, Brace, 1931). *Phänomenologie des sittlichen Bewusstseins* ["Phenomenology of the Moral Consciousness"] (Berlin: 1879) is not available in English translation. Summaries of Hartmann's views are contained in Hall, *op. cit.*, pp. 181–243, and Høffding, *op. cit.*, Vol. 2, pp. 532–540.

[6] *Philosophy of the Unconscious*, Book 2, p. 42.

gan to search for a new definition of subject matter in neo-Kantianism and found itself with major problems on its hands, it tended to review the idealistic traditions which were themselves undergoing change. The lesson of the Lotze-Fechner school was that it was possible to have a delimited idealistic definition of spiritual material which was capable of scientific study.

Neo-Hegelianism

Neo-Hegelianism is actually a form of neo-idealism, distinguished by its ties to Hegel. It was perhaps crucial to the attempt by idealists such as Lotze and Fechner to construct neo-idealism on a realistic-scientific basis that the collapse of Hegelianism had been so complete. In many respects, these thinkers were almost pre-Kantian in attitude and inclination, bearing more similarities to Spinoza and Leibnitz than to Hegel and his school. But precisely this detachment from Hegelianism was a component in the attempt to carry out their idealistic programs scientifically.

Once the fusion of idealism and scientific method had been launched, the modern forms of neo-idealism were able to make further contributions to the social sciences. This has already been made apparent in the adaptation of various philosophies of man's unconscious life to the needs of social science. For Schopenhauer and Nietzsche, science was concerned only with relatively superficial aspects of human life. To Nietzsche, the scientist was a paradigm of the hated mass man. In Eduard von Hartmann's interpretation of the significance of will for human conduct, despite some of the suspicion of science carried over from Schopenhauer and Nietzsche, the position was gradually opened to the reception of science. Under critical attack, Hartmann yielded ground and provided space for scientific method. By the time we reach the theories of Pareto and Freud, all this has been reversed and theories of the importance of man's unconscious life are advanced on strongly positivistic grounds.

Once the integration of a scientific program and idealistic theories of man's psychic life had been started by the school deriving from Lotze and Fechner, the social sciences also received new ideas from other idealistic schools, despite their anti-scientific bias. This was true of the neo-Hegelian movement.

Francis H. Bradley

The outstanding neo-Hegelian in England was Francis Herbert Bradley (1846–1924). Bradley studied at Oxford and lived in retirement as fellow of Merton College from 1876 to the end of his life. Philosophically, Bradley was convinced that true reality is spirit, which is one and identical with itself. One of the key problems to which Bradley addressed himself was the relation of this reality to the world of experience.[7] When the spirit is

[7] Important works of Bradley's are: *Ethical Studies* (London: 1876); *The Principles of Logic* (London: 1883); and *Appearance and Reality* (London: 1893).

conceived as one and self-identical, there seems to be no way of getting to experience from it. Experience becomes a world of illusion, of mere appearance. Between the eternal and the temporal, between the absolute and the contingent, mediation is impossible. Hence Bradley turns the full force of his subtle dialectical criticisms on the concept of *relation* which had been employed to hold the two worlds together. Experience concerns finite things. Every finite thing, however, presents the contradictions that it is only finite in itself in relation to other things. Thus no object of experience is self-determined and self-contained, but is embedded in external relations. Every finite thing is self-transcendent, alienated, and passing away from itself toward another thing. The finite is mere appearance. Applied to persons, this means that no person is complete in himself. He is completed only in the process that transcends the self leading to the other. Bradley's work was important in discrediting individualistic forms of the English philosophy of experience. The ideological individualism associated with the hedonistic utilitarianism of Bentham and James Mill was sharply attacked. Only by integration of the individual into a larger whole can the true self be found. The problem of the self is being posed in modern form.

Josiah Royce

The single most important idealist in the United States was Josiah Royce (1855–1916). Although he was a neo-Hegelian, he developed a highly individualized form of the position. Born and educated in California, Royce came under the influence of Joseph Le Conte, a pupil of Agassiz. His thinking was determined primarily by Kant, Hegel, the Romantics, and Schopenhauer. He was a teacher at Harvard University for thirty-four years. The first full expression of his ideas was contained in *The World and the Individual*.[8]

Royce's basic problem concerned the nature of Being. He argued that in addition to the brute facts, experience also possesses ideal properties: meanings. The purpose embodied in any idea Royce conceived as its "internal meaning." The idea also has "external meaning." The idea resembles or corresponds to facts wholly beyond itself. In the conflict of the immediate and ideal aspect of experience, Being appears as that which we first regarded as real in advance of more special definitions. It is not a transient phenomenon. Being is something "Other" than the finite ideas which seek it, for ideas seek Being as that which when completely known will fulfill them and end their doubts. As a fragment, the idea looks elsewhere for the rest of itself. An idea seeking its Other, seeks only the expression of

[8] Josiah Royce, *The World and the Individual*, 2 vols. (New York: Macmillan, 1900–1901). Royce's other principal works are: *Studies of Good and Evil* (New York: D. Appleton, 1898) ; *Outlines of Psychology* (New York: Macmillan, 1903) ; *The Philosophy of Loyalty* (New York: Macmillan, 1908) ; *The Problem of Christianity* (New York: Macmillan, 1913) ; *The Hope of the Great Community* (New York: Macmillan, 1916) ; and *Lectures on Modern Idealism* (New Haven, Conn.: Yale University Press, 1919).

its own will in an empirical conscious life. The theory of Being requires us to view every fact of nature and of man's life as a fragmentary glimpse of the Absolute life, as a revelation of the unity of the perfect whole. Science does not give us either a complete or adequate picture of reality, for it suggests that the ultimately real is material substance. When we deal with nature we deal with a realm of consciousness of which our own is a part and example.

The self, for Royce, is not a thing, but a meaning embodied in a conscious life. Its individuality implies the essential uniqueness of this life. Its unity transcends what we find presented in consciousness. The true individual self receives final expression in some form of consciousness different from that which we men now possess. For each of us, the absolute self is God. However, we still retain our individuality and our distinction from one another just so far as our life spans extend. By the very nature of their social basis, men possess mutually contrasting life-plans, each one of which can reach its own fulfillment only by recognizing other life-plans as different from its own. The inclusion of the individual will in the divine will is the assurance of individual freedom. The problem of freedom is the final problem of individuality.

In Hegel's thought, the whole, the "concrete universal," tends to swallow up the individual. Royce rejected the idea that one must choose between the life of the whole and individual freedom, but insisted that neither could be had without the other. It is only in the development of the individual that the life of the whole can properly be expressed. In extension with these ideas, Royce believed that the individual is not a closed moral unity, nor are societies made up of these. Rather, social consciousness is a necessary condition of self-consciousness. These ideas were extended into the notion that the self is a community and the community a self. The universe itself was viewed as an ideal community. In all such respects Royce made a basic contribution to the reconceptualization of the relation of the self and the community.

Wilhelm Wundt

Wilhelm Wundt (1832–1920), who taught at the universities of Heidelberg, Zurich, and Leipzig, was a man of extraordinary encyclopedic knowledge who made contributions to a whole range of theoretical and experimental sciences. He is best known for contributions to the development of experimental psychology and folk psychology. In philosophy, he contributed to the shift from positivism through neo-Kantianism to greater emphasis upon totality and organic relations. Commenting on the influence of Wundt's *Ethik* (1886), Vierkandt sums it up as follows:

> . . . He not only assailed utilitarianism but insisted upon the reality of a general will and supported Hegel in the precedence over the individual which he gave to objective forms and institutions, such as the state. He

considered psychology as more than a special discipline; to him it was the foundation of all knowledge of the intellectual and spiritual world and the intermediary between natural science and philosophy. His psychological views reflected the change from an atomistic and analytical conception to one which was more unified and organic. . . .[9]

Stimulated by Fechner and Ernst Heinrich Weber, Wundt established the Psychological Institute, from which stemmed the experimental trend in American psychology; G. Stanley Hall and James McKeen Cattell studied there.

Wundt's sociological thought is closely bound up with his psychological system. "Will," or "conation," was located at the center of his psychological interpretations as the synthesizing and integrating aspect of psychic life. This integrating power is found in the phenomenon of "apperception," which contrasts with perception: apperception adds a creative element to the external events that enter experience. This is the simplest example of the "creative synthesis" which functions throughout mental life.

Wundt draws a distinction between explanation in the natural and psychical realms. In interpreting natural phenomena, explanation is in terms of a hypothetical stable stratum. In the psychic realm, the real is directly experienced, no substratum beyond experience has any meaning. Causality has a different meaning in psychic process than in physical process. In natural events, cause and effect, action and reaction, are equal and opposite; in psychic events, there is transmutation and growth, and effects are greater than causes. While the causal principle operates differently in the psychical and the physical realms, it does not operate between them. There is rather a parallelism between the psychical and physical.

In more complex individual and social circumstances, the principle of creative synthesis is expressed in the "mutation of motives" and "heterogeneity of ends." Social forms are stable, but psychological motivation changes, and persisting forms are devoted to new purposes.

[9] *Encyclopædia of the Social Sciences* (New York: Macmillan, 1931), Vol. 15, p. 506. Wilhelm Wundt's major works include: *Grundzüge der physiologischen Psychologie* (Leipzig: W. Engelmann, 1874; 6th ed., 1908–11), the fifth revised edition (1902–1903) of which was translated by Edward B. Titchener as *Principles of Physiological Psychology* (New York: Macmillan, 1904); *Logik*, 2 vols. (Stuttgart: F. Enke, 1880–83; 4th ed., 1919–21); *Ethik* (Stuttgart: F. Enke, 1886; 4th ed., 1912), the second revised edition (1892) of which was translated by Edward B. Titchener, Julia H. Gulliver, and Margaret F. Washburn as *Ethics*, 3 vols. (New York: Macmillan, 1897–1901); *Grundriss der Psychologie* (Leipzig: 1896; 14th ed., Stuttgart: A. Kröner, 1920), of which three English translations have been made, the latest being Charles Hubbard Judd's translation of the 7th edition (1907), *Outlines of Psychology* (New York: G. E. Stechert, 1907); *Völkerpsychologie: Eine Untersuchung der Entwicklungsgesetze von Sprache, Mythus, und Sitte* ["Folk Psychology: An Investigation of the Developmental Laws of Speech, Myth, and Custom"], 10 vols. in 12 (Leipzig: W. Engelmann, 1900–20); *Sprachgeschichte und Sprachpsychologie* ["The History and Psychology of Speech"] (Leipzig: W. Engelmann, 1901); *Allgemeine Geschichte der Philosophie* ["General History of Philosophy"] (Berlin: B. G. Teubner, 1909; 2d ed., 1913); and *Elemente der Völkerpsychologie* (Leipzig: A. Kröner, 1912), translated by Edward Leroy Schaub as *Elements of Folk Psychology* (New York: Macmillan, 1916). A summary of Wundt's earlier work appears in G. Stanley Hall, *op. cit.*

Wundt employed these ideas in the analysis of the problems of folk psychology, shifting the emphasis from the intellectual to emotional and intuitive factors. Man's reaction to nature was conceived as an intuitive response described as "mythological apperception," the direct metaphorical grasp of natural events. The primitive apprehension of natural phenomena like lightning was not brought by reasoning into comparison with a snake but was apperceived as a snake. In parallel fashion, the primitive relation of individual and society was not one of reasoned receipt of society by the individual nor the rational projection of society by individuals. Rather, the individual was so closely determined by, and bound up with, his social setting as to be incapable of being understood without it. There is an unconscious functional relationship between individuals of a group so close that it is not possible to separate the elements from the psychological whole.

Three aspects of culture were thought by Wundt to be particularly subject to group penetration: language, myth, and custom. Wundt's *Völker-psychologie* explored these areas. The first two volumes examined the problems of primitive languages. This was followed by a study of art, an examination of the history of human imagination. There followed three volumes on myth and religion, two on social organization, one on law, and a final volume on culture and history. Such materials were thought to have basic value for the study of psychology.

> Psychology needs the folk-psychological material comprised in certain social sciences not less urgently than the latter require a psychological foundation. As soon as psychology begins to exploit the sources which pour in upon it from the different spheres of psychic life, the contributions of psychology itself to the interpretation of individual facts, contributions derived from the broader contemplation of psychic life, will no longer remain unrecognized. For in one respect, at least, the most refined practical tact and the richest life-wisdom cannot come up to the achievements of scientific psychology. . . . The historian, linguist, and mythologist must operate with complex concepts. Only when a bridge has been built to span the gap between the individual mind and the psychic aspects of the social process does it become possible, by retracing one's steps, to apply folk-psychological conclusions to the scientific psychologist.[10]

In his briefer work, *The Elements of Folk Psychology*, Wundt described cultural areas which succeed each other in the history of culture. The evolution of the *Zeitgeist* is divided into four stages: (1) the period of primitive man, (2) the period of totemism, (3) the period of gods and heroes, and (4) the period of humanity. The first period was one more rudimentary than any now known among existing primitive peoples; it was

[10] Translated from p. 29 of *Völkerpsychologie* (4th ed., Vol. 1) by Alexander Goldenweiser in "The Psychosociological Thought of Wilhelm Wundt," in Harry Elmer Barnes (ed.), *An Introduction to the History of Sociology* (Chicago: University of Chicago Press, 1948), p. 225, Footnote 9.

arrived at by "psychological reconstruction." The totemic period was thought to be a stage of universal gentile society and the totemic complex. The age of heroes appears when human heroes replaced the totemic or deified animal of the totemic stage. The gods were introduced when social crises led to rationalization of experience. During this period of the age of gods and heroes, the state, property, and economic and social classes appeared. Moreover, individual personality was recognized and religion took on moral properties, becoming a social force. The stage of humanity arises with the great world empires and the development of a sense of mutual interdependence, humanity, and brotherhood.

The preservation and promotion of an idealistic point of view in Wundt's work is illustrated by his idea of the difference between psychic causality and physical causality. Psychic causality has effects which are never equal and opposite to causes. A perception, he argues, is never a mere sum of sensations. The significance of a perception is the synthesis of sensations. Psychical causality is creative, while physical causality is merely mechanical. Moreover, Wundt defended the parallelism of the psychic and physical. He argued that psychic processes cannot be derived from physical ones nor physical from psychic ones in the same causal sense in which we attempt to derive physical processes from other physical ones and psychic processes from other psychic ones. Such co-existence, of course, does not preclude the presence on the physical side of certain phenomena to which no psychic phenomenon corresponds, nor on the psychic side, of certain phenomena with reference to which no accompanying physical ones can either be demonstrated or conjectured, with any degree of probability.

The neo-Hegelians, who included not only Bradley and Royce and Wundt, but persons like Dilthey, had already begun to influence the sociologists. Dilthey and Wundt, for example, influenced Tönnies, Durkheim, and, to some degree, Simmel. But their primary importance for sociology was not here. As contributors to the idealistic traditions stemming from Hegel, they represent a restructuring of "holistic" forms of idealism. Even while carrying through brilliant criticisms, as did Bradley in England, of liberal individualism, the neo-Hegelians tended to modify Hegelianism to make a basic place for the problem of personality. Furthermore, the neo-Hegelians like Dilthey and Wundt advanced the study of cultural forms such as religion, myth, ethics, and language. Neo-Hegelianism also had a strong influence on that heavily "biologized" form of idealism known as pragmatism.

Pragmatism

Pragmatism does not represent a single unified body of philosophic ideas. Nevertheless it does not completely deserve the unfriendly estimate of Ruggiero: "Pragmatism was born in America, the country of 'business,' and is, *par excellence*, the philosophy of the business man." Fixing on the conception of the instrumental nature of ideas and truth — a view presented occasionally by Peirce, frequently by James, and constantly by John Dewey, Ruggiero argues: "Pragmatism is the logical conclusion and therefore the *reductio ad absurdum* of empiricism. If reality is sensation and the concept is merely the arbitrary abbreviation of sensible experience, the sole value of the concept will lie in its character as an arbitrary but convenient fiction." He continues: "That ideas should work is all very well, but in practice they always seem to be other people's ideas: if [philosophy] has any of its own it never gives them anything to do. Philosophy has vanished and we are on the brink of comedy, if not downright charlatanism." And so far as William James accepts the identification of truth and utility, Ruggiero asserts: "All the discordant tendencies of the pragmatist thesis are united in the personality of William James; a curious patchwork of good and evil, of seriousness and extravagance. But the strictly pragmatist basis of his thought represents a stage of decadence, a sterilization of a personality whose first appearance was far more complex and robust." [11] In view of the fact that James's concept of knowledge and truth was taken as the core of pragmatism in Italy, Ruggiero's reaction is understandable. After all, it was in this same land that Mussolini welcomed the designation "pragmatism" for his own political philosophy. The instrumental conception of knowledge and truth can easily degenerate into Machiavellian political expediency.

Bertrand Russell is strongly inclined to locate the core of pragmatism in the same place as Ruggiero, though recognizing greater diversities among the pragmatists. Russell tends to disapprove it almost as much. Pragmatism, as it appears in James, he observes, is primarily a new definition of "truth." There were two other protagonists of pragmatism — F. C. S. Schiller and John Dewey. Schiller was of less importance than the other two. Between James and Dewey, there is a difference of emphasis. Dewey's outlook is scientific, and his arguments are largely derived from an examination of scientific method, but James is concerned primarily with religion and morals. According to Russell, James

> is prepared to advocate any doctrine which tends to make people virtuous and happy; if it does so, it is "true" in the sense in which he uses that word. The principle of pragmatism, according to James, was first enunciated by C. S. Peirce, who maintained that, in order to attain clearness in our thoughts of an object, we need only consider what conceivable effects of a practical kind the object may involve. . . . Ideas, we are told by James, become true in so far as they help us to get into satisfactory relations with other parts of our experience. . . . In a chapter on pragmatism and religion he reaps the harvest. "We cannot reject any hypothesis if consequences useful to life flow from it." "If the hypothesis of God works satisfactorily in the widest sense of the word, it is true." "We may well

[11] Guido de Ruggiero, *Modern Philosophy*, 1st ed. tr. by A. Howard Hannay and R. G. Collingwood (New York: Macmillan, 1921) pp. 252, 253, 254.

believe, on the proofs that religious experience affords, that higher powers exist and are at work to save the world on ideal lines similar to our own." [12]

One could hardly expect a first-rate logician like Russell to be other than shocked by the wholesale confusion of the requirements of action with the properties of thought. Moreover, even the friends of pragmatism have not always been altogether clear about what should be included in it. Kallen states that it denotes an attitude of mind rather than a system of ideas. All such systems to which it is applied have in common certain fundamentals, such as plurality and diversity of things and thoughts, the primacy of change, movement and activity, the genuineness of novelty, and belief in immediate experience as the court of last resort in validating ideas. Kallen has also argued that in accounting for the differences between true and false, right and wrong, good and bad, beauty and ugliness, pragmatists employ the Darwinian notions of spontaneous variation and the struggle for survival.[13]

The vagueness of the statement of the nature of pragmatism by its proponents and the often contradictory estimates by its opponents, taken together with the powerful influence of pragmatism on American social science, are significant. Pragmatism was one of the many attempts to reconcile some of the premises of idealism with scientific method, and unite a spiritualistic and biological conception of human development. This is evident in both of its key figures, James and Dewey.

William James

William James (1842–1910) was the eldest of five children. When he was eighteen years old and his family was living in Newport, Rhode Island, he tried his hand at art. Tiring of this, he entered the Lawrence Scientific School of Harvard University, concentrating on chemistry and anatomy. He went on to study medicine at the Harvard Medical School. He interrupted his study to accompany Louis Agassiz in exploring the Amazon. His health failed, and he returned to study medicine for a term, then went on to Germany for courses with the physiologists Hermann Helmholtz and Claude Bernard and the pathologist Rudolf Virchow. While in Germany he suffered a nervous breakdown, during which he entertained thoughts of suicide. He returned home in 1868, took the M.D. degree, and lived in a state of semi-invalidism, experiencing a prolonged period of phobic panic relieved only when he read Renouvier on free will. The materialistic determinism of nineteenth-century science overwhelmed James with a sense of psychic oppression, and he resolved to make the first act of free will the abandonment of all determinism. In this personal drama there are comparisons with Max Weber's tragic sense of the disenchantment of the world. In 1872, James was appointed instructor in physiology

[12] Bertrand Russell, *A History of Western Philosophy* (London: George Allen and Unwin, 1945; New York: Simon and Schuster, 1945), pp. 816–817.
[13] Horace M. Kallen, "Pragmatism," in *Encyclopædia of the Social Sciences*, Vol. 12, p. 307.

in Harvard College, serving in this capacity until 1876. Around 1880 he began the researches that led to the *Principles of Psychology* (1890), which was to establish the functional point of view in psychology. It also assimilated psychology to biology and treated intelligence as an instrument in the struggle to survive. While defending free will, James made use of the principles of psychophysics. With the completion of this work, he lost interest in psychology, and began to teach and write in ethics and religion, occupying himself with the existence of God, the immortality of the soul, free will and determinism, and the value of life. During these years James made increasing use of the "pragmatic rule" formulated by Peirce. The meaning of an idea, whether scientific, religious, philosophical, political-social, or personal, was to be found only in the experiential consequences to which it leads. Truth and error are identical with these consequences. This was applied to the study of religion, change, chance, freedom, variety, pluralism, and novelty. It was used against "monism" and the "block universe," against internal relations, against all finalities, completeness, and absolutes. In 1906, the Lowell Lectures were delivered in Boston. They were published as *Pragmatism: A New Name for Some Old Ways of Thinking.*[14]

The theoretical high point of James's thought may be found in the essay, "Does 'Consciousness' Exist?"[15] In it James denied that the subject–object relation is fundamental. The idea that in the occurrence of "knowing" there is a subject aware of an object or thing known had long been taken for granted. The knower was thought to be a mind or soul, the object was material or an essence or another mind. A great deal of philosophy rested on this dualism of subject and object — the distinction of mind and matter, the contemplative ideal, and the traditional notion of "truth"[16]

James came to the conclusion that there is no "entity" to be called consciousness. Those who cling to the idea are hanging on to an echo, a faint rumor left behind by the disappearance of the soul from philosophy. There is no original being, contrasted with the being composing material objects, out of which thoughts of those objects are made. This does not mean that mind does not perform a function which can be called "being conscious." The primary stuff out of which everything is composed is "pure experience." Knowing is a peculiar sort of relation between two aspects of pure experience. The subject–object relation is derivative. A given portion of experience can in one context be knower, in another known.

[14] The most important works of William James for our purposes are: *Principles of Psychology* 2 vols. (New York: Henry Holt, 1890); *The Will to Believe and Other Essays in Popular Philosophy* (New York: Longmans, Green, 1896); *Human Immortality* (Boston: Houghton Mifflin, 1898); *Talks to Teachers on Psychology and to Students on Some of Life's Ideals* (New York: Henry Holt, 1899); *Varieties of Religious Experience* (New York: Longmans, Green, 1902); *Pragmatism* (New York: Longmans, Green, 1907); *Essays in Radical Empiricism* (New York: Longmans, Green, 1912).

[15] First printed in the *Journal of Philosophy, Psychology and Scientific Methods*, Vol. 1 (September 1, 1904), pp. 477–491; reprinted in *Essays in Radical Empiricism*.

[16] See Russell's estimate, *History of Western Philosophy*, p. 812.

Pure experience is "the immediate flux of life which furnishes the material to our later reflection." [17]

At bottom, James was an idealist. The long road beginning with personal pathological reactions to the implications of materialistic determinism leads to the conception of a mentalistic proto-stuff of pure experience out of which both subject and object are mere differentiations. When one adds to this James's pragmatic rule, it is clear that he was anxious to procure a device that would permit him to accept mind as an independent reality. The rule in fact permitted him to accept anything that made him happy. Comte's mental hygiene was not nearly as effective. It is very doubtful whether even George Lundberg's semantic exorcism of mental ills has more utility as a device for self-confirmation. But in any case the conclusion is inescapable that pragmatism for James was a device for reconciling idealism with science.

John Dewey

The task of the reconciliation of idealism and science was ably carried forward by John Dewey (1859–1952), also a New Englander. Dewey graduated from the University of Minnesota (1888–1889), Michigan (1889–1894), and Chicago (1894–1904). He first won fame as director of the School of Education at Chicago, where he established an experimental school and carried out the ideas of a new pedagogy, formulating principles that have revolutionized instruction and educational practice in America. For two years he lectured on education and philosophy at the University of Peking in China. The Turkish government engaged him to draw up a report on the organization of its national schools. After 1904, when he joined the department of philosophy at Columbia University, his influence began to penetrate philosophy.

Philosophically, Dewey's starting point was found in Hegel. He made, without any sense of conflict, the transition from German idealism to pragmatism under the influence of William James. From his neo-Hegelian starting point, Dewey retained to the end the sense of the central value of intelligence and the concept of mental activity as a process. There was a sort of parallel between Dewey's movement from neo-Hegelianism to pragmatism and Marx's transition from Hegel: Marx retained the Hegelian notions of process and development, but conceived them in terms of a thoroughgoing materialism; Dewey always retained the notions of intelligence and process, but "biologized" and "instrumentalized" them. The organism is constantly reconstructing the environment as well as being determined by it. Thought is an organ of response and instrument of behavior, not an entity in the older sense. James's pragmatic rule and Dewey's instrumentalism are cut from the same cloth. Similarly, Dewey conceives of the individual as in process of development. He was also

[17] It is easy to see why Russell describes James as an unconscious Berkeleian idealist, *ibid.*, p. 813.

impressed with the social process represented by the industrial revolution. A new curriculum was needed, adequate to the practice of the arts and discipline of industrial life. If he is to live in society, man must be studied as a citizen, growing within a complex of interactions and relationships. Through education, the individual is made into an image of his fellows in a process which, while reducing his uniqueness, extends the limits of possible development. Education is the instrument of social adjustment and of political and moral reconstruction, just as thought is the instrument of adjustment in the world.

In his *Logic*, the theoretically central point of Dewey's philosophy was expressed in his conception of inquiry. "Inquiry is the controlled or directed transformation of an indeterminate situation into one that is so determinate in its constituent distinctions and relations as to convert the elements of the original situation into a unified whole." [18] Russell not unfairly observes that inquiry, "as conceived by Dewey, is part of the general process of attempting to make the world more organic. 'Unified wholes' are to be the outcome of inquiries. Dewey's love of what is organic is due partly to biology, partly to the lingering influence of Hegel. Unless on the basis of an unconscious Hegelian metaphysic, I do not see why inquiry should be expected to result in 'unified wholes.' " [19]

But this conception of organic process and the equilibrium of organic wholes is more than the framework for understanding logic. It is the framework for understanding the individual, education, and the social process as well. Thought, the need for self-development, the need for invention, the need for social change, all start with some kind of indeterminate situation or disturbed equilibrium. Every element of thought, education, social innovation, invention, or act of legislation is conceived as called forth by the indeterminate situation and functioning to restore equilibrium. A process of adjustment of activity and results is carried through in all cases, terminating only when equilibrium is restored.

Thus a kind of biological Hegelianism is crucial to every aspect of Dewey's thought. His "instrumentalism" arises as a kind of generalization of Peirce's and James's pragmatic rule; everything is estimated exclusively in terms of its equilibrium-restoring functions. Science is particularly dear to Dewey, for in all its aspects it is viewed as the most efficient of all instruments. In Dewey, as in James, a reconciliation of idealism and science seems to have been a major motive for his theories.

Summary

As the crises were experienced that accompanied the conversion of sociology from a free-lance, somewhat journalistic discipline into a professional-

---

[18] John Dewey, *Logic: The Theory of Inquiry* (New York: Henry Holt, 1938), pp. 104–105. Other works of Dewey's important to the present discussion are *Human Nature and Conduct* (New York: Henry Holt, 1922) and *Experience and Nature* (Chicago: Open Court Publishing Company, 1925).

[19] Russell, *History of Western Philosophy*, p. 823.

ized academic area of study, its responsible representatives cast about among the systems of thought of the nineteenth century for a foundation. Formalistic theories of sociology arose as one product of this enterprise, with the attempt to establish pure sociology as the study of *a priori* social forms. Perceiving that the establishment of *a priori* forms was not an empirical task, one group of formalists turned to phenomenology as a base for the formalistic program. The risks presented by formalism gradually emerged into clear view: either one succeeded in maintaining the formalistic program but at the expense of being scientific, or one remained sociologically relevant and failed to develop consistent formalism. This is no way to establish a science.

Meanwhile, however, there was renewed activity among the idealistic-minded thinkers. The group stemming from Lotze attempted to establish idealistic hypotheses on the basis of scientific method. Although the neo-Hegelians were far more critical of science, they brought pungent criticisms to bear upon special aspects of current social theories. Against an overdrawn individualism they advocated the claims of institutions, and against mechanistic claims they advanced the cause of personality. At the same time, they modified older forms of idealism by inserting the problem of personality. Finally, the pragmatists were attempting a solution to the problem on their own. William James came to pragmatism by way of reaction against the emotional implications of mechanism, and Dewey came to it by way of converting neo-Hegelianism into a practical program.

A whole series of closely related sociological theories took shape along the lines suggested by these philosophical movements. There were fluid transitions between them. They often borrowed not only from each other but from a variety of the idealistic and pragmatic trends. There were, however, some properties common to them all which made them into one general movement in sociological theory. (1) They sought a definition of sociological subject matter in terms of idealistic theories; (2) they avoided as far as possible the assumption of large-scale social units (total societies, humanity, mankind, civilization) as units of sociological analysis; they were, in one terminology, strongly "nominalistic"; (3) they had as one foremost problem the development of a theory of social persons; and (4) they brought the problem of sociological method under review.

SELECTED BIBLIOGRAPHY

CUNNINGHAM, G. WATTS, *The Idealistic Argument in Recent British and American Philosophy.* New York: Century Company, 1933.

DEWEY, JOHN, *Human Nature and Conduct.* New York: Modern Library, 1930.

FECHNER, GUSTAV, *Elemente der Psychophysik.* Leipzig: Breitkopf und Härtel, 1889.

HALL, G. STANLEY, *Founders of Modern Psychology.* New York: D. Appleton, 1912.

HARTMANN, EDUARD VON, *Philosophy of the Unconscious.* Translated by William Chatterton Coupland. New York: Harcourt, Brace, 1931.

JAMES, WILLIAM, *The Will to Believe and Other Essays in Popular Philosophy.* New York: Dover Publications, 1956.

JAMES, WILLIAM, *Pragmatism: A New Name for Some Old Ways of Thinking.* New York: Meridian Books, 1955.

LOTZE, RUDOLPH HERMANN, *Microcosmus: An Essay Concerning Man and His Relation to the World.* Translated by Elizabeth Hamilton and E. E. Constance Jones. Fourth edition. New York: Scribner's, 1897.

ROYCE, JOSIAH, *The Hope of the Great Community.* New York: Macmillan, 1916.

WERKMEISTER, WILLIAM HENRY, *A History of Philosophical Ideas in America.* New York: Ronald Press, 1949.

WUNDT, WILHELM, *Elements of Folk Psychology.* Translated by Edward Leroy Schaub. New York: Macmillan, 1916.

13

The Pluralistic Behavioral Branch
of Social Behaviorism

THE SCHOOL OF SOCIAL BEHAVIORISM COVERS A REMARKABLY VARIED AND fertile development of ideas, characterized by both theoretical and methodological ferment. At its core was a behavioristic concept of sociological subject matter, distinguishing it from positivistic organicism, conflict theory, and sociological formalism, with their structural and relational approaches. Its philosophic origins were in neo-idealism and related trends. While it retained a strong methodological positivism which separated it from sociological formalism, it recognized that the older methods were inadequate.

Social behaviorism was manifest in a series of closely equivalent but distinct and parallel forms. The oldest of these was pluralistic behaviorism. The school originally took shape in the works of Gabriel Tarde, whose position has at times been called "imitation–suggestion," but the name given by Giddings, pluralistic behaviorism, is more appropriate to it.

Gabriel Tarde

The new emphasis in sociology represented by the imitation–suggestion school is well illustrated by the fact that Gabriel Tarde is often considered to be the founder of social psychology. Tarde (1843–1904) was born at Sarlat in southern France. He studied in Paris, and became a judge in his native town, where he made quantitative studies of the cases that came before him, thus acquiring a reputation for his study of criminality. He opposed the ideas of Cesare Lombroso (1836–1909), who held that criminality is inherited and who had started a school of the biological explanation of crime. This prepared Tarde for his position as head of the Bureau of Statistics of the Ministry of Justice in Paris. He also lectured at the École des Sciences Politiques until his retirement in 1900, when he became professor of modern philosophy at the College de France.[1]

The idea of imitation for which Tarde is famous was not original with him. Hume had employed it in his essay on national character, and Bagehot had accounted for social stability in terms of it. It was also elaborated independently by William James and Josiah Royce. However, Tarde's particular use of the idea was quite new, for by means of it he fused a scientific demand for methodological precision with an idealistic definition of sociological subject matter.

Every science, he argued, deals with a variety of phenomena among which there are repetitions. It is the task of science to isolate and explain these repetitions. This is not done all at once. At first, science seizes upon bold ideas of apparent repetitions in phenomena; but these large-scale regularities are only apparent, and must be abandoned in time for the genuine subject matter of the science.

The special phenomena sociology studies are "beliefs or desires under the different names of dogmas, sentiment, laws, wants, customs, morals, etc." [2]

Psychology studies their interrelations in the single mind; sociology studies their relations between minds. The methods by which these are studied are archaeology and statistics — the latter proper to sociology, the former to history. The task of the archaeologists is to trace out the remote, almost imperceptible analogies in form, style, situation, language, legend, dress — in anything that is the vehicle of the transmission of human beliefs and desires. Statistics consists in the enumeration of acts which are as much alike as possible, but, because statistics deals with the outer manifestations of beliefs and desires, it cannot always arrive accurately at judgments of intensity. Nevertheless, in the long run the hope of

[1] Tarde's two chief works in criminology are *La Criminalité comparée* ["Comparative Criminality"] (Paris: F. Alcan, 1886; 8th ed., 1924) and *La Philosophie pénale* (Lyon: A. Storck, 1890; 4th rev. ed., 1903); the first of these is not available in English, but a translation of the fourth edition of the second was made by Rapelje Howell, *Penal Philosophy* (Boston: Little, Brown, 1912). Two other books of Tarde's which are available in English translation are: *Les Lois de l'imitation* (Paris: F. Alcan, 1890; 2d rev. ed., 1895; 4th rev. ed., 1904), the second edition of which was translated by Elsie Clews Parsons as *The Laws of Imitation* (New York: Henry Holt, 1903); and *Les Lois sociales* (Paris: F. Alcan, 1898; 6th ed., 1910), the first edition of which was translated by Howard C. Warren as *Social Laws* (New York: Macmillan, 1899). Some of Tarde's other important works, not available in English, are: *La Logique sociale* (Paris: F. Alcan, 1895); *L'Opposition universelle* (Paris: F. Alcan, 1897); *Études de psychologie sociale* ["Studies in Social Psychology"] (Paris: Giard & Brière, 1898); *L'Opinion et la foule* ["Opinion and the Mob"] (Paris: F. Alcan, 1901; 4th ed., 1922); and *Psychologie économique*, 2 vols. (Paris: F. Alcan, 1902). Excellent reviews of Tarde's work are found in two books by Michael M. Davis, *Gabriel Tarde* (New York: Columbia University Press, 1906) and *Psychological Interpretations of Society* (New York: Columbia University Press, 1909).
[2] See *Social Laws,* and *The Laws of Imitation,* p. 28.

sociological science lies in the analysis of the psychological quantities of belief and desire. Wants once initiated tend to spread in a geometric fashion, displaying a curve characterized by a slow start, a rapid expansion, and gradual leveling. Statistical curves representing development are among the most accurate items of sociological information we possess.

While the method of sociology is archaeological and statistical and the ultimate subject matter of the science consists of beliefs and desires, the specific object of interest is the inter-psychic patterns of manifestation and transmission of beliefs and desires. These are three in number: *repetition* (imitation), *opposition*, and *adaptation*.[3] An aspect of Tarde's idealism is manifest in this triad, which reflects Hegel's dialectic of thesis, antithesis, and synthesis. Of these processes, the first, repetition (imitation), accounts for the transmission, constancy, and spread of social forms; the third, adaptation (invention), is the final source of all progress and development. Inventions are any new thoughts or actions which reach expression. They arise in the minds of gifted individuals or in the conflict of imitation and existing practices. Once an invention is made, it spreads in a geometric manner from its source, opposed at every step by existing ways of doing things.

The source of all new events is in new individual ideas and inventions. Imitation is the socializing process by which an invention is spread, socially accepted, and shared. A number of factors play on invention. There is always some difficulty in combining ideas into an invention and there is always a differential ability for this task. Moreover, social conditions may favor or check mental alertness and the expression of ability. Imitation is affected by the tendency of an invention to spread from an initial center in geometric progression. Physical and biological influences (including race characteristics) may play a role in imitation, for imitations are refracted by their media. The social influences affecting imitation and invention are both logical and extra-logical. The reception of an invention is determined in part by its agreement or disagreement with inventions already accepted. Logical factors operate when an individual imitates an invention because he thinks it is more useful or efficient. But sometimes ideas are imitated before means. Imitation typically proceeds from socially superior to socially inferior. Societies and periods differ in their imitation patterns, and periods in which the past has prestige (custom imitation) alternate with periods of fashion imitation, in which the novel and foreign have prestige.

In understanding the phenomena of *opposition* in society, students have moved from the large-scale apparent similarities to the actual empirical recurrences. Early students saw opposition in terms of mythical struggles between good and evil. Later the idea of conflict of races and nations came

---

[3] Tarde devoted a book to each of these: *Les Lois de l'imitation* treats repetition, *L'Opposition universelle* treats opposition, and adaptation is taken up in *La Logique sociale*.

into view. Eventually the economists perceived the oppositions of competition. The sociologists, finally, perceived the oppositions in the individual himself, present whenever he hesitates or experiences a conflict over whether to imitate a new invention. The main types of opposition are war, competition, and discussion, and they have appeared roughly in this sequence.

In understanding *adaptation,* the first form of thought was the perception of the development of history as the integration of nation to nation, making of world history a teleological unit. But as with opposition, so here increasing precision eventually locates adaptation in the mind of the individual inventor.

The fundamental units of society for Tarde are always beliefs and desires, and the fundamental social processes repetition, opposition, and adaptation. A society is a group of persons. The only original institution was the family, which transmuted the ideas and beliefs of animal society into forms that made more complex social organization and development possible. The family was the source of all moral obligation, the source of language, worship, and art, the original political institution, the agency of social control. All specialized institutions, such as religion and the state, arose by invention within the framework of the family, and by the imitation and spread of the invention. Initially, inventions gave rise to a nobility which monopolized the advantages of the invention. Such a nobility became the point from which imitation waves could radiate. In time, the nobility was superseded by cities as the locus of inventions and source of imitation. These in turn were replaced by nations.

In *L'Opinion et la foule,* Tarde moved farther into the field of collective behavior. A "crowd" was defined as a plurality of persons gathered together in a given place and time and unified by emotion, belief, and action. The physical and mental factors associated with their contiguity account for crowd action. A "public" is a number of persons with sufficient unity of belief and emotion to act in concerted fashion, but separated from each other in time and space. For Tarde, the public is a product of modern agencies of mass communications: the printing press and the newspaper. Since the public is not in actual contiguity, it is more possible for the members of a public to deliberate. The public mind is the product of opinion produced by the impact of the printed word and gossip.

There are echoes of Bagehot in Tarde's conception of social change in terms of the alternation of epochs of custom imitation with epochs of fashion imitation. The same notions were applied to economics, leading to an anticipation of institutional economics. Custom and fashion were treated as fundamental to the study of economic development. The economics of the primitive family rested on custom imitation. It was bound by traditional forms. The spread of new consumption desires shattered the economic monopoly of the primitive family. But fashions tended to become customs, and these, in turn, were transformed into corporations, which were followed, in their turn, by a new period of fashion imitation. The two types of economic epoch differ; the one produces for use, the other for sale. We are living in a period of fashion imitation.

The properties of the school that merit the description of "social behaviorism" are already evident. While an "idealistic" definition of sociological subject matter is retained (beliefs and desires), the notion that the ultimate units of study are total societies is abandoned (as a pre-scientific analogy. Distinctions between form and content are avoided — the position is quite distinct from sociological formalism. However, like formalism, it is the vehicle for a more "liberal" conception of society. This has as a consequence the emergence of the problem of the individual personality as an area of sociological study. But in contrast to formalism, the school does not call the positivistic tradition of sociology into question. Rather, it sees the hope of sociology to lie, in part, in the development of statistical method. Like formalism, pluralistic behaviorism separates itself, despite Tarde's borrowings from Walter Bagehot, from conflict theory. Conflict is not located between groups, and certainly it is not turned into a social form. Conflict is located as the conflict of ideas in the individual mind.

Gustave Le Bon

Tarde had extended his ideas of suggestion-imitation to the problems of crowd psychology and the formation of publics. The ability of the theory to isolate new problems was already clear. Le Bon's importance lay in developing and popularizing these extensions.[4] Gustave Le Bon (1841–1931), who for a time practiced medicine, found his primary work in the study of crowd psychology.[5] In addition to having practiced medicine and written on physiology and hygiene, Le Bon was employed by the French government as an archaeologist and palaeographer in the orient, and served as editor of *Bibliothèque de philosophie scientifique*.

Whatever difficulties were later to be revealed in the principle of imitation as developed by Tarde, it was superior to any so far advanced, in simultaneously doing justice to the individual and the group, for it apparently did not require the reduction of one to the other. In France, however,

---

[4] Also important in the field is Scipio Sighele (1868–1913), whose chief work is *La Folla delinquente* ["The Delinquent Mob"] (Turin: 1891; rev. ed., 1895).

[5] A full bibliographical note on Gustave Le Bon will not be attempted. His work in crowd psychology is well represented by the following four works: *Les Lois psychologiques de l'évolution des peuples* (Paris: F. Alcan, 1894), translated into English (translator not identified) as *The Psychology of Peoples: Its Influence on Their Evolution* (New York: Macmillan, 1898; G. E. Stechert, 1912; references here are to the latter edition); *Psychologie des foules* (Paris: F. Alcan, 1895), translated into English (translator not identified) as *The Crowd* (New York: Macmillan, 1896, and later editions); *Psychologie du socialisme* (Paris: F. Alcan, 1898), translated into English (translator not identified) as *The Psychology of Socialism* (New York: Macmillan, 1899); *La Révolution française et la psychologie des révolutions* (Paris: E. Flammarion, 1912), translated by Bernard Miall as *The Psychology of Revolution* (New York: G. P. Putnam, 1913). Unavailable in English translation are Le Bon's works on archaeology, such as *La Civilisation des Arabes* ["Arabic Civilization"] (Paris: 1884) and *Les Civilisations de l'Inde* ["Indian Civilizations"] (Paris: 1887).

another strong tradition was represented by Durkheim. Hegel had viewed world history as the evolution or progress of the human spirit under the successive leaderships of the genius of one or another world power. The absolute in the form of an immanent principle of development determined the course of world history. Comte, as has been noted, was not too greatly removed from this view. He was led, in later life, to a mystically religious attitude toward society. These ideas were brought to more specific form by Moritz Lazarus (1824–1903) and Heymann Steinthal (1823–1899), who linked simpler theories to the problems of a scientific psychology. They proposed that the study of the problems of cultural history and "objective mind" should comprise the historical development of the folk mind in general and the folk minds of particular peoples. The folk community was assumed to be the fundamental communal group, with all other forms of social structures developing from it. Within the folk community, a people expressed its peculiar imagination in its art and literature; it expressed its emotion in its religion; it expressed its judgment in its codes of conduct. These notions were transmitted on to Tönnies and Durkheim. In addition to Tarde, it was Durkheim, a terminal point in this tradition, who most influenced Le Bon. Durkheim, the opponent of all forms of social nominalism, was at the other extreme of the sociological scale from Tarde, stressing the group rather than the individual in the social process. The point of emphasis for Durkheim was not ideas and beliefs invented in the individual mind and transmitted by imitation until slowed by conflict with others, but a special kind of belief, "collective representations," marked by "exteriority" and "constraint." "Collective representations" constituted a reality *sui generis* and the essential reality of society is found in its solidarity. Before he was done, Durkheim attempted to derive all other social phenomena, including science and religion, from the collective psychology of the group.

But this is merely a review to isolate the influences playing on Le Bon, who fused three primary elements in his sociological interpretations: (1) Tarde's conceptions of imitation and suggestion as basic social processes, (2) Durkheim's conception of collective mentality and the importance of group factors in social life, and (3) a racial mysticism with an anti-democratic bias.

Le Bon's racial mysticism is most fully apparent in *The Psychology of Peoples*. He takes inequality as the fundamental social fact:

> . . . people found it easy to persuade themselves that . . . inequalities were merely the outcome of differences of education, that all men are born equally intelligent and good, and that the sole responsibility for their perversion lies with the institutions they live under. This being the case, the remedy was simple in the extreme: all that had to be done was to reform the institutions and to give every man an identical education. It is in this way that institutions and education have ended by becoming the great panaceas of modern democrats, the means of remedying inequalities which clash with the important principles that are the only divinities that survive today.[6]

[6] *The Psychology of Peoples*, pp. xiv–xv.

Le Bon's whole object was to blast this democratic "myth" by describing the psychological characteristics which constitute the soul of races, and to show how the history of a people and its civilization are determined by these characteristics. Only in this way, Le Bon thought, could one smash democracy and socialism.

The moral and intellectual characters of a people, for Le Bon, form the soul of a people, an inheritance from its ancestors and a motive for its conduct. The national character, he maintains, is due to simple psychological causes. Each individual is a product not merely of his immediate parents but also of his race.

To make this argument apply, of course, it is necessary to assume the inheritance of ideas and other acquired characteristics. This Le Bon did not hesitate to do. A community of sentiments, ideas, beliefs, and interests, created by slow, hereditary accumulations, gives a high degree of identity and fixity to the mental constitution of a people. It was the cause of the greatness of Rome in ancient times, and at the present day it is the source of the greatness of England. A race is thought to possess psychological characteristics almost as fixed as its physical characteristics. There are basic inequalities among races and within any given race; the more a race approaches civilization, the greater the inequality within it. The effect of civilization is to differentiate both individuals and races. Peoples are not progressing toward equality but toward inequality. The formation of a race is due to interbreeding continued during centuries, and to a similar existence under identical conditions until the agglomeration has acquired common sentiments, common interests, and common beliefs.

While Le Bon's *Psychology of Peoples* illustrates his acceptance of a mystical biology and anti-democratic racialism, his attempt to fuse Durkheim's and Tarde's theories appears in his study of the crowd. He argues that "men are ruled by ideas, sentiments, and customs — matters which are of the essence of ourselves. Institutions and laws are the outward manifestations of our character. . . . Being its outcome institutions and laws cannot change that character." [7] However, while the complex of traits received by heredity constitutes the genius of a race, when men are assembled in a crowd for purposes of observation or action, new psychological characteristics appear, in addition to and differing from racial characteristics. Crowds have always played a part in the life of peoples, but never more important than at present. The present epoch is one of these critical moments in which the thought of man is undergoing transformation. Two fundamental factors are at the base of it: the destruction of the religious, political, and social beliefs in which all the elements of our civilization are rooted, and the creation of entirely new conditions of existence as a product of modern scientific and industrial discoveries. We have entered upon an era of crowds. This follows from the fact that the popular classes are entering political life and transforming the governing class. It follows from the growth of the

[7] *The Crowd*, p. vi.

masses in power. Civilizations are created and directed by a small intellectual aristocracy, never by crowds. Crowds are powerful only for destruction. Their rule is always tantamount to a barbarian phase of civilization.

A crowd is a gathering of people. Under certain circumstances the sentiments and ideas of the persons in the gathering take the same direction, and "conscious personality vanishes." The psychological crowd appears, forming "a single being, and is subject to the law of the mental unity of crowds." Certain conditions are necessary for predisposing individuals to subordinate themselves to the crowd mind. These are as follows: (1) the individual forming part of the crowd feels a sentiment of invisible power; (2) contagion is felt; (3) a suggestibility results. Conscious personality vanishes as discernment is lost. All feelings and thought are hypothetically determined. Intellectually the crowd is always inferior to the individual, but morally it may be good or evil, cowardly or heroic, more than is possible for any individual. Everything depends on its local bent.

Le Bon's scorn of crowds appears in the terms he successively applies to them: impulsive, mobile, irritable, suggestible, credulous, ingenuous, prone to exaggeration, intolerant, dictatorial, conservative, capable of entertaining contradictory ideas, characterized by inferior reasoning powers, possessed of an abnormally sensitive imagination, religiously tenacious of a conviction, and likely to hold fundamental convictions with great firmness while exchanging superficial opinions with amazing alacrity.[8]

The successful leaders of crowds are rhetoricians, agitators, or fanatics obsessed with an idea and dogmatic in method. The procedure of influence is reiteration rather than analysis. An idea once accepted spreads with great rapidity by contagion and imitation. Leaders of crowds maintain their control by prestige (which may have a variety of derivations). They operate by oratory, verbal extravagance, and vagueness. Crowds may be heterogeneous or homogeneous. They may be criminal crowds, criminal juries, electoral crowds, or parliamentary assemblies; as crowds, they are always the same.

In *The Psychology of Revolution*, Le Bon brought together and applied many of the ideas present in the *Psychology of Peoples* and *The Crowd*. The problems projected in *The Crowd* are fulfilled in Le Bon's theory of revolution. Crowd action is by no means identical with revolution. "The multitude is . . . the agent of a revolution; but not its point of departure. The crowd represents an amorphous being which can do nothing, and will nothing, without a head to lead it. It will quickly exceed the impulse once received, but it never creates it." [9] Revolutions are those changes which "transform the destinies of the people." [10] Revolution is the more general problem of which the crowd is an incident.

Governments are futile in the face of a true revolution, representing a

---

[8] See Harry Elmer Barnes, "The Psychosociological Theories of Gustave Le Bon," in Barnes (ed.), *An Introduction to the History of Sociology* (Chicago: University of Chicago Press, 1948), esp. pp. 489–490.

[9] *The Psychology of Revolution*, p. 24.   [10] *Ibid.*, p. 25.

change in the soul of a people. The more stable the institutions of a people are in normal times, the more violent its revolutions are likely to be. In a revolution, the people follow the dictates of their leaders. Most of the people are relatively peaceably inclined, but not all. The conception of the people as a mystic entity endowed with all powers and virtues is the creation of demagogues intent on manipulation. This popular entity is conceived as a superior personality, never having to answer for its actions and never making a mistake. The people may kill, burn, ravage, commit the most frightful cruelties, glorify its hero today and throw him into the gutter tomorrow. Actually, Le Bon argues, this mysterious fetish breaks down into two categories. The first includes peasants, traders, and workers who need tranquillity and order to exercise their callings. The second category, which plays a capital part in all national disturbances, consists of a subversive social residue dominated by a criminal mentality. Degenerates of alcoholism and poverty, thieves, beggars, destitute "casuals," indifferent workers without employment — these constitute the dangerous bulk of the armies of insurrection.[11]

Le Bon was in terror of socialism and syndicalism. Science and industry were seen as having precipitated the growth of cities, concentration of population, improvement of communication, and the extension of suffrage. All such democratizing factors and agencies opened the era of crowds. Because of their emotionality and susceptibility to suggestion, they are instruments in the hands of leaders with prestige and a readiness to utilize affirmation, repetition, contagion, and imitation in molding and directing them. One of the prime dangers of modern society is the exploitation of crowds by selfish demagogues.

The somewhat more "liberal" conception of society noted in Tarde's work also appears in Le Bon. Society is not a great organism, any part of which may not be interfered with without disaster; society is a strategy of collective actions. Once this is granted, however, Le Bon is immediately in arms with passionate defenses against inferior races, mobs, popular publics, democracy, and socialism. A sultry ideological atmosphere surrounds most of his work. Nevertheless, the general fact remains: the whole area of collective behavior has been discovered by sociology.

James Mark Baldwin

The imitation–suggestion theory founded by Tarde was extended to the interpretations of a whole series of institutions and social processes. Tarde also indicated the manner in which it could be used to analyze the problems of the crowd and the public. Le Bon further developed its implications for the crowd, extending its application to social revolution and other catastrophic social change. Baldwin's importance lay in the extension of the ideas of imitation and suggestion to the problems of the personality and the relation between self and society.

James Mark Baldwin (1861–1934), who is best known as editor and

11 *Ibid.*, p. 70.

chief author of the Dictionary of Philosophy and Psychology, helped bring about the shift in the social sciences in America away from biological organicism and evolution toward a more psychological analysis of society.[12] Baldwin was influenced not only by Tarde but by the Hegelians (particularly Josiah Royce) and the pragmatists (particularly James).

Personality study at this period was partly adapted to prevailing evolutionary doctrines. One could study the mind of the child, primitive man, and the animal as evolutionary products. G. Stanley Hall and Baldwin proposed to use the recapitulation doctrine, made significant by the evolutionists, for this purpose. From this point of view, the psychological development of the individual represents a recapitulation of the evolutionary development of the race. At the same time, the imitation-suggestion point of view tended to focus primary interest upon the environmental determination of mental life rather than on hereditary elements. In Baldwin's case, a particularly happy fusion of these two traditions occurred: the recapitulation doctrine made the mind of the child an object of major interest, and the imitation-suggestion mechanism focused attention on the factors involved in learned behavior. *The Mental Development in the Child and the Race* is a landmark in the sociological study of personality. In one of those brilliant flashes that mark a basic turn of thought, the fusion of the imitation-suggestion idea with that of recapitulation carried out the shift of interest from the historical development of the mind to the development of individual self. "The relations of individual development to race development are so intimate — the two are so identical in fact — that no topic in the one can be treated with great clearness without assuming results in the other." [13]

For all intents and purposes, one can forget about the mentality of the race, and concentrate on the more immediately observable phenomena present at first hand.

In carrying out the project of examining the development of the mentality of the child, Baldwin finds the central processes to lie in various forms of "suggestion." These were developed at length in *The Mental Development in the Child and the Race*,[14] and compactly summarized in *The Story of the Mind* in the little series of volumes quaintly described as "The Library of Useful Stories." [15]

Suggestion refers to "the fact that all sorts of hints from without disturb and modify the beliefs and actions of the individual." [16] Suggestion represents all the processes which mold psychic life. Baldwin distinguished

---

[12] James Mark Baldwin (ed.), *Dictionary of Philosophy and Psychology* (New York: Macmillan, 1901–05; corr. ed., 1925; reprinted, 1940). The other works of Baldwin with which we are concerned in the present discussion are: *The Mental Development in the Child and the Race* (New York: Macmillan, 1895; 3d rev. ed., 1906) and *The Story of the Mind* (New York: D. Appleton, 1898; 5th ed., 1912).
[13] *The Mental Development in the Child and the Race* (1906 edition), p. viii.
[14] Pp. 104–169.
[15] *The Story of the Mind* (1910 edition), pp. 148–166.
[16] *Ibid.*, p. 148.

a number of types: (1) *physiological* — the molding of behavior on the basis of environmental influence below the level of consciousness; (2) *subconscious adult suggestion* — the adult counterpart of the physiological suggestion in infants; (3) *tune suggestion* — an example of adult subconscious suggestion in which a tune heard some time previously may take possession of consciousness, serving as the counterpart of a whole series of similar types of suggestion; (4) *normal auto-suggestion* — in which the individual may consciously or unconsciously set up suggestions operating on himself (as in falling asleep in putting the baby to sleep); (5) *inhibitory suggestion* — a phenomenon present at all levels of nervous action in which inhibitory suggestions tend to suppress, check, or inhibit movement; (6) *pain suggestion* — a suggestion of a negative sort operating at all levels of mental development to suppress movement; (7) *control suggestion* — covering all cases of any kind of restraint placed on the movements of the body short of those coming from voluntary intention; (8) *contrary suggestion* — representing a special class of exaggerated instances of control suggestion, again operating at all levels of mental development and manifest in refined forms in the behavior of men of ascetic temperament with self-imposed duties of self-denial; and finally (9) *hypnotic suggestion* — referring to all instances of hypnotism. Baldwin was inclined to accept the theory that hypnosis is a special application of the principles of suggestion under deliberate manipulation.

For Baldwin, the two processes of suggestion and imitation sum up the plastic relations between individual and environment. Suggestion is the process of being acted on and imitation the response to suggestion. By locating these processes centrally to psychological development, emphasis is shifted away from all forms of hereditary determination (despite the recapitulation idea) of mental life; various psychological activities such as adaptation, consciousness, emotional expression, attitude formation, memory, recognition, imagination, and thought are seen as special emergents. Individual development consists in forming habits and adapting and modifying them. The essential property of habit is found in the tendency of an organism to continue processes proved beneficial. A habit maintains advantageous stimulations by the organism's own movements. Accommodation, on the other hand, is adaptation to more complex conditions of stimulation by the performance of more complex functions.

Continued accommodation is possible only because of habit, which conserves the past response and solidifies the structure for new accommodations. Moreover, the copy becomes, by transference from the world to the mind, capable of revival in memory. Hence, accommodation may take on a conscious basis in volition. Volition is a kind of persistent imitative suggestion arising when a copy is linked with other copies in thought and action. The residue of motive is bound up with attention. The final coordination of all motor elements is volition or choice. Imitation is the integrating principle between habit and accommodation.

In applying the suggestion–imitation formula to the development of self-hood in the child, Baldwin came to the conclusion that personality emerges in stages or "epochs of functional differentiation."

> First, the epoch of the rudimentary sense processes, the pleasure and pain process, and simple motor adaptation, called for convenience the "affective epoch": second, the epoch of presentation, memory, imitation, defensive action, instinct, which passes by gradations into, third, the epoch of complex presentation, complex motor coordination, of conquest, of offensive action, and rudimentary volition. These, the second and third together, I should characterize, on the side of consciousness, as the "epoch of objective reference": and, finally, the epoch of thought, reflection, self-assertion, social organization, union of forces, cooperation; the "epoch of subjective reference," which in human history merges into the "social and ethical epoch." [17]

There are four very distinct phases of the child's experience of persons not himself, all subsequent to his purely *affective*, or pleasure–pain, epoch. First, persons are simply *objects*, parts of the material environment; second, persons are very peculiar objects, very interesting, very active, very arbitrary, very portentous of pleasure or pain. If objects with these properties are *projects*, then persons at this stage may be called *personal projects*. They have certain peculiarities later seen to be the attributes of personality. Third, the child's own actions issuing from himself, largely by imitation in response to the requirements of this "projective" environment, having his own organism as their center and his own consciousness as their theatre, give him light on himself as *subject*. Fourth, this self-knowledge is reflected upon other persons to illuminate them as also subjects, and they to him then become *ejects* or social fellows.[18]

Analogically, Baldwin treated the suggestion–imitation formulas that link the individual mind to society as "social heredity" and the process of inter-adjustment of persons as "social selection." Socially, the man fit for social life "must be born to learn," for in society learning is the essential need. He receives his personality and constitutes a social organization in terms of his plasticity. Plasticity is the means of his progress. So he grows into the social organization, takes his place as a socius in the work of the world, and lays deep the sense of values, upon the basis of which his own contributions to the wealth of the world are brought out. He participates in and helps constitute a *milieu* in which each member of society gives and gets the same set of social suggestions. Out of this give and take, in all the interchange of suggestions, an obscure sense of social understanding grows up about ourselves generally — a *Zeitgeist*, an atmosphere, a taste, or, in minor matters, a style. The continuity of society is found in the processes of imitation or "social heredity." The innovating or inventive aspects of social process are found in genius.

[17] *Ibid.*, p. 16.   [18] *Ibid.*, p. 18.

The interrelation between self and society was nowhere more delicately summed up by Baldwin than in the concluding paragraphs of his *Mental Development,* where he suggests that the antithesis between the self and the world is not valid.

> The self is realized by taking in "copies" from the world, and the world is enabled to set higher copies only through the constant reactions of the individual self upon it. Morally I am as much a part of society as physically I am a part of the world's fauna; and as my body gets its best explanation from the point of view of its place in a zoological scale, so morally I occupy a place in the social order; and an important factor in the understanding of me is the understanding of it.[19]

The rich potential lying in the pluralistic behavioral branch of social behaviorism is dramatically revealed in Baldwin's perceptive studies. It is perhaps not unfair to say that for the first time *the study of the social person* has come into its own as a recognized branch of sociology. The conflict theorists, particularly Gumplowicz and Small, had perceived the area, but hardly invested it with full standing. Their failure to do so was inevitable: the very emphasis on the more or less complete domination of the individual by the group led to a de-emphasis on the individual.

Franklin Henry Giddings

Franklin Henry Giddings (1855–1931) was the son of a Congregational minister of Connecticut. He attended Union College, Schenectady, for the study of engineering. His education was interrupted for teaching, but he completed his degree in 1877. For the next ten years Giddings worked as a journalist. He succeeded Woodrow Wilson at Bryn Mawr College in 1888, teaching political science, economics, and the principles of charity and correction. He introduced a graduate course in sociology at Columbia University, and in 1894 he took over the newly established chair in sociology there. He was one of the founders of *The Annals of the American Academy of Political and Social Science,* and third president of the American Sociological Society.

Giddings' writings extend over a thirty-year period, and reflect a variety of influences.[20] From Comte, he drew his general picture of the main stages of the development of civilization and was, without doubt, influenced by Comte's positivism. From Darwin and Spencer, he took over a naturalistic form of evolutionism. He was strongly influenced by Ward's concept of the use of sociology for social reform. The notion of "sympathy" was taken

[19] *The Mental Development in the Child and the Race,* pp. 87–88.
[20] Among Giddings' more important works are: *The Principles of Sociology* (New York: Macmillan, 1896, 1926); *The Elements of Sociology* (New York: Macmillan, 1898, 1916); *Inductive Sociology* (New York: Macmillan, 1901); *Studies in the Theory of Human Society* (New York: Macmillan, 1922); *The Scientific Study of Human Society* (Chapel Hill, N.C.: University of North Carolina Press, 1924); and the posthumous *Civilization and Society,* edited by Howard W. Odum (New York: Henry Holt, 1932).

from Adam Smith, and "social constraint" from Durkheim and Sumner. Other elements of his thought were garnered from John Stuart Mill and Karl Pearson. However, the real core of his sociology, the ultimate conception of its nature and basic units, shows the primary influence of Tarde (possibly reinforced by Ross). Like Tarde, he was interested in the small-scale repetitions of personal acts in interaction. He was convinced that these could be — and ultimately had to be — analyzed statistically.

> Like acts by detached individuals may be competitive, or they may fall into combinations, as when animals in a pack follow the same quarry or beat off a common enemy. When it is often enough repeated, combined action becomes habitual group action.
>
> Whether they are dissimilar or similar, rivalistic or combined, simultaneous or not, equal or unequal, pluralistic reactions to a common stimulation make a strictly individualistic struggle for existence impossible. Above all is this true of the human struggle for achievement. It is a pluralistic struggle.
>
> Pluralistic behavior, in distinction from individual behavior, has its own conditions, forms, and laws.
>
> Always the character of pluralistic reactions . . . is determined by two variables, namely, (1) the strength of the stimulation, and (2) the similarity (or dissimilarity) of the reacting mechanisms.
>
> Pluralistic behavior is the subject-matter of the psychology of society, otherwise called sociology, a science statistical in method, which attempts, first, to factorize pluralistic behavior, and second, to explain its genesis, integration, differentiation, and functioning by accounting for them in terms of the variables (1) stimulation, and (2) the resemblance (more or less) to one another of reacting mechanisms.[21]

There is an essential identity between Tarde's and Giddings' formulations. Tarde was interested in repetitive and similar overt behaviors. He believed that they expressed inner beliefs and desires. Giddings states that pluralistic action is determined by the strength of stimulation. Tarde believed that a transmitted pattern of behavior is a ray of imitation reflecting the character of its transmitting medium. The second basic variable determining the character of pluralistic action, according to Giddings, was the nature of the reacting mechanisms. Just about everything that Tarde thought important is repeated except for the notion of imitation itself. Of Tarde's idea Giddings stated:

> Tarde examined imitation and all that can be shown to proceed from it with thoroughness and penetration. He gave to the world a precise and characteristic meaning, that of the action at a distance of one mind upon another, whether consciously willed or not willed, passive or active. If it were possible to demonstrate that society is but a tissue of imitations defined as intermental actions, it would be difficult to add much of interest or value to Tarde's argument.[22]

[21] *Studies in the Theory of Human Society*, pp. 251–252.
[22] *Ibid.*, p. 116.

It may be gathered from this that Giddings thought Tarde produced the single most satisfactory system of sociology outside his own: that his principles of "consciousness of kind" and "like-mindedness" were conceived as a direct substitute for Tarde's principle.

Giddings' substitutes for imitation ("like-mindedness" and "consciousness of kind"), except for a shift of emphasis, have quite the same effects as Tarde's principle. Imitation as the central principle of social life casts the primary emphasis upon interhuman action. Giddings' principles play down this interaction and emphasize parallel response to parallel stimuli. Consciousness of kind as the basis of society may be viewed simply as a special form of the similarity of stimulus coming from like individuals. "Combining with and supplementing like-response to stimulation, the consciousness of kind converts a merely instinctive cooperation into concerted action." [23]

When imitation occurs, it is as a kind of second-level principle leading to complex social forms. When an audience springs to its feet at the cry of fire, its initial action, Giddings argues, is not imitation. Example and imitation enter as complicating factors the instant that movement toward the door begins. A cool and fearless man may even prevent a panic. Inter-mental action is inter-stimulation and response. Like-mindedness, complicated by inter-mental action, may become competition or may become concerted volition. It may become solidarity. Unlike-response differentiates and individualizes; it may disintegrate.[24]

Thus Tarde emphasized the transformation of behavior in society; Giddings reversed the emphasis, and treated society largely as a product of pre-social individual similarity. It is not surprising that Giddings found himself in sharp disagreement with Baldwin's argument that *ego* and *alter* represent parallel differentiations from suggestive-imitative life. Consciousness of kind, rather, was argued to be the true source of personality. "The rise of this consciousness marks a distinct stage in the evolution of the mind of the many. Also, *it converts mere gregariousness into society;* and it transforms further the already twice amended and doubly amplified natural ego." [25]

In *Inductive Sociology* (1901), Giddings distinguished five forms of the consciousness of kind: (1) organic sympathy, (2) perception of resemblance, (3) reflective sympathy, (4) affection, and (5) desire. The nature of the particular form of like-mindedness determines all that is essential to the society, social organization, institution, or social class. The key to social life is the formation of like-response. Four like-responses are fundamental: appreciation, utilization, characterization, and socialization. On the basis of such like-response types, four fundamental types of character arise in society: the forceful, the convivial, the austere, and the rationally conscious. The four types of mind correlated with these are the ideo-motor, the ideo-emotional, the dogmatic-emotional, and the critical-intellectual. There are three primary classes: vitality classes, personality classes, and social classes.

[23] *Ibid.*, p. 117.   [24] *Ibid.*, p. 116.   [25] *Ibid.*, p. 163.

High-vitality classes have high birth rates and low death rates (rural land-owning), medium-vitality classes fall in between (business and professional), low-vitality classes have a high birth rate and high death rate (workers in the cities). Personality classes divide into genius, talented, normally endowed, and defectives. Social classes are determined by contribution to social life. The true natural aristocracy consists of philanthropists with a highly developed consciousness of kind. The pseudo-social class is composed of congenital and habitual paupers with a degenerate sense of the consciousness of kind.

Giddings was a careful student of Mill, and in his *Inductive Sociology* he followed Mill's discussion. He argued that Mill's methods of agreement and difference establish conditions and causes.[26] This, for Giddings, was preliminary to sociological study proper, which depended upon comparative and historical methods. The aim of sociological method is to determine whether a given fact belongs to a given class, and this is a product of historical method. Statistics show what is truly common to social phenomena. In fact, "standard deviation is the key to an understanding of all phenomena of evolution — variations and artificial selection." Moreover, "a coefficient of correlation is always equivalent to a generalization of law."

Such ideas developed in the *Inductive Sociology* were reformulated in a more temperate form in *The Scientific Study of Human Society* (1924). Here he argued that the scientific study of social facts requires the exercise of greatest care, becoming precise only in terms of measurement. He thought that the classification of social facts proceeds dichotomously in terms of the character inherent in them. Sociological study is eventually concerned with complex and variable phenomena (pluralistic behavior), and since it cannot be exhaustive it must utilize samples. Whereas statistics studies factors distributively, the statistical method may be legitimately supplemented by the case method, which studies factors in combination. Casual groups of persons anywhere are rich sources of sociological data. Newspaper items, families, college classes, all may be analyzed. One's discoveries include habits, reactions, consciousness of kind, reactions to the mores, and social interests. Among other things, such detailed study proves the existence of social

26 John Stuart Mill's inductive logic was a major attempt to generalize scientific procedure to all areas of experience. In trying to clarify the steps of a scientific proof, he outlined a number of procedures, of which the *method of agreement* and *method of difference* were most important. If we are interested, say, in high morale and wish to discover the causes of it, there are, Mill thought, two basic ways to proceed: comparing cases of high morale with one another or comparing cases of high morale with cases of low morale. In the first comparison, we would employ the method of difference: we would try to match instances of high morale in such a manner that they would differ item by item in every single respect except for those items causally related to high morale. On the other hand, in the comparison of cases of high morale with those of low morale, we would pursue the method of agreement: we would match the cases of high and low morale item by item for agreement in order to discover the facts which when present bring about high morale but which when absent do not. In attempting to develop experimental designs for field research, Giddings' students also went back to Mill.

telesis, the presence of purpose in human social affairs. Basic methods of measurement include averages, gradings, ratios, percentiles, modes, and coefficients of correlation.

The inconsistencies and errors in Giddings' methodological arguments are far less important than his influence. He made Columbia a center from which radiated the demand for a more rigorous, quantitatively anchored method.

E. A. Ross

It has already been necessary to examine Ross in connection with socio-logical formalism. The same journalistic sense that led him to turn to sociological formalism, which seemed to offer itself as the most plausible basis for systematizing sociology, had led him at an earlier period to the traditions of Tarde. There is little doubt that the period of Ross's sociology under the influence of Tarde was his richest; why did he ever abandon it? In the first decade of the twentieth century, a number of powerful individual voices commanded the field. Lester Ward, after his retirement from govern-ment, taught at Brown University, advocating a form of positivistic organ-icism, modified somewhat by the conflict theorists; Albion Small at Chicago was building a powerful department and teaching a form of conflict theory; Cooley was developing a branch of social behaviorism somewhat distinct from Tarde's at Michigan; and Giddings at Columbia developed a position similar to that of Tarde. Social behaviorism was the theory of the younger set. At a later period, Ross turned as naturally to Simmel as at this period he turned to Tarde. In the opinion of most students, Ross's two greatest books were done under Tarde's influence — *Social Control* (1901) and *Social Psychology* (1908).[27]

The evidences of Tarde's influence on Ross are many. They include (1) Ross's objection to taking too large units for comparative analysis, (2) his treatment of the historical method and statistical method as es-sentially complementary, and (3) his insistence on the importance of a statistical treatment of social phenomena. At this stage, his concept of society is that of Tarde.

> "Society" is, of course, a kind of fiction. There is nothing to it, after all, but people affecting one another in various ways. The thesis of this book is that from the interactions of individuals and generations there emerges a kind of collective mind evincing itself in living ideals, conventions, dogmas, institutions, and religious sentiments which are more or less happily adapted to the task of safeguarding the collective welfare from the ravages of egoism.[28]

Ross took over from Tarde, with little change, the concept of the nature and importance of imitation as well as the proposition that contrasting forms of imitation were manifest in epochs of custom and fashion imitation.

[27] For bibliographical information on Ross, see Chapter 10, Footnote 21.
[28] E. A. Ross, *Social Control* (New York: Macmillan, 1928), p. 293.

If one conceives of society as a plurality of interacting individuals, as is characteristic of social behaviorism, a series of special sub-areas leap into prominence. Some of these have been noted: the field of collective behavior emerged in the work of Le Bon and Tarde; the field of personality appeared with Baldwin. In Ross's work still another area of sociological study came into its own — the problem of social control. It is a peculiarity of the theory of social control that it poses anew the problem of the relation of the individual and society. Ross observed that the relation of the individual to society varies, among other things, with the degree of social complexity. The study of social control is the examination of the manner in which the interests of the individual and those of society are combined and ordered.

Had Ross been more of a theorist, there is little doubt that the entire topic would have been considerably more developed. As it was, a latent typology was already present in *Social Control,* a typology designed to sharpen the sorts of social conditions which affect social control. The distinction was drawn between a "natural society" and a "class-based society." A natural society is the social order appearing when basic human impulses are able to work themselves out without interference. "*Sympathy, sociability, the sense of justice,* and *resentment* are competent, under favorable circumstances, to work out by themselves a true, *natural order,* that is to say, an order without design or art." [29]

Such a natural order as a "freely competitive society" has been approximated in the societies formed in the American West during the gold rush. Persons coming to the frontiers from various cultural backgrounds worked out a society on the basis of differential abilities and a foundation of natural dependability, trust, and fairness. At the other extreme are "class-based societies" oriented toward the established interests of a particular group. "When the . . . center of such inhibition is a class living at the expense of the rest of the community, we no longer have social control in the true sense, but *class control.* This may be defined as *the exercise of power by a parasitic class in its own interest.*" [30]

Presumably the problem of social control displays its full possibilities in societies lying between these extremes — situations in which interhuman adjustment is spontaneous and unforced and situations in which control is arbitrary and coercive. Social control represents the manner in which social phenomena are ordered in the interest of society. It emerges as an issue only when society becomes more complex than the freely established order. The idea implicit in Ross's discussion seems to be that, the moment institutionalization takes place, ordering of the relations of the individuals to others cannot any longer occur spontaneously, and the problem of the regulation of the actions of the individual with respect to institutions appears. The state represents precisely a specialized institution for this purpose. "The state is, in theory at least, a channel and not a source of control. It is supposed to be

[29] *Ibid.,* p. 41.   [30] *Ibid.,* p. 256.

a device by which social power is collected, transmitted, and applied *so as to do* work. But as a matter of fact, the state, when it becomes paternal and develops on the administrative side, is able in a measure to guide the society it professes to obey." [31] In the background of social control is the problem of the relations between the interests of some and the interests of all. This may be seen in the "three laws of social control." (1) Social power is concentrated or diffused in proportion as men do or do not feel themselves in need of guidance or protection. [32] (2) The greater the ascendancy of the few, the more possible it is for social control to affect the course of the social movement.[33] (3) The more distinct, knit together, and self-conscious the influential minority, the more likely is social control to be colored with class selfishness.[34] The risk in the relation of individual and society is that the interests of some achieve ascendancy over the interests of all. In a democratic society, moneyed interests tend to dominate. In fact, the state itself, developed to oppose private interests, creates officials and may become a locus of social power.

The topic of social control is divided into the grounds of control, the means of control, and the system of control. The basic psychological materials of importance for control are sympathy, the sense of justice, sociability, and resentment. These produce the *ego* and *alter*, the sense of justice and equity, the concept of fair play. By themselves, they are sufficient to produce a natural order in which social control is not a specialized fact. The means of control include public opinion, law, belief, social suggestions (including education), custom, religion, personal ideals, ceremony, art, personality, enlightenment, illusion, social evaluation, the ethics of survival, and the ethics of elites. Finally, the problem of systems of control raises the question of the place of social control in the social order. Chiefly, in this section, Ross was occupied with the socio-ethical problem of the most desirable system of control. For him, this was the simplest and most spontaneous system possible.

Ross's *Social Psychology* was both less original and better organized than *Social Control*. It was built around the processes of suggestion–imitation and organized its subject matter into conventionality and custom imitation. It took over Tarde's laws that imitation spreads from upper to lower classes, from city to country, and other issues. Among the problems particularly interesting to Ross in this work was the part played by suggestibility in the transfer of ideas, habits, and attitudes from one group to another. The basic anchorage of Ross's interest was in the distributional uniformities of attitudes, ideas, and habits in society rather than in personality.

Ross was a strong voice in the popularization of the pluralistic behavioral branch of social behaviorism. The *Social Psychology*, moreover, not only introduced the ideas of Tarde and Le Bon to the general American audience, but represented the first complete volume in America devoted to collective behavior. Furthermore, from Tarde he derived and transmitted a strong

[31] *Ibid.*, p. 82.   [32] *Ibid.*, p. 78.   [33] *Ibid.*, p. 85.   [34] *Ibid.*, p. 86.

conviction that the future of sociology rested largely upon the development of an adequate statistical method. Though Ross did little to advance such a method, with Giddings he was one of the main persons to popularize it and dramatize its necessity.

However, Ross also illustrates the dilemma that members of the school found themselves in, once they accepted a more liberal conception of society. The organismic positivists and conflict theorists had little trouble accounting for individuals, who were considered to be socialized only to the degree that they were subordinate to the group or society. But once society is conceived as a structure of pluralistic behavior, there is no such easy solution. For this very reason, collective behavior, social control, and the sociology of personality make their appearance. While Tarde is relatively liberal, Le Bon advocates passionate conservatism. While Baldwin is primarily liberal, Giddings is primarily conservative. Ross has strong liberal tendencies overlaid with conservatism, as shown precisely by his concern with the problem of how society controls the individual.

Meanwhile, pluralistic behaviorism continued to develop in the work of the students of Giddings, two of whom will be reviewed here.[35]

W. F. Ogburn and M. F. Nimkoff

William Fielding Ogburn (1886–1959) earned his doctorate at Columbia University in 1912. He taught sociology at Reed College from 1912 to 1917, and after war service with the government he returned to academic work. He joined the faculty of the University of Chicago in 1927, staying until his retirement in 1952. From 1920–1926, he edited the *Journal of the American Statistical Association*. The most striking of all Ogburn's work was his *Social Change*.[36] Here he developed for the first time the most original and influential of his ideas, one which he continued to elaborate throughout his life.

Ogburn can be approached most simply as developing some aspects of the ideas of the pluralistic behaviorist school. This school generally tended to emphasize social influence rather than biology in the explanation of social events. Significantly, the starting point of Ogburn's analysis was a complaint against the overemphasis on biological factors in accounting for social events. More important than biology was man's "social heritage" — a term pre-

[35] Among the important students of Giddings were J. P. Lichtenberger, J. E. Gillin, W. F. Ogburn, H. W. Odum, F. S. Chapin, F. H. Hankins, Hugh S. Carter, C. E. Gehlke, Stuart A. Rice, Elbridge Sibley, Warren S. Thompson, Malcolm M. Willey, and Julian Woodard. By and large, they all remained true to the tenets of pluralistic behaviorism.
[36] W. F. Ogburn, *Social Change with Respect to Culture and Original Nature* (New York: B. W. Huebsch, 1922; Viking, 1927; rev. ed., Viking, 1950); references here are to the two Viking editions. Other important writings of Ogburn and his collaborators are: *The Social Sciences and Their Interrelations*, with Alexander Goldenweiser (Boston: Houghton Mifflin, 1927); *The Economic Development of Post-War France*, with William Jaffe (New York: Columbia University Press, 1929); *Sociology*, with Meyer F. Nimkoff (Boston: Houghton Mifflin, 1940; 3d ed., 1958); *The Social Effects of Aviation*, with Jean L. Adams and S. G. Gilfillan (Boston: Houghton Mifflin, 1946); *Technology and the Changing Family*, with Meyer F. Nimkoff (Boston: Houghton Mifflin, 1955).

ferred by Baldwin and other members of the school. "The social heritage
. . . is not solely the product of human association occurring at a particular
period . . . but is a certain surviving product over a very long period of
time." [37]

Culture is conceived as the accumulated products of human society, and
includes material objects as well as social institutions and social ways.
Cultural change is the change in these products. The fundamental factor
in cultural change is the accumulation of cultural forms which result from
invention and discovery. The basic elements of the social process are invention, diffusion, and adaptation of cultural elements. This all takes place in
a context made up of man's accumulated culture or social heritage. There is
practically nothing in this that was not stated by Tarde and others of the
school. Tarde had located the poles of the social process in repetition and
invention. In imitation, conflict, and adaptation, he located the basic model
of the spread, reception, and resistance to social influence.

What was new in Ogburn's account was the emphasis on the difference
between material culture and adaptive culture. The real sources of progressive change were found in material invention — tools, weapons, and technical
processes. Adaptive culture refers to the rest of man's social and institutional life, which is "adapted" to this material base. Many things may interfere with the adjustment of this "adaptive" culture to the material base.
(1) Those who have vested interests "derive a differential advantage under
existing conditions and . . . offer resistance to change." [38] (2) Anything
upsetting tradition tends to occasion fear. "So the mores in a culture may
embody a definite attitude for or against change." [39] (3) Slowness to
change may be due to habit. "Conservatism is . . . an attribute of a people
of a particular age and locality or . . . a trait of a special class of individuals." [40] And resistance to change may be due to (4) education or a
variety of (5) social pressures or even (6) the wish to forget the unpleasant.

> Culture once in existence persists because it has utility. Forces that
> produce changes are the discovery of new cultural elements that have
> superior utility, in which case the old utilities tend to be replaced by the
> new. The slowness of culture to change lies in the difficulties of creating
> and adopting new ideas.[41]

A social problem is created by such lack of adjustment. "Material-culture
changes force changes in other parts of culture such as social organization
and customs, but these latter parts of culture do not change as quickly.
They lag behind the material-culture changes, hence we are living in a period
of maladjustment." [42]

Ogburn seems to have been quite unhappy with this statement of social
change and account of social problems, for he immediately proceeded to

---

[37] *Social Change* (1927 edition), p. 43.   [38] *Ibid.*, p. 169.
[39] *Ibid.*, p. 173.   [40] *Ibid.*, pp. 173–174.   [41] *Ibid.*, p. 193.   [42] *Ibid.*, p. 196.

develop another. Some problems arise, he argued, not from the lack of adjustment of the various parts of culture, but from the lack of adjustment between human nature and culture. The general argument is that man's biology changes very slowly, while his culture changes quickly. "Man is the same biologically as he was in the late ice age, while his culture has suddenly become vastly different. The problem may be popularly expressed as that of cave men trying to live in a modern city. . . . Can we, being biologically the same as Cro-Magnon men, adjust ourselves to the sedentary life demanded of office workers?" [43] It seems emphatically not. It is claimed that a great many social problems such as war, crime, sexual aberrations, and disease "arise because of the inability or difficulty of the original nature of man to adapt itself to modern conditions and cultural standards." So also it is claimed that "much of our unhappiness, nervousness, and insanity is traceable to the same general causes." [44]

There are important discrepancies between the biological and cultural lag theories of social problems. There are, moreover, problems presented by the idea of *culture lag* — a term that remains meaningless until one has first decided what lags behind what. These difficulties throw significant light upon some aspects of pluralistic behaviorism. For one thing, the contrast between the implications of the two lag theories, the cultural and biological, dramatizes an issue faced by the pluralistic behaviorists. The theory of cultural lag, in posing the primacy of technology over the other aspects of culture, shows the remote penetration of modes of thought characteristic of Marxism (with its contrast between "mode" and "relations" of production) or, perhaps, Veblen (with his implicit technocracy). The cultural lag theory finds the progressive element of society to lie in science and technology in a manner characteristic of many liberal positions. However, the biological lag theory spells out the precise opposite implication, in its assertion that man's nature, having evolved much more slowly than his culture, finds many of man's most critical problems to derive from the contradictions between a stone-age biology and a twentieth-century culture. This affords a contradictory explanation of the same issues. While the first explanation of social problems attributes them to a deficient application of science, the second would view every gain of science as widening the gap between man's nature and culture and driving him into crime, homosexuality, suicide, and insanity. Whereas the culture lag theory of social problems is semi-liberal, the biological lag theory — treating human culture as the thin veneer over a fundamental savagery — is typically conservative. The uncertainty of self-identification by representatives of pluralistic behaviorism could hardly be more effectively dramatized. Meanwhile, however, Ogburn added still another area or perhaps the blurred outlines of two areas, to pluralistic behaviorism: a theory of social change and its account of social problems.

A new edition of Ogburn's *Social Change* was put out in 1950 with a

[43] *Ibid.*, p. 286.   [44] *Ibid.*, p. 287.

supplementary chapter. The first edition had appeared in no less than ten printings from 1922 to 1938. In it, Ogburn had produced one of the most widely read and discussed books in the whole of American sociology. Because it has been so much copied, attacked, and defended, the present discussion has focused on the first edition.

It is significant that in the supplementary chapter to the 1950 edition, with the mature wisdom of a man looking back on the work of nearly thirty years, Ogburn was not dissatisfied. "On re-reading the section on social evolution in *Social Change*, it is thought that the essential factors that explain social evolution are there to be found. They are there set forth quite modestly, with apologies for the scarcity of evidence." [45]

Ogburn went on to repeat some of the main arguments of the original. Cultural evolution is explained by four factors: invention, accumulation, diffusion, and adjustment.[46] Invention is either mechanical or social, resulting from the operation of three factors: mental activity, demand, and the existence of other cultural elements. Accumulation occurs when more elements are added to the cultural base than are lost. Diffusion represents the spread of inventions. Adjustment is forced when an invention interacts with other cultural elements. The most general process of such adjustment appears with the lag between material and non-material culture.

The most significant element in this re-statement of his original position is the fact that Ogburn repeated only the first of his lag hypotheses: the theory of cultural lag. While he retained the biological lag theory in the 1950 edition and did not reject it, he did not emphasize it either. Whether unconsciously or by intention, Ogburn alone can answer, but he emphasized only the more liberal of his lag theories.

The shift within Ogburn's work to the more liberal position is perhaps in part related to the unusually fruitful collaboration he undertook with Meyer F. Nimkoff.

Meyer F. Nimkoff (1904–   ) received his A.B. degree at Boston University in 1925, taking his M.A. at Southern California in 1926, and his Ph.D. in 1928. He was a professor of sociology at Bucknell University. Since 1950 he has been chairman of the sociology department of Florida State University. A major scholar in his own right, Nimkoff has written *The Family* and *Marriage and the Family*, as well as collaborating with Ogburn in *Sociology* and *Technology and the Changing Family*.

In Nimkoff's studies of the family, he argued that the inventions and discoveries of modern science and industry are the most important factors in social change and thereby also in understanding the patterns of contemporary family organization. The family reached its greatest strength in agricultural society, when plow technology was of central importance. The family's economic importance was foundational to its educational, protective, and state functions. The industrial revolution transferred many of these

[45] *Social Change* (1952 edition), p. 374.
[46] *Ibid.*, p. 377.

functions to industry and the state, bringing about compensatory forces which accent the affectional role of the family, explaining the family's increased preoccupation with happiness.[47]

It is evident from this that Nimkoff and Ogburn profoundly share the same perspective. Both are pluralistic behaviorists; both take cultural behavior as a primary point of attack on sociological issues; both are impressed by the lines of tension that may emerge between material and non-material culture, the running edge of social change. The difference between the two men in part accounts for the unusual fertility of their collaboration. This difference may be seen between *The Social Effects of Aviation* and *Technology and the Changing Family*.

In *The Social Effects of Aviation*, the thesis is advanced that there is a time sequence between an invention and its social effects, and therefore we should be able to anticipate changes from an invention like aviation. Aviation is argued to parallel automobile transportation, which affected institutions, industries, customs, and personal values. The automobile revolutionized transportation, helped eliminate the use of horses and mules, transformed rail traffic, affected modern tank warfare, redistributed population, led to the centralized school and church, helped to centralize the modern government, transformed the structure of leisure, and changed the patterns of courtship.

A parallel set of transformations is anticipated from aviation. It is expected to increase the size, speed, and variety of aircraft. There will be greater safety and efficiency. The number of passenger miles of air travel will increase. It is possible that first-class domestic mail traveling over four hundred miles and all foreign first-class mail will go by air, leading to an extension of trunk lines and a network of local feeder lines. Air cargo will rise to around 300,000,000 ton miles. A specialization of airports will occur. Private flying will increase, particularly with the development of a low-priced helicopter. However, for some time most families will still prefer the automobile. While the growth of population will be little affected by aviation, the distribution of population will change with more use of sparsely inhabited and out-of-the-way localities. Purchasing a plane will help keep the family small and stimulate location of more families in suburbia or large plots of ground. Inland towns will increase in importance. They will also tend to be decentralized. Aviation will promote the consolidated church, aid missionary work, and administration, but also contribute to secularization and decline in religious sentiment. Aviation will promote the large-scale operations of professional criminals. It will increase opportunities for smuggling and disposal of stolen goods. While it will have little effect on prostitution, it will promote large gambling centers.

Ogburn's interests always tend to be occupied primarily in the development of material culture and from there to its effects. Ogburn and Nimkoff were

---

[47] M. F. Nimkoff, *The Family* (Boston: Houghton Mifflin, 1934); *Marriage and the Family* (Boston: Houghton Mifflin, 1947).

quite conscious of this difference. They described this kind of study as "like that of a wheel, with the mechanical invention or scientific discovery at the hub and the influences upon society emanating outward like the spokes."[48] By contrast, Nimkoff's interests tend always to be in the social institutions, even when he discovers a large proportion of the forces playing upon them to originate in material culture. Here, again, Ogburn and Nimkoff phrased this very precisely in their joint study of *Technology and the Changing Family:* "In this book . . . a single institution, the family, has been chosen and upon it are recorded the influences coming from many different inventions and scientific discoveries."[49]

Among the recent changes in the family, the following were found most important: (1) the family ceases to be an economic institution, becoming a romantic and affectional structure; (2) the average age at marriage declines; (3) the trend is toward a smaller family; (4) the number of family functions declines; (5) there are more working wives; (6) the authority structure decays; (7) the accent shifts to the child; and (8) there is more disorganization.

A whole battery of factors, including such things as the use of contraceptives, the effects of the standard of living, the market for the purchase of goods, international relations and religious sanctions, causes these changes. These factors often operate in clusters. For example, "the city represents a cluster of factors, concerned with occupation, density, and ideologies that affect changes in the family."[50] The city, in turn, is said to have been caused by the application of non-human power to manufacture and transportation. These in turn were affected by the inventions of steam and steel. The family has also been affected by the invention of contraceptives. And finally, the family has been changed by ideologies regarding democracy, the welfare state, humanitarianism, and education, not so readily traceable to technology.

Ogburn was a man with a single great idea; Nimkoff has been a much more well-rounded sociologist. When they have teamed up, the effect has been to sheer away the more conservative aspects of Ogburn's thought and to convert pluralistic behaviorism into one of its general forms. The two major contemporary syntheses of pluralistic behaviorism, representing the classic phase of the doctrine, and in this respect comparable, for example, to the positions of Tönnies, Durkheim, and Redfield in positivistic organicism, are the works of F. Stuart Chapin on the one hand, and the joint work of Ogburn and Nimkoff on the other. Ogburn and Nimkoff's *Sociology*, first published in 1940 and revised in 1950 and again in 1958, is for this reason one of the most widely used and influential textbooks in North America.

When Ogburn and Nimkoff take the central clue to society to lie in culture, this could easily be misconceived, for this is no return to the tradition

---

[48] *Technology and the Changing Family*, p. iv.
[49] *Ibid.*   [50] *Ibid.*, p. 257.

of positivistic organicism. They do not propose an organismic theory of society, and culture is not conceived as some kind of superorganic entity in its own right. Culture is merely a general term for learned behavior. "Behavior transmitted by learning from one generation to another is called culture." [51] This quite corresponds to Tarde's insistence that, at bottom, society always consists of individual acts, or Giddings' belief that it represents pluralistic behavior. The same original pattern for explanation of these cultural behaviors is proposed. They are either new (inventions) or repetitions of old acts (diffused patterns or imitations) which lead to readjustments (adaptations). "A culture consists of inventions, or culture traits, integrated into a system, with varying degrees of correlation between the parts." [52]

Quite in accordance with the tradition of pluralistic behaviorism, Ogburn and Nimkoff place the point of gravity in the interdetermination of social behavior. Biological and environmental factors are mere conditions and limitations of social life, not social life itself.[53] A trend present in pluralistic behaviorism since the days when Tarde rejected biological interpretations of crime is reaffirmed. This also emphasizes the liberal aspects of the particular sociological tradition.

Pluralistic behaviorism (Tarde, Le Bon, and Ross) made the discovery of collective behavior. It is significant that once they have developed their concept of cultural behavior and discussed its biological conditions and environmental limits, Ogburn and Nimkoff place the point of analysis of social life proper in the group, the crowd, and the public.[54] The crowd and public are treated as the two polar types of group, characterized by irrational and rational behavior, respectively. They are, in a sense, the first integration of pluralistic behaviors into structural wholes.

Approached from this point, the social classes and, later, institutions arise as more complex and more stable patterns. In this fashion, by successive steps the Ogburn-Nimkoff analysis moves from cultural behavior toward the communities in which man's social life is eventually integrated. But meanwhile, again in accord with the range of the pluralistic behavioral tradition and in contrast to both positivistic organicism and conflict theory, the social individual is given an acknowledged and significant place in sociology,[55] the chief changes in the treatment of the social individual from early pluralistic behaviorism being the incorporation of numerous insights from the symbolic interactionists (such as James, Cooley, Mead, and Dewey), who are still to be discussed.

F. Stuart Chapin

Another graduate of the sociology department at Columbia University, F. Stuart Chapin (1888–   ), developed a very complete system of theory out of the principles of pluralistic behaviorism. After receiving his doctorate in 1911, Chapin taught at Wellesley College (1911–1912), Smith College

---

[51] *Sociology* (1958 edition), p. 72.   [52] *Ibid.*, p. 73.
[53] *Ibid.*, Chapters 4 and 5.   [54] *Ibid.*, Chapters 6–9.
[55] *Ibid.*, Part IV, "Personality."

(1912–1922), and the University of Minnesota. His publications have spanned a period of almost fifty years.[56]

An important part of the Tarde-Ross-Giddings tradition was the conception of statistics as the true method of sociology and the demand for more exact measures of recording and scaling data. Chapin's *Field Work and Social Research* (1920) was one of the first books in American sociology to attempt to provide a systematic inventory of the methods of sociology. Sociology, he maintained, is an inductive discipline. This inductive method consisted, in his opinion, of four parts: a working hypothesis; the collection and recording of observational facts; the classification of them into series and sequences for comparative purposes; and generalization from classified facts to some formula or law which explains their relations.[57] There were, Chapin believed, three major methods of social research: the historical method, using documentary sources; field work, consisting of case work, sampling, and complete enumeration; and statistical analysis, consisting in tabulation and the employment of graphs, ratios, averages, indexes, correlation coefficients, and the like. The various types of field-work technique were thought to be appropriate to different types of social data: case work to the study of the individual; sampling to the study of the group; and complete enumeration to the study of the entire community.

Conceptions of the statistical method have come a long way since 1920, but *Field Work and Social Research* remains a landmark among the early attempts to press statistics systematically into the service of sociological method. The pluralistic behaviorists took the lead in the promotion of statistics.

Because the pluralistic behaviorists, including Chapin, were placing their faith in the development of statistical methods as the best way to establish a properly inductive sociology, their attention was increasingly directed to the task of devising more exact measures for recording and scaling social data. Their theories forced them to the position that social life consisted at bottom not of acts, which could be counted and partly quantified, but of attitudes, values, and beliefs, which could not. Hence, if the statistical method were to fulfill its promise, these data had to be quantified. The most notable of Chapin's efforts in this direction were his living-room scale of social status and his social participation scale. His social status scale may illustrate his work along these lines.

As early as 1928 Chapin had raised the question of the possibility of measuring social status.[58] The hypothesis was posed that relations of a

---

[56] Chapin's most important works are: *An Introduction to the Study of Social Evolution* (New York: Century Company, 1913; 2d rev. ed., 1925); *Field Work and Social Research* (New York: Century Company, 1920); *Cultural Change* (New York: Century Company, 1928); *Contemporary American Institutions* (New York: Harper, 1935); and *Experimental Designs in Sociological Research* (New York: Harper, 1947).

[57] *Field Work and Social Research*, p. 17.

[58] F. Stuart Chapin, "A Quantitative Scale for Rating the Home and Social Environment of Middle Class Families in an Urban Community: A First Approximation to the Measurement of Socio-Economic Status," *Journal of Educational Psychology*, Vol. 19 (February 1928).

quantitatively exact character obtain between various factors composing social status (culture, income, material possessions, and so on). Hence, we
are able not only to measure these variables by special scales but we can
use any one scale as an index to socio-economic status as a whole. It was
assumed that the items found in a living room should permit the construction of such an index of socio-economic status. The scale was formed by
assembling such items, dropping irrelevant ones, and assigning a system of
weights to those retained. Rules for the use of the scale were carefully
standardized. A few items taken from the 1933 version of the scale [59] are
illustrative:

Schedule of Living Room Equipment

I. FIXED FEATURES

   1. Floor ————————
      Softwood, 1
      Hardwood, 2
      Composition, 3
      Stone, 4

   2. Floor covering ————————
      Composition, 1
      Carpet, 2
      Small rugs, 3
      Large rug, 4
      Oriental rug, 5

   3. Wall covering ————————
      Paper, 1
      Kalsomine, 2
      Plain paint, 3
      Decorative paint, 4
      Wooden panels, 5

However, as time went by, Chapin became increasingly convinced that the
full potential of an inductive sociology would not be achieved by statistics
alone, even when implemented by more exact scaling and measuring devices.
Returning, as did Giddings, to the methods of agreement and difference as
elaborated by John Stuart Mill, Chapin proposed the establishment of experimental designs under field conditions which would, in effect, approximate
the kind of control achieved manually in the laboratory experiment. The
aim of such experimental designs under field conditions was to provide the
basis for testing causal hypotheses. Experimental design in the field proceeds by means of two groups — an experimental group and a control
group. The key problem is securing controlled observation. "Sometimes
this control is achieved by identical individual matching; but more often it
is approximated by equating frequency distributions on a given trait." [60]
In two groups of persons, processes, or structures which have been made

[59] F. Stuart Chapin, *The Measurement of Social Status by the Use of the Social Status
Scale* (Minneapolis: University of Minnesota Press, 1933).
[60] *Experimental Designs in Sociological Research*, p. 35.

comparable in this fashion, the effect of varying factors is studied. Preferably only a single factor is varied at a time in the experimental group; the matching factor is not varied in the control group. Studies of both experimental group and control group are made before and after the experimental operation. Presumably differences between the experimental group and the control group will be causally related to the factor which has been varied. Three types of experimental designs are outlined:

1. *Cross-sectional design*, which makes controlled comparisons for a single date by procedures of selective control. . . .
2. *A projected design* of "before" and "after" study, in which an attempt is made to measure the effects of a social program or social force at some future date, thus following through the flow of events from a present date to some future date, by procedures of selective control. . . .
3. An *ex post facto design*, in which some present effect is traced backward to an assumed causal complex of factors or forces at a prior date, using for this purpose such records as are available. . . .[61]

Experimental Designs in Sociological Research is the methodological culminating point in Chapin's career.

In his two most important theoretical works, Chapin shows somewhat greater departures from the original formulations of Tarde, Giddings, and Ross than do Ogburn and Nimkoff. In *Cultural Change* (1928), for example, the attempt to include the ideas of other schools is evident. Cultural change is treated as "selectively accumulative in time, and cyclical or oscillatory in character." Moreover, the cycles "may be split up into cycles of (1) material culture and (2) non-material culture." It is selectively accumulative because there is an "adding of new elements by invention borrowing," as well as a dropping of elements.

It is clear that the ideas of invention and imitation or diffusion are complemented in this account with the added idea of cultural cycles (an idea developed by various representatives of the organismic schools). The cycles are of several types: those of first order relate to material culture and may be minor, small, and limited in time, like a business cycle or cycle of dependency in a city; or they may be major, like the rise and fall of the slave system of Rome, the manorial system of England, feudalism in France, or capitalism in modern Europe. Cycles of second order relate to non-material culture and also may be of minor degree (like the rise of religious sects, or the growth of a type of governmental structure) or of major degree (illustrated by ancestor worship, the patriarchal family, or monarchical government). Cycles of third order refer to larger cultural compositions such as national culture or civilization, and vary from minor things like the rise and fall of dynasties or classes to major types like the rise of Hellenic, Mycenaean, or Hindu culture.

Chapin believed it to be possible to develop basic hypotheses to account

[61] *Ibid.*, pp. 32–33.

for such cycles. Four were proposed: every cultural form has its own law of change; the law of each cultural form is cyclical and probably periodic; it is possible to express the law of its life cycle quantitatively; and when cycles or periods of a number of cultural forms are synchronous, there is produced a period of maturity of the cultural nation or group in which the traits are located.

This cyclical notion also leads to the assumption that there is a period of equilibrium in every cyclical change. This led Chapin to the idea that there may be present devices — social regulators — which directly implement the equilibrium. On the level of material culture, there are the well-known regulators, the stock and produce exchanges and the Federal Reserve System of bank-note issue. On the level of non-material culture, "we have as regulators of social change the various elements in the system of social control such as custom, belief, public opinion, and education, as well as law." [62]

In general, Chapin's account of social change is characterized by the addition of many elements from other traditions than that of the Tarde-Giddings school. However, it is interesting that in the continuation of his thesis he discovers that underneath the phenomenon of selective cultural accumulation and cyclical manifestation is a more fundamental group reaction pattern. This group reaction pattern has three phases in response to any new situation.

> Phase I.   The group reacts by an effort to enforce its mores. . . . But a lack of adjustment is soon felt and a shift to the second phase of the reaction pattern follows.
>
> Phase II. The group reacts by trying out different expedients. . . .
>
> Phase III. The group integrates its trial and error efforts into a stable plan. . . . [63]

At the most fundamental level of his theory of social and cultural change, the same elements as are present in Tarde's scheme of imitation, conflict, and adaptation are found. Chapin's societal reaction pattern starts the cycle with the conflict stage. In *Cultural Change*, Chapin lifts the theory of change of pluralistic behaviorism from Tarde to Ogburn to general form.

The societal reaction pattern, Chapin's point of closest affinity with the Tarde-Giddings tradition, formed the starting point for his approach to other areas — the problem of leadership, for instance. He suggested that the different phases of the societal reaction pattern required different types of leaders. In Phase I, titular or bureaucratic leaders were sufficient. But in Phase II, spontaneous natural and experimental leaders were required. In Phase III, great organizing, coordinating, consolidating, and selective leaders were needed. Culture patterns and popular psychology were also organized in terms of this schema.

[62] *Cultural Change*, p. 222.
[63] *Ibid.*, p. 228.

THE CYCLE OF THE SOCIAL PROCESS [64]

Phase	Ascendant Pattern	Leadership Type	Popular Psychology
Phase III: *Integration*	Manifest culture patterns (*i.e.*, open public, accepted patterns)	Administrators who consolidate	People are tired of social experiments
Phase II: *Experimentation*	Manifest patterns in process of formation	Innovators; experimental executives	People are anxious, looking for an answer to their problems
Phase I: *Stability* *Inertia*	Latent patterns fermenting	Titular leaders	People are complacent

In *Contemporary American Institutions*, Chapin's second major theoretical work, his affinities with the Tarde-Giddings tradition are made even more clear. He insists that sociology needs a small, concrete unit of investigation. This is a unit of individual behavior structure in terms of considerations of means–ends (that is, based on attitudes, ideas, and beliefs). To be sure, large-scale, unplanned forces may be generated as unplanned consequences of individual behaviors. These too must ultimately be brought under study. Institutions arise through the stabilization of the elements of behavior. (1) Institutions arise out of the repeated grouping of individuals in the satisfaction of basic needs (sex, hunger, fear). (2) Reciprocating attitudes and conventionalized behavior patterns appear, embodying attitudes of affection, loyalty, cooperation, domination, subordination. (3) Cultural objects embodying symbolic values are invented (idols, crosses, rings, flags). (4) Cultural implements and objects facilitating the behavior associated with the institution are constructed (buildings and furniture). (5) The knowledge gained in such experience is either preserved in written documents or transmitted orally to new generations.[65]

Two kinds of institutions (stabilized social behavior patterns) arise: diffuse or cultural (like language, art, and so on), and nucleated. Nucleated institutions have four type parts, as shown in the table on the following page. Chapin's development of the concept of institutions with a strongly empirical slant was quite in the tradition of Tarde and Giddings.

There were many other interesting aspects of Chapin's theories, including the development of a concept of latent and manifest functions (an idea that has recently become popular in other theories). He also developed a theory of the bureaucratic and professional personalities, which he tied to his theories of the societal reaction pattern and institutions. However, Chapin, like Ogburn and Nimkoff, represents the same kind of classical synthesis of the basic ideas of pluralistic behaviorism as Tönnies and Durkheim do

[64] *Contemporary American Institutions*, abbreviated from the table on p. 299.
[65] *Ibid.*, p. 14.

NUCLEATED SOCIAL INSTITUTIONS [66]

Type Part	Family	Church	Government	Business
I. Attitude and behavior patterns	Affection Love Loyalty Respect	Reverence Loyalty Fear Devotion	Subordination Cooperativeness Fear Obedience	Workmanship Thrift Cooperation Loyalty
II. Symbolic culture traits, "symbols"	Marriage Ring Crest Coat of arms Heirloom	Cross Ikon Shrine Altar	Flag Seal Emblem Anthem	Trade-mark Patent sign Emblem
III. Utilitarian culture traits (real property)	Home Dwelling Furniture	Church edifice Cathedral Temple	Public building Public works	Shop Store Factory Office
IV. Code of oral or written specifications	Marriage license Will Genealogy Mores	Creed Doctrine Bible Hymn	Charter Constitution Treaties Laws Ordinances	Contracts Licenses Franchises Articles of incorporation

for the theories of organismic positivism. He developed its method, its theory of social change, structure, leadership, and personality.

Summary

The pluralistic behavioral branch of social behaviorism contributed richly to the development of sociology. It was the bearer of strong empirical tendencies and a number of persons trained in its tenets contributed to the development of statistics and general sociological methodology. Its adherents were perhaps more centrally responsible than any other school for establishing social psychology as a special subdiscipline. Its members contributed to the theory of institutions, social change, social control, and personality, to say nothing of the field of criminology, in which Tarde was an important voice. In the works of Chapin on the one hand and those of Ogburn and Nimkoff on the other, pluralistic behaviorism was brought to its classical synthesis in a manner comparable to the classic stage of positivistic organicism in the works of Tönnies, Durkheim, and Redfield.

Perhaps the best critique of the suggestion–imitation school was the very course of its development. Its central formulas — imitation and pluralistic behavior — were too facile. It was able to do so much because it was so

[66] *Ibid.*, p. 16.

vaguely defined. For the same reason, the moment intensive analysis was turned on this central point of the theory, it tended to fall apart. When the concept of imitation is used so vaguely as to make it almost synonymous with social interaction, it will indeed "seem" to explain all forms of interaction until one examines it more closely. The profound theoretical gains made by use of the imitation formula were not due to its explanatory power but to an incidental result of its use. The explanation of social interaction was at least made in terms of the things presented in social interaction without an appeal to outside materials (like climate, environment, heredity, race, and what not). Once the harvest of this kind of analysis had been reaped, the imitation formula left no positive theory. Giddings' formula of "like-mindedness" represents the re-introduction into analysis of materials lying outside the interaction proper — introducing pre-interactional biological similarities as a factor in interaction. But this was no solution, either. Thus, it is not surprising that, by the time one reaches the work of Chapin, not too much remains of the suggestion–imitation school other than a set of definitions and a formal outline of procedure.

Imitation, upon analysis, turns out to conceal a host of problems. When imitation does in fact take place, it turns out to be a highly complex act and not a fundamental social fact at all. It is easy to imagine that "monkey see, monkey do." It is quite another thing to persuade a monkey to imitate. True imitation is learned and requires high intelligence. Suggestion, far from being identifiable with imitation, lies at the other end of the scale from imitation, presumably referring to various forms of subconscious social influence. It rarely involves repetition of the original act. The entire rich range of interhuman processes mediated by language is left out of account.

Similarly, Giddings' formula of pluralistic behavior resting on consciousness of kind assumes that social life is structured of externally similar acts. But interhuman life is not built out of unit acts like bricks, but out of complex inter-adjustments. Moreover, the theory assumes that these unit acts rest on attitudes and beliefs, the relation to which is not made clear. If this assumption is correct, it makes the statistical study resting on unit acts alone superficial. Thus, the quantification of unit acts as indices of attitudes and beliefs is not always easy to justify. In fact, the serious students of this tradition — from Bogardus to Chapin and on to Louis Guttman — have been much concerned with refining the processes of scale construction in order to justify the assumptions made by pluralistic behaviorism.

It is evident that there were tensions buried in pluralistic behaviorism, emerging between its theory and method. In a minor way, a drama similar to the tension between organicism and positivism was being played out within pluralistic behaviorism. Transformations were invited both in theory and method. These were brought about by other branches of social behaviorism.

SELECTED BIBLIOGRAPHY

BALDWIN, JAMES MARK, *The Mental Development in the Child and the Race.* Third revised edition. New York: Macmillan, 1906.

BALDWIN, JAMES MARK, *The Story of the Mind.* Fifth edition. New York: D. Appleton, 1912.

CHAPIN, F. STUART, *Cultural Change.* New York: Century Company, 1928.

CHAPIN, F. STUART, *Contemporary American Institutions.* New York: Harper, 1935.

GIDDINGS, FRANKLIN HENRY, *Studies in the Theory of Human Society.* New York: Macmillan, 1922.

LE BON, GUSTAVE, *The Crowd.* Translator not named. London: Benn, 1952.

LE BON, GUSTAVE, *The Psychology of Peoples.* Translator not named. New York: G. E. Stechert, 1912.

NIMKOFF, MEYER F., *Marriage and the Family.* Boston: Houghton Mifflin, 1947.

OGBURN, WILLIAM FIELDING, *Social Change.* Revised edition. New York: Viking, 1950.

OGBURN, WILLIAM FIELDING, and MEYER F. NIMKOFF, *Sociology.* Third edition. Boston: Houghton Mifflin, 1958.

OGBURN, WILLIAM FIELDING, and MEYER F. NIMKOFF, *Technology and the Changing Family.* Boston: Houghton Mifflin, 1955.

ROSS, EDWARD ALLSWORTH, *Social Control.* Boston: Beacon Press, 1959.

ROSS, EDWARD ALLSWORTH, *Social Psychology.* New York: Macmillan, 1929.

TARDE, GABRIEL, *Social Laws.* Translated by Howard C. Warren. New York: Macmillan, 1899.

14

Symbolic Interactionism

THE SECOND MAJOR BRANCH OF SOCIAL BEHAVIORISM IS NAMED BY ITS ADHER-
ents "symbolic interactionism." Although its problems and general solutions
to them run parallel to those of the suggestion–imitation or pluralistic behavioral theorists, there is a considerable difference of detail, and its intellectual foundations, too, are somewhat different. The suggestion–imitation
school originally took shape in Europe, most directly under the influence of
neo-idealistic philosophy and an idealistically inclined experimental psychology. Although it was influenced to some degree by pragmatism, this influence
was secondary. The symbolic interaction school took shape in America, primarily under the influence of pragmatism, and, in fact, many of its early members classified themselves as pragmatists. For them, the neo-Hegelian philosophy and idealistic experimental psychology were secondary. In the early days
of its appearance, the suggestion–imitation school was most directly characterized by the centrality given to the idea of *imitation*. Symbolic interactionism
placed the accent on *attitude* and *meaning*. The point of gravity of the suggestion–imitation school was in *mass* phenomena; symbolic interactionism
found its point of gravity in the *self* or *personality*.

William James

It is convenient to trace symbolic interactionism to the work of William
James. His brilliant *Principles of Psychology* [1] opened up new possibilities

[1] *Principles of Psychology*, 2 vols. (New York: Henry Holt, 1890). The references here
are to *Psychology* (Cleveland: World Publishing Co., 1948), which is James's own

for re-examining the relations of individual and society. Although James had taken over and accepted the instinct theory current in his day, there were other aspects of his thought which tended to modify it, including his brilliant examination of *habit*.

Habit is of considerable importance, James observed, to a creature that is plastic. "*Plasticity* . . . means the possession of a structure weak enough to yield to an influence, but strong enough not to yield all at once. Each relatively stable phase of equilibrium in such a structure is marked by what we may call a new set of habits." [2]

Among the influences of habit on behavior is the simplification of movement which makes behavior more accurate and diminishes fatigue. Moreover, habit reduces the need for conscious attention. In a creature capable of forming habits, the acquisition of a new nature is possible. " 'Habit a second nature! Habit is ten times nature,' the Duke of Wellington is said to have exclaimed; and the degree to which this is true no one probably can appreciate as well as one who is a veteran soldier himself. The daily drill and the years of discipline end by fashioning a man completely over again, as to most of the possibilities of his conduct." [3] Not only does the individual acquire a new nature through habit; habit also has the greatest importance for society.

> Habit is . . . the enormous fly-wheel of society, its most precious conservative agent. It alone is what keeps us all within the bounds of ordinance, and saves the children of fortune from the envious uprisings of the poor. It alone prevents the hardest and most repulsive walks of life from being deserted by those brought up to tread therein. It keeps the fisherman and the deck-hand at sea through the winter; it holds the miner in his darkness, and nails the countryman to his log-cabin and his lonely farm through all the months of snow; it protects us from invasion by the natives of the desert and the frozen zone. It dooms us all to fight out the battle of life upon the lines of our nurture or our early choice, and to make the best of a pursuit that disagrees, because there is no other for which we are fitted, and it is too late to begin again. [4]

James had discovered in "habit" a principle that would require the explanation of behavior in its own terms rather than through appeal to outside forces. In this way, it could operate in the same manner as imitation did for Tarde and his followers.

A second major event in James psychology was his reconceptualization of "consciousness" as a process. "States of mind" become mere momentary incidents in a process: "(1) Every 'state' tends to be part of a personal consciousness. (2) Within each personal consciousness states are always changing. (3) Each personal consciousness is sensibly continuous. (4) It is interested in some parts of its object to the exclusion of others, and

---

abridgment of the *Principles*; it was originally published by Henry Holt in 1892. For other writings of William James, see Chapter 12, Footnote 14.
[2] *Psychology*, p. 135.   [3] *Ibid.*, p. 142.   [4] *Ibid.*, p. 143.

welcomes or rejects — chooses from among them, in a word — all the while." [5] No state, once gone, can ever return again. A permanently existing idea, which makes its appearance in consciousness periodically, "is as mythological an entity as the Jack of Spades." Consciousness is the stream of thought or subjective life. It is the halo of relations around an image. In this manner, James eliminated consciousness as a kind of metaphysical substance. Through reconsideration of the importance of habit and the reduction of consciousness to a process, James opened new possibilities for the reconceptualization of the self.

One of the peculiar properties of consciousness is the fact that it always to some degree involves an awareness of the person's self. The person thus appears in thought in two ways, "partly known and partly knower, partly object and partly subject. . . . For shortness we may call one the *Me* and the other the *I*. . . . I shall therefore treat successively of (A) the self as known, or the *me*, the 'empirical ego' as it is sometimes called; and of (B) the self as knower, or the *I*, the 'pure ego' of certain authors." [6]

The empirical self or *me* in its widest sense is the sum total of all the person can call his. The "me" typically arouses feelings and emotions of self-appreciation and prompts actions of self-seeking and self-preservation. Its constituents include the material "me," the social "me," and the spiritual "me." The material "me" encompasses first of all the body and then successive circles of things associated with it, one's clothes, one's family, one's home up to and including all possessions. The social "me" is the recognition one gets from others. A man has as many social selves as there are individuals who recognize him and have images of him in mind. The individual has as many social selves as there are distinct groups about whose opinion he cares. Particularly important is the social self which exists in the mind of a person one is in love with. A man's fame, good and bad, and his honor or dishonor are names for his social selves. One of the strongest forces in life is "club opinion." The spiritual "me" refers to the collection of one's states of consciousness and psychic faculties. Next in importance after these constituents of the self are the feelings and emotions of self. These are of two sorts: self-complacency and self-dissatisfaction. The occasion for these is normally one's actual success or failure and the good or bad position one holds in the world. A man with a broadly empirical ego and powers that have uniformly brought success will rarely be visited by self-doubts. The emotions of self-satisfaction and abasement are of a primitive emotional species like pain and rage. On the basis of the constituents of the "me" and the self-emotions, self-seeking and self-preservation arise. The primitive form of such actions is biological self-preservation, but self-seeking carries beyond the biological person to social self-seeking. Because of this we are sensitive to the opinions even of persons about whom we otherwise care nothing.

The complexity of the structure of the empirical self often gives rise

[5] *Ibid.*, p. 152.   [6] *Ibid.*, p. 176.

to the necessity of choice. A rivalry and conflict of the different "me's" appears. "Not that I would not, if I could, be both handsome and fat and well dressed, and a great athlete, and make a million a year, be a wit, a *bon-vivant,* and a lady-killer, as well as a philosopher, a philanthropist, statesman, warrior, and African explorer, as well as a 'tone-poet' and saint. But the thing is simply impossible." [7] Out of the complex of rival "me's" arises the paradox of a man shamed to death because he is only the second publicist or the second oarsman in the world. Self-esteem, in fact, is a fraction of which pretensions form the denominator and success the numerator:

$$\text{Self-esteem} = \frac{\text{Success}}{\text{Pretensions}}$$

Such a fraction may be increased either by diminishing the denominator or by increasing the numerator. Among the ways of handling the ratio are the range of phenomena varying from a frantic extension of striving to ascetic withdrawal of self-expectation.

Fairly unanimous opinion arranges the different selves of a man in a hierarchical scale with the bodily "me" at the bottom, the spiritual "me" at the top, and the extra-corporeal material selves and various social selves between. But they are all important. A certain amount of bodily selfishness is required as a basis for all the other selves. In each kind of "me" — material, social, and spiritual — men distinguish between the immediate and actual and the remote and potential. One may forgo bodily enjoyment in the present for potential health later, abandon a dollar for the sake of a hundred, or make an enemy of a person in one's immediate presence for the sake of a wider circle of friends. Of all the potential selves, the potential social "me" is most interesting because of the apparent paradoxes to which it leads, as when for motives of honor and conscience one braves the condemnation of family, club and "set," or when as Protestant, one turns

DIVISIONS OF THE EMPIRICAL SELF [8]

	Material	*Social*	*Spiritual*
Self-Seeking	Bodily Appetites and Instincts. Love of Adornment, Foppery, Acquisitiveness, Constructiveness. Love of Home, etc.	Desire to Please, Be Noticed, Admired, etc. Sociability, Emulation, Envy, Love, Pursuit of Honor, Ambition, etc.	Intellectual, Moral and Religious Aspirations, Conscientiousness.
Self-Estimation	Personal Vanity, Modesty, etc. Pride of Wealth, Fear of Poverty.	Social and Family Pride, Vainglory, Snobbery, Humility, Shame, etc.	Sense of Moral or Mental Superiority, Purity, etc. Sense of Inferiority or of Guilt.

[7] *Ibid.,* p. 186.   [8] *Ibid.,* p. 195.

Catholic, or as Catholic, freethinker. The impulse to pray, James maintains, is a necessary consequence of the fact that the innermost social self tends to evolve standards which it can find approximated only in an ideal world. The progress of the social self is the substitution of higher tribunals of self-judgment for lower ones.

The self as knower, the "I" or pure ego, is a much more difficult subject of inquiry. It is that which at any moment is conscious; the "me" is only one of the things it is conscious of. One spontaneously conceives the "I" to be always the same. "This has led most philosophers to postulate behind the passing state of consciousness a permanent Substance or Agent whose modification or act it is. This Agent is the thinker; the 'state' is only its instrument or means. 'Soul,' 'transcendental Ego,' 'Spirit,' are so many names for this more permanent sort of Thinker." [9]

But James argues that various inconsistencies arise when one presupposes a unity behind the passing thought. If one assumes the existence of a stream of consciousness, things that are known together are like single pulses of that stream. The function of the supposed soul, ego, or spirit is that of a combining medium. But we never experience this; we assume it. If we stick to what we experience we have only passing states. The sense of the sameness of the self of personal identity does not require a metaphysical self. It refers to certain comparable characteristics of experience from time to time. It arises out of a resemblance of conscious states. We need no substantial identity in the thinker to account for resemblances in the various states of consciousness. Yesterday's and today's states of consciousness have no substantial identity, for when the one is here, the other is irrevocably dead and gone. But they have a *functional* identity, for both know the same objects. States of consciousness are all that psychology needs to work with. "Metaphysics or theology may prove the Soul to exist; but for psychology the hypothesis of such a substantial principle of unity is superfluous." [10]

The identity found by the "I" in its "me" is only a loosely constructed thing, an identity, on the whole, just like that which any outside observer might find in the same assemblage of facts. "We often say of a man 'he is so changed one would not know him'; and so does a man, less often, speak of himself. These changes in the *Me*, recognized by the *I*, or by the outside observers, may be grave or slight." [11] Such mutations of self divide into alterations of memory and alterations in the present bodily and spiritual self. Alterations in memory include the loss of memory — normal with advancing years — and false memories. Alterations in the present self include such things as insane delusions, alternating selves, the mediumship of the spiritualistic séance, and possession by supernatural beings. In various ways, the ratio between the "I" and "me" is transformed.

The consciousness of Self involves a stream of thought, each part of which as "I" can remember those which went before, know the things they knew,

9 *Ibid.*, p. 196.   10 *Ibid.*, p. 203.   11 *Ibid.*, p. 205.

and care paramountly for certain ones among them as "Me," and *appropriate to these* the rest. This Me is an empirical aggregate of things objectively known. The *I* which knows them cannot itself be an aggregate; neither for psychological purposes need it be an unchanging metaphysical entity like the Soul. . . . It is a *thought*, at each moment different from that of the last moment, but *appropriative* of the latter. . . .[12]

Such was the challenging manner in which James struck out the lines for a new analysis of the social self.

Charles Horton Cooley

The sociological extension of these ideas was begun by Charles Horton Cooley (1864–1929), the son of the distinguished jurist Thomas M. Cooley. He did his undergraduate work in engineering at the University of Michigan and worked for a short time as a surveyor. After some time spent in travel and study in Europe, he took his Ph.D. in economics, with a minor in sociology. He began teaching at the University of Michigan in 1892, and remained there for the rest of his life. In comparison with some of his contemporaries in sociology, he wrote very little, but his books were carefully written and have had a lasting influence.[13]

The imaginations people have of one another, Cooley maintained, "are the solid facts of society." Society is a mental phenomenon, a relation between personal ideas. "Society exists in my mind as the contact and reciprocal influence of certain ideas named 'I,' Thomas, Henry, Susan, Bridget, and so on. It exists in your mind as a similar group, and so in every mind." [14]

In a basic sense in this formulation Cooley applied to society the kind of approach that James had applied to the self. It is not surprising, then, that Cooley's conception of the self corresponds very closely to what James called the social self. "The personality of a friend, as it lives in my mind . . . is simply a group or system of thoughts associated with the symbols that stand for him." [15] Similarly, a person's own self represents some of his ideas — a notion that would be meaningless without the basic distinction introduced by James between the "I" and the "me." The social self is a core of ideas adhering to the self words "I," "me," "mine," "myself." The self consists of those things an individual conceives as belonging peculiarly to him. The core of the self is formed by an instinctive self-feeling. Imagination and habit, operating on instinctive self-feeling, create the social self. "Imagination cooperating with instinctive self-feeling

12 *Ibid.*, p. 215.
13 Cooley's books are: *Personal Competition* (New York: Macmillan, 1899); *Human Nature and the Social Order* (New York: Scribner's, 1902; rev. ed., 1922); *Social Organization* (New York: Scribner's, 1909); *Social Process* (New York: Scribner's, 1918); and the posthumous *Sociological Theory and Social Research*, introduction and notes by Robert Cooley Angell (New York: Henry Holt, 1930).
14 *Human Nature and the Social Order*, p. 84. (References are to the first edition of 1902.)
15 *Ibid.*, p. 81.

has already created a social 'I' and this has become a principal object of interest and endeavor." [16] Moreover, "habit has the same fixing and consolidating action in the growth of the self that it has elsewhere, but is not its distinctive characteristic." [17]

Cooley's famous "looking-glass self" was his particular form of what James had described as the social self. Even the elements had been developed in more detail by James. The general argument, of course, is that the social self arises reflectively in terms of the reaction to the opinions of others on the self. "A self-idea of this sort seems to have three principal elements: the imagination of our appearance to the other person; the imagination of his judgment of that appearance, and some sort of self-feeling, such as pride or mortification." [18]

If the only claim for Cooley's importance lay in the "looking-glass self," he would hardly deserve the place he holds in the development of sociology, for the idea was only a neat re-statement of James's "social self." But Cooley went beyond the "looking-glass self" to develop a general theory of society, expanding this type of social behaviorism to the explanation of groups and social organization. Cooley's foremost contribution to the theory of groups was the re-evaluation of what have been called since Cooley "primary groups." William Graham Sumner had drawn a distinction between the "in-group" and the "out-group." The conflict sociologists, such as Gumplowicz, had drawn the distinction between the prestate type of social group, characterized by a moral unity, in contrast to the social order originating in war and conquest and leading to the emergence of the state and a legal order. Tönnies had distinguished between the *Gemeinschaft* and *Gesellschaft*. There were many anticipations of Cooley's analysis. Cooley brought these conceptualizations of the group into relation with the concept of the social self, recast in terms of the needs of social behaviorism. Primary groups are "characterized by intimate face-to-face association and cooperation." Their chief properties include: (1) face-to-face association, (2) unspecified nature of associations, (3) relative permanence, (4) a small number of persons involved, and (5) relative intimacy of participants. Characteristic examples of the primary group are the family, the old-fashioned neighborhood, the play group of children, the group of elders. In such primary groups, there is an intimate fusion of individuality and group. The primary group is "fundamental in forming social nature and ideals of the individual." [19]

It is in such groups that the individual gets his earliest and most basic experiences of social unity. They are the source of the individual's ideals, which derive from the moral unity of the group itself. A subordination of the interests of the individual to the group occurs here, supplanting individual egoism and greed. The ideal of a moral whole may be analyzed into the principles of "loyalty, lawfulness, and freedom." Such principles

[16] *Ibid.*, p. 167.   [17] *Ibid.*, p. 155.   [18] *Ibid.*, p. 152.
[19] *Social Organization*, pp. 23 ff.

are fundamental, in turn, to the ideals of good faith, service, kindness, and justice. Democracy and Christianity are extensions of primary-group ideals to wider society.

Ideals such as those which make up the reflexive self and are produced by the primary group constitute the unity and structure of the social mind. *Social organization* is this unity and structure. It is partly co-extensive with public consciousness or public opinion, representing "a mutual understanding of one another's points of view on the part of individuals or groups concerned as naturally results from discussion." [20] The social mind constantly forms itself into wholes, consciously and unconsciously represented by fashions, traditions, institutions, and so on, which spread and generate more varied structures of differentiated thought symbols. Such structures of the social mind constitute types. "Any fairly distinct and durable detail of this structure may be called a social type; this being a convenient term to use when we wish to break up the whole into parts, for analysis or description. Thus there are types of personality, of political structure, of religion, of classes, of the family, of art, of language. . . ." [21]

This analysis into types was extended to institutions, which Cooley conceived as fixed phases of the public mind; to various special institutions such as the family; to the problems of public opinion; and to the social classes, which he conceived as formed on the basis of two fundamental principles: *caste* (the distribution of social functions and privileges on the basis of inheritance) and *competition* (the distribution of functions and privileges on the basis of comparative efficiency). These were the distinctions which Ralph Linton renamed "ascription" and "achievement."

The implications of his social behaviorism are kept unwaveringly in mind by Cooley: the task, as he sees it, is to explain social events by principles applying to their internal structure, not by some *deus ex machina* from the outside. In striking contrast to the pluralistic behaviorists ranging from Le Bon, through Giddings, and even at times to Ross and Ogburn, Cooley is never tempted to explain social events by the physical environment or heredity or race. Thus, when Galton's *Hereditary Genius* came into Cooley's hands, he refused to be deceived by its statistics, and cut directly to its explanatory principles. Cooley pointed out that one had no right to explain the frequent unusual men in notable families on the basis of hereditary factors alone so long as their social situations were distinctively advantageous.

The symbolic interactionists, as already illustrated by James and Cooley, were establishing a more precise definition of the ultimate materials of sociology. For Tarde these were acts of invention or imitation; for Giddings they were externally similar acts by a plurality of persons. Both wings of pluralistic behaviorism — the Tardean and the Giddings branches — stated that the ultimate subject matter of sociology consisted of ideas and beliefs. Among the more sensitive members of the school, there is

[20] *Ibid.*, p. 10.   [21] *Ibid.*, p. 22.

evidence of an uneasy feeling that between the external act and the idea or belief there may be numerous problems. Tarde, for example, cautioned that by merely counting external acts one might well lose sight of important problems of intensity. Chapin showed a strong impulse to pry apart the externally similar pluralistic behaviors and carry out an analysis in terms of *latent* and *manifest* patterns. His scale construction, too, reflects some sense of the problems that might be involved in the transition from internal beliefs to external acts.

However, with James and Cooley, the order is reversed: not external acts, but ideas and beliefs are the facts of sociology. As Cooley put it, "the imaginations people have of one another are the solid facts of society." But by putting the emphasis here, Cooley brought to light the potential tensions between the definition of subject matter by the social behaviorists and sociological method. Cooley was not against statistics. He had observed that under proper circumstances statistics could be most revealing. But everything, he insisted, depended on the "interpretation." Sometimes, he opined, the only thing exact in a statistical account is the mathematical operations involved.

If the imaginations people have of one another are the ultimate facts of society, it follows that sociological method will produce results only if it concerns them. Some form of introspection is most directly implied as proper sociological method. Cooley saw this and proposed "systematic autobiography" as the fundamental method of sociology. The underlying tension in social behaviorism between its definition of content and its method has become manifest.

W. I. Thomas

William Isaac Thomas (1863–1947) gave a characteristic re-stylization to symbolic interactionism. Thomas graduated from the University of Tennessee in 1884 and taught English and modern languages there. In 1888–89, he studied in Berlin and Göttingen, coming under the influence of the folk psychology of Lazarus and Steinthal. From 1889–95, he taught English and sociology at Oberlin College. He joined the new faculty in sociology at Chicago in 1895 taking his doctorate under Small. He remained at Chicago until 1918 when, for personal reasons, he retired. In 1923, he resumed lecturing, this time at the New School for Social Research. From 1930 to 1936, he went yearly to Sweden in connection with the Institute of Social Science at the University of Stockholm. He lectured at Harvard (1936–37). Until 1939, he lived in New Haven and then moved to Berkeley, California, where he lived until his death in 1947.

The strong influence of the pragmatic tradition, which had one of its main centers in Chicago, is manifest in *Social Origins* (1909).[22] There

[22] William I. Thomas (ed.), *Source Book for Social Origins* (Chicago: University of Chicago Press, 1909). Thomas' other books are: *Sex and Society* (Chicago: University of Chicago Press, 1907); *The Polish Peasant in Europe and America*, with Florian

Thomas argued that the sociologist is interested in those human activities demonstrating conscious control, in which man produces language, forms of government, religion, and art. The object of central interest to the sociologist is precisely the phenomena of *attention* — "the mental attitude which takes note of the outside world and manipulates it." [23] Attention is produced by a crisis, however small, which may be due to a disturbance of habit or the result of an incident or suggestion. By the time of *The Polish Peasant* (1918–20), these ideas had undergone considerable development. The purpose of sociology was conceived as one of tracing the dependence of individuals on social life and culture and of culture and social life on the individual. The subject matter of interest consists of attitudes and values, processes of consciousness determined by objective conditions, pre-existing attitudes, and definitions of the situation.[24]

Some further shift was evident in *The Unadjusted Girl* (1923), when attitude and value were reduced to secondary importance and the "definition of the situation" became the central object of study in sociology. "Preliminary to any self-determined act of behavior there is always a . . . *definition of the situation* . . . gradually a whole life-policy and the personality of the individual himself follow from a series of such definitions." Some of the most interesting of interhuman facts flow from different definitions of the situation. There is "always a rivalry between the spontaneous definitions of the situation made by the member of an organized society and the definitions which his society has provided for him." [25]

It is occasionally suggested that W. I. Thomas was influenced in these ideas by Ratzenhofer. The suggestion may be attributable to an apparent similarity between Thomas' concept of "attitudes" and Ratzenhofer's "interests"; and there is a further point of similarity in Thomas' typology of "the four wishes": the desire for new experience, the desire for security, the desire for response, and the desire for recognition. This typology was clearly modeled on the six interests advanced by Ratzenhofer and Small.[26]

Znaniecki, 5 vols. (Chicago: University of Chicago Press, 1918–20); *The Unadjusted Girl* (Boston: Little, Brown, 1923); *The Child in America*, with Dorothy Swaine Thomas (New York: Alfred A. Knopf, 1928); and *Primitive Behavior* (New York: McGraw-Hill, 1937). Thomas was also the chief author of *Old World Traits Transplanted* (New York: Harper, 1921), published under the names of Robert E. Park and Herbert A. Miller.

[23] *Source Book for Social Origins*, p. 17.

[24] See *The Polish Peasant*, I, Methodological Note.

[25] *The Unadjusted Girl*, p. 42.

[26] Thomas and Znaniecki were writing at a time when instinct theories of behavior were being scrapped. The habit of mind associated with instinct theories inclined social scientists to speak as if the various presumed organic motors of conduct (instincts, desires, wishes, interests, or drives) were the direct and primary causes of behavior, even while the alternative notion was gaining ground that these were, at best, secondary causes of conduct. The new idea was that the organic motor was not the cause of conduct in its raw form but only in the form it assumed as a product of experience. When Small classified the interests into six, he did so as a matter of convenience; the actual interests were assumed to be almost innumerable. Thomas seems to have been

Beside such derivations of Thomas' views must be placed the influence of European neo-idealism and the obvious strong ties with pragmatism. William James had dramatized the program of judging an idea in terms of its "consequences" without insisting upon too exacting an inquiry into its intrinsic truth. Although for James this seems to have been partly a device for accepting ideas that his professional standards otherwise would seem to reject, it involved a principle that could represent pure gain from a sociological point of view. If the sociologist once accepts ideas as components of interhuman conduct, he must also examine those ideas which he knows on logical or scientific grounds to be untrue if they are held by the human subjects, for they may enter as factors in the conduct of those subjects. The sociologist may not believe in magic. This, however, is no excuse for ignoring those factors in a people's conduct determined by their ideas of magic. (There is all the difference in the world between this approach and the acceptance of magic as true because it seems to have good social effects.) The importance of ideas for conduct was advanced by James and echoed by Cooley. Thomas' notions of "definition of the situation" and "attitude" — and his earlier concept of "attention" — were various forms in which he accepted this principle and founded his sociology on it. The similarity with Cooley is evident.

Again, Thomas' idea that "attention" is elicited by crises (be they as small as the mere upsetting of a habit) and that it functions to restore conduct to stability is a direct parallel of the ideas advanced by Dewey's argument that thinking is aroused by an indeterminate situation and has the function of restoring behavior to equilibrium. Similarly, the great emphasis on situation in *The Polish Peasant* is comparable to Dewey's life-long insistence on its importance in individual and social life.

Finally, Thomas' statement of the problem of sociology as one of tracing the influence of society and culture on the individual and the individual on society and culture parallels Cooley's theory and practice. For Cooley, too, had this problem in mind when he traced the effect of the primary group on the rise of the self and when he traced the effects of personal ideas upon social organization, institutions, and public opinion.

At every critical point Thomas' affinities are with the pragmatists and symbolic interactionists.

Theoretically, the most significant work of Thomas was that done in collaboration with Znaniecki; in fact, it was the greatest contribution

---

doing the same thing when he renamed the interests "wishes" and reclassified them into four. That he thought of the wishes largely as a convenient classification seems indicated by the fact that he was inclined to phrase the classification somewhat differently in different places. Moreover, at the very time when other sociologists were taking up his classification, he tended to drop it altogether, using the notion of "definition of the situation" almost alone to carry out analyses that at one time he would have carried out on the basis of the four wishes. The "four wishes" are, perhaps, best viewed as a transitional phase in modern social theory during a time when the instinct theory of conduct was being abandoned.

of both to the symbolic interactionist point of view.[27] The framework for analysis was provided by the transformations in personality and social structure in the Polish peasant community in the course of its movement to America.

> . . . the Polish peasant community has developed during many centuries complicated systems of beliefs and rules of behavior sufficient to control social life under ordinary circumstances, and the cohesion of the group and the persistence of its membership are strong enough to withstand passively the influence of eventual extraordinary occurrences, although there is no adequate method of meeting them. And if the crisis is too serious and the old unity or prosperity of the group breaks down, this is usually treated at first as a result of superior forces against which no fight is possible.
>
> But when, owing to the breakdown of the isolation of the group and its contact with a more complex and fluid world, the social evolution becomes more rapid and the crises more frequent and varied, there is no time for the same gradual, empirical, unmethodical elaboration of approximately adequate means of control, and no crisis can be passively borne, but every one must be met in a more or less adequate way, for they are too various and frequent not to imperil social life unless controlled in time.[28]

These paragraphs illustrate that, in the last analysis, the study of the Polish peasant was intended as an examination of social disorganization and a consideration of the materials necessary for rational social policy. But meanwhile the study served as a vehicle for the examination of the interrelation of personality and social order. "There are two fundamental practical problems which have constituted the center of attention of reflective social practice in all times. These are (1) the problem of the dependence of the individual upon social organization and culture, and (2) the problem of the dependence of social organization and culture upon the individual." [29]

The social theory necessary to solve these problems takes as the most fundamental data "the objective cultural elements of social life and the subjective characteristics of the members of the social group. . . . For these data we shall use now . . . the terms 'social values' and 'attitudes.' " [30] *Attitudes* represent "a process of individual consciousness which determines real or possible activity of the individual in the social world." [31] *Values* are the objects in the world to which attitudes are addressed. The consequences for behavior of the attitudinal pursuit of values are quite objective.

> Rules and actions, taken . . . with regard to the attitudes provoked by them, are quite analogous to any other values — economic, artistic, scientific, religious. . . . The rules of behavior, and the actions viewed as conforming or

---

[27] Znaniecki's contributions to social-action theory and functionalism will be discussed in Chapters 16 and 18.
[28] *The Polish Peasant*, I, p. 2.
[29] *Ibid.*, p. 20.   [30] *Ibid*, pp. 20–21.   [31] *Ibid.*, p. 22.

not conforming with these rules, constitute with regard to their objective significance a certain number of more or less connected and harmonious systems which can be generally called *social institutions,* and the totality of institutions found in a concrete social group constitutes the *social organization* of this group.[32]

In specific cases, the individuals' attitudes and values in their objective manifestation — constituting the social institutions and social organization — are always embodied in practical situations. The *situation* is the set of values and attitudes with which the individual or the group has to deal in a process of *activity* and with regard to which this activity is planned and its results appreciated. Every concrete activity consists in the solution of a situation which involves three kinds of data: (1) the objective conditions under which the individual or society has to act and which at the given moment affect the conscious status of the individual or the group; (2) the pre-existing attitudes of the individual or the group; and (3) the "definition of the situation" by the individual or group as a more or less clear conception of the conditions of consciousness and of attitudes. The individual develops his attitudes and makes his selection of the values that a situation offers on the basis of a general pattern of wishes. These wishes include: (1) the desire for new experience (art, adventure); (2) the desire for recognition (sexual response and general social appreciation, secured by devices ranging from display of ornament to the demonstration of worth through scientific attainment); (3) the desire for mastery (ownership, domestic tyranny, political despotism, based on the instinct of hate, but capable of being sublimated to laudable ambition); (4) the desire for security (exemplified negatively by the wretchedness of the individual in perpetual solitude or under social taboo).[33]

From this theoretical base, Thomas and Znaniecki developed a theory of personality which viewed personality as manifesting itself, as a whole, only in the course of its total life.[34] This evolution, however, tends toward stabilization and hence the concept of type may be applied to social personalities. Personality arises along *"typical lines of genesis* of a series of events in which attitudes [develop] from other attitudes." Such lines of genesis are dependent in part on the milieu in which the individual lives. Society imposes a frame of activities on the individual, the family, education, career, marriage. Extensive uniformities of development are found in connection with temperament and character. Temperament and character work together in a life organization, with the sphere of experience of an individual consisting of a limited number of selected and organized groups of social values which play a predominant part in his life as causes and effects of his organized attitudes. *Temperament* refers to an original group of individual attitudes existing independently of any social influences.

[32] *Ibid.,* pp. 32–33.
[33] *Ibid.,* p. 73.
[34] See Volume III of *The Polish Peasant,* "Life Record of an Immigrant."

Character is the set of organized and fixed groups of attitudes developed by social influences operating upon the temperamental base.

The individual is thus a product of interaction. In order to become a social personality in any domain, the individual must not only learn the social meanings which objects possess but also learn how to adapt himself to the demands which society puts upon him. Since meanings imply conscious thought, he must do this by conscious reflection, not by mere instinctive adaptation of reflexes. The stabilized activity arrived at in this manner becomes habitual and is thus dropped below the level of consciousness once again.

Depending on the nature of the attitudes involved in the character and in the schemes of life organization, as well as on the way they are unified and systematized, three types of life organization are developed. The set of attitudes constituting the character may be such as practically to exclude the development of any new attitudes of an individual. Such an individual's attitudes have attained so great a fixity that he is accessible only to a certain class of influences — those constituting the most permanent part of his social milieu. This may be called the "Philistine." It is opposed to the "Bohemian," whose possibilities of personal development are not closed, simply because his character remains unformed. Some of his temperamental attitudes are in their primary form, others may have become intellectualized but remain unrelated to one another and consequently do not form a stable set. The individual remains open to any and all influences. Opposed to both these types is the person whose character is settled and organized in a manner requiring inner development. This is the type of the "creative individual." In these various personality types the fundamental wishes — desire for new experience, for response, for security, for recognition — enter in varying degrees. It was Thomas' and Znaniecki's judgment that the development of the modern world, particularly the forces bringing the primary group rapidly into contact with the outside world with its new and rival schemes, tends to shatter the old organization, increasing the numbers of Philistines and Bohemians.

Just as from personal ideas Cooley moved his analysis either to the self or to social organization and institutions, so the concepts of attitude and definition of the situation were used by Thomas and Znaniecki. Particularly in the theory of social personality they made important advances beyond Cooley — this quite apart from the monumental assemblage of first-hand materials and the isolation of the case history and life history as major techniques and tools in sociological research.

W. I. Thomas' own life appears to have been a somewhat painful proof of his own theories. Following personal difficulties in which Thomas lost his job at the University of Chicago, a marked change is discernible in his intellectual activity. The academic community was the only one he had left. The possible direction of Thomas' thought, had it not been for his personal difficulties, appears in *Old World Traits Transplanted* (1921). The general intention seemed to have been to rise beyond the confines of a single minority group toward more general formulations. In later works, Thomas seemed to be inclined to drop any idea that his academic colleagues brought under critical review. The ideas of personality, the four wishes, were all largely withdrawn until little was left except the notion of "definition of the situation." Thomas even became very defensive about his use of the case history. *Primitive Behavior* was a return to the period of the *Source Book for Social Origins*. Thomas' fullest synthesis of symbolic interactionism remains the theoretical sections of the *Polish Peasant*.

At the time Thomas and Znaniecki achieved their major synthesis of symbolic interactionism, it was quite clear to both of them that their definition of sociological materials was such as to require special methods of study. How does one quantify definitions of the situation? What measurements apply to life organization? What are the weights to be assigned to temperament in contrast to character in a specific Bohemian personality? Thomas and Znaniecki advocated the life history, the detailed personal narrative, and the exhaustive study of the individual case as the methods appropriate to their materials. They made major first-hand assemblages. Having demonstrated the emancipation of sociology from dependency for its materials upon history, the *Polish Peasant* deserved the great acclaim it received. Inevitably, with the development of methodological sophistication it became clear that the case or life history is only a technique and not a self-sufficient method, but this does not obscure the importance of its development or its consistency as a technique with the particular definition of sociological subject matter of symbolic interactionism.

G. H. Mead

However, even while these developments were occurring, George Herbert Mead (1863–1931) was transforming the inner structure of the theory of symbolic interactionism, moving it to a higher level of theoretical sophistication. George Herbert Mead had been an associate of John Dewey at Michigan and continued his association at Chicago. Philosophically, he was a pragmatist. Mead had studied under Royce and was familiar with the idealist theory of personality. He was also familiar with the work of Tarde, Baldwin, and his friend Cooley. He had studied in Germany, where he became impressed by Wundt's theories of language and the gesture. From 1900 on, Mead's influence began to spread throughout the United States from his course in social psychology at the University of Chicago. Although he published many articles, he was never able to bring his ideas together into a book that satisfied him. Many of his students, out of personal devotion and a feeling for the value of the material Mead was presenting, had stenographic transcripts made of some of his lectures, and these transcripts, together with lecture notes, were carefully assembled into four volumes which were published posthumously.[35]

[35] *The Philosophy of the Present*, edited by Arthur E. Murphy (Chicago: Open Court Publishing Co., 1932) ; *Mind, Self, and Society*, edited by Charles W. Morris (Chicago: University of Chicago Press, 1934) ; *Movements of Thought in the Nineteenth Century,*

In arriving at his own peculiar interpretation of the self, Mead had the representatives of three different traditions in mind. Wundt was the heir of a German idealistic tradition which he salvaged for social science by means of his psychophysical parallelism. On the other hand, J. B. Watson represented the attempt to account for socio-psychological phenomena in purely behavioristic terms. Finally, Mead shared the pragmatism of James and Dewey. Mead made three types of criticisms of the previous theories of the self: (1) either they presupposed the mind as antecedently existing to account for mental phenomena (Wundt); (2) or they failed to account for specifically mental phenomena (Watson); and (3) they failed to isolate the mechanism by which mind and the self appeared (James and Dewey).

In his third criticism, Mead seems to have had William James particularly in mind. Mead was impressed by James's famous 1904 article "Does Consciousness Exist?", which had made a new attack on the problem of mind. In this brilliant formulation, James had brought the traditional subject–object and mind–matter dichotomies under critical review, indicating that they may not be ultimate realities but derivations from a more fundamental reality. Mead observed: "There has been of late in philosophy a growing recognition of the importance of James's insistence that a great deal has been placed in consciousness that must be returned to the so-called objective world." [36]

The properties of Mead's social psychology may be seen as arising out of a generalization of the procedure by which James brought the notion of consciousness under critical review, while at the same time attempting to be as behavioristic as Watson and using Wundt's mechanism of language to account for the inner restructuring of experience into self and other. Just as James had taken pure experience as a starting point, treating subject and object as distinctions arising within it, so Mead proposed to start analysis with an observable activity, the dynamic, on-going social process, and the social acts which are its component elements, and then to treat the mind and society as arising as discriminations within this process. Mead thus proposed to surmount both the mentalism of the introspectionists and the narrow form of behaviorism represented by Watson. "The problem that presents itself as crucial for human psychology concerns the field that is opened up by introspection; this field apparently could not be dealt with by a purely objective psychology which only studied conduct as it takes place for the observer." [37]

It has been pointed out that Thomas and Znaniecki had taken *attitudes* as the central object of analysis in *The Polish Peasant*. It is not impossible that Thomas was partly influenced in this choice by what his brilliant

edited by Merritt H. Moore (Chicago: University of Chicago Press, 1936); and *The Philosophy of the Act*, edited by Charles W. Morris (Chicago: University of Chicago Press, 1938).
[36] *Mind, Self, and Society*, p. 4. (Copyright 1934 by the University of Chicago.)
[37] *Ibid.*, p. 8.

colleague was doing in his course in social psychology. In any case, for Mead as for Thomas and Znaniecki, analysis centers in attitudes. "Present results . . . suggest the organization of the act in terms of attitudes. There is an organization of the various parts of the nervous system that are going to be responsible for acts, an organization which represents not only that which is immediately taking place, but also the later stages that are to take place." [38] However, in Mead's analysis, "attitudes" were given far more precise significance, for attitudes have the simultaneous character of representing both introspective states and the starting point of the act. "We can find in that sense in the beginning of the act just those characters which we assign to 'horse' as an idea, or if you like, as a concept." [39]

Mead devoted considerable space to the discussion of psychophysical parallelism. The importance of this approach of Wundt's to psychological problems was the attempt to do justice simultaneously to the introspectively revealed states of consciousness and external behavior. The entire importance of Mead's own position lay in his giving equal weight to both kinds of factors without requiring a schema of two irreconcilable phenomena to do it. Mead started out with Wundt's form of psychophysical parallelism and from it took the element which was to provide the mechanisms for the rise of the self within on-going activity. Wundt set out to show the parallelism between what goes on in the body and what goes on in the mind. In trying to find what was common to these two fields — what, in the psychical experience, could be referred to in physical terms — Wundt isolated a very valuable conception of the *gesture* as that which later becomes a symbol but which is to be found in its earlier states as a part of a social act. The gesture is that part of the social act which serves as a stimulus to other forms involved in the same social act.

Following Wundt, Mead took the gesture as the transitional link to language from action, and also as the phenomenon establishing the continuities of human and infrahuman social life. The gesture mediates the development of language as the basic mechanism permitting the rise of the self in the course of on-going social activity. Social life represents the interaction of creatures of the same type. Social insects and other non-human creatures, such as herding animals, and humans all have social life. Social interaction implies that the actions of one creature are in part the basis of the action of another. The "gesture" is any phase or aspect of the action of a creature which may serve to the other creatures party to the social act as a sign for the action as a whole. Baring of teeth, for example, accompanies the fighting of a creature: in the preparatory phase of attack, a dog bares its teeth and another responds to this as a sign of the attack about to begin. This phase of the action has become a sign (gesture) for the course of action that may follow. The sign has "meaning"; its meaning is precisely the potential occurrence. Gestures are the means by which non-human social action is possible.

[38] *Ibid.*, p. 11.   [39] *Ibid.*, p. 12.

But human social life is carried on not in terms of gestures but in terms of *language*. Language is a special transformation of the gestures essential to the conduct of more complex forms of social life. The gesture is an aspect of action that is taken as a sign of the course of action. If one could once isolate a class of gestures which could serve as common signs both to maker and perceiver, one would have a class of gestures making language possible. Verbal gestures represent such a class of common signs, which, being heard by the maker as well as the other parties to the social act, can serve as a common sign to all parties to the social act. The mutually understood gesture is a *significant symbol*. The continuities between gestures and language are established. In language, the gesture has been converted into a significant symbol. "Meaning" is located, in the same fashion, in the sign function of the significant symbol with respect to the future course of the social act. Language, moreover, operating with common signs on the basis of logical rules, makes possible a degree of integrated, precise, and differentiated yet plastic social behavior quite impossible to any creatures without language. In precision and integration, only the complex instinctive patterns of behavior among the social insects present any comparisons. But such instinctively produced social behaviors cannot show plasticity and variation.

> Gestures become significant symbols when they implicitly arouse in an individual making them the same responses which they explicitly arouse ... in other individuals, the individuals to whom they are addressed. . . . Only in terms of gestures as significant symbols is the existence of mind or intelligence possible; for only in terms of gestures which are significant symbols can thinking — which is simply an internalized or implicit conversation of the individual with himself by means of gestures — take place.[40]

In communication, individual and society interpenetrate to an unusual degree. "We are more or less unconsciously seeing ourselves as others see us. We are unconsciously addressing ourselves as others address us. . . . We are calling out in the other person something we are calling out in ourselves, so that unconsciously we take over these attitudes. We are unconsciously putting ourselves in the place of others and acting as others act. . . ."[41] Society, in terms of language, penetrates to the innermost recesses of thought itself. "Meaning arises and lies within the field of the relation between the gesture of a given human organism and the subsequent behavior of this organism. . . . Meaning is thus a development of something objectively there as a relation between certain phases of the social act."[42]

Meaning is not fundamentally a state of consciousness or a set of organized relations. Meaning is accounted for in terms of symbols at the most complex stage of their development. Intelligence is essentially the ability to solve the problems of present behavior in terms of its possible

---

[40] *Ibid.*, p. 47.   [41] *Ibid.*, pp. 68–69.   [42] *Ibid.*, pp. 75–76.

future consequences as implicated on the basis of past experience. It involves both memory and foresight. Meaning and mind have their origins in the social act and are made possible — in fact, necessitated — by language. Intelligence is the utilization of these instruments. The units of this process are attitudes, representing the beginning, or potential, initiation of some social act in which, along with others, the individual is involved or implicated. Thus, mind arises in the social process only when that process as a whole enters into the experience of any one individual. When this occurs, the individual becomes self-conscious and has a mind. It is by means of reflexiveness, the turning back of the experience of the individual upon himself, that the whole social process is thus brought into the experience of the individuals involved in it. Reflexiveness is the essential condition, within the social process, for the development of mind.

The reflexive property that human social experience acquires as a product of the use of language is critical for Mead's account of the rise of the self. The very definition of the self rests on this quality. A self is possible only to a creature that can be an object to itself, a characteristic possible only in society and by means of language. The underlying process producing the self consists in *role-taking*, which is present whenever significant symbols are used. One learns a significant symbol when he shares a sign referring to a common course of experience with someone else. Through the significant symbol, he is inevitably in the position of having taken the role of another. Every item of language carries with it some of the social matrix. Society penetrates the individual with every term he employs or acquires. Some aspect of society enters into the person with every different person with whom he associates. Or, by reverse, he has to become a slightly different thing to each new person. There are as many selves, in one sense, as there are persons with whom one associates, and a multivaried personality is normal. While ordinarily a person is a unified self in the community to which he belongs, at times the different requirements of social life may lead to the actual splitting up of the self and breakup of personality.

Role-taking is the basic process and the genesis of the self as one kind of unity of the social experience of the individual. The early stages of organization of social experience in terms of roles is evident in the imaginary companions which many children produce in the early stages of the formation of the self. It is a way of organizing responses called forth by others in the self. Play — at being mother, teacher, policeman, fireman — consists in taking various different roles. The child utilizes his own experiences to build a self. These are exercises in the more complex forms of role-taking that the social environment demands. In contrast to play, the organized game requires that the child take up a very specific role which reflects in its structure the roles of everyone else in the game in specific relationship to it. To perform the game role properly, the child must be able to take the role of everyone else within the game. The organization involved is put in the form of the rules of the game. But it is critical that the attitudes of all the others involved in the game be internalized. "The organized community or social group which gives to the individual his unity of self may be called 'the generalized other.' The attitude of the generalized other is the attitude of the whole community." [43]

Through the generalized other, the community exercises control over the conduct of its individual members. The two stages in the development of the self are thus (1) the organization of the particular attitudes of other individuals toward one's self and (2) the organization of the social attitudes of the generalized other toward one's self. The self reaches full development by organizing individual attitudes and generalizing them, becoming an individual reflection of the general systematic social pattern of group behavior in which all others are involved.

Mead followed James's terminology of "I" and "me" in accounting for the structure of the self. The self does not consist simply of a bare organization of social attitudes. It consists of an "I" which is aware of the social "me." The "I" is not a "me" and cannot become a "me." The "I" is the principle of action; the "I" reacts to the self that arises through the attitude of others. The "I" of the moment is present in the memory of the "me" of the next. The "I" is the response of the organism to the attitudes of the others, the "me" is the organized set of attitudes of others which one himself assumes.

> ... the "I" is always something different from what the situation itself calls for. So there is always that distinction, if you like, between the "I" and the "me." The "I" both calls out the "me" and responds to it. Taken together they constitute a personality as it appears in social experience. The self is essentially a social process going on with these two distinguishable phases. If it did not have these two phases there could not be conscious responsibility, and there would be nothing novel in experience.[44]

Just as the self arises as one kind of organization, so *society* appears as another:

> There are what I have termed "generalized social attitudes" which make an organized self possible. In the community there are certain ways of acting under situations which are essentially identical. . . . There are . . . whole series of such common responses in the community in which we live, and such responses are what we term "institutions." . . . Thus the institutions of society are organized forms of group or social activity — forms so organized that the individual members of society can act adequately and socially by taking the attitude of others toward these activities.[45]

Institutions are for society the counterpart of what the "me" is to the self.

One of the most daring of Mead's analyses appears in *Movements of Thought in the Nineteenth Century*, in which he attempted to make the

---

[43] *Ibid.*, p. 154.   [44] *Ibid.*, p. 178.   [45] *Ibid.*, pp. 260–262.

transition from the social psychology of the self to the processes of intellectual history. This study bears the same relation to Mead's work that Freud's studies of *Totem and Taboo, Civilization and Its Discontents, The Future of an Illusion,* and *Moses and Monotheism,* bear to psychoanalysis. The movement from eighteenth-century rationalism and revolution to nineteenth-century romanticism is treated by Mead as though it were a direct parallel to the stages in the development of the self. The romantic discovery of the past, for example, represents a reflexive discovery of the self. Lest this seem strange, it should be recalled that Cooley treated social organization as a kind of organized public opinion and institutions as fixed phases of the public mind. It is a perfectly logical extension of such ideas to conceive the emergence of total patterns of intellectual life in Mead's terms. The scientific acceptability of this, of course, is quite another story.

The concept of *role* emerged in central focus in Mead's work as the point of fusion for personality and social structure, moving discussion to an essentially new level of efficiency. This had been brilliantly anticipated by Simmel's splendid essay in Kantian vein, "How Is Society Possible?", in which the concept of "vocation" seemed the proper integrating point between self and society. But this was, for Simmel, a fragment in his thought; it did not arise, as for Mead, as a logical derivation from more basic propositions.

Ernst Cassirer

Ernst Cassirer (1874–1945) was born in Breslau and educated in several German universities. From 1919 to 1934 he taught at Hamburg, and he was professor of philosophy at the University of Göteborg in Sweden when he was called to Yale University in 1940. His first work to appear in English translation was *Substance and Function* (1923); after publication of his second work in English, *An Essay on Man,* and through his teaching at Yale and Columbia, his work has become increasingly well known and translated into English.[46] The special interest of Cassirer for our purposes lies in the

[46] *Substanzbegriff und Funktionsbegriff* (Berlin: B. Cassirer, 1910) was translated by William Curtis Swabey and Marie Collins Swabey as *Substance and Function* (New York: Dover Publications, 1923, 1953). The three volumes of *Philosophie der symbolischen Formen* were published between 1923 and 1929 (Berlin: B. Cassirer): Vol. 1, *Die Sprache* (1923); Vol. 2, *Das mythische Denken* (1925); Vol. 3, *Phänomenologie der Erkenntnis* (1929). This work has been translated by Ralph Manheim as *The Philosophy of Symbolic Forms* (New Haven, Conn.: Yale University Press, 1953–57); the English titles of the three volumes are *Language, Mythical Thought,* and *The Phenomenology of Knowledge.* Cassirer's *Sprache und Mythos: ein Beitrag zum Problem der Götternamen* (Leipzig: B. G. Teubner, 1925) has been translated by Susanne K. Langer as *Language and Myth* (New York: Harper, 1946). *Die Philosophie der Aufklärung* (Tübingen: J. C. B. Mohr, 1932) was translated by Fritz C. A. Koelln and James P. Pettegrove as *The Philosophy of the Enlightenment* (Princeton, N.J.: Princeton University Press, 1951). Cassirer's works in English include: *An Essay on Man: An Introduction to a Philosophy of Human Culture* (New Haven, Conn.: Yale University Press, 1944) and *The Myth of the State* (Yale University Press, 1946). For a review of Cassirer's work, see Paul A. Schilpp (ed.), *The Philosophy of Ernst Cassirer* (Evanston, Ill.: Library of Living Philosophers, 1949).

illustration his work provides of the independent development, out of neo-Kantianism and neo-idealism, of ideas which partly parallel and partly complement symbolic interactionism as it arose in America.

Human life, Cassirer maintains, is distinguished by a new method of adaptation to the environment, based on the use of the "symbolic system." "This new acquisition transforms the whole of human life. As compared with the other animals man lives not merely in a broader reality; he lives, so to speak, in a new *dimension* of reality." [47] This proposition is directly parallel to Mead, who would also agree that "language, myth, art, and religion" are parts of the symbolic universe man responds to. Cassirer continues: "Physical reality seems to recede in proportion as man's symbolic activity advances. . . . Man does not live in a world of hard facts, or according to his immediate needs and desires. He lives rather in the midst of imaginary emotions, in hopes and fears, in illusions and disillusions, in his fantasies and dreams." [48]

The whole development of human culture is dependent upon symbolic behavior; thus, for Cassirer as for Mead, the differentiation of animal reaction from human response rests on the emergence of language. As Cassirer sees it, speech arises on a substratum of the "language of the emotions." Koehler stated that chimpanzees achieve a considerable degree of expression by means of gestures: rage, terror, despair, grief, pleading, desire, playfulness, and pleasure. Human language requires something more. "The difference between *propositional language* and *emotional language* is the real landmark between the human and the animal world." [49]

A distinction may make the transition clear:

> We must carefully distinguish between *signs* and *symbols*. That we find rather complex systems of signs and signals in animal behavior seems to be an ascertained fact. . . . The famous experiments of Pavlov prove only that animals can easily be trained to react not merely to direct stimuli but to all sorts of mediate or representative stimuli. . . . Symbols — in the proper sense of this term — cannot be reduced to mere signals. Signals and symbols belong to two different universes of discourse: a signal is a part of the physical world of being; a symbol is a part of the human world of meaning. Signals are "operators"; symbols are "designators." [50]

On the basis of this difference, man is released from the immediate stimulus. Psychologists do not hesitate to speak of a creative or constructive imagination in animals. But this imagination is of a human type. The animal possesses a practical imagination and intelligence, whereas man alone has developed *symbolic imagination and intelligence*. Symbolism adds universal applicability and versatility. It makes possible relational thought. The very awareness of relations is a specific feature of human consciousness. Geometry is the classical example of the turning point in man's intellectual

[47] *An Essay on Man*, p. 24.   [48] *Ibid.*, p. 25.
[49] *Ibid.*, p. 30.   [50] *Ibid.*, pp. 31–32.

life. Even in elementary geometry we are not concerned with the apprehension of concrete individual figures. Confirming evidences for this power of abstraction are found in research on the psychopathology of language. Loss or impairment of speech caused by brain injury is never an isolated phenomenon. Such a defect tends to alter the whole character of the individual. Patients suffering from aphasia, for example, not only lose the use of words but undergo changes of personality. They may be able to perform outward tasks in a perfectly normal way but are at a complete loss in the solution of problems requiring theoretic or reflective activity. "Having lost their grip on universals, they stick to the immediate facts, to concrete situations. Such patients are unable to perform any task which can be executed only by means of a comprehension of the abstract." [51]

William James opposed the idea of the primacy of the separation of subject and object and suggested that they are differentiated out of something more primitive, "pure experience." Mead also opposed the opposition of mind and matter current in the psychologies of his day. He proposed "on-going activity" as a prior context. Wundt, who had himself employed a psychophysical parallelism, was nevertheless used as a starting point for Mead's analysis. Cassirer took a similar road, also beginning with Wundt, though he selected other elements of Wundt's thought than those which were central for Mead. He stated:

It would not be possible to speak of a discovery of the subjective in myth if the widespread view that the concepts of the I and the soul were the *beginning* of all mythical thinking were justified. Ever since Tylor in his fundamental work advocated this theory of the animistic origin of myth formation, it seems to have been accepted more and more as the secure empirical core and empirical rule of research in mythology. Wundt's approach to myth from the standpoint of ethnic psychology is entirely built on this theory; he, too, sees all mythical concepts and ideas essentially as variants of the idea of the soul, which thus becomes the empirical *presupposition* rather than the specific *aim* of the mythical world view.[52]

Cassirer's fundamental argument is similar to that of James and Mead. Just as James had taken "pure experience" as his starting point and Mead the "on-going social process," so Cassirer utilizes "mythical thinking" as a kind of matrix out of which the soul, the "I," and the self are differentiated. "A glance at the development of the various symbolic forms shows us that their essential achievement is not that they copy the outward world in the inward world or that they simply project a finished inner world outward, but rather that the two factors of 'inside' and 'outside,' of 'I' and 'reality' are *determined* and delimited from one another only in these symbolic forms and through their mediation." [53] The crucial property of every symbolic form is found in the fact that it does not have the limit between

51 *Ibid.*, p. 41.
52 *Mythical Thought* (Vol. 2 of *The Philosophy of Symbolic Forms*), p. 155.
53 *Ibid.*, pp. 155–156.

"I" and "reality" as pre-existent; rather each symbolic form creates such limits. While metaphysics and "rational psychology" have treated the concept of the soul as a possession, taking it as a substance, mythical consciousness operates the opposite way. "The concept of the soul may just as well be called the end as the beginning of mythical thinking." [54] The soul and the "I" do not arise in mythical thinking all at once. Only gradually and by all manner of detours does the new category of the "I," the idea of the person and the personality, grow from the mythical category of the soul. Within mythical consciousness, a separation begins to occur between the objective and subjective, between the world of the "I" and the world of things.

The first form of thinking is thus represented by the magical world view. For originally in the world of mythical ideas, precisely in its most immediate forms, there is a close connection with "the world of efficacy." That is, in this world of proto-thought, the world and the "I," subject and object, the subjective and objective, are blurred. "Thus, in the magical world view the I exerts almost unlimited sway over reality: it takes all reality back into itself." [55]

The soul is the first mythical form in which the "I" is apprehended. Inevitably, since the soul arises as the first differentiation of the "I" in primitive mythical consciousness, it is seen as a kind of demonic being. The personal self is conceived only vaguely at this stage. As we go back to the more primitive levels of mythical thinking, the sharpness, clarity, and definiteness of the subjective and personal existence diminish. Primitive thinking is actually characterized by the peculiarly fluid and fugitive character of its intuition and concept of personal existence. There is as yet no soul which is seen as an independent unitary substance separate from the body; the soul is life itself, immanent in the body and necessarily attached to it. Inevitably a man's spittle, his excrement, his nails, cuttings of his hair remain in a sense vehicles of his life and soul, and it may be a part of magical lore to collect these to control the soul.

Cassirer's formula for the emergence of the self is similar to that of James and Mead, though his starting point and appeal to Wundt are made on different grounds. For Cassirer, materials are found in the entire field of mythology and magic. Typically the materials of Egyptian mythology contained in the Book of the Dead are employed to trace the evolution of the self from the primitive magico-ethical principle of demonic possession to a more complex concept of the self as an ethical autonomy. "If the intuition of the I is to be freed from this confinement, if the I is to be apprehended in ideal freedom as an ideal unity, a new approach is needed. The decisive turn occurs when the accent of the soul concept shifts — when the soul ceases to be considered as the mere vehicle or cause of vital phenomena and is taken rather as the subject of the ethical consciousness." [56] The Book of the Dead mirrors the progress from the mythical to the ethical self.

[54] *Ibid.*, p. 156.   [55] *Ibid.*, p. 157.   [56] *Ibid.*, p. 166.

Man rises from magic to religion, from the fear of demons to the worship of gods, and this apotheosis is not so much outward as inward. Now man apprehends not only the world but himself, in new spiritual form. Continuation of this process makes possible the apprehension of the personality in its contemporary sense.

Furthermore, it is not the self alone that gradually arises through mythical forms to consciousness, but the community as well. Mythical consciousness and religious feeling, according to this analysis, embrace an even more fundamental contrast. For more basic than a contrast between subject and object is a contrast between the "I" and the "thou." "Subjectivity" has its correlate not in some external thing, but rather in a "thou" or "he," from which on the one hand it distinguishes itself, but with which on the other hand it groups itself. Thus is formed the true antithesis which the "I" requires in order to find and define itself. For here, again, the individual feeling and consciousness of self stand not only at the beginning but at the end of the process of development. In the earliest stages to which we can trace back this development, we find the feeling of *self* immediately fused with a definite mythical-religious feeling of *community*. The "I" feels and knows itself only as a member of a community, grouped with others into the unity of a family, a tribe, a social organism. "Only in and through this social organism does it possess itself; every manifestation of its own personal existence and life is linked, as though by invisible magic ties, with the life of the totality around it." [57]

Just as the self is apprehended only by stages through a series of mythical conceptions, each becoming more differentiated, precise, and rational, so in the progressive apprehension of community there are stages which take the form of a mystic feeling of the unity of all life in one community, mythical class formation, and totemism. Here, again, it may be noted that, in contrast to Mead, Cassirer opens up the approach to these issues through mythology and ethnographic studies of primitives. Mythical-religious consciousness follows not from the empirical content of the social form but is one of the most important prior factors in the feeling of community and social life. The linkage between religion and community was original. The orgiastic cults of the world merely restored men to that sense of magical identity with things lying at the deepest level of the mythic consciousness of community. In none of these cults does man stop at the mere contemplation of the natural process; he is impelled to burst through the barrier that separates him from the universe of living things, to intensify the life feeling in himself to the point of liberating himself from his generic or individual *particularity*. This liberation is achieved in wild, orgiastic dances which restore man's identity with the original source of life. The mythical narrative is an outward reflection of this inner process. In the cult of Dionysus, for instance, this process can be seen in the form of the cult which gives rise to the story of Dionysus-Zagreus, who is overpowered by the

[57] *Ibid.*, p. 175.

Titans, torn to pieces, and devoured, so that the one divine being is broken into the multiplicity of forms.

Thus, starting with mythic consciousness as the proto-reality, language, art, religion, and science are all seen by Cassirer as activities differentiating these materials. Human culture is the process of man's progressive self-liberation. Language, art, religion, science, are various phases in this process. In each, man discovers a new power to build up a world of his own, an "ideal" world. Philosophy cannot give up its search for a fundamental unity in this ideal world. At the same time, it must not confound this unity with simplicity nor overlook the tensions and frictions between the various powers of man, which cannot be reduced to a common denominator. They incline in different directions and obey different rules. Nevertheless, they do not denote discord, for these functions complete and complement one another. Each one opens a new horizon and shows us a new aspect of humanity.

Jean Piaget

The psychologist Jean Piaget (1896–   ) was born in Neuchâtel, Switzerland, and educated at the University of Neuchâtel, where he took his Ph.D. in zoology in 1918. His biological studies led to an early interest in the structure and processes of the human mind, and in 1918 he went to Zurich to study psychology. Shortly afterwards, he went to Paris, where he worked with Théodore Simon, co-author of the Binet-Simon intelligence tests. In 1921, Piaget returned to Switzerland, where he began his connection with the Institut des Sciences de l'Éducation, now an associate institute of the University of Geneva for the scientific study of the child and the training of teachers; Piaget was made its co-director in 1933. In 1926, Piaget became a professor of philosophy at the University of Neuchâtel; in 1929, professor of psychology at the University of Geneva; and in 1937, professor of general psychology at Lausanne University. Piaget has been a prolific writer, and his books have been very quickly translated into English. They include: *The Language and Thought of the Child* (1923), *Judgment and Reasoning in the Child* (1924), *The Child's Conception of the World* (1926), *The Child's Conception of Physical Causality* (1927), *The Moral Judgment of the Child* (1932), *The Origins of Intelligence in Children* (1935), *The Construction of Reality in the Child* (1937), *Play, Dreams and Imitation in Childhood* (1945), *The Psychology of Intelligence* (1947), *The Child's Conception of Space* (1948), and *The Child's Conception of Number* (1950).[58]

There seems to be little evidence that Cassirer, Mead, and Piaget ever had much direct influence on one another. This makes all the more interest-

---

[58] The dates given in parentheses are those of the original French publication, not of the translations. Because Piaget's output has been so enormous, and because it is difficult to single out a few titles as more significant than the others, a complete bibliographical footnote will not be attempted here.

ing their convergence on a common point of view. Symbolic interaction-ism appears independently in a number of forms as a kind of common solution to problems presented by the sociological tradition. Because of the sheer volume of Piaget's studies, it would be impossible to examine them all. Two will be reviewed here because of their parallels to American forms of symbolic interactionism.

Mead had found the game to be of particular importance for the formation of both the self and the social order. Piaget makes a similar case for the significance of games in *The Moral Judgment of the Child:* [59]

> Children's games constitute the most admirable social institutions. . . . If we wish to gain any understanding of child morality, it is obviously with the analysis of such facts as these that we must begin. All morality consists in a system of rules, and the essence of all morality is to be sought for in the respect which the individual acquires for these rules.[60]

The simplest social games contain rules elaborated by children themselves. Little boys who are beginning to play are gradually trained by the older ones in respect for the rules. The game permits the study of the process of socialization; the practice of the rules and the way children of different ages apply them; consciousness of rules and the ideas which children of different ages form of them as something obligatory and sacred or as some-thing subject to personal choice; the heteronomy or autonomy of the rules.

Piaget found that the rules of children's games such as those of marbles constitute a social reality independent of individuals (in Durkheim's sense) and transmitted, like language, from one generation to another. This set of customs is more or less plastic, for individual innovations, just as in the case of language, succeed only when they meet a general need and when they are collectively sanctioned as conforming to the spirit of the game. Piaget maintains that when children are studied in terms of their use and awareness of the rules of their games, four stages may be distinguished. In the first stage the rules are used habitually and without awareness. This may be described as a purely *motor* stage. So far as it enters awareness at all, use of rules may result in the formation of ritualistic schemas. The second, *egocentric*, stage begins when the child receives examples of codi-fied rules from the outside world. Sometime between the ages of two and five the child starts to imitate such examples even though he continues to play by himself or to play with others without trying to win. Between the ages of seven and eight, an incipient *cooperative* stage begins, in which each tries to win and all concern themselves with the question of mutual con-trol and unification of the rules, even though there is considerable discrep-ancy in the children's information about the rules. Finally, between eleven

---

[59] Jean Piaget, *The Moral Judgment of the Child* (New York: Harcourt, Brace, 1932), translated by Marjorie Gabain from *Le Jugement moral chez l'enfant* (Paris: F. Alcan, 1932).
[60] *Ibid.*, p. 1.

and twelve appears the stage of *codification of the rules*, during which every detail of procedure in the game becomes fixed and the child gains an awareness of the rules of reasoning which will enable him to apply the rules to any situation that may arise.

The child's emerging *consciousness* of the rules, though elusive in detail, is clear enough on the whole. It develops through three general stages, not completely identical with the practice of the rules. During the first stage, the rules are not yet coercive because they are purely motor or received unconsciously. This is followed by a stage in which the rules are regarded as sacred and untouchable, emanating from adults. Every suggested alteration appears as a transgression. Finally, the rule is looked on as a law resting on mutual consent — a law that must be respected if one is to be loyal but which one may alter by enlisting general opinion on one's side.

In the course of trying to understand the game and adapt himself to it, the child brings order into his behavior, which becomes schematized and ritualized. Particularly important is the fact that symbolism is grafted on the child's motor schemas. These symbols are initially enacted in play rather than thought out, and they imply a certain amount of imagination. Both rites and symbols lie in the conditions of pre-verbal intelligence. Two fundamental kinds of moral judgment already make their appearance during the second and third type of consciousness of the rules. Correlated with the egocentric practice of the rules is a feeling of respect for elders, corresponding to a theoretical judgment which turns a rule into something mystical and transcendental. To the rational practice of rules, there corresponds a theoretical judgment which attributes to the rules an autonomous character.

In connection with his derivation of morality from the practices in children's games, Piaget brought under review the socio-ethical theories of three modern thinkers: (1) Durkheim, who treated society as something standing above individuals and as the source from which all authority emanates; (2) M. Bovet, who derived morality from inter-individual relations; [61] (3) James Mark Baldwin, who derived the ethical self as an emergent from interactive life. All these theories, according to Piaget, express part of the truth, with Baldwin perhaps closest to a comprehensive view. Piaget's own conclusion [62] was that the morality prescribed by society for the individual was not homogeneous. Society is not a single thing. Society is the sum of social relations, among which two types may be distinguished: relations of *constraint* and relations of *cooperation*. Relations of constraint come from the outside as a system of rules with obligatory content; relations of cooperation arise in the consciousness of ideal norms. From the outside, the child's world tends primarily to be structured on the basis of ties of authority and unilateral respect; from within, however, relations of cooperation arise between equals, expressing an equilibrium

[61] "Les Conditions de l'obligation de la conscience," *L'Année psychologique*, 1912.
[62] *The Moral Judgment of the Child*, pp. 402 ff.

limit rather than a static system. Externally, experience is under the constraint of duty; internally, experience is ordered by spontaneous pursuit of the good and autonomous rationality, which are the fruits of reciprocity.

If one accepts from Mead's type of analysis the idea that capacity to take roles is essential to the social efficacy of the individual and that such roles form a common point of approach for personality and social structure, then the affinities of Mead's and Piaget's analyses are clear. For Mead's roles are codified in "the rules of the game," which were the object of analysis for Piaget. The rules, the learning of which Piaget was interested in, define role behaviors and the development of the "moral life" of the child from moral realism to moral democracy — this last, a close parallel to Mead's conception of the movement from the particular to the generalized other. It also parallels Cooley's concept of democracy as the extension of the ideals of the primary group. The two analyses are complementary. To Mead's theory of role-consolidation and development of the self, Piaget adds new perspectives on the ethical evolution of the self.

Piaget also turned his attention to the problem, so central to Mead's analysis, of language. Here, again, Piaget's treatment is an extension of symbolic interactionism with reference to the imitation–suggestion school. Piaget's latest discussion of these problems appears in *Play, Dreams and Imitation in Childhood*.[63] The focus of this study is on the symbolic function of the mind. The symbolic function is considered as a mechanism common to the various systems of representation — both verbal and non-verbal — and as a mechanism whose existence is a prerequisite for conceptual interaction between individuals and consequently for the acquisition of collective meaning. Piaget is clearly aware of the danger of circularity in deriving language from social interaction and social interaction from language. He adds that he in no way disputes the social nature of collective meanings but shows that it implies cooperation and reciprocity. "The social fact is for us a fact to be explained, not to be invoked as an extra-psychological factor. Hence it seems to us that the study of the symbolic function must cover all the initial forms of representation, from imitation and ludic or oneric symbols to verbal schemas and elementary pre-conceptual structures." [64]

The problem posed by Piaget is identical with Mead's attempt to make the transition from the "gesture" to the "significant symbol." Piaget believes that in play and imitation it is possible to trace the transition from sensory-motor assimilation and accommodation to the sort of mental assimilation and accommodation which characterizes the beginnings of representation. Representation begins when there is simultaneous differentiation and

---

[63] Jean Piaget, *Play, Dreams and Imitation in Childhood* (New York: W. W. Norton, 1951), translated by C. Gattegno and F. M. Hodgson from *La Formation du symbole chez l'enfant* (Neuchâtel: Delachaux & Niestlé, 1945).
[64] *Ibid.*, p. 4.

coordination between "signifiers" and "signified." The first differentiation between these is provided by imitation and the mental image derived from it. These images extend accommodation to external objects. The meanings of the symbols originate in assimilation, the dominating factor in play. At the sensory-motor level, an image develops which is capable of going beyond the immediate present. Assimilation and accommodation finally come together in a combination made necessary by this advance beyond the immediate present. The constitution of the symbolic function is a product of the union between actual or mental imitation and an absent model and the "meanings" provided by the various forms of assimilation. Thus language, a system of collective signs, becomes possible and acquires the set of individual symbols through which the sensory-motor schemas can be transformed into concepts or may integrate new concepts. The symbol results from pre-representational schematism. The ego inevitably follows as a symbolically integrated structure. The various forms of representation may interact. There is representation when an absent model is imitated in symbolic play, in imagination, and even in dreams. The system of concepts and logical relations, both in their intuitive and operational forms, implies representation.

Basic to all Piaget's explanations is a conception of the individual life process. This has two major aspects or phases: the assimilation of objects to individual activity, on the one hand, and the accommodation of activity to the object world on the other. The two processes of assimilation and accommodation are polar phases of the total life process. They are not always in equilibrium and may even operate in partial autonomy from one another. One of the fundamental facts of the life process is the establishment of an equilibrium between assimilation and accommodation. The first phase of individual development is described by Piaget as one of sensory-motor adjustment. Sensory-motor adjustment consists in the development of an assimilating activity which tends to incorporate external objects in its schemas while at the same time accommodating the schemas to the external world. This is the first and basic form of life adjustment. Imitation is not taken as an original form of activity but as secondary, including a component of intelligence. Imitation appears when the subject's schemas of action are modified without use of the external world that modified it. Imitation is a continuation of the effort at accommodation. The linkage of imitation with representation arises in the fact that representation involves the image of an object. Representation is a kind of interiorized imitation. This corresponds to Mead's idea of thinking as internalization of the social process. Representation appears as a phase of the continuation of the effort at accommodation.

On the other hand, every act of intelligence represents an equilibrium between assimilation and accommodation, and while imitation is a continuation of accommodation for its own sake, it may be said roughly that play is essentially assimilation, or the primacy of assimilation over accommodation. Play is functional, or reproductional, assimilation. Primitive play begins by being almost identical with the set of sensory-motor behaviors of which it is only one pole. With the interiorization of schemas, play becomes more distinct from adaptive behavior (intelligence). In contrast to objective thought, which seeks to adapt itself to external reality, imaginative play symbolically transposes things to the child's activity without rules or limitations. Thus, in the early stages of representation the property of the symbol as a "signifier" is a continuation of imitation. What the symbol signifies may vary from adequate adaptation to free satisfaction. With the socialization of the child, play acquires rules or gradually adapts symbolic imagination to reality in the form of constructions which are still spontaneous but which imitate reality.

For Piaget, imitation, symbolic play, and cognitive representation demonstrate the progressive establishment of equilibrium between assimilation and accommodation on a new basis. There is an equilibrium at the stage of sensory-motor adjustment level, but only assimilation and accommodation are involved. Representation, however, goes beyond the present, extending the field of adaptation in space and time. It evokes what lies outside the immediate perceptual field. The collective institution of language is the main factor in both the formation and socialization of representations. The "signifier," for Piaget, is a product of accommodation continued as imitation, that is, as images of interiorized imitations. The "signified" is the product of assimilation which, by integrating the object in earlier schemas, provides it with a meaning. Thus, representation involves a double interplay of assimilations and accommodations, past and present, tending toward equilibrium. The process is slow, occupying the whole of childhood.

Hans Gerth and C. Wright Mills

The work of two very vigorous young theorists may indicate the continued development of symbolic interactionism and the way in which it can be adapted to special purposes. Hans Gerth (1908–   ) is a social psychologist and political sociologist at the University of Wisconsin, where for some years he has taught a famous course in social stratification. He was born in Kassel, Germany, and educated at Heidelberg under Karl Mannheim. Later, he studied at London and Frankfurt, where he took his Ph.D. in 1933. Since coming to the United States as a refugee, he has become one of the primary translators of Max Weber (*From Max Weber: Essays in Sociology; The Religion of China; Ancient Judaism*). C. Wright Mills (1916–   ) took his Ph.D. at the University of Wisconsin in 1941 under Hans Gerth and Howard Becker. He has made significant contributions to the study of social stratification in such works as *The New Men of Power; The Puerto Rican Journey; White Collar: The American Middle Classes;* and *The Power Elite.* Since 1946, Mills has been professor of sociology at Columbia University.

The unusual talents of Hans Gerth and C. Wright Mills were linked in

their joint study, *Character and Social Structure*,[65] their most complete theoretical statement so far. Gerth and Mills trace their affinities primarily to
Mead and Freud. "Behaviorism's most fruitful outcome was George Mead's
work, especially his daring effort to anchor personal consciousness itself
in the social process. Mead's concept of the generalized other, and Freud's
super-ego — their closest point of contact — enable us to link the private
and the public, the innermost acts of the individual with the widest kinds
of social-historical phenomena." [66]

In both views they find serious limitations: they feel that Mead had neither
an adequate theory of emotions and motives nor a dynamic theory of the
affective life of man; on the other hand, Freud's notion of the personality
tends, they think, to be socially inflexible. Furthermore, neither Freud
nor Mead presents a conception of social structure relevant to social-psychological problems. However, the authors think, when properly integrated,
Freud and Mead provide a model of character structure and the most
fruitful set of ideas available in modern social science adequate for the
treatment of social structure as developed by Marx, Sombart, Weber, and
Mannheim.

To Gerth and Mills, the primary requirements for an adequate theory
of symbolic interactionism include: the integration and systematization of
Mead and Freud; the development of an adequate theory of motivation;
and the development of a social-psychologically relevant conception of social structure.

The two fundamental concepts by which Gerth and Mills unite personality
and social structure are drawn from Mead: *role* and *institution*. "Role" is
taken to refer to units of behavior which by their occurrence stand out as
regularities and which are oriented to the conduct of other actors. "Institutions" are taken as organizations of roles carrying different degrees of
authority, one or more of which serves to maintain the entire system of
roles.[67] The man, as a person, is composed of the roles he performs and
the effects of these roles on him. Society, as social structure, is composed
of roles, variously combined.

The integration and systematization of Mead and Freud constitute Gerth's
and Mills's concept of *character*. A character is a psychic structure formed
on a foundation of organic potential. A psychic structure is an integration
of perception, emotion, and impulse. Inner feelings become emotions by
being linked to socially recognized gestures of which the person is aware
and which he relates to himself. For sensation to become perception, certain meanings must be added. For impulses to become purposes, the objects
so specified must be defined and learned.

Language is important for all these transformations, for it is through lan-

---

[65] Hans Gerth and C. Wright Mills, *Character and Social Structure: The Psychology
of Social Institutions* (New York: Harcourt, Brace, 1953; London: Routledge and
Kegan Paul, 1953). Mills's books will be discussed in Chapter 16.
[66] *Ibid.,* p. xvi.   [67] *Ibid.,* pp. 10 ff.

guage that experience is composed in terms of the expectations of others. Character arises when, in the course of social experience through language, the organic materials of the individual are stylized into roles. And with roles, everything necessary for the concepts of institution and social structure is at hand.

Before turning to Gerth's and Mills's concept of social structure, it is worthy of note that in their conception of character they have actually taken precious little from Freud. Of such conceptions as the unconscious, conscious, censor, id, superego, ego, repression, sublimation, auto-eroticism, narcissism, Oedipus complex, Electra complex, dream symbolism, they make practically no use. Rather, the materials formed by social roles into character are conceived in pre-Freudian terms. The materials for behavior are conceived originally to break down into sensation, feeling, and impulse, which by language are transformed into perception, emotion, and purpose. Freud actually receives little more than lip service.

Just as Mead is primarily important for the Gerth and Mills concept of character, so is he central to their view of social structure. For Marx, Sombart, Weber, and Mannheim seem to have as little to do with their idea of social structure as Freud did for their idea of personality. Institutions are clusters of roles anchored in an authoritative role. The parental authority of the head of a household, for example, rests on awards and punishments emanating from this role and maintaining the entire role pattern. Institutions are in turn classified in terms of objective function, and the two ideas of institutional *order* and *sphere* are introduced. An "institutional order" consists of all institutions in the social structure which have similar consequences and ends or which serve similar objective functions. The following institutional orders form the skeleton structure of the total society.

(1) The *political* order consists of those institutions within which men acquire, wield, or influence the distribution of power and authority within social structures.

(2) The *economic* order is made up of those establishments by which men organize labor, resources, and technical implements in order to produce and distribute goods and services.

(3) The *military* order is composed of institutions in which men organize legitimate violence and supervise its use.

(4) The *kinship* order is made up of institutions which regulate and facilitate legitimate sexual intercourse, procreation, and the early rearing of children.

(5) The *religious* order is composed of those institutions in which men organize and supervise the collective worship of God or deities, usually at regular occasions and at fixed places.[68]

The institutional orders, however, are not sufficient to characterize social structure completely, for there are several "spheres" of social conduct

[68] *Ibid.*, p. 26.

which characterize all institutional orders, such as technology, symbols, status, and education. *Symbols* include the signs, emblems, ceremonies, language, music which sustain the order. *Technology* includes tools, apparatus, machines, instruments, and physical devices. *Status* consists of agencies for and means of distributing prestige, deference, or honor. And the *educational* sphere includes activities concerned with the transmission of skills and values to persons who have not yet acquired them.

The picture of social structure that emerges is one characterized by nine institutional orders interlaced by four spheres. A person, for example, may be a teacher, with his behavior thus forming part of the educational *sphere;* at the same time, since he makes his living by teaching, his behavior forms a part of the economic *order.* In view of such institutional overlap, it sometimes requires considerable ingenuity to decide just what institutional affiliation a given item of behavior has. One must assume that, at least under some conditions, orders and spheres may change places and become spheres and orders to each other.

Despite the economical formulation given by Gerth and Mills to the concepts of character and social structure, their greatest innovations in symbolic interactionism do not lie here. The conception of roles, after all, and of their importance for the formation of personality has been basic to symbolic interactionism from the outset. Furthermore, the conception of roles as the unit elements of institutions is not new either, having been formulated by Mead. Even the idea of institutions as authoritatively instituted role groupings is not new; it was formulated by Znaniecki. The idea of institutional systems is at least as old as Herbert Spencer, and the distinction between orders and spheres was drawn by Max Weber. The contribution of Gerth and Mills at this level is primarily one of unusual compactness of formulation.

On the other hand, there is not the slightest doubt that their sociology of *motivation* represents a distinctly new addition to symbolic interactionism. Motivation, they argue, is equilibrium-restoring behavior and has three forms: physio-chemical, emotional, and social:

> At the level of the *organism*, we might assume that "all organic processes are initiated by the need to restore a physio-chemical equilibrium which is experienced as health." In terms of the *psychic structure* we might assume that "psychological processes are initiated by the need to restore an emotional equilibrium which is experienced as pleasure." In terms of the *person*, we might assume that conduct is motivated by the *expectations* of others, which are internalized from the roles which the persons enact. . . . Motivation thus has to do with the balance of self-image with the appraisals of others.[69]

For Freud, the psychic structure may be socially molded, but it is not the ideal subject of social modification. Sublimation implies that role-condi-

[69] *Ibid.*, p. 112.

tioned forms of psychic drives are epiphenomena of the basic drives. To Gerth and Mills, this argument is bad metaphysics, for the biological person has no more reality than the psychic person. Hence it is only on the level of the person that we can hope to deal with understandable motives. The question of understandable intentions or motives calls attention to the role of language in interpersonal conduct.

Gerth and Mills introduce here their most original conception — "vocabularies of motive." Motives, they observe, are usually thought of as subjective springs of actions lying in the psychic structure of the organism. However, they urge, since persons ascribe motives to themselves and others, motives may be considered "as the terms which persons typically use in their interpersonal relations." [70] Sociologically, they continue, a motive is a term in a vocabulary which appears to the actor and to the observer to be an adequate reason for his conduct. "Conceived in this way," they insist, "motives are acceptable justifications for present, future, or past programs of conduct." [71] Nor is this the end of the matter. "When a person confesses or imputes motives, he is not usually trying to describe his social conduct, he is . . . usually trying to influence others." [72] Vocabularies of motive, they maintain, have histories as their institutional contexts change. While the motives accompanying the institutional conduct of war are not the causes of war, they promote continued participation in warfare.

> Examine the shift from the laissez faire to the monopolistic phase of modern capitalism. The profit motive of individual gain may be widely espoused and accepted by business men during a relatively prosperous and free economic era. . . . Now, if a man finds himself unable to engage in business conduct without joining a "liberal" business organization and proclaiming its public-spirited vocabulary, it follows that this particular vocabulary of motives is an important reinforcing feature of his social conduct.[73]

Thus, according to Gerth and Mills, symbolic interactionism requires for its completion an adequate theory of motivation. Such an adequate theory of motivation, it seems, takes its stand on the assumption that people are going to do what they would do anyway. Motivation consists of specialized vocabularies, systems of terms and phrases, that have instrumental value for self-justification and deceit. To be sure, we are warned that we "must abandon the notion that merely because vocabularies of motives are acceptable they are necessarily deceptive shams." [74] This way of putting the case suggests, however, that most of the time they are. While it is suggested that various vocabularies of motive are integrated with different levels of psychic structure and that unconscious motives refer to unverbalized conduct, it is difficult to escape the view that, for Gerth and Mills, "vocabu-

[70] *Ibid.*, pp. 114–115.   [71] *Ibid.*, p. 115.
[72] *Ibid.*, p. 117.   [73] *Ibid.*, p. 118.   [74] *Ibid.*, p. 119.

laries of motive" are at bottom always social strategies. "No one vocabulary of motives is accepted by everyone, so the alert individual must use one or the other tentatively, until he finds the way to integrate his conduct with others, to win them as allies of his act." [75] Presumably for this purpose one might find such handbooks as Dale Carnegie's *How to Win Friends and Influence People* extremely helpful.

Summary

The conceptual foundations of symbolic interactionism are found primarily in pragmatism, although strong additional influence comes from neo-idealism, both in its older and in its neo-Hegelian version. In America the primary lines of development extend from William James, through Cooley and W. I. Thomas, to George Herbert Mead. From Mead, in turn, symbolic interactionism has had influence upon almost every contemporary sociologist. The continued evolution of its theoretical structure is evident in the work of Gerth and Mills.

Though symbolic interactionism has found its strongest development in America, it represents a structural trend in sociological thought. Two very significant Europeans illustrate this: Piaget and Cassirer.

Symbolic interactionism achieved a more precise definition of sociological subject matter than pluralistic behaviorism. It opened up the problem of the linguistic structuring of interhuman behavior. It developed more adequate theories of personality and made major strides toward the linkage of personality and social structure. It is also of interest to observe, incidentally, that its picture of society was far more uniformly "liberal" than was true for pluralistic behaviorism. This is true not only for James, Cooley, Thomas, and Mead, with their Jeffersonian ideal of a small-town democracy, but also for Piaget and Cassirer, who preserve socio-political conceptions of an Enlightenment model.

Moreover, closely related to the more theoretically consistent notions of sociological subject matter, the members of this branch of social behaviorism brought statistical methods under serious question as solely adequate to sociology, preferring some sort of comparative case method or even, as in the case of Cooley, systematic autobiography (introspection).

SELECTED BIBLIOGRAPHY

CASSIRER, ERNST, *The Philosophy of Symbolic Forms.* Translated by Ralph Manheim. Three volumes. New Haven, Conn.: Yale University Press, 1953–57.

CASSIRER, ERNST, *An Essay on Man: An Introduction to a Philosophy of Human Culture.* New York: Doubleday, 1953.

COOLEY, CHARLES HORTON, *Human Nature and the Social Order.* Revised edition. New York: Scribner's, 1922.

[75] *Ibid.,* p. 122.

COOLEY, CHARLES HORTON, *Social Organization.* New York: Scribner's, 1929.

GERTH, HANS, and C. WRIGHT MILLS, *Character and Social Structure: The Psychology of Social Institutions.* New York: Harcourt, Brace, 1953.

JAMES, WILLIAM, *Psychology.* Cleveland: World Publishing Co., 1948.

MEAD, GEORGE H., *Mind, Self, and Society.* Edited by Charles W. Morris. Chicago: University of Chicago Press, 1934.

PIAGET, JEAN, *The Moral Judgment of the Child.* Translated by Marjorie Gabain. New York: Harcourt, Brace, 1932.

PIAGET, JEAN, *Play, Dreams and Imitation in Childhood.* Translated by C. Gattegno and F. M. Hodgson. New York: W. W. Norton, 1951.

THOMAS, WILLIAM I., and FLORIAN ZNANIECKI, *The Polish Peasant in Europe and America.* Two-volume edition. New York: Dover Publications, 1958.

THOMAS, WILLIAM I., *The Unadjusted Girl.* Boston: Little, Brown, 1923.

15

*The Social-Action Branch
of Social Behaviorism*

SOCIAL-ACTION THEORY, THE THIRD SIGNIFICANT BRANCH OF SOCIAL BEHAVIOR-
ism, was an independent response to the same problems that gave rise to
pluralistic behaviorism and symbolic interactionism. It represented a special
theoretical solution to the general problems of the school. For their analysis
of personality, social structure, and collective behavior, the pluralistic behavioral branch found their starting points in such notions as imitation,
innovation, suggestion, diffusion, conflict of innovations, and consciousness
of kind; the symbolic interactionist branch took attitudes, mutual expectations, language viewed as an interbehavioral mechanism, and social roles as
critical to their approach to the same issues. There were many links between these two branches: Baldwin was influenced by James; Cooley was
influenced by Baldwin; Chapin was in part influenced by Cooley; Piaget
stood astride the traditions and was influenced by Baldwin. But despite such
influences across boundaries, the properties of the two branches remain
quite distinct.

Reciprocal influences also characterize social-action theory. Gerth and
Mills, for example, were as much influenced by it as some other symbolic interactionists were by pluralistic behaviorism. But the unit of analysis of
social-action theory — *meaningful social action* — is distinct, as are a series
of related concepts. This branch of social behaviorism has worked out its
problems in a theoretically distinctive manner. Its outstanding figure is
Max Weber.

Max Weber

Max Weber (1864–1920) was the son of a middle-class German liberal who was prominent in the politics of the National Liberal Party in the Bismarck era. Max Weber studied law and was appointed *Privatdozent* at the University of Berlin. In 1893, he became professor of economics at the University of Freiburg, moving from there to the chair of economics at Heidelberg, where he succeeded the famous economist Karl Knies. In 1900, he suffered a nervous breakdown and for many years lived as a private scholar in a state of semi-invalidism in Heidelberg. During World War I, he resumed teaching duties.[1]

Weber tried to synthesize the Kantian and neo-Kantian, and idealistic and neo-idealistic traditions in Germany. A simplified model may be set up for considering the problems with which he wrestled and the kind of decision he won from them by contrasting a neo-idealist and a neo-Kantian: Dilthey and Rickert. In reaction to what he thought were crass oversimplifications of the positivists (like Comte), Dilthey, the neo-idealist, objected to the use of the instruments proper to the physical sciences in the domain of the cultural sciences. Dilthey sharpened the distinction between the physical and

[1] The first fairly complete editions of Weber's works were published shortly after his death: *Gesammelte Aufsätze zur Religionsoziologie* ["Collected Works in the Sociology of Religion"], 3 vols. (Tübingen: J. C. B. Mohr, 1920–21); *Gesammelte politische Schriften* ["Collected Political Writings"] (Munich: Drei Masken Verlag, 1921); *Gesammelte Aufsätze zur Wissenschaftslehre* ["Collected Works on Scientific Theory"] (Tübingen: J. C. B. Mohr, 1922); *Wirtschaft und Gesellschaft* ["Economy and Society"], 2 vols. (Tübingen: J. C. B. Mohr, 1922); *Wirtschaftsgeschichte* ["Economic History"] (Munich: Duncker & Humblot, 1924); *Gesammelte Aufsätze zur Soziologie und Sozialpolitik* ["Collected Works in Sociology and Social Politics"] (Tübingen: J. C. B. Mohr, 1924); and *Gesammelte Aufsätze zur Sozial- und Wirtschaftsgechichte* ["Collected Works in Social and Economic History"] (Tübingen: J. C. B. Mohr, 1924).

Weber's works are gradually finding their way into English translation. Because in many instances a given book in English translates only a section from a larger work, and because a single book in English may translate material from more than one of Weber's German works, to present a complete correlation of English translations with German originals would take up more space than we can here allow. The following English translations are listed in the order of their appearance in America: *General Economic History*, tr. by Frank H. Knight from *Wirtschaftsgeschichte* (New York: Greenberg, 1927; reissued by The Free Press, 1950); *The Protestant Ethic and the Spirit of Capitalism*, tr. by Talcott Parsons from parts of *GAzW*, *GpS*, and *WuG* (New York: Scribner's, 1930, 1958); *From Max Weber: Essays in Sociology*, tr. and ed. by Hans Gerth and C. Wright Mills (New York: Oxford University Press, 1946); *The Theory of Social and Economic Organization*, tr. by A. M. Henderson and Talcott Parsons from *WuG* (New York: Oxford University Press, 1947); *The Methodology of the Social Sciences*, tr. by Edward A. Shils and Henry A. Finch from *GAzW* (Glencoe, Ill.: The Free Press, 1949); *The Religion of China*, tr. by Hans Gerth from *GAzR* (Glencoe, Ill.: The Free Press, 1951); *Ancient Judaism*, tr. by Hans Gerth and Don Martindale from *GAzR* (Glencoe, Ill.: The Free Press, 1951); *Max Weber on Law in Economy and Society*, tr. by Edward A. Shils and Max Rheinstein from *WuG* (Cambridge, Mass.: Harvard University Press, 1954); *The City*, tr. by Don Martindale and Gertrud Neuwirth from *WuG* (Glencoe, Ill.: The Free Press, 1958); *The Religion of India*, tr. by Hans Gerth and Don Martindale from *GAzR* (Glencoe, Ill.: The Free Press, 1958); and *The Rational and Social Foundations of Music*, tr. by Don Martindale, Johannes Riedel, and Gertrud Neuwirth from *WuG* (Carbondale, Ill.: Southern Illinois University Press, 1958).

the cultural sciences. He argued that human thought in each has a distinct form, a distinct method. The physical sciences deal with *facts;* the cultural sciences with *meanings.* In the physical sciences, thought takes the form of *explanation;* in the cultural sciences, it takes the form of *understanding.* Explanation establishes causal laws and approaches its object from the outside, or externally; understanding links meaning with meaning and grasps its object immediately in acts of intuition. The objectives of explanation and interpretation differentiate the physical and the cultural sciences from one another. The method of explanation in natural science is experiment; the method of understanding in the cultural sciences consists in interpretation by means of ideal types or configurations of meaning.

Rickert, as a neo-Kantian, was quite opposed to Dilthey's conceptions and he drew his distinctions in a very different way. To a Kantian, the realm of science is the explanation of phenomena — and it does not matter whether the phenomena concern the individual or the physical world. Phenomena are phenomena and science is science. Dilthey was making introspective psychology into a science different in kind from physics. The way in which all science explains is by establishing causal laws among phenomena, and psychology is no different except for its historical recency. It has not reached the same stage of precision as physics. Rickert thus returns psychology — in fact all the social sciences — to science. Rickert, however, introduced distinctions along a new dimension. The real contrast, he believes, is between history and science. Science is the analysis of nature in terms of causal laws; history is the analysis of nature as a pattern of unique events. While the critical concepts of science are *laws,* the critical conceptions of history are unique *configurations of value.*

These arguments were developed in great variety and detail and advanced by a variety of persons besides Dilthey and Rickert, but this simplified picture may show the conceptual task Weber tackled. If one were to assume that Dilthey and Rickert both have a point, how could one bring their ideas together? Weber's answer may be approached most simply in terms of a tabular comparison of Dilthey and Rickert:

DILTHEY (NEO-IDEALIST)		RICKERT (NEO-KANTIAN)	
Discipline	*Appropriate Type of Knowledge*	*Discipline*	*Appropriate Type of Knowledge*
Cultural Science	Intuitive, meaningful	History	Unique determinations with respect to values
Natural Science	Causal-law explanations	Science	Causal-law explanations

One of the chief differences between Dilthey as a neo-idealist and Rickert as a neo-Kantian is Dilthey's idea that the cultural and social sciences deal with a *differentiated* content, as contrasted with Rickert's belief that science deals with phenomena which are not so differentiated. On the other hand, as a neo-idealist, Dilthey believes that the cultural sciences deal with the human spirit, which is in constant process of change and development. This process of change and development — a characteristic of the content of the cultural sciences — is perceived by Rickert not as a property of content, but as a distinction in method. Nature is all of one piece, but nature may be studied as science or as history, requiring a different formation of concepts in each case.

The neo-idealists were concerned with the world as a field for action; the neo-Kantians were dealing with the world as an object of knowledge. Weber was influenced by these ideas. Practically, the science of the world as a field for action is politics, the theory and art of bringing to pass irrevocable action changes. Social change is a unique process of development which is understood both as history and as science. Science achieves its full explanatory power only by becoming value-free and independent of our preferences. This very freedom from one of the immediate properties of action makes science indispensable for action. Ideas from both Dilthey and Rickert were fused in this account.

The neo-Kantian influence of thinkers like Rickert is seen in Weber's idea that reality is ultimately not reducible to a system of laws. No body of laws can exhaust a science of culture. Nor can one ever hope to achieve complete predictability, since prediction is successful only within limited or closed systems. Moreover, relation to values is fundamentally necessary to apprehension of the unique. At the same time, this clear neo-Kantianism is modified. The idealists thought of the development of the human spirit as a genuinely creative *process*. Even the values change. Weber agrees that the objective of history can never be founded on a universal system of values. Historical change moves toward unknown ends, always permitting new activities and revealing new spiritual possibilities.

Neo-Kantianism was modified by Weber in still another way. He was not ready to view phenomena as identical simply because of the fact that they are phenomena, whether in the natural or cultural sciences. With the idealists, Weber held that the role of cultural sciences is to apprehend "meanings." An objective in the cultural sciences is to "understand" a process having to do with the special kind of evidence associated with the grasp of meaningful relations. Meaningful relations are such as obtain between motives and acts and between means and ends. These appear in our own actions, and interpretive sociology must grasp them in the behavior of others as well in the behavior of ourselves. It has been penetratingly observed that at this point Weber reverses Durkheim's formula, which, in its crass positivism, treats social facts as things. Interpretive sociology treats the historical world not as a collection of objects but as a process of development of human lives.[2]

[2] See Raymond Aron, *German Sociology*, tr. by Mary and Thomas Bottomore (Glencoe, Ill.: The Free Press, 1957), p. 76.

At the same time, this broad concession to the neo-idealists was again modified: Weber was not willing to argue that science is in principle different in the cultural and the natural sciences, such that method in the first is immediate, in the second mediate. Intuition, he insisted, has the same role in the cultural sciences as it does in the natural sciences. There is no more immediate apprehension of objects in the cultural sciences than in the natural. And again, as a concession to the neo-Kantians, the role of science in the field of cultural data is only completed when causal connections are established. Weber's synthesis of the neo-idealist and neo-Kantian positions is summarized in the following scheme of possible disciplines:

Discipline	Kind of Data Studied (item on top being primary)	Type of Explanation Employed	Nature of Resultant Explanation
Cultural History	Meanings, factual conditions	Meaningful interpretations, causal explanation	Unique sequences of cultural development
Cultural Science	Meanings, factual conditions	Meaningful interpretations, causal explanations	Causal laws of cultural phenomena
Natural Science	Facts, explored by meanings	Causal explanations	Laws of natural phenomena
Natural History	Facts, explored by meanings	Meaningful interpretations, causal explanation	Unique sequences of physical development

Weber's Methodology. It is unfortunate that Weber never developed his methodology apart from the theoretical and philosophical issues that have just been reviewed. This has not promoted the clear isolation of theoretical and philosophical issues from methodological issues. It is partly the reason for the numerous conflicting interpretations that have arisen in connection with Weber's method of the ideal type.

The methodological problems of early sociology, including those which Weber faced, were in considerable measure a product of the conditions of sociology's origin. The science arose as an attempt to apply various theories derived from philosophy to empirical social materials taken from history. Although many early sociologists paid lip service to laboratory experimentation as the ideal method of science, none of them was able to see quite how it could be employed, and some thought it would be an abomination if it were. These same early sociologists could not rely upon the statistical method, for it had not yet been developed. Under the circumstances, sociological method took its only possible form: it employed a *comparative* method, based on historical data. Its historical data were soon amplified by others from ethnography.

However, two circumstances almost guaranteed the abuse of the early forms of the comparative method. Because of the sultry ideological atmosphere of early sociology, it was a foregone conclusion that early sociologists would be inclined to employ historical and ethnographic materials merely to illustrate conclusions which they had already reached in advance. The early unilinear evolutionists, for example, usually assumed that their own societies represented the high point of social evolution, and that some one of the primitive groups described by the ethnographers represented approximately the point from which every society had started. Their task, as they saw it, consisted in arranging available ethnographic and historical evidence in a series between these points. Facts were ripped from a variety of social contexts and strung together like beads on a chain.

The second circumstance that encouraged the abuse of the early comparative method was the lack of standards, other than those supplied by common sense, for deciding what constituted a legitimate comparison. The standards of common sense have a rough workability in their sphere. However, once thought moves outside the sphere of common experience, the standards of common sense are inadequate. A science tends quickly to move beyond such spheres, whereupon its growth assumes the form of a spiral of theoretical refinement and increasing methodological precision.

When these two circumstances — the ideological atmosphere and the lack of any but common-sense standards for comparison — both operated together, early sociology began to develop such an array of conflicting explanations of the same things as to bring the whole science into question. In the search for a solution to the problem of standards, the relation between science and history had to be re-examined.

Dilthey and Rickert, as we have seen, took different positions on this relationship. Weber pursued a course somewhere between the two. With Dilthey, he accepted meanings and values as basic subject matter of sociology. With Rickert, he viewed science as science, whether it deals with mental, social, or physical phenomena. In opposition to Dilthey, he did not believe that the isolation of the meanings of social events puts sociology in a different class from those disciplines which establish causal laws. In opposition to Rickert, he did not place science and history in opposite camps, leaving sociology the character of a purely formal science. Rather, Weber accepted the traditional situation of sociology as a scientific discipline, working with materials from history. He believed that a properly developed *typological* procedure was the primary device for increasing the methodological precision of sociology.

The problem for comparative method is to get cases that can actually be compared. Weber's solution was the "ideal type." As he conceived them, "ideal types" are hypothetically concrete individuals (personalities, social situations, changes, revolutions, institutions, classes, and so on), constructed out of their relevant components by the researcher for the purpose of instituting precise comparisons. Thus, for example, the ideal types of "church" and "sect" represent two idealized types of arrangment of the critical elements of religious institutions which may help the student in the analysis of the rise of Protestantism; "Protestantism" and "Christianity" themselves are ideal types. Ideal types are not general or abstract concepts, but hypothetical individuals; as hypothetical individuals, ideal types consist of a selection of items which could appear in reality. To this extent, they are like stereotypes. But stereotypes are evaluative concepts, designed to close rather than to open analysis. Finally, ideal types are not averages, which are arithmetic computations appropriate only to the analysis of quantitative variations along a single dimension.[3]

As "hypothetical individuals," ideal types do not come ready made, but must be framed by the researcher. This has led some students to strange conclusions about the scientific process. It has been argued that ideal types are "if . . . then" propositions. However, since ideal types are imaginary individuals, the argument really makes no more sense than to maintain that if wishes were horses, beggars would ride. Even more startling is the suggestion that we compare actual individuals with the (admittedly imaginary) ideal typical individuals to see how much they deviate from them. This is nothing but a form of intellectual acrobatics, for actual individuals ought to deviate from the ideal type just as much as one made them deviate in the first place.

Weber had little interest in such mental gymnastics. To him, the framing of ideal types was an incident in the attempt to understand the empirical world. If that world presented itself to the student in tidy packages, ready for generalization, the framing of types would be unnecessary. However, the world usually presents the individual case as a tangle of incidents appearing in varying degrees of relief. Thought moves against the problems of the actual world with its puny tools and surmounts its obstacles more like a patient mountain climber than a spectacular trapeze artist entertaining an audience.

The ideal type is a strategy in empirical explanation. It is framed in terms of the scientific knowledge available to the researcher at the time of his study and in terms of the empirical situations he is trying to understand. The moment understanding is won, an ideal type has lost its utility, except, perhaps, as a pedagogical device for the instruction of untried scientists or as a diagnostic instrument for practitioners.

There are two criteria for constructing an ideal type: objective possibility

---

[3] For Weber's views on the ideal type, see *The Methodology of the Social Sciences*, pp. 89 ff. For a review of Weber's study and a comparison of his views with those of recent American sociologists, see Don Martindale, "Sociological Theory and the Ideal Type," in Llewellyn Gross (ed.), *Symposium on Sociological Theory* (Evanston, Ill.: Row, Peterson, 1959), pp. 57–91.

and adequate causation. An item to be included in an ideal type is acceptable only if it does not violate the existing scientific knowledge already in the possession of the researcher. The elements of a type must be, in this sense, "objectively possible." Furthermore, the whole purpose of the type is to isolate configurations of facts which have causal influence on the course of social events. The causal relevance of any single item can vary from zero to one hundred per cent. Any item included in a type is subject to the test of adequate causation: that is, it should be causally relevant to the result. For example, if we are studying the sociology of religion and if we find it expedient to set up types of religion, we ought to include as an item of a given religious type its theodicy only if theodicy is causally relevant to socio-religious behavior.

Once a type has been formulated — and no social or natural science is without them — it should permit us to compare various kinds of situations more precisely than we could without it. If the ideal type does not do this, it should be eliminated. Moreover, we do not play games with nature. We compare different empirical configurations, not empirical configurations and types. When a new level of understanding is gained, the type has done its work. Further understanding may then suggest the formation of new types. However, any single ideal type is destined to be scrapped.

Weber's Applied Sociology. One whole block of Weber's studies may perhaps best be described as applied sociology, or the employment of sociology for the purposes of understanding the historical world or solving problems that lie in the present.

It was Weber's view that Western capitalistic civilization is unique. It has properties not duplicated by any other civilization. One of the thematic elements holding all of Weber's sociological researches together was the problem of the nature, causes, and effects of *rationality* as one of the most fundamental respects in which our civilization is distinct.[4] Only in the West, for example, has science, the most rational mode of thought, become the norm of all thought. Although partial anticipations have appeared elsewhere, something was always lacking. Precise knowledge and refined observation appeared in India, China, Babylonia, and Egypt. But Babylonian astronomy lacks a mathematical foundation, Indian geometry lacks the rational proof, medicine was developed in India but without a biochemical foundation, and a rational chemistry was absent everywhere except in the West.

Fully developed historical scholarship appeared only in the West. China had no historical method like that of Thucydides. Indian political thought had no systematic method or rational concepts. Nor did a rational jurisprudence develop elsewhere as it did in the West under the influence of Roman law and a series of special economic and political conditions.

The contrast even extends to the arts. Musical sensitivity has been highly developed by other peoples. Polyphonic music is widely diffused over the

[4] See Weber's introduction to *The Protestant Ethic and the Spirit of Capitalism.*

earth. But the rational tone intervals, while calculated and known else-where, do not appear outside the West in systems of rational harmonious music in the forms of counterpoint and harmony with the formation of tone material on the basis of three triads with the harmonic third. Also peculiar to the West are chromatics and enharmonics interpreted in terms of harmony, the orchestra built around the string quartet, the system of notation, and a music possible only with print.

In architecture, only in the West had the pointed arch and cross-arched vault been rationally employed for distributing pressure and roofing many kinds of spaces. The arch has been employed as a constructive principle in great monumental buildings and made into the foundation of a style. This is parallel to the use of perspective as a rational device for representation in painting.

While printing appears in China, only in the West does a literature de-signed only for print appear. In the universities, meanwhile, the rational, systematic, and specialized pursuit of science is unique. The Western state is the only political association with a rational, written constitution, ration-ally ordered law, and a government bound by rational laws and administered by trained officials.

Capitalism, with its pursuit of profit by means of continuous, rational, capitalistic enterprise, is peculiar to the West. Capitalism is a form of eco-nomic action resting on expectation of profit by utilization of opportunities for exchange and formally peaceful chances for profit. Various elements of capitalism have appeared outside the West in many forms and places: capitalistic acquisition, with rational pursuit of profits resting on calculations in terms of capital; the conduct of activity in terms of balances with the ascertainment of profit and loss; the capitalistic entrepreneur. But the Occi-dent not only developed these to a greater quantitative extent but added numerous additional properties, such as the rational capitalistic organization of free labor, rational industrial organization attuned to a regular market, rational bookkeeping, legal separation of corporate and personal property, and the integration of science into its service.

An extensive number of Weber's studies in applied sociology had these problems in view. They include his studies of the agrarian history of the ancient world, the study of the condition of the worker in large-scale in-dustry, his study of trading companies in the Middle Ages, the decline of the ancient world, the agrarian problems of East Germany, the Protestant ethic and the psychology of capitalism, the rational and social foundations of music.

Weber's Pure or Theoretical Sociology. As in his applied sociology, in his pure sociology Weber had the neo-Kantian formalists and the neo-ideal-ists in mind. He borrowed something from each, and arrived at a unique formulation of his own. With the neo-Kantians, Weber was convinced that sociology required a precise formulation as a scientific discipline. With the idealists, he was convinced that the field must be defined in terms of content rather than forms. In contrast to the neo-Kantians, Weber insists that sociology must study not mere forms but *social action* itself. He agrees, however, that the unit of analysis, once determined, is subject to genuine scientific study by the same methods in all science. With the idealists, Weber agrees that sociology deals with "meanings," but he does not agree that these require a non-scientific procedure. Weber's own formulation brings both issues together. "Sociology (in the sense in which this highly ambiguous word is used here) is a science which attempts the interpretive understanding of social action in order thereby to arrive at a causal explanation of its course and effects." Like the idealist, one "interprets," but it is with the aim of arriving at causal knowledge, which the neo-Kantians had maintained to be essential to science. This appears again in the concept of action. "Action is social in so far as, by virtue of the subjective meaning attached to it by the acting individual (or individuals), it takes account of the behavior of others and is thereby oriented in its course." [5]

This is certainly unambiguous enough. Weber assumes that the subjectively intended meaning present in an action is a causal component of it. Sociology is concerned with action only so far as it possesses meanings. Such meanings may be of two types, either (1) the actually existing meaning in the concrete case or (2) a theoretically conceived pure type attributed to the hypothetical actors. Meaning does not necessarily refer to an objectively correct meaning or one true in a metaphysical sense. The meaning is the one held by actors in situations and not the meaning the situation may have to a scientist or a metaphysician. (Cooley's "ideas that people have of one another" and Thomas' "definitions of the situation" are parallel.)

Two fundamental questions about such meanings were of concern to Weber. First, one must recognize the fact that meaningful behavior blurs off into non-meaningful forms. Many types of traditional behavior are so habitual as to be almost meaningless. On the other hand, many magical experiences are so personal as hardly to be communicable. Weber perceived this problem as one for interpretation. To the degree that behavior is rational (in a logical or scientific sense or according to logical or scientific standards), it is understandable directly without further ado. Beyond this, empathic understanding (sympathetic understanding of behavior on the basis of one's own) is of great assistance in explaining conduct. One does not have to have been Caesar to understand Caesar. Empathic understanding, however, was not for Weber, as it was for the neo-idealists, the true method of cultural science; rather, he viewed the employment of sympathetic empathy, the "method of *Verstehen*," as only of secondary significance. Weber's actual procedure consisted primarily in the construction of typologies of behavior and the institution of comparative study on the basis of such typologies.

Weber's second question about meaning is of greater significance, for it

[5] *The Theory of Social and Economic Organization*, p. 88.

concerns the causal importance of meaning: to what extent does meaning cause conduct? One must recognize the existence of a range of experience in which meaning is variably present. To be devoid of meaning is not identical with being lifeless or non-human. An artifact like a machine can be understood only in terms of its meaning for human action. A thing is devoid of meaning only if it cannot be related to action in the role of means or ends. A category of facts devoid of meaning but important for explaining action includes various psychophysical phenomena such as fatigue, habit, euphoria, etc. Understanding may be of a direct type, as when we understand the meaning of a proposition such as two plus two equals four when we hear or read it, or it may be explanatory, as when we understand why an actor performs a given act in terms of his motive. Understanding in terms of motive consists in placing the act in a more inclusive context of activity, as when we understand a man's actions when he works on sheets of paper in making out his income tax. Furthermore, modern psychologists isolate types of behavior in which the motives are unconscious and not known to the actor.

The study of human behavior shows that meaning is only one of the causal components of action. In some behavior, meaning is prominent; in other behavior, meaning is at best only marginally present. Sometimes isolation of the meaningful element of conduct is difficult. The conscious motives may well conceal, even from the actor himself, the real motives which constitute the driving force of his action. Many life situations which appear superficially to be very similar must sometimes be understood or interpreted very differently in terms of the meanings involved.

In view of these facts, Weber maintains, *Verstehen* is never a complete method in itself. Verification of subjective interpretation by comparison with the concrete course of events is indispensable. Unfortunately, this type of verification is feasible with relative accuracy only in cases susceptible to psychological experimentation. The approaches to a satisfactory degree of accuracy are exceedingly various, even in the limited number of cases of mass phenomena which can be statistically described and unambiguously interpreted. For the rest, there remains only the possibility of comparing the largest possible number of historical or contemporary cases which, while otherwise similar, differ in the one decisive point of their relation to the particular motive or factor being investigated. Interpretation of behavior in terms of motives varies in degree. A motive is a complex of subjective meaning which seems to the actor himself or to the observer an adequate ground for the conduct in question. An adequate explanation of behavior on the level of meaning refers to the subjective interpretation of a course of conduct so far as, according to the habitual modes of thought and feeling of ordinary persons, it is satisfactorily explained. A correct causal interpretation of a concrete course of action is arrived at when the overt action and motives have both been correctly apprehended and at the same time their relation has become meaningfully comprehensible. An explanation of conduct in terms of everyday motives is "adequate on the level of meaning." It represents a common-sense explanation of conduct which may or may not coincide with the causally adequate explanation of conduct to which the sociologist or psychologist as scientist aspires.

Throughout his analyses Weber thus assumes that subjectively intended meaning is a causal component in conduct. This is his most general hypothesis. It includes all others. Weber carefully located sociology in terms of its concern with meaning. Comparative psychology is useful in distinguishing between mechanical and instinctive factors in conduct, on the one hand, and meanings, on the other. But while helpful in differentiating animal and human behavior, it is not sociology. Similarly, the proposals of the Austrian economist and sociologist Othmar Spann to investigate all social phenomena in terms of their objective purpose and function is treated as pre-sociological, for true sociology is concerned with subjectively intended meanings. So, too, for Weber, all analyses of non-meaningful uniformities such as Gresham's law are non-sociological. Specifically, sociology is concerned with social action (which also includes failure to act and passive acquiescence in action). Action is non-social if it is oriented solely to the behavior of inanimate objects. Subjective attitudes constitute social action only so far as they are oriented to the behavior of others. Thus, the crowd studies by Le Bon are largely outside the sphere of social action; they are "actions conditioned by crowds." Similarly, Tarde's imitations are at best borderline social actions. But throughout all analysis, sociology is never to be confused with history, for it is a generalizing science, seeking abstract concepts, and not simply the causal analysis and explanation of individual actions. Conscious interhuman behavior is the unwaveringly conceived object of study.

In his assumption that subjectively intended meanings are a causal component of conduct, Weber was by no means unique. Comparable assumptions are made by all other members of other branches of social behaviorism. Tarde thought the real causes of social regularities were "beliefs" and "desires," which were seen as the mainsprings of imitation. In his "will to believe," William James had insisted that a belief has consequences even if its truth is unknown. Thomas abstracted a socially relevant orientation from James's proposition in his insistence that one could not adequately account for social events except in terms of the "definitions of the situation" of the parties involved. Cooley had treated "the imaginations people have of one another" as the solid facts of society, and Mead sharply opposed the behaviorism of Watson on the grounds that it left out of account the role of "attitude" and "meaning." Thus, in assuming that meaning is a causal component of behavior, Weber shared a basic supposition with other representatives of social behaviorism. In fact, this assumption is one of the generally distinguishing properties of the school. Because he clarified the issue, Weber has often been singled out as somehow or other a pure subjectivist — a charge which is paralleled by the idea that Weber had no other idea of method than *Verstehen* or empathy. If Weber is objectionable on this score, so too is every other member of the social-behaviorist school.

The basic device by means of which Weber made the transition from social action to general social life was a typology of action. Action was classified into four types in terms of the arrangement of its inner conscious components. Action is *zweckrational* ("rationally purposeful") when it is addressed to a situation with a plurality of means and ends in which the actor is free to choose his means purely in terms of efficiency; action is *wertrational* ("rational in terms of values") when the means are chosen for their efficiency but the ends are fixed in advance; action is *affective* when emotional factors determine the means and ends of action; and action is *traditional* when both means and ends are fixed by custom.

It is perhaps unfortunate that Weber chose to express his basic analysis of meaningful action in the form of a typology. A meaning is a consciously perceived relation between means and ends. Such a meaning may be organized in a number of ways: by efficiency, by advance fixing of the ends and means (as in religiously correct goals and religiously proper means to reach them), by the presence of emotion, or by the determination of tradition and custom. However, though tending to obscure his analytical framework, Weber's action typology is of tremendous importance for another reason. Weber was strongly nominalistic. To him, only individuals and individual actions exist. Any regularities in interhuman conduct represent no more than the stabilization of behavior in terms of rationality, ethical fixity, emotionality, or habit. To be sure, behavior will always display an admixture, for people are not merely rational or emotional; they are both, and the question is often one of determining which will be paramount. But only individual acts exist; there are no new super-individual entities. A *way* of acting is not a new *thing*.

Some of the most theoretically exciting problems of Weber's sociology were buried in his typology. It is evident that the various different ways of stabilizing or regularizing meaningful conduct are in tension. Rationalization can make its way, often, only by breaking down traditional patterns of conduct; a fixity of ends may promote a vast rationalization within some areas of life (as the Protestant sects promoted the rational psychology of capitalism); affective behavior almost always yields the social field to other types of action, becoming generally relevant only during mob actions and periods of revolution. The possible tension between these different modes of stabilizing meaningful action compare to the tension between Bagehot's "cake of custom" and the agitational and disrupting influences of modern science and war; between Tarde's imitation and disrupting innovations; between Sumner's stabilizing folkways and mores and innovating incidents; between W. I. Thomas' habitual solutions to social problems and crises. Throughout Weber's empirical studies there is an amazing array of empirical judgments concerning just what did or did not, in the given case, stabilize conduct on a rational, ethical, affective, or traditional model. Undoubtedly had he lived to carry out the program of a pure sociology, the analysis of issues such as those just raised would have been one of the most fundamental of his theoretical problems.

The next major theoretical step in Weber's sociology was the introduction of the concept of *social relation*. This is the fundamental concept for making the transition from individual acts to patterns of behavior. It is the critical concept by which one moves eventually from social action either to the social person or to social groups, institutions, and communities.

The concept "social relationship" is used to denote the behavior of a plurality of actors insofar as, in its meaningful content, the action of each takes account of that of the others and is oriented by this. The social relationship consists in the existence of a probability that there will be, in some meaningfully understandable sense, a course of social action. There must be a minimum of mutual orientation of action, though the content of action be most varied. The meaning involved is either the actual one or of a theoretically conceived pure type. The meaning need not be the same for all parties. The social relationship may be temporary or permanent. The moment there is no longer a chance that certain kinds of behaviors will occur, no "relation" can be said to exist. By "the United States government" we mean that some people act in certain ways. We need not reify this action. If people did not act this way, there would be no United States. Weber needed the concept of social relation to account for the recurrence of social action. For example, A dominates B, who is subordinate to A. This action of domination and subordination may occur between A and B in many different areas of their lives on many occasions. For analytical convenience, we may wish to isolate the arrangement or form of the action without reference to the varied occasions and content of the social actions between A and B. We "abstract" this arrangement and with a new economy of thought say that a dominance–subordination relation holds between A and B. Weber needed the concept of social relationship in order to make the transition from his concept of social action to that of social structure.

Just as from his concept of social action Weber turned to a typology of social actions resting on empirically observed regularities, so he turned directly from his concept of social relationship to categories of empirical uniformities in social practice. He distinguished: (1) usage — an actual uniformity of social relations; (2) custom — usage resting on long familiarity or habit; (3) rational usage — when the uniformity is determined by the rational actions of actors under similar conditions; (4) fashion — a usage determined by the presence of novelty in the corresponding behavior; (5) convention — usage springing from desires for social prestige, usage determined by normative patterns; and (6) law — usage determined by the presence of designated enforcing authorities. These are empirically observed categories of social relations.

Weber's concept of social relationship and his distinctions between empirical uniformities of social relationship were used in defining a "legitimate order," an added notion required to isolate the group. Action involving social relationships may be oriented by the actors to a belief (*Vorstellung*) in the existence of a "legitimate order." The probability that action will be so oriented is called the "validity" (*Geltung*) of the order in question. The legitimacy of such an order may be guaranteed from disinterested motives, for emotional reasons, because of rational belief in the absolute validity of the order as an expression of ultimate values, for religious reasons, or because of self-interest. Such a system of order is conventional if it is guaranteed by the fact that deviation will result in relatively general and significant reactions of disapproval. Such an order is called *law* when conformity is upheld by sanction of physical means in the hands of men designated to perform the function. The idea of legitimate order is needed to account for patterns of social relationship of an extensive sort. "Validity" of such an order is the probability of its being upheld. As in Weber's definition of social relationship, this is a sop to his fear of reification. Basically important is the manner in which the order is upheld — whether by moral disapproval (convention) or by legally constituted authorities (law). A significant feature of the analysis of legitimate orders is the way that it ties in with the problem of meaning. The bases of legitimacy of an order are said to lie in tradition, rational belief in an absolute value, emotional certainty, or its establishment in a manner accepted as legal.

Having developed the case for extensive systems of social relations as integrated in conventional and legal orders, Weber turned to specific problems of social relationship such as conflict and solidarity and open and closed relationships, all of which are critically important for understanding the organized group. A social relationship is treated as conflicting so far as the action embodying it is determined by the intention of carrying the actor's will against the opposition of others. Conflicting relationships vary from relatively peaceable forms like competition (formally peaceful attempts to gain control over opportunities desired by others) to bloody forms of conflict. Social relationships are communal so far as the orientation of action is based on the subjective feeling of the parties that they belong together. This kind of relationship varies from relatively rational associations (market exchange) to communal relationships of great intensity. Social relationships, whether communal or associative, are open to outsiders to the degree that, in terms of the subjective meaning, the social action relevant to the order is available to them. There are many degrees of openness and closure.

It has been noted that no theoretical bridge has been provided explicitly by Weber between the concepts of legitimate order and conflicting, solidary, open, and closed relationship. The discussion of these four kinds of relationship presupposes the operation of legitimate orders. Thus, generally, it may be supposed that conflict and solidarity represent subsidiary forms of social relation occurring within the framework of conventional and legal orders. A competitive social relationship, for example, represents a regulated conflict. The regulation is provided either by a conventional or a legal order.

With the substructuring of social relationships and their formation into solidary systems with comparative closure, the problems of representation and responsibility become crucial. And these ideas form the final transition for Weber to the concept of the *corporate group* and its types. A social relationship which is either closed or limits the admission of outsiders by rules, is a "corporate group" (*Verband*) so far as its order is enforced by the action of specific individuals whose regular function this is, i.e., a chief or head (*Leiter*) and usually also an administrative staff. Corporate groups may be self-governing or subject to the law of other groups. The types of order in corporate groups may be established by voluntary agreement or by imposition and acquiescence. The systems of order governing action in corporate groups may be administrative or regulative. The types of organization of corporate groups, including the voluntary association and compulsory association, are organizations of power and imperative control.

Just as in Weber's thought the transition is made from social action to the far reaches of social structure, so there are transitions from social action to the characteristics of culture, social change, and socially relevant forms of individually manifest behaviors ("callings"). In this case, a complex block of social changes characteristic of modern Western culture are traced to a transformed subjective interpretation of the meaning of everyday action.

The concept of "calling" or "vocation" served Weber in the same manner that the concept of "role" served symbolic interactionism — as the point of contact between personality structure and social structure. Vocation represents a peculiar accentuation and development of individual abilities relevant to social structure in a specific way. Two of Weber's most brilliant studies of social roles are his "Politics as a Vocation" and "Science as a Vocation." [6]

Weber found it fruitful to analyze a vocation (role): (1) historically; (2) distributively and statistically — and in terms of its integration with other social roles and the sources of recruitment into it; and (3) intrinsically, in terms of the inner psychological requirements of the role itself.

Scattered throughout Weber's work are many other studies of social roles. Such was his study of the Brahman, the Chinese literati, the Junker, and the scriptural prophet. However, this is only part of the story. Weber's analysis moves as easily and challengingly in the field of social structure as in the area of the formation of the social person. The more purely sociological studies occur in the course of his studies in three great subdisciplines of sociology that trace their contemporary forms primarily to him — the sociology of religion, political sociology, and the sociology of law.

Weber's political sociology contains some of his most interesting analyses of social structure and change. His discussion of the legitimation of power

---

[6] Both of these were originally speeches delivered at Munich University in 1918. They appear in *From Max Weber: Essays in Sociology*, pp. 127–156.

belongs here. He developed a typology paralleling the fundamental modes
of stabilizing social action. Power may be legitimized *rationally*, on the
basis of the belief in the legality of the rules; it may be legitimized
charismatically, when it is thought to rest on the magical or other personal
properties of an individual; or it may be legitimized *traditionally*, claiming
to rest on immemorial custom. The forms of legitimation of authority may
be further subdivided in various ways which are critical for the discrimination of various kinds of states and other structures of power.

Various modes of administration also are possible. Of particular interest
among them was Weber's study of bureaucracy. Modern officialdom rests
on the principle of fixed official jurisdictional areas ordered by rules, laws,
or regulations. Authority to give commands is distributed in a stable manner,
delimited in terms of the rules affecting the means placed at the disposal
of officials. Methodical provision is made for the regular and continuous
fulfillment of these duties and the exercise of the corresponding rights.
Generally only persons with proper qualifications are employed. The bureaucratic type of administration, articulated in such terms, is critically
important to all modern types of large-scale social structure: the modern
state, ecclesiastical institutions, great banks and other large commercial
enterprises, even modern hospitals and labor unions.

To the area of political sociology also belong Weber's studies of class,
status, and party. *Class* was defined objectively in economic terms by
Weber as consisting of a plurality of persons sharing a common component
in their life chances, consisting of opportunities for the possession of
goods and income as represented by the conditions of the commodity and
labor markets. Multiple forms of class organization, class consciousness,
and class action, as well as class struggle, are possible in terms of this
economic component in people's life chances. Weber defined *status groups*,
by contrast, as communities consisting in a plurality of persons whose life
fate is determined by a specific positive or negative social estimation of
honor. Status honor is normally expressed in a style of life expected of all
those belonging to the circle. It is decisively manifest in the sharing of table
and marriage community but it may organize and distribute a great
range of items of deportment. Among the most significant of events in
modern social life is the interplay of class and status. *Caste* was treated
by Weber, in terms strongly suggesting the extension of the brilliant discussion by Bouglé, as a ritualistically closed, magically tabooed class and
status situation in which the entire community is sealed into mutually antagonistic endogamously closed groups, the ranks of which are determined
by social distance from the Brahman caste. *Parties* were treated as plural-
ities organized purely for the acquisition of power. Parties may exist in a
social club as well as a state. As against the actions of classes and status
groups (which tend to traditionalize conduct), the actions of parties always
mean a societalization (a tendency toward the rationalization of social action). Party actions are always directed toward a goal in a planned

manner. Parties may represent interests determined through class or status position and they may recruit their following from one or the other (although they need not be exclusively recruited from one or the other). They may represent ephemeral or enduring structures. Their means of attaining power may be varied, ranging from the use of outright violence to bribery or canvassing for votes.

Also belonging in considerable measure to Weber's political sociology was his theory of *social change*, though, to be sure, it was much broader than this. Social change finds its point of focus in the conflict of three general principles: traditionalism, rationality, and charisma. Much of the evolution of human social structures has been played out in terms of the tension between traditionalization and the disruptive influence of rationalization. But both of these principles have frequently appeared in tension with the charismatic principle — the following of some individual because of his presumed magical or supernatural or other purely personal properties and powers (Jesus, Buddha, Confucius, Alexander the Great, Napoleon, Joseph Smith, Hitler). Charisma, in turn, by its highly personal nature must be transformed (routinized) into a rational or traditional form if the movement and structures it establishes are not to perish.

In the opinion of some sociologists, Max Weber was the greatest social scientist of the first half of the twentieth century. Certainly Weber formed the starting point for the careers of many major contemporary sociologists; among leading social scientists who took their point of departure in considerable measure from Weber are Karl Mannheim, Hans Speier, Hans Gerth, Talcott Parsons, Robert Merton, C. Wright Mills. There have been many others. A full appreciation of the richness of Weber's work can be gained only through a knowledge of his empirical studies, in which the theoretical and methodological concepts described here were combined with a truly extraordinary scholarship to bring historical data into a new and sharper focus.* Many of the significant trends in contemporary social science are continuations of work begun by Max Weber. Among these are stratification theory, the study of bueaucracy and large-scale organization, the study of legitimate authority, the sociology of law, the sociology of politics, the sociology of religion, and the sociology of music.

Thorstein Veblen

Thorstein B. Veblen (1857–1929) quite independently developed some aspects of a social-action theory. Veblen was born in Wisconsin and graduated from Carleton College in 1880. He studied at Johns Hopkins and at Yale and Cornell universities. In 1893, he was appointed reader in political economy at the University of Chicago, becoming instructor and assistant

---

* Appearing since this account was completed is Reinhard Bendix's *Max Weber: An Intellectual Portrait* (Garden City, N.Y.: Doubleday, 1960). Since it contains simplified paraphrases of many of Weber's works, it should make an ideal introduction to Weber for undergraduates.

professor. He was associate professor of economics at Stanford University from 1906 to 1909, lecturer in economics at the University of Missouri from 1911 to 1918, and lecturer in the New School for Social Research beginning in 1918. For ten years he was managing editor of *The Journal of Political Economy*. He died at Menlo Park, California, August 3, 1929.[7]

Veblen's approach to social-action theory was anchored in his peculiar cultural and intellectual interests. Born the son of Norwegian immigrants in a Wisconsin farm community, he was brought up in an atmosphere where the Norwegian language, religious organization, and social customs prevailed — in tension with the Americanizing influences of town and city. There was also tension between the midwestern farmers and eastern capitalists. His early reading was dominated by Herbert Spencer, but his interests were broad and he was also influenced by Hume, Kant, and the nineteenth-century idealists. When he studied classical economics, he brought to the study a special grouping of interests. The formal framework for Veblen's thought was provided by the evolutionary hypothesis, which he seems to have derived originally from Spencer. Unlike Spencer, he was critically oriented toward current economic activity — a position which is understandable in the light of his cultural background. He was also critically oriented toward classical economic theory, which he held responsible for economic tensions. The general project carried through all Veblen's works was an evolutionary presentation and institutional criticism of the existing economic system and its sustaining theories.

Just as Veblen subscribed to an evolutionary construction for his developmental studies, he subscribed to an instinct theory in his analysis of behavior. Men are assumed to be moved by an instinct for practical efficiency and by the desire to emulate and surpass. But neither evolutionism nor instinct theory touches the real basis of Veblen's thought, for one can dispense with both and still say everything he wished to say.

Veblen actually held a type of social-action theory. The units into which his analysis ultimately resolves are inter-individual actions. These actions embody human purposes, intentions, and aims. There are, for Veblen, two fundamental types: predatory and constructive. Veblen's concept of social action was not as rich as Weber's: his types were not complete and somewhat different, but he approached analysis the same way and applied his analysis to the same kinds of problems.

Weber wished to explain the tremendous growth of rationality in all spheres of Occidental life. Rationality, particularly scientific rationality,

7 Thorstein Veblen's works with major sociological import are: *The Theory of the Leisure Class* (New York: Macmillan, 1899) ; *The Theory of Business Enterprise* (New York: Scribner's, 1904); *The Instinct of Workmanship* (New York: Macmillan, 1914); *Imperial Germany and the Industrial Revolution* (New York: Macmillan, 1915) ; *The Higher Learning in America* (New York: B. W. Huebsch, 1918) ; *The Place of Science in Modern Civilization* (New York: B. W. Huebsch, 1919) ; *The Engineers and the Price System* (New York: B. W. Huebsch, 1921) ; *Absentee Ownership and Business Enterprise in Recent Times* (New York: B. W. Huebsch, 1923) ; and the posthumously published *Essays in Our Changing Order*, edited by Leon Ardzrooni (New York: Viking, 1934).

was of central interest to Veblen. Weber, in his interest in the reconstruction of economic theory on more adequate grounds, reviewed the traditional concept of social classes, examined the factors frustrating full achievement of rationality, and investigated the interrelations among institutions. All these problems were of concern to Veblen as well. Both thinkers were suspicious of all tendencies to reify abstractions. Both wished to promote a value-free science.

In Veblen's view, man's nature is developed by selective necessity. In man's own apprehension, he is a center of impulsive teleological activity. In every act, he seeks the accomplishment of some specific end. Thus, by nature, man has a taste for effective work and a distaste for useless effort. Action is guided by a sense of merit, serviceability, or efficiency, and a sense of the demerit in futility, waste, and incapacity. This attitude or propensity is called the *instinct of workmanship*. Wherever comparison of persons with respect to efficiency occurs, the instinct of workmanship issues into an emulative comparison of persons. The extent to which this occurs is related to the temperament of the population. Where such a comparison is habitual, visible success becomes an end sought for its own utility and as a basis for esteem. Esteem is gained and dispraise is avoided by making one's efficiency manifest. The result is that the instinct of workmanship works out in an emulative demonstration of force. So far as tangible evidence of prowess such as trophies finds a place in men's habits of thought as an essential feature of the paraphernalia of life, aggression may in fact become the accredited form of action. Booty may serve as *prima facie* evidence of success. An invidious distinction arises then between exploit and acquisition, on the one hand, and industrial employment, on the other. Labor then acquires a character of irksomeness by virtue of the indignity imputed to it.[8]

A surprising number of the basic elements of social-action theory are contained here. Veblen's "instinct of workmanship" corresponds with Weber's *zweckrational* (rational-purposeful) type of social action. Although Weber locates tension between rational and both affective and traditional types of action while Veblen locates it between the instinct of workmanship and the instinct of aggression, the differences are more apparent than real. Even though he does not formally incorporate it into his theories, Veblen looked upon the instinct of efficiency as the great rationalizer in human affairs, disrupting traditional and outmoded solutions to problems of all sorts. Similarly, while Weber did not isolate "aggressive social action" as one of his types (it is contained by implication in others), one of the problems of constant interest to him was the multiple points of intersection between the two ways of making a living: peaceable, by economic activities; or exploitative, by politics and war. Veblen's suggestion that rationalizing social actions (the instinct of workmanship) find some social environments

---

[8] For Veblen's own summary of these views, see his introduction to *The Theory of the Leisure Class.*

more favorable than others compares in some measure to Weber's discussion of the social atmosphere produced by inner-worldly ascetic Protestantism. (Veblen, incidentally, like Weber himself, was in some measure a product of the Protestant ethic). Similarly the interplay between life styles of status groups (Veblen's "invidious distinctions") and class and party was a common problem for both men.

According to Veblen, the emergence of a leisure class coincided with the beginnings of ownership. The earliest form of ownership was that of women by the able-bodied men in the community and began with the seizure of female captives in the cultural stage of lower barbarism. The extension of the practice led to slavery. Ownership of women in turn was extended to ownership of the products of their industry, an ownership of things as well as people. While the normal aim of acquisition and accumulation was consumption of the goods acquired, a new aim now appeared — ownership for reasons of emulation. Ownership is transformed into an institution unrelated to subsistence, and the incentive becomes invidious — to secure the distinctions attaching to wealth. Wealth has now become intrinsically honorable, conferring honor on its possessor. It is imposed upon people whether they will or no, for only individuals with aberrant temperaments can maintain their self-esteem in the long run when faced with the disesteem of their fellows. Thus, when possession of property becomes the basis of popular esteem, it becomes a prerequisite of complacency or self-respect. The end sought by accumulation is to rank high in pecuniary strength in comparison with the rest of the community. In the nature of the case, the desire for wealth can hardly be satisfied in the individual instance.[9] Furthermore, wealth also confers power, which becomes another motive for accumulation. Relative success is tested by an invidious pecuniary comparison with other men as the conventional goal of action.

If undisturbed by other elements, even this pecuniary struggle would tend to make men industrious and frugal. Where men live by their labor — at least among the lower classes — they take emulative pride in a reputation for efficiency in work. Things tend to be otherwise in the superior pecuniary class, which, while also having incentives to diligence and thrift, find their action overshadowed by pure demands of pecuniary emulation. Wealth and power must be put in evidence, for esteem is awarded only on the basis of evidence.

One of the most direct ways of proving one's wealth and power is by conspicuous display of leisure. It becomes the conventional mark of superior pecuniary achievement and the conventional index of reputability. In theory, at least, the leisure class has existed from the beginning of predatory

9 Veblen assumes that the desire for wealth, like other socially reconstructed drives, has no "natural" limits. The desires for food and for sex satisfaction have built-in limits at the point of physiological satiation. At this point, still more food or sexual activity may not only cease to be utilities, but they may become positive disutilities. However, the desire for wealth has no built-in satiation point, and it may become more inflamed the more it is appeased.

culture. Taking on new and fuller meaning with each stage of pecuniary culture, it early assumed the form of conspicuous exemption from all useful employment. Government and war as predatory activities became the monopoly of the leisure class. These activities reveal the nature of the leisure class most characteristically, for they are the precise opposite of gainful industry. The chase and sport are the pure exercise of the predatory impulse; they are typical. Abstention from labor is honorific and meritorious, the prerequisite of decency. Labor becomes disreputable in the eyes of the community, morally impossible to the noble and incompatible with a worthy life.

Around the leisured class a secondary, pseudo-leisured class appears, abjectly poor, living a life of precarious want and discomfort but morally unable to stoop to gainful pursuit — the decayed gentleman and lady who have "seen better days."

Meanwhile, "leisure" connotes the non-productive consumption of time. A whole cluster of symbols advertise the leisure class: trophies, systems of rank, titles, degrees and insignia, heraldic devices, medals, and honorary decoration. The criteria of past performances of leisure take the form of quasi-scholarly accomplishments and a knowledge of processes and incidents not conducive to furtherance of human life — knowledge of dead languages; occult science; correct spelling, syntax, and prosody; the forms of domestic music, equipage, of games, sports and fancy bred horses.

One incidental function of manners is the demonstration of the amount of time spent in learning them. Manners are symbolic and conventionalized survivals representing former acts of dominance or personal service expressive of status relations. In the last analysis, manners are vouchers of a life of leisure. Refined tastes, manners, habits of life are useful evidence of gentility, for good breeding requires time, application, and expenses and cannot be compassed by those whose time and energy are taken up with work. The conspicuous leisure which is made manifest in decorum grows into a laborious drill in deportment and an education in taste and discrimination.

The development of the concept of the leisure class formed the central object of Veblen's early work. But having once established its central property, he proceeded to trace its manifestations through practically every area of life. Thus, for example, the leisure class manifests itself through endless variants of conspicuous consumption. The noble becomes a connoisseur of creditable viands of various degrees of merit, of manly beverages and trinkets, of seemly apparel and architecture, of weapons, games, dancers, and narcotics, of all objects addressed to a cultivated aesthetic faculty. High-bred manners and ways of living are items in conformity with the norm of conspicuous leisure and consumption. A pecuniary standard of taste comes to dominate all features of life to a point where the domestic life of most classes is relatively shabby compared to the éclat of the portion of their lives carried on before the eyes of others. People tend to screen their private lives from observation. They lower the birth rate of the class to meet the requirements of reputable expenditure. A lowered birth rate is one of the prices of a standard of living resting on conspicuous waste. The high standards of pecuniary decency among the superior classes is transmitted to the scholarly classes, which as a result spends a large proportion of its substance in conspicuous waste. The resulting pecuniary canons of taste are everywhere evident. Prescriptive expensiveness is manifest even in objects not observable to outsiders, such as articles of underclothing, some articles of food, kitchen utensils, and household apparatus one would expect to be designed for service rather than evidence. The canons of expensiveness have penetrated the deepest levels of taste. In the end, a beautiful object which is not expensive is not accounted beautiful. Veblen maintains that the standards of the leisure class penetrate the very structure of higher learning itself to such a degree that many of its peculiar features are traceable to the leisure-class scheme of life.

If money-making is accepted as the criterion of success, then the more successful the technology, the more it becomes possible for the processes of invidious comparisons and conspicuous consumption to operate. But the significance of money-making goes further; this was merely the starting point of Veblen's thought. Money-making also leads to the cultivation of a type of rationality epitomized in modern accounting. It leads to a peculiar psychology and philosophy of human behavior. The classical economists, in Veblen's view, were nothing more than formulators of a money-determined philosophy of behavior; they were led to ignore other institutional factors. Money-making promotes and obstructs the process of making a living. It leads to the production of raw materials, their transformation into usable goods, their transport and distribution. It leads, as well, to a series of bargains, in which each individual seeks to take as much as he can for himself from others.

Industrial efficiency requires division of labor and exchange. The capitalistic economy is the most productive men have so far designed. Its devices, such as business accounting, are adequate to its needs. Industry requires capital and credit, the capitalist and banker. The recurrent crises and depressions which reduce the flow of goods are due to business rather than industry; there are no technological reasons for them. Business enterprises are run for profit rather than for need, and the alternation of prosperity and depression are the result.

Thus, the theme of the tension between the instinct of workmanship and the consequences of pecuniary emulation is expanded by Veblen into the contrast between the productive and predatory aspects of modern capitalism — the productiveness of industry and the predatory modes of procedure of business and finance. The phenomena of industrial crisis and depression are treated in terms of the interrelation between the predatory and productive phases of economy. These are the main themes of *The Theory of Business Enterprise* (1904).

Veblen's *The Instinct of Workmanship* (1914) represents his fullest treatment of the positive elements in his thought. Man's most profound impulse, his instinct of workmanship, is to create rather then to destroy. The most significant of all aspects of human civilization has been the development of technology from the New Stone Age to modern machine industry. Technology is the manifestation of the instinct of workmanship.

Veblen's concept of technology led him toward a form of technocracy. Even by training, businessmen are incapable of understanding the engineers. Technology becomes increasingly a matter of applied science. The graduates of engineering schools know how to make things, organize production, increase output. Less and less are businessmen even able to talk their language. The engineers talk in terms of physical science, business men in terms of natural rights and ownership. The engineers cannot understand why pecuniary interests should curtail production. Veblen saw the task of modern society to be one of setting the engineers free in a process that will create a new system of institutions.

Veblen is significant in a number of respects. In the first place, it is important to clear up the curious contradiction in treating Veblen as one of the most creative minds produced by twentieth-century America and at the same time providing neither a clear institutional nor a clear theoretical place for him. From the beginning, Veblen's economics was more than an analysis of economic phenomena; it comprehended higher learning, science and civilization, political economy, and stratification. Even his interests in economic phenomena included many issues that fell outside the sphere of traditional economics. He tended to be classified as an economist by the sociologists and as a sociologist by the economists. His proper field, it appears, is sociology; it is high time sociologists claimed him for their own.

The reason why Veblen's theoretical importance tended to be obscured was the general sociological rather than specifically economic nature of his theories. Economists thought of his work as tangential to the main business of economics. And as long as sociologists have treated him as an economist, they have not — and frequently still do not — look at Veblen's work as a type of sociological theory. Hence, one of America's most original theorists is at times denied recognition as a theorist. However, as the preceding review has tried to show, Veblen was developing a form of social-action theory which in many points bears comparison with that of Max Weber. This is particularly interesting inasmuch as the framing of social-action theory by Weber in Germany and by Veblen and other institutional economists in America was going on independently. Similar solutions to similar problems were being elaborated in different parts of the Western world.

John R. Commons

John Rogers Commons (1862–1945) illustrates the emergence of social-action theory in still another form. Born in Hollandsburg, Ohio, he studied at Oberlin College and Johns Hopkins, later teaching at Wesleyan University, Oberlin, the University of Indiana, Syracuse University, and the University of Wisconsin. He did basic work in value and distribution, the history of economic thought, public utilities, immigration, housing, labor legislation, social insurance, trade unionism, industrial government, labor history, monopoly prices, index numbers, business cycles, tariffs, civil service and administration, municipal government, and proportional representation. He worked with and for a variety of public bodies and foundations. With Richard T. Ely, who brought him to the University of Wisconsin in 1904, he prepared the *Documentary History of American Industry* (1909–11) in eleven volumes; the two men can be said to have created the field of American labor history.[10]

Social-action theory seems to have been a logical step for persons who were both impressed by and at the same time critical of classical economics. Among the most obvious characteristics of the classical theory of capitalism were: its conceptualization of economic phenomena in terms of rational individual behavior; its opposition to the reification of patterns of economic action and to reification generally (the classical economists persistently opposed treating the state as an entity above and superior to men, insisting on treating it as the ways men act); its interpretation of economic activity primarily from the standpoint of production and the market (these being the spheres in which rationalization is carried through).

If one accepts the general analysis of economic life in terms of these ideas and at the same time is critically oriented toward it, there are definite lines along which such opposition tends to develop. One may accept the idea that rational individual action is significant but explore the economic relevance of various types of non-rational economic behavior as well. One may go along with the classical economists in their reluctance to reify patterns of individual action but complete the study and modify the classical economic picture by a fuller analysis of non-economic social actions. One may accept the idea that technological, productive, and exchange institutions are important but also explore economic and social factors represented by consumption processes. This is precisely what seems to have happened in the studies of the institutional economists, including Weber. They accept the concept of rational social action as a starting point but expand the concept of social action to include non-rational types. They are reluctant to reify institutions but still examine other than economic relational complexes. Accepting the importance of production, they examine the influences of consumption and non-economic processes as well.

[10] Commons' most original works containing his general sociological as well as specifically economic theories are: *Races and Immigrants in America* (New York: Macmillan, 1907); *History of Labor in the United States*, by Commons and others, 4 vols. (New York: Macmillan, 1918–35); *Industrial Government* (New York: Macmillan, 1921); *The Legal Foundations of Capitalism* (New York: Macmillan, 1924); *Institutional Economics: Its Place in Political Economy* (New York: Macmillan, 1934); and the posthumously published *The Economics of Collective Action*, with a biographical sketch by Selig Perlman, manuscript edited, introduction, and supplementary essay by Kenneth H. Parsons (New York: Macmillan, 1950).

It is interesting to note the parallel between the American institutional economists and Max Weber in this respect. The classical economic concept of "capitalism" was reduced by Weber to an ideal type. To rational social action, he added a number of additional types. He explored the bearing of religion, politics, and other institutional complexes on the economic. He added the idea of status group (a consumption-oriented stratum) to class (a market-based stratum). He examined the interrelations between economy and law. Weber, of course, was trained in law and economics.

Veblen, as has been noted, developed a social-action theory out of classical economics, pragmatism, and neo-idealism. His most influential teacher at Carleton had been the classical economic theorist John Bates Clark. Some things taken from classical economics were always retained by Veblen — his admiration for scientific technology, production, and the manifestations of rational social action based on the instinct of workmanship. For Veblen this was the basic constructive force of human society. But Veblen modified the concept of action of classical economics by locating, along with rational social action, actions resting on emulation. Countering the productive forces are those predatory modes of achieving power which rest on exploitation. Modifying the constructive effects of scientific technology are the destructive effects of the conspicuous consumption patterns of the leisure class. Veblen's starting point is parallel to Weber's and he rises to his concept of the leisure class by a process not unlike those leading to Weber's concept of status group.

There is no need to multiply examples, but it is relevant to note that a close affinity exists between social behaviorism generally and institutional economic analysis. Tarde was anchored not in the social-action but suggestion–imitation school. Nevertheless, when he turned to economic phenomena, he tended to develop some economic interpretations quite parallel to those of the institutionalists. Tarde's invention and imitation could, on occasion, operate somewhat like Weber's contrast between rational and traditional social actions. The total patterns of economy, for Tarde, were determined by the properties of the epochs of custom or fashion imitation. Moreover, in the nature of the case, Tarde's principle of imitation brought consumption patterns more completely under analysis than was true for the classical economists.

John R. Commons also expanded into fields outside the classical economic framework and rose theoretically to a general theory of social action. Commons' opposition to reification is evident in his very definition of economic institutions as "collective action in control of individual action." Characteristically, the actions of working men became as important as the establishment of capitalistic structures. He observed them forming trade unions, cooperative buying clubs, cooperative workshops. His attitude toward the workers is stated compactly by Selig Perlman: "As self-determining beings, the workers and their movements were to set their *own* objectives, their *own* values, and were entitled to claim from the intellectuals expert aid in the road they should take to attain the goals set by leaders risen in their midst." [11] The degree to which Commons subscribed fundamentally to a social-action theory is brought out by Kenneth Parsons: "Commons devoted his life to devising and using methods of investigation and understanding which explicitly recognize that human activity is volitional." [12]

Commons conceived social life as based on judgments and actions of persons. Social events rest upon the human will, individually and collectively. Critically central is his conception of social relationships. He proceeded from a postulate of the economy as a social organization, rather than as a mechanism or organism. As a social organization, the economy is the way participants act. Organization is achieved through the stabilization and regularization of activity. Activity is regularized or controlled in a society of citizens (persons with legally recognized wills of their own) by the working rules which define the limits within which individuals may exercise their own wills.

Individuals are not self-sufficient, independent entities; they are what they are through their participation in the institutions or going concerns of which they are members. Commons noted the way in which membership in labor unions lifted workers from a level of fear and servility to a new dignity, commensurate with the rights of economic citizenship, and he formulated his conception of an institution as "collective action in control, liberation, and expansion of individual action."

Although Commons ended up with the main essentials of a general theory of social action, he did not arrive at them all at once. Shortly after going to Wisconsin in 1905, he was called in by the state to study the problem of industrial accidents. Working conditions were hazardous and legal liability for accidents followed the common-law rule of negligence. Where accidents were held by the courts to be due to corporation negligence, the usual recourse for the police and courts was to arrest and often imprison the foreman or superintendent. The persons of the stockholders were beyond the reach of the law. Relations between industry and labor were particularly bitter over these affairs. Commons proposed the elimination of criminal prosecutions for accident liability and the substitution of accident compensation commensurate with the injury as a penalty on the company. He also helped employers form their own mutual insurance company, by which the benefits of safe employment would accrue to the employers responsible for safety improvements. The insight gained in helping draft a public utility law for Wisconsin about 1910 led Commons to a study of the economic principles followed by the courts. The result was *The Legal Foundations of Capitalism* (1924). Here again the parallel with Weber is direct, for Weber was led in somewhat similar manner to a study of law and his work on a sociology of law.

The understanding of economic action could not be complete without an

[11] *The Economics of Collective Action*, p. 3.
[12] *Ibid.*, p. 13.

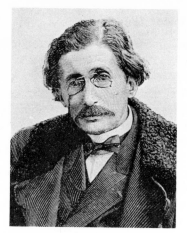

Gabriel Tarde

Gustave Le Bon

James Mark Baldwin

Charles Horton Cooley

Franklin H. Giddings

Meyer F. Nimkoff

William F. Ogburn

F. Stuart Chapin

William James

George H. Mead

W. I. Thomas

Jean Piaget

Ernst Cassirer

C. Wright Mills

Hans Gerth

William H. Whyte, Jr.

David Riesman

Max Weber

Thorstein Veblen

John R. Commons

Robert MacIver

Karl Mannheim

understanding of its ties with legal action. Commons observed that out of economic transactions come practices which serve as guides to the courts in their resolution of economic conflicts brought to it.

> A transaction occurs at a point of time. But transactions flow one into another over a period of time, and this flow is a process. The courts have fully developed the notion of this process in the concept of a "going concern," which they have taken over from the customs of business and which is none other than a technological process of production and consumption of physical things and a business process of buying and selling, borrowing and lending, commanding and obeying, according to shop rules or working rules or laws of the land.[13]

Commons was led to the concept of economic and legal activity as forming an interrelated working whole. He formulated a theory of the interrelations between group customs and the common law, of the rise of new social classes, and of their struggle for recognition. He showed how in the struggle around the "rent bargain," the English barons had reduced the King of England from theoretical owner to a mere recipient of a land tax fixed by collective bargaining between their representatives and his. Similarly, through their participation in the piepowder courts at the fairs, English merchants were able to impose the customs of their group upon the presiding judges. From this beginning, in a process extending over several centuries through judges increasingly appreciative of the growing importance of the merchants of the Commonwealth and through a continuous custom-making, adapted to changing conditions, by that merchant class, came the law merchant. The unremitting activity of the merchant class, the willingness of the judges to absorb pressures from below, and ultimately a judicial sifting of these merchant customs and the selective acceptance of some of them finally resulted in the incorporation of the law merchant in the common law. The basic mechanism by which this was accomplished was the expansion of the meaning of *property* from the mere physical object to embrace the incorporeal and the intangible forms.

By 1924, Commons had worked beyond the traditional conception of exchange through an exhaustive analysis of social relations. The concept of social action had been broken out of its framework in classical economics and conceived in a wider social framework and expanded to include customary actions in addition to rational ones.

The concept of "transaction" increasingly came into central focus in Commons' thought and found expression in his *Institutional Economics* (1934). Transactions were distinguished into three types in terms of the kind of issue and social relations involved: bargaining, rationing, and managing. Commons' analysis of rationing transactions was a pioneer work, which showed the fundamental differences in social organization implied by

---

[13] *The Legal Foundations of Capitalism*, p. 8. Quoted from the 1957 edition (Madison, Wisc.: Wisconsin University Press, 1957).

the adoption of price and production rationing in the place of the usual (market) bargaining relations. With the outbreak of the war and the necessity for curbing the exercise of individual choices and bargaining through a system of rationing, Commons' analyses were of value for the administration of price controls. (Again this type of analysis is directly paralleled by those of Max Weber.)

In his last book, *The Economics of Collective Action*, all the essentials of Commons' theory of social action are assembled. His very definition of the field parallels Weber's. "The early nineteenth century economists patterned their work upon the materialistic sciences of physics and chemistry, instead of on a volitional science of the human will as developed by the courts."[14] Paralleling the emphasis on subjectively intended meaning is Commons' emphasis on will:

> The human will is the "will in action." Whether one is earning a living, getting rich, or avoiding a loss, one is always confronted with alternatives in every choice of action taken. It is not merely a choice between one act, or direction, and another; it is a choice between alternative objects, and also a choice as to degrees of power or control exerted in the alternative actually chosen in the performance. . . .[15]

The degrees of power or control in individual action are reckoned by the courts in terms of performance, forbearance, and avoidance. The kinds of collective action may be conceived in terms of the types of pressure, influence, or sanctions that may be used: moral power, economic power, or physical power. A church, for example, exercises moral power. A labor union exercises economic power. Political bodies like a state attempt to monopolize the exercise of legitimate physical force (sovereignty). The tie between the various forms of power is found in the fact that the sanctions of sovereignty establish property.

Commons operated with a typology of transactions which partly paralleled Weber's typology of social action. Three types of transactions were distinguished. Besides voluntary exchange of physical commodities by individuals, there are *rationing* transactions by the "policy-makers" of the organization (boards of directors of corporations or similar directors of labor unions and administrative political governments) in laying down working rules; *managerial* transactions between superiors and inferiors (mainly wage earners and salary earners in the production of wealth); and *bargaining* transactions on the markets, transferring ownerships of corporeal property and the new kinds of incorporeal and intangible property of bonds and stocks of corporations.

A transaction for Commons is a two-sided relation of wills, or joint action, which issues in an agreed upon performance to be executed according to working rules. Common's concept of institutions is parallel to Weber's

14 *The Economics of Collective Action*, p. 36.
15 *Ibid.*, p. 43.

notion of relation. An institution is collective action in control, liberation, and expansion of individual action. Moreover, one need not and should not reify organization. The point of gravity lies in transactions and working rules, in the problems of organization, and in the way collective action becomes organized into going concerns. Such forms of collective action are not something different from what people do. The organization of activity is simply the more stabilized aspect of activity. The form is a part of the process. Such an institution as the "state" is simply "the collective action of politicians." In fact there are three predominant kinds of collective action in the twentieth century — "corporations, labor unions, and political parties." Their interplay creates the destiny of modern man. They are manifest in units or "going concerns," which perform the same function in Commons' thought as "corporate groups" did in Weber's.

This summary of Commons' ideas hardly gives a full idea of his great sociological relevance. *The Legal Foundations of Capitalism* is a brilliant major contribution to the sociology of law. His studies of the immigrant and labor are major substantive studies of their kind. The full richness of his theory has only been suggested. It is perhaps unfortunate that Commons has been classed as an institutional economist rather than a sociologist and thus been insulated from full influence on American sociology. The single major sociologist in contemporary America working within the Commons framework is Manford Kuhn, from whom, it is to be hoped, the extension of this phase of sociological theory will come.

Robert M. MacIver

Robert Morrison MacIver (1882–   ), one of the foremost contemporary social-action theorists in America, was born in Stornoway, Scotland. He was educated at the Nicholson Institution of Stornoway and attended Edinburgh University, receiving his M.A. in 1903, his D. Phil. in 1915. In 1907 he became lecturer in political science in Aberdeen University and in 1915 was made professor of political science at the University of Toronto. During World War I he was vice-chairman of the Dominion of Canada Labor Board. He taught at Barnard College in 1927 and became a member of the Columbia University faculty in 1929, where he remained until his retirement in 1950. He was a Fellow of the American Philosophical Society, a Trustee of the Russell Sage Foundation and has been President of the American Sociological Society.

As early as 1917, in *Community*, MacIver had developed the main essentials of his position.[16] He consciously perceived his affinities with the social behaviorists. His only real disagreement with Gabriel Tarde and

[16] Robert M. MacIver, *Community: A Sociological Study* was first published in 1917 (London: Macmillan), and was subsequently printed in 1920, 1924, 1927, 1928 (first American edition), 1931, and 1936; the references here are to Macmillan's English edition of 1927. The other two books of interest in the present discussion are: *Society: A Textbook of Sociology* (New York: Farrar & Rinehart, 1937) and *Social Causation* (Boston: Ginn, 1942).

E. A. Ross was that he thought they defined "social facts" too broadly. MacIver's own definition centers in interhuman acts in which conscious willing is present. *"Whenever living beings enter into, or maintain willed relations with one another, there society exists.* All such willed relations are the primary social facts, and their consequences are secondary social facts. . . . Society is present *in a greater or less degree"* wherever such conscious willing is found.[17]

Social facts consist in the relation of wills to one another. Social facts are grouped into two great classes: social relations, which represent interaction of wills; and social institutions, which are the general forms of such relations. Sociology as a science is devoted to the discovery of the laws holding between social facts (wills in interrelation). Social laws are a unique kind within the cosmos. The laws of the inanimate world state invariable concomitance or sequence while the laws of living facts are unstable, relative, and changeable. The keynote to the vital is its teleological nature. Among the properties of life is its urge to increase in knowledge of itself. The teleological law becomes clearer as life develops. The task of sociology is "the discovery and formulation of the laws we have called free — as well as of those secondary laws which reveal the immediate interrelations of men's purposes." [18]

MacIver is very critical of the value of statistics for social research. Such statistics as totals, averages, and ratios are not social facts to MacIver's mind; to be of any use to sociological analysis, they must be interpreted. In their zeal for measurement, he thinks, some sociologists tend to overlook the fact that measurement touches only certain quantitative aspects of things. The most vital of sociological data we can often rate and grade but hardly quantify. MacIver's own method has consisted in imaginative reconstruction, a form of comparative method.

In *Community,* largely following Tönnies' distinction between *Gemeinschaft* and *Gesellschaft,* MacIver was primarily concerned with developing the contrast between community as a complete system of social life based on territory and *associations* which promote specific interests. In *Society* (1937), he examined the concept of social structure in some detail, with particular attention to norms. Various social institutions such as the family, the community, social class and caste, ethnic groups, crowds, and political associations were analyzed in detail. Throughout, MacIver was particularly interested in developing his analysis from the standpoint of the fundamental role of subjective interpretation in social life. The degree to which the conceptions of "wills in relationship" and "forms of relation" are preserved may be seen from MacIver's own table of social structure, shown on the opposite page.

MacIver brought the theoretical core of his social-action theory to its fullest precision in *Social Causation* (1942), where he maintains that the fundamental task of all science is to determine causes. This is as true for

[17] *Community,* p. 4.   [18] *Ibid.,* p. 21.

SCHEMATIC VIEW OF THE SOCIAL STRUCTURE *

A Groupings or Organizations (persons in relationships)	B Forms or Systems (modes or conditions of interpersonal relations)
I. *Inclusive territorial unities* Generic type: *Community* Specific types: Tribe Nation Neighborhood Village City	I. *Folkways and mores* Specific types: Custom Ceremony Ritual Creed Fashion
II. *Interest-conscious unities without definite organization* Generic type (a): *Social class* Specific types: Caste Elite Competitive class Corporate class Generic type (b): *Crowd* Specific types: Like-interest crowd Common-interest crowd	II. *Institutions* Generic type (a): Established *conditions* of social relations Example: Property Generic type (b): Established *modes* of social relations Example: Marriage Specific types under (a) and (b): Political Economic Religious Familial Educational *Note.* Types under B-I and B-II need not be mutually exclusive.
III. *Interest-conscious unities with definite organization* Generic type: *Association* Specific type (a): *Primary group* Varieties: Family Play group Club Specific type (b): *Large-scale association* Varieties: State Church Economic corporation, etc.	III. *Functional systems* Generic type (a): *Institutional complex* Generic type (b): *Interest complex* *Note.* Under III-b we include the two great orders of *culture* and *civilization*. These should be regarded not as parts but as foundations of the social structure.

* From R. M. MacIver, *Society: A Textbook of Sociology* (New York: Farrar & Rinehart, 1937), p. 144.

social as for physical science. However, he argues, there are a number of distinct levels of causal analysis and two types of non-causal analysis. He distinguishes the problems posed by these different levels of analysis as modes of the question "Why?":

(1) The Why of invariant order is directed to the physical nexus. It represents universal causality.

(2) The Why of organic function is directed to the biological nexus and represents the causality of organic being.

(3) The Why of psychological behavior is directed to the psychological nexus and represents the causality of conscious being.

(4) The Why of social conjecture is directed to the social nexus and also forms a part of the causality of conscious being.

(5) The Why of inference is a non-causal type, directed to the logical nexus.

(6) The Why of obligation is also of a non-causal nexus, directed to normative nexes.[19]

The task for a scientist is to identify, first, the proper causal mode. Next, "we identify the situation or type of situation in which the phenomenon occurs, as against a comparable situation or type of situation from which it is absent, and engage ourselves to discover how the phenomenon is related to the differential organizations of the situation containing it." [20]

Scientific study has two major steps: identifying the causal level of the phenomenon in question, and instituting comparative study. The first task, the identification of level, occurs for sociology when we recognize the "teleological aspects of social phenomena." There is, MacIver observes, a school of social scientists who refuse to admit that there are significant differences of subject matter characteristic of the social sciences. There are other scientists who recognize the differences between physical and social subject matter but who deny that such differences require differential methods or approaches. To such scientists, the lack of exact quantification in the social sciences seems evidence solely of their backwardness. But, MacIver insists, we as human beings are immersed in the strivings, purposes, and goals that constitute the peculiar dynamics of this area of reality. The chain of social causation "needs mind for its existence." There is no point in applying to social systems the causal formula of classical mechanics. "On the other hand we have the advantage that some of the factors . . . in social causation . . . *understandable as causes,* are validated as causal by our own experience." [21]

Once the identification of causal level has been completed we are ready for the verification process. In social affairs we have only very limited power of experimentation. We are compelled to resort to comparison of cases and particularly the device of imaginative reconstruction. In our everyday relations we apply it continually in the assessment of the behavior of our fellows. In fact, we could hardly carry on any kind of human existence, and we certainly could not enter into effective relations with others, if we did not reconstruct, from overt but often subtle evidences, the hidden system of thoughts, attitudes, desires, motivations that lie behind them.

The task of the sociologist is to establish causal laws in the "realm of conscious being" — not an easy task. In this realm, the sociologist encounters every type of law. The nexus of invariant law is everywhere. So,

---

[19] *Social Causation,* paraphrased from pp. 12–23.
[20] *Ibid.,* p. 251.   [21] *Ibid.,* pp. 263–264.

too, is the nexus of organic life. Within human organic life, the nexus of consciousness is manifest and within that the social. "Consequently, when the social scientist pursues *his* x to its specific causal nexus, he is embarrassed by the discovery that his causal factors belong to all the diverse orders of being." In a series of emergent levels of reality the sociologist finds his special problem. "Always we are confronted with diverse factors that belong to different dynamic orders and are incomparable and scientifically intractable as such." [22]

Thus, while sociology is concerned with the psychological and social realms, which emerge out of the biological and physical, the latter continue to have causal effects on sociological events. Within the general psychological nexus, three subforms of psychological nexus must be distinguished: objective, motivation, and design. In psychological activity, according to MacIver, we encounter for the first time the relation of means and ends, the emergence into consciousness of the relation of organs and functions. As this realm of activity becomes socially articulated, two interdependent systems of order become distinct — the system of apparatus or means, and the system of values or ends. These are designated as the technological order and the cultural order. The social order itself is the scheme of relationships between social beings.

All these orders, systems, and realms form the factors selectively unified in the processes of individual and group behavior. In every conscious act they enter into "dynamic conjucture." Their unity in experience is provided by some conscious decision, with or without calculation, representing a "dynamic assessment of a situation."

All conscious behavior presents a twofold process of selective organization. On the one hand, the value system of the individual, his active cultural complex, his personality, is focused in a particular direction, toward a particular goal. On the other hand, certain aspects of external reality are selectively related to the controlling valuation. From mere externals, human values may transform elements of external reality into instruments.

The social facts of interest to sociologists are those arising out of the individual and collective dynamic assessments. These give rise to events of three main types: (1) *distributive* phenomena, directly expressive of like or converging assessments of a number of people as they issue in separate activities of a like nature, and constituting an aggregate or ratio of the same order, such as a crime rate or opinion trend; (2) *collective* phenomena, directly expressing convergent assessments of a number of people, and issuing in conjoint action, such as legal enactments or organizational policy; (3) *conjunctural* phenomena, arising from variant assessments and activities of interdependent individuals and groups, and resulting in unpurposed results such as the business cycle, or the capitalistic system.

Thus, for MacIver, every social fact represents a product, directly or indirectly, of individual meanings and decisions. The components of a social

[22] *Ibid.*, p. 270.

fact represent all those phenomena from the diverse spheres and realms of being which are fused by the meaning or dynamic assessment in the particular case. In MacIver's own formulation, a conscious action develops a dynamic relation of particularized aspects of various systems. These comprise:

1. A set of objectives (including conscious drives) arising within a particular cultural complex and finding particular expression in the process of dynamic assessment.
2. A set of techniques, derived from the apparatus of civilization, and applied to the specific objectives.
3. A set of social relations, organized conformably to the particular objectives and constituting an agency if not a goal of action.
4. A set of biophysical conditions relevant to the particular action.[23]

How closely MacIver's scheme of social-action theory follows those of other representatives hardly needs to be pointed out. Like Commons, Weber, and Veblen, MacIver is concerned with meaningful action. "Dynamic assessments" are like Commons' "acts of will" or Weber's "subjectively intended meaning." Even MacIver's "imaginative reconstruction" parallels Weber's discussion of the "ideal type." Like Weber, MacIver also made basic contributions to political sociology.

Summary

Social-action theory was the third significant branch of social behaviorism. It arose in Germany as a parallel response to the forces which led to pluralistic behaviorism in France (which spread and developed further in North America) and to symbolic interactionism in North America. The founder of social-action theory was Max Weber.

Weber attempted to synthesize the twin traditions of neo-Kantianism and neo-idealism. He defined his subject matter in ways bearing similarities to Dilthey, but maintained the scientific character of the science with Rickert. Weber avoided a purely formal definition of the subject matter of sociology. At the same time, he retained the strong nominalistic epistemology and liberalism of the neo-Kantians.

"Meaningful social action" was the ultimate object matter of sociology, according to Weber. A typology of rational, evaluative, affectional, and traditional types of action was proposed for social analysis. Relations were isolated as the patterns that may be discerned in recurrent actions. They formed the transitional concept to social structure. A social structure at bottom consists only of a complex pattern of social relations. Social structures are formed into various kinds and integrated in communities. A pattern of social relations stabilized in the individual life is a "calling," the parallel concept in Weber's theories to "role" in symbolic interactionism.

[23] *Ibid.*, condensed from pp. 330–331.

In North America a number of developments, largely independent of Weber, among social scientists describing themselves as "institutional economists" parallel the social-action theories of Weber. The two most important examples are Veblen and Commons. Veblen advanced the concepts of "conspicuous consumption" and "the instinct of workmanship," which operated in a manner parallel to Weber's typology. Commons' theory of "transactions," in terms of which he analyzed economic, political, and administrative behavior, was even closer to Weber. A parallelism in other respects appears in the fact that Commons, like Weber, was led toward the development of a sociology of law, a brilliant example of which was *The Legal Foundations of Capitalism.*

However, American developments of social-action theory were by no means confined to economists who had studied abroad. MacIver broke with positivistic organicism to establish sociology on a liberal and neo-idealistic foundation. Numerous comparisons to Weber's sociology appear throughout MacIver's works. In his most theoretical book, *Social Causation,* the definition of sociology as the study of "individual and collective dynamic assessments" is similar to Weber's "meaningful social actions." Even the method of imaginative reconstruction proposed by MacIver for comparative study is similar to Weber's use of ideal types. Finally, like Weber, MacIver went on to develop a political sociology.

SELECTED BIBLIOGRAPHY

COMMONS, JOHN R., *Races and Immigrant in America.* New edition. New York: Macmillan, 1920.

COMMONS, JOHN R., *The Legal Foundations of Capitalism.* Madison, Wisconsin: Wisconsin University Press, 1957.

COMMONS, JOHN R., *The Economics of Collective Action.* New York: Macmillan, 1950.

MACIVER, ROBERT M., *Community: A Sociological Study.* New York: Macmillan, 1936.

MACIVER, ROBERT M., *Society: A Textbook of Sociology.* New York: Farrar & Rinehart, 1937.

MACIVER, ROBERT M., *Social Causation.* Boston: Ginn, 1942.

VEBLEN, THORSTEIN, *The Theory of the Leisure Class.* New York: Modern Library, 1934.

WEBER, MAX, *General Economic History.* Translated by Frank H. Knight. Glencoe, Ill.: The Free Press, 1950.

WEBER, MAX, *The Protestant Ethic and the Spirit of Capitalism.* Translated by Talcott Parsons. New York: Scribner's, 1958.

WEBER, MAX, *From Max Weber: Essays in Sociology.* Translated and edited by Hans Gerth and C. Wright Mills. New York: Oxford University Press, 1946.

WEBER, MAX, *The Theory of Social and Economic Organization.* Translated by A. M. Henderson and Talcott Parsons. New York: Oxford University Press, 1947.

WEBER, MAX, *The Methodology of the Social Sciences.* Translated by Edward A. Shils and Henry A. Finch. Glencoe, Ill.: The Free Press, 1949.

WEBER, MAX, *Max Weber on Law in Economy and Society.* Translated by Edward A. Shils and Max Rheinstein. Cambridge, Mass.: Harvard University Press, 1954.

16

Further Developments in Social-Action Theory

SOCIAL-ACTION THEORY HAS NOT YET HAD ITS DECISIVE HISTORIAN. PERHAPS when he appears he will explain the unusually fitful character of its development. One of the reasons for this irregular development may be the fact that for so many years Max Weber operated outside the universities as an independent scholar. Apparently the existence of an established plant and the constant meeting of teacher and student are an almost irreplaceable element in the continuity of a school. The generation of scholars trained by a single teacher may serve to transmit the ideas of a school and preserve them until their properties can be explored. A significant contribution is made to the continuity of a school even by those individuals who do not particularly advance it, but who form a context against which new developments can responsibly emerge.

The establishment of a tradition in considerable measure based upon Max Weber was under way in the work of Karl Mannheim during the days of the Weimar Republic, but it was cut short by the rise of Nazism and Mannheim's emigration to England. The precipitous events leading up to World War II shifted Mannheim's interests to the problem of saving Western civilization from the forces he thought would destroy it.

Meanwhile, only gradually in the 1930's (through the work of Talcott Parsons) and more rapidly since World War II (largely through the work of Mannheim's former students) has Max Weber been generally introduced to American sociology. The development of social-action theory continues to have an erratic career.

Karl Mannheim

Karl Mannheim (1893–1947) was born of a Hungarian father and a German mother. He studied at Budapest, Freiburg, Paris, and Heidelberg. He was strongly influenced by Marxism (Karl Marx and György Lukács), neo-Kantianism (having taken courses with Heinrich Rickert), phenomenology (he was familiar with Max Scheler and a student of Edmund Husserl), and finally Max Weber, who more than anyone else provided him with his basic integrating framework. Mannheim, in fact, was the primary intellectual heir of the Max Weber tradition in Germany under the Weimar Republic, and was in the process of developing one of the fullest statements ever made of a sociology of knowledge, as indicated by *Ideology and Utopia* (1929) and his article, "Wissenssoziologie" (1931),[1] when the political events of 1933 forced him into English exile, where he became a professor at the University of London. He now turned his talents to the diagnosis and solution of the problems of European social history. His views appear in *Man and Society in an Age of Reconstruction* (1940) and *Diagnosis of Our Time* (1943). Devoted students have since got out the incompleted fragments of his earlier works.[2]

While Mannheim's immersion in social-action theory was profound, the only part of that theory that he worked into a unified new form was its sociology of knowledge. His original contributions developed on the basis of social-action theory. His rejection of all "organismic," "conflict," and "formal" definitions of social reality locates him in the category of social behaviorism. With Weber, he conceived society as a network of meaningful individual acts. Also with Weber, he worked with polar concepts of traditionalism and rationality, analyzing the composition of inter-individual actions. With the Marxians, Mannheim was convinced that class-based actions are among the most significant in modern times. With Weber and partly opposed to the Marxians, he was not willing to conceive the ideas associated with class-based actions as merely epiphenomenal, as a kind of superstructure. Mannheim was familiar with Weber's study of the role of the Protestant ethic on the rise of capitalism; the kind of relation it presupposed between ideas and social structures was also basic to his own interpretations.

---

[1] In Alfred Vierkandt (ed.), *Handwörterbuch der Soziologie* (Stuttgart: F. Enke, 1931), pp. 659–680.

[2] Mannheim's chief works are: *Ideology and Utopia* (New York: Harcourt, Brace, 1936), translated by Louis Wirth and Edward Shils from *Ideologie und Utopie* (Bonn: F. Cohen, 1929), "Wissenssoziologie," *loc. cit.*, and a special introduction by Mannheim; *Man and Society in an Age of Reconstruction* (New York: Harcourt, Brace, 1940), translated by Edward A. Shils from *Mensch und Gesellschaft in Zeitalter des Umbaus* (Leiden: A. W. Sijthoff, 1935); *Diagnosis of Our Time* (New York: Oxford University Press, 1944); *Freedom, Power, and Democratic Planning* (New York: Oxford University Press, 1950); *Essays on the Sociology of Knowledge*, edited by Paul Kecskemeti (New York: Oxford University Press, 1952); *Essays on Sociology and Social Psychology*, edited by Paul Kecskemeti (New York: Oxford University Press, 1953); and *Essays on the Sociology of Culture*, edited by Ernest Manheim and Paul Kecskemeti (New York: Oxford University Press, 1956).

For Mannheim, knowledge has the function of adapting man to his environment. But because the environment is not always the same, knowledge cannot be expected to be the same or always to operate in quite the same way. Mannheim takes as established the fact that the social environment of modern man is organized into various classes. The most important aspect of history is the competition for political and economic power by the various classes. As an adaptive instrument, knowledge is class organized.

The treatment of knowledge as class-based perspectives raises two critical problems: is knowledge true? is it merely relative? Mannheim was of the view that there is one type of theoretical knowledge which rests on the criteria of science, and hence has nothing to do with class perspective. This knowledge, however, is special and limited. All the rest of our knowledge (popular, traditional, religious, philosophical, and qualitatively scientific) is class-based, having purely practical validity.

Since the great bulk of man's knowledge is class-based, it must be relative to its particular perspective. Apparently it can never claim general validity. But Mannheim was not willing to go this far. There could, he argued, be a genuine qualitative knowledge of social affairs which was of general validity. He called his position "relationism" rather than relativism. He maintained that unanimity and the broader point of view represented by intellectuals coming from different social strata made true knowledge possible. His critics, however, have been unconvinced, pointing out that if all knowledge is true only for a perspective, then unanimity itself will make no difference. Moreover, a perspective which synthesizes other perspectives merely multiplies the alternatives. The truth is no synthesis of lies. Mannheim's perspectivism, if consistent, applies also to his own views, making them true only for a perspective as well. His relationism degenerates into a relativism after all.

While there are theoretical problems unsolved in Mannheim's formulation, there is no doubt about the skill with which he isolated and characterized the ideological perspectives of some of the major political and economic classes of modern history. Tracing ideological analysis to Marx, Mannheim went beyond Marx in drawing a distinction between two major types of ideology. An ideology is a set of ideas which function in the promotion and defense of interests. It is akin to fiction or perhaps to what Marx called "false consciousness" — a state of mind which falsifies everything coming within its sphere. Such sets of ideas either defend patterns of interest strategically placed in the given social order, in which case they are "ideologies," or they promote the interests of underprivileged groups of the given society and locate their social objectives in the future, in which case they are "utopias." Four major examples of utopian mentality were developed by Mannheim in *Ideology and Utopia*: (1) the orgiastic chiliasm of the Anabaptists, (2) the liberal-humanitarian idea, (3) the conservative idea, and (4) the socialist-communist utopia.

(1) At the threshold of modern times, among the Hussites, the followers of Thomas Münzer, and the Anabaptists, the ferment of change was manifest.

Among these oppressed peasant strata of medieval society, the dream of a new and better world took the form of "chiliasm," the belief that the millennium was at hand. This belief rose to great intensity, leading to predictions of a second coming of Christ and the intense expectation of the immediate advent of the millennial kingdom. Some of these groups prophesied the actual date, and their members sold their holdings for anything they could get, purchased ascension robes, and walked out into the hills in prayer, awaiting the appointed hour. The peculiar properties of the chiliastic mentality, according to Mannheim, lie in this kind of detachment of social aspiration from both past and future, leading to the heightened ecstatic anticipation of social and personal self-realization in the immediate present.

(2) The liberal-humanitarian idea is the utopia of the modern bourgeoisie. In contrast to the chiliast, the liberal does not sever all relationships with historical existence. His positive acceptance of culture gives the liberal an ethical approach to human affairs. The liberal conception of unilinear progress has two sources. One source is Western capitalism. The bourgeois ideal of reason was intended to bridge the gap between the imperfection of things as they occurred in a state of nature and the requirements of reason. The other source of the idea of progress is found in German pietism. The ebbing away of chiliasm left in its stead a mood of waiting and anticipation. In all these respects, the liberal-humanitarian idea is the utopia of the rising bourgeois stratum of modern times.

(3) While the liberal always tends toward theorizing, the conservative does not. The conservative mentality is a structure in harmony with a reality which it has temporarily mastered. It does not reflect on the historical process. The conservative mentality comes to consciousness only when goaded by opposing theories; it discovers its idea *ex post facto*. The original conservative social classes, in fact, did not succeed in developing a theoretical interpretation of their position. This interpretation was achieved by a body of ideologists who attached themselves to the conservatives. These are represented, for Mannheim, by the conservative romantics, particularly Hegel. Hegel set up a conservative counterpart to the liberal idea. To the conservatives, the liberal ideas of the Enlightenment were something vaporous, mere opinion. Conservatism was presented as resting on no merely formal norms but as manifest in the concrete content of the prevailing laws of the state. In the objectification of culture, art, and science, spirituality unfolds itself and the idea expresses itself in tangible fullness.

(4) The anchorage of the socialist-communist utopia was neither in the dispossessed peasants, the rising liberal members of the bourgeoisie, nor the power elite, but in the proletarian groups of modern society. Their utopia took form, in the first instance, in the attempt to radicalize the liberal idea or to overcome anarchism in a most extreme form. Its conservative antagonist was considered only secondarily; communism fights

revisionism more energetically than it fights conservatism. As it took shape, it increasingly envisioned the possibility of pitched battles that would sweep away the structure of existing society, followed by a withering away of the state and a new classless social order.

Scattered throughout Mannheim's writings, there were many rich additional observations on these and other ideological formations.

It has been noted that the advent of national socialism and World War II shifted Mannheim's attention away from the systematic development of such ideas to the diagnosis of the crises of our civilization and their cure. In the course of this practical reflection, some of his theories of social change and social structure were brought partly into order.[3] Mannheim increasingly visualized the problem of our age as that of finding a workable solution to social life between the extremes of a planless *laissez-faire* democracy and the totalitarian organization of society. History, he thought, has displayed three kinds of order. "Three essential historical stages can be distinguished here: (1) man at the stage of horde solidarity, (2) man at the stage of individual competition, (3) man at the stage of super-individual group solidarity." [4]

The task of bringing order into the social world eventually falls, according to Mannheim, on the society's elites. Modern democratic-liberal societies, on the other hand, are still in the second historical stage. "Cultural life in modern, liberal mass-society is ruled mainly by the laws peculiar to an unregulated social order, whereas in a dictatorially governed mass society it is the institutions which have the greatest influence on social life." [5] The most critical question, then, is what is happening to the elites of democratic society. "We may distinguish the following main types of elites: the political, the organizing, the intellectual, the artistic, the moral, and the religious." [6] It was Mannheim's thesis that the crisis of liberal-democratic society is due to the presence of forces tending to destroy both the reality and the prestige of elite groups. These forces are: (1) the growing number of elite groups and the consequent diminution of their power, (2) the destruction of the exclusiveness of the elite groups, (3) the change in the principle of selection of these elites, and (4) the change in the internal composition of the elites. The fundamental task is to rally the elite groups and achieve a planned social order while avoiding the negative values both of *laissez-faire* anarchism and dictatorial absolutism. Planning, Mannheim seems to agree with Weber, means among other things the extension of rational bureaucratic organization to new areas of life. However, such an extension presents a danger, for once the work of passive democratization by bureaucracy is carried through, the possibility of absolutism is at hand. "But this can only happen if there is no power greater

---

[3] See particularly *Man and Society in an Age of Reconstruction, Diagnosis of Our Time,* and *Freedom, Power, and Democratic Planning.*
[4] *Man and Society in an Age of Reconstruction,* p. 68.
[5] *Ibid.,* p. 81.
[6] *Ibid.,* pp. 82–83.

than bureaucracy, for the problem of the democratic constitution of a planned society mainly consists in avoiding bureaucratic absolutism." [7] There were times when Max Weber had envisioned the future of Western civilization in terms of an increased tension between charisma and bureaucratization. There are more than echoes of the Weber position in Mannheim's final theory of social structure and change.

Fellow Travelers

There is little doubt about the imaginative challenge contained in social-action theory. It is perhaps not surprising, for this reason, that a number of the major contemporary sociologists worked for a time as fellow travelers with social-action theory before moving on toward a new theory of their own. At least three of them made contributions to social-action theory before leaving it. They deserve discussion in the present chapter, even though the full discussion of their work remains for later chapters. These are Florian Znaniecki, Talcott Parsons, and Robert K. Merton.

Florian Znaniecki

Florian Znaniecki (1882–1958) was born to a well-to-do Polish family in Russian-dominated territory. After being dismissed from the University of Warsaw for his active support of Polish nationalism, he went abroad to study at the University of Geneva (1905) and from there to Zurich and the Sorbonne, finally completing his Ph.D. at the University of Cracow in 1910. Between 1910 and 1914, while at work helping Poles to migrate, he became acquainted with W. I. Thomas, and he was invited to join Thomas at the University of Chicago in 1914, where the famous collaboration on *The Polish Peasant* began. Znaniecki taught at Columbia University (1916–1917) and Chicago (1917–1919). In 1920 he became professor of philosophy at the new University of Poznań after Poland received her independence. He was instrumental in getting sociology established in the university and he founded the Polish Institute of Sociology. In 1929 he established a Polish sociological review. He remained at Poznań until 1939. With the outbreak of World War II and conquest of Poland, he was invited to America once again to teach at Columbia University. In 1941 he became professor of sociology at the University of Illinois, where he remained until his retirement in 1951. He was president of the American Sociological Society in 1955.

Znaniecki has already been treated in connection with *The Polish Peasant.*[8]

---

[7] *Ibid.*, p. 380.

[8] In addition to *The Polish Peasant*, which has already been discussed in Chapter 14, Znaniecki's important works include: *The Laws of Social Psychology* (Chicago: University of Chicago Press, 1925); *The Method of Sociology* (New York: Farrar & Rinehart, 1934); *Social Actions* (New York: Farrar & Rinehart, 1936); *The Social Role of the Man of Knowledge* (New York: Columbia University Press, 1940); and *Cultural Sciences: Their Origin and Development* (Urbana. Ill.: University of Illinois Press, 1952).

Znaniecki's work on this great classic made him a contributor to the development of the symbolic-interactionist branch of social behaviorism. Znaniecki also contributed something to social-action theory, though his eventual theoretical significance lies elsewhere.

With other members of the social-action school, Znaniecki finds that social and cultural data possess a special property. "This essential character of cultural data we call the *humanistic coefficient,* because such data, as objects of the student's theoretic reflection, already belong to somebody else's active experience and are such as this active experience makes them." [9] Not only does Znaniecki define the field by something corresponding to Commons' "act of will," Weber's "meaning," and MacIver's "dynamic assessment," but he argues at one period that the smallest units into which social material may be analyzed are social actions.[10] Eventually Znaniecki was to drop social actions as the primary units for the analysis of social and cultural life, with the result that his later work belongs to another branch of sociological theory. But in his earlier work, he developed a unique analysis of the elements of social action.

The objects of social action are "values" — meaningful objects with a partly sensory, partly spiritual character. These values have a positive or negative axiological significance. Most values are organized into cultural systems and constructed and maintained by active tendencies. Such tendencies are empirically determinable by the values achieved. When not active, a tendency is potential — it is an "attitude." Action breaks down into: (1) the humanistic coefficient (meanings), (2) primary social values or the social object (people), (3) secondary social values (things), (4) the method, and (5) the social result or reaction. The method makes use of social instruments, the means utilized by the social agent to influence the object. The social method as a whole is the manner in which the social instrument is utilized. The social reaction is the action of the social object, which may not coincide with the intentions of the agent. To illustrate these concepts, let us say that a father believes he ought to discipline his son for some misbehavior — experimenting with cigarettes, for example. These ideas are the humanistic coefficient. The father is the social agent. The son is the primary social value or social object. The various objects and rewards made available by the social relation between father and son are secondary social values. The father's social method of disciplining his son could consist, for instance, in the use of his hand as a social instrument for the application of force to the seat of his son's pants, or it could be the exercise of his power not to grant the son's allowance until he perceived the error of his ways. The social reaction is the change brought about in the son's behavior.

Znaniecki's contribution to social-action theory is more important than this relatively conventional analysis (of social action into ideas, means, ends,

[9] *The Method of Sociology,* p. 37.
[10] *Social Actions* (1936), Chapter 1, and particularly pp. 33 ff.

and other persons) would suggest. In a manner quite in the spirit of Weber, Znaniecki suggested in his analysis of the component elements of vocations that one of the most fruitful approaches to the problems of the sociology of knowledge is the examination of the social role of the man of knowledge. According to Znaniecki, individual specialization in any kind of cultural activity is socially conditioned. The concept of social role was developed to designate this kind of phenomenon. A social role assumes the existence of a complex of values between the person performing the role, the social person, and others in the social circle. The person is an object of positive value to his circle. He is conceived as an organic and psychosocial entity or "self." He is the kind of person the circle needs if he has the qualities required by the role. In the social circle, the person has a status, role-based rights, and social functions related to the role requirements.

So long as the average knowledge of the ordinary person is adequate to social requirements, the intellectual role does not emerge as a specialized one. But even in the primitive world, the technically excellent person tended to be consulted in times of difficulty. In addition to the technical expert in general social matters, one of the earliest advisors was the priest, who was supposed to possess direct or indirect control over the magico-religious forces of the community. His role was perhaps more differentiated in primitive circles than the technical advisor, who — like Odysseus — might be old and traveled.

The role of the technological advisor may be specialized in terms of theoretical and practical requirements. His task is that of diagnosis. When diagnosis of the problem has been made, the problem remains of carrying out a plan. The technological specialist in diagnosis and planning fore-shadows the role of the scientist. Regardless of how he achieves his position (inheritance, election, appointment, force), he can maintain it only so long as his diagnosis and plan are attended by success.

In modern times, there has been continuous evolution of the social role of the technological expert. It has been separated from the role of the technological leader, who makes the decisions about practical applications. A phase of the work of the expert may be technological experiment. He may even be expected to invent alternatives to the patterns of action or advancement of the leader's plan. (Modern captains of industry maintain laboratories for such purpose). A specifically modern development is the emergence of the independent inventor (becoming a recognizable role only in the second half of the nineteenth century). His role is a lonely one. He is often destined to be laughed at and have his visions viewed as curiosities.

The other types of intellectual roles trace ultimately back to that of the priest. Further evolution of the priestly role leads to the sage, the intellectual leader of the conservative order. He is thought to be wiser than others. His function is to rationalize the tendencies of his party, to prove by scientific arguments its rightness. Beginnings of differentiation in the role of the cultural man of knowledge lead to the appearance of the social technologist. Machiavelli's *The Prince* is perhaps the first consistent work in pure cultural technology.

On a tribal level, there are two possible origins of sacred schools: secret associations and individual medicine men (shamans, wizards, magicians). The invention of writing to transmit sacred and secret knowledge was probably the work of such schools, where it served the interests of training in sacred ritual. The lore of such schools is usually claimed to be derived from a divine source; it is knowledge about divine or mysterious things and is usually concerned with description of a sacred text.

The social role of the religious scholar is performed within the sacred school, where his task is to perpetuate the sacred law. The secularization of schools and scholars develops out of conflicts and internal schisms which are due to contacts and rivalry with outside sacred schools. A distinction between sacred and secular truth comes to be made. Sacred schools must either isolate themselves or adopt secular criteria of truth. The second process was important in the rise of the Western universities. Theological faculties, on the other hand, isolated themselves.

The rivalry between schools casts significance on the fighter for truth who is interested in the logical victory for the system in which he believes. Znaniecki explains the scholar's low estimation of empirical evidence on historical grounds. Empirical evidence was appealed to for thousands of years as a criterion of truth before secular scholarship developed. The tendency to discredit empirical evidence was a phase of the creation of the standard of rational evidence. Scholars prepared the way for a scientific standardization of empirical data as materials for inductive theory. Among additional types, specialists in eclectic and historical knowledge appear, rejected by all schools because of their failure to adapt their inner evaluations to the school's requirements but valued because they provide materials for the busy fighters for truth.

In this manner Znaniecki added to the growing body of studies of specific roles, a project required by the dynamic development of all branches of social behaviorism.

Talcott Parsons

Talcott Parsons (1902–   ) is another of those persons whose work belongs in part to social-action theory. Parsons graduated from Amherst College in 1924 and studied under Hobhouse, Ginsberg, and Malinowski at the London School of Economics (1924–1925). He spent one year at Heidelberg University (1925–1926). After a year of teaching at Amherst College, he received his doctorate from Heidelberg University in 1927. From 1927 to 1931, Parsons taught in the economics department at Harvard University. In 1931, he began to teach in sociology, and became professor of sociology in 1944. In 1946 he was appointed chairman of the new

Department of Social Relations. In 1949 he was president of the American Sociological Society.

It will be necessary to examine the more important phase of Parsons' theoretical work in another connection, but for a time, it is clear, he was under the influence of social-action theory. Parsons' Ph.D. thesis was based in part on the work of Max Weber. In his translation of *The Protestant Ethic*, he did much to introduce Max Weber's sociology to the American audience. Parsons' first book, *The Structure of Social Action*, rested on social-action theory.[11] It was only later that he changed his theoretical approach. In his preface, Parsons had made his intentions quite clear: he intended "a study in social *theory*, not *theories*." His aim was to present "a *single* body of systematic theoretical reasoning the development of which can be traced through a critical analysis of the writings of this group [the selected persons considered in the study] . . . they have all, in different respects, made important contributions to this single coherent body of theory. . . . This body of theory, the 'theory of social action' is not simply a group of concepts with their logical interrelations. It is a theory of empirical science the concepts of which refer to something beyond themselves." [12]

Part I of Parsons' study was a presentation of what Parsons describes as the "positivistic theory of action." The entire work was conceived in polemical opposition to positivism. The principle features of the positivistic theory of action as listed by Parsons are: (1) the emphasis upon rationality; (2) the identification of rationality with the procedures of modern science; (3) the analysis of elements in terms of an "atomism" of unit acts (that is, the treatment of unit acts as the atoms or analytical units of social events); (4) the treatment of ends (goals of action) as given and as if they varied randomly in relation to the actor; (5) the treatment of irrationality as a lack of knowledge. The entire burden of Parsons' argument is to develop the "voluntaristic theory of social action," which corrects the limitations of the positivistic theory of action. Parsons' procedure is to conduct an elaborate critique of several social thinkers in order to show that various concepts emerged in their systems which, when synthesized, form the "voluntaristic theory." Part II of his study is described as "the emergence of a voluntaristic theory of action from the positivistic tradition"; here Parsons analyzes some features of the work of Alfred Marshall, Vilfredo Pareto, and Emile Durkheim. Part III of the study examines

[11] Parsons' major works to date are: *The Structure of Social Action* (New York: McGraw-Hill, 1937; Glencoe, Ill.: The Free Press, 1949); *Essays in Sociological Theory, Pure and Applied* (Glencoe, Ill.: The Free Press, 1949; rev. ed., 1954); *The Social System* (Glencoe, Ill.: The Free Press, 1951); *Toward a General Theory of Action*, with Edward A. Shils and others (Cambridge, Mass.: Harvard University Press, 1951); *Working Papers in the Theory of Action*, with Robert F. Bales and Edward A. Shils (Glencoe, Ill.: The Free Press, 1953); *Family, Socialization and Interaction Process*, with Robert F. Bales and others (Glencoe, Ill.: The Free Press, 1955); and *Economy and Society*, with Neil J. Smelser (Glencoe, Ill.: The Free Press, 1956).

[12] *The Structure of Social Action*, p. v.

"the emergence of a voluntaristic theory of action from the idealistic tradition," and consists primarily in an analysis of some features of the thought of Max Weber. In Part IV, Parsons brings the "voluntaristic theory of action" together.

According to Parsons, the starting point for the modern theory of action was the idea of the intrinsic rationality of action. This concept supposed that action consists of "ends," "means," and "conditions." Rationality of action consisted in a scientifically determinable relation of means to the conditions of the situation. Parsons maintains that two positivistic positions (a rationalistic and anti-rationalistic) tended to alter the place of rationality in action. The one erased the distinction between ends, means, and conditions of action, making it a process of adaptation to the situation. The other tradition of positivism eliminated rationality altogether.

Parsons maintains that Marshall took a step away from the positivistic theories of actions by refusing to accept the independence of wants. Moreover, he refused to accept the idea that the concrete actions of economic life are solely explainable as means to the satisfaction of wants — they are also exercises of faculties helping in the development of character. Pareto's contribution to voluntarism, according to Parsons, centers in his introduction of the concepts of "residues" and "non-logical action." Pareto proved that ultimate ends of action belong to a non-logical category and that logical action is intermediate to them. Moreover, Parsons insists, Pareto proved that values are not exhausted by the kinds classical economics could accept. Durkheim's contribution is conceived to be the presentation of a fuller understanding of the non-natural normative element of action. The decisive step in Durkheim's analysis was the distinction of social constraint from naturalistic causation. The social milieu constitutes a set of conditions beyond the control of a given concrete individual, but not beyond the control of human agency in general. In fact, from this point of view its most conspicuous aspect turns out to be a system of normative rules backed by sanctions. Finally, Max Weber was seen as giving full appreciation to the value element of action in that he advanced a theory of the role of value elements in the form of a combination of religious interests in their relation to systems of metaphysical ideas.[13] Weber's ghost must have winced at this.

Parsons' general argument was that these four writers, taken together, have managed to discover the main elements for a new theory of action. When these are synthesized, the result is a new departure in theory. "This generalized system of theoretical categories common to the writers here treated is, taken as a total system, a *new* development of theory and is not simply taken over from the traditions on which they built." [14]

The elements for this new generalized system of action are four in number: (1) heredity and environment, as the ultimate conditions of action; (2) means and ends; (3) ultimate values; and (4) zeal or "effort" —

[13] *Ibid.*, p. 715.   [14] *Ibid.*, p. 720.

the "name for the relating factor between the normative and the conditional elements of action." [15] The product of this laborious analysis, covering over seven hundred pages on Pareto, Durkheim, Marshall and Weber, bears a close similarity to the findings of another great Western thinker in search of science:

> We have stated, then, what is the nature of the science we are searching for, and what is the mark which our search and our whole investigation must reach.

> Evidently we have to acquire knowledge of the original causes (for we say we know each thing only when we think we recognize its first cause), and causes are spoken of in four senses. In one of these we mean the substance, i.e., the essence (for the "why" is reducible finally to the definition, and the ultimate "why" is a cause and principle); in another the matter or substratum, in a third the source of the change, and in the fourth the cause opposed to this, the purpose and the good (for this is the end of all generation and change).[16]

If it were not for the independent value of the review of such basic thinkers as Durkheim, Pareto, Marshall, and Weber, it could well be questioned whether it is worth seven hundred pages of turgid analysis to discover Aristotle's doctrine of the four causes.

Despite consorting with organicists like Durkheim and Pareto at this stage, Parsons genuinely belongs in the social-action school. He accepts the idea that the ultimate units of social life are meaningful social actions. He even accepts Weber's nominalism (rejecting it later), when he agrees that structures are "as if" entities, representing economies of analysis.

With tremendous daring, Parsons argues that the value of this system may be demonstrated by the fact that it makes analytical laws in sociology possible. In fact, he urges, there already exists one such law of wide scope and great importance:

> The law may be tentatively formulated as follows: "In any concrete system of action a process of change so far as it is at all explicable in terms of those elements of action formulated in terms of the intrinsic means-ends relationship can proceed only in the direction of approach toward the realization of the rational norms conceived as binding on the actors in the system." That is, more briefly, such a process of action can proceed only in the direction of an increase in the value of the property rationality.[17]

This analytical law discovered by action theory is comparable, according to Parsons, to the second law of thermodynamics.

Parsons seems to be saying that the fundamental law of sociology discovered by social-action theory is a tautology — at least the statement that "so far as it is at all explicable" in terms of the action scheme, the

15 *Ibid.*, p. 719.
16 Aristotle, *Metaphysics*, Book I, Sec. 3.
17 *The Structure of Social Action*, p. 751.

action "can proceed only in the direction of approach toward the realization of rational norms," seems to say that the more rational an action becomes the more understandable it is. If it was Parsons' intention with delicate irony to take this method of telling us that all laws to which social-action theory can aspire are tautologies, one would have to agree that sociology is indeed intrinsically different from physical science. But some uncertainty is caused by Parsons' further suggestion that the law of rational tendencies in social action is like the second law of thermodynamics. This would mean that all social actions move in fact in the direction of increasing rationality. In this second interpretation of the "law of rationalization," one would have to agree, again, that sociology is a special kind of science: one which formulates empirically false generalizations as laws.

But these uncertainties arise, perhaps, because Parsons, while beginning his career in action theory, was on his way to other things. His concern with Durkheim and Pareto is symptomatic, for they are not social-action theorists at all but two types of organismic positivists. The minor ambiguities that have been found in Parsons' formulation of social-action theory are not important in themselves but for what they signify — a deep dissatisfaction with social-action theory.

Robert K. Merton

Among the recent sociological theorists whose work belongs in part to social-action theory is Robert Merton (1910–   ). Merton was born in Philadelphia and received his A.B. at Temple University in 1931. His M.A. and Ph.D. were taken at Harvard University (1932, 1936). He began his teaching career as assistant in sociology at Harvard in 1934 and became instructor in 1936. In 1939 he went to Tulane as associate professor and served as professor and chairman in 1940 and 1941. Since 1941 he has been on the faculty of Columbia University, becoming associate professor in 1944, and full professor in 1947. He has been Associate Director of the Bureau of Applied Social Research and has been President of the American Sociological Society.

Merton's original affinities with social-action theory appear in his first book, *Science, Technology and Society in Seventeenth Century England.*[18] In this and a series of related articles, reprinted in *Social Theory and Social Structure*, Merton implicitly accepted the social-action framework from Weber and continued along the lines of analysis set down by Weber in *The Protestant Ethic and the Spirit of Capitalism*.

Weber had developed hypotheses concerning the relation between early ascetic Protestantism and capitalism and had suggested that this same ascetic

[18] Published as Vol. 4, Pt. 2 of *Osiris*, "Studies in the History and Philosophy of Science" (Bruges [Belgium]: The Saint Catherine Press, 1938). Major works of Merton's are: *Mass Persuasion*, with the assistance of Marjorie Fiske and Alberta Curtis (New York: Harper, 1946) ; *Social Theory and Social Structure* (Glencoe, Ill.: The Free Press, 1949; rev. ed., 1957) ; and *Continuities in Social Research*, with Paul F. Lazarsfeld and others (Glencoe, Ill.: The Free Press, 1950).

Protestantism helped motivate and canalize the activities of men in the direction of experimental science. Merton set out to examine and verify the
hypothesis. The general argument and mode of verification is typified by
Merton's own statement that even a cursory examination of the writings of
members of the British Royal Society discloses that certain elements of the
Protestant ethic had pervaded the realm of scientific endeavour and had
left their indelible stamp upon the attitudes of scientists toward their
work. Discussions of the why and wherefore of science were found to
bear a point-to-point correlation with the Puritan teachings on the same
subject. Religion was not, and perhaps could not be, compartmentalized
and delimited. Thus, in Boyle's highly commended apologia for science,
*Some Considerations Touching the Usefulness of Experimental Natural
Philosophy* (1664), it is maintained that the study of nature is to the
greater glory of God and the good of man. This motif recurs constantly.
The juxtaposition of the spiritual and the material is characteristic. The
culture rested securely on a substratum of utilitarian norms which constituted the measuring rod of the desirability of various activities. The
definition of action designed for the greater glory of God was tenuous and
vague, but utilitarian standards could easily be applied. The spirit of
seventeenth-century English science was traced to the Protestant ethic.

That Merton has been receptive to other branches of social behaviorism
as well as the social-action branch may be seen by his interpretation of
W. I. Thomas' "definition of the situation" as a "self-fulfilling prophecy." [19]
Thomas, following William James and Charles Peirce, had noted that ideas,
even if false (like magic), still have consequences for action. In Thomas'
formulation, "definitions of the situation" became basic facts of social
actions. Merton's reconceptualization of "definitions of the situation" as
self-fulfilling prophecies shows his receptivity to the idea. As a stable
financial structure, a bank rests on interlocking definitions of the situation.
But if the depositors define the situation otherwise and start a run on the
bank, they are in danger of producing the very result they fear — the
failure of the bank. The self-fulfilling prophecy is a false definition of
the situation evoking a new behavior which makes the originally false
conception come true. Such self-fulfilling prophecies go far toward explaining race and ethnic conflict: for example, the Negro is often excluded from
the unions on the grounds that he is a strike breaker, forcing him to
become a strike breaker to get a job. The principle operates throughout
social life.

Still other positive responses by Merton to one or another branch of
social behaviorism are shown by his interest in various social roles, such
as the technical expert, adviser, and bureaucrat, and by his attempt to
expand the conception of the "generalized other" of Mead into the concept
of a "reference group" — that group which the individual takes as the
basis for his own comparative self-judgments and which may be not at

[19] *Social Theory and Social Structure* (1949 edition), p. 179.

all equivalent to the group in which he actually finds himself. "Reference group" is to "generalized other" what "self-fulfilling prophecy" is to "definition of the situation."

However, despite such obviously close ties with social behaviorism, Merton feels that his own most progressive and original theory belongs to the development of functionalism. Serious discussion of Merton must be postponed for that context.

New Recruits

It is an interesting fact which invites explanation that, while some of the most able of the older generation of sociologists who began their careers in social-action theory have abandoned the position, the generation of theorists now coming into their prime numbers some extremely vigorous exponents of the theory. They have not developed or tried to develop well-rounded social-action theories, but have carried out unusually penetrating criticisms of American society in social-action terms.

William H. Whyte, Jr.

William H. Whyte, Jr. (1917–   ) is a social scientist by avocation rather than vocation. A graduate of Princeton (1939), he worked for a time for the Vick Chemical Company (1939–1941). He was a writer for *Fortune* magazine (1946–1951), and since 1951 one of its editors. In 1952 he published *Is Anybody Listening?*, a collection of articles on communication. In 1953 he won the Benjamin Franklin Award for the best magazine article on United States life. The study of importance here is *The Organization Man*.[20]

The Organization Man is a study of the ideology, the social ethos, of the new middle class, the corporation men, the junior executives, the doctor headed for the corporate clinic, the physics Ph.D. in a government laboratory, the intellectual on a foundation-sponsored team project, the engineering graduate in the huge drafting room, the young apprentice in a Wall Street law factory. These strata form the first and second echelons of social and institutional leadership in American society. Their values form the central point of reference for the values of America.

The problems studied by Whyte were brought into focus by social-action theorists. It was Weber who opened up both the study of the bearing of the Protestant ethic on the development of capitalism and the modern trend toward bureaucratic rationalization of almost every area of life. The single most significant trend in America, Whyte feels, is the development of big organization both in politics (the civil service corporation) and in business (the large corporation). Emerging from them is a managerial hierarchy that may dominate the whole of American life. Historically, on the other hand, we are a people who adhere to the Protestant ethic.

[20] New York: Simon and Schuster, 1956.

Our ethical heritage is in tension with the realities of the present. More than any other people, Americans have publicly worshipped individualism. The observation of how basic this individualism is to the nature of American life extends back to de Tocqueville over a hundred years ago.

The norms of the corporation are described by Whyte as a social ethic, a contemporary body of thought making morally legitimate the pressures of society against the individual — pressures which violate every aspect of individuality in the older sense. Its major propositions are reduced by Whyte to three: the belief that the group is a source of creativity, the belief in belongingness as the ultimate need of the individual, and a faith in the application of science to achieve this belongingness. As Whyte sums this up:

> Man exists as a unit of society. Of himself, he is isolated, meaningless; only as he collaborates with others does he become worth while, for by sublimating himself in the group, he helps produce a whole which is greater than the sum of its parts. There should be, then, no conflict between man and society. What we think are conflicts are misunderstandings, breakdowns in communication. By applying the methods of science to human relations we can eliminate these obstacles to consensus and create an equilibrium in which society's needs and the needs of the individual are one and the same.[21]

This, Whyte observes, is a utopian faith. It coincides with none of the types of mentality outlined by Mannheim. The social ethic as described by Whyte is a new kind of conservatism unique to modern man.

The decline of the Protestant ethic and the rise of the triad of ideas — scientism, belongingness, and togetherness — are the crucial ideas in terms of which Whyte traces the social history of the typical member of the new middle class: his training, his very neuroses, the new methods of personality testing, the bureaucratization of the scientist, his image in fiction, and his life in New Suburbia (the organization man's home).

The Organization Man is one of the outstanding books of contemporary social science.

David Riesman

A second penetrating critic of modern American society belonging primarily in the social-action school is David Riesman (1909–   ). He took his A.B. degree at Harvard in 1931, becoming a law clerk to Justice Brandeis after graduation (1935–1936). He was professor of law at the University of Buffalo from 1937 to 1942, and deputy assistant district attorney of the New York Court. During World War II he worked with the Sperry Gyroscope Company, afterward becoming professor of social sciences first at the University of Chicago and since 1958 at Harvard.

There is no evidence that Riesman had very extensive acquaintance with

---

[21] *Ibid.,* p. 7.

Max Weber. He was, however, quite familiar with men strongly influenced by Weber, such as Erich Fromm. From such students, Riesman took over a number of concepts central to social-action theory and transformed them into tools for the analysis of American society and character. The best of these studies are *The Lonely Crowd* and *Faces in the Crowd.*[22]

Weber had analyzed social acts into rational, evaluative, affective, and traditionalistic. He had suggested that both character structure and social structure are capable of analysis on the basis of this typology. He even indicated that a given type of action may predominate in a single role (or calling) or in a personality. In the study of *The Protestant Ethic and the Spirit of Capitalism,* Weber had demonstrated the unusual place played by evaluative social actions derived from Protestantism, both in personalities and in social change. The socio-religious ends of the typical Protestant force a peculiar rationalism on life, together with personal responsibility for his own social and economic destiny. The inner-worldly asceticism of such persons was important both to the rise of capitalism (Weber) and the rise of science (Merton).

Unfamiliarity with the full range of social-action theory occasionally leads Riesman to some rather bizarre hypotheses, such as the derivation of personality structures resting on an inner-worldly asceticism (Riesman's "inner-directed" personalities) from population growth. "The society of transitional population growth develops in its typical members a social character whose conformity is insured by their tendency to acquire early in life an internalized set of goals. These I shall term *inner-directed* people and the society in which they live *a society dependent on inner-direction.*"[23] It is hard to say whether this is worse as sociology or demography. The two other types of personality (also derived from population) are *tradition-directed* and *other-directed.*[24]

In a "tradition-directed" society (Tönnies' *Gemeinschaft*), social change is minimal. Conformity is assured by inculcating the young with automatic obedience to tradition in a role defined from birth. Obedience is taught by the clan, age, and sex group.

In an "inner-directed" society, a new pattern of conformity resting on internalized controls appears. The parent is in control rather than the extended family. The inner-directed type of person has special attitudes toward work, the self, leisure, and history. The concept of inner-direction is central to goals such as wealth, fame, goodness, and achievement. This is a personality driven by the Protestant ethic.

[22] *The Lonely Crowd* was written by Riesman in collaboration with Reuel Denney and Nathan Glazer (New Haven, Conn.: Yale University Press, 1950) ; *Faces in the Crowd* was written in collaboration with Nathan Glazer (New Haven, Conn.: Yale University Press, 1952). Other works of Riesman's are: *Thorstein Veblen: A Critical Interpretation* (New York: Scribner's, 1953) ; *Individualism Reconsidered and Other Essays* (Glencoe, Ill.: The Free Press, 1954) ; and *Constraint and Variety in American Education* (Lincoln, Neb.: University of Nebraska Press, 1956).

[23] *The Lonely Crowd*, p. 9.

[24] For a compact discussion of these types, see *Faces in the Crowd*, pp. 5–6.

The "other-directed" personality is a cause and consequence of contemporary industrial society and the rise of the new middle class. There is a preoccupation with consumption rather than production, a concern for the "human factor" in productive spheres, a weakening of parental control over children, and a new set of attitudes toward work, consumption, sex, politics, and the self. Interpersonal relations loom large, for the point of social control lies outside rather than inside the individual.

Tradition-direction is a primitive condition, appropriate to Redfield's "folk society." The important part of Riesman's typology is equivalent to the contrast introduced by Whyte between the Protestant ethic and the social ethic. In fact, their aims are identical — the critical examination of contemporary American society and culture. However, while Whyte carries out a controlled study of the organization man proper, the point of gravity in Riesman's analysis is in general middle-class institutions, leisure patterns, and culture.

The inner-directed man of the nineteenth century is seen to be on the decline. His place is being taken by the other-directed man. This change affects all basic institutions. For example, the parental role changes with the shift from bringing up children to "bringing up father." Similarly, the roles of teacher and of peer group are transformed.

The entire problem may be epitomized, according to Riesman, in the altered meaning and function of leisure. The inner-directed man pursued his hobbies by himself and used his leisure as a phase of his own personality development. The other-directed man has far greater leisure at his disposal, but finds himself trapped in a lonely crowd of others like himself, desperately trying to have fun. Parallel changes are found in every area of middle-class American life. The political individualist disappears, being replaced by the team of policy writers and the opinion poll. The newspapers and magazines are no longer the stages of the rugged individualist, but run on the basis of anonymous findings of market research. Even work, the field of salvation proper for the old inner-directed types, becomes confounded with leisure, while leisure has become arduous.

While Riesman has used only relatively superficial features of social-action theory, there is no doubt about the imagination with which middle-class American social life and culture are integrated in terms of his typology of societal and personality types.

C. Wright Mills

Although Whyte and Riesman are not primarily sociologists, the new recruits to social-action theory are not confined to non-sociologists. C. Wright Mills was well trained in the Max Weber tradition in the course of his work with Hans Gerth, and his contribution, in collaboration with Gerth, to symbolic interactionism has already been discussed. In the books to be considered here — *White Collar* and *The Power Elite* — Mills's use of social-action theory represents a more or less direct extension of the theories of Max Weber.[25]

White Collar is an attack on the same problems as *Organization Man* and *The Lonely Crowd.* However, it does not approach these problems from the standpoint of the composition, structure, and inner motivations of the crucial social roles or from the standpoint of typical personality structure and leisure patterns. Mills's study is more traditionally sociological. He attacks the issues by way of class analysis. In a burning satirical style, reminiscent of Veblen, Mills traces the contours of that mindless monster, the new middle class. Even if the middle class has a history, it is a "history without events; whatever common interests they have do not lead to unity; whatever future they have will not be of their own making." [26]

Compared to the old hierarchies, the new white collar pyramids are youthful and feminine bureaucracies, freshly scrubbed like a Lux-girl picture of the American way of life. These white collar masses, however, are managed by people more like the old middle classes with their independence and spirit of free enterprise. In phrases reminiscent of Weber's essay on bureaucracy, Mills describes the situation of the new white collar persons. They follow clearly defined lines of authority, all related to the purpose of the enterprise. Their power is located in the office. All relations within the enterprise are impersonal, formal, and hierarchical. Expectations are calculated and enforced by governing rules and explicit sanctions. Appointment is by examination and on the basis of trained competence. They are vocationally secure, with life tenure and regularized promotion schemes.

The phenomena that create these automatons — industrialism, corporateness, and bureaucracy — also, according to Mills, penetrate the old social classes. Even the formerly free professions yield to the process, as illustrated by the doctor, lawyer, and professor, whom Mills describes in scathing stereotypes. Once through medical school, the young doctors face the hospital, which they find contains departments, hierarchies, and grades. The main qualification comes to be "personality" — adaptability to the organization. And if the doctor as medical bureaucrat appears as the prototype of modernity, the lawyer is no better off. The young graduate lawyer faces bureaucratic incorporation in a law factory. His best hope is to become a businessman and proprietor in his own right. He may also then "become the . . . general manager of a factory of law, with forty lawyers trained by Harvard, Yale, Columbia, and two hundred clerks,

[25] Works by Mills which have not been previously noted (see Footnote 65, Chapter 14, and Footnote 1, Chapter 15) are: *The New Men of Power*, with the assistance of Helen Schneider (New York: Harcourt, Brace, 1948) ; *The Puerto Rican Journey* (New York: Harper, 1950) ; *White Collar* (New York: Oxford University Press, 1951) ; *The Power Elite* (New York: Oxford University Press, 1956) ; and *The Sociological Imagination* (New York: Oxford University Press, 1959).
[26] *White Collar*, p. ix.

secretaries, and investigators to assist him." [27] Most lawyers will never make it. And as for the modern professor, Mills's scorn is boundless. The professionalization of knowledge has narrowed the grasp of the individual professor. In fact, "like the pharmacist who sells packaged drugs with more authority than the ordinary storekeeper, the professor sells packaged knowledge with better effect than the layman. He brings to the market the prestige of his university position. . . . This halo of disinterestedness has more than once been turned to the interests of companies who purchase the professor's knowledge and the name of his university." [28] Throughout, Mills sees the victory of "the technician over the intellectual." [29]

All this might seem to be enough to drive promising young men and women out of the professions were it not for the fact that Mills's contempt is even greater for other middle-class types, such as sales personnel. "Salesgirls in large department stores of big cities often attempt to borrow prestige from customers, but in the big store of strangers, the attempt often fails, and, in fact, sometimes boomerangs into a feeling of powerless depression. The hatred of customers . . . is one result." [30]

America itself becomes a great salesroom. "The personality market, the most decisive effect and symptom of the great salesroom, underlies the all-pervasive distrust and self-alienation so characteristic of metropolitan people. . . . Men are estranged from one another as each secretly tries to make an instrument of the other, and in time a full circle is made: one makes an instrument of himself, and is estranged from It also." [31]

In Kafka-like terms Mills sums up his conception of the white collar worker as like an item in an enormous file. Smaller hierarchies fit into larger ones. A formal order is expressed by titles expressing diminishing gradations of status and rank. Personal life and leisure are distorted by the vain attempt to rid one's self of the tensions this mindless existence generates. "Urban masses look forward to vacations not 'just for the change,' and not only for a 'rest'. . . . on vacation one can *buy* the feeling, even if only for a short time, of higher status." [32] In fact, "like those natives who starve until whales are tossed upon the beach, and then gorge, white-collar workers may suffer long privation of status until the month-end or year-end, and then splurge in an orgy of prestige gratification and consumption." [33]

Concentrating, as it does, only selectively upon some of the middle classes (for example, the clergy is never mentioned) and then concentrating only upon the negative and extreme aspects of middle-class roles, *White Collar* creates a kind of Frankenstein monster. However, the aim of *White Collar* seems to have been more to satirize and caricature than to develop an objective sociological picture. As one middle-class position after another is savagely run through, no positive social value is seen in any middle-class role.

The limitations of *White Collar* make of *The Power Elite* an essentially

---

[27] *Ibid.*, p. 123.   [28] *Ibid.*, p. 133.   [29] *Ibid.*, p. 10.   [30] *Ibid.*, p. 173.
[31] *Ibid.*, pp. 187–188.   [32] *Ibid.*, p. 257.   [33] *Ibid.*, p. 258.

greater book, though for some reason the reviews have been more negative.

In his analysis of political institutions, Weber developed his theory of class, status group, and political party. Political parties, Weber had indicated, live in a house of power. They represent the association of those whose common ultimate aspiration is to gain and hold power. The operation of this objective may lead to the cutting of all other lines of association, be they class, status, ethnic association, or any of a plurality of institutional anchorages.

It is Mills's thesis that at the top of the structure of American society there is a "power elite . . . composed of men whose positions enable them to transcend the ordinary environments of ordinary men." [34] They are the persons in command of the major hierarchies and organizations: the big corporations, the state, the military establishment. Major national power, Mills asserts, now lies in the economic, political, and military domain. The economy, once scattered in small productive units, is now "dominated by two or three hundred giant corporations, administratively and politically interrelated, which together hold the keys to economic decisions." [35] The political order has become a centralized executive establishment, and the military order has become the largest and most expensive feature of government, which, "although well versed in smiling public relations, now has all the grim and clumsy efficiency of a sprawling bureaucratic domain." [36]

There is, Mills observes, a tendency for the consolidation of both the power and prestige of the power elite:

> . . . one feature of these hierarchies of corporation, state, and military establishment is that their top positions are increasingly interchangeable. One result of this is the accumulative nature of prestige. Claims for prestige, for example, may be initially based on military roles, then expressed in and augmented by an educational institution run by corporate executives, and cashed in, finally, in the political order, where, for General Eisenhower and those he represents, power and prestige finally meet at the very peak.[37]

According to Mills, the power elite grows at the expense of the destruction of local society and its strata. It is more and more completely represented by the metropolitan "four hundred." And even the metropolitan four hundred changes in composition, assuming the cheap tinsel brilliance of the world of the professional celebrity. "Both the metropolitan 400 and the institutional elite must now compete with and borrow prestige from these professionals in the world of the celebrity." [38] The professional celebrity (male or female) is a product of the star system. Ironically, they are celebrated because they are displayed as celebrities. The star of the silver screen has displaced the golden debutante.

The corporate rich, the war lords, the political directorate, all are at the top of a mass society, which they manipulate by advertising and propa-

[34] *The Power Elite*, p. 3.   [35] *Ibid.*, p. 7.
[36] *Ibid.*   [37] *Ibid.*, p. 10.   [38] *Ibid.*, p. 71.

ganda. The *public* is transformed into a *mass* which, for Mills, means that (1) fewer people express opinions than receive them, (2) communications are so organized that the individual receiving opinions is unable to answer back immediately with any effect, (3) opinion is controlled by the authorities who dominate the channels of communication, (4) the mass has no institutions for developing autonomous opinions. "In a mass society, the dominant type of communication is the formal media, and the publics become mere *media markets:* all those exposed to the contents of given mass media." [39]

Meanwhile, the power elite at the top are characterized by a peculiar moral ethos. "The higher immorality is a systematic feature of the American elite; its general acceptance is an essential feature of the mass society." [40] This involves a weakening of older values and an organization of irresponsibility. The higher circles in America today contain, on the one hand, the laughing, erotic, dazzling glamor of the professional celebrity, and on the other, the prestige aura of power, authority, might, and wealth. "These two pinnacles are not unrelated. . . . The professionals, in the main, are either glossy little animals or frivolous clowns; the men of power, in the main, rarely seem to be models of representative men. . . . America — a conservative country without any conservative ideology — appears now before the world a naked and arbitrary power, as, in the name of realism, its men of decision enforce their often crackpot definitions upon world reality. The second-rate mind is in command of the ponderously spoken platitude." [41]

Whether at bottom the entire social world — or perhaps only the United States — is only pure, cold, expedient, moral-less, cynical, and ruthless power, as Mills seems to indicate, is open to question, but the signal service performed by him in posing once again the central significance of the problem of the sociology of power is not to be denied. This is true, even though — as in *White Collar — The Power Elite* substitutes deeply etched caricatures for objective analysis. Despite its apparently overdrawn concept of a conspiracy at the top, *The Power Elite* is one of the most significant studies of our time.

Summary

A common problem and a set of general solutions characterize all branches of social behaviorism. Generally, they all took their initial shape during the period from 1890 to 1910. This was precisely the period of the academic institutionalization of sociology. Sociology was faced during these critical years with dropping its claims to be a kind of universal science and defending a specific definition of its tasks. During the same period, another model for the new field was being provided by sociological formal-

---

[39] *Ibid.*, p. 304.   [40] *Ibid.*, p. 343.   [41] *Ibid.*, p. 360.

ism — a model which was unsatisfactory to those sociologists who believed that an adequate definition of their field must include reference not simply to forms but to social content. Hence, an appeal was made to traditions other than the neo-Kantian and phenomenological. Various branches of the neo-Hegelian, neo-idealistic, and pragmatic philosophies were invoked for a new approach to social matters.

With the excesses of organicism before their eyes, the sociologists who were seeking a specialized definition of sociology could hardly accept the existence of large-scale, ill-defined social entities with vast and vaguely-defined powers. The founders of social behaviorism shared with the formalists a deep suspicion of reification.

The theorists of the new schools of social behaviorism all shared a profound concern for providing sociology with an adequate method. This was in reaction to the formalists as well as the organicists. The formalists, after all, were tending to define sociology in terms that would have turned it into a kind of introspective product. But the social behaviorists were interested in establishing sociology as an empirical science. Significantly, every branch of social behaviorism made some contribution to sociological method. The suggestion–imitation school under Tarde, Ross, and Giddings made active demands for the construction of sociology as a statistical science. Persons trained under these men were to be among the most active sociologists in advancing the employment of statistics and attempting to construct scales for the underlying social materials. Some members of the symbolic interaction school were foremost among those promoting the use of case-history and life-history materials. This was of tremendous importance in advancing the assemblage of first-hand data by sociology. Finally, sociological method was a common preoccupation of all social-action theorists, and they made fundamental contributions to it. Weber's ideal type may illustrate both the preoccupation with method by social-action theorists and the attempt to construct devices to make the comparative method more precise.

Among the conjoint and common products of all the branches of social behaviorism were: (1) the introduction of the social person as an object of sociological study, and (2) the establishment of social psychology as one of the fundamental branches of sociology. Were it only for these effects, social behaviorism would have left its permanent mark on sociology.

Although all three branches of social behaviorism contributed to this study of the social person, special consequences were brought about by each branch. The suggestion–imitation theory is of particular importance in calling attention to the problems of invention and diffusion of social items. Uniform patterns of equivalent behavior were of particular interest. Thus, with this branch, fads, fashions, crazes, social movements, crowds, mobs, and publics came into their own as objects of sociological study. Inevitably the phenomena of invention of all kinds assumed special significance and the mechanisms of communication, both technical and social, came under review. The methodological significance of the school in leading eventually to such things as the public opinion survey and the attempts to scale social-psychological materials, as well as to utilize statistical devices for study, have already been commented on.

All three branches of social behaviorism show a parallelism and trend toward the development of full systems of sociology. But symbolic inter- actionism and social-action theory do not account for collective behavior as well as the suggestion–imitation school, which, for its part was less competent to develop a theory of social persons and a concept of social structure. But in the development of the theory of social persons, symbolic interactionism outruns the other trends. When the very topic of social persons is mentioned the names of symbolic interactionists spring to mind: James, Cooley, Thomas, and, above all, Mead. Baldwin, of course, deserves mention, but, then, he was strongly influenced by William James. Among the concepts brought to greater refinement and transmitted on to the sociologi- cal tradition by the symbolic interactionists were the concept of language as a fundamental social mechanism, the concepts of the stylization of personality by primary groups and by play and game situations, the concept of roles, and the concept of the self as formed in terms of social structure.

Social-action theory, too, took account of collective behavior and developed a concept of social persons (as seen in its elevation of the concepts of "calling" and "vocation" and in such studies as those of the technical expert, bureaucrat, intellectual, scientist), but it excelled the other branches of social behaviorism in its account of social structure and social change. Various of its members brought the processes of social change involved in the growth of patterns of rationalization in Western social structure under serious review. The relation between religious values and economic and scientific behavior were examined. The problems presented by modern bureaucratization in all areas of life were clarified. The structural anchorage of leadership in relation to legitimate order was explored in the forms of legalistic, traditional, and charismatic leaders. The sociology of law and political sociology, as well as the sociology of religion and the study of social stratification, were established as special subdisciplines of sociology.

Taken all together a rather amazing array of the progressive trends in modern sociology have been the work of the social behaviorists.

The general position has been taken throughout this study that perhaps the best of all criticisms of any school of sociological theory is the full presenta- tion of its varieties. It is assumed that a theory continues to "develop" — which means also that older forms of the theory are rejected — only if some of its basic problems remain unsolved. The abandonment of a theory usually means that a temporary stalemate has been reached. The suggestion– imitation branch of social behaviorism, for example, took the phenomena of suggestion and imitation as fundamental social processes. But further anal- ysis showed them to be neither original nor fundamental. Imitation, when it occurs, is a highly complex and rather special learned product. Suggestion, assumed to be fundamental, was the attempt to construe social life on the model of a kind of primitive herding tendency. The abandonment of them as the sole or fundamental social processes was inevitable.

Symbolic interactionism, on the other hand, while giving powerful and exciting insights into the role of language in socialization, isolating a basis in behavior for the notion of meaning, and presenting interesting insights into the social structuring of the self and the roles that integrate self and social structure, has given only a very partial and restricted interpretation to the nature of symbolic mechanisms and a quite inadequate account of social structure. In view of the promotion by symbolic interactionism in its early days of the use of case and life histories and of personal documents of all kinds, the frequent charge that symbolic interactionism has no adequate research base and the lamentations over the fact that "George Mead has not been made researchable" are beside the point.

The deficiencies in the social-action branch of social behaviorism lie primarily in the failure to provide genuine theoretical transitions from the fundamental concept of social action to social structure — the area where the position has displayed its greatest power. Fundamentally, a typology such as the one that Weber used to make the transition is no substitute for theory construction.

Perhaps the difficulties noted in the various branches of social behaviorism are by no means fundamental. Any one of them may yet find its Aristotle who will bring it to full form. Perhaps a new formulation will appear, having as its base, not any one branch of social behaviorism, but social behaviorism as a whole. This last is suggested by work such as that of Gerth and Mills, who clearly started with social-action theory but later, in their formulations, made a new start on the basis of symbolic interactionism, relying on social-action theory for the explanation of social structure. Even Merton, before his departure from social behaviorism, showed a strong inclination to use elements from various branches of the theory: social action from Max Weber, definition of the situation (self-fulfilling prophecy) from W. I. Thomas, the generalized other (in the modified form of reference group) from G. H. Mead, and homophily from Giddings ("consciousness of kind").

On the other hand, the trend is clearly afoot by many of the most sensitive of the former adherents of social behaviorism to abandon the school altogether and to launch a new development in theory construction. At the same time, some of the most vigorous young social scientists in North America have made brilliant use of social-action theory.

SELECTED BIBLIOGRAPHY

MANNHEIM, KARL, *Ideology and Utopia.* Translated by Louis Wirth and Edward Shils. New York: Harcourt, Brace, 1949.

MERTON, ROBERT K., *Science, Technology and Society in Seventeenth Century England.* Bruges, Belgium: The Saint Catherine Press, 1938.

MILLS, C. WRIGHT, *White Collar*. New York: Oxford University Press, 1951.

MILLS, C. WRIGHT, *The Power Elite*. New York: Oxford University Press, 1956.

PARSONS, TALCOTT, *The Structure of Social Action*. Second edition. Glencoe, Ill: The Free Press, 1949.

RIESMAN, DAVID, REUEL DENNEY and NATHAN GLAZER, *The Lonely Crowd*. Garden City, N.Y.: Doubleday-Anchor Books, 1953.

RIESMAN, DAVID, and NATHAN GLAZER, *Faces in the Crowd*. New Haven, Conn.: Yale University Press, 1952.

RIESMAN, DAVID, *Constraint and Variety in American Education*. Garden City, N.Y.: Doubleday-Anchor Books, 1958.

WHYTE, WILLIAM H., JR., *The Organization Man*. Garden City, N.Y.: Doubleday-Anchor Books, 1957.

ZNANIECKI, FLORIAN, *The Method of Sociology*. New York: Farrar & Rinehart, 1934.

ZNANIECKI, FLORIAN, *Social Actions*. New York: Farrar & Rinehart, 1936.

ZNANIECKI, FLORIAN, *The Social Role of the Man of Knowledge*. New York: Columbia University Press, 1940.

Sociological Functionalism

17

The Nature and Origins of Sociological Functionalism

DESPITE THE TREMENDOUS SOCIOLOGICAL GAINS MADE BY THE VARIOUS branches of social behaviorism, many prominent sociologists seem to feel that it is no final answer. The ranks of social behaviorism have been decimated, and by persons who made significant contributions to it.

Why is social behaviorism being abandoned? It is too early to be sure. Often if the child who runs away from home knew why, he would realize that he need not go. The reasons why a scientific change is made often become fully clear only when the change has been successful. Defining precisely what is wrong is an aspect of establishing a new solution. One may, at best, hazard some rough guesses.

The three main branches of social behaviorism — pluralistic behaviorism, symbolic interactionism, and social-action theory — presented quite independent solutions to the same set of problems. Their points of strength are quite different. Theoretically the weakest and methodologically the strongest branch of social behaviorism is the pluralistic behavioral branch. Its members strongly promoted and helped to develop modern sociological statistics. They have been very busy developing various kinds of scales for measuring sociologically significant items. In part, their method could be so widely applied because their theory was so inexact. The precise definition of the object to be studied revealed it to be unmeasurable by existing instruments. By assuming that overt, countable behaviors are an accurate index to inner beliefs and desires, measurement and statistics could be advanced with no embarrassing questions asked. As the school evolved, its theories tended more and more to become a mere set of definitions.

The second major branch of social behaviorism — symbolic interaction-ism — was strong (theoretically) precisely where pluralistic behaviorism was weak. But unfortunately it was weak (methodologically) where pluralistic behaviorism was strong. There is no doubt that its conceptual-ization of sociological subject matter as consisting in "attitudes," "roles," "language as a social mechanism," "the looking-glass self," "the generalized other," "reference groups," "life organization," and so on, was a tremen-dous improvement in subtlety and precision over the conceptions of plural-istic behaviorism. To be sure, its methods showed some development — from the mere proposal of systematic autobiography of Cooley to the attempt to set down standards for case and life histories of Thomas and Znaniecki. Nevertheless, there were areas of theory left relatively undeveloped (large-scale social organization, for example), and its methods were even-tually brought under severe attack. One of the sure signals that a given person is ready to depart from the ranks of this branch of social behaviorism is the announcement that "it is a shame that no one has made George Herbert Mead (or Cooley, or Thomas, etc.) researchable."

The third branch of social behaviorism, social-action theory, has suffered from a number of difficulties. The partial failure to visualize the full range of the school has not promoted its detachment from the powerful personality of Max Weber. For example, though J. R. Commons was a fundamental contributor to social-action theory, and though he also did much to develop social science methods, he has had few sociological fol-lowers. Furthermore, since Weber had a strong personal tendency to retain ideas "in solution" until they were fully matured, hesitating to define them formally, the only indication of many of his most vital conceptions is con-tained in his types. When the abstract concept is buried in the type, it stands in the way of clear conceptualization of ideas and helps to blur the lines between concept and methodological device. Finally, the cloud under which the comparative method has fallen has not encouraged the frank projection of theory on its basis. Thus, with some irony, though half a dozen new subdivisions of contemporary sociology take their point of departure in large measure from social-action theory, particularly Weber's, the theory itself tends to be abandoned.

When one takes the three branches as a whole, the weaker their theory, the stronger their method; the stronger their theory, the weaker their method. It is little wonder that there are desertions from the ranks. These desertions are almost universally made in the name of sociological func-tionalism.

The Meaning of Functionalism

One of the major reference points in social science discussions of "func-tionalism" is Horace Kallen's article in the *Encyclopaedia of the Social Sciences*.[1] He traces it to a movement in late nineteenth-century philosophy

[1] Vol. 6, pp. 523–524.

under the influence of Darwinism on the biological and social sciences. Its distinguishing properties are found to be in its concern with relations and activities rather than substances. Characteristic notions identifying functionalism are: transformation, dynamic patterns, and process, growth, expansion, emergence.

According to Kallen, activity or function in the past had been treated as a dependent variable or faculty of a fixed structure or form. Now all this was reversed and function was regarded as the independent variable while form or structure was demoted to second place. To illustrate this notion with an extreme example, whereas in the past it was assumed that a man had a pair of legs (structure) and he walked, now it is assumed that a man walks (function) and this activity produces a pair of legs.

Functionalism, Kallen continues, has influenced every discipline. In psychology, it led to the substitution of the stream of consciousness for states of mind; in logic, it replaced the "laws of thought" with the "theory of scientific method"; in philosophy, it led to the rise of instrumentalism and pragmatism. Functionalism came to be conceived as a going process and as a means to an end. However, to Kallen the real animus of functionalism is the conception of function without purpose. In this form it is said to be a component in the thought of Bergson,[2] Dreisch,[3] and Marx, the basic feature of Gestalt psychology, and a distinguishing property of social reform and innovating movements exalting functionalism such as guild socialism, syndicalism, communism, and fascism, as well as the theoretical ideal of Bergson's *élan vital* and the dialectical materialism of Marx. A manifestation of the same movement appears in pluralism in political theory, institutionalism in economics, functionalism in anthropology (a functionalism which sees religion, the arts, and the sciences reduced to specific habits, materials, meanings, and activities within the context of a cultural situation), and functional architecture, in which form arises out of the uses for which it is intended and re-enforces those uses.

One may conclude from this review that "functionalism" in the many senses of the term here given is completely meaningless, for it has been applied to just about every new departure, however slight, in thought or experience since the mid-nineteenth century. The real synonyms of the term when so used are "contemporary" or "modern." Clearly, so long as the term "function" is used in this vague sense, it is useless for designating any particular departure in social theory. If one is to understand sociological functionalism, this vague, overgeneralized formulation of the meaning of functionalism must be made more precise.

There are a number of possible meanings of "function" that could be employed for serious sociological theory construction. Among the more

[2] Henri Bergson (1859–1941) was a French philosopher who devoted himself to the substitution of durational for non-temporal values and the values of motion and change for static values in the interpretation of events.

[3] H. Dreisch was a German biologist-philosopher, whose work *Der Vitalismus als Geschichte und als Lehre* (Leipzig: 1905) had an important influence on Gestalt psychology.

important of these are: (1) function in a mathematical sense, (2) function as useful activity, (3) function as appropriate activity, and (4) function as system-determined and system-sustaining activity.

(1) A function in mathematics is a variable whose values are determined by those of one or more other variables. If x and y are two variables, and if to each value of x corresponds one and only one value of y, y may be said to be a single-valued function of x: $y = f(x)$. In this expression, x is the independent and y the dependent variable. If more than one value of y corresponds to a value of x, the variable y is a many-valued function of x. Historically, the theory of functions goes back to the publication of Descartes' work on analytical geometry (1637). The evolution of the theory of functions is central to the development of mathematics.

Although the needs of a positivistic sociology would be brilliantly met if one were able to express all social relations as mathematical functions, even the most daring positivist has not been willing to go this far. What tentative gestures have been made in this direction have not been very successful, producing mere empty notations (Stuart Dodd) or metaphysical oversimplifications of social relations (G. K. Zipf) or make-believe and pseudo-simple social arrangements (Nicolas Rashevsky) or speculative structures (Norbert Weiner). The work of most of the recent functionalists has been at the opposite pole from this meaning.

(2) The term "function" has often been used to mean "useful activity"; in fact, it is sometimes used even for "activity." This usage is reflected in popular speech. Public and institutional ceremonies and activities (Fourth of July fireworks, Veterans' Day parades, the church socials or picnics, the annual outing of the Royal Order of Moose, the city and county picnic) are said to be "functions." In this sense, the term "function" is useless for sociological analysis, for it would encompass every activity of people in one manner or other.

The term has more bite to it, however, when it is conceived as *"useful activity"*: the germs of a theory of interhuman activity have been introduced. Two subforms of "functional" theory become distinguishable at this point. A function may be conceived not merely as a useful activity but as (a) "need fulfillment" or (b) "purpose realization." In the first sense, functional analysis of social life is the proposal to analyze all activities (functions) in terms of a system of presumed needs. In the second sense, a theory of social life is proposed by which activities are to be interpreted in terms of their instrumental value in achieving purposes. In the first sense, one occasionally hears Sumner called a functionalist because the starting point of his analysis was the assumption of the rise of customary regularities (folkways) as stable solutions to needs. Or, at times, the proposal is made to treat Freud as a functionalist because individual and social behavior were conceived to arise in the fulfillment of powerful unconscious needs. The first usage has led to proposals to reduce sociology to psychology. In the second sense, analyses of human activity in terms of means and ends, as well as all "instrumental" analyses of activity, have been claimed to be "functional." The conflicts over a "teleological" interpretation of social conduct emerge repeatedly over this usage. Apart from these issues, it is highly doubtful whether the use of the concept "function" in either or both senses warrants description of the theorist as a functionalist.

(3) The third usage treats function as "appropriate activity," a concept by no means identical with "useful activity." An activity can be quite useful either in fulfilling a need or in implementing a purpose without being "appropriate." A distorted craving for recognition may, in the opinion of a psychiatrist, drive the individual to megalomania. There is no doubt in the psychiatrist's mind about the relation between need and activity. When he describes this as a "functional disorder," he is judging its appropriateness with respect to otherwise "normal" operations of the system of behavior. There are analogies in biology where a functional disease is a morbid change in the function of an organ without a structural transformation in the tissues involved. Instrumental activity is also occasionally judged in terms of appropriateness. A businessman's purposes may be all too clear when he drives himself at (note the judgment of appropriateness) a "killing" pace.

Repeated cases have arisen in sociology of conceptions of functionalism which rest on the idea of "appropriate activity." For example, Robert Merton distinguishes between latent and manifest functions.[4] In the context, it is strongly suggested that a manifest function is somehow like the "manifest content" of Freudian dream analysis — the apparent, surface content of the dream in contrast to its hidden meanings to the dreamer. This would seem to make of the manifest function the conscious, overt one; the latent function the hidden, secret one. Examples are given of the manifest functions of the elected public officials in contrast to the nonofficial activities of the ward heelers, fixers, and bosses. But there is nothing unconscious or unintentional about the activities of a political boss — quite the contrary. It is usually difficult to find an activity that is not quite cold-bloodedly intended. The latent–manifest distinction actually refers to judgments of appropriateness.

(4) The fourth major meaning of function is that of a "system-determined and system-maintaining activity." The critical property of this position is the view that social life is fundamentally incorporated in systems. In these systems, any item is to be judged in terms of its determination by the system and its place in maintaining the system. This is clearly a more inclusive meaning than either the second or the third. In fact, these meanings are sometimes taken up into the fourth.

Putting aside the mathematical conception of function, which the theorists calling themselves sociological functionalists do, the other three notions are utilized in various combinations. This has not been any great boon to precision. The critical questions are which concept of "function" and what

[4] *Social Theory and Social Structure* (Glencoe, Ill.: The Free Press, 1949, 1957).

manner of use constitute grounds for interpreting functionalism as a special departure in sociological theory.

The conception of function as "useful activity" in both of its subforms ("need fulfillment" and "purpose realization") is very widely distributed. Probably there is no sociologist who does not view the various items of social practice, customs, social roles, institutions, and social organization as satisfying needs and realizing purposes. Functionalism cannot mean this, for in applying to all sociologists it would discriminate none. For example, it would not discriminate functionalism from social behaviorism. There are ways of reducing structures to needs and assigning instrumental purposes to them that involve various kinds of errors, but that is another matter.

Clearly it is only when "function" is used in the third sense (as "appropriate activity") and in the fourth (as "system-determined and system determining") activity that one has moved into the sphere of a special system of theory. The properties of sociological functionalism can be seen most directly in terms of their ties with organicism.

Sociological Functionalism and Sociological Organicism

Sociological functionalism departs from social behaviorism in an essential manner. Social behaviorism was haunted by the fear of reification. In all of its major branches, it arose in polemical opposition to entities which seemed to it to be hypostatized abstractions. Tarde announced his conviction that a new science begins by assuming the existence of large-scale "apparent" regularities, but can genuinely advance only with the discovery of the real, small-scale repetitions. Tarde was always opposed to Durkheim, who seemed to him to believe in the reality of fictions. Max Weber was never more insistent than in his view that relations and structures represent no more than the probabilities of the occurrence of specific social actions. A state, for example, was treated as no more than a way people act. When they no longer act that way the state does not exist. The programs of the pragmatists and symbolic interactionists also began with a strong reaction against all metaphysical entities. This was nowhere clearer than in William James's rejection of both subject and object and of consciousness as an entity in his essay "Does Consciousness Exist?". Thus, in two fundamental points, functionalism represents a departure from social behaviorism: (1) in its concept of the primacy of a system, and (2) in its idea that all units (such as those of the social behaviorists) are only secondarily relevant, and then from the standpoint of the system in which they are found.

The present interpretation, it may be noted, stands in direct contrast to the formulation of Kingsley Davis in his presidential address to the American Sociological Association in 1959:

For more than thirty years now "functional analysis" has been debated among sociologists and anthropologists. Perhaps the time has come for the debate to be either settled or abandoned. My view is that it should be abandoned, because it rests on the false assumption that there is a special method or body of theory called functional analysis which can be distinguished from other methods or theories *within* sociology and social anthropology.[5]

To be sure, Davis does correctly touch the theoretical core of functionalism:

> Turning from the sheer variety of conceptions to the traits most frequently cited as characterizing functional analysis, we find that functionalism is most commonly said to *do* two things: to relate the parts of society to the whole, and to relate one part to another.[6]

However, this formulation is not quite precise, for it is in its view of the causal priority of the whole over the part that functionalism begins to be distinct as a special theory. Hence, when Davis assumes that there is no school of functionalism because every sociologist is a functionalist, an injustice is done both to the actual varieties of theory in contemporary sociology and to the theoretical distinctness of functionalism.

In fact, functionalism represents a radical break with social behaviorism, treating as primary precisely a kind of item which social behaviorism had rejected as reification, and automatically tending to move sociological functionalism back to ideas against which social behaviorism was a reaction. This brings functionalism close to organicism. Such was Albion Small's considered judgment after his review of two early organicists, Spencer and Schäffle:

> Spencer does not succeed in making his interpretation of society . . . as more than an *organization of mechanisms*. Schäffle's central conception of society is of an *organization of work*. Of course, mechanism implies work, and work implies mechanism. Moreover, language has grown up in such connection with the working processes of life that we cannot talk of mechanism without talking of work, and *vice versa*. For that reason, the ideas of mechanism, structure, and work (function) are in both of these systems, as certainly as they are in either. They have different degrees of importance in the two systems. The relative prominence of *structure* in the one system, and the relative importance of *function* in the other, give them the rank, respectively, of a first step and a second step in approach to adequate analysis of human association.[7]

Small was convinced that these theories and concepts had done their work, and while they had left a permanent residue, they had been surpassed. Social functions themselves require a sphere of relations by which they may

---

[5] Kingsley Davis, "The Myth of Functional Analysis as a Special Method in Sociology and Anthropology," *American Sociological Review*, Vol. 24 (December 1959), p. 757.
[6] *Ibid.*, p. 758.
[7] Albion W. Small, *General Sociology* (Chicago: University of Chicago Press, 1905), pp. 167–168.

be approximately explained. Functions are aspects of processes, not parts of mechanisms. To know social functions it is necessary to become acquainted with the social processes within which they are incidents. Hence, Small thought that while "social structure" and "social functions" had been conceptual centers for ambitious sociological systems, these systems were not serious competitors for leadership in social theory. They had had their day, and social theorists could not now be fully equipped without thinking through the problems which those systems tried to solve. However, "the concepts 'social structure' and 'social function,' or some substitute which we cannot imagine, will always be indispensable in analysis of the social reality. The principal deposit of permanent value left by the two types of sociological theory developed around the two notions 'structure' and 'function,' consists of the two conceptions, as elementary terms in more adequate explanation." [8]

These comments of Small made in 1905 already tie the basic problems of functionalism at the turn of the century to organicism. It is significant that the estimate by Timasheff fifty years later also traces functionalism primarily to the organicists.[9] He notes that the conception of the integration of parts into wholes and of the interdependence of the different elements of society appeared in Comte's *consensus universalis,* in Spencer's integration compensating for differentiation, in Cooley's organic theory, and in Pareto's conception of society as equilibrium. He notes moreover that the estimate of a social item in terms of its contribution to the whole was characteristic of Durkheim and W. I. Thomas.

The organic type of system is the primary model of functional interpretation. To link non-organicists like Cooley or Thomas with functionalism is not unjust, for they were strongly influenced by organicism. However, they were not functionalists. The true founders of functionalism were the positivistic organicists.

What is really in need of explanation more than the ties of functionalism with positivistic organicism is the extreme shyness of contemporary functionalists in admitting their ancestry. One would think — so sensitive are they to genealogical questions — that their forefathers way back were all cattle rustlers. In fact, it seems they will admit influences from biology, from psychology, from cultural anthropology — anything but their own field.

Of course, this is not actually difficult to explain. Organicism of the older type fell into disrepute. The functionalists are understandably reluctant to commit the same errors. But these are not best avoided by ignoring the tradition. There were, after all, creative possibilities in the organismic point of view in both its biological and non-biological forms. The peculiar tensions arising in the conjunction of organismic theory and positivistic

---

[8] *Ibid.,* p. 176.
[9] See Nicholas S. Timasheff, *Sociological Theory: Its Nature and Growth,* rev. ed. (New York: Random House, 1957), pp. 221–223.

method were important in the very establishment of the science. The functionalistic return to the organismic point of view is itself proof that its creative potential has not been exhausted. In ancient mythologies there sometimes appears the figure of a strange giant who gains his strength from contact with the earth. He is almost unbeatable by normal types of hand-to-hand combat, for when he is hurled to earth he gains strength from the contact and comes back with redoubled energy. In sociology, the organic point of view seems to have some of this property; cast down in the form of positivistic organicism, it arises with redoubled vigor in the form of functionalism.

In the long run, if functionalistic sociological theory is to succeed where other theories have failed, it will not be by ignoring its origins but by facing up to them, extracting the positive values and meeting the criticisms that brought organicism into disrepute.

It is quite unnecessary here to review the anticipations of functionalism contained in organicism. An entire chapter has been devoted to the tracing of the development and forms of organicism. Every one of them has important relevance for functionalism.

There are, however, two points to be noted: (1) in functionalism, sociology has seen the first school of theory that is not derived from some philosophic current: (2) functionalism has some peculiarities that set it off from older types of organicism. With respect to the first point, the fact that sociology has reached a point of development in which new movements can take their points of departure within it without particular reference to outside currents of thought may be most significant. A kind of critical density of collective experience has been built up to a point where the discipline can show the properties of autonomous development. This observation, to be sure, is speculative, but it may be the surest indication we have of the approaching maturity of the science.

The second point is less speculative and of more relevance to theory formation. The fundamental explanatory model of functionalism is that of the organic system. This was the organizing conception of sociology in the first place. But if functionalism involved merely a return to the organic model, without adding anything new, it would have to be dismissed as an unprogressive tendency. However, as far as one can tell, this is not the case.

Organicism, indeed, worked with the concept of the organic system, but it was dominated by the conception of large-scale, total organic structure. For Comte, no less a structure was conceived as forming an organic system than "humanity" or, as he put it, "chiefly the white race." Spencer conceived of "society" as his unit. This, too, was the unit of analysis for Durkheim. These are large-scale systems with a vengeance.

Functionalism represents a departure from this kind of organicism in three ways: (1) the concept of "organic system" is generalized (without commitment in advance to the acceptance of only one type or only of vast total forms); (2) the concept of "system" is given explicit central theoretical status, becoming the point from which all analyses of structure and process are made; (3) the critical system is not identified with historical society.

Sociological Functionalism and Psychological Configurationism

While there has been some reluctance on the part of sociological functionalists to recognize their ties with sociological organicism, there has been frequent explicit recognition of their ties with psychological configurationism.

The organismic basis of Gestalt and configuration theory in psychology has long been made explicit. Raymond Wheeler, for example, frankly takes this as its crucial element. In fact, psychology, he believes, tends to be ultimately either mechanistic or organismic. The last two periods in the history of psychology dominated by the mechanistic pattern occurred roughly from 1710 to 1790 and from 1830 to 1910. Accordingly, the last two organismic periods occurred between 1790 and 1830 and from 1910 to the present. Prior to the twentieth century, periods of organismic thought have been vitalistic in nature, and certain of the organismic trends within this century have been vitalistic.[10]

Mechanistic theories, whether in psychology or elsewhere, locate their fundamental and derived elements in quite a different manner from organismic ones. Mechanistic theories usually prefer an atomic pattern. An element, a particle, an individual thing, or a unit is taken as fundamental. Organismic theories, on the other hand, locate what is essential not in parts or elements, but in systems, patterns, or wholes. The part or element is secondary and derived from the whole. Organismic types of theories are not confined to psychology and sociology but turn up even in physical science in the idea of systems of positively and negatively charged particles or systems of energy obeying laws of equilibrium; they appear in biology where the basic fact is conceived as the organism as a whole, not the cell.

The problems posed by mechanism and organicism in psychology were quite distinct. The atomists needed mechanisms or expedients to put the parts together. Hence, there is emphasis upon such concepts as bonds, attractions, repulsions, affinities, sociations, contacts. Scientific laws pertain to the mechanisms by which complexes are formed; otherwise laws are merely statistical.

While organicism visualizes the parts as being in relation with one another and as possessing form and order, nevertheless these parts are reduced in importance. The *whole* with its parts in interrelation in time and space becomes the primary fact. There were many anticipations of this organismic concept of a continuity over time, and unity in time and space: Wundt's

[10] Raymond H. Wheeler, "Gestalt Psychology," in Philip Lawrence Harriman (ed.), *The Encyclopedia of Psychology* (New York: Philosophical Library, 1946), p. 239. The two opposed ways of explaining the phenomena of life are "mechanism" and "vitalism." Mechanism offers a physicochemical explanation of life, whereas vitalism maintains that there is a fundamental difference between animate and inanimate matter.

concept of apperception, Fechner's search for a systematic relationship between mind and body, James's shift of emphasis from states of mind to the "stream of consciousness," the British concept of "conation," Ehrenfels' work on "Gestaltqualitäten," and Dilthey's work on psychological wholes are all frequently cited as anticipations of the rise of the recent forms of the organismic point of view in psychology.

In America, the shift to functionalistic psychology was strongly advanced by William James. His treatment of consciousness, the will, the emotions, and memory all moved in this direction. As already noted, in his treatment of consciousness he proposed to substitute the concept of process or "stream of consciousness" for the old notions of mind as a substance and of consciousness as states. In his treatment of the will, he was convinced that mechanistic statements are inadequate. While he drops the "soul," he retains the will as a group of integrating functions in experience. His treatment of emotions (paralleling those of Carl Lange) rejected the idea that emotions exist apart from bodily, physiological changes; rather, they are a product of such changes. In James's formulation, we see a bear, we run, and are afraid, or we lose our fortune, we weep, and are sorry. Memory, too, was treated neither as a fixed faculty nor as a miscellaneous property of separate items but as a general property of brain structure.[11]

Functional psychology in America is often traced to the paper by John Dewey in 1896 on *The Reflex Arc Concept in Psychology*. Dewey criticized the division of the reflex arc into stimulus and response, maintaining that the minimal unit that could profitably be considered in isolation, if one were to analyze behavior, was the entire reflex, the key to which is its function. Functionalism, as the new developments in psychology were called, found its distinctiveness in dealing with operations rather than elements. It considered consciousness to be a biologically adaptive activity. It was concerned with interrelations in all spheres of behavior and adaptation.[12]

Of all the movements toward functionalism in psychology, the Gestaltist has proven to be the most significant to sociology. It had its beginnings in Max Wertheimer's theories and research carried on at Frankfurt am Main in 1912. In the early nineteenth century, Joseph Plateau had invented the stroboscope, permitting the projection of a series of different pictures on the eye, each picture being slightly different from the previous one. Wertheimer reduced the experiments to two pictures each with a single line, the first vertical, the second sloping. By varying the length of the blank interval between the pictures, he could study the conditions under which the illusion of movement arises. When the interval was 1/5 of a second or longer, the observer saw first one line, then another. When the interval was as short as 1/13 of a second the two lines appeared to stand side by side.

[11] For a summary of James's theories, see Gardner Murphy, *An Historical Introduction to Modern Psychology* (New York: Harcourt, Brace, 1929), pp. 207–223.
[12] J. C. Flügel, *A Hundred Years of Psychology, 1833–1933* (New York: Macmillan, 1933), pp. 230–231.

Between these limits, the observer had the impression of a single line moving from one position to another. Since there was no justification for this in the objective stimuli, Wertheimer theorized that the experience represented one that could not be reduced to simpler terms. It was similar to, and yet it was not, an elementary sensation. It was a phenomenon *sui generis* which he called the *phi-phenomenon*.[13]

Beginning with this important discovery, Wertheimer, Köhler,[14] and Koffka[15] developed the early forms of the Gestalt position. The earliest researches of the school (particularly those of Köhler and Koffka) were directed to the phenomena of perception in opposition to associationistic psychology. In experiments with chickens, for example, the creatures were taught to peck at feed on a gray rather than on a white or black background. If the same chickens were then placed in a new situation where the gray on which they had learned to eat represented the darkest of three colors, the chickens responded not to the original color to which they had been conditioned but to the medium color. The perceptual situation formed a whole, a *Gestalt*.

Among the most famous of the studies by members of the school were those carried out on chimpanzees by Köhler when he was isolated at Teneriffe during World War I. The apes were presented with all sorts of situations — bananas just out of reach outside the cage but with sticks available so that the creature could spear them or paw them in; bananas outside the cage but to which a string within their reach was attached; fruit suspended from the ceiling but with boxes that could be piled up to reach it. In contrast to the random trial-and-error behavior of rats, studied by American psychologists, in which the successes were gradually learned, the problem-solving under these conditions had a different form. Initially, there was often some trial behavior on the part of the chimpanzees. When this did not succeed the chimpanzee seemed to give up and ignore the banana just outside reach. However, sometimes the creature behaved for all the world as if he suddenly had an idea, as when without hesitation the creature picked up a stick and speared an inaccessible fruit. Solutions were remembered and used without the need for relearning. Insight and goal-directed behavior appeared as responses within a whole situation. The contrast between the experimental trends among German and American psychologists led Bertrand Russell to the famous quip that rats studied by German psychologists had been observed to sit down and think and evolve the answer out of their inner consciousness while rats studied by American psychologists had been noted to rush about with great bustle and pep, finally achieving the desired results by chance.

Among the most impressive results of Köhler's experiments were those in

13 *Ibid.*, pp. 241–242.
14 Wolfgang Köhler, *The Mentality of Apes*, tr. by Ella Winter (New York: Harcourt, Brace, 1925); *Gestalt Psychology* (New York: Liveright, 1929).
15 Kurt Koffka, *Principles of Gestalt Psychology* (New York: Harcourt, Brace, 1935).

which the chimpanzees learned to pile several boxes on top of one another in order to reach a suspended fruit. And perhaps the most striking case of all was the instance of one creature chewing the end of one of two small sticks and fitting it to another to actually make an instrument capable of reaching the banana beyond the reach of either one. In the animal's conscious experience, the elements of the situation were rearranged. A configuration appeared, organizing the elements of the situation as means and ends. Insight in these simple cases is the perception of the possibility of a new arrangement.

The concept of organic wholes is preserved throughout Gestalt theory. Koffka argues that "the term *Gestalt* is a short name for a category of thought comparable to other general categories like substance, causality, function." The essence of the problems faced by Gestalt theory are found in: "first, the problem of the relation between a whole and its parts; and, second, the problem of harmony, adaptation or teleological perfection of certain morphological structures and types of behavior." [16] Koffka believed that the role of Gestalt theory has in part been the restoration of organic conceptions in biology. In psychology, Gestaltists theorized that the main properties of systems are the movement toward coherence and integration, called the "law of *Prägnanz*." This means that in any behavioral system the best possible equilibrium will be achieved; the actual organization will be as good as the conditions allow with respect to closure, articulation, and consistency of the particular behaviors and of the total behavioral field. The chief content of Gestalt theory is the idea of the relation of parts and wholes involving the recognition of intrinsic real dynamic whole-properties which, it is argued, may legitimately be called meaningful. Gestalt theory generally is the attempt to find coherent functional wholes within phenomena and to treat them as primary realities and to understand the behavior of these wholes, as well as their parts, from the whole rather than from the parts.

Gestalt theory by no means exhausted the organismic tendency in modern psychology. Dewey, who has already been examined, pulled together the unsystematic functionalistic elements in William James. His *Human Nature and Conduct* approached the field of social psychology from the standpoint of the concept of "habit," explored so brilliantly in William James's *Principles of Psychology*. In Dewey's treatment, habit assumes the form of a central behavioral function. "Habits," he said, "may be profitably compared to physiological functions, like breathing, digesting." [17] Habits were even proposed as the reference point for problems of morality. "To get a rational basis for moral discussion we must begin with recognizing that functions and habits are ways of using and incorporating the environment in which the latter has its say as surely as the former." [18] As the functional form in

---

[16] Kurt Koffka, "Gestalt," in the *Encyclopædia of the Social Sciences*, Vol. 6, p. 642.
[17] John Dewey, *Human Nature and Conduct* (New York: Henry Holt, 1922), p. 14.
[18] *Ibid.*, p. 15.

which both the individual and the environment are involved, habits are inevitably social. This fact has been obscured by a metaphysical tradition of individual free will and responsibility. Close analysis shows the very will itself to represent merely the manifestation of habit, for habits are "demands for certain kinds of activity; and they constitute the self. In any intelligible sense of the word will, they *are* the will. They form our effective desires and they furnish us with our working capacities." [19]

To date, sociological functionalism has not gone outside the social sciences to philosophy for first-hand inspiration. This, however, does not mean that the traditions of Western thought have been without influence upon it. As a development out of positivistic organicism in sociology and functional and Gestalt psychology, sociological functionalism draws its inspiration indirectly from idealistic philosophy of the nineteenth century and to some lesser extent from nineteenth-century biology.

It is precisely the older and more traditional forms of idealism that come into question, not so much the scientifically modified forms or those types re-stylized under the influence of Kantianism. Sociological functionalism responds indirectly to those philosophic traditions and directly to those social science traditions in which organismic models of thought are paramount. Social behaviorism, too, in all its branches drew something from idealism, but it was a very different type of thing — the kind of thing the functionalists denounce as atomistic, mechanistic, or elementaristic.

The attention in some detail to the Gestalt sources of sociological functionalism is in part necessary because one of the major branches of the theory proceeded directly from it.

Sociological and Anthropological Functionalism

The rather curious phenomenon already observed of an unwillingness on the part of sociological functionalists to admit their sociological origins, even while they have freely admitted influence from some types of psychology, is also manifest in their relations to anthropology. A number of the sociological functionalists quite frankly trace their origins to anthropology. This has its ironic twist, inasmuch as anthropological functionalism was developed in considerable measure under the influence of sociology.

Functionalism would seem in advance to be a much more "natural" position for anthropology than for sociology. The two critical properties of functionalism as a system of social theory are the analysis of interhuman behavior from the standpoint of the primacy of interbehavioral systems and the study of various elements or incidents as system-determined.

One can easily understand Albion Small's sage judgment that this is very good as a provisional starting point for sociological analysis of modern society. But to Small, modern society is enormously complex. What is impressive about it is not its character as a system but its infinitely varied

[19] *Ibid.*, p. 25.

encounters. Any group, he agrees, is a system, but he is never inclined to treat it as an ultimate fact, for social life is the phenomenon of the endless establishment and destruction of groups. Hence, Small's judgment was that once we have made the important first step possible with functionalism, it is time to get down to business.

The case would seem offhand to be somewhat different for the anthropologists, dealing with numerous relatively isolated, often preliterate tribes that have frequently occupied the same river valley or island or mountain plateau for centuries. The natural unit of study is the tribal community which is often almost completely closed culturally and socially. If ever the conception of the primacy of the system were relevant, it would seem to be here. It would also seem plausible to consider the single most significant aspect of any "part" the degree to which it is system-determined and system-sustaining. Yet, this point of view was rather slow to develop in ethnology.

One could not touch ideological motives more directly than in the speed with which the functionalistic point of view emerged in early sociology (in the form of organicism) and the slowness of its appearance in ethnology, where it would seem more natural. In early sociology, organicism corresponded directly to conservative needs. It found society to be a delicately adjusted system, not something fools should be permitted to tamper with, but something even angels fear to touch.

The speed with which modern functionalists rush to their own defense when there has been no attack, denying that functionalism has any conservative ideological implications, is fairly direct testimony of their sensitivity to the conservative implications of organicism. Sociological functionalism as a maiden branch of theory has made its debut with pronouncements of its virginal character and with excited defenses of its honor.

By contrast, the functionalistic theory made its way very slowly in ethnology because there were no ideological reasons making it desirable. A Western scholar studying a contemporary preliterate tribe was under no obligation in presenting his researches to prove that "order" was after all the natural state of social affairs. He could be frankly curious in an uncommitted manner. The emergence of anthropological functionalism thus waited for a sociologist like Durkheim, infused with organismic suppositions, to take the ethnographic materials collected by others (as he did with the ethnographic reports on Australia) and subject them to functionalistic analysis. The rich suggestiveness of his analysis was something of a shock to the anthropologists of his day. One was not supposed to come to brilliant interpretative conclusions without ever having been near the field. In some measure this was possible only because in this area the kinds of questions asked by the organicists were relatively new. (This, of course, is not to underestimate Durkheim's brillance.) In this connection, it is incidentally clear that Radcliffe-Brown drew the correct conclusion as to why Durkheim was able to make as much of a contribution as he did. Radcliffe-Brown quite appropriately took Durkheim as the starting point for his functionalism.

Prior to the influence of Durkheim, ethnology was concerned with the common properties of man (psychic unity of mankind) or with the evolutionary search for origins, rather than the analysis of integral organismic units. Moreover, when the evolutionary hypothesis was shattered, it was replaced by diffusionism, which tended to concentrate study on the migration of traits and trait complexes from some place of invention, rather than on the "functional integration of elements" in a tribal community.

There were, of course, anticipations of functionalism, found for example in the works of J. J. Bachofen and Fustel de Coulange. It is not surprising that so sensitive a student as Boas should have appreciated some aspects of functionalism. In 1887 he opposed the usual practice of museum exhibits of a synoptic form. He argued that when a specimen is isolated it becomes impossible to understand its meaning. A rattle may be a musical instrument or a ritualistic object. A people's productions have to be studied as a whole if informing styles are to be discerned.[20] Boas insisted that before equating phenomena, we must first be sure of their comparability, which can be determined only from their context.

In deriving his concept from Durkheim, A. R. Radcliffe-Brown (1881–1955) frankly acknowledged the relation between functionalism and organicism:

> The concept of function applied to human societies is based on an analogy between social life and organic life. The recognition of the analogy and of some of its implications is not new. In the nineteenth century the analogy, the concept of function, and the word itself appear frequently in social philosophy and sociology. So far as I know the first systematic formulation of the concept as applying to the strictly scientific study of society was that of Émile Durkheim in 1895.[21]

In Radcliffe-Brown's conception, Durkheim defined the function of social institutions as the satisfaction of the needs of the social organism. Radcliffe-Brown believed that one must avoid teleological interpretations. Hence, he suggested that for the term "needs" the phrase "necessary conditions of existence" should be substituted. The concept of function applied to social science involves the assumption that there are necessary conditions of existence for human societies which are discoverable by scientific study.

By further elaboration of the organic analogy, Radcliffe-Brown developed the meaning of function to refer to "the life of an organism . . . conceived as the *functioning* of its structure. . . . Through the continuity of the functioning . . . the continuity of . . . structure is preserved. If we consider

---

[20] See Robert H. Lowie, *The History of Ethnological Theory* (New York: Farrar & Rinehart, 1937), p. 142.
[21] A. R. Radcliffe-Brown, *Structure and Function in Primitive Society* (Glencoe, Ill.: The Free Press, 1952), p. 178.

any recurrent part . . . its *function* is the part it plays in, the contributions it makes to, the life of the organism as a whole. . . . the function of a recurrent physiological process is . . . a correspondence between it and the needs . . . of the organism." [22] Radcliffe-Brown believed that there were three questions raised by organic systems: morphology (the study of structure), physiology (the study of function), and evolution (or development). All three questions, he thought, apply to social life. We can recognize the existence of a social structure; individuals as the essential units are connected by a definite set of social relations in an integrated whole. The continuity of structure is maintained by the process of social life. The social life of the community is the *functioning* of the social structure.

There is, however, a difficulty involved in the application of the functional point of view to society. An animal organism can be seen as a structural unit. In human society, however, social structure as a whole can only be observed in its functioning. Hence social morphology cannot be established independently of a social physiology. Moreover, an animal organism does not change its structural type in the course of its life. But a society may change its structural type without any breach of continuity. Throughout, the function of any unit or partial activity is the contribution which a partial activity makes to the total activity. We can further distinguish in the social organism the equivalent to biological health and disease. "The Greeks of the fifth century B.C. thought that one might apply the same notion to society, to the city-state, distinguishing conditions of *eunomia*, good order, social health, from *dysnomia*, disorder, social ill health." [23] At all times it brings the problems of interrelations into central focus.

Among contemporary ethnologists, the most important single functionalist besides Radcliffe-Brown was Bronislaw Malinowski (1884–1942). In his most general statement, Malinowski identifies functionalism with the study of interrelations. The functional conception of culture, he maintains, is critical to theory and method. To study details detached from their setting must inevitably stultify theory, field work, and practical handling alike.[24] Culture, for Malinowski, is the social heritage of man, comprising all inherited artifacts, goods, technical processes, ideal habits, and values. Even social organization cannot really be understood except as a part of culture. Culture does not in any way contradict the psychological nature of social reality. The ultimate medium of culture is the individual mind and social organization. "Culture is a reality *sui generis* and must be studied as such. . . . Culture is a well organized unity divided into two fundamental aspects — a body of artifacts and a system of customs." [25]

Malinowski was opposed quite explicitly to both evolutionary and diffusionist interpretations of culture. Evolutionary interpretations, he argued, rest

[22] *Ibid.*, p. 179.   [23] *Ibid.*, p. 182.
[24] Bronislaw Malinowski, *The Dynamics of Culture Change* (New Haven, Conn.: Yale University Press, 1945), p. 41.
[25] Bronislaw Malinowski, "Culture," in the *Encyclopædia of the Social Sciences*, Vol. 4, p. 623.

on the concept of survivals and attempt to reconstruct the past. Diffusionism attempts to reconstruct the history of culture by tracing out its diffusion
on the basis of imitation or taking over of artifacts. To both of these
views, he opposed the functionalist theory.

> The primary concern of functional anthropology is with the function of
> institutions, customs, implements, and ideas. It holds that the cultural
> process is subject to laws and that the laws are to be found in the function
> of the real elements of culture. The atomizing or isolating treatment of
> cultural traits is regarded as sterile, because the significance of culture
> consists in the relation between its elements, and the existence of accidental
> or fortuitous culture complexes is not admitted.[26]

The foundations for a functional theory of culture were laid down
by Malinowski as follows: (1) it is accepted, first of all, as an axiom that
human beings have needs for food, reproduction, shelter, etc.; (2) it is assumed that human drives are physiological but restructured by acquired
habit; (3) culture is conceived as a conditioning apparatus which through
training in skills and norms amalgamates nature with nurture; (4) it is
taken as fundamental that man never deals with his difficulties alone; he
organizes into families, communities, tribes, with authority and leadership
culturally defined; (5) the symbolism of language is a component in all
technology and social organization; (6) cultural satisfaction of primary
biological needs imposes secondary imperatives on man; (7) the functional
theory postulates that the system of production, distribution, and consumption must be carried on even in the most primitive of communities.[27]

The real units of culture are *institutions,* which are sets of activities
organized around some need. They are groups of people united for the
pursuit of an activity by means of a material endowment and a technical
outfit. They are organized on a definite legal or customary charter; linguis-
tically formulated in myth, legend, rule, and maxim; and trained or prepared
for the carrying out of its task.[28]

In the analysis of any item, say the construction of a seagoing craft,
there are certain stable elements of form determined by the nature of the
activity to which the craft is instrumental. Variations, however, occur
within the limits imposed by the primary function, which causes the primary
characteristics of an artifact to remain stable. The form of cultural objects
is determined by direct bodily needs on the one hand and by instrumental
uses on the other. The cultural mode of satisfaction of biological needs
creates new conditions and thus imposes new cultural imperatives. Thus,
sooner or later the act of "placing an object, custom, or idea, within
its natural setting, brings us to an institution, that is to an organized,
purposeful system of human effort and achievement." [29] Among illustra-

---

[26] *Ibid.,* p. 625.
[27] *The Dynamics of Culture Change,* pp. 42–44.
[28] *Ibid.,* p. 50.   [29] *Ibid.,* p. 51.

tions of functional analysis of various cultural items, magic, myth, sorcery, and play are typical. Magic, for example, is explained as a functional product of human needs, arising whenever there is an unbridgeable gap between man's knowledge and his powers of practical control and under circumstances in which he is forced to continue his activity. Magical practices and beliefs reassure the individual and permit life to continue. Religion, too, is explained as due to deep although derived needs of the individual and of the community. Primitive religion is largely concerned with sanctifying the crises of human life: birth, puberty, marriage, death. Sorcery is interpreted as a normally conservative force used at times for intimidation but usually for the enforcement of customary law or the wishes of those in power. Play, games, sports, and art are conceived as devices which tear man out of his ordinary rut, mitigating the strain and discipline of workaday life and restoring man to full capacity for routine work. And, finally, culture itself is an instrumental reality which came into existence to satisfy the needs of man in a manner surpassing any direct adaptation to the environment.

Robert Lowie, who was an anthropological social behaviorist, was distinctly annoyed by Malinowski's functionalism:

> In messianic mood Malinowski is forever engaged in two favorite pastimes. Either he is battering down wide open doors; or he is petulantly deriding work that does not personally attract him. In the same spirit, Malinowski thumbs his nose at technology, flouts distribution studies, sneers at reconstruction of the past. The only worthy aim is to study "The part which is played by any one factor of a culture within the general scheme." In short, Malinowski's functionalism treats each culture as a closed system except insofar as its elements respond to vital biological urges.[30]

Firth has recently brought anthropological functionalism under review. Firth thinks that Malinowski's functionalism was superior to that of Radcliffe-Brown in treating the individual. He had two major objections to the latter's formulation: (1) there was, he thought, a residual teleological element in it; and (2) Radcliffe-Brown had suggested that a social system may display functional unity or a tendency toward functional integration.[31]

If Radcliffe-Brown's functionalism is inferior to Malinowski's, it must surely be for reasons other than those given by Firth. He differs from Malinowski, most certainly, in a more frank acknowledgment of the organismic origins of functionalism, in recognizing the tendency of functional analysis to become teleological, and in proposing the functional integration of social systems as a "working hypothesis." Malinowski does none of these things. His functionalism has, thus, a much more dogmatic cast. If one accepts the grounds given, Radcliffe-Brown's functionalism is

[30] *The History of Ethnological Theory*, pp. 234–235.
[31] Raymond Firth, "Function," in William L. Thomas, Jr., and Jean S. Stewart (eds.), *Yearbook of Anthropology* (New York: Werner-Gren Foundation for Anthropological Research, 1955), p. 240.

to be treated as inferior because of its greater theoretical honesty. But however this may be, both Radcliffe-Brown and Malinowski gave recognition to that trend in ethnology which cuts itself loose from evolutionism and diffusionism in their pure forms and elevates the problem of system integration and the study of interrelations into primary focus.

Ruth Benedict's *Patterns of Culture* rests frankly on functional grounds. The significance of cultural behavior is not exhausted when it is seen to be social, man-made, and variable. A culture is conceived to be a more or less consistent pattern of thought and action with characteristic purposes. "This integration of culture is not in the least mystical. It is the same process by which a style in art comes into being and persists." [32] This necessity for functional studies of culture is traced by Benedict to Malinowski, with clear recognition of its organismic properties. "Malinowski . . . criticizes the usual diffusion studies as post-mortem dissections of organisms." [33] And confirmation of the value of functional analysis is found in the theories of Wilhelm Stern, who insisted that the undivided totality of the person must be the point of departure for psychological study. He criticizes atomistic studies, which he finds have been almost universal in introspective and experimental psychology, and he substitutes investigation into the configurations of personality. Gestalt psychology is felt by Benedict to have done some of the most striking work in "justifying the importance of this point of departure from the whole rather than from its parts," [34] and Wilhelm Dilthey is also cited as justifying functional analyses of philosophical systems. "He sees them as great expressions of the variety of life, moods, *Lebensstimmungen*, integrated attitudes the fundamental categories of which cannot be resolved into one another." [35] Finally, Oswald Spengler is treated as particularly valuable for promoting the idea "that these cultural configurations have, like an organism, a span of life they cannot overpass." [36]

Benedict's inventory of the sources and justifications of her functionalistic approach to culture have been reviewed to re-enforce a point that has already been made. The reluctance of sociological functionalists to admit their ties with organismic social theory on the one hand and idealistic philosophy on the other cannot be accepted as long as they continue to trace their affinities only or primarily to anthropology. Radcliffe-Brown frankly made his point of departure from Durkheim and extolled the virtues of the organismic hypothesis, which was the core of functionalism for him. Malinowski works directly out of Radcliffe-Brown. Benedict lists a whole series of organismic social theorists and idealistic philosophers as the sources of her functionalism: Dilthey, Nietzsche, Spengler. Incidentally, she also frankly recognizes the ties with Gestalt or configuration psychology as well. And once again the organismic hypothesis is brought forward.

It is of no particular value to trace any further here the forms of

---

[32] Ruth Benedict, *Patterns of Culture* (Boston: Houghton Mifflin, 1934), p. 47.
[33] *Ibid.*, p. 50.   [34] *Ibid.*, p. 51.   [35] *Ibid.*, p. 52.   [36] *Ibid.*, p. 53.

anthropological functionalism.[37] There is little doubt that powerful func-tionalistic themes run through the "culture and personality" studies.[38] Murdock, in a somewhat defensive manner, has insisted that functionalism genuinely traces to Sumner and Keller.[39] This, of course, is correct only insofar as Sumner and Keller share the tradition of organismic positivism. To this extent, they belong among the persons who foreshadow contemporary functionalism. The only mistake is to single them out as if they were exclusive sources.

> . . . William Graham Sumner . . . foreshadows functionalism. . . . He insisted on what is now a commonplace . . . that culture is adaptive, satisfying individual and societal needs and altering over time in response to changing conditions of life. He was the first to promulgate explicitly the doctrine of cultural relativity, shocking his contemporaries by asserting that even slavery, cannibalism, and infanticide are adaptive and socially justifiable in societies that normally practice them.[40]

To be sure, the same could be said about Comte.

Summary

Social behaviorism has tended to re-enact a drama similar to that of positivistic organicism. From the very beginning, positivistic organicism was saddled with a problem: it attempted to combine an idealistic definition of society with a positivism of method. The tensions that emerged between these two factors forced the rapid internal evolution of the school. In the end the attempt to reconcile them broke down, and positivistic organicism fell apart into its separate components.

Conflict theory preserved the positivism of the first school of sociology, but varied its definition of social reality. The formal school of sociology varied both the definition of social reality and the positivism of its method. The reasons why these were abandoned by many sociologists have been traced.

Social behaviorism did not accept the old organismic definition of society, but in reaction to the formalists, it returned to a more idealistic position. At the same time, there was a powerful tendency to establish sociology on a more positivistic foundation. Social behaviorism was thus saddled with a special form of the same tensions that had characterized positivistic organicism. The tense interplay of these factors was at the basis of the

[37] Some others may be found in Walter Buckley, "Structural-Functional Analysis in Modern Sociology," in Howard Becker and Alvin Boskoff (eds.), *Modern Sociological Theory* (New York: Dryden, 1957), pp. 236–259.

[38] See, for example, Abram Kardiner, Ralph Linton, Cora du Bois, and James West, *The Psychological Frontiers of Society* (New York: Columbia University Press, 1945).

[39] George Peter Murdock, *Social Structure* (New York: Macmillan, 1949), pp. x, 10, 126, 198, and "Sociology and Anthropology," in John Gillin (ed.), *For a Science of Social Man* (New York: Macmillan, 1954), p. 16.

[40] Murdock, "Sociology and Anthropology," *loc. cit.*

rapid evolution of both theory and method. The more precise one made the theory, the more difficult the methodological problem tended to become. There is little doubt that these new tensions have been some of the components in the movement of many former members of one or another branch of social behaviorism into functionalism.

At least four major conceptions of function must be distinguished to understand modern discussions: function in a mathematical sense, function as useful activity, function as appropriate activity, and function as system-determined and system-sustaining activity. Only the last of these provides uniqueness to functionalism as a type of sociological theory.

In the simplest terms, the difference between social behaviorism and sociological functionalism is that the former was a type of social nominalism, the latter a modern form of social realism. As it is sometimes expressed, social behaviorism is a form of social atomism; sociological functionalism is a form of social organicism. The key ideas of functionalism are the concept of the primacy of system and the idea that all units of the system are only secondarily relevant.

The origins of sociological functionalism are threefold: from early sociology, from the functionalistic branch of psychology, and from social anthropology. It is a pleasant irony that contemporary sociological functionalists have gone to anthropology to discover their own origins.

SELECTED BIBLIOGRAPHY

BUCKLEY, WALTER, "Structural-Functional Analysis in Modern Sociology," in Howard Becker and Alvin Boskoff (eds.), *Modern Sociological Theory.* New York: Dryden, 1957. Pages 236–259.

FIRTH, RAYMOND, "Function," in William L. Thomas, Jr., and Jean S. Stewart (eds.), *Yearbook of Anthropology.* New York: Werner-Gren Foundation for Anthropological Research, 1955.

KALLEN, HORACE, "Functionalism," in *Encyclopædia of the Social Sciences.* New York: Macmillan, 1931. Volume 6.

KOFFKA, KURT, *Principles of Gestalt Psychology.* New York: Harcourt, Brace, 1935.

KÖHLER, WOLFGANG, *The Mentality of Apes.* Translated by Ella Winter. New York: Harcourt, Brace, 1925.

MALINOWSKI, BRONISLAW, *The Dynamics of Culture Change.* New Haven, Conn.: Yale University Press, 1945.

MURPHY, GARDNER, *An Historical Introduction to Modern Psychology.* Revised edition. New York: Harcourt, Brace, 1949.

RADCLIFFE-BROWN, A. R., *Structure and Function in Primitive Society.* Glencoe, Ill.: The Free Press, 1952.

SMALL, ALBION W., *General Sociology*. Chicago: University of Chicago Press, 1925.

WHEELER, RAYMOND H., "Gestalt Psychology," in Philip Lawrence Harriman (ed.), *The Encyclopedia of Psychology*. New York: Philosophical Library, 1946.

18

Macro-Functionalism in Contemporary Sociology

TWO MAJOR SCHOOLS OF SOCIOLOGICAL FUNCTIONALISM ARE IN PROCESS OF development at the present time. Since all the essentials of functionalism are manifest in both, it is rather inappropriate to expend the term "functionalism" on only one. For want of better terms they will be described here as "macro-functionalism" and "micro-functionalism." This distinction is made purely in terms of the size of the unit chosen as the basic type of system for the branch of the theory in question. The macro-functionalists basically presume the existence of relatively large-scale systems, the micro-functionalists of fairly small-scale systems. The first branch of functionalistic theory had its origins primarily in sociological organicism (though its exponents are often more inclined to trace their origins to anthropology); the second branch of functionalism had its origins primarily in Gestalt psychology. The employment by the macro-functionalists of relatively large-scale systems as the basic referents of its theory is in part understandable in terms of its origins. The organismic sociological theory from which it derives had been anchored in the study of entire societies conceived as superorganisms. The relatively small-scale systems assumed by micro-functionalism (often designated as "group dynamics") are also partly understandable in terms of its derivations. The original systems assumed by Gestalt theory consisted of such things as acts of perception within a perceptual situation and acts of judgment within specific empirical context. As they develop, the macro-functionalists tend to direct analysis toward smaller, less inclusive systems, whereas the micro-functionalists tend to expand analysis to embrace larger, more inclusive systems. Whether the two schemes of functionalism can ever be brought together in a single formulation waits to be seen.

Since functionalism is anchored so deeply in organicism, practically every item said to be peculiar to functionalism has been anticipated by the organicists. Functionalism at best represents merely a regrouping of and re-emphasis upon ideas that were already present. This is one of the reasons why the moment a functionalistic program is formulated it tends to look like either an old error or something that has always been known.

Theoretically, interest attaches in functionalism not to some presumed special "functional method" but to its characteristic ideas.[1] When functionalism is taken to mean "interrelation," it has to be dismissed as a special theory. If there were no more to functionalism than this, every school of sociological thought would have to be described as functionalistic. So long as functionalism is taken to mean "teleological analysis," it has to be dismissed as questionable metaphysics or as a mere shorthand or economy of statement for ideas which could be re-expressed in more exact form. Functionalism reaches its distinctive subject matter when it takes the organism-like *system* as its peculiar object of study and conceives of this as the primary subject matter of sociological analysis, studying all other items as system-determined and system-maintaining.

Because the very ideas distinctive to functionalism are those which bring it closest to organicism, special importance attaches to the criteria by which one draws the line between organicism and functionalism. To be sure, organicism has largely declined as a distinctive form of sociological theory; functionalism has taken its place. A purely terminological distinction is of no value for theory. Besides, Toynbee, Sorokin, and Spengler are clearly organicists. Sorokin, at least, does not describe himself as a functionalist. (It is noteworthy, however, that modern functionalists find support among these three — as Benedict did from Spengler.)

The position is taken here that so far as the organic system serves as the model of theory, the organicists and functionalists are identical. However, the distinctive property of the positivistic organicists was that their supersensory organisms represented actual historical configurations: it is our own society which is "sensate" for Sorokin; it is Western civilization that is in process of organic decline for Spengler.

The transition from positivistic organicism to functionalism is made when the theoretical explanations of the sociologist turn from social criticism of actual historical societies or civilizations, conceived as organisms, to abstract formulation and the development of the concept of system as an explanatory principle of theory. It goes without saying that the transition from positivistic organicism to functionalism is rather fluid. Functionalism is a program of theory construction; positivistic organicism was a program

---

[1] Carl G. Hempel once and for all disposes of the so-called functional method in "The Logic of Functional Analysis," in Llewellyn Gross (ed.), *Symposium on Sociological Theory* (Evanston, Ill.: Row, Peterson, 1959), pp. 271–310.

of action. The anticipations of functionalism among the organicists are taken to represent those ideas that aided in the abstraction, analysis, and description of components of the idea of organic system. (Of course, if anyone wished to take organicism and functionalism to represent the applied and theoretical aspects of the same enterprise, there could hardly be much dispute.) Positivistic organicism left to functionalism (and sociology generally) a whole general heritage of concepts, including "structure," "social organization," "social order," and "function" itself, as well as a great number of detailed analyses of structures and the activities they sustain. But over and beyond this heritage, certain sociologists contributed to the abstraction and precision of the concept of organic system itself. Some of these (like Durkheim) have already been noted.

Vilfredo Pareto

Since the organismic positivists as a whole are the ancestors of sociological functionalism, there is a high level of arbitrariness in isolating one — as Radcliffe-Brown does in Durkheim, Murdock does in Sumner, Benedict does in Spengler — and treating him as the precursor of sociological functionalism. Tönnies, or Schäffle, or any of dozens of others could serve equally well.

The case is different, however, for the sociological functionalists proper. They are the persons who isolated and gave abstract formulation to the critical concept of organic system, making it a unit of sociological analysis. They proposed to analyze all other elements in terms of their system unit. Pareto was a voluntaristic organicist. At the same time, he is a transitional figure between organicism and sociological functionalism. He clearly perceived and gave abstract formulation to the concept of system. The form of a society, according to Pareto, is determined by all the elements acting upon it and which society, in turn, reacts upon. A reciprocal determination arises, among such elements as: soil, climate, flora, fauna; geological, mineralogical, and other similar conditions; elements external to a given society at a given time, such as the influences of other societies upon it and the effects of the previous situation within it; and internal elements like race, proclivities, interests, aptitudes for thought and observation, state of knowledge, and so on.[2] But however few or many the elements, Pareto maintains that they form a system. By "the social system" he means that state which a society takes both at a specified moment and in the successive transformations which it undergoes within a period of time. The real state of the system is determined by its conditions, which are of such a nature that if some modification in its form is introduced artificially a reaction will take place tending to restore the changing form to its original state. If that were not the case, the form, with its normal changes, would not be

2 Vilfredo Pareto, *The Mind and Society*, translated by Andrew Bongiorno and Arthur Livingston (New York: Harcourt, Brace, 1935), Vol. 4, *The General Form of Society*, p. 1433.

determined but would be a mere matter of chance.[3] More specifically, "equilibrium" is defined as some state X such that, if subjected to some artificial modification different from those it usually undergoes, a reaction at once occurs tending to restore it to its real, normal state.

Quite in accord with the conception of the primacy of the complex whole, Pareto maintains that we cannot simplify a society or one of its sub-parts beyond a certain point without falling into error:

> The economic system is made up of certain molecules set in motion by tastes and subject to ties (checks) in the form of obstacles to the acquisition of economic values. The social system is much more complicated, and even if we try to simplify it as far as we possibly can without falling into serious errors, we at least have to think of it as made up of certain molecules harboring residues, derivations, interests, and proclivities, and which per-form, subject to numerous ties, logical and non-logical actions. In the economic system the non-logical element is relegated entirely to tastes and disregarded, since tastes are taken as data of fact. One might wonder whether the same thing might not be done for the social system, whether we might not relegate the non-logical element to the residues, then take the residues as data of fact and proceed to examine the logical conduct that originates in the residues.[4]

But, Pareto maintains, residues are not, like tastes, merely sources of con-duct. They function throughout the whole course of conduct, developing from the source. Thus, a science based on the hypothesis that logical in-ferences are drawn from certain given residues would yield a type of social phenomenon having little or no contact with reality. Society is a pre-logical phenomenon. Individuals, the molecules of the social system, are possessed of certain sentiments manifested by residues. These sentiments, and not the rationalizations of them, determine the forms of social life.

Pareto clearly adheres to the concept of society implied by the organicists, identifying it with actual society, but his abstract formulation of the concept of equilibrium is a movement in the direction of functionalism.

Florian Znaniecki

While Sumner and a number of other early sociologists tended to make the idea of system primary and the implicit cause of all other social phenomena, and while Pareto brought the idea into a sharper formulation in the notion of equilibrium, Znaniecki abstracted and generalized the concept of system itself. Znaniecki, to be sure, made contributions to more than one branch of social behaviorism (symbolic interactionism with Thomas and social-action theory), but he found his peculiar identification in functionalism.

Znaniecki maintains that the scientific problem of selecting relevant from

---

[3] *Ibid.*, p. 1453.
[4] *Ibid.*, p. 1442. Pareto's concepts of "residue" and "derivation" have already been discussed. (See pp. 101–104.)

irrelevant factors is solved by the "principle of a closed system." As Znaniecki sees it, the idea of a closed system guides the physicist and the astronomer, the chemist and the geologist, the biologist and the philologist, the economist and the art student, in the choice and determination of their respective data. Reality is constituted by innumerable and various *closed systems*, "each of which is composed of a limited number of elements more intimately inter-related with one another than with any objects which do not belong to the system, and each possessing a specific internal structure which isolates it in certain respects from external influences." [5] Once he isolated the idea, Znaniecki retained it as his central theoretical principle, only re-naming the idea in defense against critics.

> A term has been used . . . to denote . . . systems, the term "closed systems." It was applied particularly to mechanical and thermodynamic systems. Years ago we borrowed this term and tried to apply it to social systems; but this application was misunderstood by social scientists, since closed system . . . means a system isolated from external influence. . . . this is obviously not true of a living organism . . . nor yet . . . of a cultural system. We shall adopt, therefore, a *limited system* to denote any combination of particular interdependent components with an inner order of its own.[6]

The first important contribution Znaniecki made to functionalism was the generalization of this notion. The system of concern to sociologists is not — as is still true for Pareto — "society." Society may, indeed, be a system. But the distinctive property of Znaniecki's view is the concept of the *plurality* of systems. In fact, Znaniecki maintains, one of the problems to be determined is whether the given system is included in others and itself includes others. The sun and planets may be viewed as a system or as an element of a wider sidereal system. Critical to his theory is the idea that every empirical object is either a system or an element in a system or both.

The first task of the scientist is to circumscribe the system in question and determine the elements belonging to it. For this purpose, special tests are often necessary. This task of circumscription partly overlaps with that of description. If the system as circumscribed at the outset proves to be too comprehensive, the scientist will need to break it up into smaller systems or else group many objects into larger units which behave in like respects. Moreover, we are interested in the relation to the system of any object chosen for study; we are not interested in its total unique qualities. The system itself provides standards of selection. "A system is relatively isolated from external influences owing to its structure, *i.e.* to the total combination of forces which keep its elements connected in a way none of them are connected with any outside objects." [7]

[5] Florian Znaniecki, *The Method of Sociology* (New York: Farrar & Rinehart, 1934), p. 12. (Znaniecki's major works are listed in Footnote 8, Chapter 16.)
[6] Florian Znaniecki, *Cultural Sciences: Their Origin and Development* (Urbana, Ill.: University of Illinois Press, 1952), pp. 163–164.
[7] *The Method of Sociology*, p. 16.

The central task of analysis is to move from detailed causal relations within the system to the increasingly inclusive picture of more comprehensive changes. After two changes within the same system or two interacting systems have been causally connected, we can try to formulate the connection in terms of *functional dependence*. The functional relationship is not a substitute for the causal relationship, but merely a more exact and more certain kind of causal relationship.[8]

The transition was made by Znaniecki from social-action theory to sociological functionalism by way of subsuming the concept of social action under the concept of system. In this manner the entire approach to social process proposed by Znaniecki is dominated by the concept system. In his *Laws of Social Psychology*, it is proposed to establish general laws regarding (1) interrelations between the elements of the system and (2) transformations to new systems due to outside factors. Social action, conceived as a system, has a situation, a tendency, other parties to the social act, goals, instruments, and methods. In terms of these elements, Znaniecki thought it was possible to establish a whole series of laws. A few illustrations may reveal the continuous domination of the discussion by the idea of system:

1. When activity continues to turn up negative values, a desire for stability arises in the given line of behavior.
2. When activity continues to turn up positive values, a desire for new experience arises in the given line of behavior.
3. When social action resting on positive tendencies meets unexpected negative values, the positive tendency tends to turn into a negative one.
4. If a social action resting on a negative tendency meets with unexpected positive values, the tendency becomes positive.
5. If an action is socially represented by a negative reaction of an individual or group not the original object of the action, the original positive tendency becomes anti-social.
6. If an action is socially sublimated by a positive social reaction on the part of an individual or group not the original object of the action, the original tendency becomes a conformist one.
7. If the object of a social action becomes inaccessible, the tendency becomes idealistic.
8. If the object of a social action becomes more accessible, the tendency becomes more sensual and less idealistic.
9. If, during a system of actions, new social objects are substituted for the original ones, the tendency is generalized.
10. When a contrast of situation makes goals self-contradictory, the tendency ceases to be directed toward achievement, changing into sentimental valuation.
11. If the psychological conflict between a present and virtual action is solved by accommodating the virtual situation to the present situation, the present tendency becomes rationalistic.
12. If in an action the situation becomes egocentric through introduction of the reflected self, the tendency becomes self-seeking.[9]

[8] *Ibid.*, pp. 20–21.
[9] See Florian Znaniecki, *The Laws of Social Psychology* (Chicago: University of Chicago Press, 1925), pp. 112–270.

It may be seen that Znaniecki in part carried out the program of theory construction he proposed. The laws of social psychology are codified as laws of system integration and system transformation. He suggests the reformulation of the whole field of social action in terms of systems. The suggestion was also made that personality systems are one type of system among others. In all this, Znaniecki made extensive movements in the direction of a functionalistic theory. Znaniecki argued that previous to his own discussion, sociology had been variously conceived as (1) the theory of social actions, (2) the theory of social relations, (3) the theory of social persons, and (4) the theory of social groups. From Znaniecki's standpoint, these disciplines lose their independence and become merely branches of social theory.

> It is . . . high time for the sociologists to drop the superannuated claims of making a "synthetic" or "fundamental" science of societies and culture, and to realize that whatever positive scientific results they can show to their credit have been achieved only by concentrating on those kinds of specific data we have characterized . . . as social actions, social relations, social persons, and social groups.
> The logical reason for uniting these data within the domain of one science and separating this domain from those of other sciences is founded on the fact that all of them as cultural systems have an essential *similarity of composition*, while they differ in composition from all other cultural systems — technical, economic, religious, linguistic.[10]

Znaniecki's attempt to reconstruct social theory on the basis of his functionalism may also be seen with respect to the study of the social role of the man of knowledge. The study was partly influenced by social behaviorism, and has been discussed as such in Chapter 16. At the same time, the study treats culture as a *system* of knowledge, the participation in which is determined by men's activities in social systems. The social role is conceived as linking cultural and social systems. "In sociology a conceptual framework for dealing with these problems has been gradually developing in the course of monographic investigations. In recent years the term 'social role' has been used by many sociologists to denote the phenomena in question."[11] Role is treated as a complex of values relating the person performing the role ("social person") and a number of other persons ("the social circle"). The person is conceived as an organic psychological entity (a "self"). The self is a system incorporated in a more comprehensive system. In terms of the social circle, the person is required to display the kinds of qualities the social circle needs. Thus, in the social circle he possesses status. He has rights tied in with his role and performs a function, a requirement of the role. Hence, social roles are a class of social system linking two others — "social circles" and "culture." Znaniecki thus

---

[10] *The Method of Sociology*, p. 130.
[11] Florian Znaniecki, *The Social Role of the Man of Knowledge* (New York: Columbia University Press, 1940), p. 13.

was inclined to remove the concept of role from symbolic interactionism, re-interpreting it in functionalistic terms.

Robert Merton

Merton's initial contributions to sociology were made in the social-action branch of social behaviorism — most completely in the extension of Weber's analysis of the Protestant ethic to the development of rational models of behavior under the influence of the inner-worldly asceticism of Protestantism. In his own original theorizing, Merton has abandoned the framework of social behaviorism for what he views as the more promising functionalistic theory. "Functional analysis is at once the most promising and possibly the least codified of contemporary approaches to problems of sociological interpretation. Having developed on many intellectual fronts at the same time, it has grown in shreds and patches rather than in depth. The accomplishments of functional analysis are sufficient to suggest that its larger promise will ultimately be fulfilled. . . ." [12]

It is interesting to note that the persons from whom Merton explicitly derives functional analysis are primarily anthropologists: Radcliffe-Brown, Malinowski and Clyde Kluckhohn. The theory was approached by way of a distinction between five different meanings of the term function:

(1) Function as public occasion or gathering.
(2) Function as occupation.
(3) Function as activities assigned to the incumbent of a social status, e.g., to the occupant of an office.
(4) Mathematical function.
(5) Functions as biological or social procedures which help maintain the system.[13]

It is Merton's preference for the fifth of these meanings that ties his treatment most closely to those of the anthropologists and moves him into the circle of functionalistic theory proper. In his continued discussion, however, Merton indicates that over and beyond these five meanings there are still others. He notes that the term is frequently used alternatively with "purpose," "motive," "design," "primary concern," and "aim." It is a mistake, he feels, to confuse functions with subjective feelings. Social functions have *"observable objective consequences."* The *motives* for entering into marriage, for example, should not be equated with functions. Nor are the reasons advanced by people for their behavior the same as the observed consequences of their behavior. One could not ask for a more direct rejection of social-action theory of Weber's type. Essentially, Merton has retained two basic meanings of "function": (1) as an organic type of system; (2) as the consequences of any design, aim, purpose within an organic type of system.

[12] Robert K. Merton, *Social Theory and Social Structure* (Glencoe, Ill.: The Free Press, 1949), p. 21. References here to this work are all to the first edition of 1949. Merton's major works are listed in Footnote 18, Chapter 16.
[13] *Ibid.*, p. 23.

Merton took his own point of departure from what he called the "prevailing postulates" of functional analysis. He assumes that other functionalists believe that "standardized social activities or cultural items are functional for the *entire* social or cultural system; second that *all* such social and cultural items fulfill sociological functions; and third, that these items are consequently *indispensable*." [14] Although Merton has selected quotations from Radcliffe-Brown and Malinowski to "prove" the generality of these as "prevailing postulates of functional analysis," his assumption hardly holds in an unqualified sense for Sumner or Pareto and decidedly not for Znaniecki. As against these "postulates," Merton makes a number of points: (a) functional unity is not a postulate beyond the reach of empirical test, and degree of integration is an empirical variable; (b) social usages and incidents may be functional for some groups and dysfunctional for others, and the notion that they are functional for the entire society must therefore be modified; (c) the postulate of universal functionalism must be modified, for persisting cultural forms have a net balance of functional consequences for the entire society, or a unit or subgroup of it; (d) the postulate that an item is functionally indispensable must also be modified, for the same item may have multiple functions and the same function may be fulfilled by alternative items; one substitutes the concept of functional alternatives or substitutes; (e) the nature of a particular item must be spelled out for the particular case, and functional analysis calls for a specification of the social units served by functions, for some items may have variable functions, some consequences of which are dysfunctional.

Merton emphatically denies that functional analysis is "ideological." Although this denial is implicit in his criticism of the "postulates of functionalism," he developed his position explicitly in a "paradigm" for functional sociological analysis. In Merton's view, functional analysis primarily applies to standardized items (such as social roles, institutions, social process, cultural items, social norms, group organization). It operates with some concept of motivation of individuals in social systems. It works with an idea of multiple consequences and a net balance of items. It distinguishes between motives and objective consequences, utilizing two main concepts: *manifest functions* as objective consequences, contributing to the adjustment or adaptation of the system, which are intended and recognized by participants in the system; and *latent functions* as consequences which are neither intended nor recognized. An item may be functional in a "society," but a given item may be functional for some units, dysfunctional for others. A series of units may be affected by an item: status, subgroups, larger systems, cultural systems. Functional analysis works with the assumption that there are foundational requirements of the system under observation. It also requires a knowledge of mechanisms through which the function operates (such as role-segmentation, insulation of institutional demands,

[14] *Ibid.*, p. 27.

hierarchic order of values, social division of labor, ritual and ceremonial enactments). A range of possible variation must be taken into account with respect to any given item in terms of functional equivalents or substitutes. The range of variation in an item which can fulfill designated functions is limited by the structural context of the item. And, finally, functional analysis must also cover dysfunctions, which imply strain, stress, and tension on a structural level, and which account for dynamics and change.

The descriptive protocol for functional analysis should include the location of the participants in the pattern provided by social structure, the alternative modes of behavior which are excluded by emphasis on the observed pattern, the emotional and cognitive meanings attached by participants to the pattern, a distinction between motivations for participating in the pattern and objective behavior involved in the pattern, and regularities of behavior not recognized by the participants but associated with the central pattern.

In terms of the previous discussion it may be noted that the additions made by Merton to functional analyses are basically two in number, though they have partial anticipations. (1) To the concept of function Merton added the concept of dysfunction. The anticipations of this concept, of course, are clear enough. Durkheim had believed that not only may a given society display a degree of "solidarity," but quite the opposite, a degree of *anomie*. The same idea was picked up by Radcliffe-Brown in his distinction between a social condition of order and health, or *eunomia*, in contrast to a condition of social ill-health, or *dysnomia*. Merton's "dysfunction" extends this concept to the unit of the functional system.

It should be observed that the concept of "dysfunctions" carries with it rather special risks. When any unit, activity, structure, or organization is described as "dysfunctional," such a description can easily take the form of an implicit value judgment unless the system is specified. When a primitive makes a canoe he employs the technology at his disposal. It will prove to be seaworthy only if the materials and technical processes of its construction are "adequate" for this purpose. Canoe-making may be attended by a good deal of specialized magic, without which the primitive would not even consider launching his canoe. In terms of improving its sailability — say, by adding a kind of magical leak-proofing — the magic attendant on canoe-making is quite "dysfunctional." However, there is nothing dysfunctional about its psychological function of reassurance in the face of uncertainty attendant upon putting out to sea in a cockle shell.

It may be noted, too, that when the term "dysfunctional" is introduced, the meaning of "function" tends to shift — even if ever so slightly — toward the meaning of "appropriate."

(2) Merton's second major addition to the theory of sociological functionalism was the distinction contained in the concepts of "manifest" and "latent" function. Here, again, there are direct anticipations in sociology. In his study of social institutions, F. Stuart Chapin had treated one of

the decisive properties of institutions as the appearance, organization, and integration of formal structures. He indicated, however, that this does not mean that informal behavior loses its importance. In fact, though the institutionalization of formal problems introduces efficiencies, new needs develop that the formal patterns cannot or will not absorb. Moreover, the complex of informal patterns may become integrated into a complex of their own. In Chapin's own illustration, the folkways of drinking are expressed by a demand for liquors. When (as in the case of the prohibition amendment) liquor is prohibited, a network of relations among politics, crime, and vice arises in the fulfillment of the demands related to the folkways surrounding drinking. There is, thus, a fundamental distinction between formal and informal relations and *manifest* and *latent* functions. "The formalism of creed and doctrine, although a check on freedom, was not designed to suppress personal initiative. Thus the essence of the latent pattern is not its anti-social nor yet its ethical significance, but lies rather in the fact that it is a configuration of segments of behaviors undirected by the separate purposes of the individuals who contribute to its formation." [15]

Merton, however, took the distinction not from Chapin but from Freud, who initially introduced it to refer to manifest and latent dream content, anchored in conscious and unconscious motivation. Moreover, Merton gave the distinction a quite different interpretation from that of Chapin and closer to that of Freud. *Manifest functions* are those objective consequences contributing to the adjustment or adaptation of the system which are intended and recognized by the participants in the system; *latent functions*, correlatively, are those which are neither intended nor recognized.[16]

As a major illustration of the value of a distinction between manifest and latent functions for sociological analysis, Merton cited bossism and machine politics. To understand the role of bossism and the machine in political behavior, we must look at two types of sociological variables. (1) The *structural context* of politics makes it practically impossible for morally approved structures to fulfill essential social functions; the way is thus left open for the political machines. (2) Moreover, these are *subgroups* whose distinctive needs are left unsatisfied except for the latent functions which the machine in fact fulfills.

Functional deficiencies of the official structure lead to alternative unofficial structures which satisfy existing needs more efficiently. Deprived social classes are satisfied by the political machine more adequately than by the official structure. For a second group, business (both big and small), the political boss serves the function of providing privileges which entail immediate economic gain. The demand for special privileges is built into the structure of society and the boss fulfills diverse functions for this second sub-

[15] F. Stuart Chapin, *Contemporary American Institutions* (New York: Harper, 1935), p. 47.
[16] *Social Theory and Social Structure*, p. 51.

group of business-seeking-privilege. The political machine also provides channels of social mobility for persons otherwise excluded from the conventional avenues of personal advancement. The machine mediates the needs of "illegitimate business," which often differs only in degree from legitimate business. "To seek social change, without due recognition of the manifest and latent functions performed by the social organization undergoing change, is to indulge in social ritual rather than social engineering." [17]

In actual fact, Merton quite violates his definitions of manifest and latent function as conscious and unconscious, intended and unintended consequences respectively. In the first place, it must be noted that this formulation again tends to draw Merton's concept of function into the framework of "purposiveness." But, beyond this, the examples simply do not fit the definition. It is rather curious to assume that the incumbent in the office intends his actions (manifest functions of politics) while the political boss does not (latent functions of the boss) or that the official is conscious of his actions, the political boss is not.

Perhaps the single most significant example of a functional analysis is Merton's study of "Social Structure and Anomie." [18] In this study he proposed to analyze the social and cultural sources of deviant behavior. His aim more specifically was to examine the manner in which social structures exert a definite pressure upon certain persons in society to engage in nonconformist rather than conformist conduct. Social and cultural structures, Merton indicates, define certain goals and objectives as legitimate. In addition, they determine and regulate acceptable modes of reaching these goals. In our society, there is an exceptionally strong emphasis upon specific goals, without a corresponding emphasis on institutional procedures. When this process reaches its extreme form, demoralization or a state of "anomie" develops. Contemporary American culture is an extreme type in which great emphasis upon success goals occurs without equivalent emphasis upon the institutional means of achieving these goals. American culture enjoins the acceptance of three cultural axioms: "First, all should strive for the same lofty goals since these are open to all; second, present seeming failure is but a way-station to ultimate success; and third, genuine failure consists only in lessening or withdrawal of ambition." [19]

In the acceptance of these success goals and the prescribed means to them, Merton considers five possible types of adaptation, as illustrated on the following page. In a stable society, the majority of people both *conform* to cultural goals and accept the legitimate institutional means for achieving them. However, where there is unusual emphasis upon success goals without equal emphasis on the means for achieving them, the situation tends to change. Many individuals may accept the success goals, but not the institutionalized means; under such circumstances, the line between business-like striving and shady practice may grow quite vague. In America,

[17] *Ibid.*, p. 80.   [18] *Ibid.*, pp. 125–149.   [19] *Ibid.*, p. 132.

A Typology of Modes of Individual Adaptation [20]

Modes of Adaptation	Cultural Goals	Institutional Means
I. Conformity	+	+
II. Innovation	+	−
III. Ritualism	−	+
IV. Retreatism	−	−
V. Rebellion	±	±

in the course of the accumulation of their fortunes, the Robber Barons often employed *innovations* in this sense which were institutionally questionable. A *ritualistic* adaptation, by contrast, accepts the institutional means for achieving social goals in the given society but avoids psychological strains by rejecting the social goals a society may prescribe. For example, in some sections of American society where one's social status depends on achievement, a highly competitive struggle may ensue. By permanently lowering the level of one's aspirations, one may seek to allay the anxieties which such striving produces. Many lower-middle-class Americans have had recourse to this kind of conduct. *Retreatism* is a type of adaptation to social life that rejects both social goals and the means for achieving them. It is said to typify the activities of many psychotics, artists, pariahs, vagabonds, tramps, chronic drunkards and drug addicts. *Rebellion*, while superficially similar to retreatism, is quite different, for it is characterized by a combination of rejection and acceptance both of social goals and the institutional means for achieving them. The revolutionary who would both set up a new society and a new set of institutional means for achieving the goals of the new society epitomizes the rebel in pure form.

As an example of functional analysis, this essay by Merton represents a general improvement over Durkheim's assignment of anomie as a state of "social ill-health" to society. It isolates specific features of society in their possible combination (ends and means) as a basis for the location of adaptation possibilities. It may, incidentally, be noted that David Riesman's typology (in *The Lonely Crowd*) of personality types (inner-directed and other-directed men) is surpassed by this more precise schematization of types of personality adaptation. At the same time, in this example of functional analysis the fundamental unit — the system forming the basis for estimates of the functional significance of items — is no less than American society itself. This is fully developed functionalism, in which the system determines the elements.

George C. Homans

The wave of theory construction in a functionalistic vein signaled by the publication of Merton's essay in 1949 was followed by the appearance

[20] *Ibid.*, p. 133.

of George Homans' *The Human Group* [21] in 1950 — one of the major recent examples of functionalistic theory construction. George C. Homans (b. 1910) received his A.B. degree at Harvard in 1932. He was Junior Fellow from 1934 to 1939, and an instructor in sociology at Harvard from 1939 to 1946, and professor since 1953. Because of its thoroughness, if for no other reason, Homans' work will undoubtedly remain for some time as one of the most effective statements of the functionalistic theory. Early in the book he sets down the rules for theory construction and included among them — almost menacingly — is the precept: "Once you have started to talk, do not stop until you have finished." [22]

Essentially the book accomplishes two tasks: (1) the development of a general functionalistic theory of sociology, and (2) the illustration of the theory by the analysis of a series of concrete cases in terms of it: (a) The Bank Wiring Observation Room from F. J. Roethlisberger and William J. Dickson's *Management and the Worker;* (b) the Norton Street Gang from William Foote Whyte's *Street Corner Society;* (c) The Family in Tikopia from Raymond Firth's *We, The Tikopia;* (d) The Social Disintegration of Hilltown from D. L. Hatch's *Changes in the Structure and Function of a Rural New England Community Since 1900;* (e) The Social Conflict in an Electrical Equipment Company from C. M. Arensberg and D. Macgregor, *Determination of Morale in an Industrial Company.*

With the considered ease of a man who has thought through his task and is sure of himself, Homans shows no sense of urgency in advancing his theory but carefully presents the social situation described between members of the bank-wiring team studied in the Western Electric researches. Homans then "induces" his theory from this study. This done, he carefully illustrates ("tests") it in a series of extended examinations of the remaining empirical cases. Thus, the basic theory is not broached until well into the first quarter of the book.

The distinctive property of functional analysis is the utilization of some concept of system as primary for sociological analysis. The first requirement of a comprehensible analysis is the clear definition of the system presumed. Nothing will render a functional analysis ambiguous more quickly or completely than uncertainty as to just what, in the particular case, constitutes the system. Once one has isolated the system, the next task is to identify its components. And once the components have been identified, the relation between these components becomes primary. Merton had insisted that functionalism could work with units (systems) less than total societies. He did not, however, identify these. Furthermore, in the most highly imaginative case of functional analysis he conducted ("Social

[21] George C. Homans, *The Human Group* (New York: Harcourt, Brace, 1950). Other major works by Homans are: *An Introduction to Pareto,* written with Charles P. Curtis, Jr. (New York: Alfred A. Knopf, 1934) ; and *English Villagers of the Thirteenth Century* (Cambridge, Mass.: Harvard University Press, 1941).
[22] *The Human Group,* p. 17. This and the following quotations are used with the permission of Harcourt, Brace & Company and Routledge & Kegan Paul.

Structure and Anomie"), he said nothing explicitly about the system under consideration or its elements. By implication, the system is considered to be American society, and its component elements for the particular study were (1) success goals and (2) institutional means to successes. Homans was quite clear about the system under consideration and its elements. Merton was quite understandably lyrical in his introduction to the study: "despite my occasional disagreement with certain details in the book . . . I should like to express this considered judgment: not since Simmel's pioneering analyses of almost half a century ago has any single work contributed so much to a sociological theory of the structure, processes, and functions of small groups as George Homans' *The Human Group*." [23]

The system with which he is concerned is identified by Homans as the group, which he does not hesitate to expand to comprise the whole of the city of Hilltown. He is equally clear about the elements into which such a system is analyzable: (1) *activity* — what the members of the group do as members; (2) *interaction* — the relation of the activity of one member of the group to that of another; (3) *sentiment* — the sum of the feelings of group members with respect to the group; and (4) *norms* — the code of behavior adopted consciously or unconsciously by the group. It may be noted that these are quite remarkably like the elements which Znaniecki thought characterized a social system — tendency, attitude, value, social instrument, social method, social reaction.

In his consideration of the manner in which these form a system, Homans closely follows the division suggested by Pareto in his concept of external in contrast to internal system. The group is defined as a plurality of people in interaction. The activities, interactions, and sentiments of the members, together with mutual relations of these elements when the group is active, constitute a social system. If one were to arrange various organized wholes, from a thermodynamic system like hot coffee in a thermos bottle to the system of the human body, in a scale of their "organicity," social systems would come somewhere in between.[24] The group as a social system first forms an external system, determined by the needs of the group and the conditions of the environment. The environment is broken down into three main aspects: physical, technical, and social. The external system represents the group so far as it is conditioned by the environment, and it is called external because it is conditioned by the environment. It is a system because the elements of behavior are mutually dependent. The external system, plus another set of relations called the *internal* system, make up the total social system.

Homans is not only quite explicit about his system unit — the group (and community) as a social system made up of (a) an external and (b) an internal system — and his units of analysis for the study of systems, — activity, sentiment, interaction, norms; he is also clear that there is a

[23] *Ibid.*, p. xxiii.   [24] *Ibid.*, p. 87.

series of relations of mutual dependence between the elements of the external system.

(1) Between sentiment and activity: both motives and associated activities persist, both continuously recreated, but if either side of the relationship is changed, the other will be affected. For example, if one has just eaten and his hunger (sentiment) is appeased, he is not likely to go down to the restaurant and order a meal (activity).

(2) Between activity and interaction: if the scheme of activities is changed, the scheme of interaction will also change and vice versa.

(3) Taken as a whole, the elements form a pyramid of interaction. Whatever changes occur in the scheme of activities of a group, the scheme of interaction between the leaders of various levels and their followers tend to keep the same general pyramidal form. For instance, military units tend to keep their same non-commissioned officers when they are on a field problem or at home base.[25]

The model for developing these ideas is a specific subgroup in a modern factory. It may be noted that in all such cases the task of a specialized group in the factory is fixed by its place in the factory production schedule as a whole. It makes complete sense to speak of the output of the group as if it were a more or less fixed requirement placed on the group — it often is precisely that.

It may be noted, however, that there are some risks involved in conceiving the "external system" of all groups in terms of the situation of a subgroup in a factory. The concept of external system is extended to other groups which do not fit into such a tightly organized scheme imposed by an outside source. A primitive family, among the Tikopia for example, does not have clear-cut externally imposed production requirements; its relations to the external environment are much more various and plastic. Nothing could be more absurd than to treat it as if it were a kind of cog in a cosmic social machine. While the sub-unit of a factory has to maintain a given level of externally required output, the precise counterpart of this simply does not occur in a street corner gang of young men during a depression who hang around the streets, bowling alleys, and settlement houses because they have nothing else to do. To treat such a gang as maintaining a level of output in bowling scores is not a little farfetched.

Homans maintains that on the basis of the external system an internal system appears. The "external system" represents the behavior of a group so far as that behavior represents one possible answer to the question: how does the group survive in its particular environment? By contrast, the "internal system" represents the elaboration of group behavior that simultaneously arises out of the external system and reacts upon it. "We call the system 'internal' because it is not directly conditioned by the environment and we speak of it as an 'elaboration' because it includes forms or behavior not included under the heading of the external system." [26]

[25] *Ibid.*, pp. 99–104. (Paraphrased)   [26] *Ibid.*, p. 109.

The further interrelations between the various elements of the group as a social system produce effects that create the internal system. There seem to be two general processes: (a) integration of the specifically social system and (b) differentiation of its sub-components.

The integration of the specifically social system arises in the further interrelations of the basic variables.

> (1) Mutual dependence of interaction and sentiment: persons who interact frequently with one another tend to like one another. [This apparently holds in all cases except those where the individuals grow to hate one another.]
> (1a) If the frequency of interaction between two or more persons increases, the degree of liking for one another will increase and vice versa. [Except, again, where absence makes the heart grow fonder.]
> (1b) A decrease in the frequency of interaction between the members of a group and outsiders, accompanied by an increase in the strength of their negative sentiments toward outsiders, will increase the frequency of interaction and the strength of positive sentiments among group members.
> (2) Mutual dependence between sentiment and activity: persons who feel sentiments of liking for one another will express those sentiments in activities over and above any activities of the external system, and these activities may further strengthen the sentiments of liking.
> (3) Mutual dependence of activity and interaction: much of social activity — dances, parties — is enjoyed less for the sake of the activity itself, which may be trivial, than for the possibilities of social interaction it affords.
> (4) Standardization as a product of interrelation: the more frequently persons interact with one another, the more alike in some respects their activities and sentiments tend to become.[27]

The integration of a specifically social (internal) system is evident in the appearance of a new item or element in the schema of social systems, norms. A norm is an idea in the minds of the members of a group concerning what one ought to do under given circumstances. Norms are one of the most important parts of the culture of the group, emerging from activities and playing back on them. The members of a group are often more nearly alike in the norms they hold than in their overt behavior.

The integration of the specifically social products of interaction and the formation of a normatively integrated scheme is the first distinctive process in the emergence of the internal system. Differentiation within the group is the second. Here, again, the end result (the formation of subgroups within the larger group) is derived by Homans from the relation between the basic elements of action.

> (1) Mutual dependency of interaction and sentiment: the more frequently persons interact, the stronger their sentiments of friendship for one another are likely to be [except for contrary cases].
> (2) Sentiment and activity: persons who feel sentiments of liking for one another will express those sentiments in activities after work [at times, at least].

[27] *Ibid.*, pp. 111–120. (Paraphrased)

(3) Activity and interaction: persons who interact with one another frequently are often more like one another in their activities than they are like persons with whom they interact less frequently.[28]

These are all general relations already adduced to account for the appearance of an integrated internal system over and beyond the external system. It is Homan's view that they continue to operate to differentiate the subgroup. Moreover, a great deal of the behavior of the internal system is expressive or symbolic. The behavior of a clique is expressive of its identity. The cliques are subject to a social ranking, as are the individuals within them. Social ranking is primarily based on the relation between cliques. But it applies also to a person not tied in with the cliques, who is typically downgraded because he is not a member.

In all this, there is a reaction of the internal system back upon the external system. Homans introduces the concept of "feedback" — taken from the property of electrical circuits arranged in such a way that current at a certain point in the circuit is partly fed back by an appropriate hookup into an earlier point in the circuit, an arrangement which permits the circuit to build up more rapidly to its full load and carry that load without fluctuations. Feedback and build-up go on continuously. In the social system, Homans maintains, one of the distinctive properties is the feedback of the internal into the external system, with the process of build-up going on continuously. "Beneficent or vicious circles — 'spirals' would be a better word — are characteristic of all organic phenomena. We can say that the feedback of the internal system may be either favorable or unfavorable to the group, making its action or the environment more or less effective, provided we have adopted a definite basis for judgment." [29]

With these notions Homans' functionalistic theory is essentially complete, the rest of his study consisting primarily in the application of these ideas to a variety of groups such as a street corner gang and a primitive family. Homans' study of a New England city, "Hilltown," concerns a negative "spiral"; here he applies his "feedback" principle, tracing a process of disintegration which begins in a less favorable socio-economic situation (in the external system) and which leads to a declining system of interaction; he tries to demonstrate the "negative feedback" from a weakening internal system into the external system. Economic opportunities were reduced; population declined (after 1890); schism appeared in the church; social life weakened; norms became less binding; the boys turned to petty theft, the girls to prostitution; a state of anomie prevailed.

Homans' study of an electrical equipment company, on the other hand, presents more serious problems, for it represents a case of conflict, not one of a declining spiral from external system to internal system and back to external system. There is neither a decline of external system nor a lack of intensity in the various subgroups. In this case, a series of increasing

[28] *Ibid.*, pp. 132–135. (Paraphrased)   [29] *Ibid.*, pp. 153–154.

irreconcilable discrepancies arose between design engineers and supervisors. As the two groups worked at cross-purposes, without clear lines of authority, the situation became explosive. Conflict arose because there was no coordinating structure that could consistently operate. The role of leadership is found in supplying such decisive coordination.

The ties of functionalism with organicism are testified to, once again, as Homans turns his analysis from the small group, considered as an organic system, to the problems of the birth of civilization in the manner of Spengler, Toynbee, and Sorokin. Man remained at the level of the comparatively small group, he argues — the tribe, village, small group, in which members have first-hand knowledge of all the others — for many millenia before written history. Such small groups have survived and produced a surplus of goods and have made morale, leadership, and cooperation between increasingly larger groups possible. Civilization, in Homans' view, was erected on the foundation of such small groups.

> In our view, and here we are following Toynbee . . . ancient Egypt and Mesopotamia were civilizations. So were classical India and China . . . so is our own Western civilization. . . . These societies on the grand scale have had many characteristics in common. At its height, each has been inventive: it has devised and used a more powerful technology than any at the command of the tribes coming before and after it. Each has been coterminous geographically with a communications network . . . Each . . . developed new formal organizations, in law, government, warfare, and religion. . . . almost every one of the civilizations has worked out and adopted a single body of values and beliefs.[30]

But, alas, after thriving for a time each civilization has collapsed. Homans suggests why. "Our own theory, in its main lines, would run as follows. At the level of the tribe or group, society has always found itself able to cohere. We infer, therefore, that a civilization, if it is in turn to maintain itself, must preserve at least a few of the characteristics of the group. . . . Civilizations have failed in failing to solve this problem."[31] Psychiatry, Homans argues, proves that membership in a group sustains a man, enabling him to maintain his equilibrium under the ordinary shocks of life. If he leaves a group under stress he may develop disorders of thought, feeling, and behavior. His thinking will be obsessive and unrealistic, anxious, negativistic, and his behavior will be compulsive. This is particularly important at the time of the death of a civilization. There is a net increase in the number of isolated individuals lacking the old feeling of belongingness. "Each of the sociologists — Durkheim, Le Bon, Figgis, Brooks Adams — who began, just before World War I, to point out the signs of decay in our society, used the same metaphor. They said that society was becoming a dust heap of individuals without links to one another."[32]

Thus, as civilization advances, a process like that in the Electrical Equip-

[30] *Ibid.*, p. 455.   [31] *Ibid.*, p. 456.   [32] *Ibid.*, p. 457.

ment Company or Hilltown occurs. The technical and economic adapta... of society to its environment changes. Since the internal system is co... tinuous with the external, the relations between groups in society are disturbed and a negative spiral downward begins. The circulation of elites and rise of the most effective leaders may be involved. Able men devote their skills to making money, intrigue, using force, or exploiting the increasing antagonisms between groups. Effective communication flows naturally toward the leader, but when these events occur the communication channels are disrupted, transmitting inaccurate information. No one is responsible for paying attention to the whole. The small group controls persons who threaten to depart. Groups divide; society splits into warring camps, difficulties of communication appear, the spontaneous control by groups disappears in favor of control by force imposed by the central power. Society is in a complete state of anomie.

Throughout Homans' work it is assumed that society is organized into systems. These are not simply small groups. They may be large groups, communities, societies, or entire civilizations. It is assumed, however, that they are all systems of the same type and identical laws apply within them.

Every system has two subsystems: the external and internal. The model for this is the subgroup of a modern factory, where the distinction makes some sense. The extension of the pattern to all systems up to and including civilization represents the attempt to model the social universe after the pattern of the factory subgroup. This results in curious distortions of judgment, such as treating the bowling scores of the Norton Street gang like a factory output. A tantalizing sense of duplication adheres to the entire discussion. It reminds one of those medieval theories which treated the personality as a small man inside the big man, with the former behaving in an identical manner to the latter. Even if one accepts the rather strained assumption that the whole of the social world operates like a factory subgroup, the theory is subject to radical modification. If one does not admit that there are two systems, but sticks to the only one that is sometimes apparent, matters are worse.

The proposal to isolate the various elements of the system is a decided advance, but the difficulty with using such elements as "tendency," "sentiment," "activity," and "interaction" is that they do not appear to be distinct. Activity is not one thing and interaction another. The activity is interaction. The same mysterious sense of duplication appears here. If activity and interaction are merely two ways of describing the same thing, what possible meaning can adhere to a set of principles describing their interrelation? A good number of the presumed principles obtaining between the variables are gratuitous or tautological. At the same time, to the extent that the theory rests on indistinct variables and nonexistent systems, it is metaphysically irrefutable.

These shortcomings, however, should not obscure the clear gain in theoretical precision involved in any attempt to define more precisely the system and the nature and mode of operation of its work is a significant step forward.

of functionalistic theory is shown by the appearance, ...omans' study, of Talcott Parsons' first full-scale system- ...to functionalistic theory construction with *The Social System* ...,. As noted earlier, Parsons' first work on sociology was social be- navioristic. The degree to which he departed from this early social be- haviorism is in part indicated by the attack on *The Social System* by C. Wright Mills, one of the most vigorous of the contemporary social behaviorists. Unfortunately, Mills confines his attack primarily to quoting abstract and often clumsy statements and translating them into simpler language.

> Is grand theory, as represented in *The Social System*, merely verbiage or is it also profound? My answer to this question is: it is only about 50 per cent verbiage; 40 per cent is well-known textbook sociology. The other 10 per cent, as Parsons might say, I am willing to leave open for your own empirical investigations. My own investigations suggest that the remaining 10 per cent is of possible — although rather vague — ideological use.[33]

In the present discussion, the attempt is made to demonstrate both the fact that the materials of *The Social System* represent an internal develop- ment in Parsons' own outlook and a stage in the formulation of contempo- rary functionalism.

Parsons, to be sure, had already broached the problem of functionalist theory construction in the early forties and again in an address to the annual meeting of the American Sociological Society (1947) on "The Position of Sociological Theory," where he had urged the advisability of developing a "structural-functional theory." Such a theory would analyze action into cognitive, goal-directed, and affective elements. It would, more- over, complete itself by "an analysis of the functional prerequisites of the social system," which must somehow provide for the "minimum biological and psychological needs of a sufficient proportion of its component mem- bers." On a more strictly social level, two functional prerequisites were found. "One lies in the problem of order . . . the second focus is on the adequacy of motivation. The system can only function if a sufficient propor- tion of its members perform the essential social roles with an adequate degree of effectiveness." Moreover, Parsons urged, the structure of social systems needs to be studied. One aspect of this is found in "institutions," the second in "differentiation." The most promising lead in solving these problems is thought to lie in the "demonstration of the existence of certain invariant points of reference about which differentiated structures focus." [34]

---

[33] C. Wright Mills, *The Sociological Imagination* (New York: Oxford University Press, 1959), p. 49.

[34] Talcott Parsons, *Essays in Sociological Theory, Pure and Applied* (Glencoe, Ill.: The Free Press, 1949), pp. 6, 7. Parsons' major works are cited in Footnote 11, Chapter 16.

However, it is in *The Social System* that Parsons undertakes a major program of functionalistic theory construction. This program was frankly based on Pareto. "The title, *The Social System*, goes back, more than to any other source, to the insistence of the late Professor L. J. Henderson on the extreme importance of the concept of system in scientific theory, and his clear realization that the attempt to delineate the social system as a system was the most important contribution of Pareto's great work. This book therefore is an attempt to carry out Pareto's intuition, using . . . the 'structural-functional' level of analysis." [35]

In this work Parsons took a definite step away from the conception of "social action" as a kind of atomic unit out of which societies are composed and treated action itself as a system. A social system was conceived as a new whole composed of a plurality of interacting persons "motivated in terms of a tendency to the 'optimization of gratification' and whose relation to their situations, including each other, is defined and mediated in terms of a system of culturally structured and shared symbols." [36] A social system is one of three ways in which social action is structured. The other two are the personality systems of the individual actors and cultural systems.

The action system of the individual has two basic aspects: gratificational and orientational. The "gratificational" is called by Parsons "cathectic," the "orientational" is called "cognitive." That is, human action is thought by Parsons to display both desires and ideas. The objects that may satisfy needs are many; for example, there are numerous items that can satisfy hunger. "Cognitive mapping has alternatives of judgment or interpretation as to what objects are or what they 'mean.' There must be ordered selec- tion among such alternatives. The term 'evaluation' will be given to this process of ordered selection." [37] That is, action is to be analyzed into desires, ideas, and values or norms. An action system containing these elements is one of three types: (a) a social system, (b) a personality system, or (c) a cultural system.

A society is the sociologically decisive type of social system according to Parsons. As he phrases it in his own inimitable language:

Because empirical organization of the system is a fundamental focus, the norm, as it were, must be the conception of an empirically self-subsistent social system. If we add the consideration of duration sufficiently long to transcend the life span of the normal human individual, recruitment by biological reproduction and socialization of the oncoming generation be- come essential aspects of such a social system. A social system of this type, which meets all the essential functional prerequisites of long term persist- ence from within its own resources will be called a *society*. It is not essential to the concept of a society that it should not be in any way empirically interdependent with other societies, but only that it should contain all the

[35] Talcott Parsons, *The Social System* (Glencoe, Ill.: The Free Press, 1951), p. vii.
[36] *Ibid.*, pp. 5–6.　　　　[37] *Ibid.*, p. 7.

structural and functional fundamentals of an independently subsisting system. Any other social system will be called a "partial" social system.[38]

In other words, society is a large-scale, persistent, self-sufficient system of social interaction which must train its own members since it lasts longer than the individual.

If the fundamental unit of Homans' analysis is the group, the basic unit of Parsons' analysis is the society. The society is conceived as a system of interaction and the relations between the actors represent its structure. Its dependent sub-units are "status-roles." Participation by an actor in the social system means that he is "located" relative to other actors. This is his "status." In this position he does various things, and what he does is called his "role." There are two other possible units of society: the *actor*, who, as member of the social system, represents a bundle of statuses and roles; and the social *act*. However, the system is superior to its units. The collectivity as a composite unit "cuts across the individual actor as a composite unit." Thus, "status-role" is the proper unit of the social system rather than the actor or the action.

The functional prerequisites of social systems are the things needed if it is to remain stable. An action system may be centered in personality, society, or culture. Thus, the minimum conditions of stability or orderly development of a social system may be represented in terms of the following:

I. Functional prerequisites with respect to the individual: the minimum needs of the majority of the actors must be met.

II. Functional prerequisites with respect to the society: a minimum control over potentially disruptive behavior must be maintained.

III. Functional prerequisites with respect to culture: the social system is made possible by language and culture; hence, there must be sufficient cultural resources to internalize a level of personality adequate for a social system.[39]

According to Parsons, an action system brings motivational and symbolic elements into an ordered system. This order is normative and either instrumental or intrinsic. The norms are critical to *roles*, which organize the expectations of the individual in relation to a particular interaction context and govern interaction with one or more "alters" in complementary roles. The roles are critical to *institutions*, which are role integrates of strategic structural significance in the social system. A collectivity is the organization of a series of institutions. The degree to which normative patterns as role integrates are institutionalized varies from complete integration to anomie. Throughout, the normative ordering of need satisfaction is the basic phenomenon of the dynamics of social systems.

The parallels between Homans' account and Parsons' are fundamental. Homans analyzes his basic systems (groups) into sentiments, activity, and

---

[38] *Ibid.*, p. 19.   [39] *Ibid.*, pp. 26–27. (Paraphrased)

interaction. These arose in response to the external environment. The interrelation between these elements led to the development of a new element, the "norms," which formed the integration point of the internal system. Parsons analyzes his basic systems (societies) into status-roles. But the individuals who act in these status-roles have ideas and beliefs which are normatively ordered. In fact, the normative ordering of ideas and beliefs is already the critical aspect of status-roles. They are as central for Parsons' "society" as they were for Homans' "internal system." As the elements of integration, the distinctively "social" elements of the social system, norms are equally basic for Parsons and Homans.

Just as Homans found in the norms the point of integration of the internal system, but went on to account for differentiation within the internal system (the formation of subgroups), so Parsons, at the precisely equivalent place in his analysis, states that "the next step is to begin to lay the groundwork for dealing systematically with the differentiation of roles." [40] Parsons carries out this phase of analysis somewhat differently from Homans. Parsons has treated as the distinctive features of action the presence of ideas, desires, and values; or, as he phrases it, the organization of action-orientations consists "of the three modes of motivational orientation, cognitive, cathectic and evaluative." Parsons proposes that role differentiation occurs in terms of the relative predominance of one or another mode over the others. Moreover, just as there are types of role differentiation, so there are types of institutionalization relative to the social system. The central institutions are critical to the pattern. These are *relational* institutions. In terms of collective integration, the functional problem in social systems is the regulation of interests, giving rise to *regulative* institutions. *Cultural* institutions, the third type, pattern cultural orientations. Relational institutions define reciprocal role-expectations, regulative institutions define the legitimate means to be employed in the pursuit of interests, and cultural institutions define obligations with regard to cultural patterns. Relational institutions, in Parson's theory the most fundamental of all, lie at the very core of society.

Parsons' most unique contribution to sociological functionalism appears at this point in his conception of what he calls the "pattern-alternatives of value-orientations." These represent the possibilities in which the normative elements of relational institutions are defined. As he states the case: "It should again be emphasized that we are here dealing with the foci for the patterning of relational institutions." [41]

In any given action, Parsons maintains, the actor aims at optimum gratification. However, no action system can be organized or integrated without the renunciation of some gratifications. One cannot realistically want everything, one has to be neutral about some things. "The polarity of affectivity–neutrality formulates the patterning out of action with respect to this basic alternative." [42] Secondly, the individual faces a choice of

[40] *Ibid.*, p. 46.   [41] *Ibid.*, p. 59.   [42] *Ibid.*, p. 60.

pursuing interests private to himself or shared with others. The one alternative may be called "self-orientation," the other, "collectivity-orientation." [43] Thirdly, the given action may be determined either by ideas or feeling. "The primacy of cognitive values then may be said to imply a *universalistic* standard of role-expectation, while that of appreciative values implies a *particularistic* standard." [44] Moreover, in any action there are alternatives with respect to the properties of social objects. "There is one dilemma which is of the most generalized significance. . . . With respect to characteristics of the object it is that of the focus on its qualities or attributes as distinguished from focus on its performances." [45] In other words, one may value the other party to the social action on the basis of what he is (ascription) or what he does (achievement). There remains, according to Parsons, one further action alternative — that which defines the scope of ego's interest in the object. One possibility open to the actor is the definition of the role "as orienting to the social object in *specific* terms" in contrast to orientation in a *"diffuse"* mode.[46]

The five "pattern variables," as Parsons calls these dichotomies, may be grouped in various ways. When this is done, "their permutations and combinations should yield a system of types of possible role-expectation pattern, on the relational level, namely defining the pattern of orientation to the actors in the role relationship. This system will consist of thirty-two types, which may in turn be grouped into a number of more fundamental ones." [47]

It is useful to summarize Parsons' argument:

  I. Parsons breaks with the social-action branch of social behaviorism, reducing social action to the status of a dependent unit of one of three kinds of system.
  II. The fundamental elements of action are conceived to be ideas, desires, and values (cathectic, cognitive, and evaluative orientation).
  III. Action as a system is differentiated into three subsystems: personality, social system, culture.
  IV. A social system is, if total rather than partial, a society.
     a. It is a large-scale, persistent, independent system of social action.
     b. The primary units into which it is analyzed are role-statuses: positions plus the activities appropriate to them.
     c. The functional prerequisites of a society are those minimum requirements with respect to individuals, social systems, and culture without which the society could not exist.
     d. Institutions are large-order units formed out of status-roles when they are integrated and standardized.
     e. A collectivity is formed around a core of central institutions.
  V. Social norms form the central element in status-roles and institutions.
  VI. Institutions are of three types: relational (defining reciprocal role expectations); regulative (defining legitimate means to values); and cultural (defining cultural requirements).
     a. Of these, relational institutions are most critical for establishing the character of a society.

[43] *Ibid.*   [44] *Ibid.*, p. 62.   [45] *Ibid.*, p. 63.
[46] *Ibid.*, pp. 65–66.   [47] *Ibid.*, p. 47.

VII. Pattern alternatives of value orientation define relational role-expectation patterns. There are five of these pairs:
   a. Affectivity vs. Affective Neutrality
   b. Self-Orientation vs. Collectivity-Orientation
   c. Universalism vs. Particularism
   d. Achievement vs. Ascription
   e. Specificity vs. Diffuseness

Parsons' most original contribution to functionalistic social theory appears in his proposal to generate possible societies by counting the permutations and combinations of what he calls the "pattern alternatives of value orientation in role-expectation problems."

Parsons assumes that social structure is made up of institutions, institutions of roles, and roles of mutual expectations. This is not new, having been encountered many times before (Znaniecki, Mead, Gerth and Mills, Merton, and so on). He has assumed that the actions which compose roles are analyzable into ideas, emotions, and values. This idea, too, is not new. It has been actively promoted in sociology by Gerth and Mills, W. I. Thomas, Znaniecki, and many others. The idea is as old as medieval psychology — in fact, as old as Aristotle.

Many times in human history the various elements of action have been conceived dichotomously. It has been observed that the scope of one's sympathies may be very general or very specific; one may be emotionally engaged over an issue or quite lukewarm or even neutral. So far as one's actions may involve others, one may be selfish or unselfish, egoistic or altruistic. In short one's ideas, feelings, or values and the presence or absence of others in an act have at various times been categorized dichotomously.

Parsons' novelty consists in treating five of such dichotomous categorizations of action as (1) exhaustive and as (2) defining a society — or at least defining relational-expectations or roles, which in turn define a society. If one grants this, Parsons is quite correct. By counting the permutations and combinations of this system of dichotomies, one will have established a system of possible societies. There are two fundamental points at which this scheme may break down. Either these dichotomous classifications are not exhaustive and/or they are insufficient to define a society.

However, that the full originality of Parsons' formulation is by no means exhausted by these interesting proposals appears when the resulting theoretical scheme is used to assess empirical uniformities. The scheme permits the discovery of how limited reality is, for "in certain crucial areas of social structure we do not find that empirically observable structures cover anything like the whole range of theoretically possible variability." [48] It seems, however, that the barrenness of reality can serve some value. At least it can save us the necessity of investigating all this theory. The existence of such clusterings as we find, in fact, "serves a

[48] *Ibid.*, p. 152.

two-fold purpose for the sociologist. On the one hand it justifies his short-cutting investigation of the *whole* range of structural possibilities and concentrating on a fraction of them." [49] Even more, it may aid in the formulation of laws showing why the theory doesn't apply. "It can serve as a highly important lead into the formulation, and hence testing, of fundamental dynamic generalization, of laws of social process, since the explanation of *why* the logically possible range of variability is empirically restricted can be found only in terms of such laws." [50]

The application to fact of this theoretically generated system turns up a surprise. "From a purely taxonomic point of view any considerable prominence of kinship in social structures generally would seem highly problematical." [51] This strongly suggests to Parsons a kind of conflict of facts with theory. "The fact that kinship looms large in every known society means that a great many other logically possible permutations of the structural elements have either been eliminated or relegated to secondary positions in the social structure." [52]

This formulation of functionalistic theory by no means represents Parsons' final statement of the theory. He has continued to advance the analysis and it will be useful to return later to some other phases of his formulations.

Marion J. Levy

The sudden ferment in functionalistic sociological theory continued, and a year after the appearance of Parsons' *The Social System,* Marion Levy brought out *The Structure of Society.*[53] Marion J. Levy was born in Galveston, Texas, in 1918. He received his A.B. degree at Harvard in 1939, and his Ph.D. degree in 1947. He has been on the staff at Princeton since 1947. In *The Structure of Society,* Levy attempted to synthesize structural-functional analysis. His formulation has interest for its attempt to bring the views of Merton and Parsons together. Levy conceives a "function" as a condition or state of affairs resulting from the operation of a structure through time. A "structure" is conceived as a pattern or observed uniformity of action. A "functional requisite" is defined as a generalized condition necessary for the maintenance of the unit with which it is associated, given the level of generalization of the definition of the unit and the setting of the unit. A "structural requisite" is defined as a pattern of action necessary for the continued existence of the unit with which it is associated.

In addition to functional and structional requisites, Levy also defines functional and structural prerequisites. A "functional prerequisite" is conceived as a function that must pre-exist if a given unit in its setting is to come into being. A "structural prerequisite" is conceived as a structure that must pre-exist if a given unit is to come into existence in its setting.

[49] *Ibid.*   [50] *Ibid.*
[51] *Ibid.*, p. 153.   [52] *Ibid.*, pp. 153–154.
[53] Marion J. Levy, *The Structure of Society* (Princeton, N.J.: Princeton University Press, 1952).

Still further the concepts of eufunction, dysfunction, eustructure, and dys-structure were added. A "eufunction" is a condition or state of affairs resulting from the operation of a structure of a given unit through time which increases or maintains adaptation or adjustment to the unit's setting, thus making for the persistence of the unit, as defined, of which the structure concerned is a part. A "dysfunction" is a condition, or state of affairs, that results from the operation of a structure of a given unit through time and which lessens the adaptation or adjustment to the unit's setting, making for a lack of persistence of the unit of which the structure concerned is a part or aspect. A "eustructure" is a structure the operation of which results in eufunctions. A "dysstructure" is a structure the operation of which results in dysfunctions.

To these distinctions, that between manifest and latent function and structure is added. A factor is "manifest" if it is intended and recognized by participants in the system. A factor is "latent" if it is neither intended nor recognized. Also, functions may be intended but unrecognized, and unintended but recognized.

A concrete structure is a pattern that defines the character of units which are in theory capable of physical separation from other units of which they are parts. Patterns defining the character of membership units are of this type. Analytical structures are patterned aspects of action that are not even theoretically capable of concrete separation from other patterned aspects of action.

Institutions are a particular type of normative pattern, conformity to which is generally expected and failure to conform to which is generally met with moral indignation of those persons involved in the same general social system. There are different degrees of institutionalization, and differences in conformity and the degree to which conformity is expected. There are also differences in sanctioning and in the degree to which failure to conform is met with moral indignation. Crucial and strategic institutions are defined by the fact that they are structural requisites of the system in which they appear. An institution is strategic to the degree to which it is the institutionalized form of all or a portion of structural requisites, and the pattern concerned may be altered without destroying the structural requisite involved. A tradition is an institution the perpetuation of which is institutionalized.

A society is a system of action in operation which involves a plurality of individuals recruited at least in part by the sexual reproduction of members of the plurality, at least in theory self-sufficient for the action of the plurality, and capable of existing longer than the life span of an individual of the type involved. The members of society are the plurality of interacting individuals involved in the system and acting in terms of the system. An individual is better or more poorly integrated as a member of society to the degree that he accepts and orients his action without conflict to the structures in general but particularly to the crucial and strategic institutions of that society. The four conditions that may terminate a society are (a) biological extinction or dispersion of the members, (b) apathy of the members, (c) the war of all against all, and (d) absorption of the society into another. A social change is any alteration which occurs in a system of action of a given type which is not subject to explanation solely in terms of heredity of that species and its environment. A culture is the system of action of a society considered apart from its operation.

A given function is a requisite of any society if in its absence the relationship between the unit under discussion and its setting in the most general terms can be shown to be such that one or some combination of the four conditions for the termination of a society would result. Among the functional requisites of any society are:

(1) Provision for an adequate physiological relationship to the setting for the sexual requirement. Maintaining a sufficient number and sufficient kinds of members for the adequate functioning of society.

(2) Role differentiation and role assignment. A role is any position differentiated in terms of a given social structure, whether the position be institutionalized or not.

(3) Communication. Communication is the activity or process by which ideas and/or feeling states are conveyed.

(4) Shared cognitive orientations.

(5) A shared set of goals.

(6) A regulation of the choice of means.

(7) Regulation of affective expression.

(8) Adequate socialization. There is adequate socialization if there is a sufficient number of adequately socialized individuals for the structural requisites of the society to operate.

(9) Effective control of disruptive behavior.

(10) Adequate institutionalization. Institutionalization is adequate if its conformity and sanction aspects are carried sufficiently far to permit the persistence of the minimal normative structures involved in other functional requisites.

It may be noted that Levy has brought the formulations of Merton and Parsons together with unusual compactness. The definitions of function, dysfunction, and latent and manifest function are all directly equivalent to those of Merton. The analysis of society, institution, and of the functional prerequisites of society are quite in the tradition of Parsons. Other than the attempt to fill in the blanks and work the ideas together, no basic innovations are attempted. Thus, so far as critical considerations apply to the functionalistic theories of Merton and Parsons, they would seem to apply to this formulation as well.

Not the least interesting of the novelties is Levy's conception of the field:

> Structural-functional analysis is not something new. . . . It has a pedigree that stretches indefinitely far back . . . The only "new" aspect of it is its formidable new name, "structural-functional analysis." Simply speaking,

it consists of nothing more complicated than phrasing empirical questions in one of the following several forms or some combination of them: (1) What observable uniformities . . . may be discovered in the phenomena studied? (2) What conditions . . . may be discovered? or (3) When processes . . . may be discovered to take place in terms of observable uniformities, what resultant conditions may be discovered? [54]

This is rather startling in view of the evident purpose Levy had in mind of synthesizing, by way of a uniform vocabulary, the positions of Merton and Parsons. This statement denies that sociological functionalism is a special movement in sociological theory. This is hardly the position of either Parsons or Merton or any of the functionalists reviewed. Sociological functionalism, it seems, sometimes has to be protected against its friends.

For the reasons developed above (see pp. 444 ff.), the conceptions — as I interpret them — of *function* as the effects of the operation of a structure, *eufunction* as those functions which increase or maintain adaptation or adjustment, and *dysfunction* as those which do not, are neither very enlightening nor do they constitute a distinctive theory. If one considers the activities of the human body, they may be grouped into two types: those internal to the operation of the body, on the one hand, and overt behavior, such as walking, on the other. The heart beats, the blood pulses through the arteries and veins, the lungs alternately expand and contract, oxygen is absorbed, carbon dioxide is released, and so on. Each one of these events may be conceived as making for adaptation or adjustment. But if one once starts walking, the entire system is thrown off balance. The pulse increases, the breath comes a bit faster, and so on. Presumably, in Levy's terms, the operations of heart, lungs, blood, etc., are "eufunctions" but walking is not. If one is correct in assuming that Levy intends his distinctions to be exhaustive, whatever is not a eufunction is a dysfunction, and walking, in this context, is transferred to the field of pathology. It is not suggested that Levy intends this, but it calls attention to the consequences of a simplistic conception of function. Moreover, it is related to a basic deficiency in this version of functionalism — the failure consistently to isolate the system forming the fundamental unit of analysis. In view of this, the elaborate mechanical baggage of terms (eufunction, dysfunction; eustructure, dysstructure) is rather beside the point — or perhaps "dysfunctional"?

The Parsonians

Parsons' first full statement of a functionalistic position was reviewed earlier. However, it was not his final statement, for he has continued to develop his theories. Further, he has formed the center of a very active school. In the interesting study, *Working Papers in the Theory of Action*,[55]

[54] *Ibid.*, p. 27.
[55] Talcott Parsons, Robert F. Bales, and Edward A. Shils, *Working Papers in the Theory of Action* (Glencoe, Ill.: The Free Press, 1953).

Robert F. Bales and Edward Shils joined their talents to those of Parsons in the development of functionalistic theory. Robert F. Bales was born in Ellington, Missouri, in 1916. He received a B.S. degree from the University of Oregon in 1938, and a Ph.D. degree in 1945 from Harvard, where he has continued to teach.

A Macro-Functionalist Theory of Personality. The problem of developing a macro-functionalistic theory of personality was broached by Parsons in a paper on "The Superego and the Theory of Social Systems." He proposed linking the theories of Freud and Durkheim, utilizing as the link between them the interaction of two or more persons considered as a system. This, he suggests, corrects both Freud and Durkheim. Freud failed to consider the fact that the individual's interactions with others form a system; Durkheim failed to see that the social system consisted in the interaction of personalities. Two interacting persons, Parsons suggests, are objects to each other cognitively and emotionally. The third way which the person orients himself to an object is by evaluations, which constitute the normative aspect of action — the integration of the conceptual and emotional into a system over time.

The only way in which a stable mutually oriented system of interaction on the human level can arise is on the basis of a common culture, consisting of shared symbols, the meanings of which are mutually understood. This symbol system is important in the socialization of the child. The elements of common culture have significance for all the modes of orientation of action.

Only when a sufficiently developed cognitive reference system and a system of expressive symbolism have been internalized is the foundation laid for the development of the superego. Culture is a system of generalized symbols and meanings. In order for its integration with the emotional life of an individual, which constitutes internalization, to occur, the individual's own affective organizations must be generalized at a high order. The mechanism by which this occurs is through emotional communication with others, sensitizing the individual to the attitudes of others. It is not only the superego which is internalized; also internalized are the systems of cognitive categorizations of the object world and the system of expressive symbolism.

To summarize Parsons' general argument:

  I. Social interaction is a system analyzable into three kinds of elements:
    (a) ideas, (b) emotions and drives, and (3) values and norms.
 II. Human culture consists, in part, of the system of common symbols with common meanings that make interaction possible.
    A. If interaction is complete, it must involve all three types of elements.
    B. Culture must consist of symbol systems adequate to all three categories of elements. These are:
    1. A cognitive reference system.
    2. A common moral standard.
    3. A system of expressive symbolism.

III. Socialization consists in the structuring of individual behavior on the basis of the symbol systems of common culture.

IV. Freud had already perceived that socialization represents the structuring of individual personality on the basis of the internalization of cultural norms.

V. A complete theory of personality requires the recognition that under the influence of common culture something more than common moral standards are internalized. Such a complete theory establishes the following links:

Cultural Objects	*Internalized Subject and Social Objects*
1. Cognitive reference system	Internalized self-object images
2. Cultural moral standards	Superego
3. Expressive symbolism	Symbolically organized affect

In brief, Parsons believes that the functionalistic theory of personality represents a modified form of Freudianism. His analysis differs from the Freudian theory primarily in the fact that it contemplates the formation of personality not only on the basis of the internalization of common moral standards, which Freud himself had originally seen as providing the personality with a superego, but it involves as well the internalization from the culture of concepts of self and symbols for emotional expression. (Freud, I suspect, would retort that he always said personality is made up of an *ego* and *id* as well as a *superego*.)

It is significant that Parsons turns to Freud rather than to one or any of the branches of social behaviorism for a theory of personality adequate for functionalism.

A Functionalistic Theory of Symbolism. In another of the papers, Parsons proposes the development of a functionalistic theory of symbolism. He feels that there has been a failure to develop "a coherent treatment of the *content* as distinguished from the meanings of expressive symbolism." [56] Parsons argues that a symbol always has both cognitive and expressive meanings. The former primarily refers to the situational object, the latter to the actor's own motivations or intentions.

Cognitive symbolism involves the actor as knower. Expressive symbolism involves the actor as a motivated agent. Expressive symbols mediate the action of the actor and others in a social situation.

A plurality of actors in an interactive situation are mutually interdependent for gratification. "We may now introduce another generalization or postulate. This is that two or more objects which are cathected with the same *quality* of cathectic significance, which in expressive terms have the same order of meaning for the ego, will tend to become symbolically associated with each other." [57] Moreover, insofar as one's own preference is an expression of his motivation, it becomes susceptible to interpretation by himself and the others in the social act as an expressive sign or symbol

[56] *Ibid.,* p. 31.   [57] *Ibid.,* p. 36.

of his motivation. However, "it must not be forgotten that when we speak of communication here there is always a cognitive component, but the distinctive feature of expressive symbolism is its communication of 'affect' or of 'feeling.' " [58] There remains only one further point. "A set of expressive signs or symbols . . . comes to be organized as a system. As such, a principal condition of its serving the communicative function in either its cognitive or its expressive aspects is necessarily that the interacting actors are oriented to conformity with normative standards. The 'conventions' of the symbolic system must be observed if there is to be effective communication, just as in the case of language." [59]

Reduced to its simplest terms, Parsons argues: (1) that functionalism requires a new theory of symbolism; (2) such a theory of symbolism must take account of the fact that human interaction requires a "language of emotions" as well as a "language of ideas"; (3) such a language of emotions permits the communication of motives and emotions ("It is crucial that *what* is communicated is not only *understanding of motives* in the cognitive sense, but is *mutuality of affective meanings*.") ; [60] (4) for full use as a communicative device, this "language of emotions" must rest upon symbolic conventions.

This particular paper seems intended to take over the Freudian system of emotional symbolism into functionalistic theory. Parsons appears to contemplate the possibility that there are two quite distinct sets of symbols: one for ideas, one for emotions. The latter are formed into distinct systems, and based on distinct linguistic conventions. At least this seems to be the implication of a statement such as the following: "This organization of expressive symbols, according to appreciative standards on a cultural level, is not merely 'external' to the actor but becomes, by 'internalization,' a constitutive part of his own personality structure." [61] To anyone brought up in the belief that the communication and "expression" of ideas are merely different uses of ordinary language, this seems rather mysterious. Perhaps before long we can expect from Parsons a dictionary of the emotions, a grammar of the emotions, and a logic of the emotions.

The Dimensions of Action-Space. In the joint paper on "The Dimensions of Action-Space," Parsons and Bales took a major step toward demonstrating the identity of their two brands of functionalism and went a step further in developing Parsons' concept of pattern variables. Bales has for some time made studies of small groups, some of the results of which were published in *Interaction Process Analysis*.[62] The fundamental theoretical ideas of the joint paper are summarized by Bales and Parsons:

> The essential approach was to think of the small group as a functioning social system. It was held that such a system would have four main "func-

[58] *Ibid.*, p. 38.   [59] *Ibid.*   [60] *Ibid.*   [61] *Ibid.*, p. 39.
[62] Robert F. Bales, *Interaction Process Analysis* (Reading, Mass.: Addison-Wesley Press, 1950).

tional problems," which were described, respectively, as those of *adaptation* to conditions of the external situation, of *instrumental* control over parts of the situation in the performance of goal oriented tasks, of the management and *expression* of sentiments and tensions of the members, and of preserving the social *integration* of members with each other as a solidary collectivity.[63]

Meanwhile, Parsons, in collaboration with Edward Shils,[64] developed the scheme of pattern variables reviewed earlier. These were conceived of as "dilemmas" in choice situations. Two of them (affective expression versus affective neutrality, and specificity versus diffuseness) are here said to concern the dilemmas the actor faces in deciding how his *attitudes toward objects shall be organized.* Furthermore, a second set of dilemmas (those of universalism versus particularism and of ascribed quality versus performance) represent dilemmas the actor faces in deciding how *objects themselves shall be organized* in relation to each other and in relation to the motivational interests of the actor. Parsons and Bales maintain that the fifth pattern variable, that of self-orientation versus collectivity-orientation is not paired with any other, and does not as such belong either to the attitudinal classification or to object categorization. This is because it is concerned with problems internal to the system of interaction rather than with problems internal to each act.[65]

These further comments on the pattern variables have an extremely deceptive property. In the actions of ordinary mortals, one is not faced with a dilemma whether to be or not to be emotionally involved. As a matter of fact he *is* or he *is not* emotionally involved. There may be a series of dilemmas in action occurring over alternative goals: whether to marry or pursue a career, whether to pursue one career rather than another, whether to lie and protect a friend or tell the truth and expose him. But to describe the pattern variables — the dichotomous classifications of various properties of the means, ends, or norms of action — as "dilemmas of action choice" is surrealism. Ordinary mortals sometimes have conflicts in their choices, but Parsons and Bales have problems as to whether to choose to choose.

It is the argument of Parsons and Bales that their "two sets of categories, or paradigms," though independently arrived at, may be brought together into a single formulation. They argue that the basic conception underlying both original schemes is that of a process described by comparison with a hypothetical system in a state of moving equilibrium. New elements are being added, either by perception and cognition, by personalities, or by a change in the situation. If the system is to regain equilibrium, there must be a process of adjustment to the disturbance.

[63] *Working Papers in the Theory of Action*, p. 64.
[64] See especially Talcott Parsons and Edward A. Shils (eds.), *Toward a General Theory of Action* (Cambridge, Mass.: Harvard University Press, 1951).
[65] *Working Papers in the Theory of Action*, p. 66.

Thus, it is maintained that the two schemes may be fused forthwith and the pattern variables conceived as dimensions of a four-dimensional space. "The suggestion was first made by [Robert R.] Bush that what we have here are the *dimensions of a four-dimensional* space in the mathematical sense of that term. We would like to assume from here on that this interpretation is correct and attempt to develop the implications of this assumption for the nature of the variables involved and of the theoretical system in which they belong." [66] Thus, Bales's "four functional problems" and Parsons' "pattern variables" are now fused and conceived as dimensions of space. Any activity is treated as a change of location in such a social space. The unit of observation for such change of location is taken to be the behavioral role. "This is the unit of observation in the interaction process but it is *not* the unit or particle of the *system* of action in the theoretical sense." [67] Where the system being studied is a system of social interaction, the unit is a role; if it is a personality system, it is a need-disposition.

Action now is conceived as a change of location on the dimensions of action-space. However, since we are dealing with systems in equilibrium, a tendency toward constancy or "inertia" must be assumed. The maintenance of a system is attributed to "boundaries" of the theoretical action-space. Three of these are particularly important:

  I. The first is involved in the conception of the goal attainment of a system unit-act.
 II. The second boundary condition concerns the dimension of tension, which may decline to a zero point.
III. The third boundary-feature of the system is assimilation to the environment.[68]

Parsons and Bales urge that the disintegration of a boundary-maintaining system represents disappearance of differences between internal states and the environment. This is death in the biological sense. Corresponding to the reification of dichotomous classification of the elements of action is the reification of functional prerequisites.

It becomes increasingly clear, with the conception of the pattern variables as dimensions of action-space, the conception of motivation as a change of location on these coordinates, and the conception of actions as a part of boundary-maintaining systems, that the model of classical mechanics is basic to the argument. This is made quite explicit. The laws of equilibrium in social systems are expressed as:

1. *The Principle of Inertia:* A given process of action will continue unchanged in rate and direction unless impeded or deflected by opposing motivational forces.
2. *The Principle of Action and Reaction:* If, in a system of action, there is a change in the *direction* of a process, it will tend to be balanced by a *com-*

66 *Ibid.*, p. 85.   67 *Ibid.*, p. 87.
68 *Ibid.*, pp. 91–92. (Paraphrased)

Bronislaw Malinowski

A. R. Radcliffe-Brown

Kurt Lewin

Florian Znaniecki

Leon Festinger

Talcott Parsons

Robert Merton

George C. Homans

Robert F. Bales

Marion J. Levy

plementary change which is equal in motivational force and opposite in direction.

3. *The Principle of Effort:* Any change in the rate of an action process is directly proportional to the *magnitude* of the motivational force applied or withdrawn.

4. *The Principle of System-Integration:* Any *pattern* element (*mode of organization* of components) within a *system* of action will tend to be confirmed in its place within the system or to be eliminated from the system (extinguished) as a function of its contribution to the integrative balance of the system.[69]

This seems to be nothing less than a return to the social physics of Berkeley.

The same fusion of Bales's "functional problems" and of the Shils–Parsons "pattern variables" into dimensions of action-space forms the theoretical foundation of the paper by all three of these authors, "Phase Movement in Relation to Motivation, Symbol Formation, and Role Structure," in which motivation and related problems are investigated. The whole elaborate baggage of concepts is developed to trace the changing nature of the motivation of an act. The extensively elaborate account that results bears a direct similarity to the very simple one with which John Dewey had acquainted the world at least half a century earlier. He had stated that some tension situation always represents the beginning of an act. If the tension cannot be ignored, or if it grows worse, it leads to the institution of a problem, the location of the conditions causing the tension, and the developing of a plan of action to clear it up. When the plan is tried out, it either solves the problem or leads to a new plan. When the tension is resolved, the organism is in a state of satisfaction. One's emotions have gone through a series of stages. Initially one was at rest. Some tension disturbed the peace. A solution was sought and found. One returns to a state of rest. The identical argument seems to be contained in the Parsons–Bales–Shils study of phase movement in relation to motivation. The three authors conclude that the processes accompanying motivation are a clockwise movement through the dimensions of action-space.

Summary

The two major sub-schools of functionalism today are macro- and micro-functionalism. The chief difference between them lies in the size of the organic unit they take to be fundamental. The macro-functionalists focus on large-scale social systems, the micro-functionalists on the small group.

The deepest roots of macro-functionalism are found in positivistic organicism. The transition to macro-functionalism was made possible by the abstraction and generalization of the concept of "system." The performance of this task was the work of Pareto and Znaniecki. Pareto developed the concept of an external and internal system, and Znaniecki developed the

[69] *Ibid.*, pp. 102–103.

concept of a closed system. The general features of macro-functionalism have evolved rapidly in the works of Robert Merton, Talcott Parsons, George Homans, Marion Levy, and the Parsonians, including Shils and Bales.

SELECTED BIBLIOGRAPHY

BALES, ROBERT F., *Interaction Process Analysis*. Reading, Mass.: Addison-Wesley Press, 1950.

HOMANS, GEORGE C., *The Human Group*. New York: Harcourt, Brace, 1950.

LEVY, MARION J., *The Structure of Society*. Princeton, N.J.: Princeton University Press, 1952.

MERTON, ROBERT K., *Social Theory and Social Structure*. Revised edition. Glencoe, Ill.: The Free Press, 1957.

PARETO, VILFREDO, *The Mind and Society*. Four volumes. Translated by Andrew Bongiorno and Arthur Livingston. New York: Harcourt, Brace, 1935.

PARSONS, TALCOTT, *Essays in Sociological Theory, Pure and Applied*. Second edition. Glencoe, Ill.: The Free Press, 1954.

PARSONS, TALCOTT, *The Social System*. Glencoe, Ill.: The Free Press, 1951.

PARSONS, TALCOTT, ROBERT F. BALES, and EDWARD A. SHILS, *Working Papers in the Theory of Action*. Glencoe, Ill.: The Free Press, 1953.

ZNANIECKI, FLORIAN, *The Laws of Social Psychology*. Chicago: University of Chicago Press, 1925.

ZNANIECKI, FLORIAN, *Cultural Sciences: Their Origin and Development*. Urbana, Ill.: University of Illinois Press, 1952.

19

Micro-Functionalism: Group Dynamics

THE FORM OF FUNCTIONALISTIC SOCIOLOGICAL THEORY THAT HAS JUST BEEN
sketched has been called macro-functionalism to distinguish it from the
second branch of the theory. Functionalism is characterized by its conception of the primacy of system. It is therefore appropriate to describe
the subtypes of functionalism in terms of the kind of system isolated.
Historically, the predecessors of the macro-functionalists were the positivistic organicists. Society in almost all cases represented their primary
unit of analysis. The macro-functionalists attempt repeatedly to give an
exact definition of "society" (as, for example, a total, independent, self-
sufficient system, persisting for time periods longer than the individual life).
There is little question that, in terms of their derivations and emphasis,
the macro-functionalists rest their case on the large-scale social system
(typically the society). At the same time, with the increasing attempts to
generalize the concept of system (beginning seriously with the work of
Znaniecki) and with the application of the concept to a wide variety of
social phenomena at different levels of complexity, the macro-functionalists
tend to narrow the compass of their critical systems. Still, even while criticizing the anthropologists for working with systems of too large a scale,
Merton tended to take the society-sized unit as his analytical model. And
Parsons, in *The Social System*, took society as his unitary system, although
he later fused his idea of systems with Bales's smaller units. Starting with
societies as their unitary system, the macro-functionalists tend to extend
analysis downward to include less inclusive systems.

The micro-functionalists, on the other hand, seem to be in process of working out a general functional sociological theory from the opposite direction. The origins of this branch of functionalism were in Gestalt psychology, which, as has been noted, originated in the reassertion of teleological explanations in human psychology against the mechanistic theories of the associationists. Against associationistic atomism (or as some prefer, "elementarism"), it asserted the presence of design in consciousness — an idea quickly broadened to include the concept of totality. The problems that soon came under investigation were those involved in the relationship between various kinds of psychological wholes and their parts and the problem of the adaptation of behavior to structures.

It has been pointed out that the starting point of the position can be traced to the work of Christian von Ehrenfels, who called attention to the fact that a melody is instantly recognized though transposed into a different key. He postulated a *Gestaltqualität* to account for this phenomenon, suggesting that order arises from a spontaneous process which forms functional wholes. The physical environment affects the organism through the senses. The resulting impressions are organized into distributions within the organism. Subjected to stresses, they are released by a form of energy within the distribution. Relations of closure, articulation, and consistency characterize these wholes.

The importance of the early formulations by Ehrenfels is due to the clarity with which the concept of system was perceived and formulated. From these beginnings the Gestalt psychologists soon came to protest against the exclusively neurological explanation of learning. A configurational interpretation of learning was brilliantly advanced in Köhler's theories and experiments with chimpanzees. Step by step, it moved toward a general organismic conception of human nature. It found analogical parallels between physical systems of energy (like the gravitational system) and organismic systems and developed the principle of the dynamics of energy systems. While macro-functionalism has tended to come to grips with the basic properties of systems under the more or less vague idea of "functional prerequisites," the Gestaltists early attempted an exact formulation.

I. *The Principle of Field Properties.* The units studied by science are systems in which parts are conjoined into something more than the qualities of the parts, which acquire their character through a field of properties. Relation of parts has the properties of a gradient in an organism.

II. *The Principle of Conditioned Action.* The movement of any body within a system is determined by the system as a whole, like an object in a gravitational system or the cell in a multi-cellular organism.

III. *The Principle of Differentiation.* Living systems are generated in undifferentiated cells. Growth occurs through a differentiation of parts as structure is specialized into organs.

IV. *The Principle of Unitary Evolution.* Differentiation is not an additive process. The whole is primary.

V. *The Principle of Least Action.* Energy is redistributed in a system by way of the shortest distance from high to low potential.

VI. *The Principle of Maximum Work.* When a system of energy is in equilibrium its maximum energy is distributed within the field as potential energy. When the balance is disturbed the energy is converted into kinetic energy exerted to restore the balance.

VII. *The Principle of Reciprocal Unitary Reaction.* The whole integrates its elements into a harmonious and complete system. When the unit member retains some autonomy in the exercise of its special differentiated function this is in accordance with impulse emanating from the whole.[1]

As Levine has pointed out, the Gestaltists view every system of energy as in constant alternation from quiescence to activity, balance to disequilibrium and back. And nature itself is conceived as an energy system.

In a situation where the macro-functionalists were appealing to Gestalt theory for support, it is little surprising that Gestaltists should develop their own brand of sociological functionalism. The charismatic leader who led the Gestaltists into the promised land was Kurt Lewin.

Kurt Lewin

Kurt Lewin (1890–1947), a German Gestalt psychologist, and his associates Ronald Lippitt and R. K. White, demonstrated the possibility of extending the Gestalt point of view into social situations in a series of studies, conducted at the University of Iowa Child Welfare Research Station, of the effect of democratic, authoritarian, and *laissez-faire* types of leaders upon groups. In 1945, Lewin formed the Research Center for Group Dynamics at the Massachusetts Institute of Technology. After Lewin's death, Dorwin Cartwright, the present director of the Research Center, carried on the work with the assistance of Ronald Lippitt and others. In 1948 the Center was moved to the University of Michigan. The Center has actively pursued the functionalistic sociology originally shaped in Lewin's work.[2]

The steps by which Lewin made the transition from Gestalt psychology to a micro-functionalistic Sociology are quite logical. Gestalt psychology had continually expanded its investigations until it was ready to develop a theory of personality. When Lewin took this step, he found that it almost automatically raised the question of the bearing of the social and cultural milieu (field) on the person. When his field theory of personality was followed by the study of the effects of leader types on group atmospheres,

[1] Paraphrased from the very clear summary of Albert J. Levine, *Current Psychologies* (Cambridge, Mass.: Science-Art Publishers, 1940), pp. 94–99.

[2] Kurt Lewin's major works are: *A Dynamic Theory of Personality: Selected Papers,* translated by Donald K. Adams and Karl E. Zener (New York: McGraw-Hill, 1935); *Principles of Topological Psychology,* translated by Fritz Heider and Grace M. Heider (New York: McGraw-Hill, 1936); *The Conceptual Representation and the Measurement of Psychological Forces* (Durham, N.C.: Duke University Press, 1938); *Resolving Social Conflicts: Selected Papers on Group Dynamics, 1935–1946,* edited by Gertrud Weiss Lewin (New York: Harper, 1948); and *Field Theory in Social Science: Selected Theoretical Papers,* edited by Dorwin Cartwright (New York: Harper, 1951).

the link to a general theory of groups had been provided. With the founding of the Research Center for Group Dynamics, the very name confirmed the transition. The fundamental objectives of the center were phrased as advancing knowledge and formulating theories about the forces underlying group life, affecting the relations between groups, and acting on personality and individual adjustment. Lewin's studies of personality and topological psychology preceded his elaboration of a theory of general sociological functionalism. In fact, since they form a natural bridge to his sociology, they are of basic interest.

Gestalt theory, which originated with the notion of perception as an act determined by the perceptual field, was fruitfully extended to learning, now conceived as the dynamic reorganization and instituting of a new order in behavior. The next logical step was the conception of personality as a dynamic energy system, at any moment moving toward a state of equilibrium, but undergoing change in time. Lewin was led to this conception in the course of the study of the effects of unfinished tasks and satiation on behavior. The perception of an object or event can cause the formation of a definite tense psychical system which did not previously exist in that form. Such an experience produces an intention or awakens a desire which did not exist previously. An already existing state of tensions, on the other hand, may go back to a purpose or need or a half-finished activity directed toward a certain object or event experienced as an attraction or repulsion. Such objects are said to possess "valence." Valences of this kind operate simultaneously with other experiences as field forces. They steer the psychical processes, particularly the action mechanism, or "motorium." Certain activities are caused in part by imbalances leading to satiation processes or the carrying out of intentions and hence the reduction of tensions in the basic system involved to an equilibrium at a lower level of tension. Such phenomena permit an understanding of the fact that every single everyday experience of the past may influence the present psychical life, though this influence may be so mild as to approach zero. Individual psychic experiences, actions, emotions, purposes, wishes, hopes are imbedded in definite psychical structures, spheres of personality, and whole processes. Such belonging to definite psychical systems is characteristic of the basic psychological tensions and energies. The ego or self may be viewed as one system or complex of systems, a functional part-region of the psychical totality. "The psychical totality which is Mr. X is at least different from that of Mr. R and from that of the child Q. This difference, which constitutes the individuality (*Eigenart*) of the persons involved . . . is probably evident in some way as always the same special, characteristic individuality, in each of its processes, parts and expressions." [3]

The formation of definite psychical systems is related to the ontogenetic development of the mind. The tendency to equilibrium, the dynamic firmness of boundaries and relative segregation of psychical systems, come

[3] *A Dynamic Theory of Personality*, p. 56.

into central focus in personality study. The psychical processes may often be deduced from the tendency to equilibrium. The transition from a state of rest to motion is due to disturbance of the equilibrium. The process of re-establishment of a new state ensues. The process is a movement toward equilibrium for the system as a whole. Part processes may proceed in opposite directions. A state of equilibrium does not mean that the system is without tension. Systems can come to equilibrium in a state of tension. An unfinished task does not cripple the whole motorium but remains a special tension system that may operate in experience for a long time. There are systems of considerable functional firmness in the psyche. In the adult there are, as a rule, a great number of relatively separate tension systems. They form reservoirs of energy for action. Without their considerable independence, ordered action would be impossible.

The formation of personality thus represents the constant evolution of a psychical system toward equilibrium under many sorts of interruptions and disturbances. The difference between the adult and child personality lies in the formation of complex, relatively independent tension systems in the psychic structure of the adult. These provide various kinds of tendencies toward action that define individuality in the particular case.

In arriving at his theory of personality, Lewin did not concentrate on intelligence but on will and need. His original experimental subjects were mentally retarded children in Berlin, including samples of morons and imbeciles from age two to six. Control experiments were performed on normal children. Experiments concerned the problems of satiation, unsatisfied need, and substitute action. Satiation represents the transfer of a positive valence to a negative or neutral one. Interrupted tasks produce tension systems. Release of tension may occur through resumption of the task or substitution of psychologically equivalent action.

Individuals were found to differ in the degree of differentiation of psychic material, differences in tension systems, and differences in psychic content. From childhood on, the individual is subject to differentiation in his psychical regions and in his life spheres (family, friendships, profession). The child displays fewer psychic substructures and is more a unitary system. The subsystems are developed differentially as between people. They may be many and closely knit or few and loosely integrated. In extreme cases, they may take the form of split personality. Structures are also differentiated in terms of their rigidity and plasticity: they may be elastic, hard, brittle, or fluid. Such properties determine the individual's capacity for adaptation. Tension is present in need satisfaction. Individuals differ in their tension systems. Some tensions change slowly, others rapidly, and the state of tension is a general persistent quality of the individual. Finally, goals, ideas, and meanings of the individual's life rest on cultural forms of the environment. This aspect of personality is most influenced by culture.

The differences between macro- and micro-functionalism are well illustrated by the very different stages at which the problem of personality is raised. It turns up only relatively late for the macro-functionalists, who work to it from the problem of society. For the micro-functionalists, on the other hand, it is raised early, serving as a step toward a general sociological theory.

For Lewin, "topology" provided the means for formulating the general principles of *fields,* considered in abstraction from any applications, but providing a theory general enough to be applied to ever more encompassing fields.[4] Topology is a branch of geometry which deals with problems of continuity rather than size or shape. A circle is not the same as an oval or of any variety of figures with closed lines. It is, however, similar with respect to closure. It is different if there is a hole punched in it. Or, again, a closed sphere with a hole in it is topologically different from one with two holes in it. Topological space is a set of objects or points with definite relation to one another. A rectangle is a space with a set of points organized in a certain structure. The peculiarities of topological space lie in the following: it deals with open sets (sets without limits); it includes the ideas of the surroundings of a point; it comprises the idea of "region" (an area with points), which may be open or closed. A "cut" is some division of a region. A "manifold" is a smooth surface without singularities. Space may be divided into sub-wholes which structure it, and so on.

Lewin believed that the first prerequisite for a scientific representation of the psychological field is the finding of a geometry adequate to represent the spatial relations of psychological facts. Perhaps for psychology, as for physical space, more than one geometry might be found useful. There is, Lewin felt, at least one geometry which permits a mathematical interpretation of terms like "approach" and "withdrawal" without being psychologically meaningless. Such a geometry is found in the "hodological space," a finitely structured space, whose parts are composed of certain units or regions. Direction and distance are defined by paths which can be coordinated to psychological locomotion. Such a geometry, Lewin thought, permits an adequate representation of the step-by-step character of most psychological processes. It also permits one to ascribe different psychological directions to locomotions in the same physical direction if the goal of those locomotions is different, a fact particularly important for the problem of roundabout routes. The hodological space furthermore permits the description of the structure relations within the person as well as in his psychological environment. The degree of differentiation within the person and the presence of the peripheral and central layers can thus be defined. Hodological space may also be used to describe the structure of groups and their changes.[5]

Behavior is conceived as a function of the person and his environment. The totality of facts determining the behavior of a person are conceived

4 See his *Principles of Topological Psychology.*
5 See *Field Theory in Social Science,* pp. 25–26.

topologically as his psychological life-space. The relations between the person and his situations are perceived as positions with spatial properties. Behavior is expressed in terms of the topological notions of region, correctedness, separateness, and boundaries. Within life-space, some regions are forbidden, some are free. Forbidden regions are separated by boundaries which are as solid as the discipline supporting them. Lewin translated many familiar ideas into the analogical framework of his topological psychology. The *role* of an individual is translated into a psychological position. Activity in connection with roles is translated into locomotion in relation to position. *Attitudes* are treated as tendencies toward locomotion of varying force. *Goals* are conceived as "force fields," distributed in "regions," with "boundaries" representing barriers, difficulties, or aversions. *Frustration* is treated as an overlapping of two or more force fields. *Fear* has the same dimensions as aversion, being a force away from a field. Fear is usually related to a psychological future. *Power* is the possibility of inducing forces of a certain magnitude in another person. *Values* have positive or negative valence. They induce force fields in individuals.[6] It is not difficult to see that when topological concepts were developed on the basis of such elastic analogies Lewin would indeed find it easy to apply his "hodological space" to behavior, to personality, and to groups.

By 1935 Lewin had begun to expand his field theory into sociological form. This is apparent in his study of the "Psycho-Sociological Problems of a Minority Group,"[7] a study of the effects of marginality on the Jews. The transition to a sociology was made simply by expanding the conception of what may constitute the behavior field or background. Pointing out that judgment, understanding, and perception are impossible except against a background which determines the meaning of an event, Lewin reasoned that general properties of the background may have more or less permanent effects on personality. A child growing up in a family group often responds to it as his most basic background. Instability in the background of the child may lead to instability in the adult; the child who lacks clarity about his belongingness to a group may never be completely certain. The individual belongs to many groups — say, upper middle class, merchant, member of a small family, member of a specific church, of special clubs, etc. During the course of his life, the groups to which a person belongs are not all equally dominant at the same time.

There are persons whose whole life-situation is characterized by uncertainty about their belonging, as a result of their standing near the margin of groups. This is true of the *nouveaux riches* or of other persons crossing the boundaries of social classes. It is typical of members of religious or national minority groups everywhere when they try to enter the main group. Typically, persons crossing the boundary between groups are borderline, belonging to both new and old. "It is for example one of the

6 *Ibid.*, pp. 39–41.
7 Reprinted in *Resolving Social Conflicts*, pp. 145 ff.

greatest theoretical and practical difficulties of the Jewish problem that Jewish people are often, in a high degree, uncertain of their relation to the Jewish group." [8] Among minorities there are single individuals or sections of the main group who see their chief hope in crossing the line that separates them from others. One speaks, thus, of "assimilation." Since the Jews live in Diaspora, the Jewish group is numerically a small minority in all nations. The character of the group is further determined by the strength of the boundary separating it from other groups. In the period of the ghetto, there were clear strong boundaries between Jewish and other groups. The Jews had to live in restricted territories. One of the important facts of social life is the amount of "space of free movement." The boundaries of the ghetto imposed a strict limitation on the very bodily locomotion of the Jews, in addition to limiting social locomotion.

During the period of the ghetto, the following traits characterized the Jewish group. It was compact, spacially and socially, representing a closed region which rarely included foreign sections. Belonging to the group was clearly marked. A yellow badge was imposed from without. The boundary between the Jewish group and other groups was strong, almost impassable. The space of free movement was very limited, creating a state of high tension for the individual and the group. Such isolated groups are usually extremely conservative, even retarded, and this conservatism preserves the group intact.

In contrast to this was the situation of the Jewish group in Germany before the First World War. The Jewish group was no longer compact. Jews were not compelled to live in special districts, and where they did, the group could contain foreign elements. The boundary between Jewish and other groups was no longer a boundary by law; it had lost much of its strength and concreteness. It was passable for some individuals. The space of free movement for social action had expanded. Some restrictions remained, but the possibilities were greater. There were pronounced tendencies toward progressivism and radicalism. The weakening of the boundary of the group involved more points of contact with others, and devices for maintaining separate identity (yellow badge) disappeared. With the increasing space of free movement, the tension under which the group lived decreased.

With the intermingling of Jewish and non-Jewish groups, the Jew has more often to face the pressures against the Jews as an individual. Two kinds of forces play on him: those coming from his own wishes and hopes and those socially induced. The very nearness of the goal of assimilation with the outside creates strong forces in its direction. Multiple forms of conflict situations emerge, creating tensions which lead to restlessness, unbalanced behavior, overemphasis in one direction or another. "Indeed the Jews are commonly characterized as being restless. The most productive type of restlessness is over-exertion in work. Some of the best work of Jewish peo-

[8] *Ibid.*, p. 148.

ple in the last century was partly due to this over-activity." [9] This restlessness is not an inborn trait of the Jew but a result of his situation. It is notably absent from the Jews in Palestine. The conflict is especially severe for young members of well-to-do families.

If one is going to expand the concepts of life-situation, space of free movement, boundaries, and location to account for the total relations of minority groups to the outside world and their bearing upon the problems of individual behavior, there is no good reason why the same concepts should not be extended to the general problems of personality and culture. Lewin does not hesitate to examine the social psychological differences between the United States and Germany. His attack on the problems was quite reasonably made by way of education, whose processes, he thought, depend to a high degree on the spirit of the larger social body in which the persons are living. Any change in the political, economic, or social structure of this larger group, like the nation, deeply affects not only the organization of education, but its whole spirit and technique as well. The concept of life-space has been broadened to include the "general cultural atmosphere." And Lewin is not at all of the opinion "that such general characteristics as 'freedom,' 'authority,' and 'social atmosphere' are too vague and too delicate to be grasped through any really strict concepts." [10] In fact, Lewin finds that between the United States ("freedom") and Germany ("authoritarian") there is such a general difference in social atmospheres manifest in the amount of free space of movement and structure. Generally, the educational situation in the United States as compared to Germany seems to Lewin to be characterized by regions of very different degrees of freedom and sharply determined boundaries of these regions. The educational atmosphere in German institutions, as well as in German homes, is more homogeneous, lacking regions of such high degree of freedom, and having less strictly defined limits than are found in a similar institution or home life in the United States. Totalitarian Germany tended to increase the homogeneity in education. The structure of education in the two countries was taken as an expression of the cultures as a whole. The aim of socialization was very different. In America Lewin found a quite exceptional emphasis upon personal achievement. The result, however, is not the elimination of homogeneity in America but the creation of a rather special kind of social difference.

Lewin found that the average "social distance" between individuals seems to be smaller in the United States so far as surface or "peripheral" regions of the personality are concerned. People meet easily and invite visitors home, for the American feels less need for privacy in certain regions of life. It is possible even to find the office door of the president of a college open all day. In America only the central regions of personality tend to be separated between persons.

By contrast, Lewin finds that in Germany, while the surface layer of

[9] *Ibid.*, p. 156.   [10] *Ibid.*, p. 5.

personality is open to others, there is a hard boundary not far below the surface. If, however, one ever penetrates this sort of shell all the inner layers of personality may be open. The personality of the American for Lewin has open surface layers but a relatively inaccessible hard core and the personality of the average German has a hard surface but no particularly special boundaries within.

The great homogeneity — on surface levels — in America is explained in terms of this difference. In America there can be relatively close relations between persons without a deep personal friendship. At the same time, for this reason, there is less danger of personal friction. Moreover, since the peripheral layers of personality include what one may call "motoric" or "executive" elements, such a person is an action type. Thus, the American emphasizes achievement more than status. Lewin finds affinity between such ideologies as German idealism and American pragmatism and the characteristics of other areas of life in Germany and America.

The experimental traditions in which Gestalt psychology was anchored were of great importance for the development of a sociology from such beginnings, for if the first thought was how to extend the conceptions of system and system-determined social areas, the second was how to prove one's extensions experimentally. Lewin and Lippitt urge that it is possible to investigate experimentally such fundamental socio-psychological problems as group ideology, group conflicts and their spontaneous substructuring, the stability of spontaneous group structures versus authoritarian structure, minority problems, renegades and scapegoats, and double loyalty conflicts. To do so, "one has to create a set up where group life might be studied under rather free but well defined conditions. Instead of utilizing the groups in schools, clubs, factories, one should create groups experimentally because only in this way the factors influencing group life will not be left to chance but will be in the hands of the experimenter." [11] Thus, the wave of modern experimental studies by micro-functionalists was begun by Lewin and Lippitt in their study of group atmosphere.

In this instance, two experimental mask-making clubs of ten- and eleven-year-olds were formed, using children who had little initial relation to one another. The attempt was made to create a total group atmosphere and study its effects. In the experimentally-created authoritarian group, all policy was determined by the leader, techniques for attaining the goal were dictated by the leader one at a time, authority was autocratic, and the leader praised and criticized individual activities and remained aloof and impersonal. In the experimentally-created democratic group, all policy was determined by the group (encouraged by the leader), perspective and explanation were given in general and advice given when needed, individuals were free to work with whomever they chose, and the leader attempted to praise and criticize the group as a whole.

[11] Kurt Lewin and Ronald Lippitt, "An Experimental Approach to the Study of Autocracy and Democracy: A Preliminary Note," *Sociometry*, Vol. 1 (January–April, 1938), p. 292.

The experimental results of the study were: (1) the appearance of a higher state of tension in the autocratic group, with more social interaction, less stable group structure, more ascendency, and the development of scapegoats; (2) the appearance of more cooperative behavior in the democratic group, more objectivity, more constructive suggestions and objective criticism; (3) the appearance of more primary-group feeling in the democratic group and a stronger feeling of group property and group goals.

That Lewin had made full transition to sociology was clear to him by 1939. "I am persuaded that it is possible to undertake experiments in sociology which have as much right to be called scientific experiments as those in physics and chemistry." [12] Moreover, the focus of study has become the group. The experimental task will consist in creating groups and social climates or styles of living. "The sociologist I hope will therefore forgive him when he cannot avoid handling also the so-called sociological problems of groups and group life." [13] Such groups are sociological wholes; "the unity of these sociological wholes can be defined operationally in the same way as a unity of any other dynamic whole, namely, by the interdependence of its parts." [14]

Lewin's interest in the group became increasingly more absorbing. The social group came to be viewed as a fundamental determinant of life-space. The essence of the group was found in the interdependence of its parts. It represents a dynamic whole such that a change in the state of any sub-part changes the state of all other sub-parts. The degree of interdependence of the sub-parts varies from a loose "mass" to a compact unit, determined, among other factors, by size, organization, and intimacy of the group. A group may be a part of a more inclusive group, like a family in a community. The individual usually is a member of overlapping groups. The importance of any one of these groups may vary from person to person. For Lewin, the group is the ground on which a person stands, determining his readiness to fight or to submit and other important characteristics of his behavior. Upon it rests much of his general security. If a person is not clear about his belongingness, or if he is not well established within his group, his life-space will show the characteristics of an unstable ground.

The group is also a means to the individual. From early childhood the individual is accustomed to using a group relation as a means to achieving various physical and social goals. The prestige a person acquires through belonging to a group (family, university, club, etc.) is one of the important vehicles to further achievement. Outsiders treat him as a part of this group.

It follows, also, that the change in the circumstances of an individual is to

[12] Kurt Lewin, "Experiments in Social Space," *Harvard Educational Review*, Vol. 9 (1939), pp. 21–32. Reprinted in *Resolving Social Conflicts*, from which the quotation here is taken (p. 71).
[13] *Ibid.*, p. 72.   [14] *Ibid.*, p. 73.

a great extent directly due to a change in the situation of the group of which he is a part. An attack upon his group, a rise or decline of his group, means an attack upon him, a rise or decline of his position. It teaches him ideas and goals which are group derived.

For the individual, the group is a part of the life-space in which he moves about. To reach or maintain a certain group status is one of the vital goals of the individual. His status in the group, the amount of space of free movement within it, and similar group properties are important in determining the life-space of the individual.

Belonging to a group, however, does not mean that an individual loses his identity within it. He has his personal goals, and he needs sufficient space of free movement in the group to pursue them. For the individual, the problem becomes how to satisfy his individual needs without losing membership and status in the group. If the space of free movement of the individual in the group is too small, the individual will be unhappy. Intense frustration may force him to leave the group — it may even destroy the group. The adjustment of the individual to the group rests on the character of the group, the position of the individual within it, and the character of the person.

By this period Lewin's shift to sociology was complete. The group was established as the fundamental "system" in this branch of sociological functionalism.

Some Primary Areas of Study by the Micro-Functionalists

If there were no more to Lewin than his elaborate and often overdrawn physical analogies, he could be dismissed without too much concern. His work, however, has become the starting point for much research. His extended analogies permitted Lewin to weave together an elaborate set of ideas on various levels of precision from psychology, sociology, and common sense. The analogies themselves frequently suggested new problems and areas of inquiry. And when these ideas were appended to a talent for experimental manipulation, promising leads were opened. Moreover, the establishment of the Research Center for Group Dynamics, the success in getting funds, and the luck and skill in assembling a talented group of dedicated young men has given to micro-functionalism a combination of the properties of a crusade and a gold rush. The clear proof that there was gold in the hills of small-group research led many students outside the immediate circle of the original group-dynamics program to join the trend.

The type of research situation suggested by Lewin proved to be so manipulable that research students applying it have far outrun the developments of systematic theory. In one of the most interesting anthologies of studies by the micro-functionalists, Cartwright and Zander say:

No statement is available which systematically summarizes the results of these various investigations, nor is there easily at hand a collection of the more significant articles which describe the methods and findings of research on group dynamics. . . . The preparation of an integrative summary seemed to us to be premature. To achieve theoretical consistency at the present time, we should have to omit important findings which do not as yet fit readily into a single theory and we should have to present large segments of theory for which adequate empirical testing has not yet been provided.[15]

Although Cartwright and Zander, in assembling the outstanding products of micro-functionalism, decline the opportunity to theorize, the very categories found most convenient for summarizing the research studies indicate the primary pattern of thought.

Among the main sections of the book there is: (1) a section on the formation of groups and development of group cohesiveness; (2) a section on group pressures and standards; (3) a section on group goals and group locomotion toward them; (4) a section on group structure; and (5) a section on group leadership. In terms of its origins and development, the research of micro-functionalism rests directly on its most fundamental concept: the primacy of the organic-type system. The fundamental organic-type system which they select as their central object of study is the *group*. Thus, Cartwright and Zander could hardly have chosen a more fundamental organization of the research materials than one beginning with the formation of the group and the development of its unifying properties, followed by a series of analyses of group characteristics, structure, movement, and order of the group.

Group Cohesiveness

The ultimate affinity of micro-functionalists with macro-functionalism and sociological organicism appears in the fact that they have all been preoccupied with the property of "groupness." They even tend to use the same analogies and distinguish between "healthy" and "unhealthy" group states.

And just as Durkheim long ago made the kind and state of "solidarity" the central point of approach to society conceived as an organic system, so the micro-functionalists have been preoccupied with "cohesiveness." They even talk about it in the same way.

> What do we mean intuitively when we speak of the cohesiveness of a group? A number of meanings quickly come to mind. We think, for example, of a group that has a strong feeling of "we-ness," meaning that the members are more likely to talk in terms of "we" than "I." We think, too, of a group where everyone is friendly or where loyalty to fellow members is high. A cohesive group might be characterized as one in which the members all work together for a common goal, or where everyone is ready to take responsibility for group chores.[16]

[15] Dorwin Cartwright and Alvin Zander (eds.), *Group Dynamics* (Evanston, Ill.: Row, Peterson, 1953), p. x.
[16] *Ibid.*, pp. 73–74.

No macro-functionalist or organicist could object to this. The varied studies of the micro-functionalists bear on the nature of cohesiveness, the factors associated with it, and its role in group formation.

If one takes as the most significant property of functionalism the conception of the primacy of some kind of system, and if one takes as the most critically defining property of micro-functionalism the conception of the group as the decisive system, there are hardly more important questions than those referring to the property of the group as a group (cohesiveness), the forces strengthening or weakening it, the limits of group formation with the breakdown of the group into splinter groups. By far the great majority of the experimental studies of the micro-functionalists have been on these themes — the oldest and most traditional subject matter of sociology. However, the conception of groups as systems is by no means, despite some claims, an exclusive discovery of micro-functionalistic theory.

The properties of functionalism as a distinctive formation in sociological theory fully appear with the revival of the second organismic thesis of the primacy of the whole over the parts.

The Primacy of the Whole Over the Parts

The group conceived as the fundamental system of social life has been the primary object of analysis by micro-functionalism. Quite in organismic vein is the preoccupation with group-maintaining and group-restoring processes, the determination of the parts by the whole:

> Some groups consciously and deliberately set out to exert pressures for uniformity of behavior and attitude among their members. We expect them to do so when we join them. Thus churches, political parties, character building agencies, school clubs, and others are eager to influence the membership to behave in accordance with certain norms, and everyone grants them the privilege of trying to do so.[17]

According to the micro-functionalists, two kinds of effects are produced by uniformities among members: uniformities may help the group to accomplish its purposes, and they may help the group maintain itself as a group. As with group cohesiveness, an ardently pursued experimental program has been carried out by the micro-functionalists.

Lewin had conceived the group as constituting a kind of action-space. Consistent with this analogy, motion becomes a change of position on a hypothetical set of coordinates. The group-dynamics students have retained these analogies. Thus, Cartwright and Zander ask:

> What do we mean when, in everyday language, we assert that a group does or does not "get somewhere" or "accomplish something"? These terms seem to imply that a group can be said to have a location, that it may change its location from time to time, and that certain locations are preferred by all or some segment of the members to other locations. . . . With these concepts we may ask concerning any group at any given time (a) whether, or

[17] *Ibid.*, pp. 137–138.

to what degree, it has a goal; (b) whether it has more than one goal, and, if so, whether these goals are compatible or conflicting; (c) whether as a result of some group activity group locomotion has occurred; and (d) whether any given locomotion was toward or away from the group's goals.[18]

Four concepts of group goals are developed: (1) group goals as a composite of similar individual goals, (2) group goals as individual goals for the group, (3) group goals as dependent upon a particular interrelation among motivational systems of several individuals, and (4) group goals as an inducing agent.

The micro-functionalists have also continued the study of group structure. It is maintained that an adequate description of any group will reveal that it has not one structure but several, and any particular individual has one or more positions in each of these structures. The structure of a group consists in distinguishable parts or portions and their arrangement with respect to one another. Three kinds of factors produce stable differentiations within groups: (1) requirements for efficient group performance, (2) the abilities and motivations of individuals, and (3) physical and social characteristics of the group's environment. The structure of the group may be informal or highly formalized.

The Movement Toward Macro-Functionalism

The micro-functionalists fall into three subgroups, one headed by Bales, one guided by Cartwright and Zander, and the third headed up by Leon Festinger, Henry W. Riecken, and Stanley Schachter. There are some evidences that all these subgroups are moving toward a liaison with macro-functionalism. The combined work of Parsons and Bales has already been discussed. An interesting example of the movement from the laboratory and the small *ad hoc* group to the field is portrayed in the study by Festinger, Riecken, and Schachter, *When Prophecy Fails.*[19]

Leon Festinger was born in New York in 1919. After taking his B.S. degree at City College, he went to the State University of Iowa, where he came under the influence of Kurt Lewin. He received his Ph.D. in psychology in 1942 and worked as psychologist at the Psychopathic Hospital in Iowa from 1940 to 1942. Between 1942 and 1951, Festinger taught at Iowa, the University of Rochester, the Massachusetts Institute of Technology (where he was program director of the Research Center for Group Dynamics), and the University of Michigan. From 1951 to 1955 he was professor of psychology at the University of Minnesota, and since 1955, professor at Stanford University. Henry Riecken was born in Brooklyn in 1917, re-

---

[18] *Ibid.*, pp. 306–307.
[19] Leon Festinger, Henry W. Riecken, and Stanley Schachter, *When Prophecy Fails* (Minneapolis: University of Minnesota Press, 1956). Copyright 1956 by the University of Minnesota.

ceiving his A.B. degree at Harvard in 1939 and his Ph.D. in 1950. He was lecturer in social psychology at Harvard from 1950 to 1954, and has been professor of sociology at the University of Minnesota since 1954. Stanley Schachter was born in New York City in 1922. He received his M.A. and Ph.D. degrees at Michigan in 1950. He joined the staff of the University of Minnesota in 1952. Thus, while forming one of the sub-branches of micro-functionalism, these three young men are well acquainted at first hand with the other two branches. Riecken has been associated with Bales and Festinger, and Schachter with Cartwright and Zander. *When Prophecy Fails* thus potentially has significance not only as a liaison point between micro- and macro-functionalism but as a transfer point in the movement of the small-group theorists into general sociology.

The object of study for these three social scientists was the reaction of a social group to unfulfilled prophecies and the failure of messiahs to appear according to prediction. At times, the most immediate response to a disappointed expectation is the attempt to reaffirm it. The authors set down five conditions for such a response: the belief must be deeply held; the person must be committed to it; the belief must be sufficiently precise for events to contradict it; the disconfirming evidence should be recognized; and the individual must have social support.[20]

Major examples in American experience of successive readjustment to a fervently held prophecy were provided by the Anabaptists, particularly the Millerites. When the end of the world and second coming of Christ had been predicted, the Millerites sold their New England farms, purchased ascension robes, and went out in prayer on the appointed hour to meet their maker. At first they simply refused to accept the fact that the end of the world did not come, and in an abortive way they changed the date. But these dates also passed and, alas, the movement eventually disintegrated.

When the investigators read in the newspapers of a midwestern town that a suburban housewife, on the basis of messages received from the planet "Clarion," had predicted the town's destruction by a flood, they seized upon this as an opportunity to study the response to an unfulfilled prophecy. They immediately called upon the woman, and discovered her to be a neurotic, suffering from a long preoccupation with the exotic, and in contact with several other such marginal individuals with a few gullible hangers-on.

The skill of the investigators in handling small-group situations could not be more clearly demonstrated than in their success in creating the semblance of a social movement out of these marginal neurotics and their handful of fellow travelers. For one thing, the very fact that investigators with intelligence and training were interviewing, apparently in all seriousness, the two main spirits of the prophecy (a Mrs. Keech and a Dr. Armstrong) tended to act as an authenticating sounding board for them.

[20] *Ibid.*, p. 4.

Furthermore, the requirements of having observers "inside" the movement clearly helped provide a nucleus of clientele for the "movement."

> We have already reported the difficulty our observer experienced in arousing Dr. Armstrong's interest in him; all his efforts to stimulate an invitation to the "advanced" group meetings were having no success. Time was passing. . . . We therefore decided upon a stratagem suggested to us by Dr. Armstrong's inquiry to our observer as to whether he had ever had any "psychic experiences." We decided to equip our representative with an "experience" with the supernatural.[21]

This worked so well that the investigators decided to repeat the trick.

> Forewarned by his difficulties in approaching the Armstrongs through the medium of the elementary Seekers, we decided to arm our female observer with a "psychic experience." . . . Mrs. Armstrong's reaction . . . was enthusiastic. She welcomed the observer warmly, and at once began to enlighten her visitor about the protectors from outer space.[22]

The presence of an attentive set of investigators, apparently taking all this seriously, on the one hand, and the presence within the group of a number of participant-observers, actively contributing to the mutual self-deception of this little group and providing a solid core for its continued activity, had their effect. The investigators succeeded so well that they managed to persuade the rest of the community that the prophets were a genuine menace.

> On December 24 . . . as they caroled and waited for a spaceman to visit, they were ringed about by a crowd of some 200 unruly spectators, and . . . the police were flooded with complaints against Mrs. Keech ranging from disturbing the peace to contributing to the delinquency of minors. . . . A warrant was sworn out making specific charges against Mrs. Keech and Dr. Armstrong. . . . The police themselves seem to have been reluctant to set legal machinery into motion. They telephoned Mrs. Keech's husband to inform him of the warrant and warned him that, unless the meetings and gatherings at his home were at once brought to an end, they would serve the warrant. Furthermore, they strongly hinted that, once legal action began, the community could try to commit Mrs. Keech to a mental hospital.[23]

Dr. Armstrong, it seems, was no easy dupe, for

> within minutes of receiving the warning from the police in Lake City on December 26, the Armstrongs had packed their bags, tumbled their two younger children into the car, and were on the road back to Collegeville.[24]

In the end the investigators were quite disappointed with their prophets from outer space:

> While circumstances combined to pull the steadfast adherents apart, the

[21] *Ibid.*, p. 239.   [22] *Ibid.*, p. 240.   [23] *Ibid.*, p. 230.   [24] *Ibid.*, pp. 231–232.

group failed to win a single new convert. . . . Their ideas were not without popular appeal. . . . Had they been more effective, disconfirmation might have portended the beginning, not the end.[25]

To be sure, the hypotheses of *When Prophecy Fails* are almost platitudinous. When a man is committed to a course of action on the basis of a powerful set of beliefs, even in the face of the demonstration of their error, he will often rationalize fanatically rather than give up his beliefs. The single most interesting thing about the study — apart from the demonstration of the unusual skill of the investigators in manipulating people in small-group situations — is the almost complete absence of any reference to the ancient sociological studies bearing on the problem. The problem of group illusion is one of the oldest in the sociology of knowledge. No reference or use was made of any of the numerous studies. Even the special problem coming into focus in this study had been described by Karl Mannheim as a peculiar ideological type — *chiliasm*. No reference appears either to Mannheim or to other students of the chiliastic mentality.

Similarly, no consideration whatever was given to the many sociological factors that have bearing on the potential or lack of potential for a social movement. The class and status anchorage of such ideology was ignored. One of the things that made Mannheim's study so fruitful was his perception of the fact that the chiliasm of the European Anabaptists was anchored in the frustrated hopes of peasants, trapped between the middle ages and the modern world, and lacking the institutions to make their aspirations manifest; here, at least, was a class and status situation that the chiliastic mentality could articulate. No consideration was given to equivalent social anchorage in *When Prophecy Fails*. Moreover, the failure of the group to win new converts is attributed exclusively to the ineptness of Mrs. Keech and Dr. Armstrong. Even the obvious role of a powerful, organized, modern urban world in preventing such a possibility is admitted only indirectly. Yet a single threat from the police could send Dr. Armstrong scampering from the scene.

All these considerations indicate how important for micro-functionalism the book, *When Prophecy Fails*, really is. It illustrates profoundly the kind of sociological problems that must be faced the moment this branch of sociological theory ceases to deal with purely *ad hoc* groups.

Summary

It is difficult to escape the impression that with sociological functionalism the field has come full circle. The concept of organicism has been refurbished and upholstered with new analogies and terminology, but returned to a central place as the key to the understanding of interhuman life. To be sure, the concept of organic system has been given more abstract

---

[25] *Ibid.*, pp. 232–233.

formulation and its properties have been drawn out in somewhat more detail. That is to be expected.

The similarities between sociological functionalism and positivistic organicism do not stop here. A strong movement back toward greater positivism of method is apparent throughout functionalism. The traditionalism is strongest precisely among the groups that have presented the most cultic and exclusive character — the micro-functionalists. In the first place, they have been preoccupied with the most traditional of sociological themes: the unity of the group mentality, its morale, the nature of the "group will," as Tönnies would say, or as Durkheim would put it, "solidarity." The micro-functionalists call this "cohesiveness" and have devoted the larger block of their studies to it. Furthermore, the similarities do not stop here, for the micro-functionalists have actively promoted a program of experimentalism, thus restoring a positivism of method to an organicism of theory.

Sorokin has described the group-dynamics section of the micro-functionalists as having a "discoverer's complex" and of being "new Columbuses."[26] The only thing wrong with the statement is that it is sometimes a bit tactless to say some sorts of truths in public. In any case, the irritation his characterization has caused is a bit hard to understand. Once Sorokin made the matter public, one would expect the members of the cult to welcome the opportunity to return to the general scientific community, frankly basing their researches on traditional grounds.[27]

A question perhaps even more difficult to answer is whether there are ideological grounds for the shift to functionalism. It will be recalled that positivistic organicism was powerfully affected by ideological currents. It was the conservative answer to socialism. The conflict theorists (in contrast to the conflict ideologists, who were either relatively extreme reactionaries or extreme radicals) were largely conservative. Sociological formalism, by contrast, promoted a frankly liberal "Enlightenment" model of society. Some branches of the social behaviorists were uncertain: the pluralistic behaviorists seem to have experienced considerable frustration as they wavered between a relatively liberal and relatively conservative point of view. Some, like Giddings, were consistently conservative; others, like Ross, wavered. Ogburn even invented two interpretations of social problems, one for each mood. On the other hand, the symbolic-interactionist and social-action branches of social behaviorism were fairly consistently liberal.

As one moves from school to school in the development of sociology, ideological factors decline in importance. But even so, it is not at all

26 See Pitirim Sorokin, *Fads and Foibles in Modern Sociology* (Chicago: Henry Regnery, 1956).

27 It should be noted that not all adherents of the group-dynamics movement have ignored their sociological origins. Bales and his associates, for example, are quite self-consciously identified with traditional sociology, as can be seen in such works as A. P. Hare, E. F. Borgatta, and R. F. Bales (eds.), *Small Groups: Studies in Social Interaction* (New York: Alfred A. Knopf, 1955) and Edgar F. Borgatta and Henry J. Meyer (eds.), *Sociological Theory: Present-Day Sociology from the Past* (New York: Alfred A. Knopf, 1956).

clear that the latest development in sociological theory is completely free from any ideological coloration whatsoever. The excited protests by some of the functionalists concerning their inviolability suggests that the gentlemen protest too much. Moreover, there are two major reasons for wondering whether sociological functionalism does not have some residual "conservative" significance. Organicism has almost always been acceptable to the conservatives. The very topics that have occupied the forefront of functionalist research are of a kind usually dear to the conservative: "morale," "cohesiveness," "solidarity," how groups control their deviates, why this is to be expected, and so on. Furthermore, the very dates of the steep rise of interest in functionalism among sociological theorists also suggest that it may have some ideological import. It arose after 1940 and with particular speed after World War II. Moreover, its ranks have been increasingly swelled by deserters from social behaviorism — an evidently liberal position. The rise of sociological functionalism thus coincides with the return of the Republican Party to power, the return to religion, the rise of McCarthyism, and other typical manifestations of a postwar conservative reaction. Whether these are just accidental correlations or not, it is certainly true that ideological factors are now far less important for the structure of sociological theory than was once the case.

Sociological functionalism is in a very real sense a new name for an old trend. It is distinctive in being the first major departure in sociological theory that did not draw its inspiration directly from philosophy. The organismic and idealistic philosophy that influenced it did so directly through the social sciences. In order of importance these were, despite a reluctance to admit it: (1) positivistic organicism in sociology, (2) functionalistic and Gestalt psychology, and (3) functionalistic anthropology.

Four basic meanings of functionalism have been outlined here: the mathematical conception, function as useful activity for need fulfillment and/or purpose implementation, function as appropriate activity, and function as system-produced and system-maintaining activity. The first meaning of functionalism is specifically set aside as an objective by all schools. The second meaning of function appears universally and is insufficient to define a functionalistic program. Modern forms of functionalist sociological theory are primarily built out of combinations of the third and fourth meanings: function as appropriate activity (as in the distinctions between function and dysfunction, eunomia and anomie, and manifest and latent functions) and function as system-produced and system-maintaining activity.

The mere use of some variety of the concept "function" thus is distinguished from the advocacy of a brand of functionalist sociological theory. Such a theory is characterized as the interpretation of social interaction from the standpoint of functions in the two senses noted above. There are many differences among individuals and between the two sub-branches, but two major theoretical propositions hold all branches of functionalist theory together: (1) the fundamental unit of interpretation of interhuman life is an organic-type system; (2) the parts, elements, aspects, or phases of this organic-type system are in a functional relation to the whole, both determining the whole and being determined by the whole.

Two major sub-schools of modern functionalist sociological theory are distinguished as: the macro-functionalists (comprising such persons as Znaniecki, Merton, Parsons, Homans, Shils, Levy) and the micro-functionalists (comprising such persons as Lewin, Bales, Cartwright, Zander, Schachter, Festinger and numerous others). The macro-functionalists focus primarily on large-scale systems and work out of the traditions of sociology and anthropology. Their tendency has been to extend the concept "system" downward, from presumed unities as large as the society and civilization to the group. The micro-functionalists have worked their way up from the *Gestalten* of perception and behavior through personality to the group. This latter movement represents the evolution of Gestalt psychology into a full-fledged sociology.

The two movements have drawn more closely together than some members of either seem to realize. While micro-functionalism has tended to develop its terminology concerning the systems of interest to it from topological psychology, preferring such expressions as "field," "valence," "boundaries," "sector," "tension system," etc., the macro-functionalists have been showing inclinations to meet them half way. And at least Parsons, Bales, and Shils have begun to conceive dichotomous distinctions applying to action alternatives as "dimensions of action-space." Motivation is increasingly conceived as a movement or locomotion. The term "boundaries" has become ever more important. The events in a social system have even been represented in terms of classical mechanics.

Sociological functionalism is still in full course of development, and it is not yet clear whether it will be able to develop a complete sociological theory, or what form this theory will eventually take.

SELECTED BIBLIOGRAPHY

BALES, ROBERT F., *Interaction Process Analysis*. Reading, Mass.: Addison-Wesley Press, 1950.

CARTWRIGHT, DORWIN, and ALVIN ZANDER (eds.), *Group Dynamics*. Evanston, Ill.: Row, Peterson, 1953.

COCH, LESTER, and JOHN R. P. FRENCH, JR., "Overcoming Resistance to Change," *Human Relations*, Vol. 1 (1948). Pages 512–532.

DARLEY, JOHN G., NEAL GROSS, and WILLIAM E. MARTIN, "Studies in Group Behavior: Factors Associated with the Productivity of Groups," *Journal of Applied Psychology*, Vol. 36 (December 1952). Pages 396–403.

FESTINGER, LEON, STANLEY SCHACHTER, and KURT BACK, *Social Pressures in Informal Groups*. New York: Harper, 1950.

GROSS, NEAL, and WILLIAM E. MARTIN, "On Group Cohesiveness," *American Journal of Sociology*, Vol. 57 (May 1952). Pages 546–554.

HARE, A. P., E. F. BORGATTA, and R. F. BALES (eds.), *Small Groups: Studies in Social Interaction.* New York: Alfred A. Knopf, 1955.

LEWIN, KURT, "Frontiers in Group Dynamics," *Human Relations,* Vol. 1 (1947). Pages 5–41, 143–153.

LEWIN, KURT, *Resolving Social Conflicts.* Edited by Gertrud Weiss Lewin. New York: Harper, 1948.

LEWIN, KURT, *Field Theory in Social Science.* Edited by Dorwin Cartwright. New York: Harper, 1951.

LIPPITT, RONALD, *Training in Community Relations.* New York: Harper, 1949.

RIECKEN, HENRY W., "Some Problems of Consensus Development," *Rural Sociology*, Vol. 17 (September 1952). Pages 245–252.

SCHACHTER, STANLEY, "Deviation, Rejection, and Communication," *Journal of Abnormal and Social Psychology*, Vol. 46 (April 1951). Pages 190–207.

PART SEVEN

Conclusion

20

Toward Theoretical Integration

THE PRESENT REVIEW OF THE NATURE AND SCHOOLS OF SOCIOLOGICAL THEORY opened with an abbreviated historical location of sociology within Western thought — a more complicated issue than may appear at first glance. Either a people know enough about themselves and their world to survive or one does not hear about them for long. When a new discipline arises, it does so in considerable measure by a regrouping of what is already present. In some ways this is its most difficult problem, for it requires a relearning. This means that items have to be torn out of contexts where they are at least in some degree successful. Complex pressures act on them at every step to restore them to their original condition. Human behavior is amazingly plastic, but when it is sustained by collective habit it is extraordinarily fixed. If it were not for this, it would be impossible to account for the fact that with all historical time to develop in, sociology is only about one hundred years old. Over and again, this customary fixation is demonstrated.

The disciplines that have collected knowledge in one form or another about interhuman behavior are many. They have taken shape at different times. Common-sense knowledge is present in all societies, but it is highly particularized and norm-bound. Various kinds of knowledge or information about interhuman conduct, particularly where it touches the hazardous and unknown, have been aggregated by magic and religion.

An especially significant movement in Western thought, in part re-uniting knowledge into new patterns out of both common-sense lore and religion, was represented by classical Greek philosophy. It was a secularized movement in abstract knowledge. It made a world historical discovery in the rational proof, which made thought, at least so far as it was logical, dependent only upon its internally established criteria. In the Greek world, Aristotelian logic and Euclidean geometry were two great monuments to this discovery. Even after this, the ideal was preserved in Western thought of integrating the whole of thought into a single comprehensive logical system. Philosophy, which bore this vision, has remained the general discipline from which all special sciences have developed. Sociology has in part drawn its materials and ideas independently from common sense, but primarily it has drawn its inspiration and original perspectives from philosophy.

However, while sociology has repeatedly represented a departure from philosophy — in the nature of the case, so far as it aspired to scientific standing — it could not get its facts from philosophy. In the development of Western thought, history was the discipline that assumed the task of assembling objective empirical knowledge about actual social events. Special interest thus attaches to the development of historiography, the emergence of responsible objective method in historical study. The product of this enterprise was a growing body of objective empirical social facts which for a long time were the only data sociology had.

Though Greek philosophy discovered the rational proof, and though the Greek and Roman historians advanced historiography to a stage not reached in other civilizations, the time was not ripe for the emergence of sociology. It was only reasonable that science would emerge as a discipline studying the physical world long before it was extended to the social world. For science to emerge, a systematic methodology had to be developed adequate to the needs of empirical knowledge, comparable to the rational proof for philosophy. This was provided in the workshops of the Renaissance artists, where experimental method was applied to every conceivable practical problem. In this context the foundation of the natural sciences was laid, and before the end of the Renaissance even the possibility of a social science was clearly envisioned in the work of Francis Bacon.

With the growth of the physical, and later chemical and biological, sciences and their splendid gains in one area after another, and with their gradual institutionalization in industry and in the universities, it was inevitable that the possibilities of a social science would be conceived. Repeatedly from the seventeenth century on, the possibility of social science was envisioned and various partial developments occurred. But only in the nineteenth century, with a noisy series of reciprocal influences, did the social sciences take form as a most vital family of disciplines.

A single chapter dealing with the historical derivation of a discipline cannot be much more than illustrative of the problems involved, but there is an extremely significant value even in this. Sociology has ties with the farthest reaches of Western thought. One occasionally encounters resistance to tracing the ties of sociology with other disciplines. Insofar as such resistance arises out of the desire to make sociology into a completely autonomous discipline, it is laudable. Nevertheless, it is misguided. The fuller one's understanding of an idea, the less likely one is to commit old errors. It was with this thought in mind that throughout this study one theoretical movement after another in sociology was traced to its primary philosophical sources.

When the various schools of sociological theory are brought under review, one might be led to assume that sociology has found its fountain of youth — at least it is forever starting over. It seems to approach everything except maturity. However, the successive appearance of one school of theory after another has not been a random phenomenon, for the schools have arisen in response to the changing needs of the field. Sociology did not arise as a special discipline but as a general movement in nineteenth-century philosophical thought; it became a special discipline in the course of events.

To some extent, the successive schools of thought may be conceived as stages in the growth of the discipline as a whole. However, the figure of speech involved in the conception of the schools of sociological theory as phases or stages in the historical development of the discipline should not be overworked — the latest formation in sociological theory is not necessarily the best. There are genuine theoretical alternatives. And while there have been basic gains under the influence of each separate school, this is not to say that the problems of theory can be solved by the eclectic process of fitting together a piece from each. The appearance of a given school of theory has ordinarily signalized the operation of new demands that the older formations of theory have not been able to satisfy.

Positivistic Organicism

Sociology, as we have seen, arose as a general movement in nineteenth-century philosophic thought. A peculiar property of this movement was the attempt to fuse organicism and positivism — two philosophic forms that had ordinarily been in conflict. This peculiar combination implemented the penetration of the scientific point of view into the study of social phenomena. Sociology thus achieved success in an area that had defied penetration by repeated movements in Occidental thought from the seventeenth century on. It established society as an object of science.

The eventual establishment of sociology as a discipline seems to have been inevitable. When in the course of human events a new technique or skill appears, it tends to expand to the natural limits of its utility. For example, a mode of agriculture which proves to be successful tends to be employed to the limits of the environment in which it affords success. In the strategies of modern research, this tendency of any thought system to extend to its natural limits has been expressed in terms of "limits," "barriers," and the "breakthrough" of new techniques. The solution of the problems involved in setting up a chain reaction in the course of the construction of the atom bomb represents such a research "breakthrough." A level of technology has been attained and new horizons of development are opened up, to be brought to a halt only when the outer limits to which the technique may extend are reached. This process of surmounting the limits of the prevailing technology and opening new horizons for expansion has occurred many times in human history. An invention like pottery-making is applied to an amazing array of objects: dishes, bowls, pots, jugs, vases. It is released into purely aesthetic spheres, and the pottery figurine or other art object appears designed to be viewed or used in magic. Then by way of the brick, the drain tile or pipe, the floor, wall, and roof tile, pottery-making skills are pressed into the service of large-scale construction.

The peculiar dynamism of Occidental culture is partly bound up with the place of science in it. Science, however, is not simply one more technique or process, but the institutionalization of the mother wit from which all techniques spring. The extension of a procedure that affords success is understandable. Even an insect has a range for adaptive learning — tiny to be sure — within the limits set by its instincts. It is inevitable that a complexly plastic, intelligent creature like man should try out his bag of tricks in any problematic situation. If multiple trials lead the rat in the maze gradually to drop those motions that do not promote success in its solution, it is only to be expected that the human animal should find the limits in his techniques at the point where they no longer yield success. And, similarly, it is to be expected that this is the only "natural" place to stop. Science, having yielded tremendous successes in some areas of human activity, was certain to be extended to others, and sphere after sphere of nature has yielded to the penetration of science. Science has achieved a degree of control over nature unimaginable in the early history of mankind.

While with the ordinary process or technique there are fairly determinable limits of application, science is again peculiar. Science establishes its own criteria of acceptability, and all outside limitations are alien to it. It is self-correcting. There are no limits natural to it in quite the same sense as is true of so many historical styles, or processes, or ways of life. Perhaps the day will come when even the limitations imposed by the planet itself will be transcended. It is not surprising that, after its initial successes in mastering external nature, science should turn to man himself.

It was not until the synthesis of organicism and positivism was hit upon, however, that the combination of elements was made that permitted the full "breakthrough" for social science. Both organicism and positivism had previous histories. They had ordinarily tended to be opposed tendencies in thought. Organicism, anchored in idealistic philosophy, consists in the conceptualization of the world on the basis of organismic and spiritual models. The organismic concept has usually been tied to strongly anti-

encourages the examination of historical events from the standpoint of how they worked under the conditions of the time rather than from an arbitrary perspective. However, it does not promote very serious study, for it is committed in advance to the idea that whatever has existed has been both inevitable and the best that could be done at the time. It promotes the easy justification of antiquated institutions. It proposes that the inordinate luxury of ancient class systems was essential to human progress because it furnished the leisure time necessary for intellectual growth. Slavery and war performed essential services to mankind by disciplining the masses and habituating them to steady work. Even infanticide and cannibalism were ancient forms of social welfare (Sumner and Keller). Whatever occurred was the best that could be done and a necessary stage in further progress. Based as it was on such superficial rationalizations of the *status quo*, it is little wonder that positivistic organicism was soon discovered to be working with concepts remarkably vague. "Society," for example, was thought of as a superorganism the parts of which were interdependent organs of the whole. Society was rather vaguely equated with "humanity" by Comte, though he qualified this to include mainly the white race. Society or humanity presumably included the past members of the human race and generations yet unborn. It was certainly a mystical entity. Spencer perceived a difficulty in the concept of society and described it as a plurality of people in a territory and insisted that its real essence lay in its interactive life. But if "society" is defined in terms of population and territory, it will tend to blur insensibly with the "state." Society is thus made identical with one of its institutions. On the other hand, if society is made identical with interaction, the concept can only remain completely obscure until one has specified a limited unit of interaction. A major step forward in defining this most central concept of organicism was made in Tönnies' and Durkheim's societal types. At least they set up some kind of criteria by which one could tell in some cases when one has moved from one society to another. Moreover, they implied that society is some kind of "total" unit of interaction, although this was never made explicit.

The ambiguity in isolating with precision the limits of the superorganic systems which form the objects of sociological study was further revealed when the organicists turned to the problem of social change. They did not, as a rule, hesitate to take various institutions out of context and fit them into arbitrary sequences, presumably representing stages in the development of that particular institution. The overwhelming impression grows that they were not interested in change but in the inevitability of the present. Such a procedure was, of course, completely inconsistent with the basic organicism of the school. The precise nature of the "integral wholeness" of societies as superorganisms has not been very exactly determined.

Thus the fundamental conceptual areas (social structure and social change) of the school are ambiguous and the explanations are oversimplified. The world to which they refer is rather a bloodless one. "Harmony" and

empirical tendencies. Positivism, on the other hand, had been linked with strongly anti-traditionalistic conceptions of society and social behavior. Customs, traditional institutions, ideologies, were ordinarily conceived by the positivistic thinkers as blind, irrational encrustations and ancient errors. Pre-sociological positivism found its affinities in mechanistic theories of society. It was more often bound up with programs for the reform of legislation or criminal procedure or some other aspect of social relations than with the objective study of social behavior per se. Thus the organismic-idealistic tradition tended to be anti-empirical and anti-scientific; the positivistic-empirical tradition tended to be simplistic and reformist in its social theories. When the French Revolution began to display its excesses, the conservative mind of Europe saw the confirmation of its worst fears of the scientific-mechanical theory of society. At the same time a new ground movement in European thought was represented by the various kinds of scientific-minded socialism.

The conservative organismic conceptions of society appeared as a reaction to the excesses of the French Revolution. Such organismic conceptions had an explicit conservative import. They were intended to put a stop to the sort of tampering with society which characterized the French revolutionaries. Society was an organism, a living entity, the organs of which were not to be arbitrarily interfered with. At the same time, such was the skill of the particular formula which the nineteenth century developed that a positivism of method was taken over and pressed into the service of the organismic theory of society.

Sociology was born as the conservative answer to socialism. The skill in fusing the organismic theory of society with the positivistic conception of method was undeniable. An image of society was presented which required respect for its wholeness, untouchability, and integrity. At the same time, by appropriating the scientific method and pressing it into the service of the organismic theory, the teeth had been pulled from reformist, revolutionary, and socialistic programs.

Conventionally, sociology is traced to the works of Comte and Spencer. It would be a mistake, however, to assume that sociology would not have arisen if it were not for their work. The same combination of organicism and science was being suggested by many other students of the time. De Bonald, de Maistre, to some degree Hegel, and, as A. W. Small correctly noted, the historical jurists such as Savigny were all suggesting the same combination. Comte and Spencer were merely more adept popularizers of the combination. Between them, Comte and Spencer adapted the new point of view to the respective needs of their countries: Comte provided the conservative formula for a country in reaction to the excesses of the French Revolution; Spencer provided the conservative formula for a country that had seen the first full triumph of the industrial revolution and had developed a *laissez-faire* economy and wished to preserve it intact. The differences between Comte and Spencer are contained in the contrasting social contents they wished to preserve: while Comte is a great admirer of a society based on caste, Spencer wishes to preserve individuality of a special kind; while Comte conceives of a paternalistic state which will coordinate all features of social and personal life other than those regulated by the family, Spencer desires the weakest central government which is compatible with the security of property, and which will interfere as little as possible with the individual businessman.

The ideological properties of early sociology thus are undeniable. Only a conservative ideology was able to establish the discipline. The linkage between science and reformist social attitudes (e.g., scientific socialism) was severed. In renouncing political activism, sociology became respectable enough to be received into the ivy-covered halls of the universities. It was received as a scientific justification of the existing social order.

The statement that early sociology was in part a conservative ideology is neither an attack on nor a defense of sociology. To the degree that the field remains an ideology (conservative or liberal), it is prevented from becoming a science. It is in the nature of a science that the ultimate acceptability of any generalization rests on the objective criteria established by the discipline. The emergence of sociology as a conservative ideology certainly helped in the establishment of the discipline as a legitimate area of study for stable young men (rather than as a breeding ground for wild-eyed radicals), but sociology could remain and grow only to the degree that it developed professional and scientific standards.

If positivistic organicism accomplished no more than the establishment of the new field, it would be worthy of review. But it went considerably beyond this and developed concepts which have remained a more or less permanent property of sociology. The three most general concepts dominating organicism were: (1) the conception of the task of sociology as the study of the interrelations among various types of social phenomena; (2) the idea that such social relations are a special kind of whole–part relation; (3) the idea that the fundamental units (the superorganic wholes) studied by sociology are societies. A number of derived and secondary ideas were developed around these. Society as the basic unit of analysis was conceived to represent (a) a *structure* and (b) a set of *functions*. The main branches of sociological study were established as specialized inquiries: (c) *social statics* is the comparative study of social structure, while (d) *social dynamics* is the specialized study of social functions and change. Within the total system represented by society, various (e) *subsystems* are to be found (Spencer thought these were the sustaining, distributing, and coordinating systems). The ultimate parts of society are (f) *institutions*. Because the total arrangement of elements in any given society as a system may be different, we must distinguish between (g) *societal types* (militaristic–industrial — Spencer; mechanical–organic — Durkheim; *Gemeinschaft–Gesellschaft* — Tönnies; and so on). Social change is basically (h) *evolutionary* in form,

occurring in the first instance with reference to total societies, which evolve through stages in a unidirectional form, and also to the parts or institutions.

The positivistic organicists not only handed on to sociology in general such concepts as society, interrelation, structure, function, institution, societal type, social statics or organization, and social change, but they also provided descriptions and made assemblages of materials around these various concepts. Even though these ideas have often been transformed in the hands of later sociologists, many of them still form a basic substratum of sociological thought.

Conflict Theory

Long before positivistic organicism had reached its fullest and most balanced expression, a new formation in sociological theory was evident. Conflict theory corrected some of the excesses of organicism and supplied some of the elements it missed altogether.

The conservative ideology seems to be dominated by a preoccupation with the problem of order. Ideas, said Comte, may govern the world or throw it into chaos, and he set to work to tidy up his conception of the sciences as a first step toward setting the world in order. Nothing upset Spencer more quickly than the suggestion that the social order be tampered with. He dreamed of a course of development in which theological-militaristic society everywhere gives way to an industrial-peaceable order. Durkheim invented the term "anomie" to represent the state of social disorder. Pareto made the concept of equilibrium the central clue in sociological study and admired the "lions," who represent the class in which the "residue for the persistence of aggregates" is dominant and who are quick, if necessary, to use the most brutal force to crush innovation and revolt and establish order. In fact, disorder was typically explained by the positivistic organicists as the work of a little group of agitators: revolutionaries (Comte), reformers, radicals, and socialists (Spencer), innovators and liberals of all types, the "foxes" (Pareto). Just as the organicists were strongest in interpreting such matters as social solidarity, equilibrium conditions in social organisms, and the interrelations of social phenomena conceived as dependent parts of organismic wholes, so there is no topic on which they were weaker than on that of social conflict. They appear to have ignored it whenever possible and, when this was impossible, to have disposed of the subject as quickly as they could.

The counterpart of their underestimation of the degree of conflict is their overestimate of the amount of harmony and order. Some of the most critical concepts of the positivistic organicists thus are strangely lacking in density. They have a thin, simplistic character. For example, the idea that society develops through a series of necessary stages, each essential to the following in a progressive series, has interesting implications. It

"integration" are the watchwords of positivistic organicism. War, conflict, struggle are politely bowed out of existence. Conflict theory added a new dimension of realism to sociology.

When conflict is taken as the central clue to social phenomena rather than organic integration, the result is more than a simple change of emphasis. Order itself ceases to be a primary social fact and becomes a kind of terminal point, an end product. The ideas of "humanity" and "society" as rather vague, all-embracing wholes vanish from the writings of the conflict theorists; in their place appears the compact special group, organized often for war or defense, in active tension with others. Moreover, the ideas of "origins," of "original society," and of "orderly sequences" in the development of mankind tend to disappear. The problem of the origins of society loses importance in the face of the significance attached to group conflict and defense and the functions of conflict in the organization of more complex forms of social life. Since any real struggle has its ups and downs and is subject to the fortunes of wars in which not every battle is won, the idea of orderly stages in social development is by-passed by conflict theory. The sharpening of the conception of the social group which resulted from perceiving it as a balance of forces rather than an integration of organs led to a sharpened sensitivity to the different patterns of behavior in the in-group in contrast to the out-group. These ideas emerged as one of the vital new additions to sociology. The regulative rules of society took on new meanings when they were seen as the ordering of affairs that would otherwise take the form of conflict. This school of theory sharpened the distinction between morality and law, deriving them from very different sources. Morality was seen as spontaneous social order emerging in the in-group; law was the ordering of norms imposed forceably by a conquering out-group.

The conflict theory of society re-evaluated the importance of specific institutions in the total social order. Organicism assigned major importance to the family and economic institutions. This was not always accomplished in the same manner: Spencer, for example, would have liked to eliminate the state altogether, if that were possible; Comte was not particularly moved by such a program and would simply have replaced the state with a bureau of sociologists. For Spencer, economic institutions were paramount; for Comte, greatest importance was attached to the family and to religion. With conflict theory, however, the emphasis was shifted to the state. The state was seen as the institution which arises out of conquest. All forms of developed society beyond the primitive tribe were thought to occur through conquest, as a result of which the state appears.[1]

Conflict theory made a new and more complete analysis of the problems of stratification than was the case for organicism. Moreover, it advanced a theoretical explanation of them. Classes were generally and vaguely

---

[1] Unless otherwise noted, the reference in the present discussion is to sociological forms of conflict theory rather than to conflict ideologies like Marxism and social Darwinism.

assumed by the positivistic organicists to be economic phenomena, representing social differentiation on the basis of wealth, which in turn makes leisure possible. The conflict theorists, on the other hand, saw social classes as originating primarily through conquest. The institution arises as a by-product of successful conquest out of the distinctions between masters and slaves. Some of the conflict theorists suggested that differentiation of classes occurs secondarily by way of economic specialization.

In America, in the form of conflict theory represented by Small and Vold, the culminating point of the doctrine is found in the concept of process. The social process, moreover, is treated as the constant formation and destruction of groups. The fundamental elements into which process is eventually analyzable are conceived of as *interests*.

The general import of conflict theory for sociology was a tremendous increase in realism and sophistication. Conflict was removed from the limbo to which it had been consigned and made into the core of the social process. Whole new areas of study were added to the field and old areas given new depth. The search for origins was thrust aside, the attempt to build unilinear evolutionary stages was abandoned. The older concepts of society and humanity were replaced by more dynamic concepts of groups. In short, whatever the errors and mistakes to which various forms of conflict theory were subject, there was much pure gain for the field as a whole.

Formal Sociology

The early forms of positivistic organicism and conflict theory had in one sense done their work well. They had established the field as a recognized discipline. They had given it sufficient respectability to lead to the establishment of specific university courses. Sociology was not only institutionalized — established as an interhuman pattern independent of any given personality — but was institutionalized in a special way. It was professionalized — transformed into a structure of relations under the normative control of members themselves. It established its own scientific societies and journals, implementing its professionalization.

Institutionalization affected both sociology's external relations and internal structure. Externally, institutionalization meant that sociology had come in off the streets. It had abandoned its more public situation and entered the circle of more organized structures. This meant, among other things, that the pressing need declined for ideological justification in the community at large. One of the surest indications of a new freedom from the pressure for immediate ideological justification was that, for the first time, the liberal and "Enlightenment" conceptions of society made their appearance in the official circles of sociology. A discipline never loses its ideological properties all at once, but so far as it becomes a true science, they tend to decline. The liberal ideological element of formalism is far less important to it than was the conservatism of positivistic organicism and conflict theory, and in each school that has followed, the ideological element has grown weaker.

Even more significant than this were the internal transformations accompanying professional institutionalization. Sociology had to give up all claim to being a general social science or even the queen of the sciences. Its attention turned inward toward establishing a precise delimited field and a special definition of its material.

This new enterprise was signaled by a sudden outbreak of self-consciousness. No sociological treatise was produced in the early years of professional institutionalization that did not spend many pages on the task of defining itself and tracing its detailed relations to near-by disciplines. The first chapter of this book is an echo of this process.

More than this, sociologists plunged into the philosophic tradition out of which they had come for renewed inspiration and guidance. To this end, the byways of Kantianism were explored and the subtleties of phenomenology were traced. Out of this came the definition of sociology as the study of social forms in abstraction from content. And the proof that this was a real innovation is shown by the fact that the changed definition of subject matter threw open the entire problem of the relation of theory and method. Forms were being defined in a manner which would not make them accessible to the normal methods of inductive research. Hence the new formulation of theory and method set in motion a course of development that leads from neo-Kantian formalism to various forms of phenomenology.

Among the most general gains of sociological formalism was the opening of the entire problem of *social relations,* which led toward a more detailed study of social events than had hitherto been undertaken. It suggested a new kind of comparison — not the comparisons of total societies, or of the comparative institutions of different societies, but the comparison of social relations wherever they may appear. One now began to compare, for example, superiority and subordination between two friends, a husband and wife, a skilled laborer and his assistant, a teacher and student, and so on.

The new interest in comparing relations in abstraction from content permitted sociology to attain a somewhat higher level of generality. It was accompanied by a wholesale de-emphasis on social history, a fact which was eventually to re-open the whole question of the relations between sociology and history. But meanwhile many of the materials that had been assembled by the early forms of positivistic organicism and conflict theory were reorganized in the framework of formalism. The prospects of a non-historical systematic sociology were clearly envisioned. The institution of new detailed comparisons between social groups leads to the demand for new facts.

There were consequences flowing from the employment by the formalists of liberal conceptions of society. The organic models of society and civilization were brought under critical review. The conception of society as a legal ordering of independent wills was substituted, casting legal relations into peculiar prominence and modifying the conception of law and the state that had been promoted by conflict theory. Political sociology and the sociology of law were given a new importance.

As a result of these new emphases, the individual began to assume greater prominence in sociological thought than he had for previous theories. Moreover, neo-Kantian and phenomenological methodological problems forced the sociologist to face up to the possible role and values of empathic understanding in sociological research. Both of these developments were preparing the field for the full emergence of social psychology as a subdiscipline of the science.

Social Behaviorism

Following close upon the heels of sociological formalism, and largely coextensive with it, was social behaviorism. This great school of sociological theory with its three vital branches, pluralistic behaviorism, symbolic interactionism, and social-action theory, continued the effort to find a more precise definition of sociological subject matter. It continued, too, the relative ideological freedom of the formalists. There has been some conflict in the minds of its adherents (particularly the pluralistic-behavioral branch) between a conservative and liberal image of society, but by and large the liberal image has predominated.

With this great school of sociological theory, sociology may be said to have come fully of age. Its characterizing features were found in the attempt to find a specific definition of sociological subject matter without recourse to the formalistic expedients. The very terms it has made famous are like emblems of the richly rewarding researches of its various schools: imitation, invention, innovation, attitude, role, definition of the situation, vocation, looking-glass self, generalized other, and many more. It has created whole subdisciplines and practically made over others to such a degree as to give them its peculiar stamp: collective behavior, social control, the sociology of personality, the sociology of politics, the sociology of religion, the sociology of law, the sociology of class and bureaucracy, the sociology of art, culture, and knowledge. These studies were either created by the social behaviorists or almost completely re-stylized by them. Their contributions to method have also been rich and varied: the pluralistic behaviorists have been the primary group promoting the development of statistical method in sociology; the symbolic interactionists have contributed much to the employment of case and life histories as devices in an improved comparative method; the social-action theorists have continued to develop the ideal type as the device promoting precision in the comparative method. Social behaviorism is at present still in the full tide of its development.

Sociological Functionalism

With sociological functionalism, it is difficult to escape the impression that the circle is complete and sociology has returned to the point of view of its founders. Although the ideological element in sociology has continued to weaken, there are some indications of a return to a modified conservatism. This, however, is not nearly as important as the very evident rebellion against the atomism or elementarism of social behaviorism. A revised organicism is the keynote to the new development. The concept of system is formulated in general form and made central to interpretations.

There is another respect, however, in which sociological functionalism is a return to the world of the fathers. By and large, social behaviorism had trouble with method. Pluralistic behaviorism strongly advocated the development of sociological statistics, but it ran quickly into trouble, for the problems to which it wished to apply these methods did not always yield to statistical study. Its activities were regrouped, taking the form of construction of attitude scales. There is, for all the gains, a frustrating feature of all this: each renewed effort has tended to result in a retreat to a more primitive stage of activity. Meanwhile, the other branches of social behaviorism have often been actively anti-statistical. At the same time, an atmosphere has arisen making the comparative method unacceptable. The result is that all the richest theoretical findings of social behaviorism have occurred without methodological standing.

Both branches of sociological functionalism — macro-functionalism, developing out of sociological organicism and anthropology, and micro-functionalism, developing out of Gestalt psychology — show a strong inclination to return to the positivistic tradition of the founders. The micro-functionalists, in particular, have been the bearers of a strong tradition of sociological experimentation.

Sociological functionalism is too recent a development to have revealed the full panoply of its potentialities. Indications are already present that sociological functionalism is dissatisfied with the social behaviorists' theory of personality and their theory of language. Presumably it will invite radical transformations in many areas.

Alternative Ways to Review Sociological Theory

The present study has carried out the analysis of sociological theory by schools. This is not the only possible approach; there are at least three other ways in which the materials of sociological theory could be presented: by way of the requirements of analytical theory construction; topically; and by national configuration.

Analytical Theory Construction

Among the significant developments in twentieth-century thought have been the rapid evolution in mathematics and logic, the development of analytical philosophy — the adherents of which have carried out a critique of concept formation in numerous disciplines from the standpoint of contemporary logic and mathematics — and the development of the philosophy of science.

From the classical world, science inherited the ideal of a rationally closed system of concepts. However, the ideas to which these ideals of rational closure applied were empirical. If a science ever completely achieves its objectives, it represents a set of ideas which are formed into a logically closed system and which completely explain the facts to which they are addressed. Thus, a scientific theory, including sociological theory, is subject both to logical and empirical requirements.

In one way or another, logical and empirical requirements have formed a basis for judgments made throughout the present study. It has been asked: what ideas are of central importance to the theory concerned? what ideas are secondary and derived? It has also been asked: to what kinds of evidence has the theory been addressed? It has even been asked: what kind of methodological ties hold the theory and method together in the given case? From the standpoint of strict logical requirements, however, these questions have been raised in a relatively unsystematic manner. No attempt has been made to carry through the logical analysis of a given theory with any degree of completeness. To have carried through such a full logical critique of the various theories would have infinitely extended the analysis. After all, there are five major schools of sociological theory. None of them has less than two branches. Precisely because theory construction among sociologists has tended to be carried out in an unconscious manner, there have often been sharp differences between persons belonging to a single branch. To carry out anything approaching a complete logical critique of even one of the schools of theory would require a volume at least the size of the present one. And even if one were to contemplate five additional volumes, the present study would still represent a necessary first step.

Before the logical critique of any particular school of theory is carried out, it is of value first to make a provisional assemblage of materials. The present study has the value, as a kind of necessary first step, of bringing the whole field under review. An intensive study of a single part is more fruitful as a second stage of analysis.

That the schools are true alternative formations of theory has been established beyond any doubt. They form independent systems of concepts that cannot be arbitrarily intermixed. This fact appears over and again whenever one type of theory attempts to account for evidence of another branch. Furthermore, similar observations hold for the branches of a school. They offer alternatives that are genuine: idealistic organicism, bio-organicism, and voluntaristic organicism, for example, are not simply translatable into one another. Neither are the pluralistic-behavioral, symbolic-interactionist, and social-action branches of social behaviorism. Often the fact that they represent conflicting alternatives is an aspect of the inner development of a school as a whole, as in the case of the neo-Kantian and phenomenological branches of sociological formalism. But all this has been treated sufficiently already. The more specific task of carrying out a logically complete analysis of the separate schools and their branches remains.

The task of applying the standards of modern logic and analytical philosophy to the existing schools of theory may well become one of the primary problems of future sociological theorists. The number of persons who subscribe to this possibility is evident from the appearance of the first sociological symposium to take its stand on analytical theory construction.[2]

The Topical Analysis of Theoretical Material

Another quite different approach has become familiar in books on sociological theory which partly carry out their analysis by topics. It is not at all difficult to make up an interesting array of topics as the vehicle of analysis. Thus, for example, one can review the developments in the study of the city, rural society, industry, bureaucracy, social class, the sociology of law, of art, of knowledge, political sociology, the sociology of religion, social organization, social change, social psychology, criminology, and any of a number of additional ones.

Such organizations of material by topic are often as exciting and valuable as they are theoretically useless. To be sure, theoretical insights of one sort or another are often contained in them — but this may be true of many kinds of books. The real value of topical organizations of material is for dealing with problems of content. A topical treatment brings ideas and research findings together from many studies and organizes them in terms of some properties of the topic itself.

Thus, the point of gravity in such studies lies in the material or some properties of the material. The development of a body of logically consistent propositions is not at issue. If theory comes into consideration in such a topical study, it is usually as a disturbing element. The only conceivable manner in which such a topical treatment could have basic theoretical meaning is to forget about the requirements of the topic and, rather, raise the question of what happens to the topic as we move from one theory to the next. To be sure, if the day ever comes when there is no longer a plurality of sociological theories but only one sociological theory, only a topical organization of material will be relevant.

National Treatments of Theory

Almost as popular in treatises on theory as a topical treatment of subject matters is the treatment of theoretical development by country. Characteristically, there are series of portraits, say, of German, French,

[2] Llewellyn Gross (ed.), *Symposium on Sociological Theory* (Evanston, Ill.: Row, Peterson, 1959).

English, and sometimes even Italian, Slavic, Russian, and Japanese sociological theory. What occurs here is in one sense at the opposite end of the scale from a topical treatment of theory. Emphasis is not on content but on special historical sequences.

There are undoubtedly early stages in the growth of a discipline when it has a national image. It is inconceivable, for example, to find the theories of Spencer emerging in France in place of those of Comte and vice versa. Both were conservatives. Both preferred the organismic point of view for socially conservative purposes. However, what they wanted to conserve was very different. What can happen to social theory when analyzed as a na· tional image is shown by these two persons. Comte belongs to the sociology of France, Spencer to the sociology of England.

In general, however, when national determination of the discipline is emphasized, it is at the expense of the unity of theory. One would have to disassemble conflict theory and return Gumplowicz and Ratzenhofer to Austria, Bagehot to England, Oppenheimer to Germany, and Small and Vold to the United States. One would have to break up the phenomenological branch of formalism and return Vierkandt to Germany and Switzerland and Gurvitch to France. The story is the same whenever the unity of theory is violated in the interest of tracing national development.

Mistaken impressions are conveyed by this procedure. The Nazis had ideological reasons for promoting the concept of a true German science, just as the Russians have ideological motives in distinguishing between "true" science and "decadent Western" types. And while few if any students have wished to convey such an impression in organizing sociological theory by country, this mode of organizing the materials has promoted the search for national images rather than the search for the universal properties of science.

There are, of course, very significant values to be gained from an exam· ination of the national contributions to the growth of a science, so long as one avoids the old myths that the nation imprints its soul upon its science. Each nation represents a special context within which the science develops, tending to encourage some kinds of inquiries and discourage others. If such influences are permitted exclusively to determine the fate of the science, it will be transformed into an instrument of the nation, as happened in Nazi Germany and Soviet Russia; the process is everywhere present, but only here was it brought to its logical conclusion. The study of national developments in science can sometimes serve to illumine otherwise dark areas, revealing why some leads were overlooked, why irrationalities are preserved in the heart of a rational enterprise, how the competition of alternative national claims may assist in the emancipation of science from any national context whatsoever. But such historical images are no substitute for the task of isolating the basic schools of theory.

Toward Integration

As one traces the evolution of sociology from school to school, true theoretical alternatives appear. Problems are posed, new theories are instituted. The relations of theory and method have to be re-thought over and again. But all this time, the standards of science have been at work. Step by step, item by item, the propositions of the science have either been confirmed, disconfirmed, or left in doubt. It is in the nature of the case that the moment an item of knowledge is confirmed, it loses interest for the scientist. The scientist shows more concern for one lost sheep than for the ninety and nine that remain in the fold.

Precisely because interest continually shifts to the unsolved problems, while the gains become the common property of all, it is easy to lose sight of genuine growth. During the past century, sociology was established as a recognized area of study. It was institutionalized and professionalized. It reached a stage where it emancipated itself from second-hand data and began to gather its materials first hand. It has established one area after another, gradually fixing a territory agreed upon by all members of all schools.

A common stock of terms, concepts, and empirical generalizations is increasingly shared by all schools; indeed, the ability to explain the established "facts" of the field becomes a kind of first step in determining the acceptability of a theory. One of the most significant evidences of this is the fact that each new formation of theory remains inconclusive until it is able to explain successfully those facts explained by its rivals. One can trace, in this way, successive explanations of "law" as one moves from sociological formalism to the social-action branch of social behaviorism. Many of the critical materials of positivistic organicism and conflict theory received a common treatment and were reduced to "forms" or "relations" by the formalists. This was in part why it seemed to offer the possibility of the first truly systematic sociology. The problem of personality is noted by the conflict theorists, seriously broached by the formalists, and given full treatment in the symbolic-interactionist and social-action branches of social behaviorism. It is noteworthy that both the macro- and micro-functionalists pick up the problem once again. But the successive re-stylization of a growing body of common materials has been noted many times in the course of this study. Here it is significant only as solid evidence of general growth.

Even the topic of the integration — or, as it is sometimes called, "convergence" — of sociological theory has been increasingly posed. So far, unfortunately, statements have usually approached the problem wrong end to — in terms of the distinctive features of the theory rather than from the standpoint of the humble platform of basic agreement. To force convergence at other levels is to blur the distinctive lines of theory formation.

From the perspective developed here, it is possible to offer neither easy solutions for the integration of theory nor utopian hopes for sociology as a boon to mankind. It is not even possible to offer that sop to the Western conscience — all things yield to hard work. In the cooperation of reason and energy, when the tinder is at hand and the sparks are struck from mother wit, sociology may yet find the ingredients for its synthesis. Sociology may yet produce a Newton or a Maxwell who will take the materials cast up by chance and worked up with patient labor, clarify them in the crystalline formations of his logic, and fuse them in the fire of his love.

SELECTED BIBLIOGRAPHY

BECKER, HOWARD, and ALVIN BOSKOFF (eds.), *Modern Sociological Theory*. New York: Dryden, 1957.

BORGATTA, EDGAR F., and HENRY J. MEYER (eds.), *Sociological Theory: Present-Day Sociology from the Past*. New York: Alfred A. Knopf, 1956.

GURVITCH, GEORGES, and WILBERT E. MOORE, *Twentieth Century Sociology*. New York: Philosophical Library, 1945.

KOMAROVSKY, MIRRA (ed.), *Common Frontiers of the Social Sciences*. Glencoe, Ill.: The Free Press, 1957.

SOROKIN, PITIRIM, *Contemporary Sociological Theories*. New York: Harper, 1928.

SOROKIN, PITIRIM, *Fads and Foibles in Modern Sociology*. Chicago: Henry Regnery, 1956.

TIMASHEFF, NICHOLAS S., *Sociological Theory: Its Nature and Growth*. Revised edition. New York: Random House, 1957.

WHITE, LEONARD D. (ed.), *The State of the Social Sciences*. Chicago: University of Chicago Press, 1956.

Picture Credits

AUGUSTE COMTE. Brown Brothers.

HERBERT SPENCER. Brown Brothers.

LESTER WARD. Brown Brothers.

FERDINAND TÖNNIES. Courtesy of the Ferdinand Tönnies Institute, New University, Kiel.

ÉMILE DURKHEIM. Bust by Landowski, from Presses Universitaires de France. Courtesy of Jacques Halphen.

VILFREDO PARETO. Courtesy of the University of Lausanne.

SIGMUND FREUD. Keystone View Company.

ROBERT REDFIELD. Courtesy of the University of Chicago.

OSWALD SPENGLER. Professor Fritz Behn's bust of Oswald Spengler, author of *The Decline of the West*. Courtesy of Alfred A. Knopf, Inc.

ARNOLD TOYNBEE. Courtesy of Oxford University Press. Copyright by Philippe Halsman.

PITIRIM SOROKIN. Courtesy of Pitirim Sorokin.

GEORGE LUNDBERG. Photograph by James O. Sneddon, Office of Public Information, University of Washington, Seattle. Courtesy of George Lundberg.

ADAM SMITH. Board of Trustees for the National Galleries of Scotland, Edinburgh.

KARL MARX. Brown Brothers.

CHARLES DARWIN. Brown Brothers.

WILLIAM GRAHAM SUMNER. Courtesy of Yale University, New Haven, Connecticut.

WALTER BAGEHOT. The British Museum, London.

GUSTAV RATZENHOFER. Courtesy of the Photo Archives of the Austrian National Library, Vienna.

LUDWIG GUMPLOWICZ. Courtesy of Frau Doctor Wanda Lanzer, Stockholm.

ALBION SMALL. Courtesy of Colby College, Waterville, Maine.

FRANZ OPPENHEIMER. Courtesy of the Johann Wolfgang Goethe Universität, Frankfurt am Main.

GEORGE VOLD. Courtesy of George Vold.

RUDOLF STAMMLER. Courtesy of the Archiv der Martin-Luther-Universität, Halle-Wittenberg.

GEORG SIMMEL. From *Buch des Dankes an Georg Simmel*, ed. by Kurt Gassen and Michael Landmann, Duncker & Humblot, Berlin, 1958. Courtesy of the publishers.

CÉLESTIN BOUGLÉ. Bibliothèque Nationale, Paris.

EDWARD A. ROSS. Courtesy of the University of Wisconsin, Madison, Wisc.

ROBERT E. PARK. From *American Sociology* by Howard W. Odum, Longmans, Green & Co., Inc., 1951. Courtesy of the publishers.

ERNEST BURGESS. Courtesy of the University of Chicago.

HANS KELSEN. Photo by Paul Bishop. Courtesy of Hans Kelsen.

LEOPOLD VON WIESE. Courtesy of Leopold von Wiese.

ALFRED VIERKANDT. Photo by Schatzmann & Muster, Berlin. Courtesy of Martha Vierkandt.

MAX SCHELER. Courtesy of the Universität zu Köln.

GEORGES GURVITCH. Courtesy of Georges Gurvitch.

GABRIEL TARDE. Bibliothèque Nationale, Paris.

GUSTAVE LE BON. A. Harlingue, Archives Photographiques de l'Histoire, Paris.

JAMES MARK BALDWIN. Courtesy of Mrs. Philip M. Stimson.

FRANKLIN H. GIDDINGS. Columbia University, New York.

CHARLES HORTON COOLEY. University of Michigan, Ann Arbor, Michigan.

MEYER F. NIMKOFF. Courtesy of Meyer F. Nimkoff.

WILLIAM F. OGBURN. Courtesy of William F. Ogburn.

F. STUART CHAPIN. Courtesy of F. Stuart Chapin.

WILLIAM JAMES. Harvard University Library, Cambridge, Mass.

GEORGE H. MEAD. Courtesy of Arthur E. Murphy and the University of Chicago Press, Chicago.

W. I. THOMAS. From *American Sociology* by Howard W. Odum, Longmans, Green & Co., Inc., 1951.

JEAN PIAGET. Courtesy of the University of Geneva and Jean Piaget.

ERNST CASSIRER. Columbia University, New York.

C. WRIGHT MILLS. Photograph by Yaroslava. Courtesy of C. Wright Mills.

HANS GERTH. Courtesy of the University of Wisconsin, Madison, Wisc.

WILLIAM H. WHYTE, JR. Photo by Bernard Newman. Courtesy of William H. Whyte, Jr.

DAVID RIESMAN. Photograph from Arthur Siegel. Courtesy of David Riesman.

THORSTEIN VEBLEN. Kay Harris, New York.

MAX WEBER. Painting by Otto Neumann. Courtesy of the Kurpfälzisches Museum of the city of Heidelberg.

JOHN R. COMMONS. Courtesy of the University of Wisconsin, Madison, Wisc.

ROBERT MACIVER. Courtesy of Columbia University, New York.

KARL MANNHEIM. Courtesy of Mrs. Julia Pilisansky and the London School of Economics and Political Science.

BRONISLAW MALINOWSKI. Courtesy of the Harvard University News Office, Cambridge, Mass.

A. R. RADCLIFFE-BROWN. Royal Anthropological Institute, London.

KURT LEWIN. Courtesy of Gertrud Weiss Lewin.

FLORIAN ZNANIECKI. Courtesy of Mrs. Florian Znaniecki.

LEON FESTINGER. Courtesy of Leon Festinger.

TALCOTT PARSONS. Courtesy of *The Harvard Crimson*, Cambridge, Mass.

ROBERT MERTON. Courtesy of Columbia University, New York.

GEORGE C. HOMANS. Photo by Ramsey & Muspratt, Cambridge, England. Courtesy of George C. Homans.

ROBERT F. BALES. Courtesy of the Harvard University News Office, Cambridge, Mass.

MARION J. LEVY. Courtesy of Marion J. Levy.

Index

Novicow, Jacques, 80, 206

OBSERVATION: 20, 73
  controlled, 332–333
  need for, 13
Odum, Howard W., 317n., 324n.
Oedipal stage, 106
Ogburn, William F., 47, 268, 324–330, 338, 519
Oppenheimer, Franz, 196–199, 207
Opposition, 307–308
Orders, institutionalized, 371–372
Organicism: 52–53, 76, 276, 465, 528–529
  biological, 78–81
  conflict of, with positivism, 91
  in positivistic organicism, 122
  in relation to functionalism, 446–450, 518–519, 520
  separation of, from positivism, 110–118
  in views of Ward, 69–72
Origins, search for, 181
Owen, Robert, 61

PARACELSUS, 23
Pareto, Vilfredo, 101–104, 128, 423, 466–467, 484, 499, 500, 531
Park, Robert E., 86, 93, 252–256, 265, 266, 280, 348n.
Parsonians, 493–499
Parsons, Elsie Clews, 306n.
Parsons, Kenneth H., 400n., 402
Parsons, Talcott, 129, 377n., 393, 412, 421–425, 438, 484–490, 500
Particularism, 488, 489, 497
Party, political, 392–393, 433
Paton, W. R., 149
Patriarchy, 85–86
Pattern-alternatives of value-orientations: see Pattern-variables
Pattern-variables, 487–489, 497
Pearson, Karl, 171–172
Peasant, Polish, study of, 349–350
Peirce, C. S., 298
Persistence of aggregates, 103
Perlman, Selig, 400n., 401–402
Personality:
  field theory of, 503
  formation of, 505
  and interaction, 351–352
  macro-functional theory of, 494–495
  other-directed, 430

  and social structure, 350, 351
Personality study, recapitulation theory in, 314–316
Pertz, Georg H., 191
Pettegrove, James P., 212n., 359n.
Pfister, Oskar, 109n.
Phenomena, Kantian, 267–268, 286, 378
Phenomenology, 225–228, 230, 231, 535
Philosophy: 11, 16, 19–20, 27, 222, 525–526
  and sociology, 6–7
  (See also names of individual philosophies)
Phi-phenomenon, 452
Physics: 24–26
  social, 29
Physiocrats, 33–34, 142–143
Piaget, Jean, 364–369, 375
Plasticity, 340
Plateau, Joseph, 451
Plato, 7n., 11, 53–54, 76, 150
Play: 240, 241, 242, 459
  of child, 357–358, 365–366, 369
Pluralistic behaviorism, 305–337, 441, 536, 537
Plurality patterns, 257–258
Pocock, D. F., 87n.
Political machine, 474–475
Political order, 371
Political parties, 392–393, 433
Political science, 33, 35, 39, 41, 44, 46
Politics, in democracy, 201
Polybius, 13, 130–131, 148, 150
Population, Malthus on, 145–146
Positivistic organicism: 51–77, 96–97, 461, 527–531
  classic phase of, 81–92
  philosophical and social sources of, 56–61
  weaknesses of, 128–129
Positivism: 52–53, 76, 422, 529
  elements of, in positivistic organicism, 73–75, 90–92, 122
  history of, 56–60
  separation of, from organicism, 118–121
  and social reform, 60–61
  voluntaristic, 99–100
Power: 131, 137–138, 507
  sovereign, 136
Power élite, 433–434
Pragmatism, 297–302, 374
Prediction, in social science, 379

Social class: *see* Class, social

Social contract, 80, 139–140, 219–220

Social control, 322–323

Social Darwinism, 174, 187
  as conflict ideology, 162–168
  racism based on, 168–173

Social dynamics, 530

Social fact, 90–91, 195–196

Social function, 195

Sociological functionalism: *see* Functionalism, sociological

Social geography, 34, 35, 41, 45

Social history, 535

Social karyokinesis, 70

Social pathology, 79

Social process: 195, 202, 251–252, 307–308
  theory of, 185–186

Social psychology, 45, 276, 336, 354, 469–470, 536

Social reality, levels of, 277–278

Social relations:
  phenomenological, 271
  study of, 535

"Social relationship," 389–390, 405

Social research, methods of, 331; *see also* Methodology *and* Research

Social status scale, 331–332

Social structure: 195
  and personality, 350, 351
  schematic view of, 407

Social science:
  establishment of, 35
  in nineteenth century, 36–43
  objects of study of, 193
  sociology as, 45

Social solidarity: 88
  of Ibn Khaldun, 132–133

Social statistics, 530

"Social system," 466–467
  characteristics of, 488
  elements of, 478
  internal system of, 479–480, 481

Social telesis, 70, 71

Social variation, 195

Socialism: 60–61, 72, 151–153, 174, 529, 530
  Marxian, 160–162

Socialization: 202, 486, 492, 495
  in America, 509
  of child, 494, 495

"Sociation," 238, 239, 243, 259

Sociocracy, 72

Society: 4–5, 71, 154–155, 264, 414, 466–467
  active and passive, 114–115
  a priori conditions of, 237–239
  character in, 319–320
  as collective mind, 321
  conceptions of, 86
  in Comtean theory, 63–64
  as distinct from state, 532
  Durkheim on, 88–89
  evolution in concepts of, 263–264
  Freudian view of, 106–110
  inner-directed, 429, 430
  as interaction, 253–254
  Kantian theory of, 233–234
  as mental phenomenon, 344–345
  as organized social activity, 358
  and positivistic organicism, 540
  as social life, 270
  stability of, 104
  study of, 113–114
  as supersystem, 117–118
  as system of action, 491–492
  as system of social interaction, 485–487, 489
  tradition-directed, 429, 430
  types of, 97, 530
  in view of Redfield, 95
  in view of Spencer, 67–69
  as willed human relations, 406

Sociology: 27, 51, 79, 225, 254, 526
  branches of, 277
  causal factors in, 408–409
  conceptions of, 82, 83, 120–121, 181
  cultural, 274, 275
  definition of, 3–5
  early development of, 41–45, 47
  empirical, 274
  establishment of, as discipline, 211–212, 229, 231, 279, 434–435
  formal, 240, 534–536
  general, 240
  and historiography, 15–17
  history of, 526–527, 529
  as inductive discipline, 331
  interpretive, 379
  logico-experimental, 102–103
  methodology of, 280, 380–382
  neo-Kantian view of, 231, 264
  phenomenological, 271–272
  philosophical, 240
  political, 391–392
  professionalization of, 534–535, 541